PROGRAMMING MICROSOFT® WINDOWS® CE

Douglas Boling

Microsoft Press

PUBLISHED BY
Microsoft Press
A Division of Microsoft Corporation
One Microsoft Way
Redmond, Washington 98052-6399

Library of Congress Cataloging-in-Publication Data
Boling, Douglas McConnaughey, 1960–
Programming Microsoft Windows CE / Douglas McConnaughey Boling.
p. cm.
Includes index.
ISBN 1-57231-856-2
1. Microsoft Windows (Computer file) 2. Operating Systems (Computers) I. Title.
QA76.76.O63B623 1998
005.4'469--dc21 98-39279
CIP

Printed and bound in the United States of America.

1 2 3 4 5 6 7 8 9 QMQM 3 2 1 0 9 8

Distributed in Canada by ITP Nelson, a division of Thomson Canada Limited.

A CIP catalogue record for this book is available from the British Library.

Microsoft Press books are available through booksellers and distributors worldwide. For further information about international editions, contact your local Microsoft Corporation office. Or contact Microsoft Press International directly at fax (425) 936-7329. Visit our Web site at mspress.microsoft.com.

Acquisitions Editor: Eric Stroo
Project Editor: Kathleen Atkins
Technical Editor: Jim Fuchs

To Nancy Jane

Contents at a Glance

Contents

Part II Windows CE Basics

Part III Communications

Acknowledgments

I'd heard stories from authors about the travails of writing a book. Still I was unprepared for the task. While I wrote, I learned just how much of a team effort is necessary to make a book. My name appears on the cover, but countless others were involved in its creation.

First, there is the talented team at Microsoft Press. Kathleen Atkins, the project leader and editor of this book, took my gnarled syntax and confused text and made it readable. Kathleen, thanks for your words of encouragement, your guidance, and for making this book as good as it is. The book's technical editor, Jim Fuchs, was my voice in the initial editing process. His judgement was so good that I rarely had to correct an edit for technical reasons. Many thanks also go to Cheryl Penner, the copy editor and proofreader; Elizabeth Hansford, the principal compositor; and Michael Victor, who translated my stick drawings into professional illustrations. Finally, thanks to Eric Stroo, who took a chance and signed me to write this book. Eric, the sun seems to be out now.

For technical help, I was privileged to be able to mine the golden knowledge of the Microsoft Windows CE development team. Special thanks go to Mike Thomson, who put up with endless inquiries about the technical details of Windows CE. On the rare occasions that Mike didn't have the answer, he guided me to the folks who did. Among those folks who helped were Dave Campbell, Carlos Alayo, Scott Holden, Omar Maabreh, Jeff Kelley, and Jeff Blum. While these guys did the best they could, I am, of course, responsible for any mistakes introduced into the text as I interpreted their answers.

You can't write a book of this type without hardware. My thanks go to Cheryl Balbach, Scott Nelson, and the Casio Corporation for their assistance. When other companies turned me down, Casio stepped up to the plate and provided prerelease and hard-to-find hardware necessary to test my code. Thanks, Cheryl. Call me if you need any more drop testing performed.

I also owe a debt of gratitude to the folks at Vadem Ltd. It was while working at Vadem that I was initially introduced to Windows CE and, amazingly enough, allowed to contribute to the creation of one of the machines you'll see in the introduction. Thanks to Craig Colvin, who talked me into working at Vadem and is now busy designing new and innovative Windows CE products; John Zhao, the president; and Henry Fung, CTO; as well as the managers down the line, Jim Stair and Norm Farquhar.

To all of you, thanks for allowing me to disappear as the book ran behind schedule. I'd also like to thank Edmond Ku, Scott Chastain, Ron Butterworth, Anthony Armenta, and the rest of the Clio team.

One good friend deserves special mention. Jeff Prosise started me down this path when he talked me into writing my first article in 1985. When you get past his honesty, good nature, and modesty, you're left with one incredibly smart guy, devoted to his family and friends. Thanks, Jeff, for everything.

My career as a writer started at the top, *PC Magazine*. There, I'd like to thank Michael Miller, Jake Kirchner, Bill Howard, and Gail Shaffer. Other folks no longer directly tied to the magazine but whom I still regard as part of the *PC Magazine* family are Bill Machrone, Trudy Neuhaus, and Dale Lewallen.

In addition, I thank two of the masters—Charles Petzold and Ray Duncan. These guys, along with Jeff Prosise, write the best technical books on the planet.

Thanks also to the folks at *Microsoft Systems Journal* and *Microsoft Interactive Developer,* Eric Maffei, Josh Trupin, and Gretchen Bilson. A special thanks goes to Joe Flanigan, who introduced me to some of the folks on the Windows CE team at Microsoft.

I'd also like to thank a number of musical groups that helped me through long hours in front of the PC. These include but aren't limited to the Beach Boys, the Cranberries, Alan Parson's Project, Toad the Wet Sprocket, the Eagles, and Dire Straits. Thanks also to the Southland Corporation, owners of the 7-Eleven franchise, for inventing the Big Gulp and its more potent cousins, the Super Big Gulp and the Double Gulp. Thanks also to the Coca-Cola Corporation for providing the caffeine.

On a more serious note, if there's any one person whose name also deserves to be on the cover of this book, it's Nancy Jane Hendricks Boling, my wife. Nancy endured a year of being a single parent because I spent every spare moment in front of my PC and an array of Windows CE devices writing this book. Thank you, Nancy. I'm sure I didn't say it enough over the past year. I love you. Your name isn't on the cover, but the book is dedicated to you. I must also mention two other family members—our sons Andy, 2 ½ years old, and Sam, born during the writing of Chapter 9. Andy is well on his way to becoming the best big brother a boy can be. Sam, well, he has the cutest giggle. Thanks also to Amy Sekeras for taking such good care of Andy and Sam.

Finally, I lack the words to adequately say thanks to my parents, Ronald and Jane Boling. Mom and Dad, you are simply the best parents I know, have met, or ever read about. It is my goal in life to attempt to be as good a parent to my children as you are to Rob, Chris, Jay, and me. I am truly blessed to have you as parents.

Introduction

I was introduced to Microsoft Windows CE right before it was released in the fall of 1996. A Windows programmer for many years, I was intrigued by an operating system that applied the well-known Windows API to a smaller, more power-conserving operating system. The distillation of the API for smaller machines enables tens of thousands of Windows programmers to write applications for an entirely new class of systems. The subtle differences, however, make writing Windows CE code somewhat different from writing for Windows 98 or Windows NT. It's those differences that I'll address in this book.

Just What Is Windows CE?

Windows CE is the newest, smallest, and arguably the most interesting of the Microsoft Windows operating systems. Windows CE was designed from the ground up to be a small, ROM-based operating system with a Win32 subset API. Windows CE extends the Windows API into the markets and machines that can't support the larger footprints of Windows 98 and Windows NT.

Windows 98 is a great operating system for users who need backward compatibility with DOS and Windows 2.*x* and 3.*x* programs. While it has shortcomings, Windows 98 succeeds amazingly well at this difficult task. Windows NT, on the other hand, is written for the enterprise. It sacrifices compatibility and size to achieve its high level of reliability and robustness.

Windows CE isn't backward compatible with MS-DOS or Windows. Nor is it an all-powerful operating system designed for enterprise computing. Instead, Windows CE is a lightweight, multithreaded operating system with an optional graphical user interface. Its strength lies in its small size, its Win32 subset API, and its multiplatform support.

Products Based on Windows CE

The first products designed for Windows CE were handheld "organizer" type devices with 480-by-240 or 640-by-240 screens and chiclets keyboards. These devices, dubbed Handheld PCs, were first introduced at Fall Comdex 96. Fall Comdex 97 saw the release of a dramatically upgraded version of the operating system, Windows CE 2.0, with newer hardware in a familiar form—this time the box came with a 640-by-240 landscape screen and a somewhat larger keyboard.

In January 1998 at the Consumer Electronics Show, Microsoft announced two new platforms, the Palm-size PC and the Auto PC. The Palm-size PC was aimed directly at the pen-based organizer market currently dominated by the Palm Pilot. The Palm-size PC sports a portrait mode, 240-by-320 screen and uses stylus-based input. A number of Palm-size PCs are on the market today.

Figure I-1 shows both a Palm-size PC, in this case a Casio E-10, and a Handheld PC, in this case a Casio A-20.

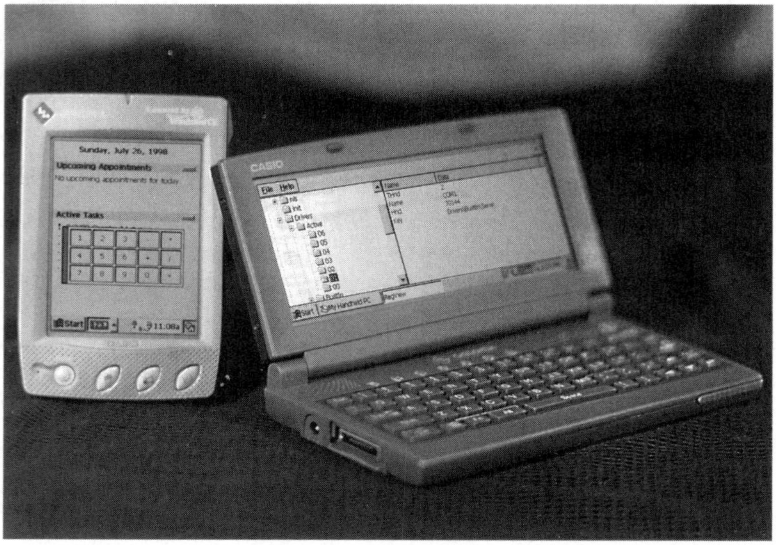

Figure I-1. *The Casio E-10 Palm-size PC and the Casio A-20 Handheld PC.*

Just as this book is being released, Microsoft has introduced the Handheld PC Professional, which is a greatly enhanced H/PC with new applications and which uses the latest version of the operating system, Windows CE 2.11.[1] This device brings the compact nature of Windows CE to devices of laptop size. The advantages of applying Windows CE to a laptop device are many. First, the battery life of a Handheld PC Pro is at least 10 hours, far better than the 2-to 3-hour average of a PC-compatible laptop. Second, the size and weight of the Windows CE devices are far more user friendly, with systems as thin as 1 inch weighing less than 3 pounds. Even with the diminutive size, a Handheld PC Pro still sports a large VGA screen and a keyboard that a normal human can use. The Vadem Clio Handheld PC Pro, shown in Figure I-2, is an example of how Windows CE is being used in newer platforms. The system

1. Windows CE 2.11 is Windows CE 2.10 with a few minor changes.

can be used as a standard laptop or "flipped" into a tablet-mode device. This device is just one example of how Windows CE is expanding into new system types.

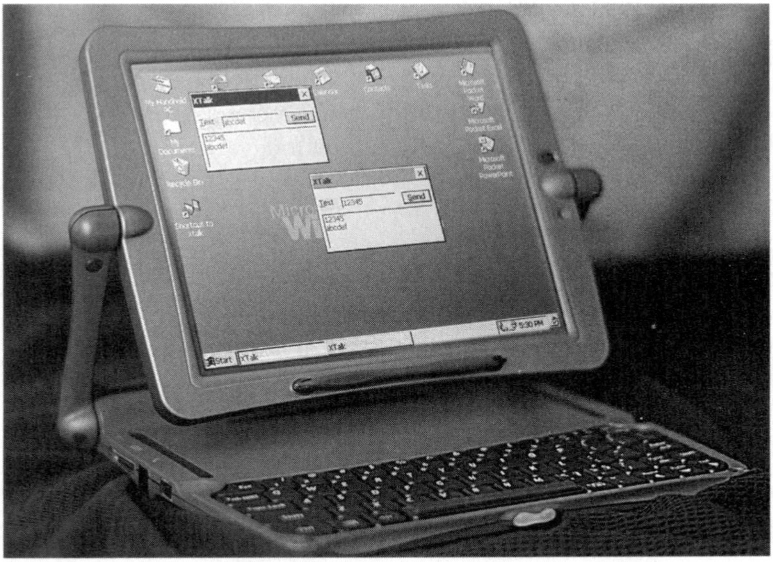

Figure I-2. *The Vadem Clio Handheld PC Pro.*

I refer to the Handheld PC Pro throughout this book under its operating system version, Windows CE 2.1, because the platform name, Handheld PC Pro, was determined very late in the process. I knew of, and in fact, had a hand in the development of a Handheld PC Pro under its code name Jupiter. However, you can't use code names in a book, so its operating system version had to suffice.

Other platforms—Auto PC, Web TV set-top boxes, and embedded platforms designed for specific tasks—are also appearing or will appear in the coming months. What's amazing about Windows CE is that the flexibility of the operating system allows it to be used in all these diverse designs while all the time retaining the same basic, well-known Win32 API.

WHY YOU SHOULD READ THIS BOOK

Programming Microsoft Windows CE is written for anyone who will be writing applications for Windows CE. Both the embedded systems programmer using Windows CE for a specific application and the Windows programmer interested in porting an existing Windows application or writing an entirely new one can use the information in this book to make their tasks easier.

The embedded systems programmer, who might not be as familiar with the Win32 API as the Windows programmer, can read the first section of the book to become familiar with Windows programming. While this section isn't the comprehensive tutorial that can be found in books such as *Programming Windows* by Charles Petzold, it does provide a base that will carry the reader through the other chapters in the book. It also can help the embedded systems programmer develop fairly complex and quite useful Windows CE programs.

The experienced Windows programmer can use the book to learn about the differences among the Win32 APIs used by Windows CE, Windows NT, and Windows 98. Programmers who are familiar with Win32 programming recognize subtle differences between the Windows 98 and Windows NT APIs. The differences between Windows CE and its two cousins are even greater. The small footprint of Windows CE means that many of the overlapping APIs in the Win32 model aren't supported. Some sections of the Win32 API aren't supported at all. On the other hand, because of its unique setting, Windows CE extends the Win32 API in a number of areas that are covered in this text.

The method used by *Programming Windows CE* is to teach by example. I wrote numerous Windows CE example programs specifically for this book. The source for each of these examples is printed in the text. Both the source and the final compiled programs for a number of the processors supported by Windows CE are also provided on the accompanying CD.

The examples in this book are all written directly to the API, the so-called "Petzold" method of programming. Since the goal of this book is to teach you how to write programs for Windows CE, the examples avoid using a class library such as MFC, which obfuscates the unique nature of writing applications for Windows CE. Some people would say that the availability of MFC on Windows CE eliminates the need for direct knowledge of the Windows CE API. I believe the opposite is true. Knowledge of the Windows CE API enables more efficient use of MFC. I also believe that truly knowing the operating system also dramatically simplifies the debugging of applications.

WHAT ABOUT MFC?

The simple fact is that Windows CE systems aren't the best platform for a general-purpose class library like MFC. The slower processors and the significantly lower memory capacity of Windows CE devices make using MFC problematic. Most Windows CE systems don't include the MFC library in their ROM. This means that the MFC and OLE32 DLLs required by MFC applications must be downloaded into the systems. The first versions of the Palm-size PCs don't even support MFC.

That said, there's a place for MFC on Windows CE devices. One such place might be if you're designing a custom application for a system you know will have the MFC and OLE32 DLLs in ROM. For those specific applications, you might want to use MFC, but only if you know the target environment and have configured the system with the proper amount of RAM to do the job.

Windows CE Development Tools

This book is written with the assumption that the reader knows C and is at least familiar with Microsoft Windows. All code development was done with Microsoft Visual C++ 5.0 and Windows CE Visual C++ for Windows CE under Windows NT 4.0.

To compile the example programs in this book, you need Microsoft Visual C++ 5.0, which is part of the integrated development environment (IDE), DevStudio, running on a standard IBM-compatible PC. You also need Microsoft Visual C++ for Windows CE, which isn't a stand-alone product. It's an add-in to Visual C++ 5.0 that incorporates components to the compiler that produce code for the different CPUs supported by Windows CE. Visual C++ for Windows CE isn't currently available through standard retail channels, but information on ordering it directly from Microsoft can be found on the Microsoft Web site. Finally, you need one of the platform SDKs for Windows CE. These SDKs provide the custom include files for each of the Windows CE platforms. These platform SDKs are available for free on the Microsoft Web site. As a convenience, I've also included the platform SDKs available at the time of the writing of this book on the accompanying CD.

While not absolutely required for developing applications for Windows CE, Windows NT 4.0 is strongly recommended for the development environment. It's possible to compile and download Windows CE programs under Windows 98, but many of the features of the integrated development environment (IDE), such as Windows CE emulation and remote debugging, aren't supported.

Visual C++ for Windows CE won't change the outward appearance of Visual C++, with the exception of a few new tools listed under the tools menu. Nor will the installation of Visual C++ for Windows CE prevent you from developing applications for other Windows operating systems. The installation of Visual C++ for Windows CE will result in new Windows CE targets such as WCE MIPS and WCE SH and WCE x86Em being added to the platforms listing when you're creating a new Win32 application. Also, a Windows CE MFC AppWizard will be added to the new projects listing to assist in creating MFC programs for Windows CE.

Target Systems

You don't need to have a Windows CE target device to experience the sample programs provided by this book. The various platform SDKs come with a Windows CE emulator that lets you perform basic testing of a Windows CE program under Windows NT. This emulator comes in handy when you want to perform initial debugging to ensure that the program starts, creates the proper windows, reacts to menu selections, and so on. However, the emulator has some limitations and there simply is no replacement for having a target Windows CE system to perform final debugging and testing for applications.

You should consider a number of factors when deciding what Windows CE hardware to use for testing. First, if the application is to be a commercial product, you should buy at least one system for each type of target CPU. You need to test against all of the target CPUs because, while the source code will probably be identical, the resulting executable will be different in size and so will the memory allocation footprint for each target CPU.

Most applications will also be written specifically for the Handheld PC or Palm-size PC, not both. Although the base operating system for both the Handheld PC and Palm-size PC is Windows CE, the hardware underneath is vastly different. The strict memory constraints of the Palm-size PC, as well as its much smaller screen, its different orientation, and its lack of a keyboard, force compromises that aren't acceptable on a Handheld PC or its larger relative, the Handheld PC Pro. Other constraints on Palm-size PC systems, such as the lack of printing and TrueType support, differentiate its environment from the Handheld PC's.

In this book, I demonstrate programs that can run on the Handheld PC, Handheld PC Pro, or Palm-size PC. The goal is to allow the lessons to be applied to all platforms. For some examples, however, the different screen dimensions mean that the example will run better on one particular system. I point out the differences and the reasons they exist. For example, some controls might exist on only one platform or the other. The shells for the two platforms—Handheld or Palm-size—are also different and need separate coverage. Finally, a small set of features in Windows CE are simply not supported on the smaller Palm-size PC platform.

WHAT'S ON THE CD

The accompanying CD contains the source code for all the examples in the book. I've also provided project files for Microsoft DevStudio so that you can open preconfigured projects. Unless otherwise noted, the examples are Windows CE 2.0 compatible so that they can run on most Windows CE systems available today. Chapter 13, "Shell Programming—Part 2" contains examples that are compiled for Windows CE 2.01, so they won't run on current Handheld PCs. There are some examples, such as the console applications in Chapter 12, that are specific to the Handheld PC Pro and other devices running Windows CE 2.10.

When you build for a specific platform, remember that it might not be backward compatible with earlier versions of Windows CE. For example, Microsoft moved some of the C library support from statically linked libraries in Windows CE 2.0 into the operating system for Windows CE 2.01, the Palm-size PC release. This reduces the size of an executable, but prevents code built for the Palm-size PC from running on a Handheld PC running Windows CE 2.0. You can, however, compile code for a Handheld PC running Windows CE 2.0 and have it run on a Palm-size PC.

In addition to the examples, the CD contains a number of folders of interest to the Windows CE programmer. I've included the platform SDKs for the Handheld PC as well as for the Palm-size PC. Unfortunately, the Handheld PC Pro SDK wasn't available in time for this release. Like the other platform SDKs, that one is available for free on the Microsoft Web site. Check out the readme file on the CD for late-breaking information about what else is included on the CD.

OTHER SOURCES

While I have attempted to make *Programming Microsoft Windows CE* a one-stop shop for Windows CE programming, no one book can cover everything. A nice complement to this book is *Inside Windows CE* by John Murray. It documents the "oral history" of Windows CE. Knowing this kind of information is crucial to understanding just why Windows CE is designed the way it is. Once you know the why, it's easy to extrapolate the what, when trying to solve problems. Murray's book is great, not just because of the information you'll learn about Windows CE but also because it's an entertaining read.

For learning more about Windows programming in general, I suggest the classic text *Programming Windows* by Charles Petzold. This is, by far, the best book for learning Windows programming. Charles presents examples that show how to tackle difficult but common Windows problems. For learning more about the Win32 kernel API, I suggest Jeff Richter's *Advanced Windows*. Jeff covers the techniques of process, thread, and memory management down to the most minute detail. For learning more about MFC programming, there's no better text than Jeff Prosise's *Programming Windows 95 with MFC*. This book is the "Petzold" of MFC programming and simply a required read for MFC programmers.

FEEDBACK

While I have striven to make the information in this book as accurate as possible, you'll undoubtedly find errors. If you find a problem with the text or just have ideas about how to make the next version of the book better, please drop me a note at *CEBook@DelValle.com*. I can't promise you that I'll answer all your notes, but I will read every one.

Doug Boling
Tahoe City, California
August 1998

Part I

WINDOWS PROGRAMMING BASICS

Chapter 1

Hello Windows CE

From Kernighan and Ritchie to Petzold and on to Prosise, programming books traditionally start with a "hello, world" program. It's a logical place to begin. Every program has a basic underlying structure that, when not obscured by some complex task it was designed to perform, can be analyzed to reveal the foundation shared by all programs running on its operating system.

In this programming book, the "hello, world" chapter covers the details of setting up and using the programming environment. The environment for developing Microsoft Windows CE applications is somewhat different from that for developing standard Microsoft Windows applications because Windows CE programs are written on PCs running Microsoft Windows NT and debugged mainly on separate, Windows CE–based target devices.

While experienced Windows programmers might be tempted to skip this chapter and move on to meatier subjects, I suggest that they—you—at least skim the chapter to note the differences between a standard Windows program and a Windows CE program. A number of subtle and significant differences in both the development process and the basic program skeleton for Windows CE applications are covered in this first chapter.

WHAT IS DIFFERENT ABOUT WINDOWS CE?

Windows CE has a number of unique characteristics that make it different from other Windows platforms. First of all, the systems running Windows CE are most likely not using an Intel x86 compatible microprocessor. Instead, a short list of supported CPUs run Windows CE. Fortunately, the development environment isolates the programmer from almost all of the differences among the various CPUs.

Nor can a Windows CE program be assured of a screen or a keyboard. Some Windows CE devices have a 240-by-320-pixel portrait-style screen while others might have screens with more traditional landscape orientations in 480-by-240, 640-by-240, or 640-by-480-pixel resolution. An embedded device might not have a display at all. The target devices might not support color. And, instead of a mouse, most Windows CE devices have a touch screen. On a touch-screen device, left mouse button clicks are achieved by means of a tap on the screen, but no obvious method exists for delivering right mouse button clicks. To give you some method of delivering a right click, the Windows CE convention is to hold down the Alt key while tapping. It's up to the Windows CE application to interpret this sequence as a right mouse click.

Fewer Resources in Windows CE Devices

The resources of the target devices vary radically across systems that run Windows CE. When writing a standard Windows program, the programmer can make a number of assumptions about the target device, almost always an IBM-compatible PC. The target device will have a hard disk for mass storage and a virtual memory system that uses the hard disk as a swap device to emulate an almost unlimited amount of (virtual) RAM. The programmer knows that the user has a keyboard, a two-button mouse, and a monitor that these days almost assuredly supports 256 colors and a screen resolution of at least 640 by 480 pixels.

Windows CE programs run on devices that almost never have hard disks for mass storage. The absence of a hard disk means more than just not having a place to store large files. Without a hard disk, virtual RAM can't be created by swapping data to the disk. So Windows CE programs are almost always run in a low-memory environment. Memory allocations can, and often do, fail because of the lack of resources. Windows CE might terminate a program automatically when free memory reaches a critically low level. This RAM limitation has a surprisingly large impact on Windows CE programs and is one of the main difficulties involved in porting existing Windows applications to Windows CE.

Unicode

One characteristic that a programmer can count on when writing Windows CE applications is Unicode. Unicode is a standard for representing a character as a 16-bit value as opposed to the ASCII standard of encoding a character into a single 8-bit value. Unicode allows for fairly simple porting of programs to different international markets because all the world's known characters can be represented in one of the 65,536 available Unicode values. Dealing with Unicode is relatively painless as long as you avoid the dual assumptions made by most programmers that strings are represented in ASCII and that characters are stored in single bytes.

A consequence of a program using Unicode is that with each character taking up two bytes instead of one, strings are now twice as long. A programmer must be careful making assumptions about buffer length and string length. No longer should you assume that a 260-byte buffer can hold 259 characters and a terminating zero. Instead of the standard char data type, you should use the TCHAR data type. TCHAR is defined to be char for Microsoft Windows 95 and Microsoft Windows 98 development and unsigned short for Unicode-enabled applications for Microsoft Windows NT and Windows CE development. These types of definitions allow source-level compatibility across ASCII- and Unicode-based operating systems.

New Controls

Windows CE includes a number of new Windows controls designed for specific environments. New controls include the command bar that provides menu- and toolbar-like functions all on one space-saving line, critical on the smaller screens of Windows CE devices. The date and time picker control and calendar control assist calendar and organizer applications suitable for handheld devices, such as the Handheld PC (H/PC) and the Palm-size PC. Other standard Windows controls have reduced function, reflecting the compact nature of Windows CE hardware-specific OS configurations.

Another aspect of Windows CE programming to be aware of is that Windows CE can be broken up and reconfigured by Microsoft or by OEMs so that it can be better adapted to a target market or device. Windows programmers usually just check the version of Windows to see whether it is from the Microsoft Windows 3.1, 95, or 98 line or Windows NT line; by knowing the version they can determine what API functions are available to them. Windows CE, however, has had four variations already in its first two years of existence: the Handheld PC, the Palm-size PC, the Handheld PC Pro, and the Auto PC. A number of new platforms are on their way, with much in common but also with many differences among them. Programmers need to understand the target platform and to have their programs check what functions are available on that particular platform before trying to use a set of functions that might not be supported on that device.

Finally, because Windows CE is so much smaller than Windows 98 or Windows NT, it simply can't support all the function calls that its larger cousins do. While you'd expect an operating system that didn't support printing, such as Windows CE on the original Palm-size PC, not to have any calls to printing functions, Windows CE also removes some redundant functions supported by its larger cousins. If Windows CE doesn't support your favorite function, a different function or set of functions will probably work just as well. Sometimes Windows CE programming seems to consist mainly of figuring out ways to implement a feature using the sparse API of Windows CE. If 2000 functions can be called sparse.

IT'S STILL WINDOWS PROGRAMMING

While differences between Windows CE and the other versions of Windows do exist, they shouldn't be overstated. Programming a Windows CE application is programming a Windows application. It has the same message loop, the same windows, and for the most part, the same resources and the same controls. The differences don't hide the similarities. For those who aren't familiar with Windows programming, here's a short introduction.

Windows programming is far different from MS-DOS–based or Unix-based programming. An MS-DOS or Unix program uses *getc*- and *putc*-style functions to read characters from the keyboard and write them to the screen whenever the program needs to do so. This is the classic "pull" style used by MS-DOS and Unix programs, which are procedural. A Windows program, on the other hand, uses a "push" model, in which the program must be written to react to notifications from the operating system that a key has been pressed or a command has been received to repaint the screen.

Windows applications don't ask for input from the operating system; the operating system notifies the application that input has occurred. The operating system achieves these notifications by sending *messages* to an application window. All windows are specific instances of a *window class*. Before we go any further, let's be sure we understand these terms.

The Window Class

A window is a region on the screen, rectangular in all but the most contrived of cases, that has a few basic parameters, such as position—*x*, *y*, and *z* (a window is over or under other windows on the screen)—visibility, and hierarchy—the window fits into a parent/child window relationship on the system *desktop*, which also happens to be a window.

Every window created is a specific instance of a window class. A window class is a template that defines a number of attributes common to all the windows of that class. In other words, windows of the same class have the same attributes. The most important of the shared attributes is the *window procedure*.

The window procedure

The behavior of all windows belonging to a class is defined by the code in its window procedure for that class. The window procedure handles all notifications and requests sent to the window. These notifications are sent either by the operating system, indicating that an event has occurred to which the window must respond, or by other windows querying the window for information.

These notifications are sent in the form of messages. A message is nothing more than a call being made to a window procedure, with a parameter indicating the nature of the notification or request. Messages are sent for events such as a window being moved or resized or to indicate a key press. The values used to indicate messages are defined by Windows. Applications use predefined constants, such as WM_CREATE or WM_MOVE, when referring to messages. Since hundreds of messages can be sent, Windows conveniently provides a default processing function to which a message can be passed when no special processing is necessary by the window class for that message.

The life of a message

Stepping back for a moment, let's look at how Windows coordinates all of the messages going to all of the windows in a system. Windows monitors all the sources of input to the system, such as the keyboard, mouse, touch screen, and any other hardware that could produce an event that might interest a window. As an event occurs, a message is composed and directed to a specific window. Instead of Windows directly calling the window procedure, the system imposes an intermediate step. The message is placed in a message queue for the application that owns the window. When the application is prepared to receive the message, it pulls it out of the queue and tells Windows to dispatch that message to the proper window in the application.

If it seems to you that a number of indirections are involved in that process, you're right. Let's break it down.

1. An event occurs, so a message is composed by Windows and placed in a message queue for the application that owns the destination window. In Windows CE, as in Windows 95 and Windows NT, each application has its own unique message queue[1]. (This is a break from Windows 3.1 and earlier versions of Windows, where there was only one, systemwide message queue.) Events can occur, and therefore messages can be composed, faster than an application can process them. The queue allows an application to process messages at its own rate, although the application had better be responsive or the user will see a jerkiness in the application. The message queue also allows Windows to set a notification in motion and continue with other tasks without having to be limited by the responsiveness of the application to which the message is being sent.

2. The application removes the message from its message queue and calls Windows back to dispatch the message. While it may seem strange that the application gets a message from the queue and then simply calls Windows back to process the message, there's a method to this madness. Having the application pull the message from the queue allows it to preprocess the message before it asks Windows to dispatch the message to

---

1. Technically, each thread in a Windows CE application can have a message queue. I'll talk about threads later in the book.

the appropriate window. In a number of cases, the application might call different functions in Windows to process specific kinds of messages.

3. Windows dispatches the message; that is, it calls the appropriate window procedure. Instead of having the application directly call the window procedure, another level of indirection occurs, allowing Windows to coordinate the call to the window procedure with other events in the system. The message doesn't stand in another queue at this point, but Windows might need to make some preparations before calling the window procedure. In any case, the scheme relieves the application of the obligation to determine the proper destination window—Windows does this instead.

4. The window procedure processes the message. All window procedures have the same calling parameters: the handle of the specific window instance being called, the message, and two generic parameters that contain data specific to each message type. The window handle differentiates each instance of a window for the window procedure. The message parameter, of course, indicates the event that the window must react to. The two generic parameters contain data specific to the message being sent. For example, in a WM_MOVE message indicating that the window is about to be moved, one of the generic parameters points to a structure containing the new coordinates of the window.

Your First Program

Enough small talk. It's time to jump into the first example, Hello Windows CE. While the entire program files for this and all examples in the book are available on the companion CD-ROM, I suggest that, at least in this one case, you avoid simply loading the project file from the CD and instead type in the entire example by hand. By performing this somewhat tedious task, you'll see the differences in the development process as well as the subtle program differences between standard Win32 programs and Windows CE programs. Figure 1-1 contains the complete source for HelloCE, my version of a hello, world program.

HelloCE.h

```
//======================================================================
// Header file
//
// Written for the book Programming Windows CE
// Copyright (C) 1998 Douglas Boling
//
```

Figure 1-1. *The HelloCE program.*

```
//======================================================================
// Returns number of elements
#define dim(x) (sizeof(x) / sizeof(x[0]))

//----------------------------------------------------------------------
// Generic defines and data types
//
struct decodeUINT {                             // Structure associates
    UINT Code;                                  // messages
                                                // with a function.
    LRESULT (*Fxn)(HWND, UINT, WPARAM, LPARAM);
};
struct decodeCMD {                              // Structure associates
    UINT Code;                                  // menu IDs with a
    LRESULT (*Fxn)(HWND, WORD, HWND, WORD);     // function
};

//----------------------------------------------------------------------
// Generic defines used by application
#define  IDC_CMDBAR 1                           // Command bar ID

//----------------------------------------------------------------------
// Function prototypes
//
int InitApp (HINSTANCE);
HWND InitInstance (HINSTANCE, LPWSTR, int);
int TermInstance (HINSTANCE, int);

// Window procedures
LRESULT CALLBACK MainWndProc (HWND, UINT, WPARAM, LPARAM);

// Message handlers
LRESULT DoCreateMain (HWND, UINT, WPARAM, LPARAM);
LRESULT DoPaintMain (HWND, UINT, WPARAM, LPARAM);
LRESULT DoHibernateMain (HWND, UINT, WPARAM, LPARAM);
LRESULT DoActivateMain (HWND, UINT, WPARAM, LPARAM);
LRESULT DoDestroyMain (HWND, UINT, WPARAM, LPARAM);
```

HelloCE.c

```
//======================================================================
// HelloCE - A simple application for Windows CE
//
// Written for the book Programming Windows CE
// Copyright (C) 1998 Douglas Boling
```

(continued)

Figure 1-1. *continued*

```
//
//======================================================================
#include <windows.h>                    // For all that Windows stuff
#include <commctrl.h>                   // command bar includes
#include "helloce.h"                    // Program-specific stuff

//----------------------------------------------------------------------
// Global data
//
const TCHAR szAppName[] = TEXT("HelloCE");
HINSTANCE hInst;                        // Program instance handle

// Message dispatch table for MainWindowProc
const struct decodeUINT MainMessages[] = {
    WM_CREATE, DoCreateMain,
    WM_PAINT, DoPaintMain,
    WM_HIBERNATE, DoHibernateMain,
    WM_ACTIVATE, DoActivateMain,
    WM_DESTROY, DoDestroyMain,
};

//======================================================================
//
// Program entry point
//
int WINAPI WinMain (HINSTANCE hInstance, HINSTANCE hPrevInstance,
                    LPWSTR lpCmdLine, int nCmdShow) {
    MSG msg;
    int rc = 0;
    HWND hwndMain;

    // Initialize application.
    rc = InitApp (hInstance);
    if (rc) return rc;

    // Initialize this instance.
    hwndMain = InitInstance (hInstance, lpCmdLine, nCmdShow);
    if (hwndMain == 0)
        return 0x10;

    // Application message loop
    while (GetMessage (&msg, NULL, 0, 0)) {
        TranslateMessage (&msg);
        DispatchMessage (&msg);
    }
    // Instance cleanup
    return TermInstance (hInstance, msg.wParam);
```

```
}
//----------------------------------------------------------------------
// InitApp - Application initialization
//
int InitApp (HINSTANCE hInstance) {
    WNDCLASS wc;

    // Register application main window class.
    wc.style = 0;                             // Window style
    wc.lpfnWndProc = MainWndProc;             // Callback function
    wc.cbClsExtra = 0;                        // Extra class data
    wc.cbWndExtra = 0;                        // Extra window data
    wc.hInstance = hInstance;                 // Owner handle
    wc.hIcon = NULL,                          // Application icon
    wc.hCursor = NULL;                        // Default cursor
    wc.hbrBackground = (HBRUSH) GetStockObject (WHITE_BRUSH);
    wc.lpszMenuName =  NULL;                  // Menu name
    wc.lpszClassName = szAppName;             // Window class name

    if (RegisterClass (&wc) == 0) return 1;

    return 0;
}
//----------------------------------------------------------------------
// InitInstance - Instance initialization
//
HWND InitInstance (HINSTANCE hInstance, LPWSTR lpCmdLine, int nCmdShow) {
    HWND hWnd;

    // Save program instance handle in global variable.
    hInst = hInstance;

    // Create main window.
    hWnd = CreateWindow (szAppName,           // Window class
                         TEXT("Hello"),       // Window title
                         WS_VISIBLE,          // Style flags
                         CW_USEDEFAULT,       // x position
                         CW_USEDEFAULT,       // y position
                         CW_USEDEFAULT,       // Initial width
                         CW_USEDEFAULT,       // Initial height
                         NULL,                // Parent
                         NULL,                // Menu, must be null
                         hInstance,           // Application instance
                         NULL);               // Pointer to create
                                              // parameters
```

(continued)

Figure 1-1. *continued*

```
    // Return fail code if window not created.
    if (!IsWindow (hWnd)) return 0;

    // Standard show and update calls
    ShowWindow (hWnd, nCmdShow);
    UpdateWindow (hWnd);
    return hWnd;
}
//----------------------------------------------------------------------
// TermInstance - Program cleanup
//
int TermInstance (HINSTANCE hInstance, int nDefRC) {

    return nDefRC;
}
//======================================================================
// Message handling procedures for main window
//

//----------------------------------------------------------------------
// MainWndProc - Callback function for application window
//
LRESULT CALLBACK MainWndProc (HWND hWnd, UINT wMsg, WPARAM wParam,
                              LPARAM lParam) {
    INT i;
    //
    // Search message list to see if we need to handle this
    // message.  If in list, call procedure.
    //
    for (i = 0; i < dim(MainMessages); i++) {
        if (wMsg == MainMessages[i].Code)
            return (*MainMessages[i].Fxn)(hWnd, wMsg, wParam, lParam);
    }
    return DefWindowProc (hWnd, wMsg, wParam, lParam);
}
//----------------------------------------------------------------------
// DoCreateMain - Process WM_CREATE message for window.
//
LRESULT DoCreateMain (HWND hWnd, UINT wMsg, WPARAM wParam,
                      LPARAM lParam) {
    HWND hwndCB;

    // Create a command bar.
    hwndCB = CommandBar_Create (hInst, hWnd, IDC_CMDBAR);
```

```
    // Add exit button to command bar.
    CommandBar_AddAdornments (hwndCB, 0, 0);
    return 0;
}
//----------------------------------------------------------------------
// DoPaintMain - Process WM_PAINT message for window.
//
LRESULT DoPaintMain (HWND hWnd, UINT wMsg, WPARAM wParam,
                     LPARAM lParam) {
    PAINTSTRUCT ps;
    RECT rect;
    HDC hdc;

    // Adjust the size of the client rectangle to take into account
    // the command bar height.
    GetClientRect (hWnd, &rect);
    rect.top += CommandBar_Height (GetDlgItem (hWnd, IDC_CMDBAR));

    hdc = BeginPaint (hWnd, &ps);
    DrawText (hdc, TEXT ("Hello Windows CE!"), -1, &rect,
              DT_CENTER | DT_VCENTER | DT_SINGLELINE);

    EndPaint (hWnd, &ps);
    return 0;
}
//----------------------------------------------------------------------
// DoHibernateMain - Process WM_HIBERNATE message for window.
//
LRESULT DoHibernateMain (HWND hWnd, UINT wMsg, WPARAM wParam,
                         LPARAM lParam) {

    // If not the active window, nuke the command bar to save memory.
    if (GetActiveWindow() != hWnd)
        CommandBar_Destroy (GetDlgItem (hWnd, IDC_CMDBAR));

    return 0;
}
//----------------------------------------------------------------------
// DoActivateMain - Process WM_ACTIVATE message for window.
//
LRESULT DoActivateMain (HWND hWnd, UINT wMsg, WPARAM wParam,
                        LPARAM lParam) {
    HWND hwndCB;
```

(continued)

Figure 1-1. *continued*

```
    // If activating and no command bar, create it.
    if ((LOWORD (wParam) != WA_INACTIVE) &&
        (GetDlgItem (hWnd, IDC_CMDBAR) == 0)) {

        // Create a command bar.
        hwndCB = CommandBar_Create (hInst, hWnd, IDC_CMDBAR);

        // Add exit button to command bar.
        CommandBar_AddAdornments (hwndCB, 0, 0);
    }
    return 0;
}
//----------------------------------------------------------------------
// DoDestroyMain - Process WM_DESTROY message for window.
//
LRESULT DoDestroyMain (HWND hWnd, UINT wMsg, WPARAM wParam,
                       LPARAM lParam) {
    PostQuitMessage (0);
    return 0;
}
```

If you look over the source code for HelloCE, you'll see the standard boilerplate for all programs in this book. I'll talk at greater length about a few of the characteristics, such as Hungarian notation and the somewhat different method I use to construct my window procedures later, in their own sections, but at this point I'll make just a few observations about them.

Just after the comments, you see the include of windows.h. You can find this file in all Windows programs; it lists the definitions for the special variable types and function defines needed for a typical program. Windows.h and the include files it contains make an interesting read because the basics for all windows programs come from the functions, typedefs, and structures defined there. The include of commctrl.h provides, among other things, the definitions for the command bar functions that are part of almost all Windows CE programs. Finally, the include of HelloCE.h gives you the boilerplate definitions and function prototypes for this specific program.

A few variables defined globally follow the defines and includes. I know plenty of good arguments why no global variables should appear in a program, but I use them as a convenience that shortens and clarifies the example programs in the book. Each program defines an *szAppName* Unicode string to be used in various places in that program. I also use the *hInst* variable a number of places and I'll mention it when I cover the *InitApp* procedure. The final global structure is a list of messages along with associated procedures to process the messages. This structure is used by the window procedure to associate messages with the procedure that handles them. Now, on to a few other characteristics common to all the programs in this book.

Hungarian Notation

A tradition, and a good one, of almost all Windows programs since Charles Petzold wrote *Programming Windows* is Hungarian notation. This programming style, developed years ago by Charles Simonyi at Microsoft, prefixes all variables in the program usually with one or two letters indicating the variable type. For example, a string array called *Name* would instead be called *szName*, with the *sz* prefix indicating that the variable type is a zero-terminated string. The value of Hungarian notation is the dramatic improvement in readability of the source code. Another programmer, or you after not looking at a piece of code for a while, won't have to look repeatedly at a variable's declaration to determine its type. The following are typical Hungarian prefixes for variables:

Variable Type	*Hungarian Prefix*
Integer	*i* or *n*
Word (16-bit)	*w* or *s*
Double word (32-bit unsigned)	*dw*
Long (32-bit signed)	*l*
Char	*c*
String	*sz*
Pointer	*p*
Long pointer	*lp*
Handle	*h*
Window handle	*hwnd*
Struct size	*cb*

You can see a few vestiges of the early days of Windows. The *lp*, or long pointer, designation refers to the days when, in the Intel 16-bit programming model, pointers were either short (a 16-bit offset) or long (a segment plus an offset). Other prefixes are formed from the abbreviation of the type. For example, a handle to a brush is typically specified as *hbr*. Prefixes can be combined, as in *lpsz*, which designates a long pointer to a zero-terminated string. Most of the structures defined in the Windows API use Hungarian notation in their field names. I use this notation as well throughout the book, and I encourage you to use this notation in your programs.

My Programming Style

One criticism of the typical SDK style of Windows programming has always been the huge *switch* statement in the window procedure. The *switch* statement parses the message to the window procedure so that each message can be handled independently. This standard structure has the one great advantage of enforcing a similar structure across almost all Windows applications, making it much easier for one programmer to understand the workings of another programmer's code. The disadvantage is that all the variables for the entire window procedure typically appear jumbled at the top of the procedure.

Over the years, I've developed a different style for my Windows programs. The idea is to break up the *WinMain* and *WinProc* procedures into manageable units that can be easily understood and easily transferred to other Windows programs. *WinMain* is broken up into procedures that perform application initialization, instance initialization, and instance termination. Also in *WinMain* is the ubiquitous message loop that's the core of all Windows programs.

I break the window procedure into individual procedures, with each handling a specific message. What remains of the window procedure itself is a fragment of code that simply looks up the message that's being passed to see whether a procedure has been written to handle that message. If so, that procedure is called. If not, the message is passed to the default window procedure.

This structure divides the handling of messages into individual blocks that can be more easily understood. Also, with greater isolation of one message-handling code fragment from another, you can more easily transfer the code that handles a specific message from one program to the next. I first saw this structure described a number of years ago by Ray Duncan in one of his old "Power Programming" columns in *PC Magazine*. Ray is one of the legends in the field of MS-DOS and OS/2 programming. I've since modified the design a bit to fit my needs, but Ray should get the credit for this program structure.

Building HelloCE

To create HelloCE from scratch on your system, start Microsoft Visual C++ and create a new Win32 application. The first change from standard Win32 programming becomes evident when you create the new project. You'll have the opportunity to select a new platform specific to Windows CE, as shown in Figure 1-2. These platforms have a WCE prefix followed by the target CPU. For example, selecting Win32 (WCE MIPS) enables compiling to a Windows CE platform with a MIPS CPU. No matter what target device you have, be sure to check the WCE x86em target. This allows you to run the sample program in the emulator under Windows NT.

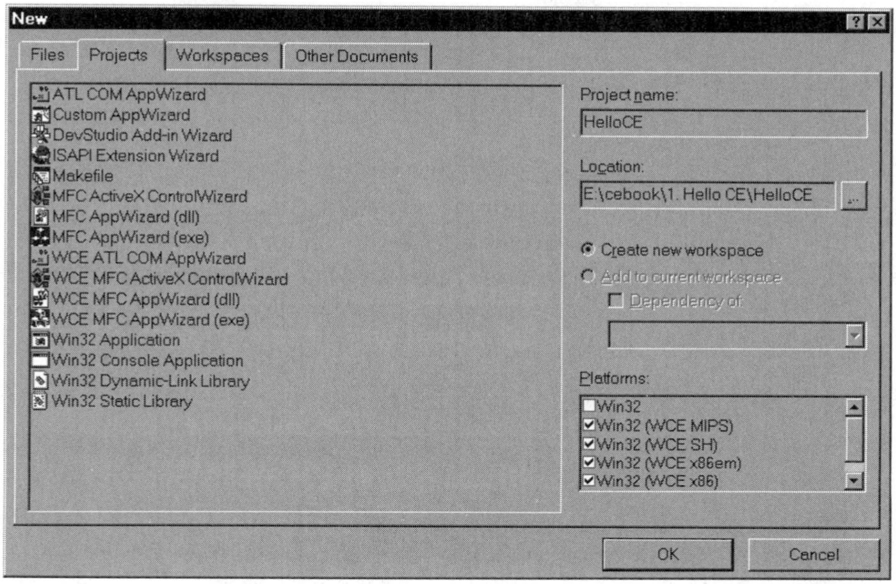

Figure 1-2. *The Platforms list box allows Visual C++ 5.0 to target Windows CE platforms.*

After you have created the proper source files for HelloCE or copied them from the CD, select the target Win32 (WCE x86em) Debug and then build the program. This step compiles the source and, assuming you have no compile errors, automatically launches the emulator and inserts the EXE into the emulator file system; you can then launch HelloCE. If you're running Windows 95 or Windows 98, the system displays an error message because the emulator runs only under Windows NT.

If you have a Windows CE system available, such as an H/PC, attach the H/PC to the PC the same way you would to sync the contents of the H/PC with the PC. Open the Mobile Devices folder and establish a connection between the H/PC and the PC. While it's not strictly necessary to have the Mobile Devices connection to your Windows CE device running because the SDK tools inside Visual C++ are supposed to make this connection automatically, I've found that having it running makes for a more stable connection between the development environment and the Windows CE system.

Once the link between the PC and the Windows CE device is up and running, switch back to Visual C++, select the compile target appropriate for the target device (for example, Win32 [WCE SH] Debug for an HP 360 HPC), and rebuild. As in the case of building for the emulator, if there are no errors Visual C++ automatically downloads the compiled program to the remote device. The program is placed in the root directory of the object store.

Running the program

To run HelloCE on an H/PC, simply click on the My Handheld PC icon to bring up the files in the root directory. At that point, a double-tap on the application's icon launches the program.

Running the program on a Palm-size PC is somewhat more complex. Because the Palm-size PC doesn't come with an Explorer program that allows users to browse through the files on the system, you can't launch HelloCE without a bit of preparatory work. You can launch the program from Visual C++ by selecting Execute from the Build menu. Or you can have Visual C++ automatically copy the executable file into the \windows\start menu\programs directory of the Palm-size PC. This automatically places the program in the Programs submenu under the Start menu. You can tell Visual C++ to automatically copy the file by setting the remote target path in the Debug tab of the Project Settings dialog box. Figure 1-3 shows this dialog box. When you've set this path, you can easily start the program by selecting it in the Start menu.

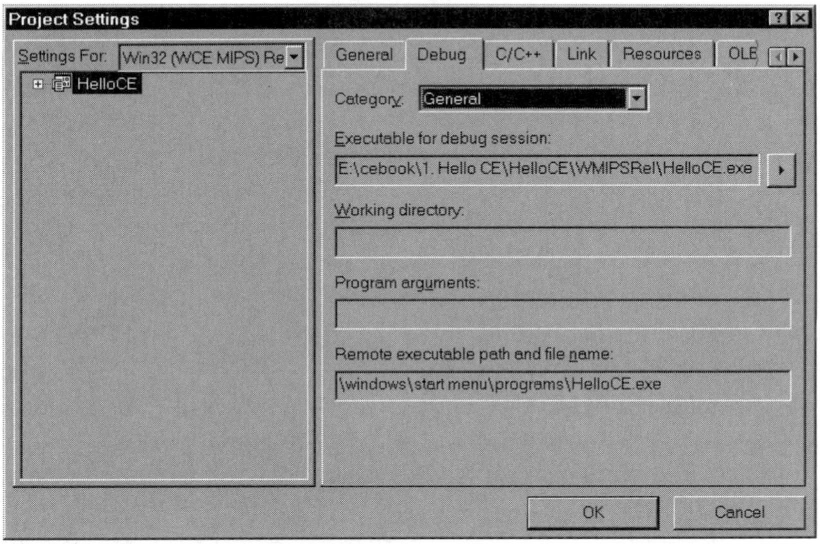

Figure 1-3. *The Project Settings dialog box in Visual C++ with the Debug tab selected.*

One "gotcha" to look out for here. If you're debugging and recompiling the program, it can't be downloaded again if an earlier version of the program is still running on the target system. That is, make sure HelloCE isn't running on the remote system when you start a new build in Visual C++ or the auto download part of the compile process will fail. If this happens, close the application and choose the Update Remote File menu command in Visual C++ to download the newly compiled file.

Palm-size PC users will notice that unlike almost all Palm-size PC programs, HelloCE has a Close button in the upper right corner of the window. By convention, the user doesn't close Palm-size PC applications; they're closed only when the system needs more memory space. The lack of a Close button in Palm-size PC applications is only a user interface guideline, not a lack of function of the version of Windows CE in the Palm-size PC. For development, you might want to keep a Close button in your application because you'll need to close the program to download a new version. You can then remove the Close button before you ship your application.

If you don't have access to an H/PC or if you want to check out Windows CE programming without the hassle of connecting to a remote device, the emulation environment is a great place to start. It's the perfect place for stepping though the code just as you would were you debugging a standard PC-based Windows program. You can set breakpoints and step though code running on a remote system, but the slow nature of the serial link as well as the difficulty in single-stepping a program on the remote system make debugging on the emulator much less painful. On the other hand, debugging on the remote system is the only way to truly test your program. While the emulator is a good first step in the debug process, nothing replaces testing on the target system.

The code

Now that you have the program up and running either in the emulator or on a Windows CE device, it's time to look at the code itself. The program entry point, *WinMain*, is the same place any Windows program begins. Under Windows CE, however, some of the parameters for *WinMain* have limits to the allowable values. *WinMain* is defined as the following:

```
int WINAPI WinMain (HINSTANCE hInstance, HINSTANCE hPrevInstance,
                    LPWSTR lpCmdLine, int nCmdShow);
```

The first of the four parameters passed, *hInstance,* identifies the specific instance of the program to other applications and to Windows API functions that need to identify the EXE. The *hPrevInstance* parameter is left over from the old Win16 API (Windows 3.1 and earlier). In those versions of Windows, the *hPrevInstance* parameter was nonzero if there were any other instances of the program currently running. In all Win32 operating systems, including Windows CE, the *hPrevInstance* is always 0 and can be ignored.

The *lCmdLine* parameter points to a Unicode string that contains the text of the command line. Applications launched from Microsoft Windows Explorer usually have no command line parameters. But in some instances, such as when the system automatically launches a program, the system includes a command line parameter to indicate why the program was started. The *lCmdLine* parameter provides us with one of the first instances in which Windows CE differs from Windows NT or Windows 98. Under Windows CE, the command line string is a Unicode string. In Windows NT and Windows 98, the string is always ASCII.

The final parameter, *nShowCmd,* specifies the initial state of the program's main window. In a standard Win32 program, this parameter might specify that the window be initially displayed as an icon (SW_SHOWMINIMIZE), maximized (SW_SHOWMAXIMIZED) to cover the entire desktop, or normal (SW_RESTORE), indicating that the window is placed on the screen in the standard resizable state. Other values specify that the initial state of the window should be invisible to the user or that the window be visible but incapable of becoming the active window. Under Windows CE, the values for this parameter are limited to only three allowable states: normal (SW_SHOW), hidden (SW_HIDE), or show without activate (SW_SHOWNOACTIVATE). Unless an application needs to force its window to a predefined state, this parameter is simply passed without modification to the *ShowWindow* function after the program's main window has been created.

On entry into *WinMain*, a call is made to *InitApp*, where the window class for the main window is registered. After that, a call to *InitInstance* is made; the main window is created in this function. I'll talk about how these two routines operate shortly, but for now I'll continue with *WinMain,* proceeding on the assumption that at the return from *InitInstance* the program's main window has been created.

The message loop

After the main window has been created, *WinMain* enters the message loop, which is the heart of every Windows application. HelloCE's message loop is shown here:

```
while (GetMessage (&msg, NULL, 0, 0)) {
    TranslateMessage (&msg);
    DispatchMessage (&msg);
}
```

The loop is simple: *GetMessage* is called to get the next message in the application's message queue. If no message is available, the call waits, blocking that application's thread until one is available. When a message is available, the call returns with the message data contained in a MSG structure. The MSG structure itself contains fields that identify the message, provide any message-specific parameters, and identify the last point on the screen touched by the pen before the message was sent. This location information is different from the standard Win32 message point data in that in Windows 9*x* or Windows NT the point returned is the current mouse position instead of the last point clicked (or tapped, as in Windows CE).

The *TranslateMessage* function translates appropriate keyboard messages into a character message. (I'll talk about others of these filter type messages, such as

IsDialogMsg, later.) The *DispatchMessage* function then tells Windows to forward the message to the appropriate window in the application.

This *GetMessage*, *TranslateMessage*, *DispatchMessage* loop continues until *GetMessage* receives a WM_QUIT message which, unlike all other messages causes *GetMessage* to return 0. As can be seen from the *while* clause, a return value of 0 by *GetMessage* causes the loop to terminate.

After the message loop terminates, the program can do little else but clean up and exit. In the case of HelloCE, the program calls *TermInstance* to perform any necessary cleanup. HelloCE is a simple program and no cleanup is required. In more complex programs, *TermInstance* would free any system resources that aren't automatically freed when the program terminates.

The value returned by *WinMain* becomes the return code of the program. Traditionally, the return value is the value in the *wParam* parameter of the last message (WM_QUIT). The *wParam* value of WM_QUIT is set when that message is sent in response to a *PostQuitMessage* call made by the application.

InitApp

The goal of *InitApp* is to perform global initialization for all instances of the application that might run. In practice, *InitApp* is a holdover from Win16 days when window classes were registered on an applicationwide basis instead of for every instance, as is done under Win32. Still, having a place for global initialization can have its uses in some applications. For a program as simple as HelloCE, the entire task of *InitApp* can be reduced to registering the application's main window class. The entire procedure is listed below:

```
int InitApp (HINSTANCE hInstance) {
    WNDCLASS wc;

    // Register App Main Window class.
    wc.style = 0;                         // Class style flags
    wc.lpfnWndProc = MainWndProc;         // Callback function
    wc.cbClsExtra = 0;                    // Extra class data
    wc.cbWndExtra = 0;                    // Extra window data
    wc.hInstance = hInstance;             // Owner handle
    wc.hIcon = NULL;                      // Application icon
    wc.hCursor = NULL;                    // Default cursor
    wc.hbrBackground = (HBRUSH) = GetStockObject (WHITE_BRUSH);
    wc.lpszMenuName =  NULL;              // Must be NULL
    wc.lpszClassName = szAppName;         // Class name

    if (RegisterClass (&wc) == 0) return 1;

    return 0;
}
```

Registering a window class is simply a matter of filling out a rather extensive structure describing the class and calling the *RegisterClass* function. The parameters assigned to the fields of the WNDCLASS structure define how all instances of the main window for HelloCE will behave. The initial field, *style*, sets the class style for the window. In Windows CE the class styles are limited to the following:

- CS_GLOBALCLASS indicates that the class is global. This flag is provided only for compatibility because all window classes in Windows CE are process global.
- CS_HREDRAW tells the system to force a repaint of the window if the window is sized horizontally.
- CS_VREDRAW tells the system to force a repaint of the window if the window is sized vertically.
- CS_NOCLOSE disables the Close button if one is present on the title bar.
- CS_PARENTDC causes a window to use its parent's device context.
- CS_DBLCLKS enables notification of double-clicks (double-taps under Windows CE) to be passed to the parent window.

The *lpfnWndProc* field should be loaded with the address of the window's window procedure. Because this field is typed as a pointer to a window procedure, the declaration to the procedure must be defined in the source code before the field is set. Otherwise, the compiler's type-checker will flag this line with a warning.

The *cbClsExtra* field allows the programmer to add extra space in the class structure to store class-specific data known only to the application. The *cbWndExtra* field is much handier. This field adds space to the Windows internal structure responsible for maintaining the state of each instance of a window. Instead of storing large amounts of data in the window structure itself, an application should store a pointer to an application-specific structure that contains the data unique to each instance of the window. Under Windows CE, both the *cbClsExtra* and *cbWndExtra* fields must be multiples of 4 bytes.

The *hInstance* field must be filled with the program's instance handle, which specifies the owning process of the window. The *hIcon* field is set to the handle of the window's default icon. The *hIcon* field isn't supported under Windows CE and should be set to NULL. (In Windows CE, the icon for the class is set after the first window of this class is created. For HelloCE, however, no icon is supplied and unlike other versions of Windows, Windows CE doesn't have any predefined icons that can be loaded.)

Unless the application being developed is designed for a Windows CE system with a mouse, the next field, *hCursor*, must be set to NULL. Almost all Windows CE systems use a touch panel instead of a mouse, so you find no cursor support in those systems. For those special systems that do have cursor support, the Windows CE doesn't support animated cursors or colored cursors.

The *hbrBackground* field specifies how Windows CE draws the background of the window. Windows uses the *brush*, a small predefined array of pixels, specified in this field to draw the background of the window. Windows CE provides a number of predefined brushes that you can load using the *GetStockObject* function. If the *hbrBackground* field is NULL, the window must handle the WM_ERASEBKGND message sent to the window telling it to redraw the background of the window.

The *lpszMenuName* field must be set to NULL because Windows CE doesn't support windows directly having a menu. In Windows CE, menus are provided by command bar or command band controls that can be created by the main window.

Finally the *lpszClassName* parameter is set to a programmer-defined string that identifies the class name to Windows. HelloCE uses the *szAppName* string, which is defined globally.

After the entire WNDCLASS structure has been filled out, the *RegisterClass* function is called with a pointer to the WNDCLASS structure as its only parameter. If the function is successful, a value identifying the window class is returned. If the function fails, the function returns 0.

InitInstance

The main task of *InitInstance* is to create the application's main window and display it in the form specified in the *nShowCmd* parameter passed to *WinMain*. The code for *InitInstance* is shown below:

```
HWND InitInstance (HINSTANCE hInstance, LPWSTR lpCmdLine, int nCmdShow) {
    HWND hWnd;
    HICON hIcon;

    // Save program instance handle in global variable.
    hInst = hInstance;

    // Create main window.
    hWnd = CreateWindow (szAppName,           // Window class
                         TEXT("Hello"),       // Window title
                         WS_VISIBLE,          // Style flags
                         0, 0,                // x, y position
                         CW_USEDEFAULT,       // Initial width
```

(continued)

```
                              CW_USEDEFAULT,       // Initial height
                              NULL,                // Parent
                              NULL,                // Menu, must be null
                              hInstance,           // App instance
                              NULL);               // Ptr to create params
    // Return fail code if window not created.
    if (!IsWindow (hWnd)) return 0;

    // Standard show and update calls
    ShowWindow (hWnd, nCmdShow);
    UpdateWindow (hWnd);

    return hWnd;
}
```

The first task performed by *InitInstance* is to save the program's instance handle *hInstance* in a global variable named *hInst*. The instance handle for a program is useful at a number of points in a Windows application. I save the value here because the instance handle is known, and this is a convenient place in the program to store it.

All Windows programmers learn early in their Windows programming lives the *CreateWindow* function call. Although the number of parameters looks daunting, the parameters are fairly logical once you learn them. The first parameter is the name of the window class of which our window will be an instance. In the case of HelloCE, the class name is a string constant, *szAppName,* which was also used in the WNDCLASS structure.

The next field is referred to as the *window text*. In other versions of Windows, this is the text that would appear on the title bar of a standard window. However, since Windows CE main windows rarely have title bars, this text is used only on the taskbar button for the window. The text is couched in a TEXT macro, which insures that the string will be converted to Unicode under Windows CE.

The style flags specify the initial styles for the window. The style flags are used both for general styles that are relevant to all windows in the system and for class-specific styles, such as those that specify the style of a button or a list box. In this case, all we need to specify is that the window be created initially visible with the WS_VISIBLE flag. Experienced Win32 programmers should refer to the documentation for *CreateWindow* because there are a number of window style flags that aren't supported under Windows CE.

The next four fields specify the initial position and size of the window. Since most applications under Windows CE are maximized (that is, they take up the entire screen above the taskbar), the size and position fields are set to default values, which are indicated by the CW_USEDEFAULT flag in each of the fields. The default value settings create a window that's maximized under the current versions of Windows CE but also compatible with future versions of the operating system, which might not maximize every window. Be careful not to assume any particular screen size for a Windows CE device because different implementations have different screen sizes.

The next field is set to the handle of the parent window. Because this is the top-level window, the parent window field is set to NULL. The menu field is also set to NULL because Windows CE supports menus through the command bar and command bands controls.

The *hInstance* parameter is the same instance handle that was passed to the program. Creating windows is one place where that instance handle, saved at the start of the routine, comes in handy. The final parameter is a pointer that can be used to pass data from the *CreateWindow* call to the window procedure during the WM_CREATE message. In this example, no additional data needs to be passed, so the parameter is set to NULL.

If successful, the *CreateWindow* call returns the handle to the window just created, or it returns 0 if an error occurred during the function. That window handle is then used in the two statements (*ShowWindow* and *UpdateWindow*) just after the error-checking *if* statement. The *ShowWindow* function modifies the state of the window to conform with the state given in the *nCmdShow* parameter passed to *WinMain*. The *UpdateWindow* function forces Windows to send a WM_PAINT message to the window that has just been created.

That completes the *InitApp* function. At this point, the application's main window has been created and updated. So even before we have entered the message loop, messages have been sent to the main window's window procedure. It's about time to look at this part of the program.

MainWndProc

You spend most of your programming time with the window procedure when you're writing a Windows program. *WinMain* contains mainly initialization and cleanup code that, for the most part, is boilerplate. The window procedure, on the other hand, is the core of the program, the place where the actions of the program's windows create the personality of the program.

```
LRESULT CALLBACK MainWndProc(HWND hWnd, UINT wMsg, WPARAM wParam,
                             LPARAM lParam) {
    INT i;
    //
    // Search message list to see if we need to handle this
    // message.  If in list, call procedure.
    //
    for (i = 0; i < dim(MainMessages); i++) {
        if (wMsg == MainMessages[i].Code)
            return (*MainMessages[i].Fxn)(hWnd, wMsg, wParam, lParam);
    }
    return DefWindowProc(hWnd, wMsg, wParam, lParam);
}
```

All window procedures, regardless of their window class, are declared with the same parameters. The LRESULT return type is actually just a long (a *long* is a 32-bit value under Windows) but is typed this way to provide a level of indirection between the source code and the machine. While you can easily look into the include files to determine the real type of variables that are used in Windows programming, this can cause problems when you're attempting to move your code across platforms. Though it can be useful to know the size of a variable type for memory-use calculations, there is no good reason, and there are plenty of bad ones, not to use the type definitions provided by windows.h.

The CALLBACK type definition specifies that this function is an external entry point into the EXE, necessary because Windows calls this procedure directly, and that the parameters will be put in a Pascal-like right-to-left push onto the program stack, which is the reverse of the standard C-language method. The reason for using the Pascal language stack frame for external entry points goes back to the very earliest days of Windows development. The use of a fixed-size, Pascal stack frame meant that the called procedure cleaned up the stack instead of leaving it for the caller to do. This reduced the code size of Windows and its bundled accessory programs sufficiently so that the early Microsoft developers thought it was a good move.

The first of the parameters passed to the window procedure is the window handle, which is useful when you need to define the specific instance of the window. The *wMsg* parameter indicates the message being sent to the window. This isn't the MSG structure used in the message loop in *WinMain*, but a simple, unsigned integer containing the message value. The remaining two parameters, *wParam* and *lParam*, are used to pass message-specific data to the window procedure. The names *wParam* and *lParam* come to us from the Win16 days, when the *wParam* was a 16-bit value and *lParam* was a 32-bit value. In Windows CE, as in other Win32 operating systems, both the *wParam* and *lParam* parameters are 32 bits wide.

It's in the window procedure that my programming style differs significantly from most Windows programs written without the help of a class library such as MFC. For almost all of my programs, the window procedure is identical to the one shown above. Before continuing, I repeat: this program structure isn't specific to Windows CE. I use this style for all my Windows applications, whether they are for Windows 3.1, Windows 95, Windows NT, or Windows CE.

This style reduces the window procedure to a simple table look-up function. The idea is to scan the *MainMessages* table defined early in the C file for the message value in one of the entries. If the message is found, the associated procedure is then called, passing the original parameters to the procedure processing the message. If no match is found for the message, the *DefWindowProc* function is called. *DefWindowProc* is a Windows function that provides a default action for all messages in the system, which frees a Windows program from having to process every message being passed to a window.

The message table associates message values with a procedure to process it. The table is listed below:

```
// Message dispatch table for MainWindowProc
const struct decodeUINT MainMessages[] = {
    WM_CREATE, DoCreateMain,
    WM_PAINT, DoPaintMain,
    WM_HIBERNATE, DoHibernateMain,
    WM_DESTROY, DoDestroyMain,
};
```

The table is defined as a constant, not just as good programming practice but also because it's helpful for memory conservation. Since Windows CE programs can be executed in place in ROM, data that doesn't change should be marked constant. This allows the Windows CE program loader to leave such constant data in ROM instead of loading a copy into RAM so that it can be modified later by the program.

The table itself is an array of a simple two-element structure. The first entry is the message value, followed by a pointer to the function that processes the message. While the functions could be named anything, I'm using a consistent structure throughout the book to help you keep track of them. The names are composed of a *Do* prefix (as a bow to object-oriented practice), followed by the message name and a suffix indicating the window class associated with the table. So, *DoCreateMain* is the name of the function that processes WM_CREATE messages for the main window of the program.

DoCreateMain

The WM_CREATE message is the first message sent to a window. WM_CREATE is unique among messages in that Windows sends it while processing the *CreateWindow* function, and therefore the window has yet to be completely created. This is a good place in the code to perform any data initialization for the window. But since the window is still being created, some Windows functions, such as *GetWindowRect,* used to query the size and position of the window, return inaccurate values. For our purposes, the procedure shown in the following code performs only one function: it creates a command bar for the window.

```
LRESULT DoCreateMain (HWND hWnd, UINT wMsg, WPARAM wParam,
                      LPARAM lParam) {
    HWND hwndCB;

    // Create a command bar.
    hwndCB = CommandBar_Create (hInst, hWnd, IDC_CMDBAR);

    // Add exit button to command bar.
    CommandBar_AddAdornments (hwndCB, 0, 0);
    return 0;
}
```

Because Windows CE windows don't support standard menus attached to windows, a command bar is necessary for menus. While HelloCE doesn't have a menu, it does require a Close button, also provided by the command bar, so the program can be terminated by the user. For this reason, the simplest form of command bar, one with only a Close button, is created. You create the command bar by calling *CommandBar_Create* and passing the program's instance handle, the handle to the window, and a constant that will be used to identify this specific command bar. (This constant can be any integer value as long as it is unique among the other child windows in the window.) Once you've created the command bar, you add a Close button by calling *CommandBar_AddAdornments*. Since all we want to do is perform the default action for this function, the parameters passed are basic: the command bar handle and two zeros. That completes the processing of the WM_CREATE message. I'll examine the command bar in depth in Chapter 5.

DoPaintMain

Painting the window, and therefore processing the WM_PAINT message, is one of the critical functions of any Windows program. As a program processes the WM_PAINT message, the look of the window is achieved. Aside from painting the default background with the brush you specified when you registered the window class, Windows provides no help for processing this message. In HelloCE, the task of the *DoPaintMain* procedure is to display one line of text in the center of the window.

```
LRESULT DoPaintMain (HWND hWnd, UINT wMsg, WPARAM wParam,
                     LPARAM lParam) {
    PAINTSTRUCT ps;
    RECT rect;
    HDC hdc;

    // Adjust the size of the client rect to take into account
    // the command bar height.
    GetClientRect (hWnd, &rect);
    rect.top += CommandBar_Height (GetDlgItem (hWnd, IDC_CMDBAR));

    hdc = BeginPaint (hWnd, &ps);
    DrawText (hdc, TEXT ("Hello Windows CE!"), -1, &rect,
              DT_CENTER | DT_VCENTER | DT_SINGLELINE);

    EndPaint (hWnd, &ps);
    return 0;
}
```

Before the drawing can be performed, the routine must determine the size of the window. In a Windows program, a standard window is divided into two areas, the nonclient area and the client area. A window's title bar and its sizing border commonly comprise the nonclient area of a window, and Windows is responsible for drawing it. The client area is the interior part of the window, and the application is responsible for drawing that. An application determines the size and location of the client area by calling the *GetClientRect* function. The function returns a RECT structure that contains left, top, right, and bottom elements that delineate the boundaries of the client rectangle. The advantage of the client vs. nonclient area concept is that an application doesn't have to account for drawing such standard elements of a window as the title bar.

When you're computing the size of the client area, you must remember that the command bar resides in the client area of the window. So, even though the *GetClientRect* function works identically in Windows CE as in other versions of Windows, the application needs to compensate for the height of the command bar, which is always placed across the top of the window. Windows CE gives you a convenient function, *CommandBar_Height*, which returns the height of the command bar and can be used in conjunction with the *GetClientRect* call to get the true client area of the window that needs to be drawn by the application.

Other versions of Windows supply a series of WM_NC*xxx* messages that enable your applications to take over the drawing of the nonclient area. In Windows CE, windows seldom have title bars and at the present time, none of them have a sizing border. Because there's so little nonclient area, the Windows CE developers decided not to expose the nonclient messages.

All drawing performed in a WM_PAINT message must be enclosed by two functions, *BeginPaint* and *EndPaint*. The *BeginPaint* function returns an *HDC*, or handle to a device context. A *device context* is a logical representation of a physical display device such as a video screen or a printer. Windows programs never modify the display hardware directly. Instead, Windows isolates the program from the specifics of the hardware with, among other tools, device contexts.

BeginPaint also fills in a PAINTSTRUCT structure that contains a number of useful parameters.

```
typedef struct tagPAINTSTRUCT {
    HDC  hdc;
    BOOL fErase;
    RECT rcPaint;
    BOOL fRestore;
    BOOL fIncUpdate;
    BYTE rgbReserved[32];
} PAINTSTRUCT;
```

The *hdc* field is the same handle that's returned by the *BeginPaint* function. The *fErase* field indicates whether the background of the window needs to be redrawn by the window procedure. The *rcPaint* field is a RECT structure that defines the client area that needs repainting. HelloCE ignores this field and assumes that the entire client window needs repainting for every WM_PAINT message, but this field is quite handy when performance is an issue because only a part of the window might need repainting. Windows actually prevents repainting outside of the *rcPaint* rectangle even when a program attempts to do so. The other fields in the structure, *fRestore*, *fIncUpdate*, and *rgbReserved*, are used internally by Windows and can be ignored by the application.

The only painting that takes place in HelloCE occurs in one line of text in the window. To do the painting, HelloCE calls the *DrawText* function. I cover the details of *DrawText* in the next chapter, but if you look at the function it's probably obvious to you that this call draws the string "Hello Windows CE" on the window. After *DrawText* returns, *EndPaint* is called to inform Windows that the program has completed its update of the window.

Calling *EndPaint* also validates any area of the window you didn't paint. Windows keeps a list of areas of a window that are *invalid* (areas that need to be redrawn) and *valid* (areas that are up to date). By calling the *BeginPaint* and *EndPaint* pair, you tell Windows that you've taken care of any invalid areas in your window, whether or not you've actually drawn anything in the window. In fact, you must call *BeginPaint* and *EndPaint*, or validate the invalid areas of the window by other means, or Windows will simply continue to send WM_PAINT messages to the window until those invalid areas are validated.

DoHibernateMain

You need *DoHibernateMain* because the WM_HIBERNATE message, unique to Windows CE, should be handled by every Windows CE program. A WM_HIBERNATE message is sent to a window to instruct it to reduce its memory use to the absolute minimum.

```
LRESULT DoHibernateMain (HWND hWnd, UINT wMsg, WPARAM wParam,
                         LPARAM lParam) {

    // If not the active window, destroy the cmd bar to save memory.
    if (GetActiveWindow () != hWnd)
        CommandBar_Destroy (GetDlgItem (hWnd, IDC_CMDBAR));

    return 0;
}
```

In the case of HelloCE, the only real way to reduce memory use is to destroy the command bar control. This is done by means of a call to *CommandBar_Destroy*.

The only case in which one should not destroy the command bar is when the window is the active window, the window through which the user is interacting with the program at the current time.

More complex Windows CE applications have a much more elaborate procedure for handling the WM_HIBERNATE messages. Applications should free up as much memory and system resources as possible without losing currently unsaved data. In a choice between performance and lower memory use, an application is better reactivating slowly after a WM_HIBERNATE message than it is consuming more memory.

DoActivateMain

While the WM_ACTIVATE message is common to all Windows platforms, it takes on new significance for Windows CE applications because among its duties is to indicate that the window should restore any data structures or window controls that were freed by a WM_HIBERNATE message.

```
LRESULT DoActivateMain (HWND hWnd, UINT wMsg, WPARAM wParam,
                        LPARAM lParam) {
    HWND hwndCB;

    // If activating and no command bar, create it.
    if ((LOWORD (wParam) != WA_INACTIVE) &&
        (GetDlgItem (hWnd, IDC_CMDBAR) == 0)) {

        // Create a command bar.
        hwndCB = CommandBar_Create (hInst, hWnd, IDC_CMDBAR);

        // Add exit button to command bar.
        CommandBar_AddAdornments (hwndCB, 0, 0);
    }
    return 0;
}
```

The lower word of the *wParam* parameter is a flag that tells why the WM_ACTIVATE message was sent to the window. The flag can be one of three values: WA_INACTIVE, indicating that the window is being deactivated after being the active window; WA_ACTIVE, indicating that the window is about to become the active window; and WA_CLICKACTIVE, indicating that the window is about to become the active window after having been clicked on by the user.

HelloCE processes this message by checking to see whether the window remains active and whether the command bar no longer exists. If both conditions are true, the command bar is re-created using the same calls used for the WM_CREATE message. The *GetDlgItem* function is convenient because it returns the handle of a child window of another window using its window ID. Remember that when the command bar, a child of HelloCE's main window, was created, I used an ID of IDC_CMDBAR (defined in HelloCE.h). That ID value is passed to *GetDlgItem* to get the command bar window handle. However, if the command bar window doesn't exist, the value returned is 0, indicating that HelloCE needs to re-create the command bar.

DoDestroyMain

The final message that HelloCE must process is the WM_DESTROY message sent when a window is about to be destroyed. Because this window is the main window of the application, the application should terminate when the window is destroyed. To make this happen, the *DoDestroyMain* function calls *PostQuitMessage*. This function places a WM_QUIT message in the message queue. The one parameter of this function is the return code value that will be passed back to the application in the *wParam* parameter of the WM_QUIT message.

```
LRESULT DoDestroyMain (HWND hWnd, UINT wMsg, WPARAM wParam,
                       LPARAM lParam) {
    PostQuitMessage (0);
    return 0;
}
```

Notice that the *DoDestroyMain* function doesn't destroy the command bar control created in *DoCreateMain*. Since the command bar is a child window of the main window, it's automatically destroyed when its parent window is destroyed.

As I've mentioned, when the message loop sees a WM_QUIT message, it exits the loop. The *WinMain* function then calls *TermInstance*, which in the case of HelloCE, does nothing but return. *WinMain* then returns, terminating the program.

Running HelloCE

After you've entered the program into Visual C++ and built it, it can be executed by a double-tap on the HelloCE icon. The program displays the Hello Windows CE text in the middle of an empty window, as shown in Figure 1-4. Figure 1-5 shows HelloCE running on a Palm-size PC. The command bar is placed by Windows CE across the top of the window. Tapping on the Close button on the command bar causes Windows CE to send a WM_CLOSE message to the window. Although HelloCE doesn't explicitly process the WM_CLOSE message, the *DefWindowProc* procedure enables default processing by destroying the main window. As the window is being destroyed, a WM_DESTROY message is sent, which causes *PostQuitMessage* to be called.

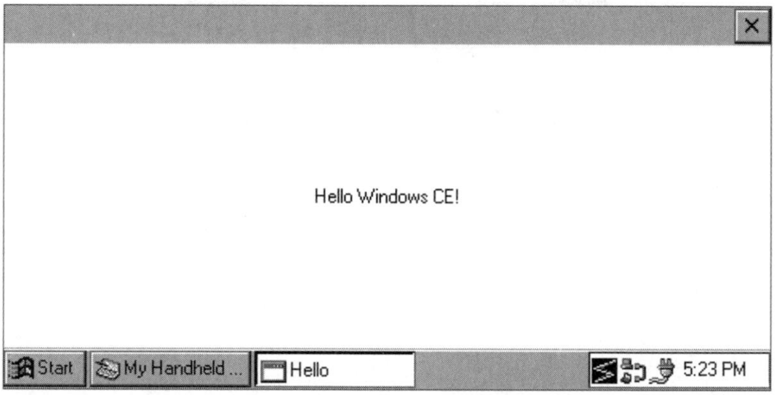

Figure 1-4. *The HelloCE window on an H/PC.*

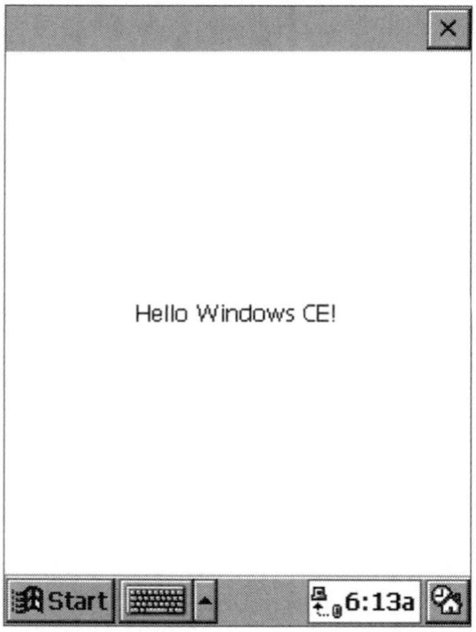

Figure 1-5. *The HelloCE window on a Palm-size PC.*

As I said, HelloCE is a very basic Windows CE program but it does gives you a skeleton of a Windows CE application upon which you can build. If you look at HelloCE.EXE using Explorer, the program is represented by a generic icon. When HelloCE is running, the button on the task bar representing HelloCE has no icon displayed next to the text. How to add a program's icon as well as how the *DrawText* function works are a couple of the topics I'll address in the next few chapters.

Chapter 2

Drawing on the Screen

In Chapter 1, the example program HelloCE had one task: to display a line of text on the screen. Displaying that line took only one call to *DrawText* with Windows CE taking care of such details as the font and its color, the positioning of the line of text inside the window, and so forth. Given the power of a graphical user interface (GUI), however, an application can do much more than simply print a line of text on the screen. It can craft the look of the display down to the most minute of details.

Over the life of the Microsoft Windows operating system, the number of functions available for crafting these displays has expanded dramatically. With each successive version of Windows, functions have been added that extend the tools available to the programmer. As functions were added, the old ones remained so that even if a function had been superseded by a new function old programs would continue to run on the newer versions of Windows. The approach in which function after function is piled on while the old functions are retained for backward compatibility was discontinued with the initial version of Windows CE. Because of the requirement to produce a smaller version of Windows, the CE team took a hard look at the Win32 API and replicated only the functions absolutely required by applications written for the Windows CE target market.

One of the areas of the Win32 API hardest hit by this reduction was graphical functions. Not that you now lack the functions to do the job—it's just that the high degree of redundancy led to some major pruning of the Win32 graphical functions.

An added challenge for the programmer is that different Windows CE platforms have subtly different sets of supported APIs. One of the ways in which Windows CE graphics support differs from that of its desktop cousins is that Windows CE doesn't support the different mapping modes available under other implementations of Windows. Instead, the Windows CE device contexts are always set to the MM_TEXT mapping mode. Coordinate transformations are also not supported under Windows CE. While these features can be quite useful for some types of applications, such as desktop publishing, their necessity in the Windows CE environment of small portable devices isn't as clear. Fortunately, as Windows CE matures we can expect more and more of the basic Win32 API to be supported.

So when you're reading about the functions and techniques used in this chapter, remember that some might not be supported on all platforms. So that a program can determine what functions are supported, Windows has always had the *GetDeviceCaps* function, which returns the capabilities of the current graphic device. Throughout this chapter, I'll refer to *GetDeviceCaps* when determining what functions are supported on a given device.

This chapter, like the other chapters in Part I of this book, reviews the drawing features supported by Windows CE. One of the most important facts to remember is that while Windows CE doesn't support the full Win32 graphics API, its rapid evolution has resulted in it supporting some of the newest functions in Win32—some so new that you might not be familiar with them. This chapter shows you the functions you can use and how to work around the areas where certain functions aren't supported under Windows CE.

PAINTING BASICS

Historically, Windows has been subdivided into three main components: the kernel, which handles the process and memory management; User, which handles the windowing interface and controls; and the Graphics Device Interface, or GDI, which performs the low-level drawing. In Windows CE, User and GDI are combined into the Graphics Windowing and Event handler, or GWE. At times, you might hear a Windows CE programmer talk about the GWE. The GWE is nothing really new—just a different packaging of standard Windows parts. In this book, I usually refer to the graphics portion of the GWE under its old name, GDI, to be consistent with standard Windows programming terminology.

But whether you're programming for Windows CE or Windows 98 or Windows NT, there is more to drawing than simply handling the WM_PAINT message. It's helpful to understand just when and why a WM_PAINT message is sent to a window.

Valid and Invalid Regions

When for some reason an area of a window is exposed to the user, that area, or *region*, as it's referred to in Windows, is marked invalid. When no other messages are waiting in an application's message queue and the application's window contains an invalid region, Windows sends a WM_PAINT message to the window. As mentioned in Chapter 1, any drawing performed in response to a WM_PAINT message is couched in calls to *BeginPaint* and *EndPaint*. *BeginPaint* actually performs a number of actions. It marks the invalid region as valid, and it computes the *clipping* region. The clipping region is the area to which the painting action will be limited. *BeginPaint* then sends a WM_ERASEBACKGROUND message, if needed, to redraw the background, and it hides the caret—the text entry cursor—if it's displayed. Finally *BeginPaint* retrieves the handle to the display device context so that it can be used by the application. The *EndPaint* function releases the device context and redisplays the caret if necessary. If no other action is performed by a WM_PAINT procedure, you must at least call *BeginPaint* and *EndPaint* if only to mark the invalid region as valid.

Alternatively, you can call to *ValidateRect* to blindly validate the region. But no drawing can take place in that case because an application must have a handle to the device context before it can draw anything in the window.

Often an application needs to force a repaint of its window. An application should never post or send a WM_PAINT message to itself or to another window. Instead, you do the following:

```
BOOL InvalidateRect (HWND hWnd, const RECT *lpRect, BOOL bErase);
```

Notice that *InvalidateRect* doesn't require a handle to the window's device context, only to the window handle itself. The *lpRect* parameter is the area of the window to be invalidated. This value can be NULL if the entire window is to be invalidated. The *bErase* parameter indicates whether the background of the window should be redrawn during the *BeginPaint* call as mentioned above. Note that unlike other versions of Windows, Windows CE requires that the *hWnd* parameter be a valid window handle.

Device Contexts

A *device context,* often referred to simply as a DC, is a tool that Windows uses to manage access to the display and printer, although for the purposes of this chapter I'll be talking only about the display. Also, unless otherwise mentioned, the explanation that follows applies to Windows in general and isn't specific to Windows CE.

Windows applications never write directly to the screen. Instead, they request a handle to a display device context for the appropriate window, and then using the handle, draw to the device context. Windows then arbitrates and manages getting the pixels from the DC to the screen.

BeginPaint, which should only be called in a WM_PAINT message, returns a handle to the display DC for the window. An application usually performs its drawing to the screen during the WM_PAINT messages. Windows treats painting as a low-priority task, which is appropriate since having painting at a higher priority would result in a flood of paint messages for every little change to the display. Allowing an application to complete all its pending business by processing all waiting messages results in all the invalid regions being painted efficiently at once. Users don't notice the minor delays caused by the low priority of the WM_PAINT messages.

Of course, there are times when painting must be immediate. An example of such a time might be when a word processor needs to display a character immediately after its key is pressed. To draw outside a WM_PAINT message, the handle to the DC can be obtained using this:

```
HDC GetDC (HWND hWnd);
```

GetDC returns a handle to the DC for the client portion of the window. Drawing can then be performed anywhere within the client area of the window because this process isn't like processing inside a WM_PAINT message; there's no clipping to restrict you from drawing in an invalid region.

Windows CE 2.1 supports another function that can be used to receive the DC. It is

```
HDC GetDCEx (HWND hWnd, HRGN hrgnClip, DWORD flags);
```

GetDCEx allows you to have more control over the device context returned. The new parameter, *hrgnClip* lets you define the clipping region, which limits drawing to that region of the DC. The *flags* parameter lets you specify how the DC acts as you draw on it. Windows CE doesn't support the following flags: DCX_PARENTCLIP, DCX_NORESETATTRS, DCX_LOCKWINDOWUPDATE, and DCX_VALIDATE.

After the drawing has been completed, a call must be made to release the device context:

```
int ReleaseDC (HWND hWnd, HDC hDC);
```

Device contexts are a shared resource, and therefore an application must not hold the DC for any longer than necessary.

While *GetDC* is used to draw inside the client area, sometimes an application needs access to the nonclient areas of a window, such as the title bar. To retrieve a DC for the entire window, make the following call:

```
HDC GetWindowDC (HWND hWnd);
```

As before, the matching call after drawing has been completed for *GetWindowDC* is *ReleaseDC*.

The DC functions under Windows CE are identical to the device context functions under Windows 98 and Windows NT. This should be expected because DCs are the core of the Windows drawing philosophy. Changes to this area of the API would result in major incompatibilities between Windows CE applications and their desktop counterparts.

WRITING TEXT

In Chapter 1, the HelloCE example displayed a line of text using a call to *DrawText*. That line from the example is shown here:

```
DrawText (hdc, TEXT ("Hello Windows CE!"), -1, &rect,
          DT_CENTER | DT_VCENTER | DT_SINGLELINE);
```

DrawText is a fairly high-level function that allows a program to display text while having Windows deal with most of the details. The first few parameters of *DrawText* are almost self-explanatory. The handle of the device context being used is passed, along with the text to display couched in a TEXT macro, which declares the string as a Unicode string necessary for Windows CE. The third parameter is the number of characters to print, or as is the case here, a –1 indicating that the string being passed is null terminated and Windows should compute the length.

The fourth parameter is a pointer to a rect structure that specifies the formatting rectangle for the text. *DrawText* uses this rectangle as a basis for formatting the text to be printed. How the text is formatted depends on the function's last parameter, the formatting flags. These flags specify how the text is to be placed within the formatting rectangle, or in the case of the DT_CALCRECT flag, the flags have *DrawText* compute the dimensions of the text that is to be printed. *DrawText* even formats multiple lines with line breaks automatically computed. In the case of HelloCE, the flags specify that the text should be centered horizontally (DT_CENTER), and centered vertically (DT_VCENTER). The DT_VCENTER flag works only on single lines of text, so the final parameter, DT_SINGLELINE, specifies that the text shouldn't be flowed across multiple lines if the rectangle isn't wide enough to display the entire string.

Device Context Attributes

What I haven't mentioned yet about HelloCE's use of *DrawText* is the large number of assumptions the program makes about the DC configuration when displaying the text. Drawing in a Windows device context takes a large number of parameters, such as foreground and background color and how the text should be drawn over the background as well as the font of the text. Instead of specifying all these parameters for each drawing call, the device context keeps track of the current settings, referred to as *attributes*, and uses them as appropriate for each call to draw to the device context.

Foreground and background colors

The most obvious of the text attributes are the foreground and background color. Two functions, *SetTextColor* and *GetTextColor*, allow a program to set and retrieve the current color. These functions work well with both four-color gray-scale screens as well as the color screens supported by Windows CE devices.

To determine how many colors a device supports, use *GetDeviceCaps* as mentioned previously. The prototype for this function is the following:

```
int GetDeviceCaps (HDC hdc, int nIndex);
```

You need the handle to the DC being queried because different DCs have different capabilities. For example, a printer DC differs from a display DC. The second parameter indicates the capability being queried. In the case of returning the colors available on the device, the NUMCOLORS value returns the number of colors as long as the device supports 256 colors or fewer. Beyond that, the returned value for NUMCOLORS is –1 and the colors can be returned using the BITSPIXEL value, which returns the number of bits used to represent each pixel. This value can be converted to the number of colors by raising 2 to the power of the BITSPIXEL returned value, as in the following code sample:

```
nNumColors = GetDeviceCaps (hdc, NUMCOLORS);
if (nNumColors == -1)
    nNumColors = 1 << GetDeviceCaps (hdc, BITSPIXEL);
```

Drawing mode

Another attribute that affects text output is the background mode. When letters are drawn on the device context, the system draws the letters themselves in the foreground color. The space between the letters is another matter. If the background mode is set to opaque, the space is drawn with the current background color. But if the background mode is set to transparent, the space between the letters is left in whatever state it was in before the text was drawn. While this might not seem like a big difference, imagine a window background filled with a drawing or graph. If text is written over the top of the graph and the background mode is set to opaque, the area around the text will be filled, and the background color will overwrite the graph. If the background mode is transparent, the text will appear as if it had been placed on the graph, and the graph will show through between the letters of the text.

The TextDemo Example Program

The TextDemo program, shown in Figure 2-1, demonstrates the relationships among the text color, the background color, and the background mode.

TextDemo.h

```
//======================================================================
// Header file
//
// Written for the book Programming Windows CE
// Copyright (C) 1998 Douglas Boling
//
//================================================================================
// Returns number of elements
#define dim(x) (sizeof(x) / sizeof(x[0]))

//----------------------------------------------------------------------
// Generic defines and data types
//
struct decodeUINT {                             // Structure associates
    UINT Code;                                  // messages
                                                // with a function.
    LRESULT (*Fxn)(HWND, UINT, WPARAM, LPARAM);
};
struct decodeCMD {                              // Structure associates
    UINT Code;                                  // menu IDs with a
    LRESULT (*Fxn)(HWND, WORD, HWND, WORD);     // function.
};

//----------------------------------------------------------------------
// Generic defines used by application
#define IDC_CMDBAR       1                      // Command bar ID

//----------------------------------------------------------------------
// Function prototypes
//
int InitApp (HINSTANCE);
int InitInstance (HINSTANCE, LPWSTR, int);
int TermInstance (HINSTANCE, int);

// Window procedures
LRESULT CALLBACK MainWndProc (HWND, UINT, WPARAM, LPARAM);

// Message handlers
LRESULT DoCreateMain (HWND, UINT, WPARAM, LPARAM);
LRESULT DoPaintMain (HWND, UINT, WPARAM, LPARAM);
LRESULT DoDestroyMain (HWND, UINT, WPARAM, LPARAM);
```

Figure 2-1. *The TextDemo program.* *(continued)*

Figure 2-1. *continued*

TextDemo.c

```
//======================================================================
// TextDemo - Text output demo
//
// Written for the book Programming Windows CE
// Copyright (C) 1998 Douglas Boling
//
//======================================================================
#include <windows.h>                 // For all that Windows stuff
#include <commctrl.h>                // Command bar includes
#include "TextDemo.h"                // Program-specific stuff

//----------------------------------------------------------------------
// Global data
//
const TCHAR szAppName[] = TEXT ("TextDemo");
HINSTANCE hInst;                     // Program instance handle

// Message dispatch table for MainWindowProc
const struct decodeUINT MainMessages[] = {
    WM_CREATE, DoCreateMain,
    WM_PAINT, DoPaintMain,
    WM_DESTROY, DoDestroyMain,
};

//======================================================================
//
// Program Entry Point
//
int WINAPI WinMain (HINSTANCE hInstance, HINSTANCE hPrevInstance,
                    LPWSTR lpCmdLine, int nCmdShow) {
    MSG msg;
    int rc = 0;

    // Initialize application.
    rc = InitApp (hInstance);
    if (rc) return rc;

    // Initialize this instance.
    if ((rc = InitInstance (hInstance, lpCmdLine, nCmdShow)) != 0)
        return rc;
```

```
    // Application message loop
    while (GetMessage (&msg, NULL, 0, 0)) {
        TranslateMessage (&msg);
        DispatchMessage (&msg);
    }
    // Instance cleanup
    return TermInstance (hInstance, msg.wParam);
}
//----------------------------------------------------------------------
// InitApp - Application initialization
//
int InitApp (HINSTANCE hInstance) {
    WNDCLASS wc;

    // Register application main window class.
    wc.style = 0;                             // Window style
    wc.lpfnWndProc = MainWndProc;             // Callback function
    wc.cbClsExtra = 0;                        // Extra class data
    wc.cbWndExtra = 0;                        // Extra window data
    wc.hInstance = hInstance;                 // Owner handle
    wc.hIcon = NULL,                          // Application icon
    wc.hCursor = NULL;                        // Default cursor
    wc.hbrBackground = (HBRUSH) GetStockObject (WHITE_BRUSH);
    wc.lpszMenuName =  NULL;                  // Menu name
    wc.lpszClassName = szAppName;             // Window class name

    if (RegisterClass (&wc) == 0) return 1;

    return 0;
}
//----------------------------------------------------------------------
// InitInstance - Instance initialization
//
int InitInstance (HINSTANCE hInstance, LPWSTR lpCmdLine, int nCmdShow){
    HWND hWnd;

    // Save program instance handle in global variable.
    hInst = hInstance;

    // Create main window.
    hWnd = CreateWindow (szAppName,           // Window class
                         TEXT("TextDemo"),    // Window title
                         WS_VISIBLE,          // Style flags
                         CW_USEDEFAULT,       // x position
                         CW_USEDEFAULT,       // y position
```

(continued)

Figure 2-1. *continued*

```
                          CW_USEDEFAULT,        // Initial width
                          CW_USEDEFAULT,        // Initial height
                          NULL,                 // Parent
                          NULL,                 // Menu, must be null
                          hInstance,            // Application instance
                          NULL);                // Pointer to create
                                                // Parameters
    // Return fail code if window not created.
    if ((!hWnd) || (!IsWindow (hWnd))) return 0x10;

    // Standard show and update calls
    ShowWindow (hWnd, nCmdShow);
    UpdateWindow (hWnd);
    return 0;
}
//----------------------------------------------------------------------
// TermInstance - Program cleanup
//
int TermInstance (HINSTANCE hInstance, int nDefRC) {

    return nDefRC;
}
//======================================================================
// Message handling procedures for MainWindow
//
//----------------------------------------------------------------------
// MainWndProc - Callback function for application window
//
LRESULT CALLBACK MainWndProc (HWND hWnd, UINT wMsg, WPARAM wParam,
                              LPARAM lParam) {
    INT i;
    //
    // Search message list to see if we need to handle this
    // message.  If in list, call procedure.
    //
    for (i = 0; i < dim(MainMessages); i++) {
        if (wMsg == MainMessages[i].Code)
            return (*MainMessages[i].Fxn)(hWnd, wMsg, wParam, lParam);
    }
    return DefWindowProc (hWnd, wMsg, wParam, lParam);
}
//----------------------------------------------------------------------
// DoCreateMain - Process WM_CREATE message for window.
//
```

```
LRESULT DoCreateMain (HWND hWnd, UINT wMsg, WPARAM wParam,
                      LPARAM lParam) {
    HWND hwndCB;

    // Create a command bar.
    hwndCB = CommandBar_Create (hInst, hWnd, IDC_CMDBAR);

    // Add exit button to command bar.
    CommandBar_AddAdornments (hwndCB, 0, 0);
    return 0;
}
//----------------------------------------------------------------------
// DoPaintMain - Process WM_PAINT message for window.
//
LRESULT DoPaintMain (HWND hWnd, UINT wMsg, WPARAM wParam,
                     LPARAM lParam) {
    PAINTSTRUCT ps;
    RECT rect, rectCli;
    HBRUSH hbrOld;
    HDC hdc;
    INT i, cy;
    DWORD dwColorTable[] = {0x00000000, 0x00808080,
                            0x00cccccc, 0x00ffffff};

    // Adjust the size of the client rect to take into account
    // the command bar height.
    GetClientRect (hWnd, &rectCli);
    rectCli.top += CommandBar_Height (GetDlgItem (hWnd, IDC_CMDBAR));

    hdc = BeginPaint (hWnd, &ps);

    // Get the height and length of the string.
    DrawText (hdc, TEXT ("Hello Windows CE"), -1, &rect,
              DT_CALCRECT | DT_CENTER | DT_SINGLELINE);

    cy = rect.bottom - rect.top + 5;

    // Draw black rectangle on right half of window.
    hbrOld = SelectObject (hdc, GetStockObject (BLACK_BRUSH));
    Rectangle (hdc, rectCli.left + (rectCli.right - rectCli.left) / 2,
               rectCli.top, rectCli.right, rectCli.bottom);
    SelectObject (hdc, hbrOld);

    rectCli.bottom = rectCli.top + cy;
```

(continued)

Figure 2-1. *continued*

```
    SetBkMode (hdc, TRANSPARENT);
    for (i = 0; i < 4; i++) {
        SetTextColor (hdc, dwColorTable[i]);
        SetBkColor (hdc, dwColorTable[3-i]);

        DrawText (hdc, TEXT ("Hello Windows CE"), -1, &rectCli,
                  DT_CENTER | DT_SINGLELINE);
        rectCli.top += cy;
        rectCli.bottom += cy;
    }

    SetBkMode (hdc, OPAQUE);
    for (i = 0; i < 4; i++) {
        SetTextColor (hdc, dwColorTable[i]);
        SetBkColor (hdc, dwColorTable[3-i]);

        DrawText (hdc, TEXT ("Hello Windows CE"), -1, &rectCli,
                  DT_CENTER | DT_SINGLELINE);
        rectCli.top += cy;
        rectCli.bottom += cy;
    }
    EndPaint (hWnd, &ps);
    return 0;
}
//----------------------------------------------------------------------
// DoDestroyMain - Process WM_DESTROY message for window.
//
LRESULT DoDestroyMain (HWND hWnd, UINT wMsg, WPARAM wParam,
                       LPARAM lParam) {
    PostQuitMessage (0);
    return 0;
}
```

The meat of TextDemo is in the *OnPaintMain* function. The first call to *DrawText* doesn't draw anything in the device context. Instead, the DT_CALCRECT flag instructs Windows to store the dimensions of the rectangle for the text string in *rect*. This information is used to compute the height of the string, which is stored in *cy*. Next, a black rectangle is drawn on the right side of the window. I'll talk about how a rectangle is drawn later in the chapter; it's used in this program to produce two different backgrounds before the text is written. The function then prints out the same string using different foreground and background colors and both the transparent and opaque drawing modes. The result of this combination is shown in Figure 2-2.

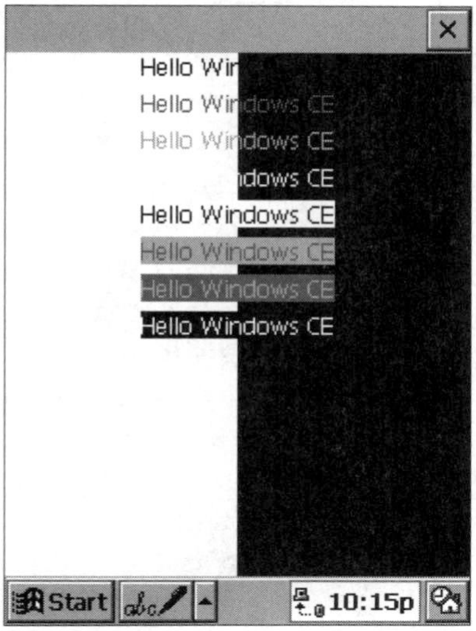

Figure 2-2. *TextDemo shows how the text color, background color, and background mode relate.*

The first four lines are drawn using the transparent mode. The second four are drawn using the opaque mode. The text color is set from black to white, so that each line drawn uses a different color, while at the same time the background color is set from white to black. In transparent mode, the background color is irrelevant because it isn't used; but in opaque mode, the background color is readily apparent on each line.

Fonts

If the ability to set the foreground and background colors were all the flexibility that Windows provided, we might as well be back in the days of MS-DOS and character attributes. Arguably, the most dramatic change from MS-DOS is Windows' ability to change the font used to display text. All Windows operating systems are built around the concept of WYSIWYG—what you see is what you get—and changeable fonts are a major tool used to achieve that goal.

Two types of fonts appear in all Windows operating systems—*raster* and *TrueType*. Raster fonts are stored as bitmaps, small pixel by pixel images, one for each character in the font. Raster fonts are easy to store and use but have one major problem: they don't scale well. Just as a small picture looks grainy when blown up to a much larger size, raster fonts begin to look blocky as they are scaled to larger and larger font sizes.

TrueType fonts solve the scaling problem. Instead of being stored as images, each TrueType character is stored as a description of how to draw the character. The font engine, which is the part of Windows that draws characters on the screen, then takes the description and draws it on the screen in any size needed. TrueType font support was introduced with Windows 3.1 but was only added to the Windows CE line in Windows CE 2.0. Even under Windows CE 2.0, though, some devices such as the original Palm-size PC, don't support TrueType fonts. A Windows CE system can support either TrueType or raster fonts, but not both. Fortunately, the programming interface is the same for both raster and TrueType fonts, relieving Windows developers from worrying about the font technology in all but the most exacting of applications.

The font functions under Windows CE closely track the same functions under other versions of Windows. Let's look at the functions used in the life of a font, from creation through selection in a DC and finally to deletion of the font. How to query the current font as well as enumerate the available fonts is also covered in the following sections.

Creating a font

Before an application is able to use a font other than the default font, the font must be created and then selected into the device context. Any text drawn in a DC after the new font has been selected into the DC will then use the new font.

Creating a font in Windows CE can be accomplished this way:

```
HFONT CreateFontIndirect (const LOGFONT *lplf);
```

This function is passed a pointer to a LOGFONT structure that must be filled with the description of the font you want.

```
typedef struct tagLOGFONT {
    LONG lfHeight;
    LONG lfWidth;
    LONG lfEscapement;
    LONG lfOrientation;
    LONG lfWeight;
    BYTE lfItalic;
    BYTE lfUnderline;
    BYTE lfStrikeOut;
    BYTE lfCharSet;
    BYTE lfOutPrecision;
    BYTE lfClipPrecision;
    BYTE lfQuality;
    BYTE lfPitchAndFamily;
    TCHAR lfFaceName[LF_FACESIZE];
} LOGFONT;
```

The *lfHeight* field specifies the height of the font in device units. If this field is 0, the font manager returns the default font size for the font family requested. For most applications, however, you want to create a font of a particular point size. The following equation can be used to convert point size to the *lfHeight* field:

*lfHeight = -1 * (PointSize * GetDeviceCaps (hdc, LOGPIXELSY) / 72);*

Here, *GetDeviceCaps* is passed a LOGPIXELSY field instructing it to return the number of logical pixels per inch in the vertical direction. The 72 is the number of *points* (a typesetting unit of measure) per inch.

The *lfWidth* field specifies the average character width. Since the height of a font is more important than its width, most programs set this value to 0. This tells the font manager to compute the proper width based on the height of the font. The *lfEscapement* and *lfOrientation* fields specify the angle in tenths of degrees of the base line of the text and the *x*-axis. The *lfWeight* field specifies the boldness of the font from 0 through 1000, with 400 being a normal font and 700 being bold. The next three fields specify whether the font is to be italic, underline, or strikeout.

The *lpCharSet* field specifies the character set you have chosen. This field is more important in international releases of software, where it can be used to request a specific language's character set. The *lfOutPrecision* field can be used to specify how closely Windows matches your requested font. Among a number of flags available, a OUT_TT_ONLY_PRECIS flag specifies that the font created must be a TrueType font. The *lfClipPrecision* field specifies how Windows should clip characters that are partially outside the region being displayed. The *lfQuality* field is set to either DEFAULT_QUALITY or DRAFT_QUALITY, which gives Windows permission to synthesize a font that, while more closely matching the other requested fields, might look less polished.

The *lfPitchAndFamily* field specifies the family of the font you want. This field is handy when you're requesting a family such as Swiss, that features proportional fonts without serifs, or a family such as Roman, that features proportional fonts with serifs, but you don't have a specific font in mind. You can also use this field to specify simply a proportional or a monospaced font and allow Windows to determine which font matches the other specified characteristics passed into the LOGFONT structure. Finally, the *lfFaceName* field can be used to specify the typeface name of a specific font.

When *CreateFontIndirect* is called with a filled LOGFONT structure, Windows creates a logical font that best matches the characteristics provided. To use the font however, the final step of selecting the font into a device context must be made.

Selecting a font into a device context

You select a font into a DC by using the following function:

```
HGDIOBJ SelectObject (HDC hdc, HGDIOBJ hgdiobj);
```

This function is used for more than just setting the default font; you use this function to select other GDI objects, as we shall soon see. The function returns the previously selected object (in our case the previously selected font), which should be saved so that it can be selected back into the DC when we're finished with the new font. The line of code looks like the following:

```
hOldFont = SelectObject (hdc, hFont);
```

When the logical font is selected, the system determines the closest match to the logical font from the fonts available in the system. For devices without TrueType fonts, this match could be a fair amount off from the specified parameters. Because of this, never assume that just because you've requested a particular font, the font returned exactly matches the one you requested. For example, the height of the font you asked for might not be the height of the font that's selected into the device context.

Querying a font's characteristics

To determine the characteristics of the font that is selected into a device context, a call to

```
BOOL GetTextMetrics (HDC hdc, LPTEXTMETRIC lptm);
```

returns the characteristics of that font. A TEXTMETRIC structure is returned with the information and is defined as

```
typedef struct tagTEXTMETRIC {
    LONG tmHeight;
    LONG tmAscent;
    LONG tmDescent;
    LONG tmInternalLeading;
    LONG tmExternalLeading;
    LONG tmAveCharWidth;
    LONG tmMaxCharWidth;
    LONG tmWeight;
    LONG tmOverhang;
    LONG tmDigitizedAspectX;
    LONG tmDigitizedAspectY;
    char tmFirstChar;
    char tmLastChar;
    char tmDefaultChar;
```

```
    char tmBreakChar;
    BYTE tmItalic;
    BYTE tmUnderlined;
    BYTE tmStruckOut;
    BYTE tmPitchAndFamily;
    BYTE tmCharSet;
} TEXTMETRIC;
```

The TEXTMETRIC structure contains a number of the fields we saw in the LOGFONT structure but this time the values listed in TEXTMETRIC are the values of the font that's selected into the device context. Figure 2-3 shows the relationship of some of the fields to actual characters.

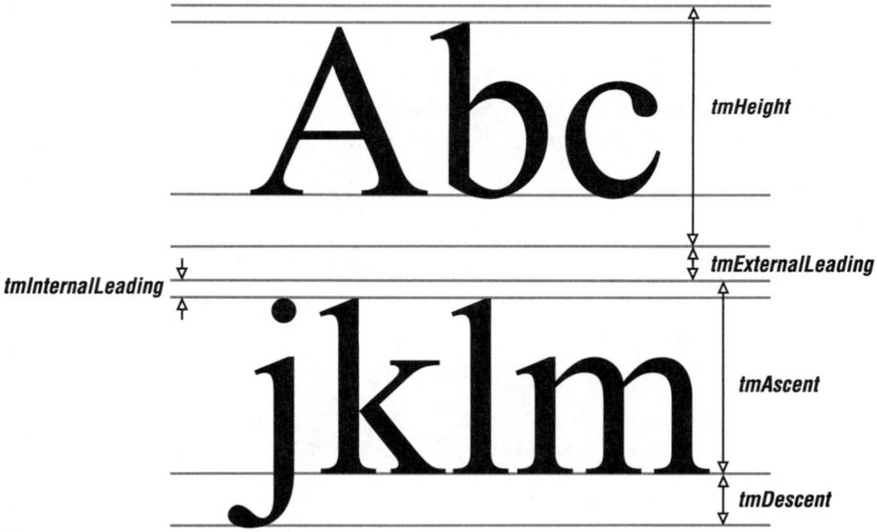

Figure 2-3. *Fields from the TEXTMETRIC structure and how they relate to a font.*

Aside from determining whether you really got the font you wanted, the *GetTextmetrics* call has another valuable purpose—determining the height of the font. Recall that in TextDemo, the height of the line was computed using a call to *DrawText*. While that method is convenient, it tends to be slow. You can use the TEXTMETRIC data to compute this height in a much more straightforward manner. By adding the *tmHeight* field, which is the height of the characters, to the *tmExternalLeading* field, which is the distance between the bottom pixel of one row and the top pixel of the next row of characters, you can determine the vertical distance between the baselines of two lines of text.

Destroying a font

Like other GDI resources, fonts must be destroyed after the program has finished using them. Failure to delete fonts before terminating a program causes what's known as a *resource leak*—an orphaned graphic resource that's taking up valuable memory but that's no longer owned by an application.

To destroy a font, first deselect it from any device contexts it has been selected into. You do this by calling *SelectObject*; the font passed is the font that was returned by the original *SelectObject* call made to select the font. After the font has been deselected, a call to

```
BOOL DeleteObject (HGDIOBJ hObject);
```

(with *hObject* containing the font handle) deletes the font from the system.

As you can see from this process, font management is no small matter in Windows. The many parameters of the LOGFONT structure might look daunting, but they give an application tremendous power to specify a font exactly.

One problem when dealing with fonts is determining just what types of fonts are available on a specific device. Windows CE devices come with a set of standard fonts, but a specific system might have been loaded with additional fonts by either the manufacturer or the user. Fortunately, Windows provides a method for enumerating all the available fonts in a system.

Enumerating fonts

To determine what fonts are available on a system, Windows provides this function:

```
int EnumFontFamilies (HDC hdc, LPCTSTR lpszFamily,
                      FONTENUMPROC lpEnumFontFamProc, LPARAM lParam);
```

This function lets you list all the font families as well as each font within a family. The first parameter is the obligatory handle to the device context. The second parameter is a string to the name of the family to enumerate. If this parameter is null, the function enumerates each of the available families.

The third parameter is something different—a pointer to a function provided by the application. The function is a callback function that Windows calls once for each font being enumerated. The final parameter, *lParam,* is a generic parameter that can be used by the application. This value is passed unmodified to the application's callback procedure.

While the name of the callback function can be anything, the prototype of the callback must match the declaration:

```
int CALLBACK EnumFontFamProc (LOGFONT *lpelf, TEXTMETRIC *lpntm,
                              DWORD FontType, LPARAM lParam);
```

The first parameter passed back to the callback function is a pointer to a LOGFONT structure describing the font being enumerated. The second parameter, a pointer to a textmetric structure, further describes the font. The font type parameter indicates whether the font is a raster or TrueType font.

The FontList Example Program

The FontList program, shown in Figure 2-4, uses the *EnumFontFamilies* function in two ways to enumerate all fonts in the system.

FontList.h

```
//======================================================================
// Header file
//
// Written for the book Programming Windows CE
// Copyright (C) 1998 Douglas Boling
//
//======================================================================
// Returns number of elements
#define dim(x) (sizeof(x) / sizeof(x[0]))

//----------------------------------------------------------------------
// Generic defines and data types
//
struct decodeUINT {                             // Structure associates
    UINT Code;                                  // messages
                                                // with a function.
    LRESULT (*Fxn)(HWND, UINT, WPARAM, LPARAM);
};
struct decodeCMD {                              // Structure associates
    UINT Code;                                  // menu IDs with a
    LRESULT (*Fxn)(HWND, WORD, HWND, WORD);     // function.
};

//----------------------------------------------------------------------
// Generic defines used by application
#define  IDC_CMDBAR 1                           // Command bar ID

//----------------------------------------------------------------------
// Program specific structures
//
#define FAMILYMAX   24
```

Figure 2-4. *The FontList program enumerates all fonts in the system.* *(continued)*

Figure 2-4. *continued*

```
typedef struct {
    int nNumFonts;
    TCHAR szFontFamily[LF_FACESIZE];
} FONTFAMSTRUCT;
typedef FONTFAMSTRUCT *PFONTFAMSTRUCT;

typedef struct {
    INT yCurrent;
    HDC hdc;
} PAINTFONTINFO;
typedef PAINTFONTINFO *PPAINTFONTINFO;

//----------------------------------------------------------------------
// Function prototypes
//
int InitApp (HINSTANCE);
HWND InitInstance (HINSTANCE, LPWSTR, int);
int TermInstance (HINSTANCE, int);

// Window procedures
LRESULT CALLBACK MainWndProc (HWND, UINT, WPARAM, LPARAM);

// Message handlers
LRESULT DoCreateMain (HWND, UINT, WPARAM, LPARAM);
LRESULT DoPaintMain (HWND, UINT, WPARAM, LPARAM);
LRESULT DoDestroyMain (HWND, UINT, WPARAM, LPARAM);
```

FontList.c

```
//======================================================================
// FontList - Lists the available fonts in the system
//
// Written for the book Programming Windows CE
// Copyright (C) 1998 Douglas Boling
//
//======================================================================
#include <windows.h>                 // For all that Windows stuff
#include <commctrl.h>                // Command bar includes
#include "FontList.h"                // Program-specific stuff

//----------------------------------------------------------------------
// Global data
//
```

```
const TCHAR szAppName[] = TEXT ("FontList");
HINSTANCE hInst;                         // Program instance handle

FONTFAMSTRUCT ffs[FAMILYMAX];
INT sFamilyCnt = 0;

// Message dispatch table for MainWindowProc
const struct decodeUINT MainMessages[] = {
    WM_CREATE, DoCreateMain,
    WM_PAINT, DoPaintMain,
    WM_DESTROY, DoDestroyMain,
};

//======================================================================
//
// Program entry point
//
int WINAPI WinMain (HINSTANCE hInstance, HINSTANCE hPrevInstance,
                    LPWSTR lpCmdLine, int nCmdShow) {
    MSG msg;
    int rc = 0;
    HWND hwndMain;

    // Initialize application.
    rc = InitApp (hInstance);
    if (rc) return rc;

    // Initialize this instance.
    hwndMain = InitInstance (hInstance, lpCmdLine, nCmdShow);
    if (hwndMain == 0)
        return 0x10;

    // Application message loop
    while (GetMessage (&msg, NULL, 0, 0)) {
        TranslateMessage (&msg);
        DispatchMessage (&msg);
    }
    // Instance cleanup
    return TermInstance (hInstance, msg.wParam);
}
//----------------------------------------------------------------------
// InitApp - Application initialization
//
```

(continued)

Figure 2-4. *continued*

```
int InitApp (HINSTANCE hInstance) {
    WNDCLASS wc;

    // Register application main window class.
    wc.style = 0;                                  // Window style
    wc.lpfnWndProc = MainWndProc;                  // Callback function
    wc.cbClsExtra = 0;                             // Extra class data
    wc.cbWndExtra = 0;                             // Extra window data
    wc.hInstance = hInstance;                      // Owner handle
    wc.hIcon = NULL,                               // Application icon
    wc.hCursor = NULL;                             // Default cursor
    wc.hbrBackground = (HBRUSH) GetStockObject(WHITE_BRUSH);
    wc.lpszMenuName =  NULL;                       // Menu name
    wc.lpszClassName = szAppName;                  // Window class name

    if (RegisterClass (&wc) == 0) return 1;

    return 0;
}
//----------------------------------------------------------------------
// InitInstance - Instance initialization
//
HWND InitInstance (HINSTANCE hInstance, LPWSTR lpCmdLine, int nCmdShow) {
    HWND hWnd;

    // Save program instance handle in global variable.
    hInst = hInstance;

    // Create main window.
    hWnd = CreateWindow (szAppName,                // Window class
                         TEXT("Font Listing"),// Window title
                         WS_VISIBLE,               // Style flags
                         CW_USEDEFAULT,            // x position
                         CW_USEDEFAULT,            // y position
                         CW_USEDEFAULT,            // Initial width
                         CW_USEDEFAULT,            // Initial height
                         NULL,                     // Parent
                         NULL,                     // Menu, must be null
                         hInstance,                // Application instance
                         NULL);                    // Pointer to create
                                                   // parameters
    // Return fail code if window not created.
    if (!IsWindow (hWnd)) return 0;
```

```
    // Standard show and update calls
    ShowWindow (hWnd, nCmdShow);
    UpdateWindow (hWnd);
    return hWnd;
}
//----------------------------------------------------------------------
// TermInstance - Program cleanup
//
int TermInstance (HINSTANCE hInstance, int nDefRC) {

    return nDefRC;
}
//======================================================================
// Font callback functions
//
//----------------------------------------------------------------------
// FontFamilyCallback - Callback function that enumerates the font
// families
//
int CALLBACK FontFamilyCallback (CONST LOGFONT *lplf,
                                 CONST TEXTMETRIC *lpntm,
                                 DWORD nFontType, LPARAM lParam) {
    int rc = 1;

    // Stop enumeration if array filled.
    if (sFamilyCnt >= FAMILYMAX)
        return 0;
    // Copy face name of font.
    lstrcpy (ffs[sFamilyCnt++].szFontFamily, lplf->lfFaceName);

    return rc;
}
//----------------------------------------------------------------------
// EnumSingleFontFamily - Callback function that enumerates fonts
//
int CALLBACK EnumSingleFontFamily (CONST LOGFONT *lplf,
                                   CONST TEXTMETRIC *lpntm,
                                   DWORD nFontType, LPARAM lParam) {
    PFONTFAMSTRUCT pffs;

    pffs = (PFONTFAMSTRUCT) lParam;
    pffs->nNumFonts++;     // Increment count of fonts in family
    return 1;
}
```

(continued)

Figure 2-4. *continued*

```
//----------------------------------------------------------------
// PaintSingleFontFamily - Callback function that draws a font
//
int CALLBACK PaintSingleFontFamily (CONST LOGFONT *lplf,
                                    CONST TEXTMETRIC *lpntm,
                                    DWORD nFontType, LPARAM lParam) {
    PPAINTFONTINFO ppfi;
    TCHAR szOut[256];
    INT nFontHeight, nPointSize;
    HFONT hFont, hOldFont;

    ppfi = (PPAINTFONTINFO) lParam;  // Translate lParam into struct
                                     // pointer.

    // Create the font from the LOGFONT structure passed.
    hFont = CreateFontIndirect (lplf);

    // Select the font into the device context.
    hOldFont = SelectObject (ppfi->hdc, hFont);

    // Compute font size.
    nPointSize = (lplf->lfHeight * 72) /
                 GetDeviceCaps(ppfi->hdc,LOGPIXELSY);

    // Format string and paint on display.
    wsprintf (szOut, TEXT ("%s   Point:%d"), lplf->lfFaceName,
              nPointSize);
    ExtTextOut (ppfi->hdc, 25, ppfi->yCurrent, 0, NULL,
                szOut, lstrlen (szOut), NULL);

    // Compute the height of the default font.
    nFontHeight = lpntm->tmHeight + lpntm->tmExternalLeading;
    // Update new draw point.
    ppfi->yCurrent += nFontHeight;

    // Deselect font and delete.
    SelectObject (ppfi->hdc, hOldFont);
    DeleteObject (hFont);
    return 1;
}
//================================================================
// Message handling procedures for MainWindow
//
```

```
//----------------------------------------------------------------------
// MainWndProc - Callback function for application window
//
LRESULT CALLBACK MainWndProc (HWND hWnd, UINT wMsg, WPARAM wParam,
                              LPARAM lParam) {
    INT i;
    //
    // Search message list to see if we need to handle this
    // message.  If in list, call procedure.
    //
    for (i = 0; i < dim(MainMessages); i++) {
        if (wMsg == MainMessages[i].Code)
            return (*MainMessages[i].Fxn)(hWnd, wMsg, wParam, lParam);
    }
    return DefWindowProc (hWnd, wMsg, wParam, lParam);
}
//----------------------------------------------------------------------
// DoCreateMain - Process WM_CREATE message for window.
//
LRESULT DoCreateMain (HWND hWnd, UINT wMsg, WPARAM wParam,
                      LPARAM lParam) {
    HWND hwndCB;
    HDC hdc;
    INT i, rc;

    // Create a command bar.
    hwndCB = CommandBar_Create (hInst, hWnd, IDC_CMDBAR);

    // Add exit button to command bar.
    CommandBar_AddAdornments (hwndCB, 0, 0);

    //Enumerate the available fonts.
    hdc = GetDC (hWnd);
    rc = EnumFontFamilies ((HDC)hdc, (LPTSTR)NULL,
        FontFamilyCallback, 0);

    for (i = 0; i < sFamilyCnt; i++) {
        ffs[i].nNumFonts = 0;
        rc = EnumFontFamilies ((HDC)hdc, ffs[i].szFontFamily,
                               EnumSingleFontFamily,
                               (LPARAM)(PFONTFAMSTRUCT)&ffs[i]);
    }
    ReleaseDC (hWnd, hdc);
    return 0;
}
```

(continued)

Figure 2-4. *continued*

```
//----------------------------------------------------------------------
// DoPaintMain - Process WM_PAINT message for window.
//
LRESULT DoPaintMain (HWND hWnd, UINT wMsg, WPARAM wParam,
                     LPARAM lParam) {
    PAINTSTRUCT ps;
    RECT rect;
    HDC hdc;
    TEXTMETRIC tm;
    INT nFontHeight, i;
    TCHAR szOut[256];
    PAINTFONTINFO pfi;

    // Adjust the size of the client rect to take into account
    // the command bar height.
    GetClientRect (hWnd, &rect);
    rect.top += CommandBar_Height (GetDlgItem (hWnd, IDC_CMDBAR));

    hdc = BeginPaint (hWnd, &ps);

    // Get the height of the default font.
    GetTextMetrics (hdc, &tm);
    nFontHeight = tm.tmHeight + tm.tmExternalLeading;

    // Initialize struct that is passed to enumerate function.
    pfi.yCurrent = rect.top;
    pfi.hdc = hdc;
    for (i = 0; i < sFamilyCnt; i++) {

        // Format output string and paint font family name.
        wsprintf (szOut, TEXT("Family: %s   "),
                  ffs[i].szFontFamily);
        ExtTextOut (hdc, 5, pfi.yCurrent, 0, NULL,
                    szOut, lstrlen (szOut), NULL);
        pfi.yCurrent += nFontHeight;

        // Enumerate each family to draw a sample of that font.
        EnumFontFamilies ((HDC)hdc, ffs[i].szFontFamily,
                          PaintSingleFontFamily,
                          (LPARAM)&pfi);
    }
    EndPaint (hWnd, &ps);
    return 0;
}
```

```
//----------------------------------------------------------------------
// DoDestroyMain - Process WM_DESTROY message for window.
//
LRESULT DoDestroyMain (HWND hWnd, UINT wMsg, WPARAM wParam,
                       LPARAM lParam) {
    PostQuitMessage (0);
    return 0;
}
```

Enumerating the different fonts begins when the application is processing the WM_CREATE message in *OnCreateMain*. Here, *EnumFontFamilies* is called with the *FontFamily* field set to NULL so that each family will be enumerated. The callback function is *FontFamilyCallback*, where the name of the font family is copied into an array of strings.

The remainder of the work is performed during the processing of the WM_PAINT message. The *OnPaintMain* function begins with the standard litany of getting the size of the area below the command bar and calling *BeginPaint*, which returns the handle to the device context of the window. *GetTextMetrics* is then called to compute the row height of the default font. A loop is then entered in which *EnumerateFontFamilies* is called for each family name that had been stored during the enumeration process in *OnCreateMain*. The callback process for this callback sequence is somewhat more complex than the code we've seen so far.

The *PaintSingleFontFamily* callback procedure, used in the enumeration of the individual fonts, employs the *lParam* parameter to retrieve a pointer to a PAINTFONTINFO structure defined in FontList.h. This structure contains the current vertical drawing position as well as the handle to the device context. By using the *lParam* pointer, FontList avoids having to declare global variables to communicate with the callback procedure.

The callback procedure next creates the font using the pointer to LOGFONT that was passed to the callback procedure. The new font is then selected into the device context, while the handle to the previously selected font is retained in *hOldFont*. The point size of the enumerated font is computed using the inverse of the equation mentioned earlier in the chapter on page 49. The callback procedure then produces a line of text showing the name of the font family along with the point size of this particular font. Instead of using *DrawText*, the callback uses a different text output function:

```
BOOL ExtTextOut (HDC hdc, int X, int Y, UINT fuOptions,
                 const RECT *lprc, LPCTSTR lpString,
                 UINT cbCount, const int *lpDx);
```

The *ExtTextOut* function has a few advantages over *DrawText* in this situation. First, *ExtTextOut* tends to be faster for drawing single lines of text. Second, instead of formatting the text inside a rectangle, *x* and *y* starting coordinates are passed, specifying the upper left corner of the rectangle where the text will be drawn. The *rect* parameter that's passed is used as a clipping rectangle, or if the background mode is opaque, the area where the background color is drawn. This rectangle parameter can be NULL if you don't want any clipping or opaquing. The next two parameters are the text and the character count. The last parameter, *ExtTextOut,* allows an application to specify the horizontal distance between adjacent character cells. In our case, this parameter is set to NULL also, which results in the default separation between characters.

Windows CE differs from other versions of Windows in having only these two text drawing functions for displaying text. Most of what you can do with the other text functions typically used in other versions of Windows, such as *TextOut* and *TabbedTextOut*, can be emulated using either *DrawText* or *ExtTextOut*. This is one of the areas in which Windows CE has broken with earlier versions of Windows, sacrificing backward compatibility to achieve a smaller operating system.

After displaying the text, the function computes the height of the line of text just drawn using the combination of *tmHeight* and *tmExternalLeading* that was provided in the passed TEXTMETRIC structure. The new font is then deselected using a second call to *SelectObject*, this time passing the handle to the font that was the original selected font. The new font is then deleted using *DeleteObject*. Finally, the callback function returns a nonzero value to indicate to Windows that it is okay to make another call to the *enumerate* callback.

Figure 2-5 shows the FontListing window. Notice that the font names are displayed in that font and that each font has a specific set of available sizes.

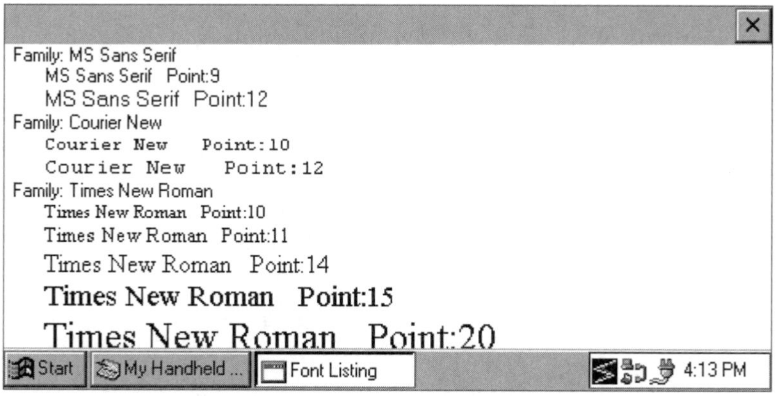

Figure 2-5. *The FontList window shows some of the available fonts for a Handheld PC.*

Unfinished business

If you look closely at Figure 2-5, you'll notice a problem with the display. The list of fonts just runs off the bottom edge of the FontList window. At this point in a book covering the desktop versions of Windows, the author might add a window style flag for a vertical scroll bar and a small amount of code, and magically, the program would have a scrollable window. But if you do that to a Windows CE main window, you end up with the look shown in Figure 2-6.

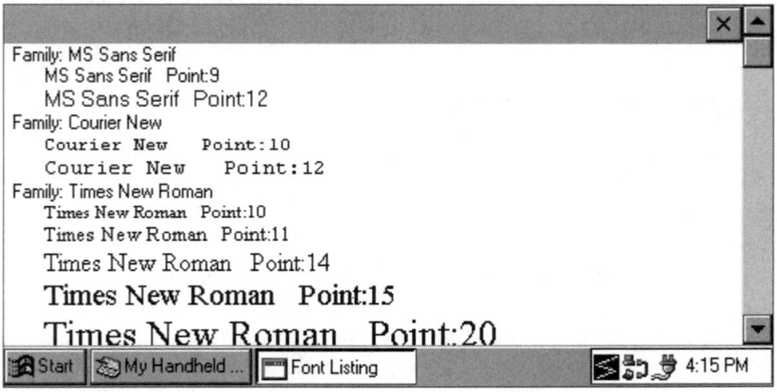

Figure 2-6. *The FontList window with a scrollbar attached to the main window.*

Notice how the scroll bar extends past the right side of the command bar up to the top of the window. The scroll bar should stop below the command bar and the command bar should extend to the right edge of the window. The problem is that the command bar lies in the client area of the window, and the default scroll bar style provided by all Windows operating systems places the scroll bar outside the client area, in the nonclient space along the edge of the window. The solution to this problem involves creating a child window inside our main window and letting it do the scrolling. But since I'll provide a complete explanation of child windows in Chapter 4, I'll hold off describing how to properly implement a scroll bar until then.

BITMAPS

Bitmaps are graphical objects that can be used to create, draw, manipulate, and retrieve images in a device context. Bitmaps are everywhere within Windows, from the little Windows logo on the Start button to the Close button on the command bar. Think of a bitmap as a picture composed of an array of pixels that can be painted onto the screen. Like any picture, a bitmap has height and width. It also has a method for determining what color or colors it uses. Finally, a bitmap has an array of bits that describe each pixel in the bitmap.

Historically, bitmaps under Windows have been divided into two types; *device dependent bitmaps* (DDBs) and *device independent bitmaps* (DIBs). DDBs are bitmaps that are tied to the characteristics of a specific DC and can't easily be rendered on DCs with different characteristics. DIBs, on the other hand, are independent of any device and therefore must carry around enough information so that they can be rendered accurately on any device.

Windows CE contains many of the bitmap functions available in other versions of Windows. The differences include a new four-color bitmap format not supported anywhere but on Windows CE and a different method for manipulating DIBs.

Device Dependent Bitmaps

A device dependent bitmap can be created with this function:

```
HBITMAP CreateBitmap (int nWidth, int nHeight, UINT cPlanes,
                      UINT cBitsPerPel, CONST VOID *lpvBits);
```

The *nWidth* and *nHeight* parameters indicate the dimensions of the bitmap. The *cPlanes* parameter is an historical artifact from the days when display hardware implemented each color within a pixel in a different hardware plane. For Windows CE, this parameter must be set to 1. The *cBitspPerPel* parameter indicates the number of bits used to describe each pixel. The number of colors is 2 to the power of the *cBitspPerPel* parameter. Under Windows CE, the allowable values are 1, 2, 4, 8, 16, and 24. As I said, the four-color bitmap is unique to Windows CE and isn't supported under other Windows platforms, including the Windows CE emulator that runs on top of Windows NT.

The final parameter is a pointer to the bits of the bitmap. Under Windows CE, the bits are always arranged in a packed pixel format; that is, each pixel is stored as a series of bits within a byte, with the next pixel starting immediately after the first. The first pixel in the array of bits is the pixel located in the upper left corner of the bitmap. The bits continue across the top row of the bitmap, then across the second row, and so on. Each row of the bitmap must be double-word (4-byte) aligned. If any pad bytes are required at the end of a row to align the start of the next row, they should be set to 0. Figure 2-7 illustrates this scheme, showing a 126-by-64 pixel bitmap with 8 bits per pixel.

The function

```
HBITMAP CreateCompatibleBitmap (HDC hdc, int nWidth, int nHeight);
```

creates a bitmap whose format is compatible with the device context passed to the function. So, if the device context is a four-color DC, the resulting bitmap is a four-color bitmap as well. This function comes in handy when you're manipulating images on the screen because it makes it easy to produce a blank bitmap that's directly color compatible with the screen.

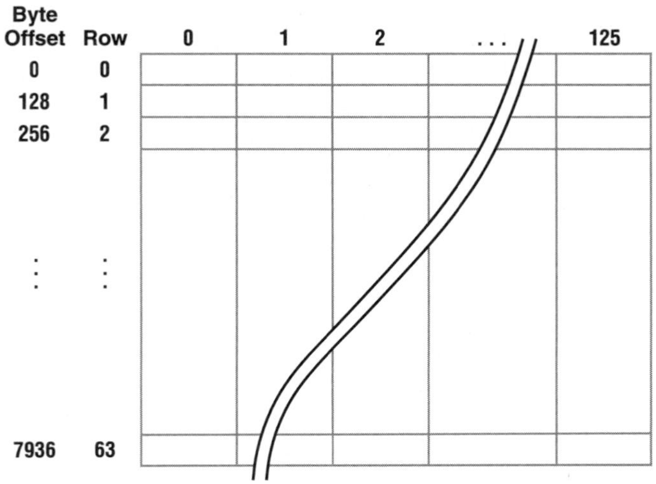

Figure 2-7. *Layout of bytes within a bitmap.*

Device Independent Bitmaps

The fundamental difference between DIBs and their device dependent cousins is that the image stored in a DIB comes with its own color information. Almost every bitmap file since Windows 3.0, which used the files with the BMP extension, contains information that can be directly matched with the information needed to create a DIB in Windows.

In the early days of Windows, it was a rite of passage for a programmer to write a routine that manually read a DIB file and converted the data to a bitmap. These days, the same arduous task can be accomplished with the following function, unique to Windows CE:

```
HBITMAP SHLoadDIBitmap (LPCTSTR szFileName);
```

It loads a bitmap directly from a bitmap file and provides a handle to the bitmap. In Windows NT and Windows 98, the same process can be accomplished with *LoadImage* using the LR_LOADFROMFILE flag, but this flag isn't supported under the Windows CE implementation of *LoadImage*.

DIB Sections

While Windows CE makes it easy to load a bitmap file, sometimes you must read what is on the screen, manipulate it, and redraw the image back to the screen. This is another case in which DIBs are better than DDBs. While the bits of a device dependent bitmap are obtainable, the format of the buffer is directly dependent on the screen format. By using a DIB, or more precisely, something called a DIB section, your program can read the bitmap into a buffer that has a predefined format without worrying about the format of the display device.

While Windows has a number of DIB creation functions that have been added over the years since Windows 3.0, Windows CE carries over only one DIB section function from Windows NT and Windows 98. Here it is:

```
HBITMAP CreateDIBSection (HDC hdc, const BITMAPINFO *pbmi,
                          UINT iUsage, void *ppvBits,
                          HANDLE hSection, DWORD dwOffset);
```

Because it's a rather late addition to the Win32 API, DIB sections might be new to Windows programmers. DIB Sections were invented to improve the performance of applications on Windows NT that directly manipulated bitmaps. In short, a DIB section allows a programmer to select a DIB in a device context while still maintaining direct access to the bits that compose the bitmap. To achieve this, a DIB section associates a memory DC with a buffer that also contains the bits of that DC. Because the image is mapped to a DC, other graphics calls can be made to modify the image. At the same time, the raw bits of the DC, in DIB format, are available for direct manipulation. While the improved performance is all well and good on NT, the relevance to the Windows CE programmer is the ease in which an application can work with bitmaps and manipulate their contents.

The parameters of this call lead off with the pointer to a BITMAPINFO structure. This structure describes the layout and color composition of a device independent bitmap and is a combination of a BITMAPINFOHEADER structure and an array of RGBQUAD values that represent the palette of colors used by the bitmap.

The BITMAPINFOHEADER structure is defined as the following:

```
typedef struct tagBITMAPINFOHEADER{
    DWORD biSize;
    LONG biWidth;
    LONG biHeight;
    WORD biPlanes;
    WORD biBitCount;
    DWORD biCompression;
    DWORD biSizeImage;
```

```
    LONG biXPelsPerMeter;
    LOG biYPelsPerMeter;
    DWORD biClrUsed;
    DWORD biClrImportant;
} BITMAPINFOHEADER;
```

As you can see, this structure contains much more information than just the parameters passed to *CreateBitmap*. The first field is the size of the structure and must be filled in by the calling program to differentiate this structure from the similar BITMAPCOREINFOHEADER structure that's a holdover from the OS/2 presentation manager. The *biWidth*, *biHeight*, *biPlanes*, and *biBitCount* fields are similar to their like-named parameters to the *CreateBitmap* call—with one exception. The sign of the *biHeight* field specifies the organization of the bit array. If *biHeight* is negative, the bit array is organized in a top-down format, as is *CreateBitmap*. If *biHeight* is positive, the array is organized in a bottom-up format, in which the bottom row of the bitmap is defined by the first bits in the array. As with the *CreateBitmap* call, the *biPlanes* field must be set to 1.

The *biCompression* field specifies the compression method used in the bit array. Under Windows CE, the only allowable setting for this field is BI_RGB, indicating that the buffer isn't compressed. The *biSizeImage* parameter is used to indicate the size of the bit array; when used with BI_RGB, however, the *biSizeImage* field can be set to 0, meaning the array size is computed using the dimensions and bits per pixel information provided in the BITMAPINFOHEADER structure.

The *biXPelsPerMeter* and *biYPelsPerMeter* fields provide information to accurately scale the image. For *CreateDIBSection,* however, these parameters can be set to 0. The *biClrUsed* parameter specifies the number of colors in the palette that are actually used. In a 256-color image, the palette will have 256 entries, but the bitmap itself might need only 100 or so distinct colors. This field helps the palette manager, the part of the Windows that manages color matching, to match the colors in the system palette with the colors required by the bitmap. The *biClrImportant* field further defines the colors that are *really* required as opposed to those that are used. For most color bitmaps, these two fields are set to 0, indicating that all colors are used and that all colors are important.

As I mentioned above, an array of RGBQUAD structures immediately follows the BITMAPINFOHEADER structure. The RGBQUAD structure is defined as follows:

```
typedef struct tagRGBQUAD { /* rgbq */
    BYTE rgbBlue;
    BYTE rgbGreen;
    BYTE rgbRed;
    BYTE rgbReserved;
} RGBQUAD;
```

This structure allows for 256 shades of red, green, and blue. While almost any shade of color can be created using this structure, the color that's actually rendered on the device will, of course, be limited by what the device can display.

The array of RGBQUAD structures, taken as a whole, describe the palette of the DIB. The palette is the list of colors in the bitmap. If a bitmap has a palette, each entry in the bitmap array contains not colors, but an index into the palette that contains the color for that pixel. While redundant on a monochrome bitmap, the palette is quite important when rendering color bitmaps on color devices. For example a 256 color bitmap has one byte for each pixel, but that byte points to a 24 bit value that represents equal parts red, green, and blue colors. So, while a 256-color bitmap can only contain 256 distinct colors, each of those colors can be one of 16 million colors rendered using the 24-bit palette entry. For convenience in a 32-bit world, each palette entry, while containing only 24 bits of color information, is padded out to a 32-bit wide entry—hence the name of the data type: RGBQUAD.

Of the remaining four *CreateDIBSection* parameters, only two are used under Windows CE. The *iUsage* parameter indicates how the colors in the palette are represented. For Windows CE, this field must be set to DIB_RGB_COLORS. The *ppvBits* parameter is a pointer to a variable that receives the pointer to the bitmap bits that compose the bitmap image. The final two parameters, *hSection* and *dwOffset*, aren't supported under Windows CE and must be set to 0. In other versions of Windows, they allow the bitmap bits to be specified by a memory mapped file. While Windows CE does support memory mapped files, they aren't supported by *CreateDIBSection*.

Drawing Bitmaps

Creating and loading bitmaps is all well and good, but there's not much point to it unless the bitmaps you create can be rendered on the screen. Drawing a bitmap isn't as straightforward as you might think. Before a bitmap can be drawn in a screen DC, it must be selected into a DC and then copied over to the screen device context. While this process sounds convoluted, there is rhyme to this reason.

The process of selecting a bitmap into a device context is similar to selecting a logical font into a device context; it converts the ideal to the actual. Just as Windows finds the best possible match to a requested font, the bitmap selection process must match the available colors of the device to the colors requested by a bitmap. Only after this is done can the bitmap be rendered on the screen. To help with this intermediate step, Windows provides a shadow type of DC, a *memory device context*.

To create a memory device context, use this function:

```
HDC CreateCompatibleDC (HDC hdc);
```

This function creates a memory DC that's compatible with the current screen DC. Once created, the source bitmap is selected into this memory DC using the same *SelectObject* function you used to select in a logical font. Finally, the bitmap is copied from the memory DC to the screen DC using one of the blit functions, *BitBlt* or *StretchBlt.*

The workhorse of bitmap functions is the following:

```
BOOL BitBlt (HDC hdcDest, int nXDest, int nYDest, int nWidth,
             int nHeight, HDC hdcSrc, int nXSrc,  int nYSrc,
             DWORD dwRop);
```

Fundamentally, the *BitBlt* function, pronounced *bit blit,* is just a fancy *memcopy* function, but since it operates on device contexts, not memory, it's something far more special. The first parameter is a handle to the destination device context—the DC to which the bitmap is to be copied. The next four parameters specify the location and size of the destination rectangle where the bitmap is to end up. The next three parameters specify the handle to the source device context and the location within that DC of the upper left corner of the source image.

The final parameter, *dwRop*, specifies how the image is to be copied from the source to the destination device contexts. The ROP code defines how the source bitmap and the current destination are combined to produce the final image. The ROP code for a simple copy of the source image is SRCCOPY. The ROP code for combining the source image with the current destination is SRCPAINT. Copying a logically inverted image, essentially a negative of the source image, is accomplished using SRCINVERT. Some ROP codes also combine the currently selected brush into the equation to compute the resulting image. A large number of ROP codes are available, too many for me to cover here. For a complete list, check out the Windows CE programming documentation.

The following code fragment sums up how to paint a bitmap:

```
// Create a DC that matches the device.
hdcMem = CreateCompatibleDC (hdc);

// Select the bitmap into the compatible device context.
hOldSel = SelectObject (hdcMem, hBitmap);

// Get the bitmap dimensions from the bitmap.
GetObject (hBitmap, sizeof (BITMAP), &bmp);
// Copy the bitmap image from the memory DC to the screen DC.
BitBlt (hdc, rect.left, rect.top, bmp.bmWidth, bmp.bmHeight,
        hdcMem, 0, 0, SRCCOPY);
```

(continued)

```
// Restore original bitmap selection and destroy the memory DC.
SelectObject (hdcMem, hOldSel);
DeleteDC (hdcMem);
```

The memory device context is created and the bitmap to be painted is selected into that DC. Since you might not have stored the dimensions of the bitmap to be painted, the routine makes a call to *GetObject*. *GetObject* returns information about a graphics object, in this case, a bitmap. Information about fonts and other graphic objects can be queried using this useful function. Next, *BitBlt* is used to copy the bitmap into the screen DC. To clean up, the bitmap is deselected from the memory device context and the memory DC is deleted using *DeleteDC*. Don't confuse *DeleteDC* with *ReleaseDC*, which is used to free a display DC. *DeleteDC* should be paired only with *CreateCompatibleDC* and *ReleaseDC* should be paired only with *GetDC* or *GetWindowDC*.

Instead of merely copying the bitmap, stretch or shrink it using this function:

```
BOOL StretchBlt (HDC hdcDest, int nXOriginDest, int nYOriginDest,
                 int nWidthDest, int nHeightDest, HDC hdcSrc,
                 int nXOriginSrc, int nYOriginSrc, int nWidthSrc,
                 int nHeightSrc, DWORD dwRop);
```

The parameters in *StretchBlt* are the same as those used in *BitBlt*, with the exception that now the width and height of the source image can be specified. Here again, the ROP codes specify how the source and destination are combined to produce the final image.

Windows CE 2.0 added a new, and quite handy, bitmap function. It is

```
BOOL TransparentImage (HDC hdcDest, LONG DstX, LONG DstY, LONG DstCx,
                       LONG DstCy, HANDLE hSrc, LONG SrcX, LONG SrcY,
                       LONG SrcCx, LONG SrcCy, COLORREF TransparentColor);
```

This function is similar to *StretchBlt* with two very important exceptions. First, you can specify a color in the bitmap to be the transparent color. When the bitmap is copied to the destination, the pixels in the bitmap that are the transparent color are not copied. The second difference is that the *hSrc* parameter can either be a device context or a handle to a bitmap, which allows you to bypass the requirement to select the source image into a device context before rendering it on the screen.

As in other versions of Windows, Windows CE supports two other blit functions: *PatBlt* and *MaskBlt*. The *PatBlt* function combines the currently selected brush with the current image in the destination DC to produce the resulting image. I cover brushes later in this chapter. The *MaskBlt* function is similar to *BitBlt* but encompasses a masking image that provides the ability to draw only a portion of the source image onto the destination DC.

LINES AND SHAPES

One of the areas in which Windows CE provides substantially less functionality than other versions of Windows is in the primitive line-drawing and shape-drawing functions. Gone are the *Chord*, *Arc*, and *Pie* functions that created complex circular shapes. Gone too is the concept of *current point*. Other versions of Windows track a current point, which is then used as the starting point for the next drawing command. So drawing a series of connected lines and curves by calling *MoveTo* to move the current point followed by calls to *LineTo*, *ArcTo*, *PolyBezierTo* and so forth is no longer possible. But even with the loss of a number of graphic functions, Windows CE still provides the essential functions necessary to draw lines and shapes.

Lines

Drawing one or more lines is as simple as a call to

```
BOOL Polyline (HDC hdc, const POINT *lppt, int cPoints);
```

The second parameter is a pointer to an array of POINT structures that are defined as the following:

```
typedef struct tagPOINT {
    LONG x;
    LONG y;
} POINT;
```

Each *x* and *y* combination describes a pixel from the upper left corner of the screen. The third parameter is the number of point structures in the array. So to draw a line from (0, 0) to (50, 100), the code would look like this:

```
POINTS pts[2];

pts[0].x = 0;
pts[0].y = 0;
pts[1].x = 50;
pts[1].y = 100;
PolyLine (hdc, &pts, 2);
```

Just as in the early text examples, this code fragment makes a number of assumptions about the default state of the device context. For example, just what does the line drawn between (0,0) and (50, 100) look like? What is its width and its color, and is it a solid line? All versions of Windows, including Windows CE, allow these parameters to be specified.

The tool for specifying the appearance of lines and the outline of shapes is called, appropriately enough, a *pen*. A pen is another GDI object and, like the others described in this chapter, is created, selected into a device context, used, deselected, and then destroyed. Among other stock GDI objects, stock pens can be retrieved using the following code:

```
HGDIOBJ GetStockObject (int fnObject);
```

All versions of Windows provide three stock pens, each 1 pixel wide. The stock pens come in 3 colors: white, black, and null. Using *GetStockObject*, the call to retrieve one of those pens employs the parameters WHITE_PEN, BLACK_PEN, and NULL_PEN respectively. Unlike standard graphic objects created by applications, stock objects should never be deleted by the application. Instead, the application should simply deselect the pen from the device context when it's no longer needed.

To create a custom pen under Windows, two functions are available. The first is this:

```
HPEN CreatePen ( int fnPenStyle, int nWidth, COLORREF crColor);
```

The *fnPenStyle* parameter specifies the appearance of the line to be drawn. For example, the PS_DASH flag can be used to create a dashed line. The *nWidth* parameter specifies the width of the pen. Finally, the *crColor* parameter specifies the color of the pen. The *crColor* parameter is typed as COLORREF, which under Windows CE 2.0 is an RGB value. The RGB macro is as follows:

```
COLORREF RGB (BYTE bRed, BYTE bGreen, BYTE bBlue);
```

So to create a solid red pen, the code would look like this:

```
hPen = CreatePen (PS_SOLID, 1, RGB (0xff, 0, 0));
```

The other pen creation function is the following:

```
HPEN CreatePenIndirect (const LOGPEN *lplgpn);
```

where the logical pen structure LOGPEN is defined as

```
typedef struct tagLOGPEN {
    UINT lopnStyle;
    POINT lopnWidth;
    COLORREF lopnColor;
} LOGPEN;
```

CreatePenIndirect provides the same parameters to Windows, in a different form. To create the same 1-pixel-wide red pen with *CreatePenIndirect*, the code would look like this:

```
LOGPEN lp;
HPEN hPen;

lp.lopnStyle = PS_SOLID;
lp.lopnWidth.x = 1;
lp.lopnWidth.y = 1;
lp.lopnColor = RGB (0xff, 0, 0);

hPen = CreatePenIndirect (&lp);
```

Windows CE devices don't support complex pens such as wide (more than one pixel wide), dashed lines. To determine what's supported, our old friend *GetDeviceCaps* comes into play, taking LINECAPS as the second parameter. Refer to the Windows CE documentation for the different flags returned by this call.

Shapes

Lines are useful but Windows also provides functions to draw shapes, both filled and unfilled. Here, Windows CE does a good job supporting most of the functions familiar to Windows programmers. The *Rectangle*, *RoundRect*, *Ellipse,* and *Polygon* functions are all supported.

Brushes

Before I can talk about shapes such as rectangles and ellipses I need to describe another GDI object that I've only mentioned briefly before now, called a *brush*. A brush is a small 8-by-8 bitmap used to fill shapes. It's also used by Windows to fill the background of a client window. Windows CE provides a number of stock brushes and also the ability to create a brush from an application-defined pattern. A number of stock brushes, each a solid color, can be retrieved using *GetStockObject*. Among the brushes available is one for each of the grays of a four grayscale display: white, light gray, dark gray, and black.

To create solid color brushes, the function to call is the following:

```
HBRUSH CreateSolidBrush (COLORREF crColor);
```

This function isn't really necessary when you're writing an application for a four-color Windows CE device because those four solid brushes can be retrieved with the *GetStockObject* call. For higher color devices however, the *crColor* parameter can be generated using the RGB macro.

To create custom pattern brushes, Windows CE supports the Win32 function:

```
HBRUSH CreateDIBPatternBrushPt (const void *lpPackedDIB,
                                UINT iUsage);
```

The first parameter to this function is a pointer to a DIB in *packed* format. This means that the pointer points to a buffer that contains a BITMAPINFO structure immediately followed by the bits in the bitmap. Remember that a BITMAPINFO structure is actually a BITMAPINFOHEADER structure followed by a palette in RGBQUAD format, so the buffer contains everything necessary to create a DIB—that is, bitmap information, a palette, and the bits to the bitmap. The second parameter must be set to DIB_RGB_COLORS for Windows CE applications. This setting indicates that the palette specified contains RGBQUAD values in each entry. The complimentary flag, DIB_PAL_COLORS, used in other versions of Windows isn't supported in Windows CE.

The *CreateDIBPatternBrushPt* function is more important under Windows CE because the hatched brushes, supplied under other versions of Windows by the *CreateHachBrush* function, aren't supported under Windows CE. Hatched brushes are brushes composed of any combination of horizontal, vertical, or diagonal lines. Ironically, they're particularly useful with grayscale displays because you can use them to accentuate different areas of a chart with different hatch patterns. These brushes, however, can be reproduced by using *CreateDIBPatternBrushPt* and the proper bitmap patterns. The Shapes code example, later in the chapter, demonstrates a method for creating hatched brushes under Windows CE.

By default, the brush origin will be in the upper left corner of the window. This isn't always what you want. Take, for example, a bar graph where the bar filled with a hatched brush fills a rectangle from (100, 100) to (125, 220). Since this rectangle isn't divisible by 8 (brushes being 8 by 8 pixels square), the upper left corner of the bar will be filled with a partial brush that might not look pleasing to the eye.

To avoid this situation, you can move the origin of the brush so that each shape can be drawn with the brush aligned correctly in the corner of the shape to be filled. The function available for this remedy is the following:

```
BOOL SetBrushOrgEx (HDC hdc, int nXOrg, int nYOrg, LPPOINT lppt);
```

The *nXOrg* and *nYOrg* parameters allow the origin to be set between 0 and 7 so that you can position the origin anywhere in the 8-by-8 space of the brush. The *lppt* parameter is filled with the previous origin of the brush so that you can restore the previous origin if necessary.

Rectangles

The rectangle function draws either a filled or a hollow rectangle; the function is defined as the following:

```
BOOL Rectangle (HDC hdc, int nLeftRect, int nTopRect,
                int nRightRect, int nBottomRect);
```

The function uses the currently selected pen to draw the outline of the rectangle and the current brush to fill the interior. To draw a hollow rectangle, select the null brush into the device context before calling *Rectangle.*

The actual pixels drawn for the border are important to understand. Say we're drawing a 5-by-7 rectangle at 0, 0. The function call would look like this:

```
Rectangle (0, 0, 5, 7);
```

Assuming that the selected pen was 1 pixel wide, the resulting rectangle would look like the one shown in Figure 2-8.

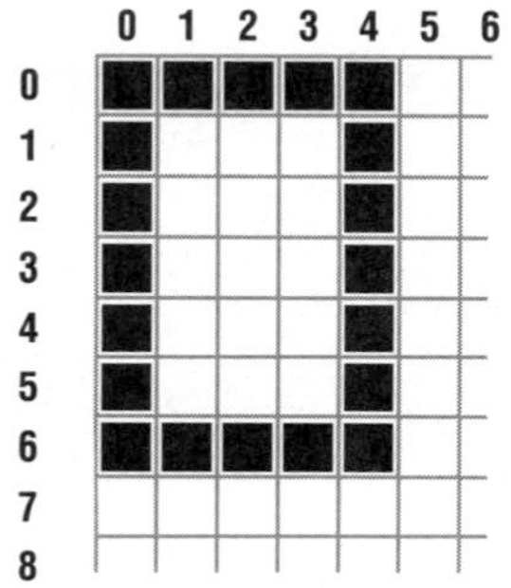

Figure 2-8. *Expanded view of a rectangle drawn with the* Rectangle *function.*

Notice how the right edge of the drawn rectangle is actually drawn in column 4 and that the bottom edge is drawn on row 6. This is standard Windows practice. The rectangle is drawn inside the right and bottom boundary specified for the *Rectangle* function. If the selected pen is wider than one pixel, the right and bottom edges are drawn with the pen centered on the bounding rectangle. (Other versions of Windows support the PS_INSIDEFRAME pen style that forces the rectangle to be drawn inside the frame regardless of the pen width.)

Circles and ellipses

Circles and ellipses can be drawn with this function:

```
BOOL Ellipse (HDC hdc, int nLeftRect, int nTopRect,
              int nRightRect, int nBottomRect);
```

The ellipse is drawn using the rectangle passed as a bounding rectangle, as shown in Figure 2-9. As with the *Rectangle* function, while the interior of the ellipse is filled with the current brush, the outline is drawn with the current pen.

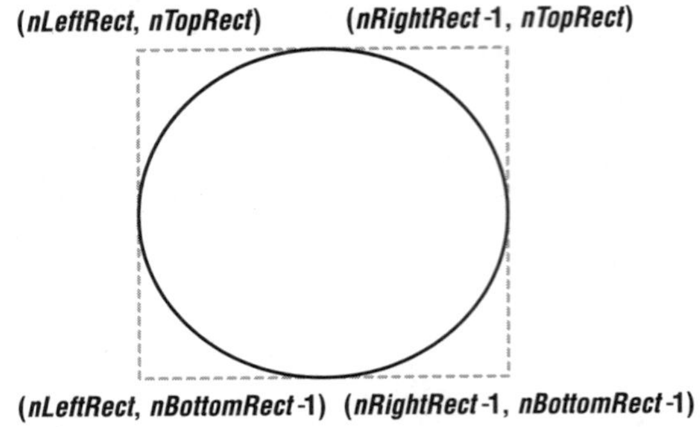

Figure 2-9. *The ellipse is drawn within the bounding rectangle passed to the* Ellipse *function.*

Round rectangles

The *RoundRect* function,

```
BOOL RoundRect (HDC hdc, int nLeftRect, int nTopRect,
                int nRightRect, int nBottomRect,
                int nWidth, int nHeight);
```

draws a rectangle with rounded corners. The roundedness of the corners is defined by the last two parameters that specify the width and height of the ellipse used to round the corners, as shown in Figure 2-10. Specifying the ellipse height and width enables your program to draw identically symmetrical rounded corners. Shortening the ellipse height flattens out the sides of the rectangle, while shortening the width of the ellipse flattens the top and bottom of the rectangle.

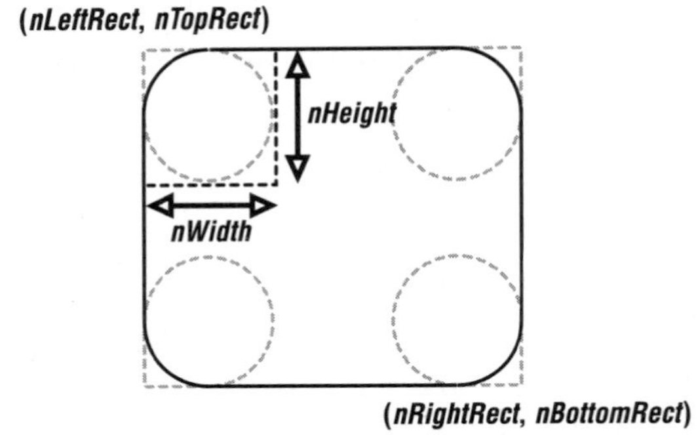

Figure 2-10. *The height and width of the ellipse define the round corners of the rectangle drawn by* RoundRect.

Polygons

Finally, the *Polygon* function,

```
BOOL Polygon (HDC hdc, const POINT *lpPoints, int nCount);
```

draws a many-sided shape. The second parameter is a pointer to an array of point structures defining the points that delineate the polygon. The resulting shape has one more side than the number of points because the function automatically completes the last line of the polygon by connecting the last point with the first. Under Windows CE 1.0, this function is limited to producing convex polygons.

The Shapes Example Program

The Shapes program, shown in Figure 2-11, demonstrates a number of these functions. In Shapes, five figures are drawn, each filled with a different brush.

Shapes.h

```
//======================================================================
// Header file
//
// Written for the book Programming Windows CE
// Copyright (C) 1998 Douglas Boling
//
//================================================================================
// Returns number of elements
#define dim(x) (sizeof(x) / sizeof(x[0]))

//----------------------------------------------------------------------
// Generic defines and data types
//
struct decodeUINT {                             // Structure associates
    UINT Code;                                  // messages
                                                // with a function.
    LRESULT (*Fxn)(HWND, UINT, WPARAM, LPARAM);
};
struct decodeCMD {                              // Structure associates
    UINT Code;                                  // menu IDs with a
    LRESULT (*Fxn)(HWND, WORD, HWND, WORD);     // function.
};

//----------------------------------------------------------------------
// Generic defines used by application
#define  IDC_CMDBAR 1                           // Command bar ID
//----------------------------------------------------------------------
// Defines used by MyCreateHatchedBrush
//
```

Figure 2-11. *The Shapes program.* *(continued)*

Figure 2-11. *continued*

```
typedef struct {
    BITMAPINFOHEADER bmi;
    COLORREF dwPal[2];
    BYTE bBits[64];
} BRUSHBMP;

#define HS_HORIZONTAL       0       /* ----- */
#define HS_VERTICAL         1       /* ||||| */
#define HS_FDIAGONAL        2       /* \\\\\ */
#define HS_BDIAGONAL        3       /* ///// */
#define HS_CROSS            4       /* +++++ */
#define HS_DIAGCROSS        5       /* xxxxx */


//----------------------------------------------------------------------
// Function prototypes
//
int InitApp (HINSTANCE);
HWND InitInstance (HINSTANCE, LPWSTR, int);
int TermInstance (HINSTANCE, int);

// Window procedures
LRESULT CALLBACK MainWndProc (HWND, UINT, WPARAM, LPARAM);

// Message handlers
LRESULT DoCreateMain (HWND, UINT, WPARAM, LPARAM);
LRESULT DoPaintMain (HWND, UINT, WPARAM, LPARAM);
LRESULT DoDestroyMain (HWND, UINT, WPARAM, LPARAM);
```

Shapes.c

```
//======================================================================
// Shapes- Brush and shapes demo for Windows CE
//
// Written for the book Programming Windows CE
// Copyright (C) 1998 Douglas Boling
//
//======================================================================
#include <windows.h>                 // For all that Windows stuff
#include <commctrl.h>                // Command bar includes
#include "shapes.h"                  // Program-specific stuff
```

```
//----------------------------------------------------------------------
// Global data
//
const TCHAR szAppName[] = TEXT ("Shapes");
HINSTANCE hInst;                     // Program instance handle

// Message dispatch table for MainWindowProc
const struct decodeUINT MainMessages[] = {
    WM_CREATE, DoCreateMain,
    WM_PAINT, DoPaintMain,
    WM_DESTROY, DoDestroyMain,
};

//======================================================================
//
// Program entry point
//
int WINAPI WinMain (HINSTANCE hInstance, HINSTANCE hPrevInstance,
                    LPWSTR lpCmdLine, int nCmdShow) {
    MSG msg;
    int rc = 0;
    HWND hwndMain;

    // Initialize application.
    rc = InitApp (hInstance);
    if (rc) return rc;

    // Initialize this instance.
    hwndMain = InitInstance(hInstance, lpCmdLine, nCmdShow);
    if (hwndMain == 0)
        return 0x10;

    // Application message loop
    while (GetMessage (&msg, NULL, 0, 0)) {
        TranslateMessage (&msg);
        DispatchMessage (&msg);
    }
    // Instance cleanup
    return TermInstance (hInstance, msg.wParam);
}
//----------------------------------------------------------------------
// InitApp - Application initialization
//
```

(continued)

Figure 2-11. *continued*

```
int InitApp (HINSTANCE hInstance) {
    WNDCLASS wc;

    // Register application main window class.
    wc.style = 0;                                  // Window style
    wc.lpfnWndProc = MainWndProc;                  // Callback function
    wc.cbClsExtra = 0;                             // Extra class data
    wc.cbWndExtra = 0;                             // Extra window data
    wc.hInstance = hInstance;                      // Owner handle
    wc.hIcon = NULL,                               // Application icon
    wc.hCursor = NULL;                             // Default cursor
    wc.hbrBackground = (HBRUSH) GetStockObject (WHITE_BRUSH);
    wc.lpszMenuName =  NULL;                       // Menu name
    wc.lpszClassName = szAppName;                  // Window class name

    if (RegisterClass (&wc) == 0) return 1;

    return 0;
}
//----------------------------------------------------------------------
// InitInstance - Instance initialization
//
HWND InitInstance (HINSTANCE hInstance, LPWSTR lpCmdLine, int nCmdShow){
    HWND hWnd;

    // Save program instance handle in global variable.
    hInst = hInstance;

    // Create main window.
    hWnd = CreateWindow (szAppName,                // Window class
                         TEXT("Shapes"),           // Window title
                         WS_VISIBLE,               // Style flags
                         CW_USEDEFAULT,            // x position
                         CW_USEDEFAULT,            // y position
                         CW_USEDEFAULT,            // Initial width
                         CW_USEDEFAULT,            // Initial height
                         NULL,                     // Parent
                         NULL,                     // Menu, must be null
                         hInstance,                // Application instance
                         NULL);                    // Pointer to create
                                                   // parameters
    // Return fail code if window not created.
    if (!IsWindow (hWnd)) return 0;

    // Standard show and update calls
```

```
    ShowWindow (hWnd, nCmdShow);
    UpdateWindow (hWnd);
    return hWnd;
}
//----------------------------------------------------------------------
// TermInstance - Program cleanup
//
int TermInstance (HINSTANCE hInstance, int nDefRC) {

    return nDefRC;
}
//======================================================================
// Message handling procedures for MainWindow
//

//----------------------------------------------------------------------
// MainWndProc - Callback function for application window
//
LRESULT CALLBACK MainWndProc (HWND hWnd, UINT wMsg, WPARAM wParam,
                              LPARAM lParam) {
    INT i;
    //
    // Search message list to see if we need to handle this
    // message.  If in list, call procedure.
    //
    for (i = 0; i < dim(MainMessages); i++) {
        if (wMsg == MainMessages[i].Code)
            return (*MainMessages[i].Fxn)(hWnd, wMsg, wParam, lParam);
    }
    return DefWindowProc (hWnd, wMsg, wParam, lParam);
}
//----------------------------------------------------------------------
// DoCreateMain - Process WM_CREATE message for window.
//
LRESULT DoCreateMain (HWND hWnd, UINT wMsg, WPARAM wParam,
                      LPARAM lParam) {
    HWND hwndCB;

    // Create a command bar.
    hwndCB = CommandBar_Create (hInst, hWnd, IDC_CMDBAR);

    // Add exit button to command bar.
    CommandBar_AddAdornments (hwndCB, 0, 0);
    return 0;
}
```

(continued)

Figure 2-11. *continued*

```
//----------------------------------------------------------------------
// MyCreateHachBrush - Creates hatched brushes
//
HBRUSH MyCreateHachBrush (INT fnStyle, COLORREF clrref) {
    BRUSHBMP brbmp;
    BYTE *pBytes;
    int i;
    DWORD dwBits[6][2] = {
        {0x000000ff,0x00000000}, {0x10101010,0x10101010},
        {0x01020408,0x10204080}, {0x80402010,0x08040201},
        {0x101010ff,0x10101010}, {0x81422418,0x18244281},
    };

    if ((fnStyle < 0) || (fnStyle > dim(dwBits)))
        return 0;
    memset (&brbmp, 0, sizeof (brbmp));

    brbmp.bmi.biSize = sizeof (BITMAPINFOHEADER);
    brbmp.bmi.biWidth = 8;
    brbmp.bmi.biHeight = 8;
    brbmp.bmi.biPlanes = 1;
    brbmp.bmi.biBitCount = 1;
    brbmp.bmi.biClrUsed = 2;
    brbmp.bmi.biClrImportant = 2;

    // Initialize the palette of the bitmap.
    brbmp.dwPal[0] = PALETTERGB(0xff,0xff,0xff);
    brbmp.dwPal[1] = PALETTERGB((BYTE)((clrref >> 16) & 0xff),
                                (BYTE)((clrref >> 8) & 0xff),
                                (BYTE)(clrref & 0xff));

    // Write the hatch data to the bitmap.
    pBytes = (BYTE *)&dwBits[fnStyle];
    for (i = 0; i < 8; i++)
        brbmp.bBits[i*4] = *pBytes++;

    // Return the handle of the brush created.
    return CreateDIBPatternBrushPt (&brbmp, DIB_RGB_COLORS);
}
//----------------------------------------------------------------------
// DoPaintMain - Process WM_PAINT message for window.
//
//#define ENDPOINTS 32
#define ENDPOINTS 64
```

```
LRESULT DoPaintMain (HWND hWnd, UINT wMsg, WPARAM wParam,
                     LPARAM lParam) {
    PAINTSTRUCT ps;
    RECT rect;
    HDC hdc;
    POINT ptArray[ENDPOINTS];
    HBRUSH hBr, hOldBr;
    TCHAR szText[128];

    // Adjust the size of the client rect to take into account
    // the command bar height.
    GetClientRect (hWnd, &rect);
    rect.top += CommandBar_Height (GetDlgItem (hWnd, IDC_CMDBAR));

    hdc = BeginPaint (hWnd, &ps);

    // Draw rectangle.
    hBr = GetStockObject (BLACK_BRUSH);
    hOldBr = SelectObject (hdc, hBr);
    Rectangle (hdc, 50, 50, 125, 150);
    SelectObject (hdc, hOldBr);

    // Draw ellipse.
    hBr = GetStockObject (DKGRAY_BRUSH);
    hOldBr = SelectObject (hdc, hBr);
    Ellipse (hdc, 150, 50, 225, 150);
    SelectObject (hdc, hOldBr);

    // Draw round rectangle.
    hBr = GetStockObject (LTGRAY_BRUSH);
    hOldBr = SelectObject (hdc, hBr);
    RoundRect (hdc, 250, 50, 325, 150, 30, 30);
    SelectObject (hdc, hOldBr);

    // Draw hexagon using Polygon.
    hBr = GetStockObject (WHITE_BRUSH);
    hOldBr = SelectObject (hdc, hBr);
    ptArray[0].x = 387;
    ptArray[0].y = 50;
    ptArray[1].x = 350;
    ptArray[1].y = 75;
    ptArray[2].x = 350;
    ptArray[2].y = 125;
```

(continued)

Figure 2-11. *continued*

```
    ptArray[3].x = 387;
    ptArray[3].y = 150;
    ptArray[4].x = 425;
    ptArray[4].y = 125;
    ptArray[5].x = 425;
    ptArray[5].y = 75;

    Polygon (hdc, ptArray, 6);
    SelectObject (hdc, hOldBr);

    hBr = MyCreateHachBrush (HS_DIAGCROSS, RGB (0, 0, 0));
    hOldBr = SelectObject (hdc, hBr);
    Rectangle (hdc, 50, 165, 425, 210);
    SelectObject (hdc, hOldBr);
    DeleteObject (hBr);

    SetBkMode (hdc, OPAQUE);
    lstrcpy (szText, TEXT ("Opaque background"));
    ExtTextOut (hdc, 60, 175, 0, NULL,
                szText, lstrlen (szText), NULL);

    SetBkMode (hdc, TRANSPARENT);
    lstrcpy (szText, TEXT ("Transparent background"));
    ExtTextOut (hdc, 250, 175, 0, NULL,
                szText, lstrlen (szText), NULL);

    EndPaint (hWnd, &ps);
    return 0;
}
//----------------------------------------------------------------------
// DoDestroyMain - Process WM_DESTROY message for window.
//
LRESULT DoDestroyMain (HWND hWnd, UINT wMsg, WPARAM wParam,
                       LPARAM lParam) {
    PostQuitMessage (0);
    return 0;
}
```

In Shapes, *OnPaintMain* draws the five figures using the different functions discussed earlier. For each of the shapes, a different brush is created, selected into the device context, and, after the shape has been drawn, deselected from the DC. The first four shapes are filled with solid grayscale shades, ranging from black to white. These solid brushes are loaded with the *GetStockObject* function. The final shape is filled with a brush created with the *CreateDIBPatternBrushPt*. The creation of this brush is segregated into a function called *MyCreateHatchBrush* that mimics the *CreateHatchBrush* function not available under Windows CE. To create the hatched brushes, a black and white bitmap is built by filling in a bitmap structure and setting the bits to form the hatch patterns. The bitmap itself is the 8-by-8 bitmap specified by *CreateDIBPatternBrushPt*. Since the bitmap is monochrome, its total size, including the palette and header, is only around 100 bytes. Notice, however, that since each scan line of a bitmap must be double-word aligned, the last three bytes of each one-byte scan line are left unused.

Finally the program completes the painting by writing two lines of text into the lower rectangle. The text further demonstrate the difference between the opaque and transparent drawing modes of the system. In this case, the opaque mode of drawing the text might be a better match for the situation because the hatched lines tend to obscure letters drawn in transparent mode. A view of the Shapes window is shown in Figure 2-12.

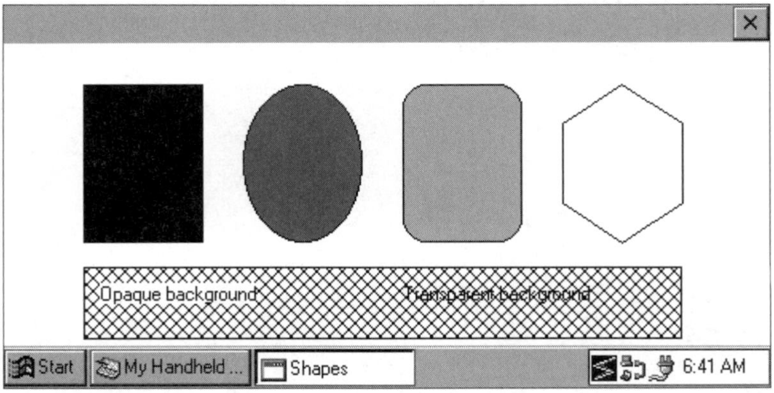

Figure 2-12. *The Shapes example demonstrates drawing different filled shapes.*

To keep things simple, the Shapes example assumes that it's running on at least a 480-pixel-wide display. To properly display the same shapes on a Palm-size PC requires a few minor changes to the coordinates used to position the shapes displayed.

I have barely scratched the surface of the abilities of the Windows CE GDI portion of GWE. The goal of this chapter wasn't to provide total presentation of all aspects of GDI programming. Instead, I wanted to demonstrate the methods available for basic drawing and text support under Windows CE. In other chapters in the book, I extend some of the techniques touched on in this chapter. I talk about these new techniques and newly introduced functions at the point, generally, where I demonstrate how to use them in code. To further your knowledge, I recommend *Programming Windows 95*, by Charles Petzold (Microsoft Press, 1996), as the best source for learning about the Windows GDI.

Now that we've looked at output, it's time to turn our attention to the input side of the system, the keyboard and touch panel.

Chapter 3

Input: Keyboard, Stylus, and Menus

Traditionally, Microsoft Windows platforms have allowed users two methods of input: the keyboard and the mouse. Windows CE continues this tradition, but replaces the mouse with a stylus and touch screen. Programmatically, the change is minor because the messages from the stylus are mapped to the mouse messages used in other versions of Windows. A more subtle but also more important change from versions of Windows that run on PCs is that a system running Windows CE might have either a tiny keyboard or no keyboard at all. This makes the stylus input that much more important for Windows CE systems.

THE KEYBOARD

While keyboards play a lesser role in Windows CE, they're still the best means of entering large volumes of information. Even on systems without a physical keyboard such as the Palm-size PC, *soft* keyboards—controls that simulate keyboards on a touch screen—will most likely be available to the user. Given this, proper handling of keyboard input is critical to all but the most specialized of Windows CE applications. While I'll talk at length about soft keyboards later in the book, one point should be made here. To the application, input from a soft keyboard is no different from input from a traditional "hard" keyboard.

Input Focus

Under Windows operating systems, only one window at a time has the input focus. The focus window receives all keyboard input until it loses focus to another window. The system assigns the keyboard focus using a number of rules but most often the focus window is the current active window. The active window, you'll recall, is the top-level window, the one with which the user is currently interacting. With rare exceptions, the active window also sits at the top of the Z-order; that is, it's drawn on top of all other windows in the system. The user can change the active window by pressing Alt-Esc to switch between programs or by tapping on another top-level window's button on the task bar. The focus window is either the active window or one of its child windows.

Under Windows, a program can determine which window has the input focus by calling

```
HWND GetFocus (void);
```

The focus can be changed to another window by calling

```
HWND SetFocus (HWND hWnd);
```

Under Windows CE, the target window of *SetFocus* is limited. The window being given the focus by *SetFocus* must have been created by the thread calling *SetFocus*. An exception to this rule occurs if the window losing focus is related to the window gaining focus by a parent/child or sibling relationship; in this case, the focus can be changed even if the windows were created by different threads.

When a window loses focus, Windows sends a WM_KILLFOCUS message to that window informing it of its new state. The *wParam* parameter contains the handle of the window that will be gaining the focus. The window gaining focus receives a WM_SETFOCUS message. The *wParam* parameter of the WM_SETFOCUS message contains the handle of the window losing focus.

Now for a bit of motherhood. Programs shouldn't change the focus window without some input from the user. Otherwise, the user can easily become confused. A proper use of *SetFocus* is to set the input focus to a child window (more than likely a control) contained in the active window. In this case, a window would respond to the WM_SETFOCUS message by calling *SetFocus* with the handle of a child window contained in the window to which the program wants to direct keyboard messages.

Keyboard Messages

Windows CE practices the same keyboard message processing as its larger desktop relations with a few small exceptions, which I cover shortly. When a key is pressed, Windows sends a series of messages to the focus window, typically beginning with a WM_KEYDOWN message. If the key pressed represents a character such as letter or number, Windows follows the WM_KEYDOWN with a WM_CHAR message. (Some keys, such as function keys and cursor keys don't represent characters, so WM_CHAR messages aren't sent in response to those keys. For those keys, a program must interpret the WM_KEYDOWN message to know when the keys are pressed.) When the key is released, Windows sends a WM_KEYUP message. If a key is held down long enough for the auto-repeat feature to kick in, multiple WM_KEYDOWN and WM_CHAR messages are sent for each auto-repeat until the key is released when the final WM_KEYUP message is sent. I used the word *typically* to qualify this process because if the Alt key is being held when another key is pressed, the messages I've just described are replaced by WM_SYSKEYDOWN, WM_SYSCHAR, and WM_SYSKEYUP messages.

For all of these messages, the generic parameters *wParam* and *lParam* are used in mostly the same manner. For WM_KEY*xx* and WM_SYSKEY*xx* messages, the *wParam* value contains the virtual key value, indicating the key being pressed. All versions of Windows provide a level of indirection between the keyboard hardware and applications by translating the scan codes returned by the keyboard into virtual key values. You see a list of the VK_*xx* values and their associated keys in Figure 3-1. While the table of virtual keys is extensive, not all keys listed in the table are present on Windows CE devices. For example, function keys, a mainstay on PC keyboards and listed in the virtual key table, aren't present on most Windows CE keyboards. In fact, a number of keys on a PC keyboard are left off the space-constrained Windows CE keyboards. A short list of the keys not typically used on Windows CE devices is presented in Figure 3-2 on page 92. This list is meant to inform you that these keys might not exist, not to indicate that the keys *never* exist on Windows CE keyboards.

VIRTUAL-KEY CODES

Constant	*Value*	*Keyboard Equivalent*
VK_LBUTTON	01	Stylus tap
VK_RBUTTON	02	Mouse right button§
VK_CANCEL	03	Control-break processing
VK_RBUTTON	04	Mouse middle button§
--	05–07	Undefined
VK_BACK	08	Backspace key
VK_TAB	09	Tab key
--	0A–0B	Undefined
VK_CLEAR	0C	Clear key

Figure 3-1. *Virtual key values in relation to the keys on the keyboard. Not all keys will be on all keyboards.* *(continued)*

Figure 3-1. *continued*

Constant	*Value*	*Keyboard Equivalent*
VK_RETURN	0D	Enter key
--	0E–0F	Undefined
VK_SHIFT	10	Shift key
VK_CONTROL	11	Ctrl key
VK_MENU	12	Alt key
VK_CAPITAL	14	Caps Lock key
--	15–19	Reserved for Kanji systems
--	1A	Undefined
VK_ESCAPE	1B	Escape key
--	1C–1F	Reserved for Kanji systems
VK_SPACE	20	Spacebar
VK_PRIOR	21	Page Up key
VK_NEXT	22	Page Down key
VK_END	23	End key
VK_HOME	24	Home key
VK_LEFT	25	Left Arrow key
VK_UP	26	Up Arrow key
VK_RIGHT	27	Right Arrow key
VK_DOWN	28	Down Arrow key
VK_SELECT	29	Select key
--	2A	Original equipment manufacturer (OEM)–specific
VK_EXECUTE	2B	Execute key
VK_SNAPSHOT	2C	Print Screen key for Windows 3.0 and later
VK_INSERT	2D	Insert *
VK_DELETE	2E	Delete †
VK_HELP	2F	Help key
VK_0–VK_9	30–39	0–9 keys
--	3A–40	Undefined
VK_A–VK_Z	41–5A	A through Z keys
VK_LWIN	5B	Windows key
VK_RWIN	5C	Windows key *

Constant	*Value*	*Keyboard Equivalent*
VK_APPS	5D	
--	5E–5F	Undefined
VK_NUMPAD0–9	60–69	Numeric keypad 0–9 keys
VK_MULTIPLY	6A	Numeric keypad Asterisk (*) key
VK_ADD	6B	Numeric keypad Plus sign (+) key
VK_SEPARATOR	6C	Separator key
VK_SUBTRACT	6D	Numeric keypad Minus sign (–) key
VK_DECIMAL	6E	Numeric keypad Period (.) key
VK_DIVIDE	6F	Numeric keypad Slash mark (/) key
VK_F1–VK_F24	70–87	F1–F24 *
--	88–8F	Unassigned
VK_NUMLOCK	90	Num Lock *
VK_SCROLL	91	Scroll Lock *
--	92–9F	Unassigned
VK_LSHIFT	A0	Left Shift‡
VK_RSHIFT	A1	Right Shift‡
VK_LCONTROL	A2	Left Control‡
VK_RCONTROL	A3	Right Control‡
VK_LMENU	A4	Left Alt‡
VK_RMENU	A5	Right Alt‡
--	A6–B9	Unassigned
VK_SEMICOLON	BA	; key
VK_EQUAL	BB	= key
VK_COMMA	BC	, key
VK_HYPHEN	BD	- key
VK_PERIOD	BE	. key
VK_SLASH	BF	/ key
VK_BACKQUOTE	C0	` key
--	C1–DA	Unassigned
VK_LBRACKET	DB	[key
VK_BACKSLASH	DC	\ key
VK_RBRACKET	DD	] key
VK_APOSTROPHE	DE	‘ key

(continued)

Figure 3-1. *continued*

Constant	*Value*	*Keyboard Equivalent*
VK_OFF	DF	Power button
--	E5	Unassigned
--	E6	OEM-specific
--	E7–E8	Unassigned
--	E9–F5	OEM-specific
VK_ATTN	F6	
VK_CRSEL	F7	
VK_EXSEL	F8	
VK_EREOF	F9	
VK_PLAY	FA	
VK_ZOOM	FB	
VK_NONAME	FC	
VK_PA1	FD	
VK_OEM_CLEAR	FE	

* Many Windows CE Systems don't have this key.

† On some Windows CE systems, Delete is simulated with Shift-Backspace

‡ These constants can be used only with *GetKeyState* and *GetAsyncKeyState*.

§ Mouse right and middle buttons are defined but are relevant only on a Windows CE system equipped with a mouse.

For the WM_CHAR and WM_SYSCHAR messages, the *wParam* value contains the Unicode character represented by the key. Most often an application can simply look for WM_CHAR messages and ignore WM_KEYDOWN and WM_KEYUP. The WM_CHAR message allows for a second level of abstraction so that the application doesn't have to worry about the up or down state of the keys and can concentrate on the characters being entered by means of the keyboard.

The *lParam* value of any of these keyboard messages contains further information about the pressed key. The format of the *lParam* parameter is shown in Figure 3-3 on the following page.

InsertDelete (Many Windows CE keyboards use Shift-Backspace for this function.)

Num LockPause

Print Screen

Scroll Lock

Function Keys

Windows Context Menu key

Figure 3-2. *Keys on a PC keyboard that are rarely on a Windows CE keyboard.*

The low word, bits 0 through 15, contains the repeat count of the key. Often, keys on a Windows CE device can be pressed faster than Windows CE can send messages to the focus application. In these cases, the repeat count contains the number of times the key has been pressed. Bit 29 contains the context flag. If the Alt key was being held down when the key was pressed, this bit will be set. Bit 30 contains the previous key state. If the key was previously down, this bit is set; otherwise it's 0. Bit 30 can be used to determine whether the key message is the result of an auto-repeat sequence. Bit 31 indicates the transition state. If the key is in transition from down to up, Bit 31 is set. The Reserved field, bits 16 through 28, is used in the desktop versions of Windows to indicate the key scan code. In almost all cases, Windows CE doesn't support this field. However, on some of the newer Windows CE platforms where scan codes are necessary, this field does contain the scan code. You shouldn't plan on the scan code field being available unless you know it's supported on your specific platform.

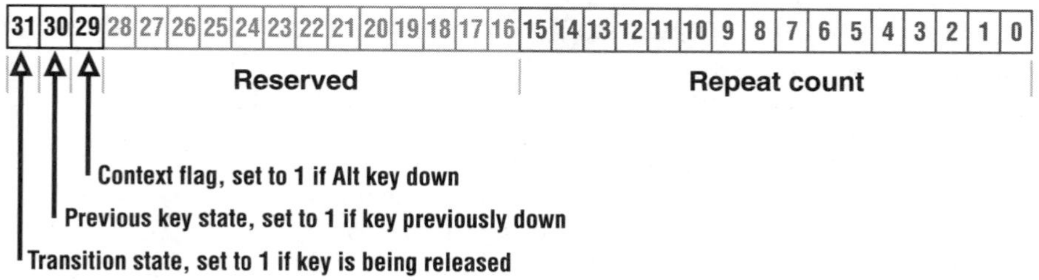

Figure 3-3. *The layout of the* lParam *value for key messages.*

One additional keyboard message, WM_DEADCHAR, can sometimes come into play. You send it when the pressed key represents a dead character, such as an umlaut, that you want to combine with a character to create a different character. In this case the WM_DEADCHAR message can be used to prevent the text entry point (the caret) from advancing to the next space until the second key is pressed so that you can complete the combined character.

The WM_DEADCHAR message has always been present under Windows, but under Windows CE it takes on a somewhat larger role. With the internationalization of small consumer devices that run Windows CE, programmers should plan for, and if necessary use, the WM_DEADCHAR message that is so often necessary in foreign language systems.

Keyboard Functions

You will find useful a few other keyboard-state-determining functions for Windows applications. Among the keyboard functions, two are closely related but often confused: *GetKeyState* and *GetAsyncKeyState*.

GetKeyState, prototyped as

```
SHORT GetKeyState (int nVirtKey);
```

returns the up/down state of the shift keys, Ctrl, Alt, and Shift, and indicates whether any of these keys is in a toggled state. If the keyboard has two keys with the same function—for example, two Shift keys, one on each side of the keyboard—this function can also be used to differentiate which of them is being pressed. (Most keyboards have left and right Shift keys, and some include left and right Ctrl and Alt keys.)

You pass to the function the virtual key code for the key being queried. If the high bit of the return value is set, the key is down. If the least significant bit of the return value is set, the key is in a toggled state; that is, it has been pressed an odd number of times since the system was started. The state returned is the state at the time the most recent message was read from the message queue, which isn't necessarily the real-time state of the key. An interesting aside: notice that the virtual key label for the Alt key is VK_MENU, which relates to the windows convention that the Alt-shift key combination works in concert with other keys to access various menus from the keyboard.

Note that the *GetKeyState* function is limited under Windows CE to querying the state of the shift keys. Under other versions of Windows, *GetKeyState* can determine the state of every key on the keyboard.

To determine the real-time state of a key, use

```
SHORT GetAsyncKeyState (int vKey);
```

As with *GetKeyState*, you pass to this function the virtual key code for the key being queried. The *GetAsyncKeyState* function returns a value subtly different from the one returned by *GetKeyState*. As with the *GetKeyState* function, the high bit of the return value is set while the key is being pressed. However, the least significant bit is then set if the key was pressed after a previous call to *GetAsyncKeyState*. Like *GetKeyState*, the *GetAsyncKeyState* function can distinguish the left and right Shift, Ctrl, and Alt keys. In addition, by passing the VK_LBUTTON virtual key value, *GetAsyncKeyState* determines whether the stylus is currently touching the screen.

An application can simulate a keystroke using the *keybd_event* function:

```
VOID keybd_event (BYTE bVk, BYTE bScan, DWORD dwFlags,
                  DWORD dwExtraInfo);
```

The first parameter is the virtual key code of the key to simulate. The *bScan* code should be set to NULL under Windows CE. The *dwFlags* parameter can have two possible flags: KEYEVENTF_KEYUP indicates that the call is to emulate a key up event while KEYEVENTF_SILENT indicates that the simulated key press won't cause the standard keyboard click that you normally hear when you press a key. So, to fully simulate a key press, *keybd_event* should be called twice, once without

KEYEVENTF_KEYUP to simulate a key down, then once again, this time *with* KEYEVENTF_KEYUP to simulate the key release.

One final keyboard function, *MapVirtualKey*, translates virtual key codes to characters. *MapVirtualKey* in Windows CE doesn't translate keyboard scan codes to and from virtual key codes, although it does so in other versions of Windows. The prototype of the function is the following:

```
UINT MapVirtualKey (UINT uCode, UINT uMapType);
```

Under Windows CE, the first parameter is the virtual key code to be translated while the second parameter, *uMapType*, must be set to 2.

Testing for the keyboard

To determine whether a keyboard is even present in the system, first call *GetVersionEx* to find out which version of Windows CE is running. All systems that run Windows CE 1.0 have a keyboard. When running under Windows CE 2.0 or later, call

```
DWORD GetKeyboardStatus (VOID);
```

This function returns the KBDI_KEYBOARD_PRESENT flag if a hardware keyboard is present in the system. This function also returns a KBDI_KEYBOARD_ENABLED flag if the keyboard is enabled. To disable the keyboard, a call can be made to

```
BOOL EnableHardwareKeyboard (BOOL bEnable);
```

with the *bEnable* flag set to FALSE. You might want to disable the keyboard in a system for which the keyboard folds around behind the screen; in such a system, a user could accidentally hit keys while using the stylus. This function is also new to Windows CE 2.0.

If you build an application to run under Windows CE 1.0, you'll need to explicitly load both *GetKeyboardStatus* and *EnableHardwareKeyboard* using *LoadLibrary* and *GetProcAddress* to determine the address of these 2.0-specific functions. If a call is made directly to a 2.0 function from an application, that application is incompatible with Windows CE 1.0 and won't load.

The KeyTrac Example Program

The following example program, KeyTrac, displays the sequence of keyboard messages. Programmatically, KeyTrac isn't much of a departure from the earlier programs in the book. The difference is that the keyboard messages I've been describing are all trapped and recorded in an array that's then displayed during the WM_PAINT message. For each keyboard message, the message name is recorded along with the *wParam* and *lParam* values and a set of flags indicating the state of the shift keys. The key messages are recorded in an array because these messages can occur faster than the redraw can occur. Figure 3-4 shows the KeyTrac window after a few keys have been pressed.

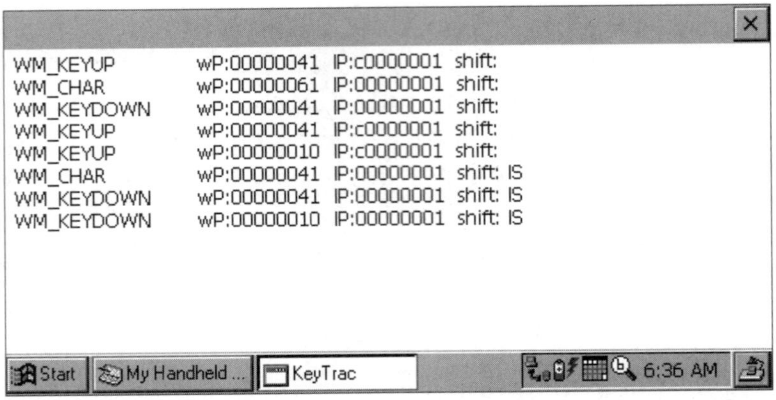

Figure 3-4. *The KeyTrac window after a Shift-A key combination followed by a lowercase* a *key press.*

The best way to learn about the sequence of the keyboard messages is to run KeyTrac, press a few keys, and watch the messages scroll down the screen. Pressing a character key such as the *a* results in three messages: WM_KEYDOWN, WM_CHAR, and WM_KEYUP. Holding down the Shift key while pressing the *a* and then releasing the Shift key produces a key-down message for the Shift key followed by the three messages for the *a* key followed by a key-up message for the Shift key. Because the Shift key itself isn't a character key, no WM_CHAR message is sent in response to it. However, the WM_CHAR message for the *a* key now contains a *0x41* in the *wParam* value, indicating that an uppercase *A* was entered instead of a lowercase *a*.

Figure 3-5 shows the source code for the KeyTrac program.

KeyTrac.h

```
//======================================================================
// Header file
//
// Written for the book Programming Windows CE
// Copyright (C) 1998 Douglas Boling
//
//======================================================================
// Returns number of elements
#define dim(x) (sizeof(x) / sizeof(x[0]))

//----------------------------------------------------------------------
// Generic defines and data types
//
```

Figure 3-5. *The KeyTrac program.*

```
struct decodeUINT {                              // Structure associates
    UINT Code;                                   // messages
                                                 // with a function.
    LRESULT (*Fxn)(HWND, UINT, WPARAM, LPARAM);
};
struct decodeCMD {                               // Structure associates
    UINT Code;                                   // menu IDs with a
    LRESULT (*Fxn)(HWND, WORD, HWND, WORD);      // function.
};

//----------------------------------------------------------------------
// Generic defines used by application
#define  IDC_CMDBAR 1                            // Command bar ID

//----------------------------------------------------------------------
// Program-specific defines and structures
//
#define FLAG_LMENU        0x0001
#define FLAG_RMENU        0x0002
#define FLAG_LCONTROL     0x0004
#define FLAG_RCONTROL     0x0008
#define FLAG_LSHIFT       0x0010
#define FLAG_RSHIFT       0x0020

typedef struct {
    UINT wKeyMsg;
    INT wParam;
    INT lParam;
    UINT wFlags;
    TCHAR szMsgTxt[64];
} KEYARRAY, *PKEYARRAY;

//----------------------------------------------------------------------
// Function prototypes
//
int InitApp (HINSTANCE);
HWND InitInstance (HINSTANCE, LPWSTR, int);
int TermInstance (HINSTANCE, int);

// Window procedures
LRESULT CALLBACK MainWndProc (HWND, UINT, WPARAM, LPARAM);

// Message handlers
LRESULT DoCreateMain (HWND, UINT, WPARAM, LPARAM);
LRESULT DoPaintMain (HWND, UINT, WPARAM, LPARAM);
LRESULT DoKeysMain (HWND, UINT, WPARAM, LPARAM);
LRESULT DoDestroyMain (HWND, UINT, WPARAM, LPARAM);
```

(continued)

Figure 3-5. *continued*

KeyTrac.c

```
//======================================================================
// KeyTrac - displays keyboard messages
//
// Written for the book Programming Windows CE
// Copyright (C) 1998 Douglas Boling
//
//======================================================================
#include <windows.h>                 // For all that Windows stuff
#include <commctrl.h>                // Command bar includes
#include "keytrac.h"                 // Program-specific stuff

//----------------------------------------------------------------------
// Global data
//
const TCHAR szAppName[] = TEXT ("KeyTrac");
HINSTANCE hInst;                     // Program instance handle

// Program-specific global data
KEYARRAY ka[16];
UINT wKeyMsg = 0;
INT nKeyCnt = 0, nFontHeight;
TCHAR szMsgTxt[64];

// Message dispatch table for MainWindowProc
const struct decodeUINT MainMessages[] = {
    WM_CREATE, DoCreateMain,
    WM_PAINT, DoPaintMain,
    WM_KEYUP, DoKeysMain,
    WM_KEYDOWN, DoKeysMain,
    WM_CHAR, DoKeysMain,
    WM_DEADCHAR, DoKeysMain,
    WM_SYSCHAR, DoKeysMain,
    WM_SYSDEADCHAR, DoKeysMain,
    WM_SYSKEYDOWN, DoKeysMain,
    WM_SYSKEYUP, DoKeysMain,
    WM_DESTROY, DoDestroyMain,
};

//======================================================================
//
// Program entry point
//
```

```
int WINAPI WinMain (HINSTANCE hInstance, HINSTANCE hPrevInstance,
                    LPWSTR lpCmdLine, int nCmdShow) {
    MSG msg;
    int rc = 0;
    HWND hwndMain;

    // Initialize application.
    rc = InitApp (hInstance);
    if (rc) return rc;

    // Initialize this instance.
    hwndMain = InitInstance (hInstance, lpCmdLine, nCmdShow);
    if (hwndMain == 0)
        return 0x10;

    // Application message loop
    while (GetMessage (&msg, NULL, 0, 0)) {
        TranslateMessage (&msg);
        DispatchMessage (&msg);
    }
    // Instance cleanup
    return TermInstance (hInstance, msg.wParam);
}
//----------------------------------------------------------------------
// InitApp - Application initialization
//
int InitApp (HINSTANCE hInstance) {
    WNDCLASS wc;

    // Register application main window class.
    wc.style = 0;                             // Window style
    wc.lpfnWndProc = MainWndProc;             // Callback function
    wc.cbClsExtra = 0;                        // Extra class data
    wc.cbWndExtra = 0;                        // Extra window data
    wc.hInstance = hInstance;                 // Owner handle
    wc.hIcon = NULL,                          // Application icon
    wc.hCursor = NULL;                        // Default cursor
    wc.hbrBackground = (HBRUSH) GetStockObject (WHITE_BRUSH);
    wc.lpszMenuName =  NULL;                  // Menu name
    wc.lpszClassName = szAppName;             // Window class name

    if (RegisterClass(&wc) == 0) return 1;

    return 0;
}
```

(continued)

Figure 3-5. *continued*

```
//----------------------------------------------------------------------
// InitInstance - Instance initialization
//
HWND InitInstance (HINSTANCE hInstance, LPWSTR lpCmdLine, int nCmdShow) {
                   HWND hWnd;

    // Save program instance handle in global variable.
    hInst = hInstance;

    // Create main window.
    hWnd = CreateWindow (szAppName,           // Window class
                         TEXT ("KeyTrac"),    // Window title
                         WS_VISIBLE,          // Style flags
                         CW_USEDEFAULT,       // x position
                         CW_USEDEFAULT,       // y position
                         CW_USEDEFAULT,       // Initial Width
                         CW_USEDEFAULT,       // Initial Height
                         NULL,                // Parent
                         NULL,                // Menu, must be null
                         hInstance,           // App instance
                         NULL);               // Pointer to create
                                              // parameters
    // Return fail code if window not created.
    if (!IsWindow (hWnd)) return 0;

    // Standard show and update calls
    ShowWindow (hWnd, nCmdShow);
    UpdateWindow (hWnd);
    return hWnd;
}
//----------------------------------------------------------------------
// TermInstance - Program cleanup
//
int TermInstance (HINSTANCE hInstance, int nDefRC) {

    return nDefRC;
}
//======================================================================
// Message handling procedures for MainWindow
//

//----------------------------------------------------------------------
// MainWndProc - Callback function for application window
//
LRESULT CALLBACK MainWndProc (HWND hWnd, UINT wMsg, WPARAM wParam,
                              LPARAM lParam) {
```

```
    INT i;
    //
    // Search message list to see if we need to handle this
    // message.  If in list, call procedure.
    //
    for (i = 0; i < dim(MainMessages); i++) {
        if (wMsg == MainMessages[i].Code)
            return (*MainMessages[i].Fxn)(hWnd, wMsg, wParam, lParam);
    }
    return DefWindowProc (hWnd, wMsg, wParam, lParam);
}
//----------------------------------------------------------------------
// DoCreateMain - Process WM_CREATE message for window.
//
LRESULT DoCreateMain (HWND hWnd, UINT wMsg, WPARAM wParam,
                      LPARAM lParam) {
    HWND hwndCB;
    HDC hdc;
    TEXTMETRIC tm;

    // Create a command bar.
    hwndCB = CommandBar_Create (hInst, hWnd, IDC_CMDBAR);

    // Add exit button to command bar.
    CommandBar_AddAdornments (hwndCB, 0, 0);

    // Get the height of the default font.
    hdc = GetDC (hWnd);
    GetTextMetrics (hdc, &tm);
    nFontHeight = tm.tmHeight + tm.tmExternalLeading;
    ReleaseDC (hWnd, hdc);

    return 0;
}
//----------------------------------------------------------------------
// DoPaintMain - Process WM_PAINT message for window.
//
LRESULT DoPaintMain (HWND hWnd, UINT wMsg, WPARAM wParam,
                     LPARAM lParam) {
    PAINTSTRUCT ps;
    RECT rect, rectOut;
    TCHAR szOut[256];
    HDC hdc;
    INT i;

    // Adjust the size of the client rect to take into account
    // the command bar height.
```

(continued)

Figure 3-5. *continued*

```
    GetClientRect (hWnd, &rect);
    rect.top += CommandBar_Height (GetDlgItem (hWnd, IDC_CMDBAR));

    // Create a drawing rectangle for the bottom line of the window.
    rectOut = rect;
    rectOut.top = rectOut.bottom - nFontHeight;

    hdc = BeginPaint (hWnd, &ps);

    if (nKeyCnt) {
        for (i = 0; i < nKeyCnt; i++) {
            // Scroll window up by one line.
            ScrollDC (hdc, 0, -nFontHeight, &rect, &rect, NULL, NULL);
            // Write key name, use opaque mode to erase background.
            ExtTextOut (hdc, 5, rect.bottom - nFontHeight, ETO_OPAQUE,
                        &rectOut, ka[i].szMsgTxt,
                        lstrlen (ka[i].szMsgTxt), NULL);
            // Write key variables.
            wsprintf (szOut, TEXT ("wParam:%08x    lParam:%08x    shift: "),
                      ka[i].wParam, ka[i].lParam);

            if (ka[i].wFlags & FLAG_LMENU)
                lstrcat (szOut, TEXT ("lA "));
            if (ka[i].wFlags & FLAG_RMENU)
                lstrcat (szOut, TEXT ("rA "));

            if (ka[i].wFlags & FLAG_LCONTROL)
                lstrcat (szOut, TEXT ("lC "));
            if (ka[i].wFlags & FLAG_RCONTROL)
                lstrcat (szOut, TEXT ("rC "));

            if (ka[i].wFlags & FLAG_LSHIFT)
                lstrcat (szOut, TEXT ("lS "));
            if (ka[i].wFlags & FLAG_RSHIFT)
                lstrcat (szOut, TEXT ("rS "));

            ExtTextOut (hdc, 125, rect.bottom - nFontHeight, 0, NULL,
                        szOut, lstrlen (szOut), NULL);
        }
        nKeyCnt = 0;
    }
    EndPaint (hWnd, &ps);
    return 0;
}
//----------------------------------------------------------------------
```

```
// DoKeysMain - Process all keyboard messages for window.
//
LRESULT DoKeysMain (HWND hWnd, UINT wMsg, WPARAM wParam,
                    LPARAM lParam) {

    if (nKeyCnt >= 16)
        return 0;

    switch (wMsg) {
        case WM_KEYUP:
            lstrcpy (ka[nKeyCnt].szMsgTxt, TEXT ("WM_KEYUP"));
            break;

        case WM_KEYDOWN:
            lstrcpy (ka[nKeyCnt].szMsgTxt, TEXT ("WM_KEYDOWN"));
            break;

        case WM_CHAR:
            lstrcpy (ka[nKeyCnt].szMsgTxt, TEXT ("WM_CHAR"));
            break;

        case WM_DEADCHAR:
            lstrcpy (ka[nKeyCnt].szMsgTxt, TEXT ("WM_DEADCHAR"));
            break;

        case WM_SYSCHAR:
            lstrcpy (ka[nKeyCnt].szMsgTxt, TEXT ("WM_SYSCHAR"));
            break;

        case WM_SYSDEADCHAR:
            lstrcpy (ka[nKeyCnt].szMsgTxt, TEXT ("WM_SYSDEADCHAR"));
            break;

        case WM_SYSKEYDOWN:
            lstrcpy (ka[nKeyCnt].szMsgTxt, TEXT ("WM_SYSKEYDOWN"));
            break;

        case WM_SYSKEYUP:
            lstrcpy (ka[nKeyCnt].szMsgTxt, TEXT ("WM_SYSKEYUP"));
            break;

        default:
            lstrcpy (ka[nKeyCnt].szMsgTxt, TEXT ("unknown"));
            break;
    }
```

(continued)

Figure 3-5. *continued*

```
    ka[nKeyCnt].wKeyMsg = wMsg;
    ka[nKeyCnt].wParam = wParam;
    ka[nKeyCnt].lParam = lParam;

    // Capture the state of the shift flags.
    ka[nKeyCnt].wFlags = 0;
    if (GetKeyState (VK_LMENU))
        ka[nKeyCnt].wFlags |= FLAG_LMENU;
    if (GetKeyState (VK_RMENU))
        ka[nKeyCnt].wFlags |= FLAG_RMENU;

    if (GetKeyState (VK_LCONTROL))
        ka[nKeyCnt].wFlags |= FLAG_LCONTROL;
    if (GetKeyState (VK_RCONTROL))
        ka[nKeyCnt].wFlags |= FLAG_RCONTROL;

    if (GetKeyState (VK_LSHIFT))
        ka[nKeyCnt].wFlags |= FLAG_LSHIFT;
    if (GetKeyState (VK_RSHIFT))
        ka[nKeyCnt].wFlags |= FLAG_RSHIFT;

    nKeyCnt++;
    InvalidateRect (hWnd, NULL, FALSE);
    return 0;
}
//----------------------------------------------------------------------
// DoDestroyMain - Process WM_DESTROY message for window.
//
LRESULT DoDestroyMain (HWND hWnd, UINT wMsg, WPARAM wParam,
                       LPARAM lParam) {
    PostQuitMessage (0);
    return 0;
}
```

Here are a few more characteristics of KeyTrac to notice. After each keyboard message is recorded, an *InvalidateRect* function is called to force a redraw of the window and therefore also a WM_PAINT message. As I mentioned in Chapter 2, a program should never attempt to send or post a WM_PAINT message to a window because Windows needs to perform some setup before it calls a window with a WM_PAINT message.

Another device context function used in KeyTrac is

```
BOOL ScrollDC (HDC hDC, int dx, int dy, const RECT *lprcScroll,
               const RECT *lprcClip, HRGN hrgnUpdate,
               LPRECT lprcUpdate);
```

which scrolls an area of the device context either horizontally or vertically, but under Windows CE, not both directions at the same time. The three rectangle parameters define the area to be scrolled, the area within the scrolling area to be clipped, and the area to be painted after the scrolling ends. Alternatively, a handle to a region can be passed to *ScrollDC*. That region is defined by *ScrollDC* to encompass the region that needs painting after the scroll.

Finally, if the KeyTrac window is covered up for any reason and then re-exposed, the message information on the display is lost. This is because a device context doesn't store the bit information of the display. The application is responsible for saving any information necessary to completely restore the client area of the screen. Since Keytrac doesn't save this information, it's lost when the window is covered up.

THE STYLUS AND THE TOUCH SCREEN

The stylus/touch screen combination is new to Windows platforms, but fortunately, its integration into Windows CE applications is relatively painless. The best way to deal with the stylus is to treat it as a single-button mouse. The stylus creates the same mouse messages that are provided by the mouse in other versions of Windows and by Windows CE systems that use a mouse. The differences that do appear between a mouse and a stylus are due to the different physical realities of the two input devices.

Unlike a mouse, a stylus doesn't have a cursor to indicate the current position of the mouse. Therefore a stylus can't *hover* over a point on the screen in the way that the mouse cursor does. A cursor hovers when a user moves it over a window without pressing a mouse button. This concept can't be applied to programming for a stylus because the touch screen can't detect the position of the stylus when it isn't in contact with the screen.

Another consequence of the difference between a stylus and a mouse is that without a mouse cursor, an application can't provide feedback to the user by means of changes in appearance of a hovering cursor. Windows CE does support setting the cursor for one classic Windows method of user feedback. The busy hourglass cursor, indicating that the user must wait for the system to complete processing, is supported under Windows CE so that applications can display the busy hourglass in the same manner as applications running under other versions of Windows, using the *SetCursor* function.

Stylus Messages

When the user presses the stylus on the screen, the topmost window under that point receives the input focus if it didn't have it before and then receives a WM_LBUTTONDOWN message. When the user lifts the stylus, the window receives a WM_LBUTTONUP message. Moving the stylus within the same window while it's down causes WM_MOUSEMOVE messages to be sent to the window. For all of these messages, the *wParam* and *lParam* parameters are loaded with the same values. The *wParam* parameter contains a set of bit flags indicating whether the Ctrl or Shift keys on the keyboard are currently held down. As in other versions of Windows, the Alt key state isn't provided in these messages. To get the state of the Alt key when the message was sent, use the *GetKeyState* function.

The *lParam* parameter contains two 16-bit values that indicate the position on the screen of the tap. The low-order 16 bits contains the *x* (horizontal) location relative to the upper left corner of the client area of the window while the high-order 16 bits contains the *y* (vertical) position.

If the user *double-taps,* that is, taps twice on the screen at the same location and within a predefined time, Windows sends a WM_LBUTTONDBLCLK message to the double-tapped window, but only if that window's class was registered with the CS_DBLCLKS style. The class style is set when the window class is registered with *RegisterClass*.

You can differentiate between a tap and a double-tap by comparing the messages sent to the window. When a double-tap occurs, a window first receives the WM_LBUTTONDOWN and WM_LBUTTONUP messages from the original tap. Then a WM_LBUTTONDBLCLK is sent followed by another WM_LBUTTONUP. The trick is to refrain from acting on a WM_LBUTTONDOWN message in any way that precludes action on a subsequent WM_LBUTTONDBLCLK. This is usually not a problem because taps usually select an object while double-tapping launches the default action for the object.

Inking

A typical application for a handheld device is capturing the user's writing on the screen and storing the result as *ink*. This isn't handwriting recognition—simply ink storage. At first pass, the best way to accomplish this would be to store the stylus points passed in each WM_MOUSEMOVE message. The problem is that sometimes small CE-type devices can't send these messages fast enough to achieve a satisfactory resolution. Under Windows CE 2.0, a new function call has been added to assist programmers in tracking the stylus.

```
BOOL GetMouseMovePoints (PPOINT pptBuf, UINT nBufPoints,
                         UINT *pnPointsRetrieved);
```

GetMouseMovePoints returns a number of stylus points that didn't result in WM_MOUSEMOVE messages. The function is passed an array of points, the size of the array (in points), and a pointer to an integer that will receive the number of points passed back to the application. Once received, these additional points can be used to fill in the blanks between the last WM_MOUSEMOVE message and the current one.

GetMouseMovePoints does throw one curve at you. It returns points in the resolution of the touch panel, not the screen. This is generally set at four times the screen resolution, so you need to divide the coordinates returned by *GetMouseMovePoints* by four to convert them to screen coordinates. The extra resolution helps programs such as handwriting recognizers.

A short example program, PenTrac, illustrates the difference that *GetMouseMovePoints* can make. Figure 3-6 shows the PenTrac window. Notice the two lines of dots across the window. The top line was drawn using points from WM_MOUSEMOVE only. The second line included points that were queried with *GetMouseMovePoints*. The black dots were queried from WM_MOUSEMOVE while the red (lighter) dots were locations queried with *GetMouseMovePoints*.

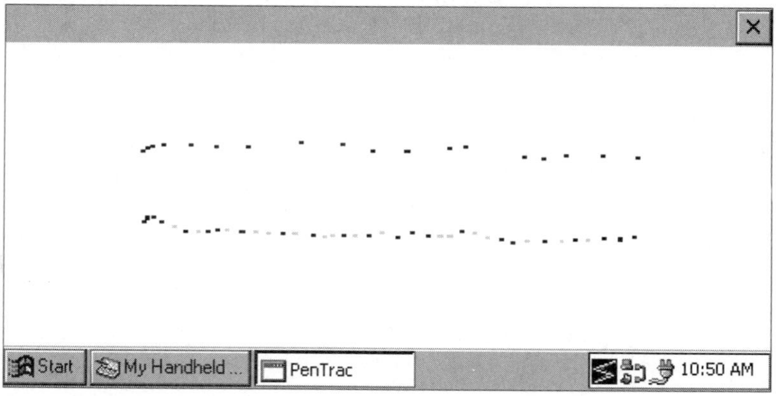

Figure 3-6. *The PenTrac window showing two lines drawn.*

The source code for PenTrac is shown in Figure 3-7. The program places a dot on the screen for each WM_MOUSEMOVE or WM_LBUTTONDOWN message it receives. If the Shift key is held down during the mouse move messages, PenTrac also calls *GetMouseMovePoints* and marks those points in the window in red to distinguish them from the points returned by the mouse messages alone.

PenTrac cheats a little to enhance the effect of *GetMouseMovePoints*. In the *DoMouseMain* routine called to handle WM_MOUSEMOVE and WM_LBUTTONDOWN messages, the routine calls the function *sleep* to kill a few milliseconds. This simulates a slow-responding application that might not have time to process every mouse move message in a timely manner.

PenTrac.h

```
//======================================================================
// Header file
//
// Written for the book Programming Windows CE
// Copyright (C) 1998 Douglas Boling
//
//======================================================================
// Returns number of elements.
#define dim(x) (sizeof(x) / sizeof(x[0]))

//----------------------------------------------------------------------
// Generic defines and data types
//
struct decodeUINT {                             // Structure associates
    UINT Code;                                  // messages
                                                // with a function.
    LRESULT (*Fxn)(HWND, UINT, WPARAM, LPARAM);
};
struct decodeCMD {                              // Structure associates
    UINT Code;                                  // menu IDs with a
    LRESULT (*Fxn)(HWND, WORD, HWND, WORD);     // function.
};

//----------------------------------------------------------------------
// Generic defines used by application
#define  IDC_CMDBAR 1                           // Command bar ID

//----------------------------------------------------------------------
// Function prototypes
//
int InitApp (HINSTANCE);
HWND InitInstance (HINSTANCE, LPWSTR, int);
int TermInstance (HINSTANCE, int);

// Window procedures
LRESULT CALLBACK MainWndProc (HWND, UINT, WPARAM, LPARAM);

// Message handlers
LRESULT DoCreateMain (HWND, UINT, WPARAM, LPARAM);
LRESULT DoPaintMain (HWND, UINT, WPARAM, LPARAM);
LRESULT DoMouseMain (HWND, UINT, WPARAM, LPARAM);
LRESULT DoDestroyMain (HWND, UINT, WPARAM, LPARAM);
```

Figure 3-7. *The PenTrac program.*

PenTrac.c

```
//======================================================================
// PenTrac - Tracks stylus movement
//
// Written for the book Programming Windows CE
// Copyright (C) 1998 Douglas Boling
//
//======================================================================
#include <windows.h>                 // For all that Windows stuff
#include <commctrl.h>                // Command bar includes
#include "pentrac.h"                 // Program-specific stuff

//----------------------------------------------------------------------
// Global data
//
const TCHAR szAppName[] = TEXT ("PenTrac");
HINSTANCE hInst;                     // Program instance handle

// Message dispatch table for MainWindowProc
const struct decodeUINT MainMessages[] = {
    WM_CREATE, DoCreateMain,
    WM_LBUTTONDOWN, DoMouseMain,
    WM_MOUSEMOVE, DoMouseMain,
    WM_DESTROY, DoDestroyMain,
};

//======================================================================
//
// Program entry point
//
int WINAPI WinMain (HINSTANCE hInstance, HINSTANCE hPrevInstance,
                    LPWSTR lpCmdLine, int nCmdShow) {
    MSG msg;
    int rc = 0;
    HWND hwndMain;

    // Initialize application.
    rc = InitApp (hInstance);
    if (rc) return rc;

    // Initialize this instance.
    hwndMain = InitInstance (hInstance, lpCmdLine, nCmdShow);
    if (hwndMain == 0)
        return 0x10;
```

(continued)

Figure 3-7. *continued*

```
    // Application message loop
    while (GetMessage (&msg, NULL, 0, 0)) {
        TranslateMessage (&msg);
        DispatchMessage (&msg);
    }
    // Instance cleanup
    return TermInstance (hInstance, msg.wParam);
}
//----------------------------------------------------------------------
// InitApp - Application initialization
//
int InitApp (HINSTANCE hInstance) {
    WNDCLASS wc;

    // Register application main window class.
    wc.style = 0;                             // Window style
    wc.lpfnWndProc = MainWndProc;             // Callback function
    wc.cbClsExtra = 0;                        // Extra class data
    wc.cbWndExtra = 0;                        // Extra window data
    wc.hInstance = hInstance;                 // Owner handle
    wc.hIcon = NULL,                          // Application icon
    wc.hCursor = NULL;                        // Default cursor
    wc.hbrBackground = (HBRUSH) GetStockObject (WHITE_BRUSH);
    wc.lpszMenuName =  NULL;                  // Menu name
    wc.lpszClassName = szAppName;             // Window class name

    if (RegisterClass (&wc) == 0) return 1;

    return 0;
}
//----------------------------------------------------------------------
// InitInstance - Instance initialization
//
HWND InitInstance (HINSTANCE hInstance, LPWSTR lpCmdLine, int nCmdShow) {
                   HWND hWnd;

    // Save program instance handle in global variable.
    hInst = hInstance;

    // Create main window.
    hWnd = CreateWindow (szAppName,           // Window class
                         TEXT ("PenTrac"),    // Window title
                         WS_VISIBLE,          // Style flags
                         CW_USEDEFAULT,       // x position
                         CW_USEDEFAULT,       // y position
```

```
                           CW_USEDEFAULT,          // Initial width
                           CW_USEDEFAULT,          // Initial height
                           NULL,                   // Parent
                           NULL,                   // Menu, must be null
                           hInstance,              // App instance
                           NULL);                  // Pointer to create
                                                   // parameters
    // Return fail code if window not created.
    if (!IsWindow (hWnd)) return 0;

    // Standard show and update calls
    ShowWindow (hWnd, nCmdShow);
    UpdateWindow (hWnd);
    return hWnd;
}
//----------------------------------------------------------------------
// TermInstance - Program cleanup
//
int TermInstance (HINSTANCE hInstance, int nDefRC) {

    return nDefRC;
}
//======================================================================
// Message handling procedures for MainWindow
//

//----------------------------------------------------------------------
// MainWndProc - Callback function for application window
//
LRESULT CALLBACK MainWndProc (HWND hWnd, UINT wMsg, WPARAM wParam,
                              LPARAM lParam) {
    INT i;
    //
    // Search message list to see if we need to handle this
    // message.  If in list, call procedure.
    //
    for (i = 0; i < dim(MainMessages); i++) {
        if (wMsg == MainMessages[i].Code)
            return (*MainMessages[i].Fxn)(hWnd, wMsg, wParam, lParam);
    }
    return DefWindowProc (hWnd, wMsg, wParam, lParam);
}
//----------------------------------------------------------------------
// DoCreateMain - Process WM_CREATE message for window.
//
```

(continued)

Figure 3-7. *continued*

```
LRESULT DoCreateMain (HWND hWnd, UINT wMsg, WPARAM wParam,
                      LPARAM lParam) {
    HWND hwndCB;

    // Create a command bar.
    hwndCB = CommandBar_Create (hInst, hWnd, IDC_CMDBAR);

    // Add exit button to command bar.
    CommandBar_AddAdornments (hwndCB, 0, 0);
    return 0;
}
//----------------------------------------------------------------------
// DoMouseMain - Process WM_LBUTTONDOWN and WM_MOUSEMOVE messages
// for window.
//
LRESULT DoMouseMain (HWND hWnd, UINT wMsg, WPARAM wParam,
                     LPARAM lParam) {
    POINT pt[64];
    POINT ptM;
    UINT i, uPoints = 0;
    HDC hdc;

    ptM.x = LOWORD (lParam);
    ptM.y = HIWORD (lParam);

    hdc = GetDC (hWnd);
    // If shift and mouse move, see if any lost points.
    if (wMsg == WM_MOUSEMOVE) {
        if (wParam & MK_SHIFT)
            GetMouseMovePoints (pt, 64, &uPoints);

        for (i = 0; i < uPoints; i++) {
            SetPixel (hdc, pt[i].x/4,   pt[i].y/4, RGB (255, 0, 0));
            SetPixel (hdc, pt[i].x/4+1, pt[i].y/4, RGB (255, 0, 0));
            SetPixel (hdc, pt[i].x/4,   pt[i].y/4+1, RGB (255, 0, 0));
            SetPixel (hdc, pt[i].x/4+1, pt[i].y/4+1, RGB (255, 0, 0));
        }
    }
    // The original point is drawn last in case one of the points
    // returned by GetMouseMovePoints overlaps it.
    SetPixel (hdc, ptM.x, ptM.y, RGB (0, 0, 0));
    SetPixel (hdc, ptM.x+1, ptM.y, RGB (0, 0, 0));
    SetPixel (hdc, ptM.x, ptM.y+1, RGB (0, 0, 0));
    SetPixel (hdc, ptM.x+1, ptM.y+1, RGB (0, 0, 0));
    ReleaseDC (hWnd, hdc);
```

```
    // Kill time to make believe we are busy.
    Sleep(25);
    return 0;
}
//----------------------------------------------------------------------
// DoDestroyMain - Process WM_DESTROY message for window.
//
LRESULT DoDestroyMain (HWND hWnd, UINT wMsg, WPARAM wParam,
                       LPARAM lParam) {
    PostQuitMessage (0);
    return 0;
}
```

Input focus and mouse messages

Here are some subtleties to note about circumstances that rule how and when mouse messages initiated by stylus input are sent to different windows. As I mentioned previously, the input focus of the system changes when the stylus is pressed against a window. However, dragging the stylus from one window to the next won't cause the new window to receive the input focus. The down tap sets the focus, not the process of dragging the stylus across a window. When the stylus is dragged outside the window, that window stops receiving WM_MOUSEMOVE messages but retains input focus. Because the tip of the stylus is still down, no other window will receive the WM_MOUSEMOVE messages. This is akin to using a mouse and dragging the mouse outside a window with a button held down.

To continue to receive mouse messages even if the stylus moves off its window, an application can call

```
HWND SetCapture (HWND hWnd);
```

passing the handle of the window to receive the mouse messages. The function returns the handle of the window that previously had captured the mouse or NULL if the mouse wasn't previously captured. To stop receiving the mouse messages initiated by stylus input, the window calls

```
BOOL ReleaseCapture (void);
```

Only one window can capture the stylus input at any one time. To determine whether the stylus has been captured, an application can call

```
HWND GetCapture (void);
```

which returns the handle of the window that has captured the stylus input or 0 if no window has captured the stylus input—although please note one caveat. *The window that has captured the stylus must be in the same thread context as the window calling the function*. This means that if the stylus has been captured by a window in another application, *GetCapture* still returns 0.

If a window has captured the stylus input and another window calls *GetCapture*, the window that had originally captured the stylus receives a WM_CAPTURECHANGED message. The *lParam* parameter of the message contains the handle of the window that has gained the capture. You shouldn't attempt to take back the capture by calling *GetCapture* in response to this message. In general, since the stylus is a shared resource, applications should be wary of capturing the stylus for any length of time and they should be able to handle gracefully any loss of capture.

Another interesting tidbit: Just because a window has captured the mouse, that doesn't prevent a tap on another window gaining the input focus for that window. You can use other methods for preventing the change of input focus, but in almost all cases, it's better to let the user, not the applications, decide what top-level window should have the input focus.

Right-button clicks

When you click the right mouse button on an object in Windows systems, the action typically calls up a context menu, which is a stand-alone menu displaying a set of choices for what you can do with that particular object. On a system with a mouse, Windows sends WM_RBUTTONDOWN and WM_RBUTTONUP messages indicating a right-button click. When you use a stylus however, you don't have a right button. The Windows CE guidelines, however, allow you to simulate a right button click using a stylus. The guidelines specify that if a user holds down the Alt key while tapping the screen with the stylus, a program should act as if a right mouse button were being clicked and display any appropriate context menu. Because there's no MK_ALT flag in the *wParam* value of WM_LBUTTONDOWN, the best way to determine whether the Alt key is pressed is to use *GetKeyState* with VK_MENU as the parameter and test for the most significant bit of the return value to be set. *GetKeyState* is more appropriate in this case because the value returned will be the state of the key at the time the mouse message was pulled from the message queue.

The TicTac1 Example Program

To demonstrate stylus programming, I have written a trivial tic-tac-toe game. The TicTac1 window is shown in Figure 3-8. The source code for the program is shown in Figure 3-9. This program doesn't allow you to play the game against the computer, nor does it determine the end of the game—it simply draws the board and keeps track of the Xs and Os. Nevertheless, it demonstrates basic stylus interaction.

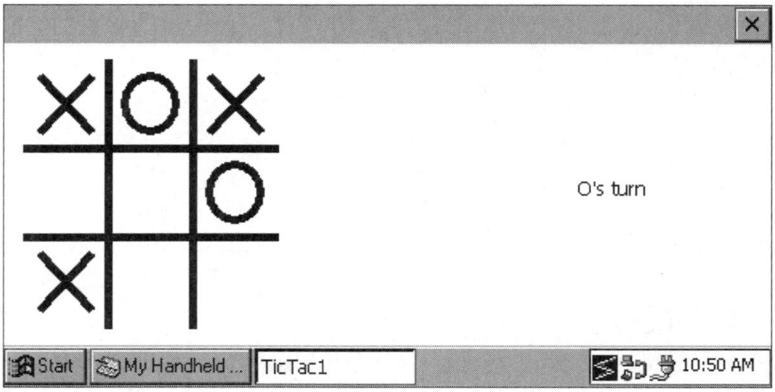

Figure 3-8. *The TicTac1 window.*

TicTac1.h

```
//======================================================================
// Header file
//
// Written for the book Programming Windows CE
// Copyright (C) 1998 Douglas Boling
//
//======================================================================
// Returns number of elements
#define dim(x) (sizeof(x) / sizeof(x[0]))

//----------------------------------------------------------------------
// Generic defines and data types
//
struct decodeUINT {                            // Structure associates
    UINT Code;                                 // messages
                                               // with a function.
    LRESULT (*Fxn)(HWND, UINT, WPARAM, LPARAM);
};
struct decodeCMD {                             // Structure associates
    UINT Code;                                 // menu IDs with a
    LRESULT (*Fxn)(HWND, WORD, HWND, WORD);    // function.
};

//----------------------------------------------------------------------
// Generic defines used by application
#define  IDC_CMDBAR 1                          // Command bar ID
```

Figure 3-9. *The TicTac1 program.* *(continued)*

Figure 3-9. *continued*

```
//----------------------------------------------------------------------
// Function prototypes
//
int InitApp (HINSTANCE);
HWND InitInstance (HINSTANCE, LPWSTR, int);
int TermInstance (HINSTANCE, int);

// Window procedures
LRESULT CALLBACK MainWndProc (HWND, UINT, WPARAM, LPARAM);

// Message handlers
LRESULT DoCreateMain (HWND, UINT, WPARAM, LPARAM);
LRESULT DoSizeMain (HWND, UINT, WPARAM, LPARAM);
LRESULT DoPaintMain (HWND, UINT, WPARAM, LPARAM);
LRESULT DoLButtonDownMain (HWND, UINT, WPARAM, LPARAM);
LRESULT DoLButtonUpMain (HWND, UINT, WPARAM, LPARAM);
LRESULT DoDestroyMain (HWND, UINT, WPARAM, LPARAM);

// Game function prototypes
void DrawXO (HDC hdc, HPEN hPen, RECT *prect, INT nCell, INT nType);
void DrawBoard (HDC hdc, RECT *prect);
```

TicTac1.c

```
//======================================================================
// TicTac1 - Simple tic-tac-toe game
//
// Written for the book Programming Windows CE
// Copyright (C) 1998 Douglas Boling
//
//======================================================================
#include <windows.h>                 // For all that Windows stuff
#include <commctrl.h>                // Command bar includes
#include "tictac1.h"                 // Program-specific stuff

//----------------------------------------------------------------------
// Global data
//
const TCHAR szAppName[] = TEXT ("TicTac1");
HINSTANCE hInst;                     // Program instance handle

// State data for game
RECT rectBoard = {0, 0, 0, 0};       // Used to place game board.
RECT rectPrompt;                     // Used to place prompt.
BYTE bBoard[9];                      // Keeps track of Xs and Os.
BYTE bTurn = 0;                      // Keeps track of the turn.
```

```
// Message dispatch table for MainWindowProc
const struct decodeUINT MainMessages[] = {
    WM_CREATE, DoCreateMain,
    WM_SIZE, DoSizeMain,
    WM_PAINT, DoPaintMain,
    WM_LBUTTONUP, DoLButtonUpMain,
    WM_DESTROY, DoDestroyMain,
};

//======================================================================
//
// Program entry point
//
int WINAPI WinMain (HINSTANCE hInstance, HINSTANCE hPrevInstance,
                    LPWSTR lpCmdLine, int nCmdShow) {
    MSG msg;
    int rc = 0;
    HWND hwndMain;

    // Initialize application.
    rc = InitApp (hInstance);
    if (rc) return rc;

    // Initialize this instance.
    hwndMain = InitInstance (hInstance, lpCmdLine, nCmdShow);
    if (hwndMain == 0)
        return 0x10;

    // Application message loop
    while (GetMessage (&msg, NULL, 0, 0)) {
        TranslateMessage (&msg);
        DispatchMessage (&msg);
    }
    // Instance cleanup
    return TermInstance (hInstance, msg.wParam);
}
//----------------------------------------------------------------------
// InitApp - Application initialization
//
int InitApp (HINSTANCE hInstance) {
    WNDCLASS wc;

    // Register application main window class.
    wc.style = 0;                             // Window style
    wc.lpfnWndProc = MainWndProc;             // Callback function
    wc.cbClsExtra = 0;                        // Extra class data
```

(continued)

Figure 3-9. *continued*

```
    wc.cbWndExtra = 0;                          // Extra window data
    wc.hInstance = hInstance;                   // Owner handle
    wc.hIcon = NULL,                            // Application icon
    wc.hCursor = NULL;                          // Default cursor
    wc.hbrBackground = (HBRUSH) GetStockObject (WHITE_BRUSH);
    wc.lpszMenuName =  NULL;                    // Menu name
    wc.lpszClassName = szAppName;               // Window class name

    if (RegisterClass (&wc) == 0) return 1;

    return 0;
}
//----------------------------------------------------------------------
// InitInstance - Instance initialization
//
HWND InitInstance (HINSTANCE hInstance, LPWSTR lpCmdLine, int nCmdShow) {
    HWND hWnd;

    // Save program instance handle in global variable.
    hInst = hInstance;

    // Create main window.
    hWnd = CreateWindow (szAppName,             // Window class
                         TEXT ("TicTac1"),      // Window title
                         WS_VISIBLE,            // Style flags
                         CW_USEDEFAULT,         // x position
                         CW_USEDEFAULT,         // y position
                         CW_USEDEFAULT,         // Initial width
                         CW_USEDEFAULT,         // Initial height
                         NULL,                  // Parent
                         NULL,                  // Menu, must be null
                         hInstance,             // App instance
                         NULL);                 // Pointer to create
                                                // parameters
    // Return fail code if window not created.
    if (!IsWindow (hWnd)) return 0;

    // Standard show and update calls
    ShowWindow (hWnd, nCmdShow);
    UpdateWindow (hWnd);
    return hWnd;
}
//----------------------------------------------------------------------
// TermInstance - Program cleanup
//
```

```
int TermInstance (HINSTANCE hInstance, int nDefRC) {

    return nDefRC;
}
//======================================================================
// Message handling procedures for MainWindow
//

//----------------------------------------------------------------------
// MainWndProc - Callback function for application window
//
LRESULT CALLBACK MainWndProc (HWND hWnd, UINT wMsg, WPARAM wParam,
                              LPARAM lParam) {
    INT i;
    //
    // Search message list to see if we need to handle this
    // message.  If in list, call procedure.
    //
    for (i = 0; i < dim(MainMessages); i++) {
        if (wMsg == MainMessages[i].Code)
            return (*MainMessages[i].Fxn)(hWnd, wMsg, wParam, lParam);
    }
    return DefWindowProc(hWnd, wMsg, wParam, lParam);
}
//----------------------------------------------------------------------
// DoCreateMain - Process WM_CREATE message for window.
//
LRESULT DoCreateMain (HWND hWnd, UINT wMsg, WPARAM wParam,
                      LPARAM lParam) {
    HWND hwndCB;

    // Create a command bar.
    hwndCB = CommandBar_Create (hInst, hWnd, IDC_CMDBAR);

    // Add exit button to command bar.
    CommandBar_AddAdornments (hwndCB, 0, 0);
    return 0;
}
//----------------------------------------------------------------------
// DoSizeMain - Process WM_SIZE message for window.
//
LRESULT DoSizeMain (HWND hWnd, UINT wMsg, WPARAM wParam,
                    LPARAM lParam) {
    RECT rect;
    INT i;
```

(continued)

Figure 3-9. *continued*

```
    // Adjust the size of the client rect to take into account
    // the command bar height.
    GetClientRect (hWnd, &rect);
    rect.top += CommandBar_Height (GetDlgItem (hWnd, IDC_CMDBAR));

    // Init the board rectangle if not yet initialized.
    if (rectBoard.right == 0) {

        // Init the board.
        for (i = 0; i < dim(bBoard); i++)
            bBoard[i] = 0;
    }
    // Define the playing board rect.
    rectBoard = rect;
    rectPrompt = rect;
    // Layout depends on portrait or landscape screen.
    if (rect.right - rect.left > rect.bottom - rect.top) {
        rectBoard.left += 20;
        rectBoard.top += 10;
        rectBoard.bottom -= 10;
        rectBoard.right = rectBoard.bottom - rectBoard.top + 10;

        rectPrompt.left = rectBoard.right + 10;

    } else {
        rectBoard.left += 20;
        rectBoard.right -= 20;
        rectBoard.top += 10;
        rectBoard.bottom = rectBoard.right - rectBoard.left + 10;

        rectPrompt.top = rectBoard.bottom + 10;
    }
    return 0;
}
//----------------------------------------------------------------------
// DoPaintMain - Process WM_PAINT message for window.
//
LRESULT DoPaintMain (HWND hWnd, UINT wMsg, WPARAM wParam,
                     LPARAM lParam) {
    PAINTSTRUCT ps;
    RECT rect;
    HFONT hFont, hOldFont;
    HDC hdc;

    // Adjust the size of the client rect to take into account
    // the command bar height.
```

```
    GetClientRect (hWnd, &rect);
    rect.top += CommandBar_Height (GetDlgItem (hWnd, IDC_CMDBAR));

    hdc = BeginPaint (hWnd, &ps);

    // Draw the board.
    DrawBoard (hdc, &rectBoard);

    // Write the prompt to the screen.
    hFont = GetStockObject (SYSTEM_FONT);
    hOldFont = SelectObject (hdc, hFont);
    if (bTurn == 0)
        DrawText (hdc, TEXT (" X's turn"), -1, &rectPrompt,
                  DT_CENTER | DT_VCENTER | DT_SINGLELINE);
    else
        DrawText (hdc, TEXT (" O's turn"), -1, &rectPrompt,
                  DT_CENTER | DT_VCENTER | DT_SINGLELINE);

    SelectObject (hdc, hOldFont);
    EndPaint (hWnd, &ps);
    return 0;
}
//----------------------------------------------------------------------
// DoLButtonUpMain - Process WM_LBUTTONUP message for window.
//
LRESULT DoLButtonUpMain (HWND hWnd, UINT wMsg, WPARAM wParam,
                         LPARAM lParam) {
    POINT pt;
    INT cx, cy, nCell = 0;

    pt.x = LOWORD (lParam);
    pt.y = HIWORD (lParam);

    // See if pen on board.  If so, determine which cell.
    if (PtInRect (&rectBoard, pt)){
        // Normalize point to upper left corner of board.
        pt.x -= rectBoard.left;
        pt.y -= rectBoard.top;

        // Compute size of each cell.
        cx = (rectBoard.right - rectBoard.left)/3;
        cy = (rectBoard.bottom - rectBoard.top)/3;

        // Find column.
        nCell = (pt.x / cx);
```

(continued)

Figure 3-9. *continued*

```
        // Find row.
        nCell += (pt.y / cy) * 3;

        // If cell empty, fill it with mark.
        if (bBoard[nCell] == 0) {
            if (bTurn) {
                bBoard[nCell] = 2;
                bTurn = 0;
            } else {
                bBoard[nCell] = 1;
                bTurn = 1;
            }
            InvalidateRect (hWnd, NULL, FALSE);
        } else {
            // Inform the user of the filled cell.
            MessageBeep (0);
            return 0;
        }
    }
    return 0;
}
//----------------------------------------------------------------------
// DoDestroyMain - Process WM_DESTROY message for window.
//
LRESULT DoDestroyMain (HWND hWnd, UINT wMsg, WPARAM wParam,
                       LPARAM lParam) {
    PostQuitMessage (0);
    return 0;
}
//======================================================================
// Game-specific routines
//
//----------------------------------------------------------------------
// DrawXO - Draw a single X or O in a square.
//
void DrawXO (HDC hdc, HPEN hPen, RECT *prect, INT nCell, INT nType) {
    POINT pt[2];
    INT cx, cy;
    RECT rect;

    cx = (prect->right - prect->left)/3;
    cy = (prect->bottom - prect->top)/3;

    // Compute the dimensions of the target cell.
    rect.left = (cx * (nCell % 3) + prect->left) + 10;
    rect.right = rect.right =  rect.left + cx - 20;
    rect.top = cy * (nCell / 3) + prect->top + 10;
```

```
    rect.bottom = rect.top + cy - 20;

    // Draw an X ?
    if (nType == 1) {
        pt[0].x = rect.left;
        pt[0].y = rect.top;
        pt[1].x = rect.right;
        pt[1].y = rect.bottom;
        Polyline (hdc, pt, 2);

        pt[0].x = rect.right;
        pt[1].x = rect.left;
        Polyline (hdc, pt, 2);
    // How about an O ?
    } else if (nType == 2) {
        Ellipse (hdc, rect.left, rect.top, rect.right, rect.bottom);
    }
    return;
}
//----------------------------------------------------------------------
// DrawBoard - Draw the tic-tac-toe board.
//  VK_MENU
void DrawBoard (HDC hdc, RECT *prect) {
    HPEN hPen, hOldPen;
    POINT pt[2];
    LOGPEN lp;
    INT i, cx, cy;

    // Create a nice thick pen.
    lp.lopnStyle = PS_SOLID;
    lp.lopnWidth.x = 5;
    lp.lopnWidth.y = 5;
    lp.lopnColor = RGB (0, 0, 0);
    hPen = CreatePenIndirect (&lp);

    hOldPen = SelectObject (hdc, hPen);

    cx = (prect->right - prect->left)/3;
    cy = (prect->bottom - prect->top)/3;

    // Draw lines down.
    pt[0].x = cx + prect->left;
    pt[1].x = cx + prect->left;
    pt[0].y = prect->top;
    pt[1].y = prect->bottom;
    Polyline (hdc, pt, 2);
```

(continued)

Figure 3-9. *continued*

```
    pt[0].x += cx;
    pt[1].x += cx;
    Polyline (hdc, pt, 2);

    // Draw lines across.
    pt[0].x = prect->left;
    pt[1].x = prect->right;
    pt[0].y = cy + prect->top;
    pt[1].y = cy + prect->top;
    Polyline (hdc, pt, 2);

    pt[0].y += cy;
    pt[1].y += cy;
    Polyline (hdc, pt, 2);

    // Fill in Xs and Os.
    for (i = 0; i < dim (bBoard); i++)
        DrawXO (hdc, hPen, &rectBoard, i, bBoard[i]);

    SelectObject (hdc, hOldPen);
    DeleteObject (hPen);
    return;
}
```

The action in TicTac1 is centered around three routines: *DrawBoard*, *DrawXO*, and *OnLButtonUpMain*. The first two perform the tasks of drawing the playing board. The routine that determines the location of a tap on the board (and therefore is more relevant to our current train of thought) is *OnLButtonUpMain*. As the name suggests, this routine is called in response to a WM_LBUTTONUP message. The first action to take is to call

```
BOOL PtInRect (const RECT *lprc, POINT pt);
```

which determines whether the tap is even on the game board. The program knows the location of the tap because it's passed in the *lParam* value of the message. The board rectangle is computed when the program starts in *OnSizeMain*. Once the tap is localized to the board, the program determines the location of the relevant cell within the playing board by dividing the coordinates of the tap point within the board by the number of cells across and down.

I mentioned that the board rectangle was computed during the *OnSizeMain* routine, which is called in response to a WM_SIZE message. While it might seem strange that Windows CE supports the WM_SIZE message common to other versions of Windows, it needs to support this message because a window is sized frequently: first right after it's created, and then each time it's minimized and restored. You might think that another possibility for determining the size of the window would be during the WM_CREATE message. The *lParam* parameter points to a CREATESTRUCT structure that contains, among other things, the initial size and position of the window. The problem with using those numbers is that the size obtained is the total size of the window, not the size of client area, which is what we need. Under Windows CE, most windows have no title bar and no border, but some have both and many have scroll bars, so using these values can cause trouble. So now, with the TicTac1 example, we have a simple program that uses the stylus effectively but isn't complete. To restart the game, we must exit and restart TicTac1. We can't take back a move nor have O start first. We need a method for sending these commands to the program. Sure, using keys would work. Another solution would be to create hot spots on the screen that when tapped, provided the input necessary. However, the standard method of exercising these types of commands in a program is through menus.

MENUS

Menus are a mainstay of Windows input. While each application might have a different keyboard and stylus interface, almost all have sets of menus that are organized in a structure familiar to the Windows user.

Windows CE programs use menus a little differently from other Windows programs, the most obvious difference being that in Windows CE, menus aren't part of the standard window. Instead, menus are attached to the command bar control that has been created for the window. Other than this change, the functions of the menu and the way menu selections are processed by the application match the other versions of Windows, for the most part. Because of this general similarity, I give you only a basic introduction to Windows menu management in this section.

Creating a menu is as simple as calling

```
HMENU CreateMenu (void);
```

The function returns a handle to an empty menu. To add an item to a menu, two calls can be used. The first,

```
BOOL AppendMenu (HMENU hMenu, UINT fuFlags, UINT idNewItem,
                 LPCTSTR lpszNewItem);
```

appends a single item to the end of a menu. The *fuFlags* parameter is set with a series of flags indicating the initial condition of the item. For example, the item might be initially disabled (thanks to the MF_GRAYED flag) or have a check mark next to it (courtesy of the MF_CHECKED flag). Almost all calls specify the MF_STRING flag, indicating that the *lpszNewItem* parameter contains a string that will be the text for the item. The *idNewItem* parameter contains an ID value that will be used to identify the item when it's selected by the user or that the state of the menu item needs to be changed.

Another call that can be used to add a menu item is this one:

```
BOOL InsertMenu (HMENU hMenu, UINT uPosition, UINT uFlags,
                 UINT uIDNewItem, LPCTSTR lpNewItem);
```

This call is similar to *AppendMenu* with the added flexibility that the item can be inserted anywhere within a menu structure. For this call, the *uFlags* parameter can be passed one of two additional flags: MF_BYCOMMAND or MF_BYPOSITION, which specify how to locate where the menu item is to be inserted into the menu.

Under Windows CE 2.0, menus can be nested to provide a cascading effect. This feature brings Windows CE up to the level of other versions of Windows, which have always allowed cascading menus. To add a cascading menu, or submenu, create the menu you want to attach using *CreateMenu* and *InsertMenu*. Then insert or append the submenu to the main menu using either *InsertMenu* or *AppendMenu* with the MF_POPUP flag in the flags parameter. In this case, the *uIDNewItem* parameter contains the handle to the submenu while the *lpNewItem* contains the string that will be on the menu item.

You can query and manipulate a menu item to add or remove check marks or to enable or disable it by means of a number of functions. This function,

```
BOOL EnableMenuItem (HMENU hMenu, UINT uIDEnableItem, UINT uEnable);
```

can be used to enable or disable an item. The flags used in the *uEnable* parameter are similar to the flags used with other menu functions. Under Windows CE, the flag you use to disable a menu item is MF_GRAYED, not MF_DISABLED. The function

```
DWORD CheckMenuItem (HMENU hmenu, UINT uIDCheckItem, UINT uCheck);
```

can be used to check and uncheck a menu item. Many other functions are available to query and manipulate menu items. Check the SDK documentation for more details.

The following code fragment creates a simple menu structure:

```
hMainMenu = CreatePopupMenu ();

hMenu = CreateMenu ();
AppendMenu (hMenu, MF_STRING | MF_ENABLED, 100, TEXT ("&New"));
AppendMenu (hMenu, MF_STRING | MF_ENABLED, 101, TEXT ("&Open"));
AppendMenu (hMenu, MF_STRING | MF_ENABLED, 101, TEXT ("&Save"));
AppendMenu (hMenu, MF_STRING | MF_ENABLED, 101, TEXT ("E&xit"));

AppendMenu (hMainMenu, MF_STRING | MF_ENABLED | MF_POPUP, (UINT)hMenu,
            TEXT ("&File"));

hMenu = CreateMenu ();
AppendMenu (hMenu, MF_STRING | MF_ENABLED, 100, TEXT ("C&ut"));
AppendMenu (hMenu, MF_STRING | MF_ENABLED, 101, TEXT ("&Copy"));
AppendMenu (hMenu, MF_STRING | MF_ENABLED, 101, TEXT ("&Paste"));
```

```
AppendMenu (hMainMenu, MF_STRING | MF_ENABLED | MF_POPUP, hMenu,
            TEXT ("&Edit"));

hMenu = CreateMenu ();
AppendMenu (hMenu, MF_STRING | MF_ENABLED, 100, TEXT ("&About"));

AppendMenu (hMainMenu, MF_STRING | MF_ENABLED | MF_POPUP, hMenu,
            TEXT ("&Help"));
```

Once a menu has been created, it can be attached to a command bar using this function:

```
BOOL CommandBar_InsertMenubarEx (HWND hwndCB, HINSTANCE hInst,
                                 LPTSTR pszMenu, int iButton);
```

The menu handle is passed in the third parameter while the second parameter, *hInst*, must be 0. The final parameter, *iButton*, indicates the button that will be to the immediate right of the menu. The Windows CE user interface guidelines recommend that the menu be on the far left of the command bar, so this value is almost always 0.

Handling Menu Commands

When a user selects a menu item, Windows sends a WM_COMMAND message to the window that owns the menu. The low word of the *wParam* parameter contains the ID of the menu item that was selected. The high word of *wParam* contains the notification code. For a menu selection, this value is always 0. The *lParam* parameter is 0 for WM_COMMAND messages sent due to a menu selection. Those familiar with Windows 3.*x* programming might notice that the layout of *wParam* and *lParam* match the standard Win32 assignments and are different from Win16 programs. So, to act on a menu selection, a window needs to field the WM_COMMAND message, decode the ID passed, and act according to the menu item that was selected.

Now that I've covered the basics of menu creation, you might wonder where all this menu creation code sits in a Windows program. The answer is, it doesn't. Instead of dynamically creating menus on the fly, most Windows programs simply load a menu template from a *resource*. To learn more about this, let's take a detour from the description of input methods and look at resources.

RESOURCES

Resources are read-only data segments of an application or a DLL that are linked to the file after it has been compiled. The point of a resource is to give a developer a compiler-independent place for storing content data such as dialog boxes, strings, bitmaps, icons, and yes, menus. Since resources aren't compiled into a program, they can be changed without having to recompile the application.

You create a resource by building an ASCII file—called a *resource script*—describing the resources. Your ASCII file has an extension of RC. You compile this file with a resource compiler, which is provided by every maker of Windows development tools, and then you link them into the compiled executable again using the linker. These days, these steps are masked by a heavy layer of visual tools, but the fundamentals remain the same. For example, Visual C++ 5.0 creates and maintains an ASCII resource (RC) file even though few programmers directly look at the resource file text any more.

It's always a struggle for the author of a programming book to decide how to approach tools. Some lay out a very high level of instruction, talking about menu selections and describing dialog boxes for specific programming tools. Others show the reader how to build all the components of a program from the ground up, using ASCII files and command line compilers. Resources can be approached the same way: I could describe how to use the visual tools or how to create the ASCII files that are the basis for the resources. In this book, I stay primarily at the ASCII resource script level since the goal is to teach Windows CE programming, not how to use a particular set of tools. I'll show how to create and use the ASCII RC file for adding menus and the like, but later in the book in places where the resource file isn't relevant, I won't always include the RC file in the listings. The files are, of course, on the CD included with this book.

Resource Scripts

Creating a resource script is as simple as using Notepad to create a text file. The language used is simple, with C-like tendencies. Comment lines are prefixed by a double slash (//) and files can be included using a *#include* statement.

An example menu template would be the following:

```
//
// A menu template
//
ID_MENU MENU DISCARDABLE
BEGIN
    POPUP "&File"
    BEGIN
        MENUITEM "&Open...",                    100
        MENUITEM "&Save...",                    101
        MENUITEM SEPARATOR
        MENUITEM "E&xit",                       120
    END
    POPUP "&Help"
    BEGIN
        MENUITEM "&About",                      200
    END
END
```

The initial ID_MENU is the ID value for the resource. Alternatively, this ID value can be replaced by a string identifying the resource. The ID value method provides more compact code while using a string may provide more readable code when the application loads the resource in the source file. The next word, *MENU*, identifies the type of resource. The menu starts with *POPUP*, indicating that the menu item *File* is actually a pop-up (cascade) menu attached to the main menu. Because it's a menu within a menu, it too has *BEGIN* and *END* keywords surrounding the description of the File menu. The ampersand (&) character tells Windows that the next character should be the key assignment for that menu item. The character following the ampersand is automatically underlined by Windows when the menu item is displayed, and if the user presses the Alt key along with the character, that menu item is selected. Each item in a menu is then specified by the *MENUITEM* keyword followed by the string used on the menu. The ellipsis following the *Open* and *Save* strings is a Windows UI custom indicating to the user that selecting that item displays a dialog box. The numbers following the *Open*, *Save*, *Exit*, and *About* menu items are the menu identifiers. These values identify the menu items in the WM_COMMAND message. It's good programming practice to replace these values with equates that are defined in a common include file so that they match the WM_COMMAND handler code.

Figure 3-10 lists other resource types that you might find in a resource file. The *DISCARDABLE* keyword is optional and tells Windows that the resource can be discarded from memory if it's not in use. The remainder of the menu is couched in *BEGIN* and *END* keywords, although bracket characters { and } are recognized as well.

Resource Type	***Explanation***
MENU	Defines a menu
ACCELERATORS	Defines a keyboard accelerator table
DIALOG	Defines a dialog box template
BITMAP	Includes a bitmap file as a resource
ICON	Includes an icon file as a resource
FONT	Includes a font file as a resource
RCDATA	Defines application-defined binary data block
STRINGTABLE	Defines a list of strings
VERSIONINFO	Includes file version information

Figure 3-10. *The resource types allowed by the resource compiler.*

Icons

Now that we're working with resource files, it's a trivial matter to modify the icon that the Windows CE shell uses to display a program. Simply create an icon with your favorite icon editor and add to the resource file an icon statement such as

```
ID_ICON ICON "tictac2.ico"
```

When Windows displays a program in Windows Explorer, it looks inside the EXE file for the first icon in the resource list and uses it to represent the program.

Having that icon represent an application's window is somewhat more of a chore. Windows CE uses a small 16-by-16-pixel icon on the taskbar to represent windows on the desktop. Under other versions of Windows, the *RegisterClassEx* function could be used to associate a small icon with a window, but Windows CE doesn't support this function. Instead, the icon must be explicitly loaded and assigned to the window. The following code fragment assigns a small icon to a window.

```
hIcon = (HICON) SendMessage (hWnd, WM_GETICON, FALSE, 0);
if (hIcon == 0) {
    hIcon = LoadImage (hInst, MAKEINTRESOURCE (ID_ICON1), IMAGE_ICON,
                       16, 16, 0);
    SendMessage (hWnd, WM_SETICON, FALSE, (LPARAM)hIcon);
}
```

The first *SendMessage* call gets the currently assigned icon for the window. The FALSE value in *wParam* indicates that we're querying the small icon for the window. If this returns 0, indicating that no icon has been assigned, a call to *LoadImage* is made to load the icon from the application resources. The *LoadImage* function can take either a text string or an ID value to identify the resource being loaded. In this case, the MAKEINTRESOURCE macro is used to label an ID value to the function. The icon being loaded must be a 16-by-16 icon because under Windows CE, *LoadImage* won't resize the icon to fit the requested size. Also under Windows CE, *LoadImage* is limited to loading icons and bitmaps from resources. Windows CE provides the function *ShLoadDIBitmap* to load a bitmap from a file.

Unlike other versions of Windows, Windows CE stores window icons on a per class basis. This means if two windows in an application have the same class, they share the same window icon. A subtle caveat here—window classes are specific to a particular instance of an application. So, if you have two different instances of the application FOOBAR, they each have different window classes, so they may have different window icons even though they were registered with the same class information. If the second instance of FOOBAR had two windows of the same class open, those two windows would share the same icon, independent of the window icon in the first instance of FOOBAR.

Accelerators

Another resource that can be loaded is a keyboard accelerator table. This table is used by Windows to enable developers to designate shortcut keys for specific menus or controls in your application. Specifically, accelerators provide a direct method for a key combination to result in a WM_COMMAND message being sent to a window. These accelerators are different from the Alt-F key combination that, for example, can be used to access a File menu. File menu key combinations are handled automatically as long as the File menu item string was defined with the *&* character, as in *&File*. The keyboard accelerators are independent of menus or any other controls, although their assignments typically mimic menu operations, as in using Ctrl-O to open a file.

Below is a short resource script that defines a couple of accelerator keys.

```
ID_ACCEL ACCELERATORS DISCARDABLE
BEGIN
    "N", IDM_NEWGAME, VIRTKEY, CONTROL
    "Z", IDM_UNDO,  VIRTKEY, CONTROL
END
```

As with the menu resource, the structure starts with an ID value. The ID value is followed by the type of resource and, again optionally, the discardable keyword. The entries in the table consist of the letter identifying the key, followed by the ID value of the command, *VIRTKEY*, which indicates that the letter is actually a virtual key value, followed finally by the *CONTROL* keyword, indicating that the control shift must be pressed with the key.

Simply having the accelerator table in the resource doesn't accomplish much. The application must load the accelerator table and, for each message it pulls from the message queue, see whether an accelerator has been entered. Fortunately, this is accomplished with a few simple modifications to the main message loop of a program. Here's a modified main message loop that handles keyboard accelerators.

```
// Load accelerator table.
hAccel = LoadAccelerators (hInst, MAKEINTRESOURCE (ID_ACCEL));

// Application message loop
while (GetMessage (&msg, NULL, 0, 0)) {
    // Translate accelerators
    if (!TranslateAccelerator (hwndMain, hAccel, &msg)) {
        TranslateMessage (&msg);
        DispatchMessage (&msg);
    }
}
```

The first difference in this main message loop is the loading of the accelerator table using the *LoadAccelerators* function. Then after each message is pulled from the message queue, a call is made to *TranslateAccelerator*. If this function translates the message, it returns TRUE, which skips the standard *TranslateMessage* and *DispatchMessage* loop body. If no translation was performed, the loop body executes normally.

Bitmaps

Bitmaps can also be stored as resources. Windows CE works with bitmap resources somewhat differently from other versions of Windows. With Windows CE, the call

```
HBITMAP LoadBitmap(HINSTANCE hInstance, LPCTSTR lpBitmapName);
```

loads a read-only version of the bitmap. This means that after the bitmap is selected into a device context, the image can't be modified by other drawing actions in that DC. To load a read/write version of a bitmap resource, use the *LoadImage* function.

Strings

String resources are a good method for reducing the memory footprint of an application while keeping language-specific information out of the code to be compiled. An application can call

```
int LoadString(HINSTANCE hInstance, UINT uID, LPTSTR lpBuffer,
               int nBufferMax);
```

to load a string from a resource. The ID of the string resource is *uID,* the *lpBuffer* parameter points to a buffer to receive the string, and *nBufferMax* is the size of the buffer. To conserve memory, *LoadString* has a new feature under Windows CE. If *lpBuffer* is NULL, *LoadString* returns a read-only pointer to the string as the return value. Simply cast the return value as a pointer to a constant Unicode string (*LPCTSTR*) and use the string as needed. The length of the string, not including any null terminator, will be located in the word immediately preceding the start of the string.

While I will be covering memory management and strategies for memory conservation in Chapter 6, one quick note here. It's not a good idea to load a number of strings from a resource into memory. This just uses memory both in the resource and in RAM. If you need a number of strings at the same time, it might be a better strategy to use the new feature of *LoadString* to return a pointer directly to the resource itself. As an alternative, you can have the strings in a read-only segment compiled with the program. You lose the advantage of a separate string table, but you reduce your memory footprint.

The TicTac2 Example Program

The final program in this chapter encompasses all of the information presented up to this point as well as a few new items. The TicTac2 program is an extension of TicTac1; the additions are a menu, a window icon, and keyboard accelerators. The TicTac2 window, complete with menu, is shown in Figure 3-11, while the source is shown in Figure 3-12.

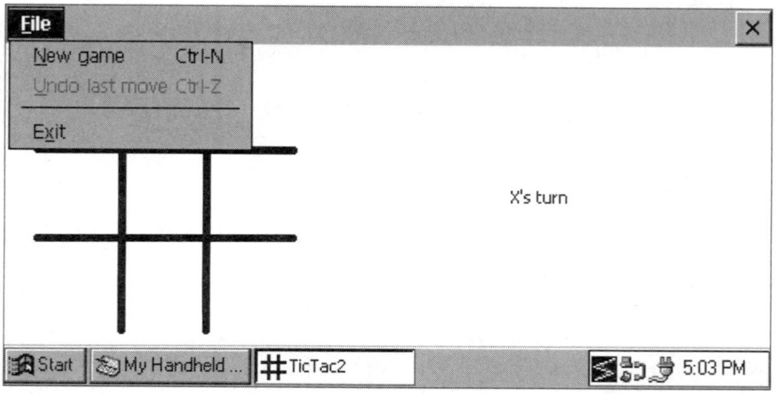

Figure 3-11. *The TicTac2 window wInsertDelete (Many Windows CE keyboards use Shift-Backspace for this function.)*

TicTac2.rc

```
//======================================================================
// TicTac2 - Resource file
//
// Written for the book Programming Windows CE
// Copyright (C) 1998 Douglas Boling
//
//======================================================================

#include "tictac2.h"

//----------------------------------------------------------------------
//
// Icon
//
ID_ICON ICON "tictac2.ico"

//----------------------------------------------------------------------
//
```

Figure 3-12. *The Tictac2 program.* *(continued)*

Figure 3-12. *continued*

```
// Menu
//
ID_MENU MENU DISCARDABLE
BEGIN
    POPUP "&File"
    BEGIN
        MENUITEM "&New game\tCtrl-N",          IDM_NEWGAME
        MENUITEM "&Undo last move\tCtrl-Z",    IDM_UNDO
        MENUITEM SEPARATOR
        MENUITEM "E&xit",                      IDM_EXIT
    END
END
//----------------------------------------------------------------------
//
// Accelerator table
//
ID_ACCEL ACCELERATORS DISCARDABLE
BEGIN
    "N", IDM_NEWGAME, VIRTKEY, CONTROL
    "Z", IDM_UNDO,  VIRTKEY, CONTROL
END
//----------------------------------------------------------------------
//
// String table
//
STRINGTABLE DISCARDABLE
BEGIN
    IDS_XTURN, " Xs turn"
    IDS_OTURN, " Os turn"
END
```

TicTac2.h

```
//======================================================================
// Header file
//
// Written for the book Programming Windows CE
// Copyright (C) 1998 Douglas Boling
//
//======================================================================
// Returns number of elements
#define dim(x) (sizeof(x) / sizeof(x[0]))

//----------------------------------------------------------------------
// Generic defines and data types
```

```
//
struct decodeUINT {                              // Structure associates
    UINT Code;                                   // messages
                                                 // with a function.
    LRESULT (*Fxn)(HWND, UINT, WPARAM, LPARAM);
};
struct decodeCMD {                               // Structure associates
    UINT Code;                                   // menu IDs with a
    LRESULT (*Fxn)(HWND, WORD, HWND, WORD);      // function.
};

//----------------------------------------------------------------------
// Generic defines used by application
#define  IDC_CMDBAR 1                            // Command bar ID

#define  ID_ICON            10                   // Icon resource ID
#define  ID_MENU            11                   // Main menu resource ID
#define  ID_ACCEL           12                   // Main menu resource ID

#define  IDM_NEWGAME        100                  // Menu item ID
#define  IDM_UNDO           101                  // Menu item ID
#define  IDM_EXIT           102                  // Menu item ID

#define  IDS_XTURN          201                  // String ID
#define  IDS_OTURN          202                  // String ID

//----------------------------------------------------------------------
// Function prototypes
//
int InitApp (HINSTANCE);
HWND InitInstance (HINSTANCE, LPWSTR, int);
int TermInstance (HINSTANCE, int);

// Window procedures
LRESULT CALLBACK MainWndProc (HWND, UINT, WPARAM, LPARAM);

// Message handlers
LRESULT DoCreateMain (HWND, UINT, WPARAM, LPARAM);
LRESULT DoSizeMain (HWND, UINT, WPARAM, LPARAM);
LRESULT DoPaintMain (HWND, UINT, WPARAM, LPARAM);
LRESULT DoInitMenuPopMain (HWND, UINT, WPARAM, LPARAM);
LRESULT DoCommandMain (HWND, UINT, WPARAM, LPARAM);
LRESULT DoLButtonUpMain (HWND, UINT, WPARAM, LPARAM);
LRESULT DoDestroyMain (HWND, UINT, WPARAM, LPARAM);
```

(continued)

Figure 3-12. *continued*

```
// Command functions
LPARAM DoMainCommandNewGame (HWND, WORD, HWND, WORD);
LPARAM DoMainCommandUndo (HWND, WORD, HWND, WORD);
LPARAM DoMainCommandExit (HWND, WORD, HWND, WORD);

// Game functon prototypes
void ResetGame (void);
void DrawXO (HDC hdc, HPEN hPen, RECT *prect, INT nCell, INT nType);
void DrawBoard (HDC hdc, RECT *prect);
```

TicTac2.c

```
//======================================================================
// TicTac2 - Simple tic-tac-toe game with menus
//
// Written for the book Programming Windows CE
// Copyright (C) 1998 Douglas Boling
//
//======================================================================
#include <windows.h>                    // For all that Windows stuff
#include <commctrl.h>                   // Command bar includes
#include "tictac2.h"                    // Program-specific stuff

//----------------------------------------------------------------------
// Global data
//
const TCHAR szAppName[] = TEXT ("TicTac2");
HINSTANCE hInst;                        // Program instance handle

// State data for game
RECT rectBoard = {0, 0, 0, 0};          // Used to place game board.
RECT rectPrompt;                        // Used to place prompt.
BYTE bBoard[9];                         // Keeps track of Xs and Os.
BYTE bTurn;                             // Keeps track of the turn.
char bLastMove;                         // Last cell changed

// Message dispatch table for MainWindowProc
const struct decodeUINT MainMessages[] = {
    WM_CREATE, DoCreateMain,
    WM_SIZE, DoSizeMain,
    WM_PAINT, DoPaintMain,
    WM_INITMENUPOPUP, DoInitMenuPopMain,
    WM_COMMAND, DoCommandMain,
    WM_LBUTTONUP, DoLButtonUpMain,
    WM_DESTROY, DoDestroyMain,
};
```

```
// Command Message dispatch for MainWindowProc
const struct decodeCMD MainCommandItems[] = {
    IDM_NEWGAME, DoMainCommandNewGame,
    IDM_UNDO, DoMainCommandUndo,
    IDM_EXIT, DoMainCommandExit,
};

//======================================================================
//
// Program entry point
//
int WINAPI WinMain (HINSTANCE hInstance, HINSTANCE hPrevInstance,
                    LPWSTR lpCmdLine, int nCmdShow) {
    MSG msg;
    int rc = 0;
    HWND hwndMain;
    HACCEL hAccel;

    // Initialize application.
    rc = InitApp (hInstance);
    if (rc) return rc;

    // Initialize this instance.
    hwndMain = InitInstance (hInstance, lpCmdLine, nCmdShow);
    if (hwndMain == 0)
        return 0x10;

    // Load accelerator table.
    hAccel = LoadAccelerators (hInst, MAKEINTRESOURCE (ID_ACCEL));

    // Application message loop
    while (GetMessage (&msg, NULL, 0, 0)) {
        // Translate accelerators
        if (!TranslateAccelerator (hwndMain, hAccel, &msg)) {
            TranslateMessage (&msg);
            DispatchMessage (&msg);
        }
    }
    // Instance cleanup
    return TermInstance (hInstance, msg.wParam);
}
//----------------------------------------------------------------------
// InitApp - Application initialization
//
int InitApp (HINSTANCE hInstance) {
    WNDCLASS wc;
```

(continued)

Figure 3-12. *continued*

```
    // Register application main window class.
    wc.style = 0;                              // Window style
    wc.lpfnWndProc = MainWndProc;              // Callback function
    wc.cbClsExtra = 0;                         // Extra class data
    wc.cbWndExtra = 0;                         // Extra window data
    wc.hInstance = hInstance;                  // Owner handle
    wc.hIcon = NULL,                           // Application icon
    wc.hCursor = NULL;                         // Default cursor
    wc.hbrBackground = (HBRUSH) GetStockObject (WHITE_BRUSH);
    wc.lpszMenuName =  NULL;                   // Menu name
    wc.lpszClassName = szAppName;              // Window class name

    if (RegisterClass(&wc) == 0) return 1;

    return 0;
}
//----------------------------------------------------------------------
// InitInstance - Instance initialization
//
HWND InitInstance (HINSTANCE hInstance, LPWSTR lpCmdLine, int nCmdShow) {
    HWND hWnd;

    // Save program instance handle in global variable.
    hInst = hInstance;

    // Create main window.
    hWnd = CreateWindow (szAppName,            // Window class
                         TEXT ("TicTac2"),     // Window title
                         WS_VISIBLE,           // Style flags
                         CW_USEDEFAULT,        // x position
                         CW_USEDEFAULT,        // y position
                         CW_USEDEFAULT,        // Initial width
                         CW_USEDEFAULT,        // Initial height
                         NULL,                 // Parent
                         NULL,                 // Menu, must be null
                         hInstance,            // Application instance
                         NULL);                // Pointer to create
                                               // parameters
    // Return fail code if window not created.
    if (!IsWindow (hWnd)) return 0;

    // Standard show and update calls
    ShowWindow (hWnd, nCmdShow);
    UpdateWindow (hWnd);
    return hWnd;
}
```

```
//----------------------------------------------------------------------
// TermInstance - Program cleanup
//
int TermInstance (HINSTANCE hInstance, int nDefRC) {

    return nDefRC;
}
//======================================================================
// Message handling procedures for MainWindow
//

//----------------------------------------------------------------------
// MainWndProc - Callback function for application window
//
LRESULT CALLBACK MainWndProc (HWND hWnd, UINT wMsg, WPARAM wParam,
                              LPARAM lParam) {
    INT i;
    //
    // Search message list to see if we need to handle this
    // message.  If in list, call procedure.
    //
    for (i = 0; i < dim(MainMessages); i++) {
        if (wMsg == MainMessages[i].Code)
            return (*MainMessages[i].Fxn)(hWnd, wMsg, wParam, lParam);
    }
    return DefWindowProc (hWnd, wMsg, wParam, lParam);
}
//----------------------------------------------------------------------
// DoCreateMain - Process WM_CREATE message for window.
//
LRESULT DoCreateMain (HWND hWnd, UINT wMsg, WPARAM wParam,
                      LPARAM lParam) {
    HWND hwndCB;
    HICON hIcon;

    // Create a command bar.
    hwndCB = CommandBar_Create (hInst, hWnd, IDC_CMDBAR);
    // Add the menu.
    CommandBar_InsertMenubar (hwndCB, hInst, ID_MENU, 0);
    // Add exit button to command bar.
    CommandBar_AddAdornments (hwndCB, 0, 0);

    hIcon = (HICON) SendMessage (hWnd, WM_GETICON, 0, 0);
    if (hIcon == 0) {
        hIcon = LoadImage (hInst, MAKEINTRESOURCE (ID_ICON),
                           IMAGE_ICON, 16, 16, 0);
```

(continued)

Figure 3-12. *continued*

```
        SendMessage (hWnd, WM_SETICON, FALSE, (LPARAM)hIcon);
    }

    // Initialize game.
    ResetGame ();
    return 0;
}
//----------------------------------------------------------------------
// DoSizeMain - Process WM_SIZE message for window.
//
LRESULT DoSizeMain (HWND hWnd, UINT wMsg, WPARAM wParam,
                    LPARAM lParam) {
    RECT rect;

    // Adjust the size of the client rect to take into account
    // the command bar height.
    GetClientRect (hWnd, &rect);
    rect.top += CommandBar_Height (GetDlgItem (hWnd, IDC_CMDBAR));

    // Define the playing board rect.
    rectBoard = rect;
    rectPrompt = rect;
    // Layout depends on portrait or landscape screen.
    if (rect.right - rect.left > rect.bottom - rect.top) {
        rectBoard.left += 20;
        rectBoard.top += 10;
        rectBoard.bottom -= 10;
        rectBoard.right = rectBoard.bottom - rectBoard.top + 10;

        rectPrompt.left = rectBoard.right + 10;

    } else {
        rectBoard.left += 20;
        rectBoard.right -= 20;
        rectBoard.top += 10;
        rectBoard.bottom = rectBoard.right - rectBoard.left + 10;

        rectPrompt.top = rectBoard.bottom + 10;
    }
    return 0;
}
//----------------------------------------------------------------------
// DoPaintMain - Process WM_PAINT message for window.
//
LRESULT DoPaintMain (HWND hWnd, UINT wMsg, WPARAM wParam,
                     LPARAM lParam) {
    PAINTSTRUCT ps;
```

```
    RECT rect;
    HFONT hFont, hOldFont;
    TCHAR szPrompt[32];
    HDC hdc;

    // Adjust the size of the client rect to take into account
    // the command bar height.
    GetClientRect (hWnd, &rect);
    rect.top += CommandBar_Height (GetDlgItem (hWnd, IDC_CMDBAR));

    hdc = BeginPaint (hWnd, &ps);

    // Draw the board.
    DrawBoard (hdc, &rectBoard);

    // Write the prompt to the screen.
    hFont = GetStockObject (SYSTEM_FONT);
    hOldFont = SelectObject (hdc, hFont);

    if (bTurn == 0)
        LoadString (hInst, IDS_XTURN, szPrompt, sizeof (szPrompt));
    else
        LoadString (hInst, IDS_OTURN, szPrompt, sizeof (szPrompt));

    DrawText (hdc, szPrompt, -1, &rectPrompt,
              DT_CENTER | DT_VCENTER | DT_SINGLELINE);

    SelectObject (hdc, hOldFont);
    EndPaint (hWnd, &ps);
    return 0;
}
//----------------------------------------------------------------------
// DoInitMenuPopMain - Process WM_INITMENUPOPUP message for window.
//
LRESULT DoInitMenuPopMain (HWND hWnd, UINT wMsg, WPARAM wParam,
                           LPARAM lParam) {
    HMENU hMenu;

    hMenu = CommandBar_GetMenu (GetDlgItem (hWnd, IDC_CMDBAR), 0);

    if (bLastMove == -1)
        EnableMenuItem (hMenu, IDM_UNDO, MF_BYCOMMAND | MF_GRAYED);
    else
        EnableMenuItem (hMenu, IDM_UNDO,  MF_BYCOMMAND | MF_ENABLED);
    return 0;
}
```

(continued)

Figure 3-12. *continued*

```
//----------------------------------------------------------------------
// DoCommandMain - Process WM_COMMAND message for window.
//
//
LRESULT DoCommandMain (HWND hWnd, UINT wMsg, WPARAM wParam,
                       LPARAM lParam) {
    WORD idItem, wNotifyCode;
    HWND hwndCtl;
    INT  i;

    // Parse the parameters.
    idItem = (WORD) LOWORD (wParam);
    wNotifyCode = (WORD) HIWORD(wParam);
    hwndCtl = (HWND) lParam;

    // Call routine to handle control message.
    for (i = 0; i < dim(MainCommandItems); i++) {
        if (idItem == MainCommandItems[i].Code)
            return (*MainCommandItems[i].Fxn)(hWnd, idItem, hwndCtl,
                                               wNotifyCode);
    }
    return 0;
}
//----------------------------------------------------------------------
// DoLButtonUpMain - Process WM_LBUTTONUP message for window.
//
LRESULT DoLButtonUpMain (HWND hWnd, UINT wMsg, WPARAM wParam,
                         LPARAM lParam) {
    POINT pt;
    INT cx, cy, nCell = 0;

    pt.x = LOWORD (lParam);
    pt.y = HIWORD (lParam);

    // See if pen on board.  If so, determine which cell.
    if (PtInRect (&rectBoard, pt)){
        // Normalize point to upper left corner of board.
        pt.x -= rectBoard.left;
        pt.y -= rectBoard.top;

        // Compute size of each cell.
        cx = (rectBoard.right - rectBoard.left)/3;
        cy = (rectBoard.bottom - rectBoard.top)/3;

        // Find column.
        nCell = (pt.x / cx);
```

```
        // Find row.
        nCell += (pt.y / cy) * 3;

        // If cell empty, fill it with mark.
        if (bBoard[nCell] == 0) {
            if (bTurn) {
                bBoard[nCell] = 2;
                bTurn = 0;
            } else {
                bBoard[nCell] = 1;
                bTurn = 1;
            }
            // Save the cell for the undo command.
            bLastMove = nCell;
            // Force the screen to be repainted.
            InvalidateRect (hWnd, NULL, FALSE);
        } else {
            // Inform the user of the filled cell.
            MessageBeep (0);
            return 0;
        }
    }
    return 0;
}
//----------------------------------------------------------------------
// DoDestroyMain - Process WM_DESTROY message for window.
//
LRESULT DoDestroyMain (HWND hWnd, UINT wMsg, WPARAM wParam,
                       LPARAM lParam) {
    PostQuitMessage (0);
    return 0;
}
//======================================================================
// Command handler routines
//
//----------------------------------------------------------------------
// DoMainCommandNewGame - Process New Game command.
//
LPARAM DoMainCommandNewGame (HWND hWnd, WORD idItem, HWND hwndCtl,
                             WORD wNotifyCode) {
    INT i, j = 0, rc;

    // Count the number of used spaces.
    for (i = 0; i < 9; i++)
        if (bBoard[i])
            j++;
```

(continued)

Figure 3-12. *continued*

```
    // If not new game or complete game, ask user before clearing.
    if (j && (j != 9)) {
        rc = MessageBox (hWnd,
                         TEXT ("Are you sure you want to clear the board?"),
                         TEXT ("New Game"), MB_YESNO | MB_ICONQUESTION);
        if (rc == IDNO)
            return 0;
    }
    ResetGame ();
    InvalidateRect (hWnd, NULL, TRUE);
    return 0;
}
//----------------------------------------------------------------------
// DoMainCommandUndo - Process Undo Last Move command.
//
LPARAM DoMainCommandUndo (HWND hWnd, WORD idItem, HWND hwndCtl,
                          WORD wNotifyCode) {

    if (bLastMove != -1) {
        bBoard[bLastMove] = 0;
        if (bTurn) {
            bTurn = 0;
        } else {
            bTurn = 1;
        }
        // Only one level of undo
        bLastMove = -1;
        InvalidateRect (hWnd, NULL, TRUE);
    }
    return 0;
}
//----------------------------------------------------------------------
// DoMainCommandExit - Process Program Exit command.
//
LPARAM DoMainCommandExit (HWND hWnd, WORD idItem, HWND hwndCtl,
                          WORD wNotifyCode) {

    SendMessage (hWnd, WM_CLOSE, 0, 0);
    return 0;
}
//======================================================================
// Game-specific routines
//
//----------------------------------------------------------------------
// ResetGame - Initialize the structures for a game.
//
```

```
void ResetGame (void) {
    INT i;

    // Initialize the board.
    for (i = 0; i < dim(bBoard); i++)
        bBoard[i] = 0;

    bTurn = 0;
    bLastMove = -1;
    return;
}
//----------------------------------------------------------------------
// DrawXO - Draw a single X or O in a square.
//
void DrawXO (HDC hdc, HPEN hPen, RECT *prect, INT nCell, INT nType) {
    POINT pt[2];
    INT cx, cy;
    RECT rect;

    cx = (prect->right - prect->left)/3;
    cy = (prect->bottom - prect->top)/3;

    // Compute the dimensions of the target cell.
    rect.left = (cx * (nCell % 3) + prect->left) + 10;
    rect.right = rect.left + cx - 20,
    rect.top = cy * (nCell / 3) + prect->top + 10,
    rect.bottom =  rect.top + cy - 20;

    // Draw an X?
    if (nType == 1) {
        pt[0].x = rect.left;
        pt[0].y = rect.top;
        pt[1].x = rect.right;
        pt[1].y = rect.bottom;
        Polyline (hdc, pt, 2);

        pt[0].x = rect.right;
        pt[1].x = rect.left;
        Polyline (hdc, pt, 2);
    // How about an O?
    } else if (nType == 2) {
        Ellipse (hdc, rect.left, rect.top, rect.right, rect.bottom);
    }
    return;
}
//----------------------------------------------------------------------
```

(continued)

Figure 3-12. *continued*

```
// DrawBoard - Draw the tic-tac-toe board.
//
void DrawBoard (HDC hdc, RECT *prect) {
    HPEN hPen, hOldPen;
    POINT pt[2];
    LOGPEN lp;
    INT i, cx, cy;

    // Create a nice thick pen.
    lp.lopnStyle = PS_SOLID;
    lp.lopnWidth.x = 5;
    lp.lopnWidth.y = 5;
    lp.lopnColor = RGB (0, 0, 0);
    hPen = CreatePenIndirect (&lp);

    hOldPen = SelectObject (hdc, hPen);

    cx = (prect->right - prect->left)/3;
    cy = (prect->bottom - prect->top)/3;

    // Draw lines down.
    pt[0].x = cx + prect->left;
    pt[1].x = cx + prect->left;
    pt[0].y = prect->top;
    pt[1].y = prect->bottom;
    Polyline (hdc, pt, 2);

    pt[0].x += cx;
    pt[1].x += cx;
    Polyline (hdc, pt, 2);

    // Draw lines across.
    pt[0].x = prect->left;
    pt[1].x = prect->right;
    pt[0].y = cy + prect->top;
    pt[1].y = cy + prect->top;
    Polyline (hdc, pt, 2);

    pt[0].y += cy;
    pt[1].y += cy;
    Polyline (hdc, pt, 2);

    // Fill in Xs and Os.
    for (i = 0; i < dim (bBoard); i++)
        DrawXO (hdc, hPen, &rectBoard, i, bBoard[i]);
```

```
    SelectObject (hdc, hOldPen);
    DeleteObject (hPen);
    return;
}
```

The biggest change in TicTac2 is the addition of a WM_COMMAND handler in the form of the routine *OnCommandMain*. Because a program might end up handling a large number of different menu items and other controls, I extend the table-lookup design of the window procedure to another table lookup for command IDs from menus and accelerators. For TicTac2, I use three command handlers, one for each of the menu items. This results in another table of IDs and procedure pointers that associates menu IDs with handler procedures. Again, this way of using a table lookup instead of the standard switch statement isn't necessary or specific to Windows CE. It's simply my programming style.

The first menu handler, *OnCommandNewGame*, simply calls the reset game routine to clear the game structures. The routine itself returns 0, which is the default value for a WM_COMMAND handler.

The *OnCommandUndo* command handler is interesting in that it isn't always enabled. TicTac2 handles an additional message WM_INITMENUPOPUP, which is sent to a window immediately before the window menu is displayed. This gives the window a chance to initialize any of the menu items. In this case, the routine *OnInitMenuPopMain* looks to see whether the *bLastMove* field contains a valid cell value (0 through 8). If not, the routine disables the Undo menu item using *EnableMenuItem*. This action also disables the keyboard accelerator for that menu item as well.

The final command handler, *OnCommandExit*, sends a WM_CLOSE message to the main window. Closing the window eventually results in Windows sending a WM_DESTROY message, which results in a *PostQuitMessage* call that terminates the program. Sending a WM_CLOSE message is, by the way, the same action that results from clicking on the Close button on the command bar.

Other changes from the first TicTac example include modification of the message loop to provide for keyboard accelerators and the addition of code in the *OnCreateMain* routine to load and assign a window icon. Also, the string prompts for whose turn it is are loaded from the resource file.

Looking at the *OnCommandNewGame* handler introduces one last new function. If the game isn't complete, the program asks the players whether they really want to clear the game board. This query is accomplished by calling

```
int MessageBox (HWND hWnd, LPCTSTR lpText, LPCTSTR lpCaption,
                UINT uType);
```

This function displays a message box, a simple dialog box, with definable text and buttons. A message box can display a message along with a limited series of buttons. Message boxes are often used to query users for a simple response or to notify them of some event. The *uType* parameter allows the programmer to select different button configurations, such as Yes/No, OK/Cancel, Yes/No/Cancel, and simply OK. You can also select an icon to appear in the message box that signals the level of importance of the answer.

A message box is essentially a poor man's dialog box. It offers a simple method of querying the user but little flexibility in how the dialog box is configured. Now that we've introduced the subject of *dialog boxes*, it's time to take a closer look at them and other types of secondary and child windows.

Chapter 4

Windows, Controls, and Dialog Boxes

Understanding how windows work and relate to each other is the key to understanding the user interface of the Microsoft Windows operating system, whether it be Microsoft Windows 98, Microsoft Windows NT, or Microsoft Windows CE. Everything you see on a Windows display is a window. The desktop is a window, the taskbar is a window, even the Start button on the taskbar is a window. Windows are related to one another according to one relationship model or another; they may be in *parent/child, sibling,* or *owner/owned* relationships. Windows supports a number of predefined window classes, called *controls*. These controls simplify the work of programmers by providing a range of predefined user interface elements as simple as a button or as complex as a multiline text editor. Windows CE supports the same standard set of built-in controls as the other versions of Windows. These built-in controls shouldn't be confused with the complex controls provided by the common control library. I'll talk about those controls in Chapter 5.

Controls are usually contained in dialog boxes (sometimes simply referred to as *dialogs*). These dialog boxes constitute a method for a program to query users for information the program needs. A specialized form of dialog, named a *property sheet*, allows a program to display multiple but related dialog boxes in an overlapping style; each box or property sheet is equipped with an identifying tab. Property sheets are particularly valuable given the tiny screens associated with Windows CE devices.

Finally, Windows CE supports a subset of the common dialog library available under Windows NT and Windows 98. Specifically, Windows CE supports versions of the common dialog boxes File Open, File Save, Color, and Print. These dialogs are somewhat different on Windows CE. They're reformatted for the smaller screens and aren't as extensible as their desktop counterparts.

CHILD WINDOWS

Each window is connected via a parent/child relationship scheme. Applications create a main window with no parent, called a *top-level window*. That window might (or might not) contain windows, called *child* windows. A child window is clipped to its parent. That is, no part of a child window is visible beyond the edge of its parent. Child windows are automatically destroyed when their parent windows are destroyed. Also, when a parent window moves, its child windows move with it.

Child windows are programmatically identical to top-level windows. You use the *CreateWindow* or *CreateWindowEx* function to create them, each has a window procedure that handles the same messages as its top-level window, and each can, in turn, contain its own child windows. To create a child window, use the WS_CHILD window style in the *dwStyle* parameter of *CreateWindow* or *CreateWindowEx*. In addition, the *hMenu* parameter, unused in top-level Windows CE windows, passes an ID value that you can use to reference the window.

Under Windows CE, there's one other major difference between top-level windows and child windows. Windows sends WM_HIBERNATE messages only to top-level windows that have the WS_OVERLAPPED and WS_VISIBLE styles. (Window visibility in this case has nothing to do with what a user sees. A window can be "visible" to the system and still not be seen by the user if other windows are above it in the Z-order.) This means that child windows and most dialog boxes aren't sent WM_HIBERNATE messages. Top-level windows must either manually send a WM_HIBERNATE message to their child windows as necessary or perform all the necessary tasks themselves to reduce the application's memory footprint. On Windows CE systems, such as the H/PC that support application buttons on the taskbar, the rules for determining the target of WM_HIBERNATE messages are also used to determine what windows get buttons on the taskbar.

In addition to the parent/child relationship, windows also have an owner/owned relationship. Owned windows aren't clipped to their owners. However, they always appear "above" (in Z-order) the window that owns them. If the owner window is minimized, all windows it owns are hidden. Likewise, if a window is destroyed, all windows it owns are destroyed. Windows CE 1.0 supports window ownership only for dialog boxes, but from version 2.0 on, Windows CE provides full support for owned windows.

Window Management Functions

Given the windows-centric nature of Windows, it's not surprising that you can choose from a number of functions that enable a window to interrogate its environment so that it might determine its location in the window family tree. To find its parent, a window can call

```
HWND GetParent (HWND hWnd);
```

This function is passed a window handle and returns the handle of the calling window's parent window. If the window has no parent, the function returns NULL.

Enumerating windows

GetWindow, prototyped as

```
HWND GetWindow (HWND hWnd, UINT uCmd);
```

is an omnibus function that allows a window to query its children, owner, and siblings. The first parameter is the window's handle while the second is a constant that indicates the requested relationship. The GW_CHILD constant returns a handle to the first child window of a window. *GetWindow* returns windows in Z-order, so the first window in this case is the child window highest in the Z-order. If the window has no child windows, this function returns NULL. The two constants, GW_HWNDFIRST and GW_HWNDLAST, return the first and last windows in the Z-order. If the window handle passed is a top-level window, these constants return the first and last topmost windows in the Z-order. If the window passed is a child window, the GetWindow function returns the first and last sibling window. The GW_HWNDNEXT and GW_HWNDPREV constants return the next lower and next higher windows in the Z-order. These constants allow a window to iterate through all the sibling windows by getting the next window, then using that window handle with another call to *GetWindow* to get the next, and so on. Finally, the GW_OWNER constant returns the handle of the owner of a window.

Another way to iterate through a series of windows is

```
BOOL EnumWindows (WNDENUMPROC lpEnumFunc, LPARAM lParam);
```

This function calls the callback function pointed to by *lpEnumFunc* once for each top-level window on the desktop, passing the the handle of each window in turn. The *lParam* value is an application-defined value, which is also passed to the enumeration function. This function is better than iterating through a *GetWindow* loop to find the top-level windows because it always returns valid window handles; it's possible that a *GetWindow* iteration loop will get a window handle whose window is destroyed before the next call to *GetWindow* can occur. However, since *EnumWindows* works only with top-level windows, *GetWindow* still has a place when iterating through a series of child windows.

Finding a window

To get the handle of a specific window, use the function

```
HWND FindWindow (LPCTSTR lpClassName, LPCTSTR lpWindowName);
```

This function can find a window either by means of its window class name or by means of a window's title text. This function is handy when an application is just starting up; it can determine whether another copy of the application is already running. All an application has to do is call *FindWindow* with the name of the window class for the main window of the application. Because an application almost always has a main window while it's running, a NULL returned by *FindWindow* indicates that the function can't locate another window with the specified window class—therefore, it's almost certain that another copy of the application isn't running.

Editing the window structure values

The pair of functions

```
LONG GetWindowLong (HWND hWnd, int nIndex);
```

and

```
LONG SetWindowLong (HWND hWnd, int nIndex, LONG dwNewLong);
```

allow an application to edit data in the window structure for a window. Remember the WNDCLASS structure passed to the *RegisterClass* function has a field, *cbWndExtra*, that controls the number of extra bytes that are to be allocated after the structure. If you allocated extra space in the window structure when the window class was registered, you can access those bytes using the *GetWindowLong* and *SetWindowLong* functions. Under Windows CE, the data must be allocated and referenced in 4-byte (integer sized and aligned) blocks. So, if a window class was registered with 12 in the *cbWndExtra* field, an application can access those bytes by calling *GetWindowLong* or *SetWindowLong* with the window handle and by setting values of 0, 4, and 8 in the *nIndex* parameter.

GetWindowLong and *SetWindowLong* support a set of predefined index values that allow an application access to some of the basic parameters of a window. Here is a list of the supported values for Windows CE.

- *GWL_STYLE* The style flags for the window
- *GWL_EXSTYLE* The extended style flags for the window
- *GWL_WNDPROC* The pointer to the window procedure for the window
- *GWL_ID* The ID value for the window
- *GWL_USERDATA* An application-usable 32-bit value

Dialog box windows support the following additional values:

- *DWL_DLGPROC* The pointer to the dialog procedure for the window
- *DWL_MSGRESULT* The value returned when the dialog box function returns
- *DWL_USER* An application-usable 32-bit value

Windows CE doesn't support the GWL_HINSTANCE and GWL_HWNDPARENT values supported by Windows NT and Windows 98.

Scroll Bars and the FontList2 Example Program

To demonstrate a handy use for a child window, we return to the FontList program from Chapter 2. As you might remember, the problem was that if a scroll bar were attached to the main window of the application, the scroll bar would extend upward, past the right side of the command bar. The reason for this is that a scroll bar attached to a window is actually placed in the nonclient area of that window. Because the command bar lies in the client space, we have no easy way to properly position the two controls in the same window.

An easy way to solve this problem is to use a child window. We place the child window so that it fills all of the client area of the top-level window not covered by the command bar. The scroll bar can then be attached to the child window so that it appears on the right side of the window but stops just beneath the command bar. Figure 4-1 shows the Fontlist2 window. Notice that the scroll bar now fits properly underneath the command bar. Also notice that the child window is completely undetectable by the user.

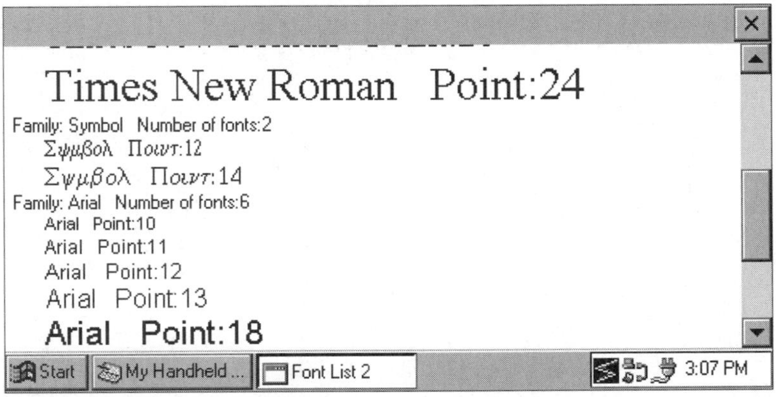

Figure 4-1. *The FontList2 window with the scroll bar properly positioned just beneath the command bar.*

The code for this fix, which isn't that much more complex than the original FontList example, is shown in Figure 4-2. Instead of one window procedure, there are now two, one for the top-level window, which I have labeled the Frame window, and one for the child window. I separated the code for these two windows into two different source files, FontList2.c and ClientWnd.c. ClientWnd.c also contains a function, *InitClient*, which registers the client window class.

FontList2.h

```
//======================================================================
// Header file
//
// Written for the book Programming Windows CE
// Copyright (C) 1998 Douglas Boling
//======================================================================
// Returns number of elements
#define dim(x) (sizeof(x) / sizeof(x[0]))

//----------------------------------------------------------------------
// Generic defines and data types
//
struct decodeUINT {                            // Structure associates
    UINT Code;                                 // messages
                                               // with a function.
    LRESULT (*Fxn)(HWND, UINT, WPARAM, LPARAM);
};
struct decodeCMD {                             // Structure associates
    UINT Code;                                 // menu IDs with a
    LRESULT (*Fxn)(HWND, WORD, HWND, WORD);    // function.
};

//----------------------------------------------------------------------
// Generic defines used by application
#define  IDC_CMDBAR 1                          // Command bar ID
#define  IDC_CLIENT 2                          // Client window ID

//----------------------------------------------------------------------
// Window prototypes and defines
//
#define FAMILYMAX   24
typedef struct {
    int nNumFonts;
    TCHAR szFontFamily[LF_FACESIZE];
} FONTFAMSTRUCT;
```

Figure 4-2. *The FontList2 program.*

```
typedef FONTFAMSTRUCT *PFONTFAMSTRUCT;

typedef struct {
    INT yCurrent;
    HDC hdc;
} PAINTFONTINFO;
typedef PAINTFONTINFO *PPAINTFONTINFO;

#define CLIENTWINDOW    TEXT ("ClientWnd")

int InitClient (HINSTANCE);
int TermClient (HINSTANCE, int);

//----------------------------------------------------------------------
// Function prototypes
//
int InitApp (HINSTANCE);
HWND InitInstance (HINSTANCE, LPWSTR, int);
int TermInstance (HINSTANCE, int);

// Window procedures
LRESULT CALLBACK FrameWndProc (HWND, UINT, WPARAM, LPARAM);
LRESULT CALLBACK ClientWndProc (HWND, UINT, WPARAM, LPARAM);

// Message handlers
LRESULT DoCreateFrame (HWND, UINT, WPARAM, LPARAM);
LRESULT DoSizeFrame (HWND, UINT, WPARAM, LPARAM);
LRESULT DoDestroyFrame (HWND, UINT, WPARAM, LPARAM);

LRESULT DoCreateClient (HWND, UINT, WPARAM, LPARAM);
LRESULT DoPaintClient (HWND, UINT, WPARAM, LPARAM);
LRESULT DoVScrollClient (HWND, UINT, WPARAM, LPARAM);
```

FontList2.c

```
//======================================================================
// FontList2 - Lists the available fonts in the system
//
// Written for the book Programming Windows CE
// Copyright (C) 1998 Douglas Boling
//======================================================================
#include <windows.h>                 // For all that Windows stuff
#include <commctrl.h>                // Command bar includes
#include "FontList2.h"               // Program-specific stuff
```

(continued)

Figure 4-2. *continued*

```
//----------------------------------------------------------------------
// Global data
//
const TCHAR szAppName[] = TEXT ("FontList2");
HINSTANCE hInst;                     // Program instance handle

// Message dispatch table for FrameWindowProc
const struct decodeUINT FrameMessages[] = {
    WM_CREATE, DoCreateFrame,
    WM_SIZE, DoSizeFrame,
    WM_DESTROY, DoDestroyFrame,
};
//======================================================================
// Program entry point
//
int WINAPI WinMain (HINSTANCE hInstance, HINSTANCE hPrevInstance,
                    LPWSTR lpCmdLine, int nCmdShow) {
    MSG msg;
    int rc = 0;
    HWND hwndFrame;

    // Initialize application.
    rc = InitApp (hInstance);
    if (rc) return rc;

    // Initialize this instance.
    hwndFrame = InitInstance (hInstance, lpCmdLine, nCmdShow);
    if (hwndFrame == 0)
        return 0x10;

    // Application message loop
    while (GetMessage (&msg, NULL, 0, 0)) {
        TranslateMessage (&msg);
        DispatchMessage (&msg);
    }
    // Instance cleanup
    return TermInstance (hInstance, msg.wParam);
}
//----------------------------------------------------------------------
// InitApp - Application initialization
//
int InitApp (HINSTANCE hInstance) {
    WNDCLASS wc;

    // Register application frame window class.
```

```
    wc.style = 0;                             // Window style
    wc.lpfnWndProc = FrameWndProc;            // Callback function
    wc.cbClsExtra = 0;                        // Extra class data
    wc.cbWndExtra = 0;                        // Extra window data
    wc.hInstance = hInstance;                 // Owner handle
    wc.hIcon = NULL,                          // Application icon
    wc.hCursor = NULL;                        // Default cursor
    wc.hbrBackground = (HBRUSH) GetStockObject (WHITE_BRUSH);
    wc.lpszMenuName =  NULL;                  // Menu name
    wc.lpszClassName = szAppName;             // Window class name

    if (RegisterClass (&wc) == 0) return 1;

    // Initialize client window class.
    if (InitClient (hInstance) != 0) return 2;
    return 0;
}
//----------------------------------------------------------------------
// InitInstance - Instance initialization
//
HWND InitInstance (HINSTANCE hInstance, LPWSTR lpCmdLine, int nCmdShow) {
    HWND hWnd;

    // Save program instance handle in global variable.
    hInst = hInstance;

    // Create frame window.
    hWnd = CreateWindow (szAppName,            // Window class
                         TEXT ("Font List 2"), // Window title
                         WS_VISIBLE,           // Style flags
                         CW_USEDEFAULT,        // x position
                         CW_USEDEFAULT,        // y position
                         CW_USEDEFAULT,        // Initial width
                         CW_USEDEFAULT,        // Initial height
                         NULL,                 // Parent
                         NULL,                 // Menu, must be null
                         hInstance,            // Application instance
                         NULL);                // Pointer to create
                                               // parameters
    // Return fail code if window not created.
    if (!IsWindow (hWnd)) return 0;

    // Standard show and update calls
    ShowWindow (hWnd, nCmdShow);
    UpdateWindow (hWnd);
    return hWnd;
}
```

(continued)

Figure 4-2. *continued*

```
//----------------------------------------------------------------------
// TermInstance - Program cleanup
//
int TermInstance (HINSTANCE hInstance, int nDefRC) {

    return nDefRC;
}
//======================================================================
// Message handling procedures for FrameWindow
//----------------------------------------------------------------------
// FrameWndProc - Callback function for application window
//
LRESULT CALLBACK FrameWndProc (HWND hWnd, UINT wMsg, WPARAM wParam,
                               LPARAM lParam) {
    INT i;
    //
    // Search message list to see if we need to handle this
    // message.  If in list, call procedure.
    //
    for (i = 0; i < dim(FrameMessages); i++) {
        if (wMsg == FrameMessages[i].Code)
            return (*FrameMessages[i].Fxn)(hWnd, wMsg, wParam, lParam);
    }
    return DefWindowProc (hWnd, wMsg, wParam, lParam);
}
//----------------------------------------------------------------------
// DoCreateFrame - Process WM_CREATE message for window.
//
LRESULT DoCreateFrame (HWND hWnd, UINT wMsg, WPARAM wParam,
                       LPARAM lParam) {
    HWND hwndCB, hwndClient;
    INT sHeight;
    LPCREATESTRUCT lpcs;

    // Convert lParam into pointer to create structure.
    lpcs = (LPCREATESTRUCT) lParam;

    // Create a command bar.
    hwndCB = CommandBar_Create (hInst, hWnd, IDC_CMDBAR);
    // Add exit button to command bar.
    CommandBar_AddAdornments (hwndCB, 0, 0);
    sHeight = CommandBar_Height (GetDlgItem (hWnd, IDC_CMDBAR));
    //
    // Create client window.  Size it so that it fits under
    // the command bar and fills the remaining client area.
    //
```

```
    hwndClient = CreateWindow (CLIENTWINDOW, TEXT (""),
                               WS_VISIBLE | WS_CHILD | WS_VSCROLL,
                               lpcs->x, lpcs->y + sHeight,
                               lpcs->cx, lpcs->cy - sHeight,
                               hWnd, (HMENU)IDC_CLIENT,
                               lpcs->hInstance, NULL);

    // Destroy frame if client window not created.
    if (!IsWindow (hwndClient))
        DestroyWindow (hWnd);
    return 0;
}
//----------------------------------------------------------------------
// DoSizeFrame - Process WM_SIZE message for window.
//
LRESULT DoSizeFrame (HWND hWnd, UINT wMsg, WPARAM wParam, LPARAM lParam) {
    RECT rect;
    INT i;

    GetClientRect (hWnd, &rect);
    i = CommandBar_Height (GetDlgItem (hWnd, IDC_CMDBAR));
    rect.top += i;

    SetWindowPos (GetDlgItem (hWnd, IDC_CLIENT), NULL, rect.left, rect.top,
                  rect.right - rect.left, rect.bottom - rect.top,
                  SWP_NOZORDER);
    return 0;
}
//----------------------------------------------------------------------
// DoDestroyFrame - Process WM_DESTROY message for window.
//
LRESULT DoDestroyFrame (HWND hWnd, UINT wMsg, WPARAM wParam,
                        LPARAM lParam) {
    PostQuitMessage (0);
    return 0;
}MM
```

ClientWnd.c

```
//======================================================================
// ClientWnd - Client window code for FontList2
//
// Written for the book Programming Windows CE
// Copyright (C) 1998 Douglas Boling
```

(continued)

Figure 4-2. *continued*

```
//======================================================================
#include <windows.h>                    // For all that Windows stuff
#include "FontList2.h"                  // Program-specific stuff

extern HINSTANCE hInst;
BOOL fFirst = TRUE;

//----------------------------------------------------------------------
// Global data
//
FONTFAMSTRUCT ffs[FAMILYMAX];
INT sFamilyCnt = 0;
INT sVPos = 0;
INT sVMax = 0;

// Message dispatch table for ClientWindowProc
const struct decodeUINT ClientMessages[] = {
    WM_CREATE, DoCreateClient,
    WM_PAINT, DoPaintClient,
    WM_VSCROLL, DoVScrollClient,
};
//----------------------------------------------------------------------
// InitClient - Client window initialization
//
int InitClient (HINSTANCE hInstance) {
    WNDCLASS wc;

    // Register application client window class.
    wc.style = 0;                              // Window style
    wc.lpfnWndProc = ClientWndProc;            // Callback function
    wc.cbClsExtra = 0;                         // Extra class data
    wc.cbWndExtra = 0;                         // Extra window data
    wc.hInstance = hInstance;                  // Owner handle
    wc.hIcon = NULL,                           // Application icon
    wc.hCursor = NULL;                         // Default cursor
    wc.hbrBackground = (HBRUSH) GetStockObject (WHITE_BRUSH);
    wc.lpszMenuName =  NULL;                   // Menu name
    wc.lpszClassName = CLIENTWINDOW;           // Window class name

    if (RegisterClass (&wc) == 0) return 1;

    return 0;
}
//----------------------------------------------------------------------
// TermClient - Client window cleanup
//
```

```
int TermClient (HINSTANCE hInstance, int nDefRC) {
    return nDefRC;
}
//======================================================================
// Font callback functions
//----------------------------------------------------------------------
// FontFamilyCallback - Callback function that enumerates the font
// families.
//
int CALLBACK FontFamilyCallback (CONST LOGFONT *lplf,
                                 CONST TEXTMETRIC *lpntm,
                                 DWORD nFontType, LPARAM lParam) {
    int rc = 1;

    // Stop enumeration if array filled.
    if (sFamilyCnt >= FAMILYMAX)
        return 0;
    // Copy face name of font.
    lstrcpy (ffs[sFamilyCnt++].szFontFamily, lplf->lfFaceName);

    return rc;
}
//----------------------------------------------------------------------
// EnumSingleFontFamily - Callback function that enumerates the font
// families
//
int CALLBACK EnumSingleFontFamily (CONST LOGFONT *lplf,
                                   CONST TEXTMETRIC *lpntm,
                                   DWORD nFontType, LPARAM lParam) {
    PFONTFAMSTRUCT pffs;

    pffs = (PFONTFAMSTRUCT) lParam;
    pffs->nNumFonts++;    // Increment count of fonts in family.
    return 1;
}
//----------------------------------------------------------------------
// PaintSingleFontFamily - Callback function that enumerates the font
// families.
//
int CALLBACK PaintSingleFontFamily (CONST LOGFONT *lplf,
                                    CONST TEXTMETRIC *lpntm,
                                    DWORD nFontType, LPARAM lParam) {
    PPAINTFONTINFO ppfi;
    TCHAR szOut[256];
    INT nFontHeight, nPointSize;
    TEXTMETRIC tm;
    HFONT hFont, hOldFont;
```

(continued)

Figure 4-2. *continued*

```
    ppfi = (PPAINTFONTINFO) lParam;  // Translate lParam into
                                     // structure pointer.

    // Create the font from the LOGFONT structure passed.
    hFont = CreateFontIndirect (lplf);

    // Select the font into the device context.
    hOldFont = SelectObject (ppfi->hdc, hFont);

    // Get the height of the default font.
    GetTextMetrics (ppfi->hdc, &tm);
    nFontHeight = tm.tmHeight + tm.tmExternalLeading;

    // Compute font size.
    nPointSize = (lplf->lfHeight * 72) /
                 GetDeviceCaps(ppfi->hdc,LOGPIXELSY);

    // Format string and paint on display.
    wsprintf (szOut, TEXT ("%s   Point:%d"), lplf->lfFaceName,
              nPointSize);
    ExtTextOut (ppfi->hdc, 25, ppfi->yCurrent, 0, NULL,
                szOut, lstrlen (szOut), NULL);

    // Update new draw point.
    ppfi->yCurrent += nFontHeight;
    // Deselect font and delete.
    SelectObject (ppfi->hdc, hOldFont);
    DeleteObject (hFont);
    return 1;
}
//======================================================================
// Message handling procedures for ClientWindow
//----------------------------------------------------------------------
// ClientWndProc - Callback function for application window
//
LRESULT CALLBACK ClientWndProc (HWND hWnd, UINT wMsg, WPARAM wParam,
                                LPARAM lParam) {
    INT i;
    //
    // Search message list to see if we need to handle this
    // message.  If in list, call procedure.
    //
    for (i = 0; i < dim(ClientMessages); i++) {
        if (wMsg == ClientMessages[i].Code)
            return (*ClientMessages[i].Fxn)(hWnd, wMsg, wParam, lParam);
    }
```

```
    return DefWindowProc (hWnd, wMsg, wParam, lParam);
}
//----------------------------------------------------------------------
// DoCreateClient - Process WM_CREATE message for window.
//
LRESULT DoCreateClient (HWND hWnd, UINT wMsg, WPARAM wParam,
                        LPARAM lParam) {
    HDC hdc;
    INT i, rc;

    //Enumerate the available fonts.
    hdc = GetDC (hWnd);
    rc = EnumFontFamilies ((HDC)hdc, (LPTSTR)NULL, FontFamilyCallback, 0);

    for (i = 0; i < sFamilyCnt; i++) {
        ffs[i].nNumFonts = 0;
        rc = EnumFontFamilies ((HDC)hdc, ffs[i].szFontFamily,
                               EnumSingleFontFamily,
                               (LPARAM)(PFONTFAMSTRUCT)&ffs[i]);
    }
    ReleaseDC (hWnd, hdc);
    return 0;
}
//----------------------------------------------------------------------
// DoPaintClient - Process WM_PAINT message for window.
//
LRESULT DoPaintClient (HWND hWnd, UINT wMsg, WPARAM wParam,
                       LPARAM lParam) {
    PAINTSTRUCT ps;
    RECT rect;
    HDC hdc;
    TEXTMETRIC tm;
    INT nFontHeight, i;
    TCHAR szOut[256];
    PAINTFONTINFO pfi;
    SCROLLINFO si;

    hdc = BeginPaint (hWnd, &ps);

    GetClientRect (hWnd, &rect);

    // Get the height of the default font.
    GetTextMetrics (hdc, &tm);
    nFontHeight = tm.tmHeight + tm.tmExternalLeading;
```

(continued)

Figure 4-2. *continued*

```
    // Initialize struct that is passed to enumerate function.
    pfi.yCurrent = rect.top - sVPos;
    pfi.hdc = hdc;
    for (i = 0; i < sFamilyCnt; i++) {

        // Format output string and paint font family name.
        wsprintf (szOut, TEXT ("Family: %s   Number of fonts:%d"),
                  ffs[i].szFontFamily, ffs[i].nNumFonts);
        ExtTextOut (hdc, 5, pfi.yCurrent, 0, NULL,
                    szOut, lstrlen (szOut), NULL);
        pfi.yCurrent += nFontHeight;

        // Enumerate each family to draw a sample of that font.
        EnumFontFamilies ((HDC)hdc, ffs[i].szFontFamily,
                          PaintSingleFontFamily,
                          (LPARAM)&pfi);
    }
    // Compute the total height of the text in the window.
    if (fFirst) {
        sVPos = 0;
        sVMax = (pfi.yCurrent - rect.top) - (rect.bottom - rect.top);

        si.cbSize = sizeof (si);
        si.nMin = 0;
        si.nMax = pfi.yCurrent;
        si.nPage = rect.bottom - rect.top;
        si.nPos = sVPos;
        si.fMask = SIF_ALL;
        SetScrollInfo (hWnd, SB_VERT, &si, TRUE);
        fFirst = FALSE;
    }
    EndPaint (hWnd, &ps);
    return 0;
}
//----------------------------------------------------------------------
// DoVScrollClient - Process WM_VSCROLL message for window.
//
LRESULT DoVScrollClient (HWND hWnd, UINT wMsg, WPARAM wParam,
                         LPARAM lParam) {
    RECT rect;
    SCROLLINFO si;
    INT sOldPos = sVPos;

    GetClientRect (hWnd, &rect);
```

```
    switch (LOWORD (wParam)) {
    case SB_LINEUP:
        sVPos -= 10;
        break;

    case SB_LINEDOWN:
        sVPos += 10;
        break;

    case SB_PAGEUP:
        sVPos -= rect.bottom - rect.top;
        break;

    case SB_PAGEDOWN:
        sVPos += rect.bottom - rect.top;
        break;

    case SB_THUMBPOSITION:
        sVPos = HIWORD (wParam);
        break;
    }
    // Check range.
    if (sVPos < 0)
        sVPos = 0;
    if (sVPos > sVMax)
        sVPos = sVMax;

    // If scroll position changed, update scrollbar and
    // force redraw of window.
    if (sVPos != sOldPos) {
        si.cbSize = sizeof (si);
        si.nPos = sVPos;
        si.fMask = SIF_POS;
        SetScrollInfo (hWnd, SB_VERT, &si, TRUE);

        InvalidateRect (hWnd, NULL, TRUE);
    }
    return 0;
}
```

The window procedure for the frame window is quite simple. Just as in the original FontList program in Chapter 2, the command bar is created in the WM_CREATE message handler, *DoCreateFrame*. Now, however, this procedure also calls *CreateWindow* to create the child window in the area underneath the command bar. The child window is created with three style flags: WS_VISIBLE, so that the window is initially visible; WS_CHILD, required because it will be a child window of the frame window; and WS_VSCROLL to add the vertical scroll bar to the child window.

The majority of the work for the program is handled in the client window procedure. Here the same font enumeration calls are made to query the fonts in the system. The WM_PAINT handler, *DoPaintClient*, has a new characteristic: it now bases what it paints on the new global variable *sVPos*, which provides vertical positioning. That variable is initialized to 0 in *DoCreateClient* and is changed in the handler for a new message, WM_VSCROLL.

Scroll bar messages

A WM_VSCROLL message is sent to the owner of a vertical scroll bar any time the user taps on the scroll bar to change its position. A complementary message, WM_HSCROLL, is identical to WM_VSCROLL but is sent when the user taps on a horizontal scroll bar. For both these messages, the *wParam* and *lParam* assignments are the same. The low word of the *wParam* parameter contains a code indicating why the message was sent. Figure 4-3 shows a diagram of horizontal and vertical scroll bars and how tapping on different parts of the scroll bars results in different messages. The high word of *wParam* is the position of the thumb, but this value is valid only while you're processing the SB_THUMBPOSITION and SB_THUMBTRACK codes, which I'll explain shortly. If the scroll bar sending the message is a stand-alone control and not attached to a window, the *lParam* parameter contains the window handle of the scroll bar.

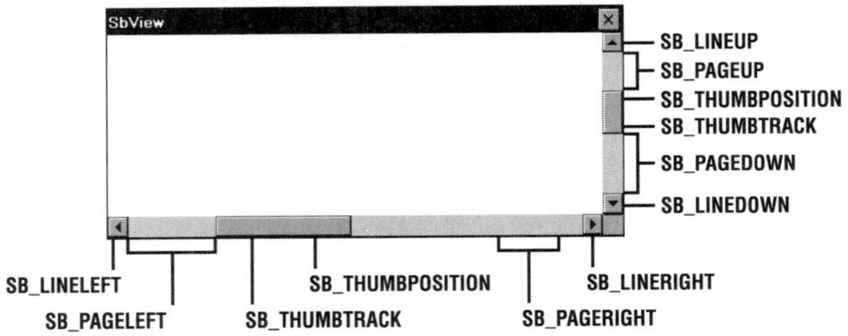

Figure 4-3. *Scroll bars and their hot spots.*

The scroll bar message codes sent by the scroll bar allow the program to react to all the different user actions allowable by a scroll bar. The response required by each code is listed in the following table, Figure 4-4.

The SB_LINE*xxx* and SB_PAGE*xxx* codes are pretty straightforward. You move the scroll position either a line or a page at a time. The SB_THUMBPOSITION and SB_THUMBTRACK codes can be processed in one of two ways. When the user drags the scroll bar thumb, the scroll bar sends SB_THUMBTRACK code so that a program can interactively track the dragging of the thumb. If your application is fast enough, you can simply process the SB_THUMBTRACK code and interactively update the display. If you field the SB_THUMBTRACK code, however, your application must be quick enough to redraw the display so that the thumb can be dragged without hesitation or jumping of the scroll bar. This is especially a problem on the slower devices that run Windows CE.

Codes	*Response*
For WS_VSCROLL	
SB_LINEUP	Program should scroll the screen up one line.
SB_LINEDOWN	Program should scroll the screen down one line.
SB_PAGEUP	Program should scroll the screen up one screen's worth of data.
SB_PAGEDOWN	Program should scroll the screen down one screen's worth of data.
For WS_HSCROLL	
SB_LINELEFT	Program should scroll the screen left one character.
SB_LINERIGHT	Program should scroll the screen right one character.
SB_PAGELEFT	Program should scroll the screen left one screen's worth of data.
SB_PAGERIGHT	Program should scroll the screen right one screen's worth of data.
For both WS_VSCROLL and WS_HSCROLL	
SB_THUMBTRACK	Programs with enough speed to keep up should update the display with the new scroll position.
SB_THUMBPOSITION	Programs that can't update the display fast enough to keep up with the SB_THUMBTRACK message should update the display with the new scroll position.
SB_ENDSCROLL	This code indicates that the scroll bar has completed the scroll event. No action is required by the program.
SB_TOP	Program should set the display to the top or left end of the data.
SB_BOTTOM	Program should set the display to the bottom or right end of the data.

Figure 4-4. *Scroll codes.*

If your application (or the system it's running on) is too slow to quickly update the display for every SB_THUMBTRACK code, you can ignore the SB_THUMBTRACK and wait for the SB_THUMBPOSITION code that's sent when the user drops the scroll bar thumb. Then you have to update the display only once, after the user has finished moving the scroll bar thumb.

Configuring a scroll bar

To use a scroll bar, an application should first set the minimum and maximum values—the range of the scroll bar, along with the initial position. Windows CE scroll bars, like their Win32 cousins, support proportional thumb sizes, which provide feedback to the user about the size of the current visible page compared to the entire scroll range. To set all these parameters, Windows CE applications should use the *SetScrollInfo* function, prototyped as

```
int SetScrollInfo (HWND hwnd, int fnBar, LPSCROLLINFO lpsi, BOOL fRedraw);
```

The first parameter is either the handle of the window that contains the scroll bar or the window handle of the scroll bar itself. The second parameter, *fnBar*, is a flag that determines the use of the window handle. The scroll bar flag can be one of three values: SB_HORZ for a window's standard horizontal scroll bar, SB_VERT for a window's standard vertical scroll bar, or SB_CTL if the scroll bar being set is a standalone control. Unless the scroll bar is a control, the window handle is the handle of the window containing the scroll bar. With SB_CTL, however, the handle is the window handle of the scroll bar control itself. The last parameter is *fRedraw*, a Boolean value that indicates whether the scroll bar should be redrawn after the call has been completed.

The third parameter is a pointer to a SCROLLINFO structure, which is defined as

```
typedef struct tagSCROLLINFO {
    UINT cbSize;
    UINT fMask;
    int   nMin;
    int   nMax;
    UINT nPage;
    int   nPos;
    int   nTrackPos;
} SCROLLINFO;
```

This structure allows you to completely specify the scroll bar parameters. The *cbSize* field must be set to the size of the SCROLLINFO structure. The *fMask* field contains flags indicating what other fields in the structure contain valid data. The *nMin* and *nMax* fields can contain the minimum and maximum scroll values the scroll bar can report. Windows looks at the values in these fields if the *fMask* parameter contains the SIF_RANGE flag. Likewise, the *nPos* field sets the position of the scroll bar within its predefined range if the *fMask* field contains the SIF_POS flag.

The *nPage* field allows a program to define the size of the currently viewable area of the screen in relation to the entire scrollable area. This allows a user to have a feel for how much of the entire scrolling range is currently visible. This field is used only if the *fMask* field contains the SIF_PAGE flag. The last member of the SCROLLINFO structure, *nTrackPos,* isn't used by the *SetScrollInfo* call and is ignored.

The *fMask* field can contain one last flag. Passing a SIF_DISABLENOSCROLL flag causes the scroll bar to be disabled, but still visible. This is handy when the entire scrolling range is visible within the viewable area and no scrolling is necessary. Disabling the scroll bar in this case is often preferable to simply removing the scroll bar completely.

Those with a sharp eye for detail will notice a problem with the width of the fields in the SCROLLINFO structure. The *nMin*, *nMax*, and *nPos* fields are integers and therefore in the world of Windows CE, are 32 bits wide. On the other hand, the WM_HSCROLL and WM_VSCROLL messages can return only a 16-bit position in the high word of the *wParam* parameter. If you're using scroll ranges greater than 65,535, use this function:

```
BOOL GetScrollInfo (HWND hwnd, int fnBar, LPSCROLLINFO lpsi);
```

As with *SetScrollInfo*, the flags in the *fnBar* field indicate the window handle that should be passed to the function. The SCROLLINFO structure is identical to the one used in *SetScrollInfo*; however, before it can be passed to *GetScrollInfo*, it must be initialized with the size of the structure in *cbSize*. An application must also indicate what data it wants the function to return by setting the appropriate flags in the *fMask* field. The flags used in *fMask* are the same as the ones used in *SetScrollInfo* with a couple of additions. Now a SIF_TRACKPOS flag can be passed to have the scroll bar return its current thumb position. When called during a WM_*x*SCROLL message, the *nTrackPos* field contains the real time position while the *nPos* field contains the scroll bar position at the start of the drag of the thumb.

The scroll bar is an unusual control in that it can be added easily to windows simply by specifying a window style flag. It's also unusual in that the control is placed outside the client area of the window. The reason for this assistance is that scroll bars are commonly needed by applications, so the Windows developers made it easy to attach scroll bars to windows. Now let's look at the other basic Windows controls.

WINDOWS CONTROLS

While scroll bars hold a special place because of their easy association with standard windows, there are a large number of other controls that Windows applications often use, including buttons, edit boxes, and list boxes. In short, controls are simply predefined window classes. Each has a custom window procedure supplied by Windows that gives each of these controls a tightly defined user and programming interface.

Since a control is just another window, it can be created with a call to *CreateWindow* or *CreateWindowEx*, or, as I will explain later in this chapter, automatically by the dialog manager during the creation of a dialog box. Like menus, controls notify the parent window of events via WM_COMMAND messages encoding events and the ID and window handle of the control encoded in the parameters of the message. Controls can also be configured and manipulated using predefined messages sent to the control. Among other things, applications can set the state of buttons, add or delete items to list boxes, and set the selection of text in edit boxes all by sending messages to the controls.

There are six predefined window control classes. They are

- *Button* A wide variety of buttons.
- *Edit* A window that can be used to enter or display text.
- *List* A window that contains a list of strings.
- *Combo* A combination edit box and list box.
- *Static* A window that displays text or graphics that a user can't change.
- *Scroll bar* A scroll bar not attached to a specific window.

Each of these controls has a wide range of function, far too much for me to cover completely in this chapter. But I'll quickly review these controls, mentioning at least the highlights. Afterward, I'll show you an example program, CtlView, to demonstrate these controls and their interactions with their parent windows.

Button Controls

Button controls enable several forms of input to the program. Buttons come in many styles, including push buttons, check boxes, and radio buttons. Each style is designed for a specific use—for example, push buttons are designed for receiving momentary input, check boxes are designed for on/off input, and radio buttons allow a user to select one of a number of choices.

Push buttons

In general, push buttons are used to invoke some action. When a user presses a push button using a stylus, the button sends a WM_COMMAND message with a BN_CLICKED (for button notification clicked) notify code in the high word of the *wParam* parameter.

Check boxes

Check boxes display a square box and a label that asks the user to specify a choice. A check box retains its state, either checked or unchecked, until the user clicks it again or the program forces the button to change state. In addition to the standard

BS_CHECKBOX style, check boxes can come in a 3-state style, BS_3STATE, that allows the button to be disabled and shown grayed out. Two additional styles, BS_AUTOCHECKBOX and BS_AUTO3STATE, automatically update the state and look of the control to reflect the checked, unchecked, and in the case of the 3-state check box, the disabled state.

As with push buttons, check boxes send a BN_CLICKED notification when the button is clicked. Unless the check box has one of the automatic styles, it's the responsibility of the application to manually change the state of the button. This can be done by sending a BM_SETCHECK message to the button with the *wParam* set to 0 to uncheck the button or 1 to check the button. The 3-state check boxes have a third, disabled state that can be set by means of the BM_SETCHECK message with the *wParam* value set to 2. An application can determine the current state using the BM_GETCHECK message.

Radio buttons

Radio buttons allow a user to select from a number of choices. Radio buttons are grouped in a set, with only one of the set ever being checked at a time. If it's using the standard BS_RADIOBUTTON style, the application is responsible for checking and unchecking the radio buttons so that only one is checked at a time. However, like check boxes, radio buttons have an alternative style, BS_AUTORADIOBUTTON, that automatically maintains the group of buttons so that only one is checked.

Group boxes

Strangely, the group box is also a type of button. A group box appears to the user as a hollow box with an integrated text label surrounding a set of controls that are naturally grouped together. Group boxes are merely an organizational device and have no programming interface other than the text of the box, which is specified in the window title text upon creation of the group box. Group boxes should be created after the controls within the box are created. This ensures that the group box will be "beneath" the controls it contains in the window Z-order.

You should also be careful when using group boxes on Windows CE devices. The problem isn't with the group box itself, but with the small size of the Windows CE screen. Group boxes take up valuable screen real estate that can be better used by functional controls. This is especially the case on the Palm-size PC with its very small screen. In many cases, a line drawn between sets of controls can visually group the controls as well as a group box can.

Customizing the appearance of a button

You can further customize the appearance of the buttons described so far by using a number of additional styles. The styles, BS_RIGHT, BS_LEFT, BS_BOTTOM, and BS_TOP, allow you to position the button text in a place other than the default center of the button. The BS_MULTILINE style allows you to specify more than one line of text in the button. The text is flowed to fit within the button. The newline character (\n) in the button text can be used to specifically define where line breaks occur. Windows CE doesn't support the BS_ICON and BS_BITMAP button styles supported by other versions of Windows.

Owner-draw buttons

You can totally control the look of a button by specifying the BS_OWNERDRAW style. When a button is specified as owner-draw, its owner window is entirely responsible for drawing the button for all the states in which it might occur. When a window contains an owner-draw button, it's sent a WM_DRAWITEM message to inform it that a button needs to be drawn. For this message, the *wParam* parameter contains the ID value for the button and the *lParam* parameter points to a DRAWITEMSTRUCT structure defined as

```
typedef struct tagDRAWITEMSTRUCT {
    UINT  CtlType;
    UINT  CtlID;
    UINT  itemID;
    UINT  itemAction;
    UINT  itemState;
    HWND  hwndItem;
    HDC   hDC;
    RECT  rcItem;
    DWORD itemData;
} DRAWITEMSTRUCT;
```

The *CtlType* field is set to ODT_BUTTON while the *CtlID* field, like the *wParam* parameter, contains the button's ID value. The *itemAction* field contains flags that indicate what needs to be drawn and why. The most significant of these fields is *itemState*, which contains the state (selected, disabled, and so forth) of the button. The *hDC* field contains the device context handle for the button window while the *rcItem* RECT contains the dimensions of the button. The *itemData* field is NULL for owner-draw buttons.

As you might expect, the WM_DRAWITEM handler contains a number of GDI calls to draw lines, rectangles, and whatever else is needed to render the button. An important aspect of drawing a button is matching the standard colors of the other windows in the system. Since these colors can change, they shouldn't be hard coded. You can query to find out which are the proper colors by using the function

```
DWORD GetSysColor (int nIndex);
```

This function returns an RGB color value for the colors defined for different aspects of windows and controls in the system. Among a number of predefined index values passed in the index parameter, an index of COLOR_BTNFACE returns the proper color for the face of a button while COLOR_BTNSHADOW returns the dark color for creating the three-dimensional look of a button.

The Edit Control

The edit control is a window that allows the user to enter and edit text. As you might imagine, the edit control is one of the handiest controls in the Windows control pantheon. The edit control is equipped with full editing capability, including cut, copy, and paste interaction with the system clipboard, all without assistance from the application. Edit controls display a single line, or by specifying the ES_MULTILINE style, multiple lines of text. The Notepad accessory, provided with the desktop versions of Windows, is simply a top-level window that contains a multiline edit control.

The edit control has a few other features that should be mentioned. An edit control with the ES_PASSWORD style displays an asterisk (*) character by default in the control for each character typed; the control saves the real character. The ES_READONLY style protects the text contained in the control so that it can be read, or copied into the clipboard, but not modified. The ES_LOWERCASE and ES_UPPERCASE styles force characters entered into the control to be changed to the specified case.

You can add text to an edit control by using the WM_SETTEXT message and retrieve text by using the WM_GETTEXT message. Selection can be controlled using the EM_SETSEL message. This message specifies the starting and ending characters in the selected area. Other messages allow the position of the caret (the marker that indicates the current entry point in an edit field) to be queried and set. Multiline edit controls contain a number of additional messages to control scrolling as well as to access characters by line and column position.

The List Box Control

The list box control displays a list of text items so that the user might select one or more of the items within the list. The list box stores the text, optionally sorts the items, and manages the display of the items, including scrolling. List boxes can be configured to allow selection of a single item or multiple items or to prevent any selection at all.

You add an item to a list box by sending an LB_ADDSTRING or LB_INSERTSTRING message to the control, passing a pointer to the string to add in the *lParam* parameter. The LB_ADDSTRING message places the newly added string at the end of the list of items while LB_INSERTSTRING can place the string anywhere within the list of items in the list box. The list box can be searched for a particular item using the LB_FIND message.

Selection status can be queried using the LB_GETCURSEL for single selection list boxes. For multiple selection list boxes, the LB_GETSELCOUNT and LB_GETSELITEMS can be used to retrieve the items currently selected. Items in the list box can be selected programmatically using the LB_SETCURSEL and LB_SETSEL messages.

Windows CE supports most of the list box functionality available in other versions of Windows with the exception of owner-draw list boxes, and the LB_DIR family of messages. A new style, LBS_EX_CONSTSTRINGDATA, is supported under Windows CE. A list box with this style doesn't store strings passed to it. Instead, the pointer to the string is stored and the application is responsible for maintaining the string. For large arrays of strings that might be loaded from a resource, this procedure can save RAM because the list box won't maintain a separate copy of the list of strings.

The Combo Box Control

The combo box is (as the name implies) a combination of controls—in this case, a single-line edit control and a list box. The combo box is a space-efficient control for selecting one item from a list of many or for providing an edit field with a list of predefined, suggested entries. Under Windows CE, the combo box comes in two styles: drop-down and drop-down list. (Simple combo boxes aren't supported.) The drop-down style combo box contains an edit field with a button at the right end. Clicking on the button displays a list box that might contain more selections. Clicking on one of the selections fills the edit field of the combo box with the selection. The drop-down list style replaces the edit box with a static text control. This allows the user to select from an item in the list but prevents the user from entering an item that's not in the list.

Since the combo box combines the edit and list controls, a list of the messages used to control the combo box strongly resembles a merged list of the messages for the two base controls. CB_ADDSTRING, CB_INSERTSTRING, and CB_FINDSTRING act like their list box cousins. Likewise the CB_SETEDITSELECT and CB_GETEDITSELECT messages set and query the selected characters in the edit box of a drop-down or a drop-down list combo box. To control the drop-down state of a drop-down or drop-down list combo box, the messages CB_SHOWDROPDOWN and CB_GETDROPPEDSTATE can be used.

As in the case of the list box, Windows CE doesn't support owner-draw combo boxes. However, the combo box supports the CBS_EX_CONSTSTRINGDATA extended style, which instructs the combo box to store a pointer to the string for an item instead of the string itself. As with the list box LBS_EX_CONSTSTRINGDATA style, this procedure can save RAM if an application has a large array of strings stored in ROM because the combo box won't maintain a separate copy of the list of strings.

Static Controls

Static controls are windows that display text, icons, or bitmaps not intended for user interaction. You can use static text controls to label other controls in a window. What a static control displays is defined by the text and the style for the control Under Windows CE, static controls support the following styles:

- *SS_LEFT* Displays a line of left-aligned text. The text is wrapped, if necessary, to fit inside the control.
- *SS_CENTER* Displays a line of text centered in the control. The text is wrapped, if necessary, to fit inside the control.
- *SS_RIGHT* Displays a line of text aligned with the right side of the control. The text is wrapped, if necessary, to fit inside the control.
- *SS_LEFTNOWORDWRAP* Displays a line of left-aligned text. The text isn't wrapped to multiple lines. Any text extending beyond the right side of the control is clipped.
- *SS_BITMAP* Displays a bitmap. Window text for the control specifies the name of the resource containing the bitmap.
- *SS_ICON* Displays an icon. Window text for the control specifies the name of the resource containing the icon.

Static controls with the SS_NOTIFY style send a WM_COMMAND message when the control is clicked, enabled, or disabled, although the Windows CE version of the static control doesn't send a notification when it's double-clicked. The SS_CENTERIMAGE style, used in combination with the SS_BITMAP or SS_ICON style, centers the image within the control. The SS_NOPREFIX style can be used in combination with the text styles. It prevents the ampersand (&) character from being interpreted as indicating the next character is an accelerator character.

Windows CE doesn't support static controls that display filled or hollow rectangles such as those drawn with the SS_WHITEFRAME or SS_BLACKRECT styles. Also, Windows CE doesn't support owner-draw static controls.

The Scroll Bar Control

The scroll bar control operates identically to the window scroll bars described previously with the exception that the *fnBar* field used in *SetScrollInfo* and *GetScrollInfo* must be set to SB_CTL. The *hwnd* field then must be set to the handle of the scroll bar control, not to the window that owns the scroll bar. Like window scroll bars, the owner of the scroll bar is responsible for fielding the scroll messages WM_VSCROLL and WM_HSCROLL and setting the new position of the scroll bar in response to these messages.

The CtlView Example Program

The CtlView example program, shown in Figure 4-5, demonstrates all the controls I've just described. The example makes use of several application-defined child windows that contain various controls. You switch between the different child windows by clicking on one of five radio buttons displayed across the top of the main window. As each of the controls reports a notification through a WM_COMMAND message, that notification is displayed in a list box on the right side of the window. CtlView is handy for observing just what messages a control sends to its parent window and when they're sent. One problem with CtlView is that it's designed for an H/PC screen, not a Palm-size PC screen. If you run CtlView on a Palm-size PC, you'll see that the controls don't all fit onto the small Palm-size PC screen.

CtlView.rc

```
//======================================================================
// Resource file
//
// Written for the book Programming Windows CE
// Copyright (C) 1998 Douglas Boling
//======================================================================

#include "CtlView.h"                    // Program-specific stuff

ID_ICON      ICON   "CtlView.ico"      // Program icon
TEXTICON     ICON   "btnicon.ico"      // Icon used in static window
STATICBMP    BITMAP "statbmp.bmp"      // Bitmap used in static window
```

CtlView.h

```
//======================================================================
// Header file
//
// Written for the book Programming Windows CE
// Copyright (C) 1998 Douglas Boling
//======================================================================
// Returns number of elements
#define dim(x) (sizeof(x) / sizeof(x[0]))
//----------------------------------------------------------------------
// Generic defines and data types
//
struct decodeUINT {                             // Structure associates
    UINT Code;                                  // messages
                                                // with a function.
    LRESULT (*Fxn)(HWND, UINT, WPARAM, LPARAM);
```

Figure 4-5. *The CtlView program.*

```
};
struct decodeCMD {                              // Structure associates
    UINT Code;                                  // menu IDs with a
    LRESULT (*Fxn)(HWND, WORD, HWND, WORD);     // function.
};

//----------------------------------------------------------------------
// Generic defines used by application
#define  IDI_BTNICON        20                  // Icon used on button

#define  ID_ICON            1                   // Icon ID
#define  IDC_CMDBAR         2                   // Command bar ID
#define  IDC_RPTLIST        3                   // Report window ID

// Client window IDs go from 5 through 9.
#define  IDC_WNDSEL         5                   // Starting client
                                                // window IDs

// Radio button IDs go from 10 through 14.
#define  IDC_RADIOBTNS      10                  // Starting ID of
                                                // radio buttons

// Button window defines
#define  IDC_PUSHBTN   100
#define  IDC_CHKBOX    101
#define  IDC_ACHKBOX   102
#define  IDC_A3STBOX   103
#define  IDC_RADIO1    104
#define  IDC_RADIO2    105
#define  IDC_OWNRDRAW  106

// Edit window defines
#define  IDC_SINGLELINE 100
#define  IDC_MULTILINE  101
#define  IDC_PASSBOX    102

// List box window defines
#define  IDC_COMBOBOX   100
#define  IDC_SNGLELIST  101
#define  IDC_MULTILIST  102

// Static control window defines
#define  IDC_LEFTTEXT   100
#define  IDC_RIGHTTEXT  101
#define  IDC_CENTERTEXT 102
#define  IDC_ICONCTL    103
#define  IDC_BITMAPCTL  104
```

(continued)

Figure 4-5. *continued*

```
// Scroll bar window defines
#define  IDC_LRSCROLL   100
#define  IDC_UDSCROLL   101

// User defined message to add a line to the window
#define MYMSG_ADDLINE   (WM_USER + 10)

typedef struct {
    TCHAR *szClass;
    INT   nID;
    TCHAR *szTitle;
    INT   x;
    INT   y;
    INT   cx;
    INT   cy;
    DWORD lStyle;
} CTLWNDSTRUCT, *PCTLWNDSTRUCT;

typedef struct {
    WORD wMsg;
    INT nID;
    WPARAM wParam;
    LPARAM lParam;
} CTLMSG, * PCTLMSG;

typedef struct {
    TCHAR *pszLabel;
    WORD wNotification;
} NOTELABELS, *PNOTELABELS;

//----------------------------------------------------------------------
// Function prototypes
//
int InitApp (HINSTANCE);
HWND InitInstance (HINSTANCE, LPWSTR, int);
int TermInstance (HINSTANCE, int);

// Window procedures
LRESULT CALLBACK FrameWndProc (HWND, UINT, WPARAM, LPARAM);
LRESULT CALLBACK ClientWndProc (HWND, UINT, WPARAM, LPARAM);

// Message handlers
LRESULT DoCreateFrame (HWND, UINT, WPARAM, LPARAM);
LRESULT DoCommandFrame (HWND, UINT, WPARAM, LPARAM);
LRESULT DoAddLineFrame (HWND, UINT, WPARAM, LPARAM);
LRESULT DoDestroyFrame (HWND, UINT, WPARAM, LPARAM);
```

```
//----------------------------------------------------------------------
// Window prototypes and defines for BtnWnd
//
#define BTNWND    TEXT ("ButtonWnd")
int InitBtnWnd (HINSTANCE);

// Window procedures
LRESULT CALLBACK BtnWndProc (HWND, UINT, WPARAM, LPARAM);

LRESULT DoCreateBtnWnd (HWND, UINT, WPARAM, LPARAM);
LRESULT DoCtlColorBtnWnd (HWND, UINT, WPARAM, LPARAM);
LRESULT DoCommandBtnWnd (HWND, UINT, WPARAM, LPARAM);
LRESULT DoDrawItemBtnWnd (HWND, UINT, WPARAM, LPARAM);
LRESULT DoMeasureItemBtnWnd (HWND, UINT, WPARAM, LPARAM);

//----------------------------------------------------------------------
// Window prototypes and defines for EditWnd
//
#define EDITWND    TEXT ("EditWnd")
int InitEditWnd (HINSTANCE);

// Window procedures
LRESULT CALLBACK EditWndProc (HWND, UINT, WPARAM, LPARAM);

LRESULT DoCreateEditWnd (HWND, UINT, WPARAM, LPARAM);
LRESULT DoCommandEditWnd (HWND, UINT, WPARAM, LPARAM);
LRESULT DoDrawItemEditWnd (HWND, UINT, WPARAM, LPARAM);
LRESULT DoMeasureItemEditWnd (HWND, UINT, WPARAM, LPARAM);

//----------------------------------------------------------------------
// Window prototypes and defines for ListWnd
//
#define LISTWND    TEXT ("ListWnd")
int InitListWnd (HINSTANCE);

// Window procedures
LRESULT CALLBACK ListWndProc (HWND, UINT, WPARAM, LPARAM);

LRESULT DoCreateListWnd (HWND, UINT, WPARAM, LPARAM);
LRESULT DoCommandListWnd (HWND, UINT, WPARAM, LPARAM);
LRESULT DoDrawItemListWnd (HWND, UINT, WPARAM, LPARAM);
LRESULT DoMeasureItemListWnd (HWND, UINT, WPARAM, LPARAM);

//----------------------------------------------------------------------
// Window prototypes and defines for StatWnd
//
```

(continued)

Figure 4-5. *continued*

```
#define STATWND    TEXT ("StaticWnd")
int InitStatWnd (HINSTANCE);

// Window procedures
LRESULT CALLBACK StatWndProc (HWND, UINT, WPARAM, LPARAM);

LRESULT DoCreateStatWnd (HWND, UINT, WPARAM, LPARAM);
LRESULT DoCommandStatWnd (HWND, UINT, WPARAM, LPARAM);
LRESULT DoDrawItemStatWnd (HWND, UINT, WPARAM, LPARAM);
LRESULT DoMeasureItemStatWnd (HWND, UINT, WPARAM, LPARAM);

//----------------------------------------------------------------------
// Window prototypes and defines ScrollWnd
//
#define SCROLLWND    TEXT ("ScrollWnd")
int InitScrollWnd (HINSTANCE);

// Window procedures
LRESULT CALLBACK ScrollWndProc (HWND, UINT, WPARAM, LPARAM);

LRESULT DoCreateScrollWnd (HWND, UINT, WPARAM, LPARAM);
LRESULT DoVScrollScrollWnd (HWND, UINT, WPARAM, LPARAM);
LRESULT DoHScrollScrollWnd (HWND, UINT, WPARAM, LPARAM);
```

CtlView.c

```
//======================================================================
// CtlView - Lists the available fonts in the system.
//
// Written for the book Programming Windows CE
// Copyright (C) 1998 Douglas Boling
//======================================================================
#include <windows.h>                 // For all that Windows stuff
#include <commctrl.h>                // Command bar includes
#include "CtlView.h"                 // Program-specific stuff

//----------------------------------------------------------------------
// Global data
//
const TCHAR szAppName[] = TEXT ("CtlView");
HINSTANCE hInst;                     // Program instance handle

// Message dispatch table for FrameWindowProc
const struct decodeUINT FrameMessages[] = {
    WM_CREATE, DoCreateFrame,
```

```
    WM_COMMAND, DoCommandFrame,
    MYMSG_ADDLINE, DoAddLineFrame,
    WM_DESTROY, DoDestroyFrame,
};

typedef struct {
    TCHAR *szTitle;
    INT   nID;
    TCHAR *szCtlWnds;
    HWND  hWndClient;
} RBTNDATA;

// Text for main window radio buttons
TCHAR *szBtnTitle[] = {TEXT ("Buttons"), TEXT ("Edit"), TEXT ("List"),
                       TEXT ("Static"), TEXT ("Scroll")};
// Class names for child windows containing controls
TCHAR *szCtlWnds[] = {BTNWND, EDITWND, LISTWND, STATWND, SCROLLWND};

INT nWndSel = 0;

//HWND hwndVisClient = 0;
//======================================================================
// Program entry point
//
int WINAPI WinMain (HINSTANCE hInstance, HINSTANCE hPrevInstance,
                    LPWSTR lpCmdLine, int nCmdShow) {
    MSG msg;
    int rc = 0;
    HWND hwndFrame;

    // Initialize application.
    rc = InitApp (hInstance);
    if (rc) return rc;

    // Initialize this instance.
    hwndFrame = InitInstance (hInstance, lpCmdLine, nCmdShow);
    if (hwndFrame == 0)
        return 0x10;

    // Application message loop
    while (GetMessage (&msg, NULL, 0, 0)) {
        TranslateMessage (&msg);
        DispatchMessage (&msg);
    }
    // Instance cleanup
    return TermInstance (hInstance, msg.wParam);
}
```

(continued)

Figure 4-5. *continued*

```
//----------------------------------------------------------------------
// InitApp - Application initialization
//
int InitApp (HINSTANCE hInstance) {
    WNDCLASS wc;

    // Register application frame window class.
    wc.style = 0;                             // Window style
    wc.lpfnWndProc = FrameWndProc;            // Callback function
    wc.cbClsExtra = 0;                        // Extra class data
    wc.cbWndExtra = 0;                        // Extra window data
    wc.hInstance = hInstance;                 // Owner handle
    wc.hIcon = NULL,                          // Application icon
    wc.hCursor = NULL;                        // Default cursor
    wc.hbrBackground = (HBRUSH) GetSysColorBrush (COLOR_STATIC);
    wc.lpszMenuName =  NULL;                  // Menu name
    wc.lpszClassName = szAppName;             // Window class name

    if (RegisterClass (&wc) == 0) return 1;

    // Initialize client window classes
    if (InitBtnWnd (hInstance) != 0) return 2;
    if (InitEditWnd (hInstance) != 0) return 2;
    if (InitListWnd (hInstance) != 0) return 2;
    if (InitStatWnd (hInstance) != 0) return 2;
    if (InitScrollWnd (hInstance) != 0) return 2;
    return 0;
}
//----------------------------------------------------------------------
// InitInstance - Instance initialization
//
HWND InitInstance (HINSTANCE hInstance, LPWSTR lpCmdLine, int nCmdShow) {
    HWND hWnd;

    // Save program instance handle in global variable.
    hInst = hInstance;

    // Create frame window.
    hWnd = CreateWindow (szAppName,             // Window class
                         TEXT ("Control View"), // Window title
                         WS_VISIBLE,            // Style flags
                         CW_USEDEFAULT,         // x position
                         CW_USEDEFAULT,         // y position
                         CW_USEDEFAULT,         // Initial width
                         CW_USEDEFAULT,         // Initial height
                         NULL,                  // Parent
```

```
                        NULL,                  // Menu, must be null
                        hInstance,             // Application instance
                        NULL);                 // Pointer to create
                                               // parameters
    // Return fail code if window not created.
    if (!IsWindow (hWnd)) return 0;

    // Standard show and update calls
    ShowWindow (hWnd, nCmdShow);
    UpdateWindow (hWnd);

    return hWnd;
}
//----------------------------------------------------------------------
// TermInstance - Program cleanup
//
int TermInstance (HINSTANCE hInstance, int nDefRC) {

    return nDefRC;
}
//======================================================================
// Message handling procedures for FrameWindow
//
//----------------------------------------------------------------------
// FrameWndProc - Callback function for application window
//
LRESULT CALLBACK FrameWndProc (HWND hWnd, UINT wMsg, WPARAM wParam,
                              LPARAM lParam) {
    INT i;
    //
    // Search message list to see if we need to handle this
    // message.  If in list, call procedure.
    //
    for (i = 0; i < dim(FrameMessages); i++) {
        if (wMsg == FrameMessages[i].Code)
            return (*FrameMessages[i].Fxn)(hWnd, wMsg, wParam, lParam);
    }
    return DefWindowProc (hWnd, wMsg, wParam, lParam);
}
//----------------------------------------------------------------------
// DoCreateFrame - Process WM_CREATE message for window.
//
LRESULT DoCreateFrame (HWND hWnd, UINT wMsg, WPARAM wParam,
                       LPARAM lParam) {
    LPCREATESTRUCT lpcs;
    HWND hwndCB, hwndChild;
    INT sHeight, i, x, y, cx, cy;
```

(continued)

Figure 4-5. *continued*

```
    // Convert lParam into pointer to create struct.
    lpcs = (LPCREATESTRUCT) lParam;
    x = lpcs->x;
    y = lpcs->y;
    cx = lpcs->cx;
    cy = lpcs->cy;
    nWndSel = 0;
    // Create a command bar.
    hwndCB = CommandBar_Create (hInst, hWnd, IDC_CMDBAR);
    // Add exit button to command bar.
    CommandBar_AddAdornments (hwndCB, 0, 0);
    sHeight = CommandBar_Height (GetDlgItem (hWnd, IDC_CMDBAR));

    // Create the radio buttons.
    for (i = 0; i < dim(szBtnTitle); i++) {
        hwndChild = CreateWindow (TEXT ("BUTTON"),
                              szBtnTitle[i], BS_AUTORADIOBUTTON |
                              WS_VISIBLE | WS_CHILD,
                              10 + (i * 85), sHeight,
                              80, 23, hWnd, (HMENU)(IDC_RADIOBTNS+i),
                              hInst, NULL);

        // Destroy frame if window not created.
        if (!IsWindow (hwndChild)) {
            DestroyWindow (hWnd);
            break;
        }
    }
    //
    // Create report window.  Size it so that it fits under
    // the command bar and fills the remaining client area.
    //
    hwndChild = CreateWindowEx (WS_EX_CLIENTEDGE, TEXT ("listbox"),
                          TEXT (""), WS_VISIBLE | WS_CHILD | WS_VSCROLL |
                          LBS_USETABSTOPS | LBS_NOINTEGRALHEIGHT,
                          cx/2, y + sHeight + 25,
                          cx/2, cy - sHeight - 25,
                          hWnd, (HMENU)IDC_RPTLIST,
                          hInst, NULL);

    // Destroy frame if window not created.
    if (!IsWindow (hwndChild)) {
        DestroyWindow (hWnd);
        return 0;
    }
```

```
    // Initialize tab stops for display list box.
    i = 25;
    SendMessage (hwndChild, LB_SETTABSTOPS, 1, (LPARAM)&i);

    //
    // Create the child windows.  Size them so that they fit under
    // the command bar and fill the left side of the child area.
    //
    for (i = 0; i < dim(szCtlWnds); i++) {
        hwndChild = CreateWindowEx (WS_EX_CLIENTEDGE,
                                    szCtlWnds[i],
                                    TEXT (""), WS_CHILD,
                                    x, y + sHeight + 25,
                                    cx/2, cy - sHeight - 25,
                                    hWnd, (HMENU)(IDC_WNDSEL+i),
                                    hInst, NULL);
        // Destroy frame if client window not created.
        if (!IsWindow (hwndChild)) {
            DestroyWindow (hWnd);
            return 0;
        }
    }
    // Check one of the auto radio buttons.
    SendDlgItemMessage (hWnd, IDC_RADIOBTNS+nWndSel, BM_SETCHECK, 1, 0);
    hwndChild = GetDlgItem (hWnd, IDC_WNDSEL+nWndSel);
    ShowWindow (hwndChild, SW_SHOW);
    return 0;
}
//----------------------------------------------------------------------
// DoCommandFrame - Process WM_COMMAND message for window.
//
LRESULT DoCommandFrame (HWND hWnd, UINT wMsg, WPARAM wParam,
                        LPARAM lParam) {
    HWND hwndTemp;
    int nBtn;
    // Don't look at list box messages.
    if (LOWORD (wParam) == IDC_RPTLIST)
        return 0;
    nBtn = LOWORD (wParam) - IDC_RADIOBTNS;
    if (nWndSel != nBtn) {

        // Hide the currently visible window.
        hwndTemp = GetDlgItem (hWnd, IDC_WNDSEL+nWndSel);
        ShowWindow (hwndTemp, SW_HIDE);

        // Save the current selection.
        nWndSel = nBtn;
```

(continued)

Figure 4-5. *continued*

```
        // Show the window selected via the radio button.
        hwndTemp = GetDlgItem (hWnd, IDC_WNDSEL+nWndSel);
        ShowWindow (hwndTemp, SW_SHOW);
    }
    return 0;
}
//----------------------------------------------------------------------
// DoAddLineFrame - Process MYMSG_ADDLINE message for window.
//
LRESULT DoAddLineFrame (HWND hWnd, UINT wMsg, WPARAM wParam,
                        LPARAM lParam) {
    TCHAR szOut[128];
    INT i;

    if (LOWORD (wParam) == 0xffff)
        wsprintf (szOut, TEXT ("      \t %s"), (LPTSTR)lParam);
    else
        wsprintf (szOut, TEXT ("id:%x \t %s"), LOWORD (wParam),
                  (LPTSTR)lParam);


    i = SendDlgItemMessage (hWnd, IDC_RPTLIST, LB_ADDSTRING, 0,
                            (LPARAM)(LPCTSTR)szOut);

    if (i != LB_ERR)
        SendDlgItemMessage (hWnd, IDC_RPTLIST, LB_SETTOPINDEX, i,
                            (LPARAM)(LPCTSTR)szOut);
    return 0;
}
//----------------------------------------------------------------------
// DoDestroyFrame - Process WM_DESTROY message for window.
//
LRESULT DoDestroyFrame (HWND hWnd, UINT wMsg, WPARAM wParam,
                        LPARAM lParam) {
    PostQuitMessage (0);
    return 0;
}
```

BtnWnd.c

```
//======================================================================
// BtnWnd - Button window code
//
// Written for the book Programming Windows CE
// Copyright (C) 1998 Douglas Boling
```

```
//======================================================================
#include <windows.h>                    // For all that Windows stuff
#include "Ctlview.h"                    // Program-specific stuff

extern HINSTANCE hInst;

LRESULT DrawButton (HWND hWnd, LPDRAWITEMSTRUCT pdi);
//----------------------------------------------------------------------
// Global data
//

// Message dispatch table for BtnWndWindowProc
const struct decodeUINT BtnWndMessages[] = {
    WM_CREATE, DoCreateBtnWnd,
    WM_CTLCOLORSTATIC, DoCtlColorBtnWnd,
    WM_COMMAND, DoCommandBtnWnd,
    WM_DRAWITEM, DoDrawItemBtnWnd,
};

// Structure defining the controls in the window
CTLWNDSTRUCT  Btns [] = {
    {TEXT ("BUTTON"), IDC_PUSHBTN, TEXT ("Button"),
     10,  10, 120,  23, BS_PUSHBUTTON | BS_NOTIFY},
    {TEXT ("BUTTON"), IDC_CHKBOX, TEXT ("Check box"),
     10,  35, 120,  23, BS_CHECKBOX},
    {TEXT ("BUTTON"), IDC_ACHKBOX, TEXT ("Auto check box"),
     10,  60, 120,  23, BS_AUTOCHECKBOX},
    {TEXT ("BUTTON"), IDC_A3STBOX, TEXT ("Auto 3-state box"),
     10,  85, 120,  23, BS_AUTO3STATE},
    {TEXT ("BUTTON"), IDC_RADIO1, TEXT ("Auto radio button 1"),
     10, 110, 120,  23, BS_AUTORADIOBUTTON},
    {TEXT ("BUTTON"), IDC_RADIO2, TEXT ("Auto radio button 2"),
     10, 135, 120,  23, BS_AUTORADIOBUTTON},
    {TEXT ("BUTTON"), IDC_OWNRDRAW, TEXT ("OwnerDraw"),
     150,  10,  44,  44, BS_PUSHBUTTON | BS_OWNERDRAW},
};
// Structure labeling the button control WM_COMMAND notifications
NOTELABELS nlBtn[] = {{TEXT ("BN_CLICKED "),      0},
                      {TEXT ("BN_PAINT   "),      1},
                      {TEXT ("BN_HILITE  "),      2},
                      {TEXT ("BN_UNHILITE"),      3},
                      {TEXT ("BN_DISABLE "),      4},
                      {TEXT ("BN_DOUBLECLICKED"), 5},
                      {TEXT ("BN_SETFOCUS "),     6},
                      {TEXT ("BN_KILLFOCUS"),     7}
};
```

(continued)

Figure 4-5. *continued*

```
// Handle for icon used in owner-draw icon
HICON hIcon = 0;
//----------------------------------------------------------------------
// InitBtnWnd - BtnWnd window initialization
//
int InitBtnWnd (HINSTANCE hInstance) {
    WNDCLASS wc;

    // Register application BtnWnd window class.
    wc.style = 0;                             // Window style
    wc.lpfnWndProc = BtnWndProc;              // Callback function
    wc.cbClsExtra = 0;                        // Extra class data
    wc.cbWndExtra = 0;                        // Extra window data
    wc.hInstance = hInstance;                 // Owner handle
    wc.hIcon = NULL,                          // Application icon
    wc.hCursor = NULL;                        // Default cursor
    wc.hbrBackground = (HBRUSH) GetStockObject (WHITE_BRUSH);
    wc.lpszMenuName =  NULL;                  // Menu name
    wc.lpszClassName = BTNWND;                // Window class name

    if (RegisterClass (&wc) == 0) return 1;

    return 0;
}

//======================================================================
// Message handling procedures for BtnWindow
//----------------------------------------------------------------------
// BtnWndWndProc - Callback function for application window
//
LRESULT CALLBACK BtnWndProc (HWND hWnd, UINT wMsg, WPARAM wParam,
                             LPARAM lParam) {
    INT i;
    //
    // Search message list to see if we need to handle this
    // message.  If in list, call procedure.
    //
    for (i = 0; i < dim(BtnWndMessages); i++) {
        if (wMsg == BtnWndMessages[i].Code)
            return (*BtnWndMessages[i].Fxn)(hWnd, wMsg, wParam, lParam);
    }
    return DefWindowProc (hWnd, wMsg, wParam, lParam);
}
//----------------------------------------------------------------------
// DoCreateBtnWnd - Process WM_CREATE message for window.
//
```

```
LRESULT DoCreateBtnWnd (HWND hWnd, UINT wMsg, WPARAM wParam,
                        LPARAM lParam) {
    INT i;

    for (i = 0; i < dim(Btns); i++) {

        CreateWindow (Btns[i].szClass, Btns[i].szTitle,
                      Btns[i].lStyle | WS_VISIBLE | WS_CHILD,
                      Btns[i].x, Btns[i].y, Btns[i].cx, Btns[i].cy,
                      hWnd, (HMENU) Btns[i].nID, hInst, NULL);
    }
    hIcon = LoadIcon (hInst, TEXT ("TEXTICON"));

    // We need to set the initial state of the radio buttons.
    CheckRadioButton (hWnd, IDC_RADIO1, IDC_RADIO2, IDC_RADIO1);
    return 0;
}
//----------------------------------------------------------------------
// DoCtlColorBtnWnd - process WM_CTLCOLORxx messages for window.
//
LRESULT DoCtlColorBtnWnd (HWND hWnd, UINT wMsg, WPARAM wParam,
                          LPARAM lParam) {
    return GetStockObject (WHITE_BRUSH);
}
//----------------------------------------------------------------------
// DoCommandBtnWnd - Process WM_COMMAND message for window.
//
LRESULT DoCommandBtnWnd (HWND hWnd, UINT wMsg, WPARAM wParam,
                         LPARAM lParam) {
    TCHAR szOut[128];
    INT i;

    // Since the Check Box button is not an auto check box, it
    // must be set manually.
    if ((LOWORD (wParam) == IDC_CHKBOX) &&
        (HIWORD (wParam) == BN_CLICKED)) {
        // Get the current state, complement, and set.
        i = SendDlgItemMessage (hWnd, IDC_CHKBOX, BM_GETCHECK, 0, 0);
        if (i == 0)
            SendDlgItemMessage (hWnd, IDC_CHKBOX, BM_SETCHECK, 1, 0);
        else
            SendDlgItemMessage (hWnd, IDC_CHKBOX, BM_SETCHECK, 0, 0);
    }

    // Report WM_COMMAND messages to main window.
```

(continued)

Figure 4-5. *continued*

```
    for (i = 0; i < dim(nlBtn); i++) {
        if (HIWORD (wParam) == nlBtn[i].wNotification) {
            lstrcpy (szOut, nlBtn[i].pszLabel);
            break;
        }
    }
    if (i == dim(nlBtn))
        wsprintf (szOut, TEXT ("notification: %x"), HIWORD (wParam));

    SendMessage (GetParent (hWnd), MYMSG_ADDLINE, wParam,
                 (LPARAM)szOut);
    return 0;
}
//----------------------------------------------------------------------
// DoDrawItemBtnWnd - Process WM_DRAWITEM message for window.
//
LRESULT DoDrawItemBtnWnd (HWND hWnd, UINT wMsg, WPARAM wParam,
                          LPARAM lParam) {

    return DrawButton (hWnd, (LPDRAWITEMSTRUCT)lParam);
}

//----------------------------------------------------------------------
// DrawButton - Draws an owner-draw button
//
LRESULT DrawButton (HWND hWnd, LPDRAWITEMSTRUCT pdi) {

    HPEN hPenShadow, hPenLight, hPenDkShadow, hOldPen;

    HBRUSH hBr, hOldBr;
    LOGPEN lpen;
    TCHAR szOut[128];
    POINT ptOut[3], ptIn[3];

    // Reflect the messages to the report window.
    wsprintf (szOut, TEXT ("WM_DRAWITEM  Action:%x  State:%x"),
              pdi->itemAction, pdi->itemState);
    SendMessage (GetParent (hWnd), MYMSG_ADDLINE, pdi->CtlID,
                 (LPARAM)szOut);

    // Create pens for drawing.
    lpen.lopnStyle = PS_SOLID;
    lpen.lopnWidth.x = 3;
    lpen.lopnWidth.y = 3;
    lpen.lopnColor = GetSysColor (COLOR_3DSHADOW);
    hPenShadow = CreatePenIndirect (&lpen);
```

```
lpen.lopnWidth.x = 1;
lpen.lopnWidth.y = 1;
lpen.lopnColor = GetSysColor (COLOR_3DLIGHT);
hPenLight = CreatePenIndirect (&lpen);

lpen.lopnColor = GetSysColor (COLOR_3DDKSHADOW);
hPenDkShadow = CreatePenIndirect (&lpen);

// Create a brush for the face of the button.
hBr = CreateSolidBrush (GetSysColor (COLOR_3DFACE));

// Draw a rectangle with a thick outside border to start the
// frame drawing.
hOldPen = SelectObject (pdi->hDC, hPenShadow);
hOldBr = SelectObject (pdi->hDC, hBr);
Rectangle (pdi->hDC, pdi->rcItem.left, pdi->rcItem.top,
           pdi->rcItem.right, pdi->rcItem.bottom);

// Draw the upper left inside line.
ptIn[0].x = pdi->rcItem.left + 1;
ptIn[0].y = pdi->rcItem.bottom - 2;
ptIn[1].x = pdi->rcItem.left + 1;
ptIn[1].y = pdi->rcItem.top + 1;
ptIn[2].x = pdi->rcItem.right - 2;
ptIn[2].y = pdi->rcItem.top+1;

// Select a pen to draw shadow or light side of button.
if (pdi->itemState & ODS_SELECTED) {
    SelectObject (pdi->hDC, hPenDkShadow);
} else {
    SelectObject (pdi->hDC, hPenLight);
}
Polyline (pdi->hDC, ptIn, 3);

// If selected, also draw a bright line inside the lower
// right corner.
if (pdi->itemState & ODS_SELECTED) {
    SelectObject (pdi->hDC, hPenLight);
    ptIn[1].x = pdi->rcItem.right- 2;
    ptIn[1].y = pdi->rcItem.bottom - 2;
    Polyline (pdi->hDC, ptIn, 3);
}

// Now draw the black outside line on either the upper left or lower
// right corner.
ptOut[0].x = pdi->rcItem.left;
ptOut[0].y = pdi->rcItem.bottom-1;
```

(continued)

Figure 4-5. *continued*

```
        ptOut[2].x = pdi->rcItem.right-1;
        ptOut[2].y = pdi->rcItem.top;

        SelectObject (pdi->hDC, hPenDkShadow);
        if (pdi->itemState & ODS_SELECTED) {
            ptOut[1].x = pdi->rcItem.left;
            ptOut[1].y = pdi->rcItem.top;
        } else {
            ptOut[1].x = pdi->rcItem.right-1;
            ptOut[1].y = pdi->rcItem.bottom-1;
        }
        Polyline (pdi->hDC, ptOut, 3);

        // Draw the icon.
        if (hIcon) {
            ptIn[0].x = (pdi->rcItem.right - pdi->rcItem.left)/2 -
                        GetSystemMetrics (SM_CXICON)/2 - 2;
            ptIn[0].y = (pdi->rcItem.bottom - pdi->rcItem.top)/2 -
                        GetSystemMetrics (SM_CYICON)/2 - 2;
            // If pressed, shift image down one pel to simulate depress.
            if (pdi->itemState & ODS_SELECTED) {
                ptOut[1].x += 2;
                ptOut[1].y += 2;
            }
            DrawIcon (pdi->hDC, ptIn[0].x, ptIn[0].y, hIcon);
        }

        // If button has the focus, draw the dotted rect inside the button.
        if (pdi->itemState & ODS_FOCUS) {
            pdi->rcItem.left += 3;
            pdi->rcItem.top += 3;
            pdi->rcItem.right -= 4;
            pdi->rcItem.bottom -= 4;
            DrawFocusRect (pdi->hDC, &pdi->rcItem);
        }

        // Clean up. First select the original brush and pen into the DC.
        SelectObject (pdi->hDC, hOldBr);
        SelectObject (pdi->hDC, hOldPen);

        // Now delete the brushes and pens created.
        DeleteObject (hBr);
        DeleteObject (hPenShadow);
        DeleteObject (hPenDkShadow);
        DeleteObject (hPenLight);
        return 0;
    }
```

EditWnd.c

```
//======================================================================
// EditWnd - Edit control window code
//
// Written for the book Programming Windows CE
// Copyright (C) 1998 Douglas Boling
//======================================================================
#include <windows.h>                 // For all that Windows stuff
#include "Ctlview.h"                 // Program-specific stuff

extern HINSTANCE hInst;
//----------------------------------------------------------------------
// Global data
//
// Message dispatch table for EditWndWindowProc
const struct decodeUINT EditWndMessages[] = {
    WM_CREATE, DoCreateEditWnd,
    WM_COMMAND, DoCommandEditWnd,
};

// Structure defining the controls in the window
CTLWNDSTRUCT  Edits[] = {
    {TEXT ("edit"), IDC_SINGLELINE, TEXT ("Single line edit control"),
     10,  10, 130,  23, ES_AUTOHSCROLL},

    {TEXT ("edit"), IDC_MULTILINE, TEXT ("Multi line edit control"),
     10,  35, 130,  90, ES_MULTILINE | ES_AUTOVSCROLL},

    {TEXT ("edit"), IDC_PASSBOX, TEXT (""),
     10, 127, 130,  23, ES_PASSWORD},
};
// Structure labeling the edit control WM_COMMAND notifications
NOTELABELS nlEdit[] = {{TEXT ("EN_SETFOCUS "), 0x0100},
                       {TEXT ("EN_KILLFOCUS"), 0x0200},
                       {TEXT ("EN_CHANGE   "), 0x0300},
                       {TEXT ("EN_UPDATE   "), 0x0400},
                       {TEXT ("EN_ERRSPACE "), 0x0500},
                       {TEXT ("EN_MAXTEXT  "), 0x0501},
                       {TEXT ("EN_HSCROLL  "), 0x0601},
                       {TEXT ("EN_VSCROLL  "), 0x0602},
};
//----------------------------------------------------------------------
// InitEditWnd - EditWnd window initialization
//
```

(continued)

Figure 4-5. *continued*

```
int InitEditWnd (HINSTANCE hInstance) {
    WNDCLASS wc;

    // Register application EditWnd window class.
    wc.style = 0;                               // Window style
    wc.lpfnWndProc = EditWndProc;               // Callback function
    wc.cbClsExtra = 0;                          // Extra class data
    wc.cbWndExtra = 0;                          // Extra window data
    wc.hInstance = hInstance;                   // Owner handle
    wc.hIcon = NULL,                            // Application icon
    wc.hCursor = NULL;                          // Default cursor
    wc.hbrBackground = (HBRUSH) GetStockObject (WHITE_BRUSH);
    wc.lpszMenuName =  NULL;                    // Menu name
    wc.lpszClassName = EDITWND;                 // Window class name

    if (RegisterClass (&wc) == 0) return 1;

    return 0;
}
//======================================================================
// Message handling procedures for EditWindow
//----------------------------------------------------------------------
// EditWndWndProc - Callback function for application window
//
LRESULT CALLBACK EditWndProc (HWND hWnd, UINT wMsg, WPARAM wParam,
                              LPARAM lParam) {
    INT i;
    //
    // Search message list to see if we need to handle this
    // message.  If in list, call procedure.
    //
    for (i = 0; i < dim(EditWndMessages); i++) {
        if (wMsg == EditWndMessages[i].Code)
            return (*EditWndMessages[i].Fxn)(hWnd, wMsg, wParam, lParam);
    }
    return DefWindowProc (hWnd, wMsg, wParam, lParam);
}
//----------------------------------------------------------------------
// DoCreateEditWnd - Process WM_CREATE message for window.
//
LRESULT DoCreateEditWnd (HWND hWnd, UINT wMsg, WPARAM wParam,
                         LPARAM lParam) {
    INT i;

    for (i = 0; i < dim(Edits); i++) {
```

```
        CreateWindow (Edits[i].szClass, Edits[i].szTitle,
                      Edits[i].lStyle | WS_VISIBLE | WS_CHILD | WS_BORDER,
                      Edits[i].x, Edits[i].y, Edits[i].cx, Edits[i].cy,
                      hWnd, (HMENU) Edits[i].nID, hInst, NULL);
    }
    return 0;
}
//----------------------------------------------------------------------
// DoCommandEditWnd - Process WM_COMMAND message for window.
//
LRESULT DoCommandEditWnd (HWND hWnd, UINT wMsg, WPARAM wParam,
                          LPARAM lParam) {
    TCHAR szOut[128];
    INT i;

    for (i = 0; i < dim(nlEdit); i++) {
        if (HIWORD (wParam) == nlEdit[i].wNotification) {
            lstrcpy (szOut, nlEdit[i].pszLabel);
            break;
        }
    }

    if (i == dim(nlEdit))
        wsprintf (szOut, TEXT ("notification: %x"), HIWORD (wParam));

    SendMessage (GetParent (hWnd), MYMSG_ADDLINE, wParam,
                 (LPARAM)szOut);
    return 0;
}
```

ListWnd.c

```
//======================================================================
// ListWnd - List box control window code
//
// Written for the book Programming Windows CE
// Copyright (C) 1998 Douglas Boling
//======================================================================
#include <windows.h>                 // For all that Windows stuff
#include "Ctlview.h"                 // Program-specific stuff

extern HINSTANCE hInst;
//----------------------------------------------------------------------
// Global data
//
```

(continued)

Figure 4-5. *continued*

```
// Message dispatch table for ListWndWindowProc
const struct decodeUINT ListWndMessages[] = {
    WM_CREATE, DoCreateListWnd,
    WM_COMMAND, DoCommandListWnd,
};

// Structure defining the controls in the window
CTLWNDSTRUCT  Lists[] = {
    {TEXT ("combobox"), IDC_COMBOBOX, TEXT (""), 10,  10, 170, 100,
     WS_VSCROLL},

    {TEXT ("Listbox"), IDC_SNGLELIST, TEXT (""),   10,  35, 100, 120,
     WS_VSCROLL | LBS_NOTIFY},

    {TEXT ("Listbox"), IDC_MULTILIST, TEXT (""), 115,  35, 100, 120,
     WS_VSCROLL | LBS_EXTENDEDSEL | LBS_NOTIFY}
};
// Structure labeling the list box control WM_COMMAND notifications
NOTELABELS nlList[] = {{TEXT ("LBN_ERRSPACE "), (-2)},
                       {TEXT ("LBN_SELCHANGE"), 1},
                       {TEXT ("LBN_DBLCLK   "), 2},
                       {TEXT ("LBN_SELCANCEL"), 3},
                       {TEXT ("LBN_SETFOCUS "), 4},
                       {TEXT ("LBN_KILLFOCUS"), 5},
};
// Structure labeling the combo box control WM_COMMAND notifications
NOTELABELS nlCombo[] = {{TEXT ("CBN_ERRSPACE    "), (-1)},
                        {TEXT ("CBN_SELCHANGE   "), 1},
                        {TEXT ("CBN_DBLCLK      "), 2},
                        {TEXT ("CBN_SETFOCUS    "), 3},
                        {TEXT ("CBN_KILLFOCUS   "), 4},
                        {TEXT ("CBN_EDITCHANGE  "), 5},
                        {TEXT ("CBN_EDITUPDATE  "), 6},
                        {TEXT ("CBN_DROPDOWN    "), 7},
                        {TEXT ("CBN_CLOSEUP     "), 8},
                        {TEXT ("CBN_SELENDOK    "), 9},
                        {TEXT ("CBN_SELENDCANCEL"), 10},
};
//----------------------------------------------------------------------
// InitListWnd - ListWnd window initialization
//
int InitListWnd (HINSTANCE hInstance) {
    WNDCLASS wc;

    // Register application ListWnd window class.
    wc.style = 0;                              // Window style
```

```
    wc.lpfnWndProc = ListWndProc;               // Callback function
    wc.cbClsExtra = 0;                          // Extra class data
    wc.cbWndExtra = 0;                          // Extra window data
    wc.hInstance = hInstance;                   // Owner handle
    wc.hIcon = NULL,                            // Application icon
    wc.hCursor = NULL;                          // Default cursor
    wc.hbrBackground = (HBRUSH) GetStockObject (WHITE_BRUSH);
    wc.lpszMenuName =  NULL;                    // Menu name
    wc.lpszClassName = LISTWND;                 // Window class name

    if (RegisterClass (&wc) == 0) return 1;

    return 0;
}
//======================================================================
// Message handling procedures for ListWindow
//----------------------------------------------------------------------
// ListWndProc - Callback function for application window
//
LRESULT CALLBACK ListWndProc (HWND hWnd, UINT wMsg, WPARAM wParam,
                              LPARAM lParam) {
    INT i;
    //
    // Search message list to see if we need to handle this
    // message.  If in list, call procedure.
    //
    for (i = 0; i < dim(ListWndMessages); i++) {
        if (wMsg == ListWndMessages[i].Code)
            return (*ListWndMessages[i].Fxn)(hWnd, wMsg, wParam, lParam);
    }
    return DefWindowProc (hWnd, wMsg, wParam, lParam);
}
//----------------------------------------------------------------------
// DoCreateListWnd - Process WM_CREATE message for window.
//
LRESULT DoCreateListWnd (HWND hWnd, UINT wMsg, WPARAM wParam,
                         LPARAM lParam) {
    INT i;
    TCHAR szOut[64];

    for (i = 0; i < dim(Lists); i++) {

        CreateWindow (Lists[i].szClass, Lists[i].szTitle,
                      Lists[i].lStyle | WS_VISIBLE | WS_CHILD | WS_BORDER,
                      Lists[i].x, Lists[i].y, Lists[i].cx, Lists[i].cy,
                      hWnd, (HMENU) Lists[i].nID, hInst, NULL);
    }
```

(continued)

Figure 4-5. *continued*

```
    for (i = 0; i < 20; i++) {
        wsprintf (szOut, TEXT ("Item %d"), i);
        SendDlgItemMessage (hWnd, IDC_SNGLELIST, LB_ADDSTRING, 0,
                            (LPARAM)szOut);

        SendDlgItemMessage (hWnd, IDC_MULTILIST, LB_ADDSTRING, 0,
                            (LPARAM)szOut);

        SendDlgItemMessage (hWnd, IDC_COMBOBOX, CB_ADDSTRING, 0,
                            (LPARAM)szOut);
    }
    // Set initial selection.
    SendDlgItemMessage (hWnd, IDC_COMBOBOX, CB_SETCURSEL, 0, 0);
    return 0;
}
//----------------------------------------------------------------------
// DoCommandListWnd - Process WM_COMMAND message for window.
//
LRESULT DoCommandListWnd (HWND hWnd, UINT wMsg, WPARAM wParam,
                          LPARAM lParam) {
    TCHAR szOut[128];
    INT i;

    if (LOWORD (wParam) == IDC_COMBOBOX) {
        for (i = 0; i < dim(nlCombo); i++) {
            if (HIWORD (wParam) == nlCombo[i].wNotification) {
                lstrcpy (szOut, nlCombo[i].pszLabel);
                break;
            }
        }
        if (i == dim(nlList))
            wsprintf (szOut, TEXT ("notification: %x"), HIWORD (wParam));
    } else {
        for (i = 0; i < dim(nlList); i++) {
            if (HIWORD (wParam) == nlList[i].wNotification) {
                lstrcpy (szOut, nlList[i].pszLabel);
                break;
            }
        }
        if (i == dim(nlList))
            wsprintf (szOut, TEXT ("notification: %x"), HIWORD (wParam));
    }
    SendMessage (GetParent (hWnd), MYMSG_ADDLINE, wParam,
                 (LPARAM)szOut);
    return 0;
}
```

StatWnd.c

```
//======================================================================
// StatWnd - Static control window code
//
// Written for the book Programming Windows CE
// Copyright (C) 1998 Douglas Boling
//======================================================================
#include <windows.h>                 // For all that Windows stuff
#include "Ctlview.h"                 // Program-specific stuff

extern HINSTANCE hInst;
//----------------------------------------------------------------------
// Global data
//
// Message dispatch table for StatWndWindowProc
const struct decodeUINT StatWndMessages[] = {
    WM_CREATE, DoCreateStatWnd,
    WM_COMMAND, DoCommandStatWnd,
};

// Structure defining the controls in the window
CTLWNDSTRUCT  Stats [] = {
    {TEXT ("static"), IDC_LEFTTEXT, TEXT ("Left text"),
     10,  10, 120,  23, SS_LEFT | SS_NOTIFY},

    {TEXT ("static"), IDC_RIGHTTEXT, TEXT ("Right text"),
     10,  35, 120,  23, SS_RIGHT},

    {TEXT ("static"), IDC_CENTERTEXT, TEXT ("Center text"),
     10,  60, 120,  23, SS_CENTER | WS_BORDER},

    {TEXT ("static"), IDC_ICONCTL, TEXT ("TEXTICON"),
     10,  85, 120,  23, SS_ICON},

    {TEXT ("static"), IDC_BITMAPCTL, TEXT ("STATICBMP"),
     170,  10,  44,  44, SS_BITMAP | SS_NOTIFY},
};

// Structure labeling the static control WM_COMMAND notifications
NOTELABELS nlStatic[] = {{TEXT ("STN_CLICKED"), 0},
                         {TEXT ("STN_ENABLE "), 2},
                         {TEXT ("STN_DISABLE"), 3},
};
//----------------------------------------------------------------------
// InitStatWnd - StatWnd window initialization
```

(continued)

Figure 4-5. *continued*

```
//
int InitStatWnd (HINSTANCE hInstance) {
    WNDCLASS wc;

    // Register application StatWnd window class.
    wc.style = 0;                               // Window style
    wc.lpfnWndProc = StatWndProc;               // Callback function
    wc.cbClsExtra = 0;                          // Extra class data
    wc.cbWndExtra = 0;                          // Extra window data
    wc.hInstance = hInstance;                   // Owner handle
    wc.hIcon = NULL,                            // Application icon
    wc.hCursor = NULL;                          // Default cursor
    wc.hbrBackground = (HBRUSH) GetStockObject (WHITE_BRUSH);
    wc.lpszMenuName =  NULL;                    // Menu name
    wc.lpszClassName = STATWND;                 // Window class name

    if (RegisterClass (&wc) == 0) return 1;

    return 0;
}
//======================================================================
// Message handling procedures for StatWindow
//----------------------------------------------------------------------
// StatWndProc - Callback function for application window
//
LRESULT CALLBACK StatWndProc (HWND hWnd, UINT wMsg, WPARAM wParam,
                              LPARAM lParam) {
    INT i;
    //
    // Search message list to see if we need to handle this
    // message.  If in list, call procedure.
    //
    for (i = 0; i < dim(StatWndMessages); i++) {
        if (wMsg == StatWndMessages[i].Code)
            return (*StatWndMessages[i].Fxn)(hWnd, wMsg, wParam, lParam);
    }
    return DefWindowProc (hWnd, wMsg, wParam, lParam);
}
//----------------------------------------------------------------------
// DoCreateStatWnd - Process WM_CREATE message for window.
//
LRESULT DoCreateStatWnd (HWND hWnd, UINT wMsg, WPARAM wParam,
                         LPARAM lParam) {
    INT i;
```

```
    for (i = 0; i < dim(Stats); i++) {

        CreateWindow (Stats[i].szClass, Stats[i].szTitle,
                      Stats[i].lStyle | WS_VISIBLE | WS_CHILD,
                      Stats[i].x, Stats[i].y, Stats[i].cx, Stats[i].cy,
                      hWnd, (HMENU) Stats[i].nID, hInst, NULL);
    }
    return 0;
}
//----------------------------------------------------------------------
// DoCommandStatWnd - Process WM_COMMAND message for window.
//
LRESULT DoCommandStatWnd (HWND hWnd, UINT wMsg, WPARAM wParam,
                          LPARAM lParam) {
    TCHAR szOut[128];
    INT i;

    for (i = 0; i < dim(nlStatic); i++) {
        if (HIWORD (wParam) == nlStatic[i].wNotification) {
            lstrcpy (szOut, nlStatic[i].pszLabel);
            break;
        }
    }
    if (i == dim(nlStatic))
        wsprintf (szOut, TEXT ("notification: %x"), HIWORD (wParam));

    SendMessage (GetParent (hWnd), MYMSG_ADDLINE, wParam,
                 (LPARAM)szOut);
    return 0;
}
```

ScrollWnd.c

```
//======================================================================
// ScrollWnd - Scroll bar control window code
//
// Written for the book Programming Windows CE
// Copyright (C) 1998 Douglas Boling
//======================================================================
#include <windows.h>                 // For all that Windows stuff
#include "Ctlview.h"                 // Program-specific stuff

extern HINSTANCE hInst;
//----------------------------------------------------------------------
// Global data
//
```

(continued)

Figure 4-5. *continued*

```
// Message dispatch table for ScrollWndWindowProc
const struct decodeUINT ScrollWndMessages[] = {
    WM_CREATE, DoCreateScrollWnd,
    WM_HSCROLL, DoVScrollScrollWnd,
    WM_VSCROLL, DoVScrollScrollWnd,
};

// Structure defining the controls in the window
CTLWNDSTRUCT  Scrolls [] = {
    {TEXT ("Scrollbar"), IDC_LRSCROLL, TEXT (""),
     10,  10, 150,  23, SBS_HORZ},

    {TEXT ("Scrollbar"), IDC_UDSCROLL, TEXT (""),
     180,  10,  23, 150, SBS_VERT},
};

// Structure labeling the scroll bar control scroll codes for WM_VSCROLL
NOTELABELS nlVScroll[] = {{TEXT ("SB_LINEUP        "), 0},
                          {TEXT ("SB_LINEDOWN      "), 1},
                          {TEXT ("SB_PAGEUP        "), 2},
                          {TEXT ("SB_PAGEDOWN      "), 3},
                          {TEXT ("SB_THUMBPOSITION"), 4},
                          {TEXT ("SB_THUMBTRACK    "), 5},
                          {TEXT ("SB_TOP           "), 6},
                          {TEXT ("SB_BOTTOM        "), 7},
                          {TEXT ("SB_ENDSCROLL     "), 8},
};
// Structure labeling the scroll bar control scroll codes for WM_HSCROLL
NOTELABELS nlHScroll[] = {{TEXT ("SB_LINELEFT      "), 0},
                          {TEXT ("SB_LINERIGHT     "), 1},
                          {TEXT ("SB_PAGELEFT      "), 2},
                          {TEXT ("SB_PAGERIGHT     "), 3},
                          {TEXT ("SB_THUMBPOSITION"), 4},
                          {TEXT ("SB_THUMBTRACK    "), 5},
                          {TEXT ("SB_LEFT          "), 6},
                          {TEXT ("SB_RIGHT         "), 7},
                          {TEXT ("SB_ENDSCROLL     "), 8},
};
//----------------------------------------------------------------------
// InitScrollWnd - ScrollWnd window initialization
//
int InitScrollWnd (HINSTANCE hInstance) {
    WNDCLASS wc;

    // Register application ScrollWnd window class.
    wc.style = 0;                              // Window style
    wc.lpfnWndProc = ScrollWndProc;            // Callback function
```

```
    wc.cbClsExtra = 0;                          // Extra class data
    wc.cbWndExtra = 0;                          // Extra window data
    wc.hInstance = hInstance;                   // Owner handle
    wc.hIcon = NULL,                            // Application icon
    wc.hCursor = NULL;                          // Default cursor
    wc.hbrBackground = (HBRUSH) GetStockObject (WHITE_BRUSH);
    wc.lpszMenuName =  NULL;                    // Menu name
    wc.lpszClassName = SCROLLWND;               // Window class name

    if (RegisterClass (&wc) == 0) return 1;

    return 0;
}
//======================================================================
// Message handling procedures for ScrollWindow
//----------------------------------------------------------------------
// ScrollWndProc - Callback function for application window
//
LRESULT CALLBACK ScrollWndProc (HWND hWnd, UINT wMsg, WPARAM wParam,
                                LPARAM lParam) {
    INT i;
    //
    // Search message list to see if we need to handle this
    // message.  If in list, call procedure.
    //
    for (i = 0; i < dim(ScrollWndMessages); i++) {
        if (wMsg == ScrollWndMessages[i].Code)
            return (*ScrollWndMessages[i].Fxn)(hWnd, wMsg, wParam, lParam);
    }
    return DefWindowProc (hWnd, wMsg, wParam, lParam);
}
//----------------------------------------------------------------------
// DoCreateScrollWnd - Process WM_CREATE message for window.
//
LRESULT DoCreateScrollWnd (HWND hWnd, UINT wMsg, WPARAM wParam,
                           LPARAM lParam) {
    INT i;

    for (i = 0; i < dim(Scrolls); i++) {
        CreateWindow (Scrolls[i].szClass, Scrolls[i].szTitle,
                      Scrolls[i].lStyle | WS_VISIBLE | WS_CHILD,
                      Scrolls[i].x, Scrolls[i].y, Scrolls[i].cx,
                      Scrolls[i].cy,
                      hWnd, (HMENU) Scrolls[i].nID, hInst, NULL);
    }
    return 0;
}
```

(continued)

Figure 4-5. *continued*

```
//----------------------------------------------------------------------
// DoVScrollScrollWnd - Process WM_VSCROLL message for window.
//
LRESULT DoVScrollScrollWnd (HWND hWnd, UINT wMsg, WPARAM wParam,
                            LPARAM lParam) {
    TCHAR szOut[128];
    SCROLLINFO si;
    INT i, sPos;

    // Update the report window.
    if (GetDlgItem (hWnd, 101) == (HWND)lParam) {

        for (i = 0; i < dim(nlVScroll); i++) {
            if (LOWORD (wParam) == nlVScroll[i].wNotification) {
                lstrcpy (szOut, nlVScroll[i].pszLabel);
                break;
            }
        }
        if (i == dim(nlVScroll))
            wsprintf (szOut, TEXT ("notification: %x"), HIWORD (wParam));
    } else {
        for (i = 0; i < dim(nlHScroll); i++) {
            if (LOWORD (wParam) == nlHScroll[i].wNotification) {
                lstrcpy (szOut, nlHScroll[i].pszLabel);
                break;
            }
        }
        if (i == dim(nlHScroll))
            wsprintf (szOut, TEXT ("notification: %x"), HIWORD (wParam));
    }
    SendMessage (GetParent (hWnd), MYMSG_ADDLINE, -1, (LPARAM)szOut);

    // Get scroll bar position.
    si.cbSize = sizeof (si);
    si.fMask = SIF_POS;
    GetScrollInfo ((HWND)lParam, SB_CTL, &si);
    sPos = si.nPos;

    // Act on the scroll code.
    switch (LOWORD (wParam)) {
    case SB_LINEUP:       // Also SB_LINELEFT
        sPos -= 2;
        break;
```

```
        case SB_LINEDOWN:     // Also SB_LINERIGHT
            sPos += 2;
            break;

        case SB_PAGEUP:       // Also SB_PAGELEFT
            sPos -= 10;
            break;

        case SB_PAGEDOWN:     // Also SB_PAGERIGHT
            sPos += 10;
            break;

        case SB_THUMBPOSITION:
            sPos = HIWORD (wParam);
            break;
        }
        // Check range.
        if (sPos < 0)
            sPos = 0;
        if (sPos > 100)
            sPos = 100;

        // Update scrollbar position.
        si.cbSize = sizeof (si);
        si.nPos = sPos;
        si.fMask = SIF_POS;
        SetScrollInfo ((HWND)lParam, SB_CTL, &si, TRUE);
        return 0;
    }
```

When the CtlView program starts, the WM_CREATE handler of the main window, *DoCreateFrame*, creates a row of radio buttons across the top of the window, a list box on the right side of the window, and five different child windows on the left side of the window. (The five child windows are all created without the WS_VISIBLE style, so they're initially hidden.) Each of the child windows in turn creates a number of controls. Before returning from the *DoCreateFrame*, CtlView checks one of the auto radio buttons and makes the BtnWnd child window (the window that contains the example button controls) visible using *ShowWindow*.

As each of the controls on the child windows are tapped, clicked, or selected, the control sends WM_COMMAND messages to its parent window. That window in turn sends the information from the WM_COMMAND message to its parent, the frame window, using the application-defined message MYMSG_ADDLINE. There the notification data is formatted and displayed in the list box on the right side of the frame window.

The other function of the frame window is to switch between the different child windows. The application accomplishes this by displaying only the child window that matches the selection of the radio buttons across the top of the frame window. The processing for this is done in the WM_COMMAND handler, *DoCommandFrame* in CtlView.c.

The best way to discover how and when these controls send notifications is to run the example program and use each of the controls. Figure 4-6 shows the CtlView window with the button controls displayed. As each of the buttons is clicked, a BN_CLICKED notification is sent to the parent window of the control. The parent window simply labels the notification and forwards it to the display list box. Because the Check Box button isn't an auto check box, CtlView must manually change the state of the check box when a user clicks it. The other check boxes and radio buttons, however, do automatically change state because they were created with the BS_AUTOCHECKBOX, BS_AUTO3STATE, and BS_AUTORADIOBUTTON styles. The square button with the exclamation mark inside a triangular icon is an owner-draw button.

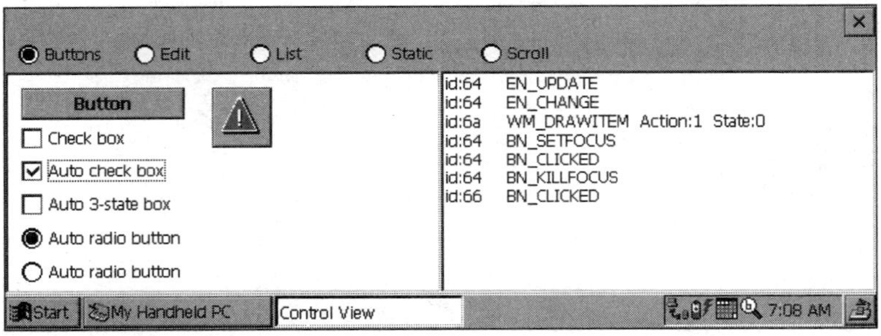

Figure 4-6. *The CtlView window with the button child window displayed in the left pane.*

The source code for each child window is contained in a separate file. The source for the window containing the button controls is contained in BtnWnd.c. The file contains an initialization routine (*InitBtnWnd*) that registers the window and a window procedure (*BtnWndProc*) for the window itself. The button controls themselves are created during the WM_CREATE message using *CreateWindow*. The position, style, and other aspects of each control are contained in an array of structures named *Btns*. The *DoCreateBtnWnd* function cycles through each of the entries in the array, calling *CreateWindow* for each one. Each child window in CtlView uses a similar process to create its controls.

To support the owner-draw button, *BtnWndProc* must handle the WM_DRAWITEM message. The WM_DRAWITEM message is sent when the button needs to be drawn because it has changed state, gained or lost the focus, or because it has been uncovered. Although the *DrawButton* function (called each time a WM_DRAWITEM message is received) expends a great deal of effort to make the button look like a standard button, there's no reason a button can't have any look you want.

The other window procedures provide only basic support for their controls. The WM_COMMAND handlers simply reflect the notifications back to the main window. The ScrollWnd child window procedure, *ScrollWndProc*, handles WM_VSCROLL and WM_HSCROLL messages because that's how scroll bar controls communicate with their parent windows.

Controls and colors

Finally, a word about colors. A large number of Windows CE devices use a gray-scale display instead of a color display, including all of the first generation H/PC and Palm-size PC systems. This has made many Windows CE developers, including me, somewhat lazy in managing color in our Windows CE programs. Now that newer Windows CE systems sport color displays, we have to think a bit more.

In CtlView, the frame window class is registered in a subtly different way from the way I've registered it in previous programs. In the CtlView example, I set the background brush for the frame window using the line

```
wc.hbrBackground = (HBRUSH)GetSysColorBrush (COLOR_STATIC);
```

This sets the background color of the frame window to the same background color I used to draw the radio buttons. The function *GetSysColorBrush* returns a brush that matches the color used by the system to draw various objects in the system. In this case, the constant COLOR_STATIC is passed to *GetSysColorBrush*, which then returns the background color Windows uses when drawing static text and the text for check box and radio buttons. This makes the frame window background match the static text background.

In the window that contains the button controls, the check box and radio button background is changed to match the white background of the button window, by fielding the WM_CTLCOLORSTATIC message. This message is sent to the parent of a static control or a button control when the button is a check box or radio button to ask the parent which colors to use when drawing the control. In CtlView, the button window returns the handle to a white brush so that the control background will match the white background of the window. Modifying the color of a push button is done by fielding the WM_CTLCOLORBUTTON message. Other controls send different WM_CTLCOLOR*xxx* messages so that the colors used to draw them can be modified by the parent window.

DIALOG BOXES

The CtlView example program demonstrates a complex use of controls. While CtlView creates these controls for demonstration purposes, controls are generally used to query user input. As CtlView demonstrates, a fair amount of code is necessary for creating and placing the controls in the windows. Fortunately, you don't need this code because Windows provides a service for exactly this purpose: dialog boxes. Dialog boxes query data from the user or present data to the user, hence the term *dialog* box.

Dialog boxes are windows created by Windows using a template provided by an application. The template describes the type and placement of the controls in the window. The Dialog Manager—the part of Windows that creates and manages dialog boxes—also provides default functionality for switching focus between the controls using the Tab key as well as default actions for the Enter and Escape keys. In addition, Windows provides a default dialog box window class, freeing applications from the necessity of registering a window class for each of the dialog boxes it might create.

Dialog boxes come in two types: *modal* and *modeless*. A modal dialog prevents the user from using the application until the dialog box has been dismissed. For example, the File Open and the Print dialog boxes are modal. A modeless dialog box can be used interactively with the remainder of the application. The Find dialog box in Microsoft Pocket Word is modeless; the user doesn't need to dismiss it before typing in the main window.

Like other windows, dialog boxes have a window procedure, although the dialog box window procedure is constructed somewhat differently from standard windows procedures. Instead of passing unprocessed messages to *DefWindowProc* for default processing, a dialog box procedure returns TRUE if it processed the message and FALSE if it didn't process the message. Windows supplies a default procedure, *DefDialogProc*, for use in specific cases—that is, for specialized modeless dialog boxes that have their own window classes.

Dialog Box Resource Templates

Most of the time, the description for the size and placement of the dialog box and for the controls is provided via a resource called a *dialog template*. You can create a dialog template in memory, but unless a program has an overriding need to format the size and shape of the dialog box on the fly, loading a dialog template directly from a resource is a much better choice. As is the case for other resources such as menus, dialog templates are contained in the resource (RC) file. The template is referenced by the application using either its name or its resource ID. Here is a dialog template for a simple dialog box:

```
GetVal DIALOG discardable 10, 10, 75, 60
STYLE  WS_POPUP | WS_VISIBLE | WS_CAPTION | WS_SYSMENU | DS_CENTER
EXSTYLE WS_EX_CAPTIONOKBTN
CAPTION "Enter line number"
BEGIN
    LTEXT "Enter &value:"  IDD_VALLABEL,   5,  10,  40,  12
    EDITTEXT                  IDD_VALUE,  50,  10,  20,  12, WS_TABSTOP
    AUTORADIOBUTTON "&Decimal", IDD_DEC,   5,  25,  60,  12,
                    WS_TABSTOP | WS_GROUP
    AUTORADIOBUTTON "&Hex",      IDD_HEX,   5,  40,  60,  12
END
```

The syntax for a dialog template follows a simple pattern similar to that for a menu resource. First is the name or ID of the resource followed by the keyword *DIALOG* identifying that what follows is a dialog template. The optional *discardable* keyword is followed by the position and size of the dialog box. The position specified is, by default, relative to the owner window of the dialog box.

The units of measurement in a dialog box aren't pixels but *dialog units*. A dialog unit is defined as one quarter of the average width of the characters in the system font for horizontal units and one eighth of the height of one character from the same font for vertical units. The goal is to create a unit of measurement independent of the display technology; in practice, dialog boxes still need to be tested in all display resolutions in which the box might be displayed. You can compute a pixel vs. dialog unit conversion using the *GetDialogBaseUnits* function but you'll rarely find it necessary. The visual tools that come with most compilers these days isolate a programmer from terms like *dialog units* but it's still a good idea to know just how dialog boxes are described in an RC file.

The *STYLE* line of code specifies the style flags for the dialog box. The styles include the standard window (WS_*xx*) style flags used for windows as well as a series of dialog (DS_*xx*) style flags specific to dialog boxes. Windows CE supports the following dialog box styles:

- *DS_ABSALIGN* Places the dialog box relative to the upper left corner of the screen instead of basing the position on the owner window.
- *DS_CENTER* Centers the dialog box vertically and horizontally on the screen.
- *DS_MODALFRAME* Creates a dialog box with a modal dialog box frame that can be combined with a title bar and System menu by specifying the WS_CAPTION and WS_SYSMENU styles.

- *DS_SETFONT* Tells Windows to use a nondefault font that is specified in the dialog template.
- *DS_SETFOREGROUND* Brings the dialog box to the foreground after it's created. If an application not in the foreground displays a dialog box, this style forces the dialog box to the top of the Z-order so that the user will see it.

Most dialog boxes are created with at least some combination of the WS_POPUP, WS_CAPTION, and WS_SYSMENU style flags. The WS_POPUP flag indicates the dialog box is a top-level window. The WS_CAPTION style gives the dialog box a title bar. A title bar allows the user to drag the dialog box around as well as serving as a site for title text for the dialog box. The WS_SYSMENU style causes the dialog box to have a Close button on the right end of the title bar, thus eliminating the need for a command bar control to provide the Close button. Note that Windows CE uses this flag differently from other versions of Windows, in which the flag indicates that a system menu is to be placed on the end of the title bar.

The *EXSTYLE* line of code specifies the extended style flags for the dialog box. For Windows CE, these flags are particularly important. The WS_EX_CAPTIONOKBTN flag tells the dialog manager to place an OK button on the title bar to the immediate left of the Close button. Having both OK and Close (or Cancel) buttons on the title bar saves precious space in dialog boxes that are displayed on the small screens typical of Windows CE devices. The WS_EX_CONTEXTHELP extended style places a Help button on the title bar to the immediate left of the OK button. Clicking on this button results in a WM_HELP message being sent to the dialog box procedure.

The *CAPTION* line of code specifies the title bar text of the dialog, providing that the WS_CAPTION style was specified so that the dialog box will have a title bar.

The lines describing the type and placement of the controls in the dialog box are enclosed in *BEGIN* and *END* keywords. Each control is specified either by a particular keyword, in the case of commonly used controls, or by the keyword *CONTROL,* which is a generic placeholder that can specify any window class to be placed in the dialog box. The *LTEXT* line of code on page 209 specifies a static left-justified text control. The keyword is followed by the default text for the control in quotes. The next parameter is the ID of the control, which must be unique for the dialog box. In this template, the ID is a constant defined in an include file that is included by both the resource script and the C or C++ file containing the dialog box procedure.

The next four values are the location and size of the control, in dialog units, relative to the upper left corner of the dialog box. Following that, any explicit style flags can be specified for the control. In the case of the *LTEXT* line, no style flags are necessary, but as you can see the *EDITTEXT* and first *AUTORADIOBUTTON* entries each have style flags specified. Each of the control keywords have subtly different syntax. For example, the *EDITTEXT* line doesn't have a field for default text. The style flags for the individual controls deserve notice. The edit control and the first of the two radio buttons have a WS_TABSTOP style. The dialog manager looks for controls with the WS_TABSTOP style to determine which control gets focus when the user presses the Tab. In this example, pressing the Tab key results in focus being switched between the edit control and the first radio button.

The WS_GROUP style on the first radio button starts a new group of controls. All the controls following the radio button are grouped together, up to the next control that has the WS_GROUP style. Grouping auto radio buttons allow only one radio button at a time to be selected.

Another benefit of grouping is that focus can be changed among the controls within a group by exploiting the cursor keys as well as the Tab key. The first member of a group should have a WS_TABSTOP style; this allows the user to tab to the group of controls and then use the cursor keys to switch the focus among the controls in the group.

The CONTROL statement isn't used in this example, but it's important and merits some explanation. It's a generic statement that allows inclusion of any window class in a dialog box. It has the following syntax:

```
CONTROL "text", id, class, style, x, y, width, height
    [, extended-style]
```

For this entry, the default text and control ID are similar to the other statements but the next field, *class*, is new. It specifies the window class of the control you want to place in the dialog box. The *class* field is followed by the *style* flags, then the location and size of your control. Finally, the CONTROL statement has a field for extended style flags. If you use Microsoft Developer Studio to create a dialog box and look at the resulting RC file using a text editor, you'll see that Developer Studio uses CONTROL statements instead of the more readable LTEXT, EDITTEXT, and BUTTON statements. There's no functional difference between an edit control created with a CONTROL statement and one created with an EDITTEXT statement. The CONTROL statement is a generic version of the more specific keywords. The CONTROL statement also allows inclusion of controls that don't have a special keyword associated with them.

Creating a Dialog Box

Creating and displaying a dialog box is simple; just use one of the many dialog box creation functions. The first two are these:

```
int DialogBox (HANDLE hInstance, LPCTSTR lpTemplate, HWND hWndOwner,
               DLGPROC lpDialogFunc);

int DialogBoxParam (HINSTANCE hInstance, LPCTSTR lpTemplate,
                    HWND hWndOwner, DLGPROC lpDialogFunc,
                    LPARAM dwInitParam);
```

These two functions differ only in *DialogBoxParam*'s additional *LPARAM* parameter, so I'll talk about them at the same time. The first parameter to these functions is the instance handle of the program. The second parameter specifies the name or ID of the resource containing the dialog template. As with other resources, to specify a resource ID instead of a name requires the use of the MAKEINTRESOURCE macro.

The third parameter is the handle of the window that will own the dialog box. The owning window isn't the parent of the dialog box because, were that true, the dialog box would be clipped to fit inside the parent. Ownership means instead that the dialog box will be hidden when the owner window is minimized and will always appear above the owner window in the Z-order.

The fourth parameter is a pointer to the dialog box procedure for the dialog box. I'll describe the dialog box procedure shortly. The *DialogBoxParam* function has a fifth parameter, which is a user-defined value that's passed to the dialog box procedure when the dialog box is to be initialized. This helpful value can be used to pass a pointer to a structure of data that can be referenced when your application is initializing the dialog box controls.

Two other dialog box creation functions create modal dialogs. They are the following:

```
int DialogBoxIndirect (HANDLE hInstance, LPDLGTEMPLATE lpTemplate,
                       HWND hWndParent, DLGPROC lpDialogFunc);

int DialogBoxIndirectParam (HINSTANCE hInstance,
                            LPCDLGTEMPLATE DialogTemplate, HWND hWndParent,
                            DLGPROC lpDialogFunc, LPARAM dwInitParam);
```

The difference between these two functions and the two previously described is that these two use a dialog box template in memory to define the dialog box rather than using a resource. This allows a program to dynamically create a dialog box template on the fly. The second parameter to these functions points to a DLGTEMPLATE structure, which describes the overall dialog box window, followed by an array of DLGITEMTEMPLATE structures defining the individual controls.

When any of these four functions are called, the dialog manager creates a modal dialog box using the template passed. The window that owns the dialog is disabled and the dialog manager then enters its own internal *GetMessage/DispatchMessage* message processing loop; this loop doesn't exit until the dialog box is destroyed. Because of this, these functions don't return to the caller until the dialog box has been destroyed. The WM_ENTERIDLE message that's sent to owner windows in other versions of Windows while the dialog box is displayed isn't supported under Windows CE.

If an application wanted to create a modal dialog box with the template shown above and pass a value to the dialog box procedure it might call this:

```
DialogBoxParam (hInstance, TEXT ("GetVal"), hWnd, GetValDlgProc,
                0x1234);
```

The *hInstance* and *hWnd* parameters would be the instance handle of the application and the handle of the owner window. The *GetVal* string is the name of the dialog box template while *GetValDlgProc* is the name of the dialog box procedure. Finally, *0x1234* is an application-defined value. In this case, it might be used to provide a default value in the dialog box.

Dialog Box Procedures

The final component necessary for a dialog box is the dialog box procedure. As in the case of a window procedure, the purpose of the dialog box procedure is to field messages sent to the window—in this case, a dialog box window—and perform the appropriate processing. In fact, a dialog box procedure is simply a special case of a window procedure, although we should pay attention to a few differences between the two.

The first difference, as mentioned in the previous section, is that a dialog box procedure doesn't pass unprocessed messages to *DefWindowProc*. Instead, the procedure returns TRUE for messages it processes and FALSE for messages that it doesn't process. The dialog manager uses this return value to determine whether the message needs to be passed to the default dialog box procedure.

The second difference from standard window procedures is the addition of a new message, WM_INITDIALOG. Dialog box procedures perform any initialization of the controls during the processing of this message. Also, if the dialog box was created with *DialogBoxParam* or *DialogBoxIndirectParam*, the *lParam* value is the generic parameter passed during the call that created the dialog box. While it might seem that the controls could be initialized during the WM_CREATE message, that doesn't work. The problem is that during the WM_CREATE message, the controls on the dialog box haven't yet been created, so they can't be initialized. The WM_INITDIALOG message is sent after the controls have been created and before the dialog box is made visible, which is the perfect time to initialize the controls.

Here are a few other minor differences between a window procedure and a dialog box procedure. Most dialog box procedures don't need to process the WM_PAINT message because any necessary painting is done by the controls or, in the case of owner-draw controls, in response to control requests. Most of the code in a dialog box procedure is responding to WM_COMMAND messages from the controls. As with menus, the WM_COMMAND messages are parsed by the control ID values. Two special predefined ID values that a dialog box has to deal with are IDOK and IDCANCEL. IDOK is assigned to the OK button on the title bar of the dialog box while IDCANCEL is assigned to the Close button. In response to a click of either button, a dialog box procedure should call

```
BOOL EndDialog (HWND hDlg, int nResult);
```

EndDialog closes the dialog box and returns control to the caller of whatever function created the dialog box. The *hDlg* parameter is the handle of the dialog box while the *nResult* parameter is the value that's passed back as the return value of the function that created the dialog box.

The difference, of course, between handling the IDOK and IDCANCEL buttons is that if the OK button is clicked, the dialog box procedure should collect any relevant data from the dialog box controls to return to the calling procedure before it calls *EndDialog*.

A dialog box procedure to handle the GetVal template previously described is shown here:

```
//======================================================================
// GetVal Dialog procedure
//
BOOL CALLBACK GetValDlgProc (HWND hWnd, UINT wMsg, WPARAM wParam,
                             LPARAM lParam) {
    TCHAR szText[64];
    INT nVal, nBase;

    switch (wMsg) {
        case WM_INITDIALOG:
            SetDlgItemInt (hWnd, IDD_VALUE, 0, TRUE);
            SendDlgItemMessage (hWnd, IDD_VALUE, EM_LIMITTEXT,
                                sizeof (szText)-1, 0);
            CheckRadioButton (hWnd, IDD_DEC, IDD_HEX, IDD_DEC);
            return TRUE;

        case WM_COMMAND:
            switch (LOWORD (wParam)) {

                case IDD_HEX:
                    // See if Hex already checked.
```

```
        if (SendDlgItemMessage (hWnd, IDD_HEX,
                BM_GETSTATE, 0, 0) == BST_CHECKED)
            return TRUE;

        // Get text from edit control.
        GetDlgItemText (hWnd, IDD_VALUE, szText,
                        sizeof (szText));
        // Convert value from decimal, then set as hex.
        if (ConvertValue (szText, 10, &nVal)) {
            // If conversion successful, set new value.
            wsprintf (szText, TEXT ("%X"), nVal);
            SetDlgItemText (hWnd, IDD_VALUE, szText);
            // Set radio button.
            CheckRadioButton (hWnd, IDD_DEC, IDD_HEX,
                              IDD_HEX);
        } else {
            MessageBox (hWnd,
                        TEXT ("Value not valid"),
                        TEXT ("Error"), MB_OK);
        }
        return TRUE;

    case IDD_DEC:
        // See if Dec already checked.
        if (SendDlgItemMessage (hWnd, IDD_DEC,
                BM_GETSTATE, 0, 0) == BST_CHECKED)
            return TRUE;

        // Get text from edit control.
        GetDlgItemText (hWnd, IDD_VALUE, szText,
                        sizeof (szText));
        // Convert value from hex, then set as decimal.
        if (ConvertValue (szText, 16, &nVal)) {
            // If conversion successful, set new value.
            wsprintf (szText, TEXT ("%d"), nVal);
            SetDlgItemText (hWnd, IDD_VALUE, szText);
            // Set radio button.
            CheckRadioButton (hWnd, IDD_DEC, IDD_HEX,
                              IDD_DEC);
        } else {
            // If bad conversion, tell user.
            MessageBox (hWnd,
                        TEXT ("Value not valid"),
                        TEXT ("Error"), MB_OK);
        }
        return TRUE;
```

(continued)

```
                case IDOK:
                    // Get the current text.
                    GetDlgItemText (hWnd, IDD_VALUE, szText,
                                    sizeof (szText));
                    // See which radio button checked.
                    if (SendDlgItemMessage (hWnd, IDD_DEC,
                            BM_GETSTATE, 0, 0) == BST_CHECKED)
                        nBase = 10;
                    else
                        nBase = 16;
                    // Convert the string to a number.
                    if (ConvertValue (szText, nBase, &nVal))
                        EndDialog (hWnd, nVal);
                    else
                        MessageBox (hWnd,
                                    TEXT ("Value not valid"),
                                    TEXT ("Error"), MB_OK);
                    break;

                case IDCANCEL:
                    EndDialog (hWnd, 0);
                    return TRUE;
            }
        break;
    }
    return FALSE;
}
```

This is a typical example of a dialog box procedure for a simple dialog box. The only messages that are processed are the WM_INITDIALOG and WM_COMMAND messages. The WM_INITDIALOG message is used to initialize the edit control using a number passed, via *DialogBoxParam*, through to the *lParam* value. The radio button controls aren't auto radio buttons because the dialog box procedure needs to prevent the buttons from changing if the value in the entry field is invalid. The WM_COMMAND message is parsed by the control ID where the appropriate processing takes place. The IDOK and IDCANCEL buttons aren't in the dialog box template; as mentioned earlier, those buttons are placed by the dialog manager in the title bar of the dialog box.

Modeless Dialog Boxes

I've talked so far about modal dialog boxes that prevent the user from using other parts of the application before the dialog box is dismissed. Modeless dialog boxes, on the other hand, allow the user to work with other parts of the application while the dialog box is still open. Creating and using modeless dialog boxes requires a bit more work. For example, you create modeless dialog boxes using different functions than those for modal dialog boxes:

```
HWND CreateDialog (HINSTANCE hInstance, LPCTSTR lpTemplate,
                   HWND hWndOwner, DLGPROC lpDialogFunc);

HWND CreateDialogIndirect (HINSTANCE hInstance, LPCDLGTEMPLATE lpTemplate,
                           HWND hWndOwner, DLGPROC lpDialogFunc);

HWND CreateDialogIndirect (HINSTANCE hInstance,
                           LPCDLGTEMPLATE lpTemplate, HWND hWndOwner,
                           DLGPROC lpDialogFunc);
```

or

```
HWND CreateDialogIndirectParam (HINSTANCE hInstance,
                                LPCDLGTEMPLATE lpTemplate, HWND hWndOwner,
                                DLGPROC lpDialogFunc, LPARAM lParamInit);
```

The parameters in these functions mirror the creation functions for the modal dialog boxes with similar parameters. The difference is that these functions return immediately after creating the dialog boxes. Each function returns 0 if the create failed or returns the handle to the dialog box window if the create succeeded.

The handle returned after a successful creation is important because applications that use modeless dialog boxes must modify their message loop code to accommodate the dialog box. The new message loop should look similar to the following:

```
while (GetMessage (&msg, NULL, 0, 0)) {
    if ((hMlDlg == 0) || (!IsDialogMessage (hMlDlg, &msg))) {
        TranslateMessage (&msg);
        DispatchMessage (&msg);
    }
}
```

The difference from a modal dialog box message loop is that if the modeless dialog box is being displayed, messages should be checked to see whether they're dialog messages. If they're not dialog messages, your application forwards them to *TranslateMessage* and *DispatchMessage*. The code shown above simply checks to see whether the dialog box exists by checking a global variable containing the handle to the modeless dialog box and, if it's not 0, calls *IsDialogMessage*. If *IsDialogMessage* doesn't translate and dispatch the message itself, the message is sent to the standard *TranslateMessage/DispatchMessage* body of the message loop. Of course, this code assumes that the handle returned by *CreateDialog* (or whatever function creates the dialog box) is saved in *hMlDlg* and that *hMlDlg* is set to 0 when the dialog box is closed.

Another difference between modal and modeless dialog boxes is in the dialog box procedure. Instead of using *EndDialog* to close the dialog box, you must call *DestroyWindow* instead. This is because *EndDialog* is designed to work only with the internal message loop processing that's performed with a modal dialog box. Finally, an application usually won't want more than one instance of a modeless dialog box displayed at a time. An easy way to prevent this is to check the global copy of the window handle to see whether it's nonzero before calling *CreateDialog*. To do this, the dialog box procedure must set the global handle to 0 after it calls *DestroyWindow*.

Property Sheets

To the user, a property sheet is a dialog box with one or more tabs across the top that allow the user to switch among different "pages" of the dialog box. To the programmer, a property sheet is a series of stacked dialog boxes. Only the top dialog box is visible; the dialog manager is responsible for displaying the dialog box associated with the tab on which the user clicks. However you approach property sheets, they're invaluable given the limited screen size of Windows CE devices.

Each page of the property sheet, named appropriately enough a *property page*, is a dialog box template, either loaded from a resource or created dynamically in memory. Each property page has its own dialog box procedure. The frame around the property sheets is maintained by the dialog manager, so the advantages of property sheets come with little overhead to the programmer. Unlike the property sheets supported in other versions of Windows, the property sheets in Windows CE don't support the Apply button. Also, the OK and Cancel buttons for the property sheet are contained in the title bar, not positioned below the pages.

Creating a property sheet

Instead of using the dialog box creation functions to create a property sheet, a new function is used:

```
int PropertySheet (LPCPROPSHEETHEADER lppsph);
```

The *PropertySheet* function creates the property sheet according to the information contained in the PROPSHEETHEADER structure which is defined as the following:

```
typedef struct _PROPSHEETHEADER {
    DWORD dwSize;
    DWORD dwFlags;
    HWND hwndOwner;
    HINSTANCE hInstance;
```

```
    union {
        HICON hIcon;
        LPCWSTR pszIcon;
    };
    LPCWSTR pszCaption;
    UINT nPages;
    union {
        UINT nStartPage;
        LPCWSTR pStartPage;
    };
    union {
        LPCPROPSHEETPAGE ppsp;
        HPROPSHEETPAGE FAR *phpage;
    };
    PFNPROPSHEETCALLBACK pfnCallback;
} PROPSHEETHEADER;
```

Filling in this convoluted structure isn't as imposing a task as it might look. The *dwSize* field is the standard size field that must be initialized with the size of the structure. The *dwFlags* field contains the creation flags that define how the property sheet is created, which fields of the structure are valid, and how the property sheet behaves. Some of the flags indicate which fields in the structure are used. (I'll talk about those flags when I describe the other fields.) Two other flags set the behavior of the property sheet. The PSH_PROPTITLE flag appends the string "Properties" to the end of the caption specified in the *pszCaption* field. The PSH_MODELESS flag causes the *PropertySheet* function to create a modeless property sheet and immediately return. A modeless property sheet is like a modeless dialog box; it allows the user to switch back to the original window while the property sheet is still being displayed.

The next two fields are the handle of the owner window and the instance handle of the application. Neither the *hIcon* or *pszIcon* fields are used in Windows CE so they should be set to 0. The *pszCaption* field should point to the title bar text for the property sheet. The *nStartPage/pStartPage* union should be set to indicate the page that should be initially displayed. This can be selected either by number or by title if the PSH_USEPSTARTPAGE flag is set in the *dwFlags* field.

The *ppsp/phpage* union points to either an array of PROPSHEETPAGE structures describing each of the property pages or handles to previously created property pages. For either of these, the *nPages* field must be set to the number of entries of the array of structures or page handles. To indicate that the pointer points to an array of PROPSHEETPAGE structures, set the PSH_PROPSHEETPAGE flag in the *dwFlags* field. I'll describe both the structure and how to create individual pages shortly.

The *pfnCallBack* field is an optional pointer to a procedure that's called twice—when the property sheet is about to be created and again when it's about to be initialized. The callback function allows applications to fine-tune the appearance of the property sheet for the rare times when it's necessary. This field is ignored unless the PSP_USECALLBACK flag is set in the *dwFlags* field.

Creating a property page

As I mentioned earlier, individual property pages can be specified by an array of PROPSHEETPAGE structures or an array of handles to existing property pages. Creating a property page is accomplished with a call to the following:

```
HPROPSHEETPAGE CreatePropertySheetPage (LPCPROPSHEETPAGE lppsp);
```

This function is passed a pointer to the same PROPSHEETPAGE structure and returns a handle to a property page. PROPSHEETPAGE is defined as this:

```
typedef struct _PROPSHEETPAGE {
    DWORD dwSize;
    DWORD dwFlags;
    HINSTANCE hInstance;
    union {
        LPCSTR pszTemplate;
        LPCDLGTEMPLATE pResource;
    };
    union {
        HICON hIcon;
        LPCSTR pszIcon;
    };
    LPCSTR pszTitle;
    DLGPROC pfnDlgProc;
    LPARAM lParam;
    LPFNPSPCALLBACK pfnCallback;
    UINT FAR * pcRefParent;
} PROPSHEETPAGE;
```

The structure looks similar to the PROPSHEETHEADER structure, leading with a *dwSize* and *dwFlags* field followed by an *hInstance* field. In this structure, *hInstance* is the handle of the module from which the resources will be loaded. The *dwFlags* field again specifies which fields of the structure are used and how they're used, as well as a few flags specifying the characteristics of the page itself.

The *pszTemplate/pResource* union specifies the dialog box template used to define the page. If the PSP_DLGINDIRECT flag is set in the *dwFlags* field, the union points to a dialog box template in memory. Otherwise, the field specifies the name of a dialog box resource. The *hIcon/pszIcon* union isn't used in Windows CE and should be set to 0. If the *dwFlags* field contains a PSP_USETITLE flag, the *pszTitle* field points to the text used on the tab for the page. Otherwise, the tab text is taken from the caption field in the dialog box template. The *pfnDlgProc* field points to the dialog box procedure for this specific page and the *lParam* field is an application-defined parameter that can be used to pass data to the dialog box procedure. The *pfnCallback* field can point to a callback procedure that's called twice— when the page is about to be created and when it's about to be destroyed. Again, like the callback for the property sheet, the property page callback allows applications to fine-tune the page characteristics. This field is ignored unless the *dwFlags* field contains the PSP_USECALLBACK flag. Finally, the *pcRefCount* field can contain a pointer to an integer that will store a reference count for the page. This field is ignored unless the flags field contains the PSP_USEREFPARENT flag.

Windows CE supports a new flag for property pages, PSP_PREMATURE. This flag causes a property page to be created when the property sheet that owns it is created. Normally, a property page isn't created until the first time it's shown. This has an impact on property pages that communicate and cooperate with each other. Without the PSP_PREMATURE flag, the only property page that's automatically created when the property sheet is created is the page that is displayed first. So, at that moment, that first page has no sibling pages to communicate with. Using the PSP_PREMATURE flag, you can ensure that a page is created when the property sheet is created even though it isn't the first page in the sheet. While it's easy to get overwhelmed with all these structures, simply using the default values and not using the optional fields results in a powerful and easily maintainable property sheet that's also as easy to construct as a set of individual dialog boxes.

Once a property sheet has been created, the application can add and delete pages. The application adds a page by sending a PSM_ADDPAGE message to the property sheet window. The message must contain the handle of a previously created property page in *lParam*; *wParam* isn't used. Likewise, the application can remove a page by sending a PSM_REMOVEPAGE message to the property sheet window. The application specifies a page for deletion either by setting *wParam* to the zero-based index of the page selected for removal or by passing the handle to that page in *lParam*.

The code below creates a simple property sheet with three pages. Each of the pages references a dialog box template resource. As you can see, most of the initialization of the structures can be performed in a fairly mechanical fashion.

```
PROPSHEETHEADER psh;
PROPSHEETPAGE psp[3];
INT i;
```

(continued)

```
// Init page structures with generic information.
memset (&psp, 0, sizeof (psp));       // Zero out all unused values.
for (i = 0; i < dim(psp); i++) {
    psp[i].dwSize = sizeof (PROPSHEETPAGE);
    psp[i].dwFlags = PSP_DEFAULT;       // No special processing needed
    psp[i].hInstance = hInst;           // Instance handle where the
}                                       // dialog templates are located
// Now do the page specific stuff.
psp[0].pszTemplate = TEXT ("Page1"); // Name of dialog resource for page 1
psp[0].pfnDlgProc = Page1DlgProc;    // Pointer to dialog proc for page 1

psp[1].pszTemplate = TEXT ("Page2"); // Name of dialog resource for page 2
psp[1].pfnDlgProc = Page2DlgProc;    // Pointer to dialog proc for page 2

psp[2].pszTemplate = TEXT ("Page3"); // Name of dialog resource for page 3
psp[2].pfnDlgProc = Page3DlgProc;    // Pointer to dialog proc for page 3

// Init property sheet header structure.
psh.dwSize = sizeof (PROPSHEETHEADER);
psh.dwFlags = PSH_PROPSHEETPAGE;     // We are using templates not handles.
psh.hwndParent = hWnd;               // Handle of the owner window
psh.hInstance = hInst;               // Instance handle of the application
psh.pszCaption = TEXT ("Property sheet title");
psh.nPages = dim(psp);               // Number of pages
psh.nStartPage = 0;                  // Index of page to be shown first
psh.ppsp = psp;                      // Pointer to page structures
psh.pfnCallback = 0;                 // We don't need a callback procedure.

// Create property sheet.  This returns when the user dismisses the sheet
// by tapping OK or the Close button.
i = PropertySheet (&psh);
```

While this fragment has a fair amount of structure filling, it's boilerplate code. Everything not defined, such as the page dialog box resource templates and the page dialog box procedures, are required for dialog boxes as well as property sheets. So, aside from the boilerplate stuff, property sheets require little, if any, work beyond simple dialog boxes.

Property page procedures

The procedures that back up each of the property pages have only a few differences from standard dialog box procedures. First, as I mentioned previously, unless the PSP_PREMATURE flag is used, pages aren't created immediately when the property sheet is created. Instead, each page is created and WM_INITDIALOG messages are sent only when the page is initially shown. Also, the *lParam* parameter doesn't point to a user-defined parameter; instead, it points to the PROPSHEETPAGE structure that defined the page. Of course, that structure contains a user-definable value that can be used to pass data to the dialog box procedure.

Also, a property sheet procedure doesn't field the IDOK and IDCANCEL control IDs for the OK and Close buttons on a standard dialog box. These buttons instead are handled by the system-provided property sheet procedure that coordinates the display and management of each page. When the OK or Close button is tapped, the property sheet sends a WM_NOTIFY message to each sheet notifying them that one of the two buttons has been tapped and that they should acknowledge that it's okay to close the property sheet.

WM_NOTIFY

While this is the first time I've mentioned the WM_NOTIFY message, it has become a mainstay of the new common controls added to Windows over the last few years. The WM_NOTIFY message is essentially a redefined WM_COMMAND message, which instead of encoding the reason for the message in one of the parameters passes a pointer to an extensible structure instead. This has allowed the WM_NOTIFY message to be extended and adapted for each of the controls that use it. In the case of property sheets, the WM_NOTIFY message is sent under a number of conditions; when the user taps the OK button, when the user taps the Close button, when the page gains or loses focus from or to another page, or when the user requests help.

At a minimum, the WM_NOTIFY message is sent with *lParam* pointing to an NMHDR structure defined as the following:

```
typedef struct tagNMHDR {
    HWND hwndFrom;
    UINT idFrom;
    UINT code;
} NMHDR;
```

The *hwndFrom* field contains the handle of the window that sent the notify message. For property sheets, this is the property sheet window. The *idFrom* field contains the ID of the control if a control is sending the notification. Finally, the *code* field contains the notification code. While this basic structure doesn't contain any more information than the WM_COMMAND message, often this structure is extended with additional fields appended to the structure. The notification code then indicates what, if any, additional fields are appended to the notification structure.

Switching pages

When a user switches from one page to the next, the Dialog Manager sends a WM_NOTIFY message with the code PSN_KILLACTIVE to the page currently being displayed. The dialog box procedure should then validate the data on the page. If it's permissible for the user to change the page, the dialog box procedure should then set the return value of the window structure of the page to PSNRET_NOERROR and return TRUE. You set the PSNRET_NOERROR return field by calling *SetWindowLong* with DWL_MSGRESULT as in the following line of code:

```
SetWindowLong (hwndPage, DWL_MSGRESULT, PSNRET_NOERROR);
```

where *hwndPage* is the handle of the property sheet page. A page can keep focus by returning PSNRET_INVALID_NOCHANGEPAGE in the return field. Assuming a page has indicated that it's okay to lose focus, the page being switched to receives a PSN_SETACTIVE notification via a WM_NOTIFY message. The page can then accept the focus or specify another page that should receive the focus.

Closing a property sheet

When the user taps on the OK button, the property sheet procedure sends a WM_NOTIFY with the notification code PSN_KILLACTIVE to the page currently being displayed followed by a WM_NOTIFY with the notification code PSN_APPLY to each of the pages that has been created. Each page procedure should save any data from the page controls when it receives the PSN_APPLY notification code.

When the user clicks the Close button, a PSN_QUERYCANCEL notification is sent to the page procedure of the page currently being displayed. All this notification requires is that the page procedure return TRUE to prevent the close or FALSE to allow the close. A further notification, PSN_RESET, is then sent to all the pages that have been created, indicating that the property sheet is about to be destroyed.

Common Dialogs

In the early days of Windows, it was a rite of passage for a Windows developer to write his or her own File Open dialog box. A File Open dialog box is complex—it must display a list of the possible files from a specific directory, allow file navigation, and return a fully justified filename back to the application. While it was great for programmers to swap stories about how they struggled with their unique implementation of a File Open dialog, it was hard on the users. Users had to learn a different file open interface for every Windows application.

Windows now provides a set of common dialog boxes that perform typical functions, such as selecting a filename to open or save or picking a color. These standard dialog boxes (called *common dialogs*) serve two purposes. First, common dialogs lift from developers the burden of having to create these dialog boxes from scratch. Second, and just as important, common dialogs provide a common interface to the user across different applications. (These days, Windows programmers swap horror stories about learning COM.)

Windows CE 2.0 provides four common dialogs: File Open, Save As, Print, and Choose Color. Common dialogs, such as Find, Choose Font, and Page Setup, that are available under other versions of Windows aren't supported under Windows CE. Applications developed for Windows CE 1.0 or for the first release of the Palm-size PC must also do without the Print and Color common dialogs, but this isn't much of a sacrifice because neither color screens nor printing is supported on those systems.

The other advantage of the common dialogs is that they have a customized look for each platform while retaining the same programming interface. This makes it easy to use, say, the File Open dialog on both the H/PC and the Palm-size PC because the dialog box has the same interface on both systems even though the look of the dialog box is vastly different on the two platforms. Figure 4-7 shows the File Open dialog on the H/PC; Figure 4-8 shows the File Open dialog box on the Palm-size PC.

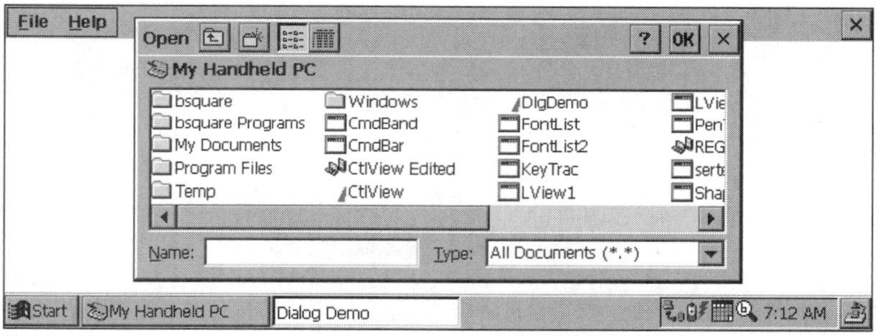

Figure 4-7. *The File Open dialog on a Handheld PC.*

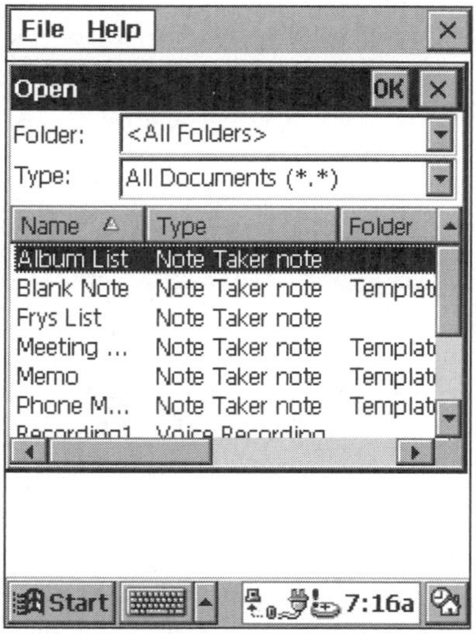

Figure 4-8. *The File Open dialog on a Palm-size PC.*

Instead of showing you how to use the common dialogs here, I'll let the next example program, DlgDemo, show you. That program demonstrates all four supported common dialog boxes.

The DlgDemo Example Program

The DlgDemo program demonstrates basic dialog boxes, modeless dialog boxes, property sheets, and common dialogs. When you start DlgDemo, it displays a window that shows the WM_COMMAND and WM_NOTIFY messages sent by the various controls in the dialogs, similar to the right side of the CtlView window. The different dialogs can be opened using the various menu items. Figure 4-9 shows the Dialog Demo window with the property sheet dialog displayed.

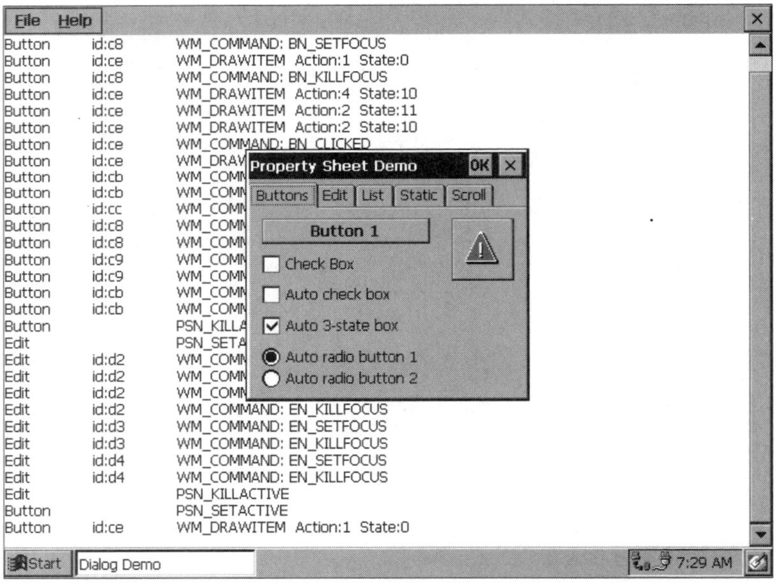

Figure 4-9. *The DlgDemo window.*

The basic dialog box is a simple "about box" launched by selecting the Help About menu. The property sheet is launched by selecting the File Property Sheet menu. The property sheet dialog contains five pages corresponding to the different windows in the CtlView example. The common dialog boxes are launched from the File Open, File Save, File Color, and File Print menu items. These last two menu items are disabled when the program is run on a Palm-size PC since those common dialog boxes aren't supported on that platform. The DlgDemo source code is shown in Figure 4-10.

DlgDemo.rc

```
//======================================================================
// Resource file
//
// Written for the book Programming Windows CE
// Copyright (C) 1998 Douglas Boling
//======================================================================

#include "windows.h"                 //
#include "DlgDemo.h"                 // Program-specific stuff

//----------------------------------------------------------------------
// Icons and bitmaps
//
ID_ICON      ICON   "DlgDemo.ico"    // Program icon
IDI_BTNICON  ICON   "btnicon.ico"    // Bitmap used in owner-draw button
statbmp      BITMAP "statbmp.bmp"    // Bitmap used in static window

//----------------------------------------------------------------------
// Menu
//
ID_MENU MENU DISCARDABLE
BEGIN
    POPUP "&File"
    BEGIN
        MENUITEM "Open...",                     IDM_OPEN
        MENUITEM "Save...",                     IDM_SAVE
        MENUITEM SEPARATOR
        MENUITEM "Color...",                    IDM_COLOR
        MENUITEM "Print...",                    IDM_PRINT
        MENUITEM SEPARATOR
        MENUITEM "Property Sheet",              IDM_SHOWPROPSHEET
        MENUITEM "Modeless Dialog",             IDM_SHOWMODELESS
        MENUITEM SEPARATOR
        MENUITEM "E&xit",                       IDM_EXIT
    END
    POPUP "&Help"
    BEGIN
        MENUITEM "&About...",                   IDM_ABOUT
    END
END

//----------------------------------------------------------------------
// Property page templates
//
```

Figure 4-10. *The DlgDemo program.* *(continued)*

Figure 4-10. *continued*

```
ID_BTNPAGE DIALOG discardable 0, 0, 125,  90
CAPTION "Buttons"
BEGIN
    PUSHBUTTON "Button 1",              IDC_PUSHBTN,   5,   5,  80,  12,
                                            WS_TABSTOP | BS_NOTIFY
    CHECKBOX "Check Box",               IDC_CHKBOX,   5,  20,  80,  12,
                                            WS_TABSTOP | BS_NOTIFY
    AUTOCHECKBOX "Auto check box"       IDC_ACHKBOX,   5,  35,  80,  12,
                                            WS_TABSTOP
    AUTO3STATE "Auto 3-state box",      IDC_A3STBOX,   5,  50,  80,  12,
                                            WS_TABSTOP
    AUTORADIOBUTTON "Auto radio button 1",
                                        IDC_RADIO1,    5,  65,  80,  12,
                                            WS_TABSTOP | WS_GROUP
    AUTORADIOBUTTON "Auto radio button 2",
                                        IDC_RADIO2,    5,  75,  80,  12
    PUSHBUTTON "",                      IDC_OWNRDRAW, 95,   5,  30,  30,
                                            BS_OWNERDRAW
END

ID_EDITPAGE DIALOG discardable 0, 0,  80,  80
CAPTION "Edit"
BEGIN
    EDITTEXT                         IDC_SINGLELINE,   5,   5,  70,  12,
                                            WS_TABSTOP
    EDITTEXT                         IDC_MULTILINE,    5,  20,  70,  40,
                                            WS_TABSTOP | ES_MULTILINE
    EDITTEXT                         IDC_PASSBOX,      5,  65,  70,  12,
                                            WS_TABSTOP | ES_PASSWORD
END

ID_LISTPAGE DIALOG discardable 0, 0,  125,  80
CAPTION "List"
BEGIN
    COMBOBOX                   IDC_COMBOBOX,      5,   5,  70,  60,
                                            WS_TABSTOP | CBS_DROPDOWN
    LISTBOX                    IDC_SNGLELIST,   5,  20,  50,  60,
                                            WS_TABSTOP
    LISTBOX                    IDC_MULTILIST,  60,  20,  50,  60,
                                            WS_TABSTOP | LBS_EXTENDEDSEL
END

ID_STATPAGE DIALOG discardable 0, 0, 130,  80
CAPTION "Static"
BEGIN
    LTEXT "Left text",               IDC_LEFTTEXT,    5,   5,  70,  20
    RTEXT "Right text",              IDC_RIGHTTEXT,   5,  30,  70,  20
```

```
    CTEXT "Center text",            IDC_CENTERTEXT,  5,  55,  70,  20,
                                           WS_BORDER
    ICON IDI_BTNICON                IDC_ICONCTL,    95,   5,  32,  32
    CONTROL "statbmp",              IDC_BITMAPCTL,  "static", SS_BITMAP,
                                                    95,  40,  32,  32
END

ID_SCROLLPAGE DIALOG discardable 0, 0,  60,  80
CAPTION "Scroll"
BEGIN
    SCROLLBAR                       IDC_LRSCROLL,   5,   5,  70,  12,
                                           WS_TABSTOP
    SCROLLBAR                       IDC_UDSCROLL,  80,   5,  12,  70,
                                           WS_TABSTOP | SBS_VERT
END
//----------------------------------------------------------------------
// Clear list modeless dialog box template.
//
Clearbox DIALOG discardable 60, 10,  70, 30
STYLE  WS_POPUP | WS_VISIBLE | WS_CAPTION | WS_SYSMENU | DS_MODALFRAME
CAPTION "Clear"
BEGIN
    DEFPUSHBUTTON "Clear Listbox"
                        IDD_CLEAR,   5,   5,  60,   20
END
//----------------------------------------------------------------------
// About box dialog box template
//
aboutbox DIALOG discardable 10, 10, 132, 40
STYLE  WS_POPUP | WS_VISIBLE | WS_CAPTION | WS_SYSMENU | DS_CENTER |
       DS_MODALFRAME
CAPTION "About"
BEGIN
    ICON    ID_ICON                   -1,   5,   5,   0,  0

    LTEXT "DlgDemo - Written for the book Programming Windows \
           CE Copyright 1998 Douglas Boling"
                                      -1,  28,   5, 100,  30
END
```

DlgDemo.h

```
//======================================================================
// Header file
//
// Written for the book Programming Windows CE
```

(continued)

Figure 4-10. *continued*

```
// Copyright (C) 1998 Douglas Boling
//======================================================================
// Returns number of elements
#define dim(x) (sizeof(x) / sizeof(x[0]))

//----------------------------------------------------------------------
// Generic defines and data types
//
struct decodeUINT {                             // Structure associates
    UINT Code;                                  // messages
                                                // with a function.
    LRESULT (*Fxn)(HWND, UINT, WPARAM, LPARAM);
};
struct decodeCMD {                              // Structure associates
    UINT Code;                                  // menu IDs with a
    LRESULT (*Fxn)(HWND, WORD, HWND, WORD);     // function.
};

//----------------------------------------------------------------------
// Generic defines used by application
#define  IDC_CMDBAR   1                         // Command bar ID
#define  IDC_RPTLIST  2                         // ID for report list box

#define  ID_ICON             10                 // Icon resource ID
#define  ID_MENU             11                 // Main menu resource ID

// Menu item IDs
#define  IDM_OPEN            100
#define  IDM_SAVE            101
#define  IDM_COLOR           102
#define  IDM_PRINT           103
#define  IDM_SHOWPROPSHEET   104
#define  IDM_SHOWMODELESS    105
#define  IDM_EXIT            106

#define  IDM_ABOUT           110

#define  IDI_BTNICON         120

// Identifiers for the property page resources
#define  ID_BTNPAGE          50
#define  ID_EDITPAGE         51
#define  ID_LISTPAGE         52
#define  ID_STATPAGE         53
#define  ID_SCROLLPAGE       54
```

```
// Button window defines
#define  IDC_PUSHBTN        200
#define  IDC_CHKBOX         201
#define  IDC_ACHKBOX        202
#define  IDC_A3STBOX        203
#define  IDC_RADIO1         204
#define  IDC_RADIO2         205
#define  IDC_OWNRDRAW       206

// Edit window defines
#define  IDC_SINGLELINE     210
#define  IDC_MULTILINE      211
#define  IDC_PASSBOX        212

// List box window defines
#define  IDC_COMBOBOX       220
#define  IDC_SNGLELIST      221
#define  IDC_MULTILIST      222

// Static control window defines
#define  IDC_LEFTTEXT       230
#define  IDC_RIGHTTEXT      231
#define  IDC_CENTERTEXT     232
#define  IDC_ICONCTL        233
#define  IDC_BITMAPCTL      234

// Scroll bar window defines
#define  IDC_LRSCROLL       240
#define  IDC_UDSCROLL       241

// Control IDs for modeless dialog box
#define  IDD_CLEAR          500

// User-defined message to add a line to the window
#define MYMSG_ADDLINE   (WM_USER + 10)

//----------------------------------------------------------------------
// Program-specific structures
//
typedef struct {
    TCHAR *pszLabel;
    DWORD wNotification;
} NOTELABELS, *PNOTELABELS;
```

(continued)

Figure 4-10. *continued*

```
//----------------------------------------------------------------------
// Function prototypes
//
int InitApp (HINSTANCE);
HWND InitInstance (HINSTANCE, LPWSTR, int);
int TermInstance (HINSTANCE, int);

// Window procedures
LRESULT CALLBACK MainWndProc (HWND, UINT, WPARAM, LPARAM);

// Message handlers
LRESULT DoCreateMain (HWND, UINT, WPARAM, LPARAM);
LRESULT DoCommandMain (HWND, UINT, WPARAM, LPARAM);
LRESULT DoAddLineMain (HWND, UINT, WPARAM, LPARAM);
LRESULT DoDestroyMain (HWND, UINT, WPARAM, LPARAM);

// Command functions
LPARAM DoMainCommandOpen (HWND, WORD, HWND, WORD);
LPARAM DoMainCommandSave (HWND, WORD, HWND, WORD);
LPARAM DoMainCommandColor (HWND, WORD, HWND, WORD);
LPARAM DoMainCommandPrint (HWND, WORD, HWND, WORD);
LPARAM DoMainCommandShowProp (HWND, WORD, HWND, WORD);
LPARAM DoMainCommandModeless (HWND, WORD, HWND, WORD);
LPARAM DoMainCommandExit (HWND, WORD, HWND, WORD);
LPARAM DoMainCommandAbout (HWND, WORD, HWND, WORD);

// Dialog box procedures
BOOL CALLBACK BtnDlgProc (HWND, UINT, WPARAM, LPARAM);
BOOL CALLBACK EditDlgProc (HWND, UINT, WPARAM, LPARAM);
BOOL CALLBACK ListDlgProc (HWND, UINT, WPARAM, LPARAM);
BOOL CALLBACK StaticDlgProc (HWND, UINT, WPARAM, LPARAM);
BOOL CALLBACK ScrollDlgProc (HWND, UINT, WPARAM, LPARAM);
BOOL CALLBACK AboutDlgProc (HWND, UINT, WPARAM, LPARAM);
BOOL CALLBACK ModelessDlgProc (HWND, UINT, WPARAM, LPARAM);
```

DlgDemo.c

```
//======================================================================
// DlgDemo - Dialog box demonstration
//
// Written for the book Programming Windows CE
// Copyright (C) 1998 Douglas Boling
//======================================================================
#include <windows.h>                 // For all that Windows stuff
#include <commctrl.h>                // Command bar includes
```

```
#include <commdlg.h>                  // Common dialog box includes
#include <prsht.h>                    // Property sheet includes

#include "DlgDemo.h"                  // Program-specific stuff

//----------------------------------------------------------------------
// Global data
//
const TCHAR szAppName[] = TEXT ("DlgDemo");
HINSTANCE hInst;                      // Program instance handle
HWND g_hwndMlDlg = 0;                 // Handle to modeless dialog box

HINSTANCE hLib = 0;                   // Handle to CommDlg lib
FARPROC lpfnChooseColor = 0;          // Ptr to color common dialog fn
FARPROC lpfnPrintDlg = 0;             // Ptr to print common dialog fn

// Message dispatch table for MainWindowProc
const struct decodeUINT MainMessages[] = {
    WM_CREATE, DoCreateMain,
    WM_COMMAND, DoCommandMain,
    MYMSG_ADDLINE, DoAddLineMain,
    WM_DESTROY, DoDestroyMain,
};

// Command message dispatch for MainWindowProc
const struct decodeCMD MainCommandItems[] = {
    IDM_OPEN, DoMainCommandOpen,
    IDM_SAVE, DoMainCommandSave,
    IDM_SHOWPROPSHEET, DoMainCommandShowProp,
    IDM_SHOWMODELESS, DoMainCommandModeless,
    IDM_COLOR, DoMainCommandColor,
    IDM_PRINT, DoMainCommandPrint,
    IDM_EXIT, DoMainCommandExit,
    IDM_ABOUT, DoMainCommandAbout,
};
//
// Labels for WM_NOTIFY notifications
//
NOTELABELS nlPropPage[] = {{TEXT ("PSN_SETACTIVE  "), (PSN_FIRST-0)},
                           {TEXT ("PSN_KILLACTIVE "), (PSN_FIRST-1)},
                           {TEXT ("PSN_APPLY      "), (PSN_FIRST-2)},
                           {TEXT ("PSN_RESET      "), (PSN_FIRST-3)},
                           {TEXT ("PSN_HASHELP    "), (PSN_FIRST-4)},
                           {TEXT ("PSN_HELP       "), (PSN_FIRST-5)},
                           {TEXT ("PSN_WIZBACK    "), (PSN_FIRST-6)},
                           {TEXT ("PSN_WIZNEXT    "), (PSN_FIRST-7)},
```

(continued)

Figure 4-10. *continued*

```
                              {TEXT ("PSN_WIZFINISH  "), (PSN_FIRST-8)},
                              {TEXT ("PSN_QUERYCANCEL"), (PSN_FIRST-9)},
};
int nPropPageSize = dim(nlPropPage);

// Labels for the property pages
TCHAR *szPages[] = {TEXT ("Button"),
                    TEXT ("Edit  "),
                    TEXT ("List  "),
                    TEXT ("Static"),
                    TEXT ("Scroll"),
};
//======================================================================
// Program entry point
//
HWND hwndMain;

int WINAPI WinMain (HINSTANCE hInstance, HINSTANCE hPrevInstance,
                    LPWSTR lpCmdLine, int nCmdShow) {
    MSG msg;
    int rc = 0;

    // Initialize application.
    rc = InitApp (hInstance);
    if (rc) return rc;

    // Initialize this instance.
    hwndMain = InitInstance (hInstance, lpCmdLine, nCmdShow);
    if (hwndMain == 0)
        return 0x10;

    // Application message loop
    while (GetMessage (&msg, NULL, 0, 0)) {
        // If modeless dialog box is created, let it have
        // the first crack at the message.
        if ((g_hwndMlDlg == 0) ||
            (!IsDialogMessage (g_hwndMlDlg, &msg))) {
            TranslateMessage (&msg);
            DispatchMessage (&msg);
        }
    }
    // Instance cleanup
    return TermInstance (hInstance, msg.wParam);
}
//----------------------------------------------------------------------
```

```
// InitApp - Application initialization
//
int InitApp (HINSTANCE hInstance) {
    WNDCLASS wc;

    // Register application main window class.
    wc.style = 0;                             // Window style
    wc.lpfnWndProc = MainWndProc;             // Callback function
    wc.cbClsExtra = 0;                        // Extra class data
    wc.cbWndExtra = 0;                        // Extra window data
    wc.hInstance = hInstance;                 // Owner handle
    wc.hIcon = NULL,                          // Application icon
    wc.hCursor = NULL;                        // Default cursor
    wc.hbrBackground = (HBRUSH) GetStockObject (WHITE_BRUSH);
    wc.lpszMenuName =  NULL;                  // Menu name
    wc.lpszClassName = szAppName;             // Window class name

    if (RegisterClass (&wc) == 0) return 1;

    // Get the Color and print dialog function pointers.
    hLib = LoadLibrary (TEXT ("COMMDLG.DLL"));
    if (hLib) {
        lpfnChooseColor = GetProcAddress (hLib, TEXT ("ChooseColor"));
        lpfnPrintDlg = GetProcAddress (hLib, TEXT ("PrintDlg"));
    }
    return 0;
}
//----------------------------------------------------------------------
// InitInstance - Instance initialization
//
HWND InitInstance (HINSTANCE hInstance, LPWSTR lpCmdLine,
                   int nCmdShow) {
    HWND hWnd;

    // Save program instance handle in global variable.
    hInst = hInstance;

    // Create main window.
    hWnd = CreateWindow (szAppName,           // Window class
                         TEXT ("Dialog Demo"), // Window title
                         WS_VISIBLE,          // Style flags
                         CW_USEDEFAULT,       // x position
                         CW_USEDEFAULT,       // y position
                         CW_USEDEFAULT,       // Initial width
                         CW_USEDEFAULT,       // Initial height
                         NULL,                // Parent
```

(continued)

Figure 4-10. *continued*

```
                          NULL,                      // Menu, must be null
                          hInstance,                 // Application instance
                          NULL);                     // Pointer to create
                                                     // parameters
    // Return fail code if window not created.
    if (!IsWindow (hWnd)) return 0;

    // Standard show and update calls
    ShowWindow (hWnd, nCmdShow);
    UpdateWindow (hWnd);
    return hWnd;
}
//----------------------------------------------------------------------
// TermInstance - Program cleanup
//
int TermInstance (HINSTANCE hInstance, int nDefRC) {
    if (hLib)
        FreeLibrary (hLib);
    return nDefRC;
}
//======================================================================
// Message-handling procedures for MainWindow
//
//----------------------------------------------------------------------
// MainWndProc - Callback function for application window
//
LRESULT CALLBACK MainWndProc (HWND hWnd, UINT wMsg, WPARAM wParam,
                              LPARAM lParam) {
    INT i;
    //
    // Search message list to see if we need to handle this
    // message.  If in list, call procedure.
    //
    for (i = 0; i < dim(MainMessages); i++) {
        if (wMsg == MainMessages[i].Code)
            return (*MainMessages[i].Fxn)(hWnd, wMsg, wParam, lParam);
    }
    return DefWindowProc (hWnd, wMsg, wParam, lParam);
}
//----------------------------------------------------------------------
// DoCreateMain - Process WM_CREATE message for window.
//
LRESULT DoCreateMain (HWND hWnd, UINT wMsg, WPARAM wParam,
                      LPARAM lParam) {
    HWND hwndCB, hwndChild;
```

```
    INT i, nHeight;
    LPCREATESTRUCT lpcs;
    HMENU hMenu;

    // Convert lParam into pointer to create structure.
    lpcs = (LPCREATESTRUCT) lParam;

    // Create a command bar.
    hwndCB = CommandBar_Create (hInst, hWnd, IDC_CMDBAR);
    // Add the menu.
    CommandBar_InsertMenubar (hwndCB, hInst, ID_MENU, 0);
    // Add exit button to command bar.
    CommandBar_AddAdornments (hwndCB, 0, 0);

    // See color and print functions not found, disable menus.
    hMenu = CommandBar_GetMenu (hwndCB, 0);
    if (!lpfnChooseColor)
        EnableMenuItem (hMenu, IDM_COLOR, MF_BYCOMMAND | MF_GRAYED);
    if (!lpfnPrintDlg)
        EnableMenuItem (hMenu, IDM_PRINT, MF_BYCOMMAND | MF_GRAYED);

    nHeight = CommandBar_Height (hwndCB);
    //
    // Create report window.  Size it so that it fits under
    // the command bar and fills the remaining client area.
    //
    hwndChild = CreateWindowEx (0, TEXT ("listbox"),
                         TEXT (""), WS_VISIBLE | WS_CHILD | WS_VSCROLL |
                         LBS_USETABSTOPS | LBS_NOINTEGRALHEIGHT, 0,
                         nHeight, lpcs->cx, lpcs->cy - nHeight,
                         hWnd, (HMENU)IDC_RPTLIST,
                         lpcs->hInstance, NULL);

    // Destroy frame if window not created.
    if (!IsWindow (hwndChild)) {
        DestroyWindow (hWnd);
        return 0;
    }
    // Initialize tab stops for display list box.
    i = 40;
    SendMessage (hwndChild, LB_SETTABSTOPS, 1, (LPARAM)&i);
    return 0;
}
//----------------------------------------------------------------------
// DoCommandMain - Process WM_COMMAND message for window.
```

(continued)

Figure 4-10. *continued*

```
//
LRESULT DoCommandMain (HWND hWnd, UINT wMsg, WPARAM wParam,
                       LPARAM lParam) {
    WORD idItem, wNotifyCode;
    HWND hwndCtl;
    INT  i;

    // Parse the parameters.
    idItem = (WORD) LOWORD (wParam);
    wNotifyCode = (WORD) HIWORD (wParam);
    hwndCtl = (HWND) lParam;

    // Call routine to handle control message.
    for (i = 0; i < dim(MainCommandItems); i++) {
        if (idItem == MainCommandItems[i].Code)
            return (*MainCommandItems[i].Fxn)(hWnd, idItem, hwndCtl,
                         wNotifyCode);
    }
    return 0;
}
//----------------------------------------------------------------------
// DoAddLineMain - Process MYMSG_ADDLINE message for window.
//
LRESULT DoAddLineMain (HWND hWnd, UINT wMsg, WPARAM wParam,
                       LPARAM lParam) {
    TCHAR szOut[128];
    INT i;

    // If nothing in wParam, just fill in spaces.
    if (wParam == -1) {
        // Print message only.
        lstrcpy (szOut, (LPTSTR)lParam);
    } else {
        // If no ID val, ignore that field.
        if (LOWORD (wParam) == 0xffff)
            // Print prop page and message.
            wsprintf (szOut, TEXT ("%s \t       \t %s"),
                      szPages[HIWORD (wParam) - ID_BTNPAGE],
                      (LPTSTR)lParam);
        else
            // Print property page, control ID, and message.
            wsprintf (szOut, TEXT ("%s \t id:%x \t %s"),
                      szPages[HIWORD (wParam) - ID_BTNPAGE],
                      LOWORD (wParam), (LPTSTR)lParam);
    }
```

```
    i = SendDlgItemMessage (hWnd, IDC_RPTLIST, LB_ADDSTRING, 0,
                            (LPARAM)(LPCTSTR)szOut);

    if (i != LB_ERR)
        SendDlgItemMessage (hWnd, IDC_RPTLIST, LB_SETTOPINDEX, i,
                            (LPARAM)(LPCTSTR)szOut);
    return 0;
}
//----------------------------------------------------------------------
// DoDestroyMain - Process WM_DESTROY message for window.
//
LRESULT DoDestroyMain (HWND hWnd, UINT wMsg, WPARAM wParam,
                       LPARAM lParam) {
    PostQuitMessage (0);
    return 0;
}
//======================================================================
// Command handler routines
//----------------------------------------------------------------------
// DoMainCommandOpen - Process File Open command
//
LPARAM DoMainCommandOpen (HWND hWnd, WORD idItem, HWND hwndCtl,
                          WORD wNotifyCode) {
    OPENFILENAME of;
    TCHAR szFileName [MAX_PATH] = {0};
    const LPTSTR pszOpenFilter = TEXT ("All Documents (*.*)\0*.*\0\0");
    TCHAR szOut[128];
    INT rc;

    // Initialize filename.
    szFileName[0] = '\0';

    // Initialize File Open structure.
    memset (&of, 0, sizeof (of));

    of.lStructSize = sizeof (of);
    of.hwndOwner = hWnd;
    of.lpstrFile = szFileName;
    of.nMaxFile = dim(szFileName);
    of.lpstrFilter = pszOpenFilter;
    of.Flags = 0;

    rc = GetOpenFileName (&of);
```

(continued)

Figure 4-10. *continued*

```
    wsprintf (szOut,
              TEXT ("GetOpenFileName returned: %x, filename: %s"),
              rc, szFileName);
    SendMessage (hWnd, MYMSG_ADDLINE, -1, (LPARAM)szOut);
    return 0;
}
//----------------------------------------------------------------------
// DoMainCommandSave - Process File Save command.
//
LPARAM DoMainCommandSave (HWND hWnd, WORD idItem, HWND hwndCtl,
                          WORD wNotifyCode) {
    OPENFILENAME of;
    TCHAR szFileName [MAX_PATH] = {0};
    const LPTSTR pszOpenFilter = TEXT ("All Documents (*.*)\0*.*\0\0");
    TCHAR szOut[128];
    INT rc;

    // Initialize filename.
    szFileName[0] = '\0';

    // Initialize File Open structure.
    memset (&of, 0, sizeof (of));

    of.lStructSize = sizeof (of);
    of.hwndOwner = hWnd;
    of.lpstrFile = szFileName;
    of.nMaxFile = dim(szFileName);
    of.lpstrFilter = pszOpenFilter;
    of.Flags = 0;

    rc = GetSaveFileName (&of);

    wsprintf (szOut,
              TEXT ("GetSaveFileName returned: %x, filename: %s"),
              rc, szFileName);
    SendMessage (hWnd, MYMSG_ADDLINE, -1, (LPARAM)szOut);
    return 0;
}
//----------------------------------------------------------------------
// DoMainCommandColor - Process File Color command.
//
LPARAM DoMainCommandColor (HWND hWnd, WORD idItem, HWND hwndCtl,
                           WORD wNotifyCode) {
    CHOOSECOLOR cc;
    static COLORREF cr[16];
    TCHAR szOut[128];
    INT rc;
```

```
    // Initialize color structure.
    memset (&cc, 0, sizeof (cc));
    memset (&cr, 0, sizeof (cr));

    cc.lStructSize = sizeof (cc);
    cc.hwndOwner = hWnd;
    cc.hInstance = hInst;
    cc.rgbResult = RGB (0, 0, 0);
    cc.lpCustColors = cr;
    cc.Flags = CC_ANYCOLOR;

    rc = (lpfnChooseColor) (&cc);

    wsprintf (szOut, TEXT ("Choose Color returned: %x, color: %x"),
              rc, cc.rgbResult);
    SendMessage (hWnd, MYMSG_ADDLINE, -1, (LPARAM)szOut);
    return 0;
}
//----------------------------------------------------------------------
// DoMainCommandPrint - Process File Print command.
//
LPARAM DoMainCommandPrint (HWND hWnd, WORD idItem, HWND hwndCtl,
                           WORD wNotifyCode) {
    PRINTDLG pd;
    INT rc;

    // Initialize print structure.
    memset (&pd, 0, sizeof (pd));

    pd.cbStruct = sizeof (pd);
    pd.hwndOwner = hWnd;
    pd.dwFlags = PD_SELECTALLPAGES;

    rc = (lpfnPrintDlg) (&pd);

    return 0;
}
//----------------------------------------------------------------------
// DoMainCommandShowProp - Process show property sheet command.
//
LPARAM DoMainCommandShowProp(HWND hWnd, WORD idItem, HWND hwndCtl,
                             WORD wNotifyCode) {

    PROPSHEETPAGE psp[5];
    PROPSHEETHEADER psh;
    INT i;
```

(continued)

Figure 4-10. *continued*

```
    // Zero all the property page structures.
    memset (&psp, 0, sizeof (psp));
    // Fill in default values in property page structures.
    for (i = 0; i < dim(psp); i++) {
        psp[i].dwSize = sizeof (PROPSHEETPAGE);
        psp[i].dwFlags = PSP_DEFAULT;
        psp[i].hInstance = hInst;
        psp[i].lParam = (LPARAM)hWnd;
    }
    // Set the dialog box templates for each page.
    psp[0].pszTemplate = MAKEINTRESOURCE (ID_BTNPAGE);
    psp[1].pszTemplate = MAKEINTRESOURCE (ID_EDITPAGE);
    psp[2].pszTemplate = MAKEINTRESOURCE (ID_LISTPAGE);
    psp[3].pszTemplate = MAKEINTRESOURCE (ID_STATPAGE);
    psp[4].pszTemplate = MAKEINTRESOURCE (ID_SCROLLPAGE);

    // Set the dialog box procedures for each page.
    psp[0].pfnDlgProc = BtnDlgProc;
    psp[1].pfnDlgProc = EditDlgProc;
    psp[2].pfnDlgProc = ListDlgProc;
    psp[3].pfnDlgProc = StaticDlgProc;
    psp[4].pfnDlgProc = ScrollDlgProc;

    // Initialize property sheet structure.
    psh.dwSize = sizeof (PROPSHEETHEADER);
    psh.dwFlags = PSH_PROPSHEETPAGE;
    psh.hwndParent = hWnd;
    psh.hInstance = hInst;
    psh.pszCaption = TEXT ("Property Sheet Demo");
    psh.nPages = dim(psp);
    psh.nStartPage = 0;
    psh.ppsp = psp;
    psh.pfnCallback = 0;

    // Create and display property sheet.
    i = PropertySheet (&psh);
    return 0;
}
//----------------------------------------------------------------------
// DoMainCommandModelessDlg - Process the File Modeless menu command.
//
LPARAM DoMainCommandModeless(HWND hWnd, WORD idItem, HWND hwndCtl,
                             WORD wNotifyCode) {
```

```
    // Only create dialog box if not already created.
    if (g_hwndMlDlg == 0)
        // Use CreateDialog to create modeless dialog box.
        g_hwndMlDlg = CreateDialog (hInst, TEXT ("Clearbox"), hWnd,
                                    ModelessDlgProc);
    return 0;
}
//----------------------------------------------------------------------
// DoMainCommandExit - Process Program Exit command.
//
LPARAM DoMainCommandExit (HWND hWnd, WORD idItem, HWND hwndCtl,
                          WORD wNotifyCode) {

    SendMessage (hWnd, WM_CLOSE, 0, 0);
    return 0;
}
//----------------------------------------------------------------------
// DoMainCommandAbout - Process the Help About menu command.
//
LPARAM DoMainCommandAbout(HWND hWnd, WORD idItem, HWND hwndCtl,
                          WORD wNotifyCode) {

    // Use DialogBox to create modal dialog box.
    DialogBox (hInst, TEXT ("aboutbox"), hWnd, AboutDlgProc);
    return 0;
}
//======================================================================
// Modeless ClearList dialog box procedure.
//
BOOL CALLBACK ModelessDlgProc (HWND hWnd, UINT wMsg, WPARAM wParam,
                               LPARAM lParam) {

    switch (wMsg) {
        case WM_COMMAND:
            switch (LOWORD (wParam)) {
                case IDD_CLEAR:
                    // Send message to list box to clear it.
                    SendDlgItemMessage (GetWindow (hWnd, GW_OWNER),
                                        IDC_RPTLIST,
                                        LB_RESETCONTENT, 0, 0);
                    return TRUE;

                case IDOK:
                case IDCANCEL:
                    // Modeless dialog boxes can't use EndDialog.
                    DestroyWindow (hWnd);
```

(continued)

Figure 4-10. *continued*

```
                    // Set hwnd value to zero to indicate that
                    // the dialog box is destroyed.
                    g_hwndMlDlg = 0;
                    return TRUE;
            }
        break;
    }
    return FALSE;
}
//======================================================================
// About dialog box procedure
//
BOOL CALLBACK AboutDlgProc (HWND hWnd, UINT wMsg, WPARAM wParam,
                            LPARAM lParam) {

    switch (wMsg) {
        case WM_COMMAND:
            switch (LOWORD (wParam)) {
                case IDOK:
                case IDCANCEL:
                    EndDialog (hWnd, 0);
                    return TRUE;
            }
        break;
    }
    return FALSE;
}
```

BtnDlg.c

```
//======================================================================
// BtnDlg - Button dialog box window code
//
// Written for the book Programming Windows CE
// Copyright (C) 1998 Douglas Boling
//======================================================================
#include <windows.h>                // For all that Windows stuff
#include <prsht.h>                  // Property sheet includes
#include "DlgDemo.h"                // Program-specific stuff

extern HINSTANCE hInst;

LRESULT DrawButton (HWND hWnd, LPDRAWITEMSTRUCT pdi);
//----------------------------------------------------------------------
// Global data
```

```
//
// Identification strings for various WM_COMMAND notifications
NOTELABELS nlBtn[] = {{TEXT ("BN_CLICKED "),       0},
                      {TEXT ("BN_PAINT   "),       1},
                      {TEXT ("BN_HILITE  "),       2},
                      {TEXT ("BN_UNHILITE"),       3},
                      {TEXT ("BN_DISABLE "),       4},
                      {TEXT ("BN_DOUBLECLICKED"), 5},
                      {TEXT ("BN_SETFOCUS "),      6},
                      {TEXT ("BN_KILLFOCUS"),      7}
};
extern NOTELABELS nlPropPage[];
extern int nPropPageSize;

// Handle for icon used in owner-draw icon
HICON hIcon = 0;
//======================================================================
// BtnDlgProc - Button page dialog box procedure
//
BOOL CALLBACK BtnDlgProc (HWND hWnd, UINT wMsg, WPARAM wParam,
                          LPARAM lParam) {
    TCHAR szOut[128];
    HWND hwndMain;
    INT i;

    switch (wMsg) {

        case WM_INITDIALOG:
            // The generic parameter contains the
            // top-level window handle.
            hwndMain = (HWND)((LPPROPSHEETPAGE)lParam)->lParam;
            // Save the window handle in the window structure.
            SetWindowLong (hWnd, DWL_USER, (LONG)hwndMain);

            // Load icon for owner-draw window.
            hIcon = LoadIcon (hInst, MAKEINTRESOURCE (IDI_BTNICON));

            // We need to set the initial state of the radio buttons.
            CheckRadioButton (hWnd, IDC_RADIO1, IDC_RADIO2, IDC_RADIO1);
            return TRUE;
        //
        // Reflect WM_COMMAND messages to main window.
        //
        case WM_COMMAND:
            // Since the check box is not an auto check box, the button
            // has to be set manually.
```

(continued)

Figure 4-10. *continued*

```
        if ((LOWORD (wParam) == IDC_CHKBOX) &&
            (HIWORD (wParam) == BN_CLICKED)) {
            // Get the current state, complement, and set.
            i = SendDlgItemMessage (hWnd, IDC_CHKBOX, BM_GETCHECK,
                                    0, 0);
            if (i)
                SendDlgItemMessage (hWnd, IDC_CHKBOX, BM_SETCHECK,
                                    0, 0);
            else
                SendDlgItemMessage (hWnd, IDC_CHKBOX, BM_SETCHECK,
                                    1, 0);
        }


        // Get the handle of the main window from the user word.
        hwndMain = (HWND) GetWindowLong (hWnd, DWL_USER);

        // Look up button notification.
        lstrcpy (szOut, TEXT ("WM_COMMAND: "));
        for (i = 0; i < dim(nlBtn); i++) {
            if (HIWORD (wParam) == nlBtn[i].wNotification) {
                lstrcat (szOut, nlBtn[i].pszLabel);
                break;
            }
        }
        if (i == dim(nlBtn))
            wsprintf (szOut, TEXT ("WM_COMMAND notification: %x"),
                      HIWORD (wParam));

        SendMessage (hwndMain, MYMSG_ADDLINE,
                     MAKEWPARAM (LOWORD (wParam),ID_BTNPAGE),
                     (LPARAM)szOut);
        return TRUE;

    //
    // Reflect notify message.
    //
    case WM_NOTIFY:
        // Get the handle of the main window from the user word.
        hwndMain = (HWND) GetWindowLong (hWnd, DWL_USER);

        // Look up notify message.
        for (i = 0; i < nPropPageSize; i++) {
```

```
                if (((NMHDR *)lParam)->code ==
                                       nlPropPage[i].wNotification) {
                    lstrcpy (szOut, nlPropPage[i].pszLabel);
                    break;
                }
            }
            if (i == nPropPageSize)
                wsprintf (szOut, TEXT ("Notify code:%d"),
                          ((NMHDR *)lParam)->code);

            SendMessage (hwndMain, MYMSG_ADDLINE,
                         MAKEWPARAM (-1,ID_BTNPAGE), (LPARAM)szOut);

            return FALSE;  // Return false to force default processing.

        case WM_DRAWITEM:
            DrawButton (hWnd, (LPDRAWITEMSTRUCT)lParam);
            return TRUE;
    }
    return FALSE;
}

//----------------------------------------------------------------------
// DrawButton - Draws an owner-draw button.
//
LRESULT DrawButton (HWND hWnd, LPDRAWITEMSTRUCT pdi) {

    HPEN hPenShadow, hPenLight, hPenDkShadow, hOldPen;
    POINT ptOut[3], ptIn[3];
    HBRUSH hBr, hOldBr;
    TCHAR szOut[128];
    HWND hwndMain;
    LOGPEN lpen;

    // Get the handle of the main window from the user word.
    hwndMain = (HWND) GetWindowLong (hWnd, DWL_USER);

    // Reflect the messages to the report window.
    wsprintf (szOut, TEXT ("WM_DRAWITEM  Action:%x  State:%x"),
              pdi->itemAction, pdi->itemState);

    SendMessage (hwndMain, MYMSG_ADDLINE,
                 MAKEWPARAM (pdi->CtlID, ID_BTNPAGE),
                 (LPARAM)szOut);
```

(continued)

Figure 4-10. *continued*

```
    // Create pens for drawing.
    lpen.lopnStyle = PS_SOLID;
    lpen.lopnWidth.x = 3;
    lpen.lopnWidth.y = 3;
    lpen.lopnColor = GetSysColor (COLOR_3DSHADOW);
    hPenShadow = CreatePenIndirect (&lpen);

    lpen.lopnWidth.x = 1;
    lpen.lopnWidth.y = 1;
    lpen.lopnColor = GetSysColor (COLOR_3DLIGHT);
    hPenLight = CreatePenIndirect (&lpen);

    lpen.lopnColor = GetSysColor (COLOR_3DDKSHADOW);
    hPenDkShadow = CreatePenIndirect (&lpen);

    // Create a brush for the face of the button.
    hBr = CreateSolidBrush (GetSysColor (COLOR_3DFACE));

    // Draw a rectangle with a thick outside border to start the
    // frame drawing.
    hOldPen = SelectObject (pdi->hDC, hPenShadow);
    hOldBr = SelectObject (pdi->hDC, hBr);
    Rectangle (pdi->hDC, pdi->rcItem.left, pdi->rcItem.top,
               pdi->rcItem.right, pdi->rcItem.bottom);

    // Draw the upper left inside line.
    ptIn[0].x = pdi->rcItem.left + 1;
    ptIn[0].y = pdi->rcItem.bottom - 3;
    ptIn[1].x = pdi->rcItem.left + 1;
    ptIn[1].y = pdi->rcItem.top + 1;
    ptIn[2].x = pdi->rcItem.right - 3;
    ptIn[2].y = pdi->rcItem.top+1;

    // Select a pen to draw shadow or light side of button.
    if (pdi->itemState & ODS_SELECTED) {
        SelectObject (pdi->hDC, hPenDkShadow);
    } else {
        SelectObject (pdi->hDC, hPenLight);
    }
    Polyline (pdi->hDC, ptIn, 3);

    // If selected, also draw a bright line inside the lower
    // right corner.
    if (pdi->itemState & ODS_SELECTED) {
        SelectObject (pdi->hDC, hPenLight);
        ptIn[1].x = pdi->rcItem.right- 3;
```

```
        ptIn[1].y = pdi->rcItem.bottom - 3;
        Polyline (pdi->hDC, ptIn, 3);
    }
    // Now draw the black outside line on either the upper left or lower
    // right corner.
    ptOut[0].x = pdi->rcItem.left;
    ptOut[0].y = pdi->rcItem.bottom-1;
    ptOut[2].x = pdi->rcItem.right-1;
    ptOut[2].y = pdi->rcItem.top;

    SelectObject (pdi->hDC, hPenDkShadow);
    if (pdi->itemState & ODS_SELECTED) {
        ptOut[1].x = pdi->rcItem.left;
        ptOut[1].y = pdi->rcItem.top;
    } else {
        ptOut[1].x = pdi->rcItem.right-1;
        ptOut[1].y = pdi->rcItem.bottom-1;
    }
    Polyline (pdi->hDC, ptOut, 3);

    // Draw the icon.
    if (hIcon) {
        ptIn[0].x = (pdi->rcItem.right - pdi->rcItem.left)/2 -
                    GetSystemMetrics (SM_CXICON)/2 - 2;
        ptIn[0].y = (pdi->rcItem.bottom - pdi->rcItem.top)/2 -
                    GetSystemMetrics (SM_CYICON)/2 - 2;
        // If pressed, shift image down one pel to simulate the press.
        if (pdi->itemState & ODS_SELECTED) {
            ptOut[1].x += 2;
            ptOut[1].y += 2;
        }
        DrawIcon (pdi->hDC, ptIn[0].x, ptIn[0].y, hIcon);
    }

    // If button has the focus, draw the dotted rect inside the button.
    if (pdi->itemState & ODS_FOCUS) {
        pdi->rcItem.left += 3;
        pdi->rcItem.top += 3;
        pdi->rcItem.right -= 4;
        pdi->rcItem.bottom -= 4;
        DrawFocusRect (pdi->hDC, &pdi->rcItem);
    }

    // Clean up. First select the original brush and pen into the DC.
    SelectObject (pdi->hDC, hOldBr);
    SelectObject (pdi->hDC, hOldPen);
```

(continued)

Figure 4-10. *continued*

```
    // Now delete the brushes and pens created.
    DeleteObject (hBr);
    DeleteObject (hPenShadow);
    DeleteObject (hPenDkShadow);
    DeleteObject (hPenLight);
    return 0;
}
```

EditDlg.c

```
//======================================================================
// EditDlg - Edit dialog box window code
//
// Written for the book Programming Windows CE
// Copyright (C) 1998 Douglas Boling
//======================================================================
#include <windows.h>                 // For all that Windows stuff
#include <prsht.h>                   // Property sheet includes
#include "DlgDemo.h"                 // Program-specific stuff

extern HINSTANCE hInst;
//----------------------------------------------------------------------
// Global data
//
// Identification strings for various WM_COMMAND notifications
NOTELABELS nlEdit[] = {{TEXT ("EN_SETFOCUS "), 0x0100},
                       {TEXT ("EN_KILLFOCUS"), 0x0200},
                       {TEXT ("EN_CHANGE   "), 0x0300},
                       {TEXT ("EN_UPDATE   "), 0x0400},
                       {TEXT ("EN_ERRSPACE "), 0x0500},
                       {TEXT ("EN_MAXTEXT  "), 0x0501},
                       {TEXT ("EN_HSCROLL  "), 0x0601},
                       {TEXT ("EN_VSCROLL  "), 0x0602},
};
extern NOTELABELS nlPropPage[];
extern int nPropPageSize;
//======================================================================
// EditDlgProc - Button page dialog box procedure
//
BOOL CALLBACK EditDlgProc (HWND hWnd, UINT wMsg, WPARAM wParam,
                           LPARAM lParam) {
    TCHAR szOut[128];
    HWND hwndMain;
    INT i;
```

```
    switch (wMsg) {

        case WM_INITDIALOG:
            // The generic parameter contains the
            // top-level window handle.
            hwndMain = (HWND)((LPPROPSHEETPAGE)lParam)->lParam;
            // Save the window handle in the window structure.
            SetWindowLong (hWnd, DWL_USER, (LONG)hwndMain);
            return TRUE;
        //
        // Reflect WM_COMMAND messages to main window.
        //
        case WM_COMMAND:
            // Get the handle of the main window from the user word.
            hwndMain = (HWND) GetWindowLong (hWnd, DWL_USER);

            // Look up button notification.
            lstrcpy (szOut, TEXT ("WM_COMMAND: "));
            for (i = 0; i < dim(nlEdit); i++) {
                if (HIWORD (wParam) == nlEdit[i].wNotification) {
                    lstrcat (szOut, nlEdit[i].pszLabel);
                    break;
                }
            }
            if (i == dim(nlEdit))
                wsprintf (szOut, TEXT ("WM_COMMAND notification: %x"),
                          HIWORD (wParam));

            SendMessage (hwndMain, MYMSG_ADDLINE,
                         MAKEWPARAM (LOWORD (wParam),ID_EDITPAGE),
                         (LPARAM)szOut);
            return TRUE;

        //
        // Reflect notify message.
        //
        case WM_NOTIFY:
            // Get the handle of the main window from the user word.
            hwndMain = (HWND) GetWindowLong (hWnd, DWL_USER);

            // Look up notify message.
            for (i = 0; i < nPropPageSize; i++) {
                if (((NMHDR *)lParam)->code ==
                                      nlPropPage[i].wNotification) {
                    lstrcpy (szOut, nlPropPage[i].pszLabel);
                    break;
```

(continued)

Figure 4-10. *continued*

```
                }
            }
            if (i == nPropPageSize)
                wsprintf (szOut, TEXT ("Notify code:%d"),
                          ((NMHDR *)lParam)->code);

            SendMessage (hwndMain, MYMSG_ADDLINE,
                         MAKEWPARAM (-1,ID_EDITPAGE), (LPARAM)szOut);

            return FALSE;  // Return false to force default processing.
    }
    return FALSE;
}
```

ListDlg.c

```
//======================================================================
// ListDlg - List box dialog window code
//
// Written for the book Programming Windows CE
// Copyright (C) 1998 Douglas Boling
//======================================================================
#include <windows.h>                 // For all that Windows stuff
#include <prsht.h>                   // Property sheet includes
#include "DlgDemo.h"                 // Program-specific stuff

extern HINSTANCE hInst;
//----------------------------------------------------------------------
// Global data
//
NOTELABELS nlList[] = {{TEXT ("LBN_ERRSPACE "), (-2)},
                       {TEXT ("LBN_SELCHANGE"), 1},
                       {TEXT ("LBN_DBLCLK   "), 2},
                       {TEXT ("LBN_SELCANCEL"), 3},
                       {TEXT ("LBN_SETFOCUS "), 4},
                       {TEXT ("LBN_KILLFOCUS"), 5},
};

NOTELABELS nlCombo[] = {{TEXT ("CBN_ERRSPACE     "), (-1)},
                        {TEXT ("CBN_SELCHANGE    "), 1},
                        {TEXT ("CBN_DBLCLK       "), 2},
                        {TEXT ("CBN_SETFOCUS     "), 3},
                        {TEXT ("CBN_KILLFOCUS    "), 4},
                        {TEXT ("CBN_EDITCHANGE   "), 5},
                        {TEXT ("CBN_EDITUPDATE   "), 6},
```

```
                        {TEXT ("CBN_DROPDOWN    "), 7},
                        {TEXT ("CBN_CLOSEUP     "), 8},
                        {TEXT ("CBN_SELENDOK    "), 9},
                        {TEXT ("CBN_SELENDCANCEL"), 10},
};

extern NOTELABELS nlPropPage[];
extern int nPropPageSize;
//======================================================================
// ListDlgProc - Button page dialog box procedure
//
BOOL CALLBACK ListDlgProc (HWND hWnd, UINT wMsg, WPARAM wParam,
                           LPARAM lParam) {
    TCHAR szOut[128];
    HWND hwndMain;
    INT i;

    switch (wMsg) {

        case WM_INITDIALOG:
            // The generic parameter contains the
            // top-level window handle.
            hwndMain = (HWND)((LPPROPSHEETPAGE)lParam)->lParam;
            // Save the window handle in the window structure.
            SetWindowLong (hWnd, DWL_USER, (LONG)hwndMain);

            // Fill the list and combo boxes.
            for (i = 0; i < 20; i++) {
                wsprintf (szOut, TEXT ("Item %d"), i);
                SendDlgItemMessage (hWnd, IDC_SNGLELIST, LB_ADDSTRING,
                                    0, (LPARAM)szOut);

                SendDlgItemMessage (hWnd, IDC_MULTILIST, LB_ADDSTRING,
                                    0, (LPARAM)szOut);

                SendDlgItemMessage (hWnd, IDC_COMBOBOX, CB_ADDSTRING,
                                    0, (LPARAM)szOut);
            }
            // Provide default selection for the combo box.
            SendDlgItemMessage (hWnd, IDC_COMBOBOX, CB_SETCURSEL, 0, 0);
            return TRUE;
        //
        // Reflect WM_COMMAND messages to main window.
        //
```

(continued)

Figure 4-10. *continued*

```
        case WM_COMMAND:
            // Get the handle of the main window from the user word.
            hwndMain = (HWND) GetWindowLong (hWnd, DWL_USER);

            // Report the WM_COMMAND messages.
            lstrcpy (szOut, TEXT ("WM_COMMAND: "));
            if (LOWORD (wParam) == IDC_COMBOBOX) {
                for (i = 0; i < dim(nlCombo); i++) {
                    if (HIWORD (wParam) == nlCombo[i].wNotification) {
                        lstrcat (szOut, nlCombo[i].pszLabel);
                        break;
                    }
                }
                if (i == dim(nlCombo))
                    wsprintf (szOut,
                              TEXT ("WM_COMMAND notification: %x"),
                              HIWORD (wParam));
            } else {
                for (i = 0; i < dim(nlList); i++) {
                    if (HIWORD (wParam) == nlList[i].wNotification) {
                        lstrcat (szOut, nlList[i].pszLabel);
                        break;
                    }
                }
                if (i == dim(nlList))
                    wsprintf (szOut,
                              TEXT ("WM_COMMAND notification: %x"),
                              HIWORD (wParam));
            }
            SendMessage (hwndMain, MYMSG_ADDLINE,
                         MAKEWPARAM (LOWORD (wParam),ID_LISTPAGE),
                        (LPARAM)szOut);
            return TRUE;

        //
        // Reflect notify message.
        //
        case WM_NOTIFY:
            // Get the handle of the main window from the user word.
            hwndMain = (HWND) GetWindowLong (hWnd, DWL_USER);

            // Look up notify message.
            for (i = 0; i < nPropPageSize; i++) {
                if (((NMHDR *)lParam)->code ==
                                   nlPropPage[i].wNotification) {
```

```
                    lstrcpy (szOut, nlPropPage[i].pszLabel);
                    break;
                }
            }
            if (i == nPropPageSize)
                wsprintf (szOut, TEXT ("Notify code:%d"),
                          ((NMHDR *)lParam)->code);

            SendMessage (hwndMain, MYMSG_ADDLINE,
                         MAKEWPARAM (-1,ID_LISTPAGE),
                         (LPARAM)szOut);
            return FALSE;  // Return false to force default processing.
    }
    return FALSE;
}
```

StaticDlg.c

```
//======================================================================
// StaticDlg - Static control dialog box window code
//
// Written for the book Programming Windows CE
// Copyright (C) 1998 Douglas Boling
//======================================================================
#include <windows.h>                 // For all that Windows stuff
#include <prsht.h>                   // Property sheet includes
#include "DlgDemo.h"                 // Program-specific stuff

extern HINSTANCE hInst;
//----------------------------------------------------------------------
// Global data
//
// Identification strings for various WM_COMMAND notifications
NOTELABELS nlStatic[] = {{TEXT ("STN_CLICKED"), 0},
                         {TEXT ("STN_ENABLE "), 2},
                         {TEXT ("STN_DISABLE"), 3},
};
extern NOTELABELS nlPropPage[];
extern int nPropPageSize;
//======================================================================
// StaticDlgProc - Button page dialog box procedure
//
BOOL CALLBACK StaticDlgProc (HWND hWnd, UINT wMsg, WPARAM wParam,
                             LPARAM lParam) {
    TCHAR szOut[128];
```

(continued)

Figure 4-10. *continued*

```
    HWND hwndMain;
    INT i;

    switch (wMsg) {

        case WM_INITDIALOG:
            // The generic parameter contains the
            // top-level window handle.
            hwndMain = (HWND)((LPPROPSHEETPAGE)lParam)->lParam;
            // Save the window handle in the window structure.
            SetWindowLong (hWnd, DWL_USER, (LONG)hwndMain);
            return TRUE;
        //
        // Reflect WM_COMMAND messages to main window.
        //
        case WM_COMMAND:
            // Get the handle of the main window from the user word.
            hwndMain = (HWND) GetWindowLong (hWnd, DWL_USER);

            // Look up button notification.
            lstrcpy (szOut, TEXT ("WM_COMMAND: "));
            for (i = 0; i < dim(nlStatic); i++) {
                if (HIWORD (wParam) == nlStatic[i].wNotification) {
                    lstrcat (szOut, nlStatic[i].pszLabel);
                    break;
                }
            }
            if (i == dim(nlStatic))
                wsprintf (szOut, TEXT ("WM_COMMAND notification: %x"),
                          HIWORD (wParam));

            SendMessage (hwndMain, MYMSG_ADDLINE,
                         MAKEWPARAM (LOWORD (wParam),ID_STATPAGE),
                         (LPARAM)szOut);
            return TRUE;

        //
        // Reflect notify message.
        //
        case WM_NOTIFY:
            // Get the handle of the main window from the user word.
            hwndMain = (HWND) GetWindowLong (hWnd, DWL_USER);

            // Look up notify message.
```

```
            for (i = 0; i < nPropPageSize; i++) {
                if (((NMHDR *)lParam)->code ==
                    nlPropPage[i].wNotification) {
                        lstrcpy (szOut, nlPropPage[i].pszLabel);
                    break;
                }
            }
            if (i == nPropPageSize)
                wsprintf (szOut, TEXT ("Notify code:%d"),
                          ((NMHDR *)lParam)->code);

            SendMessage (hwndMain, MYMSG_ADDLINE,
                         MAKEWPARAM (-1,ID_STATPAGE), (LPARAM)szOut);

            return FALSE;  // Return false to force default processing.
    }
    return FALSE;
}
```

ScrollDlg.c

```
//======================================================================
// ScrollDlg - Scroll bar dialog box window code
//
// Written for the book Programming Windows CE
// Copyright (C) 1998 Douglas Boling
//======================================================================
#include <windows.h>                    // For all that Windows stuff
#include <prsht.h>                      // Property sheet includes
#include "DlgDemo.h"                    // Program-specific stuff

extern HINSTANCE hInst;
//----------------------------------------------------------------------
// Global data
//
// Identification strings for various WM_xSCROLL notifications
NOTELABELS nlVScroll[] = {{TEXT ("SB_LINEUP         "), 0},
                          {TEXT ("SB_LINEDOWN       "), 1},
                          {TEXT ("SB_PAGEUP         "), 2},
                          {TEXT ("SB_PAGEDOWN       "), 3},
                          {TEXT ("SB_THUMBPOSITION"), 4},
                          {TEXT ("SB_THUMBTRACK     "), 5},
                          {TEXT ("SB_TOP            "), 6},
                          {TEXT ("SB_BOTTOM         "), 7},
                          {TEXT ("SB_ENDSCROLL      "), 8},
};
```

(continued)

Figure 4-10. *continued*

```
NOTELABELS nlHScroll[] = {{TEXT ("SB_LINELEFT     "), 0},
                          {TEXT ("SB_LINERIGHT    "), 1},
                          {TEXT ("SB_PAGELEFT     "), 2},
                          {TEXT ("SB_PAGERIGHT    "), 3},
                          {TEXT ("SB_THUMBPOSITION"), 4},
                          {TEXT ("SB_THUMBTRACK   "), 5},
                          {TEXT ("SB_LEFT         "), 6},
                          {TEXT ("SB_RIGHT        "), 7},
                          {TEXT ("SB_ENDSCROLL    "), 8},
};
extern NOTELABELS nlPropPage[];
extern int nPropPageSize;
//======================================================================
// EditDlgProc - Button page dialog box procedure
//
BOOL CALLBACK ScrollDlgProc (HWND hWnd, UINT wMsg, WPARAM wParam,
                             LPARAM lParam) {
    TCHAR szOut[128];
    SCROLLINFO si;
    HWND hwndMain;
    INT i, sPos;

    switch (wMsg) {

        case WM_INITDIALOG:
            // The generic parameter contains
            // the top-level window handle.
            hwndMain = (HWND)((LPPROPSHEETPAGE)lParam)->lParam;
            // Save the window handle in the window structure.
            SetWindowLong (hWnd, DWL_USER, (LONG)hwndMain);
            return TRUE;
        //
        // Reflect WM_COMMAND messages to main window.
        //
        case WM_VSCROLL:
        case WM_HSCROLL:
            // Get the handle of the main window from the user word.
            hwndMain = (HWND) GetWindowLong (hWnd, DWL_USER);

            // Update the report window.
            // Determine whether from horizontal or vertical scroll bar.
            if (GetDlgItem (hWnd, 101) == (HWND)lParam) {
                for (i = 0; i < dim(nlVScroll); i++) {
                    if (LOWORD (wParam) == nlVScroll[i].wNotification) {
                        lstrcpy (szOut, nlVScroll[i].pszLabel);
                        break;
```

```
                }
            }
            if (i == dim(nlVScroll))
                wsprintf (szOut, TEXT ("notification: %x"),
                          HIWORD (wParam));
        } else {
            for (i = 0; i < dim(nlHScroll); i++) {
                if (LOWORD (wParam) == nlHScroll[i].wNotification) {
                    lstrcpy (szOut, nlHScroll[i].pszLabel);
                    break;
                }
            }
            if (i == dim(nlHScroll))
                wsprintf (szOut, TEXT ("notification: %x"),
                          HIWORD (wParam));
        }
        SendMessage (hwndMain, MYMSG_ADDLINE,
                     MAKEWPARAM (-1, ID_SCROLLPAGE), (LPARAM)szOut);

        // Get scroll bar position.
        si.cbSize = sizeof (si);
        si.fMask = SIF_POS;
        GetScrollInfo ((HWND)lParam, SB_CTL, &si);
        sPos = si.nPos;

        // Act on the scroll code.
        switch (LOWORD (wParam)) {
        case SB_LINEUP:         // Also SB_LINELEFT
            sPos -= 2;
            break;

        case SB_LINEDOWN:       // Also SB_LINERIGHT
            sPos += 2;
            break;

        case SB_PAGEUP:         // Also SB_PAGELEFT
            sPos -= 10;
            break;

        case SB_PAGEDOWN:       // Also SB_PAGERIGHT
            sPos += 10;
            break;

        case SB_THUMBPOSITION:
            sPos = HIWORD (wParam);
            break;
        }
```

(continued)

Figure 4-10. *continued*

```
            // Check range.
            if (sPos < 0)
                sPos = 0;
            if (sPos > 100)
                sPos = 100;

            // Update scrollbar position.
            si.cbSize = sizeof (si);
            si.nPos = sPos;
            si.fMask = SIF_POS;
            SetScrollInfo ((HWND)lParam, SB_CTL, &si, TRUE);

            return TRUE;

        //
        // Reflect notify message.
        //
        case WM_NOTIFY:
            // Get the handle of the main window from the user word.
            hwndMain = (HWND) GetWindowLong (hWnd, DWL_USER);

            // Look up notify message.
            for (i = 0; i < nPropPageSize; i++) {
                if (((NMHDR *)lParam)->code ==
                        nlPropPage[i].wNotification) {
                            lstrcpy (szOut, nlPropPage[i].pszLabel);
                            break;
                }
            }
            if (i == nPropPageSize)
                wsprintf (szOut, TEXT ("Notify code:%d"),
                          ((NMHDR *)lParam)->code);

            SendMessage (hwndMain, MYMSG_ADDLINE,
                         MAKEWPARAM (-1, ID_SCROLLPAGE), (LPARAM)szOut);

            return FALSE;  // Return false to force default processing.
    }
    return FALSE;
}
```

The dialog box procedures for each of the property pages report all WM_COMMAND and WM_NOTIFY messages back to the main window where they're displayed in a list box contained in the main window. The property page dialog box procedures mirror the child window procedures of the CtlView example, the differences being that the page procedures don't have to create their controls, and they field the WM_INITDIALOG message to initialize the controls. The page procedures also use the technique of storing information in their window structures—in this case, the window handle of the main window of the example. This is necessary because the parent window of the pages is the property sheet, not the main window. The window handle is conveniently accessible during the WM_INITDIALOG message because it's loaded into the user-definable parameter in the PROPSHEETPAGE structure by the main window when the property sheet is created. Each page procedure copies the parameter from the PROPSHEETPAGE structure into the DWL_USER field of the window structure available to all dialog box procedures. When other messages are handled, the handle is then queried using *GetWindowLong*. The page procedures also field the WM_NOTIFY message so that they, too, can be reflected back to the main window.

As with CtlView, the best way to learn from DlgDemo is to run the program and watch the different WM_COMMAND and WM_NOTIFY messages that are sent by the controls and the property sheet. Opening the property sheet and switching between the pages results in a flood of WM_NOTIFY messages informing the individual pages of what's happening. It's also interesting to note that when the OK button is pressed on the property sheet, the PSN_APPLY messages are sent only to property pages that have been displayed.

The menu handlers that display the Print and Color common dialogs work with a bit of a twist. Since the Palm-size PC doesn't support these dialogs, DlgDemo can't call the functions directly. That would result in these two functions being implicitly linked at run time. Since the Palm-size PC doesn't have these common dialogs and therefore these functions, Windows CE wouldn't be able to resolve the implicit links to all the functions in the program and therefore the program wouldn't be able to load. So, instead of calling the functions directly, you explicitly link these functions in *InitApp* by loading the common dialog DLL using *LoadLibrary* and getting pointers to the functions using *GetProcAddress*. If DlgDemo is running on a Palm-size PC, the GetProcAddress function fails and returns 0 for the function pointer. In *OnCreateMain*, a check is made to see whether these function pointers are 0, and if so, the Print and Color menu items are disabled. In the menu handler functions *DoMainCommandColor* and *DoMainCommandPrint*, the function pointers returned by *GetProcAddress* are used to call the functions. This extra effort isn't necessary if you know your program will run only on a system that supports a specific set of functions, but every once in a while, this technique comes in handy.

CONCLUSION

This chapter has covered a huge amount of ground, from basic child windows to controls and on to dialog boxes and property sheets. My goal wasn't to teach everything there is to know about these topics. Instead, I've tried to introduce these program elements, provide a few examples, and point out the subtle differences between the way they're handled by Windows CE and the desktop versions of Windows.

This chapter also marks the end of the introductory section, "Windows Programming Basics." In these first four chapters, I've talked about fundamental Windows programming while also using a basic Windows CE application to introduce the concepts of the system message queue, windows, and messages. I've given you an overview of how to paint text and graphics in a window and how to query the user for input. Finally, I talked about the windows hierarchy, controls, and dialog boxes. For the remainder of the book, I move from description of the elements common to both Windows CE and the desktop versions of Windows to the unique nature of Windows CE programming. I begin this process in Chapter 5 by talking about another set of controls, the *common controls,* this time with an emphasis on controls unique to Windows CE.

Part II

WINDOWS CE BASICS

Chapter 5

Common Controls and Windows CE

As Microsoft Windows matured as an operating system, it became apparent that the basic controls provided by Windows were insufficient for the sophisticated user interfaces that users demanded. Microsoft developed a series of additional controls, called *common controls*, for their internal applications and later made the dynamic link library (DLL) containing the controls available to application developers. Starting with Microsoft Windows 95 and Microsoft Windows NT 3.5, the common control library was bundled with the operating system. (Although this hasn't stopped Microsoft from making interim releases of the DLL as the common control library was enhanced.) With each release of the common control DLL, new controls and new features are added to old controls. As a group, the common controls are less mature than the standard Windows controls and therefore show greater differences between implementations across the various versions of Windows. These differences aren't just between Microsoft Windows CE and other versions of Windows, but also between Windows NT, Windows 95, and Microsoft Windows 98. The functionality of the common controls in Windows CE tracks most closely with the common controls delivered with Windows 98, although not all of the Windows 98 features are supported.

It isn't the goal of this chapter to cover in depth all the common controls. That would take an entire book. Instead, I'll cover the controls and features of controls the Windows CE programmer will most often need when writing Windows CE applications. I'll start with the command bar and then look at the month calendar and time and date picker controls. Finally, I'll finish up with the list view control. By the end of the chapter, you might not know every common control inside and out, but you will be able to see how the common controls work in general. And you'll have the background to look at the documentation and understand the common controls not covered.

PROGRAMMING COMMON CONTROLS

Since the common controls are separate from the core operating system, the DLL that contains them must be initialized before any of the common controls can be used. Under all versions of Windows, including Windows CE, you can call the function

```
void InitCommonControls (void);
```

to load the library and register all the common control classes.

Another function added recently to the common control library and supported by Windows CE is this one:

```
BOOL InitCommonControlsEx (LPINITCOMMONCONTROLSEX lpInitCtrls);
```

This function allows an application to load and initialize only selected common controls. This function is handy under Windows CE because loading only the necessary controls can reduce the memory impact. The only parameter to this function is a two-field structure that contains a size field and a field that contains a set of flags indicating which common controls should be registered. Figure 5-1 shows the available flags and their associated controls.

Flag	*Control Classes Initialized*
ICC_BAR_CLASSES	Toolbar Status bar Trackbar Command bar
ICC_COOL_CLASSES	Rebar
ICC_DATE_CLASSES	Date and time picker Month calendar control
ICC_LISTVIEW_CLASSES	List view Header control
ICC_PROGRESS_CLASS	Progress bar control
ICC_TAB_CLASSES	Tab control
ICC_TREEVIEW_CLASSES	Tree view control
ICC_UPDOWN_CLASS	Up-down control

Figure 5-1. *Flags for selected common controls.*

Once the common control DLL has been initialized, these controls can be treated as any other control. But since the common controls aren't formally part of the Windows core functionality, an additional include file, commctrl.h, must be included.

The programming interface for the common controls is similar to standard Windows controls. Each of the controls has a set of custom style flags that configure the look and behavior of the control. Messages specific to each control are sent to configure, manipulate, and cause the control to perform actions. One major difference between the standard windows controls and common controls is that notifications of events or requests for service are sent via WM_NOTIFY messages instead of WM_COMMAND messages as in the standard controls. This technique allows the notifications to contain much more information than would be allowed using WM_COMMAND message notifications.

One additional difference when programming common controls is that most of the control-specific messages that can be sent to the common controls have predefined macros that make sending the message look as if your application is calling a function. So, instead of using an LVM_INSERTITEM message to a list view control to insert an item, as in

```
nIndex = (int) SendMessage (hwndLV, LVM_INSERTITEM, 0, (LPARAM)&lvi);
```

an application could just as easily have used the line:

```
nIndex = ListView_InsertItem (hwndLV, &lvi);
```

There's no functional difference between the two lines; the advantage of these macros is clarity. The macros themselves are defined in commctrl.h along with the other definitions required for programming the common controls. One problem with the macros is that the compiler doesn't perform the type checking on the parameters that would normally occur if the macro were an actual function. This is also true of the *SendMessage* technique, in which the parameters must be typed as WPARAM and LPARAM types, but at least with messages the lack of type checking is obvious. All in all though, the macro route provides better readability. One exception to this system of macros are the calls made to the command bar control and the command bands control. Those controls actually have a number of true functions in addition to a large set of macro-wrapped messages. As a rule, I'll talk about messages as messages, not as their macro equivalents. That should help differentiate what is a message or macro and what is a true function.

THE COMMON CONTROLS

Windows CE's special niche—small personal productivity devices—has driven the requirements for the common controls in Windows CE. The frequent need for time and date references for schedule and task management applications has led to inclusion of the date and time picker control and the month calendar control. The small screens of personal productivity devices inspired the space-saving *command bar*. Mating the command bar with the *rebar control* that was created for Internet Explorer 3.0 has produced the *command bands control*. The command bands control provides even more room for menus, buttons, and other controls across the top of a Windows CE application. You've seen glimpses of the command bar control in Chapter 1 and again in Chapters 3 and 4. It's time you were formally introduced.

The Command Bar

Briefly, a *command bar* control combines a menu and a toolbar. This combination is valuable because, as I've pointed out before, the combination of a menu and toolbar on one line saves screen real estate on space-constrained Windows CE displays. To the programmer, the command bar looks like a toolbar with a number of helper functions that make programming the command bar a breeze. In addition to the command bar functions, you can also use most toolbar messages when you're working with command bars.

The command bands control was added to Windows CE in version 2.0. A command bands control is a rebar control that, by default, contains a command bar in each band of the control. The rebar control is a fairly new common control; it's a container of controls that the user can drag around the application window. It was previously known as a *Cool Bar* when it first appeared in the common control DLL delivered with Internet Explorer 3.0. Given that command bands are nothing more than command bars in a rebar control, knowing how to program a command bar is most of the battle when learning how to program the command bands control.

Creating a command bar

You build a command bar in a number of steps, each defined by a particular function. The command bar is created, the menu is added, buttons are added, other controls are added, tool tips are added, and finally, the Close and Help buttons are appended to the right side of the command bar.

You begin the process of creating a command bar with a call to

```
HWND CommandBar_Create (HINSTANCE hInst, HWND hwndParent,
                        int idCmdBar);
```

The function requires the program's instance handle, the handle of the parent window, and an ID value for the control. If successful, the function returns the handle to the newly created command bar control. But a bare command bar isn't much use to the application. It takes a menu and a few buttons jazz it up.

Command bar menus

You can add a menu to a command bar by calling one of two functions. The first function is this:

```
BOOL CommandBar_InsertMenubar (HWND hwndCB, HINSTANCE hInst,
                               WORD idMenu, int iButton);
```

The first two parameters of this function are the handle of the command bar and the instance handle of the application. The *idMenu* parameter is the resource ID of the menu to be loaded into the command bar. The last parameter is the index of the button to the immediate left of the menu. Because the Windows CE guidelines specify that the menu should be at the left end of the command bar, this parameter should be set to 0, which indicates that all the buttons are to the right of the menu.

A shortcoming of the *CommandBar_InsertMenubar* function is that it requires the menu to be loaded from a resource. You can't configure the menu on the fly. Of course, it would be possible to load a dummy menu and manipulate the contents of the menu with the various menu functions, but here's an easier method.

The function

```
BOOL CommandBar_InsertMenubarEx (HWND hwndCB, HINSTANCE hInst,
                                 LPTSTR pszMenu, int iButton);
```

was added in Windows CE 2.0. The difference between *CommandBar_InsertMenubarEx* and *CommandBar_InsertMenubar* is the change in the third parameter, *pszMenu*. This parameter can be either the name of a menu resource or the handle to a menu previously created by the program. If the *pszMenu* parameter is a menu handle, the *hInst* parameter must be NULL.

Once a menu has been loaded into a command bar, the handle to the menu can be retrieved at any time using

```
HMENU CommandBar_GetMenu (HWND hwndCB, int iButton);
```

The second parameter, *iButton*, is the index of the button to the immediate left of the menu. This mechanism provides the ability to identify more than one menu on the command bar. However, given the Windows CE design guidelines, you should see only one menu on the bar. With the menu handle, you can manipulate the structure of the menu using the many menu functions available.

If an application modifies the menu on the command bar, the application must call

```
BOOL CommandBar_DrawMenuBar (HWND hwndCB, int iButton);
```

which forces the menu on the command bar to be redrawn. Here again, the parameters are the handle to the command bar and the index of the button to the left of the menu. Under Windows CE, you must use *CommandBar_DrawMenuBar* instead of *DrawMenuBar*, which is the standard function used to redraw the menu under other versions of Windows.

Command bar buttons

Adding buttons to a command bar is a two-step process, and is similar to adding buttons to a toolbar. First the bitmap images for the buttons must be added to the command bar. Second the buttons are added, with each of the buttons referencing one of the images in the bitmap list that was previously added.

The command bar maintains its own list of bitmaps for the buttons in an internal image list. Bitmaps can be added to this image list one at a time or as a group of images contained in a long and narrow bitmap. For example, for a bitmap to contain four 16-by-15-bit images, the dimensions of the bitmap added to the command bar would be 64 by 15 bits. Figure 5-2 shows this bitmap image layout.

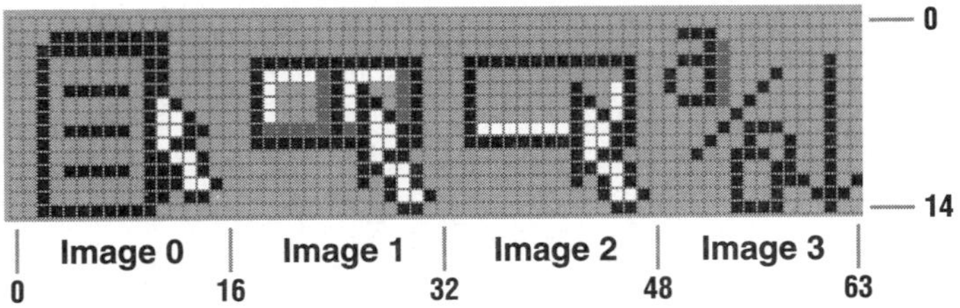

Figure 5-2. *Layout of a bitmap that contains four 16-by-15-bit images.*

Loading a image bitmap is accomplished using

```
int CommandBar_AddBitmap (HWND hwndCB, HINSTANCE hInst, int idBitmap,
                          int iNumImages, int iReserved, int iReserved);
```

This first two parameters are, as is usual with a command bar function, the handle to the command bar and the instance handle of the executable. The third parameter, *idBitmap*, is the resource ID of the bitmap image. The fourth parameter, *iNumImages*, should contain the number of images in the bitmap being loaded. Multiple bitmap images can be loaded into the same command bar by calling *CommandBar_AddBitmap* as many times as is needed.

Two predefined bitmaps provide a number of images that are commonly used in command bars and toolbars. You load these images by setting the *hInst* parameter in *CommandBar_AddBitmap* to HINST_COMMCTRL and setting the *idBitmap* parameter to either IDB_STD_SMALL_COLOR or IDB_VIEW_SMALL_COLOR. The images contained in these bitmaps are shown in Figure 5-3. The buttons on the top line contain the bitmaps from the standard bitmap while the second-line buttons contain the bitmaps from the standard view bitmap.

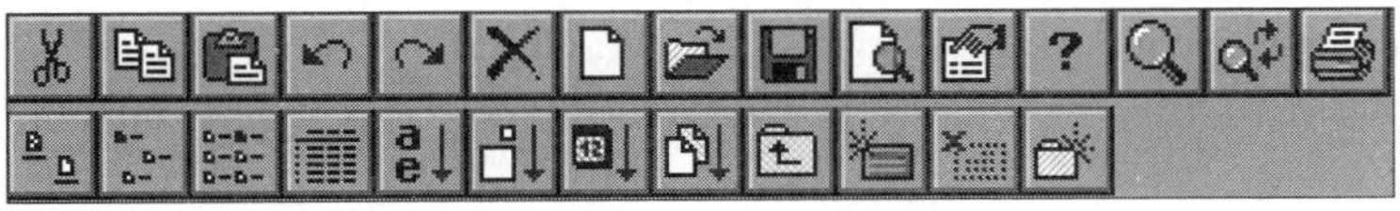

Figure 5-3. *Images in the two standard bitmaps provided by the common control DLL.*

The index values to these images are defined in commctrl.h, so you don't need to know the exact order in the bitmaps. The constants are

```
Constants to access the standard bitmap
STD_CUT                     Edit/Cut button image
STD_COPY                    Edit/Copy button image
STD_PASTE                   Edit/Paste button image
STD_UNDO                    Edit/Undo button image
STD_REDOW                   Edit/Redo button image
STD_DELETE                  Edit/Delete button image
STD_FILENEW                 File/New button image
STD_FILEOPEN                File/Open button image
STD_FILESAVE                File/Save button image
STD_PRINTPRE                Print preview button image
STD_PROPERTIES              Properties button image
STD_HELP                    Help button (Use Commandbar_Addadornments
                            function to add a help button to the
                            command bar.)
STD_FIND                    Find button image
STD_REPLACE                 Replace button image
STD_PRINT                   Print button image

Constants to access the standard view bitmap
VIEW_LARGEICONS             View/Large Icons button image
VIEW_SMALLICONS             View/Small Icons button image
VIEW_LIST                   View/List button image
VIEW_DETAILS                View/Details button image
VIEW_SORTNAME               Sort by name button image
VIEW_SORTSIZE               Sort by size button image
VIEW_SORTDATE               Sort by date button image
VIEW_SORTTYPE               Sort by type button image
VIEW_PARENTFOLDER           Go to Parent folder button image
VIEW_NETCONNECT             Connect network drive button image
VIEW_NETDISCONNECT          Disconnect network drive button image
VIEW_NEWFOLDER              Create new folder button image
```

Referencing images

The images loaded into the command bar are referenced by their index into the list of images. For example, if the bitmap loaded contained five images, and the image to be referenced was the fourth image into the bitmap, the zero-based index value would be 3.

If more than one set of bitmap images was added to the command bar using multiple calls to *CommandBar_AddBitmap*, the images' subsequent lists are referenced according to the previous count of images plus the index into that list. For example, if two calls were made to *CommandBar_AddBitmap* to add two sets of images, with the first call adding five images and the second adding four images, the third image of the second set would be referenced with the total number of images added in the first bitmap (5) plus the index into the second bitmap (2) resulting in an index value of 5 + 2 = 7.

Once the bitmaps have been loaded, the buttons can be added using one of two functions. The first function is this one:

```
BOOL CommandBar_AddButtons (HWND hwndCB, UINT uNumButtons,
                            LPTBBUTTON lpButtons);
```

CommandBar_AddButtons adds a series of buttons to the command bar at one time. The function is passed a count of buttons and a pointer to an array of TBBUTTON structures. Each element of the array describes one button. The TBBUTTON structure is defined as the following:

```
typedef struct {
    int iBitmap;
    int idCommand;
    BYTE fsState;
    BYTE fsStyle;
    DWORD dwData;
    int iString;
} TBBUTTON;
```

The *iBitmap* field specifies the bitmap image to be used by the button. This is, as I just explained, the zero-based index into the list of images. The second parameter is the command ID of the button. This ID value is sent via a WM_COMMAND message to the parent when a user clicks the button.

The *fsState* field specifies the initial state of the button. The allowable values in this field are the following:

- *TBSTATE_ENABLED* The button is enabled. If this flag isn't specified, the button is disabled and is grayed.
- *TBSTATE_HIDDEN* The button isn't visible on the command bar.
- *TBSTATE_PRESSED* This button is displayed in a depressed state.
- *TBSTATE_CHECKED* The button is initially checked. This state can be used only if the button has the TBSTYLE_CHECKED style.
- *TBSTATE_INDETERMINATE* The button is grayed.

One last flag is specified in the documentation, TBSTATE_WRAP, but it doesn't have a valid use in a command bar. This flag is used by toolbars when a toolbar wraps across more than one line.

The *fsStyle* field specifies the initial style of the button, which defines how the button acts. The button can be defined as a standard push button, a check button, a drop-down button, or a check button that resembles a radio button but allows only one button in a group to be checked. The possible flags for the *fsStyle* field are the following:

- *TBSTYLE_BUTTON* The button looks like a standard push button.
- *TBSTYLE_CHECK* The button is a check button that toggles between checked and unchecked states each time the user clicks the button.
- *TBSTYLE_GROUP* Defines the start of a group of buttons.
- *TBSTYLE_CHECKGROUP* The button is a member of a group of check buttons that act like a radio buttons in that only one button in the group is checked at any one time.
- *TBSTYLE_DROPDOWN* The button is a drop-down list button.
- *TBSTYLE_AUTOSIZE* The button's size is defined by the button text.
- *TBSTYLE_SEP* Defines a separator (instead of a button) that inserts a small space between buttons.

The *dwData* field of the TBBUTTON structure is an application-defined value. This value can be set and queried by the application using the TB_SETBUTTONINFO and TB_ GETBUTTONINFO messages. The *iString* field defines the index into the command bar string array that contains the text for the button. The *iString* field can also be filled with a pointer to a string that contains the text for the button.

The other function that adds buttons to a command bar is this one:

```
BOOL CommandBar_InsertButton (HWND hwndCB, int iButton,
                              LPTBBUTTON lpButton);
```

This function inserts one button into the command bar to the left of the button referenced by the *iButton* parameter. The parameters in this function mimic the parameters in *CommandBar_AddButtons* with the exception that the *lpButton* parameter points to a single TBBUTTON structure. The *iButton* parameter specifies the position on the command bar of the new button.

Working with command bar buttons

When a user presses a command bar button other than a drop-down button, the command bar sends a WM_COMMAND message to the parent window of the command bar. So, handling button clicks on the command bar is just like handling menu commands. In fact, since many of the buttons on the command bar have menu command equivalents, it's customary to use the same command IDs for the buttons and the like functioning menus, thus removing the need for any special processing for the command bar buttons.

The command bar maintains the checked and unchecked state of check and checkgroup buttons. After the buttons have been added to the command bar, their states can be queried or set using two messages, TB_ISBUTTONCHECKED and TB_CHECKBUTTON. (The TB_ prefix in these messages indicates the close relationship between the command bar and the toolbar controls.) The TB_ISBUTTONCHECKED message is sent with the ID of the button to be queried passed in the *wParam* parameter this way:

```
fChecked = SendMessage (hwndCB, TB_ISBUTTONCHECKED, wID, 0);
```

where *hwndCB* is the handle to the command bar containing the button. If the return value from the TB_ISBUTTONCHECKED message is nonzero, the button is checked. To place a button in the checked state, send a TB_CHECKBUTTON message to the command bar, as in

```
SendMessage (hwndCB, TB_CHECKBUTTON, wID, TRUE);
```

To uncheck a checked button, replace the TRUE value in *lParam* with FALSE.

A new look for disabled buttons

Windows CE allows you to easily modify the way a command bar or toolbar button looks when the button is disabled. Command bars and toolbars maintain two image lists: the standard image list that I described previously and a disabled image list used to store bitmaps that you can employ for disabled buttons.

To use this new feature, you need to create and load a second image list for disabled buttons. The easiest way to do this is to create the image list for the normal states of the buttons using the techniques I described when I talked about *CommandBar_AddBitmap*. (Image lists in toolbars are loaded with the message TB_LOADIMAGES.) Once that image list complete, simply copy the original image list and modify the bitmaps of the images to create disabled counterparts to the original images. Then load the new image list back into the command bar or toolbar. A short code fragment that accomplishes this chore is shown below.

```
HBITMAP hBmp, hMask;
HIMAGELIST hilDisabled, hilEnabled;

// Load the bitmap and mask to be used in the disabled image list.
hBmp = LoadBitmap (hInst, TEXT ("DisCross"));
hMask = LoadBitmap (hInst, TEXT ("DisMask"));
```

```
// Get the std image list and copy it.
hilEnabled = (HIMAGELIST)SendMessage (hwndCB, TB_GETIMAGELIST, 0, 0);
hilDisabled = ImageList_Duplicate (hilEnabled);

// Replace one bitmap in the disabled list.
ImageList_Replace (hilDisabled, VIEW_LIST, hBmp, hMask);

// Set the disabled image list.
SendMessage (hwndCB, TB_SETDISABLEDIMAGELIST, 0, (LPARAM) hilDisabled);
```

The code fragment first loads a bitmap and a mask bitmap that will replace one of the images in the disabled image list. You retrieve the current image list by sending a TB_GETIMAGELIST message to the command bar, and then you duplicate it using *ImageList_Duplicate*. One image in the image list is then replaced by the bitmap that was loaded earlier.

This example replaces only one image, but in a real-world example many images might be replaced. If all the images were replaced, it might be easier to build the disabled image list from scratch instead of copying the standard image list and replacing a few bitmaps in it. Once the new image list is created, you load it into the command bar by sending a TB_SETDISABLEDIMAGELIST message. The code that I just showed you works just as well for toolbars under Windows CE as it does for command bars.

Drop-down buttons

The drop-down list button is a more complex animal than the standard button on a command bar. The button looks to the user like a button that, when pressed, displays a list of items for the user to select from. To the programmer, a drop-down button is actually a combination of a button and a menu that is displayed when the user clicks on the button. Unfortunately, the command bar does little to support a drop-down button except to modify the button appearance to indicate that the button is a drop-down button and to send a special notification when the button is clicked by the user. It's up to the application to display the menu.

The notification of the user clicking a drop-down button is sent to the parent window of the command bar by a WM_NOTIFY message with a notification value of TBN_DROPDOWN. When the parent window receives the TBN_DROPDOWN notification, it must create a pop-up menu immediately below the drop-down button identified in the notification. The menu is filled by the parent window with whatever selections are appropriate for the button. When one of the menu items is selected, the menu will send a WM_COMMAND message indicating the menu item picked and the menu will be dismissed. The easiest way to understand how to handle a drop-down button notification is to look at the following procedure that handles a TBN_DROPDOWN notification.

```
LRESULT DoNotifyMain (HWND hWnd, UINT wMsg, WPARAM wParam,
                      LPARAM lParam) {
    LPNMHDR pNotifyHeader;
    LPNMTOOLBAR pNotifyToolBar;
    RECT rect;
    TPMPARAMS tpm;
    HMENU hMenu;

    // Get pointer to notify message header.
    pNotifyHeader = (LPNMHDR)lParam;

    if (pNotifyHeader->code == TBN_DROPDOWN) {

        // Get pointer to toolbar notify structure.
        pNotifyToolBar = (LPNMTOOLBAR)lParam;

        // Get the rectangle of the drop-down button.
        SendMessage (pNotifyHeader->hwndFrom, TB_GETRECT,
                     pNotifyToolBar->iItem, (LPARAM)&rect);

        // Convert rect into screen coordinates.  The rect is
        // considered here to be an array of 2 POINT  structures.
        MapWindowPoints (pNotifyHeader->hwndFrom, HWND_DESKTOP,
                         (LPPOINT)&rect, 2);

        // Prevent the menu from covering the button.
        tpm.cbSize = sizeof (tpm);
        CopyRect (&tpm.rcExclude, &rect);

        // Load the menu resource to display under the button.
        hMenu = GetSubMenu (LoadMenu (hInst, TEXT ("popmenu")),0);

        // Display the menu.  This function returns after the
        // user makes a selection or dismisses the menu.
        TrackPopupMenuEx (hMenu, TPM_LEFTALIGN | TPM_VERTICAL,
                          rect.left, rect.bottom, hWnd, &tpm);
    }
    return 0;
}
```

After the code determines that the message is a TBN_DROPDOWN notification, the first task of the notification handler code is to get the rectangle of the drop-down button. The rectangle is queried so that the drop-down menu can be positioned immediately below the button. To do this, the routine sends a TB_GETRECT message to the command bar with the ID of the drop-down button passed in *wParam* and a pointer to a rectangle structure in *lParam*.

Since the rectangle returned is in the coordinate base of the parent window, and pop-up menus are positioned in screen coordinates, the coordinates must be converted from one basis to the other. You accomplish this using the function

```
MapWindowPoints (HWND hwndFrom, HWND hwndTo,
                 LPPOINT lppoints, UINT cPoints);
```

The first parameter is the handle of the window in which the coordinates are originally based. The second parameter is the handle of the window to which you want to map the coordinates. The third parameter is a pointer to an array of points to be translated; the last parameter is the number of points in the array. In the routine I just showed you, the window handles are the command bar handle and the desktop window handle, respectively.

Once the rectangle has been translated into desktop coordinates, the pop-up, or context, menu can be created. You do this by first loading the menu from the resource, then displaying the menu with a call to *TrackPopupMenuEx*. That function is prototyped as

```
BOOL TrackPopupMenuEx (HMENU hmenu, UINT fuFlags, int x, int y,
                       HWND hwnd, LPTPMPARAMS lptpm);
```

The *hMenu* parameter is the handle of the menu to be displayed. The *hwnd* parameter identifies the window to receive the WM_COMMAND message if a menu item is selected. The TPMPARAMS structure contains a rectangle that won't be covered up by the menu when it is displayed. For our purposes, this rectangle is set to the dimensions of the drop-down button so that the button won't be covered by the pop-up menu. The *fuFlags* field can contain a number of values that define the placement of the menu. For drop-down buttons, the only flag needed is TPM_VERTICAL. If TMP_VERTICAL is set, the menu leaves uncovered as much of the horizontal area of the exclude rectangle as possible. The *TrackPopupMenuEx* function doesn't return until an item on the menu has been selected or the menu has been dismissed by the user tapping on another part of the screen.

Combo boxes on the command bar

Combo boxes on a command bar are much easier to implement than drop-down buttons. You add a combo box by calling

```
HWND CommandBar_InsertComboBox (HWND hwndCB, HINSTANCE hInst,
                                int iWidth, UINT dwStyle,
                                WORD idComboBox,
                                int iButton);
```

This function inserts a combo box on the command bar to the left of the button indicated by the *iButton* parameter. The width of the combo box is specified, in pixels, by the *iWidth* parameter. The *dwStyle* parameter specifies the style of the combo box.

The allowable style flags are any valid Windows CE combo box style and window styles. The function automatically adds the WS_CHILD and WS_VISIBLE flags when creating the combo box. The *idComboBox* parameter is the ID for the combo box that will be used when WM_COMMAND messages are sent notifying the parent window of a combo box event. Experienced Windows programmers will be happy to know that *CommandBar_InsertComboBox* takes care of all the "parenting" problems that occur when a control is added to a standard Windows toolbar. That one function call is all that is needed to create a properly functioning combo box on the command bar.

Once a combo box is created, you program it on the command bar the same way you would a stand-alone combo box. Since the combo box is a child of the command bar, you must query the window handle of the combo box by passing the handle of the command bar to *GetDlgItem* with the ID value of the combo box, as in the following code:

```
hwndCombobox = GetDlgItem (GetDlgItem (hWnd, IDC_CMDBAR),
                           IDC_COMBO));
```

However, the WM_COMMAND messages from the combo box are sent directly to the parent of the command bar, so handling combo box events is identical to handling them from a combo box created as a child of the application's top-level window.

Command bar tool tips

Tool tips are small windows that display descriptive text that labels a command bar button when the stylus is held down over the control. Tool tips under Windows CE are implemented in a completely different way from how they're implemented under Windows 98 and Windows NT.

You add tool tips to a command bar by using this function:

```
BOOL CommandBar_AddToolTips (HWND hwndCB, UINT uNumToolTips,
                             LPTSTR lpToolTips);
```

The *lpToolTips* parameter must point to an array of pointers to strings. The *uNumToolTips* parameter should be set to the number of elements in the string pointer array. The *CommandBar_AddToolTips* function doesn't copy the strings into its own storage. Instead, the location of the string array is saved. This means that the block of memory containing the string array must not be released until the command bar is destroyed.

Each string in the array becomes the tool tip text for a control or separator on the command bar excluding the menu. The first string in the array becomes the tool tip for the first control or separator, the second string is assigned to the second control or separator, and so on. So, even though combo boxes and separators don't display tool tips, they must have entries in the string array so that all the text lines up with the proper buttons.

Other command bar functions

A number of other functions assist in command bar management. The *CommandBar_Height* function returns the height of the command bar and is used in all the example programs that use the command bar. Likewise, the *CommandBar_AddAdornments* function is also used whenever a command bar is used. This function, prototyped as

```
BOOL CommandBar_AddAdornments (HWND hwndCB, DWORD dwFlags,
                               DWORD dwReserved);
```

places a Close button and, if you want, a Help button and an OK button on the extreme right of the command bar. You pass a CMDBAR_HELP flag to the *dwFlags* parameter to add a Help button, and you pass a CMDBAR_OK flag to add an OK button.

The Help button is treated differently from other buttons on the command bar. When the Help button is pressed, the command bar sends a WM_HELP message to the owner of the command bar instead of the standard WM_COMMAND message. The OK button's action is more traditional. When it is pressed, a WM_COMMAND message is sent with a control ID of IDOK. *CommandBar_AddAdornments* must be called after all other conrols of the command bar have been added.

A command bar can be hidden by calling

```
BOOL CommandBar_Show (HWND hwndCB, BOOL fShow);
```

The *fShow* parameter is set to TRUE to show the command bar and FALSE to hide a command bar. The visibility of a command bar can be queried with this:

```
BOOL CommandBar_IsVisible (HWND hwndCB);
```

Finally, a command bar can be destroyed using this:

```
void CommandBar_Destroy (HWND hwndCB);
```

Although a command bar is automatically destroyed when its parent window is destroyed, sometimes it's more convenient to destroy a command bar manually. This is often done if a new command bar is needed for a different mode of the application. Of course, you can create multiple command bars, hiding all but one and switching between them by showing only one at a time, but this isn't good programming practice under Windows CE because all those hidden command bars take up valuable RAM that could be used elsewhere. The proper method is to destroy and create command bars on the fly. You can create a command bar fast enough so that a user shouldn't notice any delay in the application when a new command bar is created.

Design guidelines for command bars

Because command bars are a major element of Windows CE applications, it's not surprising that Microsoft has a rather strong set of rules for their use. Many of these rules are similar to the design guidelines for other versions of Windows, such as the recommendations for the ordering of main menu items and the use of tool tips. Most of these guidelines are already second nature for Windows programmers.

The menu should be the left-most item on the command bar. The order of the main menu items should be from left to right: File, Edit, View, Insert, Format, Tools, and Window. Of course, most applications have all of those menu items but the order of the items used should follow the suggested order. For buttons, the order is from left to right; New, Open, Save, and Print for file actions; and Bold, Italic, and Underline for font style.

The CmdBar Example Program

The CmdBar example demonstrates the basics of command bar operation. On startup, the example creates a bar with only a menu and a close button. Selecting the different items from the view menu creates various command bars showing the capabilities of the command bar control. The source code for CmdBar is shown in Figure 5-4.

CmdBar.rc

```
//======================================================================
// Resource file
//
// Written for the book Programming Windows CE
// Copyright (C) 1998 Douglas Boling
//======================================================================
#include "windows.h"
#include "CmdBar.h"                        // Program-specific stuff

//----------------------------------------------------------------------
// Icons and bitmaps
//
ID_ICON       ICON   "cmdbar.ico"       // Program icon
DisCross      BITMAP "cross.bmp"        // Disabled button image
DisMask       BITMAP "mask.bmp"         // Disabled button image mask
SortDropBtn   BITMAP "sortdrop.bmp"     // Sort drop-down button image

//----------------------------------------------------------------------
// Menu
//
ID_MENU MENU DISCARDABLE
BEGIN
    POPUP "&File"
    BEGIN
        MENUITEM "E&xit",                        IDM_EXIT
    END
```

Figure 5-4. *The CmdBar program.*

```
    POPUP "&View"
    BEGIN
        MENUITEM "&Standard",                    IDM_STDBAR
        MENUITEM "&View",                        IDM_VIEWBAR
        MENUITEM "&Combination",                 IDM_COMBOBAR
    END
    POPUP "&Help"
    BEGIN
        MENUITEM "&About...",                    IDM_ABOUT
    END
END

popmenu MENU DISCARDABLE
BEGIN
    POPUP "&Sort"
    BEGIN
        MENUITEM "&Name",                        IDC_SNAME
        MENUITEM "&Type",                        IDC_STYPE
        MENUITEM "&Size",                        IDC_SSIZE
        MENUITEM "&Date",                        IDC_SDATE
    END
END

//----------------------------------------------------------------------
// About box dialog template
//
aboutbox DIALOG discardable 10, 10, 160, 40
STYLE  WS_POPUP | WS_VISIBLE | WS_CAPTION | WS_SYSMENU |
       DS_CENTER | DS_MODALFRAME
CAPTION "About"
BEGIN
    ICON  ID_ICON,                   -1,   5,   5,  10,  10
    LTEXT "CmdBar - Written for the book Programming Windows \
           CE Copyright 1998 Douglas Boling"
                                     -1,  40,   5, 110,  30
END
```

CmdBar.h

```
//======================================================================
// Header file
//
// Written for the book Programming Windows CE
// Copyright (C) 1998 Douglas Boling
//======================================================================
// Returns number of elements
```

(continued)

Figure 5-4. *continued*

```
#define dim(x) (sizeof(x) / sizeof(x[0]))

//----------------------------------------------------------------------
// Generic defines and data types
//
struct decodeUINT {                             // Structure associates
    UINT Code;                                  // messages
                                                // with a function.
    LRESULT (*Fxn)(HWND, UINT, WPARAM, LPARAM);
};
struct decodeCMD {                              // Structure associates
    UINT Code;                                  // menu IDs with a
    LRESULT (*Fxn)(HWND, WORD, HWND, WORD);     // function.
};

//----------------------------------------------------------------------
// Generic defines used by application
#define  IDC_CMDBAR          1                  // Command band ID
#define  ID_ICON             10                 // Icon resource ID
#define  ID_MENU             11                 // Main menu resource ID
#define  IDC_COMBO           12                 // Combo box on cmd bar ID

// Menu item IDs
#define  IDM_EXIT            101                // File menu
#define  IDM_STDBAR          111                // View menu
#define  IDM_VIEWBAR         112
#define  IDM_COMBOBAR        113
#define  IDM_ABOUT           120                // Help menu

// Command bar button IDs
#define  IDC_NEW             201
#define  IDC_OPEN            202
#define  IDC_SAVE            203
#define  IDC_CUT             204
#define  IDC_COPY            205
#define  IDC_PASTE           206
#define  IDC_PROP            207

#define  IDC_LICON           301
#define  IDC_SICON           302
#define  IDC_LIST            303
#define  IDC_RPT             304
#define  IDC_SNAME           305
#define  IDC_STYPE           306
#define  IDC_SSIZE           307
#define  IDC_SDATE           308
```

```
#define  IDC_DPSORT          350

#define  STD_BMPS            (STD_PRINT+1)      // Number of bmps in
                                                // std imglist
#define  VIEW_BMPS           (VIEW_NEWFOLDER+1) // Number of bmps in
                                                // view imglist

//----------------------------------------------------------------------
// Function prototypes
//
int InitApp (HINSTANCE);
HWND InitInstance (HINSTANCE, LPWSTR, int);
int TermInstance (HINSTANCE, int);

// Window procedures
LRESULT CALLBACK MainWndProc (HWND, UINT, WPARAM, LPARAM);

// Message handlers
LRESULT DoCreateMain (HWND, UINT, WPARAM, LPARAM);
LRESULT DoCommandMain (HWND, UINT, WPARAM, LPARAM);
LRESULT DoNotifyMain (HWND, UINT, WPARAM, LPARAM);
LRESULT DoDestroyMain (HWND, UINT, WPARAM, LPARAM);

// Command functions
LPARAM DoMainCommandExit (HWND, WORD, HWND, WORD);
LPARAM DoMainCommandVStd (HWND, WORD, HWND, WORD);
LPARAM DoMainCommandVView (HWND, WORD, HWND, WORD);
LPARAM DoMainCommandVCombo (HWND, WORD, HWND, WORD);
LPARAM DoMainCommandAbout (HWND, WORD, HWND, WORD);

// Dialog procedures
BOOL CALLBACK AboutDlgProc (HWND, UINT, WPARAM, LPARAM);
```

CmdBar.c

```
//======================================================================
// CmdBar - Command bar demonstration
//
// Written for the book Programming Windows CE
// Copyright (C) 1998 Douglas Boling
//======================================================================
#include <windows.h>                 // For all that Windows stuff
#include <commctrl.h>                // Command bar includes
#include "CmdBar.h"                  // Program-specific stuff
```

(continued)

Figure 5-4. *continued*

```
//----------------------------------------------------------------------
// Global data
//
const TCHAR szAppName[] = TEXT ("CmdBar");
HINSTANCE hInst;                        // Program instance handle

// Message dispatch table for MainWindowProc
const struct decodeUINT MainMessages[] = {
    WM_CREATE, DoCreateMain,
    WM_COMMAND, DoCommandMain,
    WM_NOTIFY, DoNotifyMain,
    WM_DESTROY, DoDestroyMain,
};

// Command Message dispatch for MainWindowProc
const struct decodeCMD MainCommandItems[] = {
    IDM_EXIT, DoMainCommandExit,
    IDM_STDBAR, DoMainCommandVStd,
    IDM_VIEWBAR, DoMainCommandVView,
    IDM_COMBOBAR, DoMainCommandVCombo,
    IDM_ABOUT, DoMainCommandAbout,
};

// Standard file bar button structure
const TBBUTTON tbCBStdBtns[] = {
//  BitmapIndex       Command    State        Style        UserData String
    {0,               0,         0,           TBSTYLE_SEP,        0,   0},
    {STD_FILENEW,     IDC_NEW,   TBSTATE_ENABLED,
                                              TBSTYLE_BUTTON,     0,   0},
    {STD_FILEOPEN,    IDC_OPEN,  TBSTATE_ENABLED,
                                              TBSTYLE_BUTTON,     0,   0},
    {STD_FILESAVE,    IDC_SAVE,  TBSTATE_ENABLED,
                                              TBSTYLE_BUTTON,     0,   0},
    {0,                 0,       0,           TBSTYLE_SEP,        0,   0},
    {STD_CUT,         IDC_CUT,   TBSTATE_ENABLED,
                                              TBSTYLE_BUTTON,     0,   0},
    {STD_COPY,        IDC_COPY,  TBSTATE_ENABLED,
                                              TBSTYLE_BUTTON,     0,   0},
    {STD_PASTE,       IDC_PASTE, TBSTATE_ENABLED,
                                              TBSTYLE_BUTTON,     0,   0},
    {0,                 0,       0,           TBSTYLE_SEP,        0,   0},
    {STD_PROPERTIES,  IDC_PROP,  TBSTATE_ENABLED,
        TBSTYLE_BUTTON,    0,   0}
};
```

```
// Standard view bar button structure
const TBBUTTON tbCBViewBtns[] = {
//   BitmapIndex        Command     State          Style         UserData String
    {0,                 0,          0,             TBSTYLE_SEP,         0,  0},
    {VIEW_LARGEICONS, IDC_LICON, TBSTATE_ENABLED | TBSTATE_CHECKED,
                                                   TBSTYLE_CHECKGROUP, 0,  0},
    {VIEW_SMALLICONS, IDC_SICON, TBSTATE_ENABLED,
                                                   TBSTYLE_CHECKGROUP, 0,  0},
    {VIEW_LIST,         IDC_LIST,  0,              TBSTYLE_CHECKGROUP, 0,  0},
    {VIEW_DETAILS,      IDC_RPT,   TBSTATE_ENABLED,
                                                   TBSTYLE_CHECKGROUP, 0,  0},
    {0,                 0,         TBSTATE_ENABLED,
                                                   TBSTYLE_SEP,         0,  0},
    {VIEW_SORTNAME,     IDC_SNAME, TBSTATE_ENABLED | TBSTATE_CHECKED,
                                                   TBSTYLE_CHECKGROUP, 0,  0},
    {VIEW_SORTTYPE,     IDC_STYPE, TBSTATE_ENABLED,
                                                   TBSTYLE_CHECKGROUP, 0,  0},
    {VIEW_SORTSIZE,     IDC_SSIZE, TBSTATE_ENABLED,
                                                   TBSTYLE_CHECKGROUP, 0,  0},
    {VIEW_SORTDATE,     IDC_SDATE, TBSTATE_ENABLED,
                                                   TBSTYLE_CHECKGROUP, 0,  0},
    {0,                 0,         0,              TBSTYLE_SEP,         0,  0},
};
// Tooltip string list for view bar
const TCHAR *pViewTips[] = {TEXT (""),
                            TEXT ("Large"),
                            TEXT ("Small"),
                            TEXT ("List"),
                            TEXT ("Details"),
                            TEXT (""),
                            TEXT ("Sort by Name"),
                            TEXT ("Sort by Type"),
                            TEXT ("Sort by Size"),
                            TEXT ("Sort by Date"),
};

// Combination standard and view bar button structure
const TBBUTTON tbCBCmboBtns[] = {
//   BitmapIndex        Command     State          Style         UserData String
    {0,                 0,          0,             TBSTYLE_SEP,         0,  0},
    {STD_FILENEW,       IDC_NEW,    TBSTATE_ENABLED,
                                                   TBSTYLE_BUTTON,      0,  0},
    {STD_FILEOPEN,      IDC_OPEN,   TBSTATE_ENABLED,
                                                   TBSTYLE_BUTTON,      0,  0},
    {STD_PROPERTIES,    IDC_PROP,   TBSTATE_ENABLED,
                                                   TBSTYLE_BUTTON,      0,  0},
```

(continued)

Figure 5-4. *continued*

```
    {0,                 0,          0,          TBSTYLE_SEP,        0,  0},
    {STD_CUT,           IDC_CUT,    TBSTATE_ENABLED,
                                                TBSTYLE_BUTTON,     0,  0},
    {STD_COPY,          IDC_COPY,   TBSTATE_ENABLED,
                                                TBSTYLE_BUTTON,     0,  0},
    {STD_PASTE,         IDC_PASTE,  TBSTATE_ENABLED,
                                                TBSTYLE_BUTTON,     0,  0},
    {0,                 0,          0,          TBSTYLE_SEP,        0,  0},
    {STD_BMPS + VIEW_LARGEICONS,
                        IDC_LICON,  TBSTATE_ENABLED | TBSTATE_CHECKED,
                                                TBSTYLE_CHECKGROUP, 0,  0},
    {STD_BMPS + VIEW_SMALLICONS,
                        IDC_SICON,  TBSTATE_ENABLED,
                                                TBSTYLE_CHECKGROUP, 0,  0},
    {STD_BMPS + VIEW_LIST,
                        IDC_LIST,   TBSTATE_ENABLED,
                                                TBSTYLE_CHECKGROUP, 0,  0},
    {STD_BMPS + VIEW_DETAILS,
                        IDC_RPT,    TBSTATE_ENABLED,
                                                TBSTYLE_CHECKGROUP, 0,  0},
    {0,                 0,          0,          TBSTYLE_SEP,        0,  0},
    {STD_BMPS + VIEW_BMPS,
                        IDC_DPSORT,TBSTATE_ENABLED,
                                                TBSTYLE_DROPDOWN,   0,  0}
};

//======================================================================
// Program entry point
//
int WINAPI WinMain (HINSTANCE hInstance, HINSTANCE hPrevInstance,
                    LPWSTR lpCmdLine, int nCmdShow) {
    HWND hwndMain;
    MSG msg;
    int rc = 0;

    // Initialize application.
    rc = InitApp (hInstance);
    if (rc) return rc;

    // Initialize this instance.
    hwndMain = InitInstance (hInstance, lpCmdLine, nCmdShow);
    if (hwndMain == 0)
        return 0x10;

    // Application message loop
    while (GetMessage (&msg, NULL, 0, 0)) {
```

```
        TranslateMessage (&msg);
        DispatchMessage (&msg);
    }
    // Instance cleanup
    return TermInstance (hInstance, msg.wParam);
}
//----------------------------------------------------------------------
// InitApp - Application initialization
//
int InitApp (HINSTANCE hInstance) {
    WNDCLASS wc;
    INITCOMMONCONTROLSEX icex;

    // Register application main window class.
    wc.style = 0;                             // Window style
    wc.lpfnWndProc = MainWndProc;             // Callback function
    wc.cbClsExtra = 0;                        // Extra class data
    wc.cbWndExtra = 0;                        // Extra window data
    wc.hInstance = hInstance;                 // Owner handle
    wc.hIcon = NULL,                          // Application icon
    wc.hCursor = NULL;                        // Default cursor
    wc.hbrBackground = (HBRUSH) GetStockObject (WHITE_BRUSH);
    wc.lpszMenuName =  NULL;                  // Menu name
    wc.lpszClassName = szAppName;             // Window class name

    if (RegisterClass (&wc) == 0) return 1;

    // Load the command bar common control class.
    icex.dwSize = sizeof (INITCOMMONCONTROLSEX);
    icex.dwICC = ICC_BAR_CLASSES;
    InitCommonControlsEx (&icex);
    return 0;
}
//----------------------------------------------------------------------
// InitInstance - Instance initialization
//
HWND InitInstance (HINSTANCE hInstance, LPWSTR lpCmdLine, int nCmdShow){
    HWND hWnd;

    // Save program instance handle in global variable.
    hInst = hInstance;

    // Create main window.
    hWnd = CreateWindow (szAppName,           // Window class
                         TEXT ("CmdBar Demo"), // Window title
                         WS_VISIBLE,          // Style flags
```

(continued)

Figure 5-4. *continued*

```
                            CW_USEDEFAULT,          // x position
                            CW_USEDEFAULT,          // y position
                            CW_USEDEFAULT,          // Initial width
                            CW_USEDEFAULT,          // Initial height
                            NULL,                   // Parent
                            NULL,                   // Menu, must be null
                            hInstance,              // Application instance
                            NULL);                  // Pointer to create
                                                    // parameters
    // Return fail code if window not created.
    if (!IsWindow (hWnd)) return 0;

    // Standard show and update calls
    ShowWindow (hWnd, nCmdShow);
    UpdateWindow (hWnd);
    return hWnd;
}
//----------------------------------------------------------------------
// TermInstance - Program cleanup
//
int TermInstance (HINSTANCE hInstance, int nDefRC) {
    return nDefRC;
}
//======================================================================
// Message handling procedures for MainWindow
//----------------------------------------------------------------------
// MainWndProc - Callback function for application window
//
LRESULT CALLBACK MainWndProc (HWND hWnd, UINT wMsg, WPARAM wParam,
                              LPARAM lParam) {
    INT i;
    //
    // Search message list to see if we need to handle this
    // message.  If in list, call procedure.
    //
    for (i = 0; i < dim(MainMessages); i++) {
        if (wMsg == MainMessages[i].Code)
            return (*MainMessages[i].Fxn)(hWnd, wMsg, wParam, lParam);
    }
    return DefWindowProc (hWnd, wMsg, wParam, lParam);
}
//----------------------------------------------------------------------
// DoCreateMain - Process WM_CREATE message for window.
//
```

```
LRESULT DoCreateMain (HWND hWnd, UINT wMsg, WPARAM wParam,
                      LPARAM lParam) {
    HWND hwndCB;

    // Create a minimal command bar that only has a menu and an
    // exit button.
    hwndCB = CommandBar_Create (hInst, hWnd, IDC_CMDBAR);

    // Insert the menu.
    CommandBar_InsertMenubar (hwndCB, hInst, ID_MENU, 0);

    // Add exit button to command bar.
    CommandBar_AddAdornments (hwndCB, 0, 0);
    return 0;
}
//----------------------------------------------------------------------
// DoCommandMain - Process WM_COMMAND message for window.
//
LRESULT DoCommandMain (HWND hWnd, UINT wMsg, WPARAM wParam,
                       LPARAM lParam) {
    WORD idItem, wNotifyCode;
    HWND hwndCtl;
    INT  i;

    // Parse the parameters.
    idItem = (WORD) LOWORD (wParam);
    wNotifyCode = (WORD) HIWORD (wParam);
    hwndCtl = (HWND) lParam;

    // Call routine to handle control message.
    for (i = 0; i < dim(MainCommandItems); i++) {
        if (idItem == MainCommandItems[i].Code)
            return (*MainCommandItems[i].Fxn)(hWnd, idItem, hwndCtl,
                                              wNotifyCode);
    }
    return 0;
}
//----------------------------------------------------------------------
// DoNotifyMain - Process WM_NOTIFY message for window.
//
LRESULT DoNotifyMain (HWND hWnd, UINT wMsg, WPARAM wParam,
                      LPARAM lParam) {
    LPNMHDR pNotifyHeader;
    LPNMTOOLBAR pNotifyToolBar;
```

(continued)

Figure 5-4. *continued*

```
    RECT rect;
    TPMPARAMS tpm;
    HMENU hMenu;

    // Get pointer to notify message header.
    pNotifyHeader = (LPNMHDR)lParam;

    if (pNotifyHeader->code == TBN_DROPDOWN) {

        // Get pointer to toolbar notify structure.
        pNotifyToolBar = (LPNMTOOLBAR)lParam;

        if (pNotifyToolBar->iItem == IDC_DPSORT) {

            // Get the rectangle of the drop-down button.
            SendMessage (pNotifyHeader->hwndFrom, TB_GETRECT,
                         pNotifyToolBar->iItem, (LPARAM)&rect);

            // Convert rect into screen coordinates.  The rect is
            // considered here to be an array of 2 POINT structures.
            MapWindowPoints (pNotifyHeader->hwndFrom, HWND_DESKTOP,
                             (LPPOINT)&rect, 2);

            // Prevent the menu from covering the button.
            tpm.cbSize = sizeof (tpm);
            CopyRect (&tpm.rcExclude, &rect);

            hMenu = GetSubMenu (LoadMenu (hInst, TEXT ("popmenu")),0);
            TrackPopupMenuEx (hMenu, TPM_LEFTALIGN | TPM_VERTICAL,
                              rect.left, rect.bottom, hWnd, &tpm);
        }
    }
    return 0;
}
//----------------------------------------------------------------------
// DoDestroyMain - Process WM_DESTROY message for window.
//
LRESULT DoDestroyMain (HWND hWnd, UINT wMsg, WPARAM wParam,
                       LPARAM lParam) {
    PostQuitMessage (0);
    return 0;
}
//======================================================================
// Command handler routines
//----------------------------------------------------------------------
// DoMainCommandExit - Process Program Exit command.
//
```

```
LPARAM DoMainCommandExit (HWND hWnd, WORD idItem, HWND hwndCtl,
                          WORD wNotifyCode) {

    SendMessage (hWnd, WM_CLOSE, 0, 0);
    return 0;
}
//----------------------------------------------------------------------
// DoMainCommandViewStd - Displays a standard edit-centric cmd bar
//
LPARAM DoMainCommandVStd (HWND hWnd, WORD idItem, HWND hwndCtl,
                          WORD wNotifyCode) {
    HWND hwndCB;

    // If a command bar exists, kill it.
    if (hwndCB = GetDlgItem (hWnd, IDC_CMDBAR))
        CommandBar_Destroy (hwndCB);

    // Create a command bar.
    hwndCB = CommandBar_Create (hInst, hWnd, IDC_CMDBAR);

    // Insert a menu.
    CommandBar_InsertMenubar (hwndCB, hInst, ID_MENU, 0);

    // Insert buttons.
    CommandBar_AddBitmap (hwndCB, HINST_COMMCTRL, IDB_STD_SMALL_COLOR,
                          STD_BMPS, 0, 0);

    CommandBar_AddButtons (hwndCB, dim(tbCBStdBtns), tbCBStdBtns);

    // Add exit button to command bar.
    CommandBar_AddAdornments (hwndCB, 0, 0);
    return 0;
}
//----------------------------------------------------------------------
// DoMainCommandVView - Displays a standard edit-centric cmd bar
//
LPARAM DoMainCommandVView (HWND hWnd, WORD idItem, HWND hwndCtl,
                           WORD wNotifyCode) {
    INT i;
    HWND hwndCB;
    TCHAR szTmp[64];
    HBITMAP hBmp, hMask;
    HIMAGELIST hilDisabled, hilEnabled;

    // If a command bar exists, kill it.
    if (hwndCB = GetDlgItem (hWnd, IDC_CMDBAR))
        CommandBar_Destroy (hwndCB);
```

(continued)

Figure 5-4. *continued*

```
    // Create a command bar.
    hwndCB = CommandBar_Create (hInst, hWnd, IDC_CMDBAR);

    // Insert a menu.
    CommandBar_InsertMenubar (hwndCB, hInst, ID_MENU, 0);

    // Insert buttons, first add a bitmap and then the buttons.
    CommandBar_AddBitmap (hwndCB, HINST_COMMCTRL, IDB_VIEW_SMALL_COLOR,
                          VIEW_BMPS, 0, 0);

    // Load bitmaps for disabled image.
    hBmp = LoadBitmap (hInst, TEXT ("DisCross"));
    hMask = LoadBitmap (hInst, TEXT ("DisMask"));

    // Get the current image list and copy.
    hilEnabled = (HIMAGELIST)SendMessage (hwndCB, TB_GETIMAGELIST, 0, 0);
    hilDisabled = ImageList_Duplicate (hilEnabled);

    // Replace a button image with the disabled image.
    ImageList_Replace (hilDisabled, VIEW_LIST, hBmp, hMask);

    // Set disabled image list.
    SendMessage (hwndCB,  TB_SETDISABLEDIMAGELIST, 0,
                 (LPARAM)hilDisabled);

    // Add buttons to the command bar.
    CommandBar_AddButtons (hwndCB, dim(tbCBViewBtns), tbCBViewBtns);

    // Add tooltips to the command bar.
    CommandBar_AddToolTips (hwndCB, dim(pViewTips), pViewTips);

    // Add a combo box between the view icons and the sort icons.
    CommandBar_InsertComboBox (hwndCB, hInst, 75,
                               CBS_DROPDOWNLIST | WS_VSCROLL,
                               IDC_COMBO, 6);
    // Fill in combo box.
    for (i = 0; i < 10; i++) {
        wsprintf (szTmp, TEXT ("Item %d"), i);
        SendDlgItemMessage (hwndCB, IDC_COMBO, CB_INSERTSTRING, -1,
                            (LPARAM)szTmp);
    }
    SendDlgItemMessage (hwndCB, IDC_COMBO, CB_SETCURSEL, 0, 0);

    // Add exit button to command bar.
    CommandBar_AddAdornments (hwndCB, 0, 0);
    return 0;
}
```

```
//----------------------------------------------------------------------
// DoMainCommandVCombo - Displays a combination of file and edit buttons
//
LPARAM DoMainCommandVCombo (HWND hWnd, WORD idItem, HWND hwndCtl,
                            WORD wNotifyCode) {
    HWND hwndCB;

    // If a command bar exists, kill it.
    if (hwndCB = GetDlgItem (hWnd, IDC_CMDBAR))
        CommandBar_Destroy (hwndCB);

    // Create a command bar.
    hwndCB = CommandBar_Create (hInst, hWnd, IDC_CMDBAR);

    // Insert a menu.
    CommandBar_InsertMenubar (hwndCB, hInst, ID_MENU, 0);

    // Add two bitmap lists plus custom bmp for drop-down button.
    CommandBar_AddBitmap (hwndCB, HINST_COMMCTRL, IDB_STD_SMALL_COLOR,
                          STD_BMPS, 0, 0);
    CommandBar_AddBitmap (hwndCB, HINST_COMMCTRL, IDB_VIEW_SMALL_COLOR,
                          VIEW_BMPS, 0, 0);
    CommandBar_AddBitmap (hwndCB, NULL,
                          (int)LoadBitmap (hInst, TEXT ("SortDropBtn")),
                          1, 0, 0);

    CommandBar_AddButtons (hwndCB, dim(tbCBCmboBtns), tbCBCmboBtns);

    // Add exit button to command bar.
    CommandBar_AddAdornments (hwndCB, 0, 0);
    return 0;
}
//----------------------------------------------------------------------
// DoMainCommandAbout - Process the Help | About menu command.
//
LPARAM DoMainCommandAbout(HWND hWnd, WORD idItem, HWND hwndCtl,
                          WORD wNotifyCode) {

    // Use DialogBox to create modal dialog box.
    DialogBox (hInst, TEXT ("aboutbox"), hWnd, AboutDlgProc);
    return 0;
}
//======================================================================
// About Dialog procedure
//
```

(continued)

Figure 5-4. *continued*

```
BOOL CALLBACK AboutDlgProc (HWND hWnd, UINT wMsg, WPARAM wParam,
                            LPARAM lParam) {

    switch (wMsg) {
        case WM_COMMAND:
            switch (LOWORD (wParam)) {
                case IDOK:
                case IDCANCEL:
                    EndDialog (hWnd, 0);
                    return TRUE;
            }
        break;
    }
    return FALSE;
}
```

Each of the three command bars created in CmdBar demonstrate different capabilities of the command bar control. The first command bar, created in the routine *DoMainCommandVStd* creates a vanilla command bar with a menu and a set of buttons. The button structure for this command bar is defined in the array *tbCBStdBtns,* which is defined near the top of CmdBar.C.

The second command bar, created in the routine *DoMainCommandVView,* contains two groups of checkgroup buttons separated by a combo box. This command bar also demonstrates the use of a separate image for a disabled button. The list view button, the third button on the bar, is disabled. The image for that button in the image list for disabled buttons is replaced with a bitmap that looks like an X.

The *DoMainCommandVCombo* routine creates the third command bar. It uses both the standard and view bitmap images as well as a custom bitmap for a drop-down button. This command bar demonstrates the technique of referencing the images in an image list that contains multiple bitmaps. The drop-down button is serviced by the *OnNotifiyMain* routine where a pop-up menu is loaded and displayed when a TBN_DROPDOWN notification is received.

Command Bands

Command bands appeared in Windows CE 2.0 and are a valuable feature, especially in their capacity to contain separate bands that can be dragged around by a user. Each individual band can have a "gripper" that can be used to drag the band to a new position. A band can be in a minimized state, showing only its gripper and, if you want, an icon; in a maximized state, covering up the other bands on the line; or restored, sharing space with the other bands on the same line. You can even move bands to a new row, creating a multiple-row command band.

The standard use of a command bands control is to break up the elements of a command bar—menu, buttons, and other controls—into separate bands. This allows users to rearrange these elements as they see fit. Users can also expose or overlap separate bands as needed in order to provide a larger total area for menus, buttons, and other controls.

Creating a command bands control

Creating a command bands control is straightforward, if a bit more involved than creating a command bar control. You create the control by calling

```
HWND CommandBands_Create (HINSTANCE hinst, HWND hwndParent, UINT wID,
                          DWORD dwStyles, HIMAGELIST himl);
```

The *dwStyles* parameter accepts a number of flags that define the look and operation of the command bands control. These styles match the rebar styles; the command bands control is, after all, closely related to the rebar control.

- *RBS_AUTOSIZE* Bands are automatically reformatted if the size or position of the control is changed.
- *RBS_BANDBORDERS* Each band is drawn with lines to separate adjacent bands.
- *RBS_FIXEDORDER* Bands can be moved but always remain in the same order.
- *RBS_SMARTLABELS* When minimized, a band is displayed with its icon. When restored or maximized, the band's label text is displayed.
- *RBS_VARHEIGHT* Each row in the control is vertically sized to the minimum required by the bands on that row. Without this flag, the height of every row is defined by the height of the tallest band in the control.
- *CCS_VERT* Creates a vertical command bands control.
- *RBS_VERTICALGRIPPER* Displays a gripper appropriate for a vertical command bar. This flag is ignored unless CCS_VERT is set.

Of these styles, the RBS_SMARTLABLES and RBS_VARHEIGHT are the two most frequently used flags. The RBS_SMARTLABLES flag lets you choose an attractive appearance for the command bands control without requiring any effort from the application. The RBS_VARHEIGHT flag is important if you use controls in a band other than the default command bar. The CCS_VERT style creates a vertical command bands control, but because Windows CE doesn't support vertical menus, any band with a menu won't be displayed correctly in a vertical band. As you'll see, however, you can hide a particular band when the control is orientated vertically.

IMAGE LISTS FOR COMMAND BANDS CONTROLS

I touched on image lists earlier. Command bars and toolbars use image lists internally to manage the images used on buttons. Image lists can be managed in a stand-alone image list control. This control is basically a helper control that assists applications in managing a series of like-size images. The image list control in Windows CE is identical to the image list control under Windows NT and Windows 98, with the exception that the Windows CE version can't contain cursors for systems built without mouse/cursor support. For the purposes of the command bands control, the image list just needs to be created and a set of bitmaps added that will represent the individual bands when they're minimized. An example of the minimal code required for this is shown here:

```
himl = ImageList_Create (16, 16, ILC_COLOR, 2, 0);
hBmp = LoadBitmap (hInst, TEXT ("CmdBarBmps"));
ImageList_Add (himl, hBmp, NULL);
DeleteObject (hBmp);
```

The *ImageList_Create* function takes the dimensions of the images to be loaded, the format of the images (ILC_COLOR is the default), the number of images initially in the list, and the number to be added. The two images are then added by loading a double-wide bitmap that contains two images and calling *ImageList_Add*. After the bitmap has been loaded into the image list, it should be deleted.

Adding bands

You can add bands to your application by passing an array of REBARBANDINFO structures that describe each band to the control. The function is

```
BOOL CommandBands_AddBands (HWND hwndCmdBands, HINSTANCE hinst,
                            UINT cBands, LPREBARBANDINFO prbbi);
```

Before you call this function, you must fill out a REBARBANDINFO structure for each of the bands to be added to the control. The structure is defined as

```
typedef struct tagREBARBANDINFO{
    UINT cbSize;
    UINT fMask;
    UINT fStyle;
    COLORREF clrFore;
    COLORREF clrBack;
    LPTSTR lpText;
    UINT cch;
    int iImage;
```

```
    HWND hwndChild;
    UINT cxMinChild;
    UINT cyMinChild;
    UINT cx;
    HBITMAP hbmBack;
    UINT wID;
    UINT cyChild;
    UINT cyMaxChild;
    UINT cyIntegral;
    UINT cxIdeal;
    LPARAM lParam;
} REBARBANDINFO;
```

Fortunately, although this structure looks imposing, many of the fields can be ignored because there are default actions for uninitialized fields. As usual with a Windows structure, the *cbSize* field must be filled with the size of the structure as a fail-safe measure when the structure is passed to Windows. The *fMask* field is filled with a number of flags that indicate which of the remaining fields in the structure are filled with valid information. I'll describe the flags as I cover each of the fields.

The *fStyle* field must be filled with the style flags for the band if the RBBIM_STYLE flag is set in the *fMask* field. The allowable flags are the following:

- *RBBS_BREAK* The band will start on a new line.
- *RBBS_FIXEDSIZE* The band can't be sized. When this flag is specified, the gripper for the band isn't displayed.
- *RBBS_HIDDEN* The band won't be visible when the command band is created.
- *RBBS_GRIPPERALWAYS* The band will have a sizing grip, even if it's the only band in the command band.
- *RBBS_NOGRIPPER* The band won't have a sizing grip. The band therefore can't be moved by the user.
- *RBBS_NOVERT* The band won't be displayed if the command bands control is displayed vertically due to the CCS_VERT style.
- *RBBS_CHILDEDGE* The band will be drawn with an edge at the top and bottom of the band.
- *RBBS_FIXEDBMP* The background bitmap of the band doesn't move when the band is resized.

For the most part, these flags are self-explanatory. Although command bands are usually displayed across the top of a window, they can be created as vertical bands and displayed down the left side of a window. In that case, the RBBS_NOVERT style allows the programmer to specify which bands won't be displayed when the command band is in a vertical orientation. Bands containing menus or wide controls are candidates for this flag because they won't be displayed correctly on vertical bands.

You can fill the *clrFore* and *clrBack* fields with a color that the command band will use for the foreground and background color when your application draws the band. These fields are used only if the RBBIM_COLORS flag is set in the mask field. These fields, along with the *hbmBack* field, which specifies a background bitmap for the band, are useful only if the band contains a transparent command bar. Otherwise, the command bar covers most of the area of the band, obscuring any background bitmap or special colors. I'll explain how to make a command bar transparent in the section, "Configuring individual bands."

The *lpText* field specifies the optional text that labels the individual band. This text is displayed at the left end of the bar immediately right of the gripper. The *iImage* field is used to specify a bitmap that will also be displayed on the left end of the bar. The *iImage* field is filled with an index to the list of images contained in the image list control. The text and bitmap fields take added significance when paired with the RBS_SMARTLABELS style of the command band control. When that style is specified, the text is displayed when the band is restored or maximized and the bitmap is displayed when the band is minimized. This technique is used by the H/PC Explorer on its command band control.

The *wID* field should be set to an ID value that you use to identify the band. The band ID is important if you plan on configuring the bands after they have been created or if you think you'll be querying their state. Even if you don't plan to use band IDs in your program, it's important that each band ID be unique because the control itself uses the IDs to manage the bands. This field is checked only if the RBBIM_ID flag is set in the *fMask* field.

The *hwndChild* field is used if the default command bar control in a band is replaced by another control. To replace the command bar control, the new control must first be created and the window handle of the control then placed in the *hwndChild* field. The *hwndChild* field is checked only if the RBBIM_CHILD flag is set in the *fMask* field.

The *cxMinChild* and *cyMinChild* fields define the minimum dimensions to which a band can shrink. When you're using a control other than the default command bar, these fields are useful for defining the height and minimum width (the width when minimized) of the band. These two fields are checked only if the RBBIM_CHILDSIZE flag is set.

The *cxIdeal* field is used when a band is maximized by the user. If this field isn't initialized, a maximized command band stretches across the entire width of the control. By setting *cxIdeal*, the application can limit the maximized width of a band, which is handy if the controls on the band take up only part of the total width of the control. This field is checked only if the RBBIM_IDEALSIZE flag is set in the *fMask* field.

The *lParam* field gives you a space to store an application-defined value with the band information. This field is checked only if the RBBIM_LPARAM flag is set in the *fMask* field. The other fields in the REBARBANDINFO apply to the more flexible rebar control, not the command band control. The code below creates a command bands control, initializes an array of three REBARBANDINFO structures, and adds the bands to the control.

```
// Create a command bands ctl.
hwndCB = CommandBands_Create (hInst, hWnd, IDC_CMDBAND, RBS_SMARTLABELS |
                              RBS_VARHEIGHT, himl);

// Init common REBARBANDINFO structure fields.
for (i = 0; i < dim(rbi); i++) {
    rbi[i].cbSize = sizeof (REBARBANDINFO);
    rbi[i].fMask = RBBIM_ID | RBBIM_IMAGE | RBBIM_SIZE | RBBIM_STYLE;
    rbi[i].fStyle = RBBS_FIXEDBMP;
    rbi[i].wID = IDB_CMDBAND+i;
}
// Init REBARBANDINFO structure for each band.
// 1. Menu band.
rbi[0].fStyle |= RBBS_NOGRIPPER;
rbi[0].cx = 130;
rbi[0].iImage = 0;

// 2. Standard button band.
rbi[1].fMask |= RBBIM_TEXT;
rbi[1].cx = 200;
rbi[1].iImage = 1;
rbi[1].lpText = TEXT ("Std Btns");

// 3. Edit control band.
hwndChild = CreateWindow (TEXT ("edit"), TEXT ("edit ctl"),
                          WS_VISIBLE | WS_CHILD | WS_BORDER,
                          0, 0, 10, 5, hWnd, (HMENU)IDC_EDITCTL,
                          hInst, NULL);

rbi[2].fMask |= RBBIM_TEXT | RBBIM_STYLE | RBBIM_CHILDSIZE | RBBIM_CHILD;
rbi[2].fStyle |= RBBS_CHILDEDGE;
rbi[2].hwndChild = hwndChild;
rbi[2].cxMinChild = 0;
rbi[2].cyMinChild = 25;
rbi[2].cyChild = 55;
rbi[2].cx = 130;
rbi[2].iImage = 2;
rbi[2].lpText = TEXT ("Edit field");

// Add bands.
CommandBands_AddBands (hwndCB, hInst, 3, rbi);
```

The command bands control created above has three bands, one containing a menu, one containing a set of buttons, and one containing an edit control instead of a command bar. The control is created with the RBS_SMARTLABELS and RBS_VARHEIGHT styles. The smart labels display an icon when the bar is minimized and a text label when the band isn't minimized. The RBS_VARHEIGHT style allows each line on the control to have a different height.

The common fields of the REBARBANDINFO structures are then initialized in a loop. Then the remaining fields of the structures are customized for each band on the control. The third band, containing the edit control, is the most complex to initialize. This band needs more initialization since the edit control needs to be properly sized to match the standard height of the command bar controls in the other bands.

The *iImage* field for each band is initialized using an index into an image list that was created and passed to the *CommandBands_Create* function. The text fields for the second and third bands are filled with labels for those bands. The first band, which contains a menu, doesn't contain a text label because there's no need to label the menu. You also use the RBBS_NOGRIPPER style for the first band so that it can't be moved around the control. This fixes the menu band at its proper place in the control.

Now that we've created the bands, it's time to see how to initialize them.

Configuring individual bands

At this point in the process, the command bands control has been created and the individual bands have been added to the control. We have one more task, which is to configure the individual command bar controls in each band. (Actually, there's little more to configuring the command bar controls than what I've already described for command bars.)

The handle to a command bar contained in a band is retrieved using

```
HWND CommandBands_GetCommandBar (HWND hwndCmdBands, UINT uBand);
```

The *uBand* parameter is the zero-based band index for the band containing the command bar. If you call this function when the command bands control is being initialized, the index value correlates directly with the order in which the bands were added to the control. However, once the user has a chance to drag the bands into a new order, your application must obtain this index indirectly by sending a RB_IDTOINDEX message to the command bands control, as in

```
nIndex = SendMessage (hwndCmdBands, RB_IDTOINDEX, ID_BAND, 0);
```

This message is critical for managing the bands because many of the functions and messages for the control require the band index as the method to identify the band. The problem is that the index values are fluid. As the user moves the bands around, these index values change. You can't even count on the index values being consecutive. So, as a rule, never blindly use the index value without first querying the proper value by translating an ID value to an index value with RB_IDTOINDEX.

Once you have the window handle to the command bar, simply add the menu or buttons to the bar using the standard command bar control functions and messages. Most of the time, you'll specify only a menu in the first bar, only buttons in the second bar, and other controls in the third and subsequent bars.

The following code completes the creation process shown in the earlier code fragments. This code initializes the command bar controls in the first two bands. Since the third band has an edit control, you don't need to initialize that band. The final act necessary to complete the command band control initialization is to add the close box to the control using a call to *CommandBands_AddAdornments*.

```
// Add menu to first band.
hwndBand = CommandBands_GetCommandBar (hwndCB, 0);
CommandBar_InsertMenubar (hwndBand, hInst, ID_MENU, 0);

// Add std buttons to second band.
hwndBand = CommandBands_GetCommandBar (hwndCB, 1);
CommandBar_AddBitmap (hwndBand, HINST_COMMCTRL, IDB_STD_SMALL_COLOR,
                      15, 0, 0);
CommandBar_AddButtons (hwndBand, dim(tbCBStdBtns), tbCBStdBtns);

// Add exit button to command band.
CommandBands_AddAdornments (hwndCB, hInst, 0, NULL);
```

Saving the band layout

The configurability of the command bands control presents a problem to the programmer. Users who rearrange the bands expect their customized layout to be restored the next time the application is started. This task is supposed to be made easy using the following function.

```
BOOL CommandBands_GetRestoreInformation (HWND hwndCmdBands,
                     UINT uBand, LPCOMMANDBANDSRESTOREINFO pcbr);
```

This function saves the positioning information from an individual band into a COMMANDBANDSRESTOREINFO structure. The function takes the handle of the command bands control and an index value for the band to be queried. The following code fragment shows how to query the information from each of the bands in a command band control.

```
// Get the handle of the command bands control.
hwndCB = GetDlgItem (hWnd, IDC_CMDBAND);

// Get information for each band.
for (i = 0; i < NUMBANDS; i++) {
```

(continued)

```
    // Get band index from ID value.
    nBand = SendMessage (hwndCB, RB_IDTOINDEX, IDB_CMDBAND+i, 0);

    // Initialize the size field and get the restore information.
    cbr[i].cbSize = sizeof (COMMANDBANDSRESTOREINFO);
    CommandBands_GetRestoreInformation (hwndCB, nBand, &cbr[i]);
}
```

The code above uses the RB_IDTOINDEX message to convert known band IDs into the unknown band indexes required by *CommandBands_GetRestoreInformation*. The data from the structure would normally be stored in the system registry. I'll talk about how to read and write registry data in Chapter 7, "Files, Databases, and the Registry."

The restore information should be read from the registry when the application is restarted, and used when creating the command bands control.

```
// Restore configuration to a command band.
COMMANDBANDSRESTOREINFO cbr[NUMBANDS];
REBARBANDINFO rbi;

// Initialize size field.
rbi.cbSize = sizeof (REBARBANDINFO);

// Set only style and size fields.
rbi.fMask = RBBIM_STYLE | RBBIM_SIZE;

// Set the size and style for all bands.
for (i = 0; i < NUMBANDS; i++) {
    rbi.cx = cbr[i].cxRestored;
    rbi.fStyle = cbr[i].fStyle;

    nBand = SendMessage (hwndCB, RB_IDTOINDEX, cbr[i].wID, 0);
    SendMessage (hwndCB, RB_SETBANDINFO, nBand, (LPARAM)&rbi);
}

// Only after the size is set for all bands can the bands
// needing maximizing be maximized.
for (i = 0; i < NUMBANDS; i++) {
    if (cbr[i].fMaximized) {
        nBand = SendMessage (hwndCB, RB_IDTOINDEX, cbr[i].wID, 0);
        SendMessage (hwndCB, RB_MAXIMIZEBAND, nBand, TRUE);
    }
}
```

This code assumes that the command bands control has already been created in its default configuration. In a real-world application, the restore information for the size and style could be used when first creating the control. In that case, all that would remain would be to maximize the bands depending on the state of the *fMaximized* field in the COMMANDBANDSRESTOREINFO structure. This last step must take place only after all bands have been created and properly resized.

One limitation of this system of saving and restoring the band layout is that you have no method for determining the order of the bands in the control. The band index isn't likely to provide reliable clues because after the user has rearranged the bands a few times, the indexes are neither consecutive nor in any defined order. The only way around this problem is to constrain the arrangement of the bands so that the user can't reorder the bands. You do this by setting the RBS_FIXEDORDER style. This solves your problem, but doesn't help users if they want a different order. In the example program at the end of this section, I use the band index value to guess at the order. But this method isn't guaranteed to work.

Handling command band messages

The command bands control needs a bit more maintenance than a command bar. The difference is that the control can change height, and thus the window containing the command bands control must monitor the control and redraw and perhaps reformat its client area when the control is resized.

The command bands control sends a number of different WM_NOTIFY messages when the user rearranges the control. To monitor the height of the control, your application needs to check for a RBN_HEIGHTCHANGE notification and to react accordingly. The code below does just this:

```
// This code is inside a WM_NOTIFY message handler.
LPNMHDR pnmh;

pnmh = (LPNMHDR)lParam;
if (pnmh->code == RBN_HEIGHTCHANGE) {
    InvalidateRect (hWnd, NULL, TRUE);
}
```

If a RBN_HEIGHTCHANGE notification is detected, the routine simply invalidates the client area of the window forcing a WM_PAINT message. The code in the paint message then calls

```
UINT CommandBands_Height (HWND hwndCmdBands);
```

to query the height of the command bands control and subtracts this height from the client area rectangle.

As with the command bar, the command bands control can be hidden and shown with a helper function:

```
BOOL CommandBands_Show (HWND hwndCmdBands, BOOL fShow);
```

The visibility state of the control can be queried using

```
BOOL CommandBands_IsVisible (HWND hwndCmdBands);
```

The CmdBand Example Program

The CmdBand program demonstrates a fairly complete command bands control. The example creates three bands: a fixed menu band, a band containing a number of buttons, and a band containing an edit control. Transparent command bars and a background bitmap in each band are used to create a command bands control with a background image.

You can use the View menu to replace the command bands control with a simple command bar by choosing Command Bar from the View menu. You can then recreate and restore the command bands control to its last configuration by choosing Command Bands from the View menu. The code for the CmdBand program is shown in Figure 5-5 .

CmdBand.rc

```
//======================================================================
// Resource file
//
// Written for the book Programming Windows CE
// Copyright (C) 1998 Douglas Boling
//======================================================================
#include "windows.h"                 //
#include "CmdBand.h"                 // Program-specific stuff

//----------------------------------------------------------------------
// Icons and bitmaps
//
ID_ICON         ICON   "cmdband.ico"    // Program icon
CmdBarBmps      BITMAP "cbarbmps.bmp"   // Bmp used in cmdband image list
CmdBarEditBmp   BITMAP "cbarbmp2.bmp"   // Bmp used in cmdband image list
CmdBarBack      BITMAP "backg2.bmp"     // Bmp used for cmdband background

//----------------------------------------------------------------------
// Menu
//
ID_MENU MENU DISCARDABLE
BEGIN
    POPUP "&File"
    BEGIN
        MENUITEM "E&xit",                       IDM_EXIT
    END
    POPUP "&View"
```

Figure 5-5. *The CmdBand program.*

```
    BEGIN
        MENUITEM "Command Bar",                IDM_VIEWCMDBAR
        MENUITEM "Command Band",               IDM_VIEWCMDBAND
    END
    POPUP "&Help"

    BEGIN
        MENUITEM "&About...",                  IDM_ABOUT
    END
END
//----------------------------------------------------------------------
// About box dialog template
//
aboutbox DIALOG discardable 10, 10, 160, 40
STYLE  WS_POPUP | WS_VISIBLE | WS_CAPTION | WS_SYSMENU | DS_CENTER |
       DS_MODALFRAME
CAPTION "About"
BEGIN
    ICON  ID_ICON,                     -1,   5,   5,  10,  10
    LTEXT "CmdBand - Written for the book Programming Windows \
           CE Copyright 1998 Douglas Boling"
                                       -1,  40,   5, 110,  30
END
```

CmdBand.h

```
//======================================================================
// Header file
//
// Written for the book Programming Windows CE
// Copyright (C) 1998 Douglas Boling
//======================================================================
// Returns number of elements
#define dim(x) (sizeof(x) / sizeof(x[0]))

//----------------------------------------------------------------------
// Generic defines and data types
//
struct decodeUINT {                            // Structure associates
    UINT Code;                                 // messages
                                               // with a function.
```

(continued)

Figure 5-5. *continued*

```
    LRESULT (*Fxn)(HWND, UINT, WPARAM, LPARAM);
};
struct decodeCMD {                              // Structure associates
    UINT Code;                                  // menu IDs with a
    LRESULT (*Fxn)(HWND, WORD, HWND, WORD);     // function.
};
//----------------------------------------------------------------------
// Defines used by application
//
#define  IDC_CMDBAND         1                  // Command band ID
#define  IDC_CMDBAR          2                  // Command bar ID

#define  ID_ICON             10                 // Icon ID
#define  ID_MENU             11                 // Main menu resource ID
#define  IDC_EDITCTL         12

#define  IDB_CMDBAND         50                 // Base ID for bands
#define  IDB_CMDBANDMENU     50                 // Menu band ID
#define  IDB_CMDBANDBTN      51                 // Button band ID
#define  IDB_CMDBANDEDIT     52                 // Edit control band ID

// Menu item IDs
#define  IDM_EXIT            100

#define  IDM_VIEWCMDBAR      110
#define  IDM_VIEWCMDBAND     111

#define  IDM_ABOUT           120
#define  NUMBANDS            3
//----------------------------------------------------------------------
// Function prototypes
//
int CreateCommandBand (HWND hWnd, BOOL fFirst);
int DestroyCommandBand (HWND hWnd);

int InitApp (HINSTANCE);
HWND InitInstance (HINSTANCE, LPWSTR, int);
int TermInstance (HINSTANCE, int);

// Window procedures
LRESULT CALLBACK MainWndProc (HWND, UINT, WPARAM, LPARAM);

// Message handlers
LRESULT DoCreateMain (HWND, UINT, WPARAM, LPARAM);
LRESULT DoPaintMain (HWND, UINT, WPARAM, LPARAM);
LRESULT DoNotifyMain (HWND, UINT, WPARAM, LPARAM);
```

```
LRESULT DoCommandMain (HWND, UINT, WPARAM, LPARAM);
LRESULT DoDestroyMain (HWND, UINT, WPARAM, LPARAM);

// Command functions
LPARAM DoMainCommandViewCmdBar (HWND, WORD, HWND, WORD);
LPARAM DoMainCommandVCmdBand (HWND, WORD, HWND, WORD);
LPARAM DoMainCommandExit (HWND, WORD, HWND, WORD);
LPARAM DoMainCommandAbout (HWND, WORD, HWND, WORD);

// Dialog procedures
BOOL CALLBACK AboutDlgProc (HWND, UINT, WPARAM, LPARAM);
```

CmdBand.c

```
//======================================================================
// CmdBand - Dialog box demonstration
//
// Written for the book Programming Windows CE
// Copyright (C) 1998 Douglas Boling
//======================================================================
#include <windows.h>                  // For all that Windows stuff
#include <commctrl.h>                 // Command bar includes

#include "CmdBand.h"                  // Program-specific stuff

//----------------------------------------------------------------------
// Global data
//
const TCHAR szAppName[] = TEXT ("CmdBand");
HINSTANCE hInst;                      // Program instance handle

// Message dispatch table for MainWindowProc
const struct decodeUINT MainMessages[] = {
    WM_CREATE, DoCreateMain,
    WM_PAINT, DoPaintMain,
    WM_NOTIFY, DoNotifyMain,
    WM_COMMAND, DoCommandMain,
    WM_DESTROY, DoDestroyMain,
};
// Command message dispatch for MainWindowProc
const struct decodeCMD MainCommandItems[] = {
    IDM_VIEWCMDBAR, DoMainCommandViewCmdBar,
    IDM_VIEWCMDBAND, DoMainCommandVCmdBand,
    IDM_EXIT, DoMainCommandExit,
    IDM_ABOUT, DoMainCommandAbout,
};
```

(continued)

Figure 5-5. *continued*

```
// Command band button initialization structure
const TBBUTTON tbCBStdBtns[] = {
//  BitmapIndex       Command  State              Style          UserData  String
    {STD_FILENEW,     210,     TBSTATE_ENABLED, TBSTYLE_BUTTON, 0,      0},
    {STD_FILEOPEN,    211,     TBSTATE_ENABLED, TBSTYLE_BUTTON, 0,      0},
    {STD_FILESAVE,    212,     TBSTATE_ENABLED, TBSTYLE_BUTTON, 0,      0},
    {0,               0,       TBSTATE_ENABLED, TBSTYLE_SEP,    0,      0},
    {STD_CUT,         213,     TBSTATE_ENABLED, TBSTYLE_BUTTON, 0,      0},
    {STD_COPY,        214,     TBSTATE_ENABLED, TBSTYLE_BUTTON, 0,      0},
    {STD_PASTE,       215,     TBSTATE_ENABLED, TBSTYLE_BUTTON, 0,      0},
    {0,               0,       TBSTATE_ENABLED, TBSTYLE_SEP,    0,      0},
    {STD_PROPERTIES, 216,      TBSTATE_ENABLED, TBSTYLE_BUTTON, 0,      0},
};

// Command bar initialization structure
const TBBUTTON tbCBViewBtns[] = {
//  BitmapIndex     Command  State                       Style          UserData String
    {0,                 0, 0,
                                                TBSTYLE_SEP,           0, 0},
    {VIEW_LARGEICONS, 210, TBSTATE_ENABLED | TBSTATE_CHECKED,
                                                TBSTYLE_CHECKGROUP, 0, 0},
    {VIEW_SMALLICONS, 211, TBSTATE_ENABLED,
                                                TBSTYLE_CHECKGROUP, 0, 0},
    {VIEW_LIST,       212, TBSTATE_ENABLED,
                                                TBSTYLE_CHECKGROUP, 0, 0},
    {VIEW_DETAILS,    213, TBSTATE_ENABLED,
                                                TBSTYLE_CHECKGROUP, 0, 0},
    {0,                 0, 0,                   TBSTYLE_SEP,           0, 0},
    {VIEW_SORTNAME,   214, TBSTATE_ENABLED | TBSTATE_CHECKED,
                                                TBSTYLE_CHECKGROUP, 0, 0},
    {VIEW_SORTTYPE,   215, TBSTATE_ENABLED,
                                                TBSTYLE_CHECKGROUP, 0, 0},
    {VIEW_SORTSIZE,   216, TBSTATE_ENABLED,
                                                TBSTYLE_CHECKGROUP, 0, 0},
    {VIEW_SORTDATE,   217, TBSTATE_ENABLED,
                                                TBSTYLE_CHECKGROUP, 0, 0}
};

// Array that stores the band configuration
COMMANDBANDSRESTOREINFO cbr[NUMBANDS];
INT nBandOrder[NUMBANDS];
//======================================================================
// Program entry point
//
int WINAPI WinMain (HINSTANCE hInstance, HINSTANCE hPrevInstance,
                    LPWSTR lpCmdLine, int nCmdShow) {
```

```
    HWND hwndMain;
    MSG msg;
    int rc;

    // Initialize application.
    rc = InitApp (hInstance);
    if (rc) return rc;

    // Initialize this instance.
    hwndMain = InitInstance (hInstance, lpCmdLine, nCmdShow);
    if (hwndMain == 0)
        return 0x10;

    // Application message loop
    while (GetMessage (&msg, NULL, 0, 0)) {
        TranslateMessage (&msg);
        DispatchMessage (&msg);
    }
    // Instance cleanup
    return TermInstance (hInstance, msg.wParam);
}
//----------------------------------------------------------------------
// InitApp - Application initialization
//
int InitApp (HINSTANCE hInstance) {
    WNDCLASS wc;
    INITCOMMONCONTROLSEX icex;

    // Register application main window class.
    wc.style = 0;                             // Window style
    wc.lpfnWndProc = MainWndProc;             // Callback function
    wc.cbClsExtra = 0;                        // Extra class data
    wc.cbWndExtra = 0;                        // Extra window data
    wc.hInstance = hInstance;                 // Owner handle
    wc.hIcon = NULL,                          // Application icon
    wc.hCursor = NULL;                        // Default cursor
    wc.hbrBackground = (HBRUSH) GetStockObject (WHITE_BRUSH);
    wc.lpszMenuName =  NULL;                  // Menu name
    wc.lpszClassName = szAppName;             // Window class name

    if (RegisterClass (&wc) == 0) return 1;

    // Load the command bar common control class.
    icex.dwSize = sizeof (INITCOMMONCONTROLSEX);
    icex.dwICC = ICC_COOL_CLASSES;
    InitCommonControlsEx (&icex);
```

(continued)

Figure 5-5. *continued*

```
    return 0;
}
//----------------------------------------------------------------------
// InitInstance - Instance initialization
//
HWND InitInstance (HINSTANCE hInstance, LPWSTR lpCmdLine, int nCmdShow){
    HWND hWnd;

    // Save program instance handle in global variable.
    hInst = hInstance;

    // Create main window.

    hWnd = CreateWindow (szAppName,                    // Window class
                         TEXT ("CmdBand Demo"), // Window title
                         WS_VISIBLE,            // Style flags
                         CW_USEDEFAULT,         // x position
                         CW_USEDEFAULT,         // y position
                         CW_USEDEFAULT,         // Initial width
                         CW_USEDEFAULT,         // Initial height
                         NULL,                  // Parent
                         NULL,                  // Menu, must be null
                         hInstance,             // Application instance
                         NULL);                 // Pointer to create
                                                // parameters
    // Return fail code if window not created.
    if (!IsWindow (hWnd)) return 0;

    // Standard show and update calls
    ShowWindow (hWnd, nCmdShow);
    UpdateWindow (hWnd);
    return hWnd;
}
//----------------------------------------------------------------------
// TermInstance - Program cleanup
//
int TermInstance (HINSTANCE hInstance, int nDefRC) {
    return nDefRC;
}
//======================================================================
// Message handling procedures for MainWindow
//----------------------------------------------------------------------
// MainWndProc - Callback function for application window
```

```
//
LRESULT CALLBACK MainWndProc (HWND hWnd, UINT wMsg, WPARAM wParam,
                              LPARAM lParam) {
    INT i;
    //
    // Search message list to see if we need to handle this
    // message.  If in list, call procedure.
    //
    for (i = 0; i < dim(MainMessages); i++) {
        if (wMsg == MainMessages[i].Code)
            return (*MainMessages[i].Fxn)(hWnd, wMsg, wParam, lParam);
    }

    return DefWindowProc (hWnd, wMsg, wParam, lParam);
}

//----------------------------------------------------------------------
// DoCreateMain - Process WM_CREATE message for window.
//
LRESULT DoCreateMain (HWND hWnd, UINT wMsg, WPARAM wParam,
                      LPARAM lParam) {

    CreateCommandBand (hWnd, TRUE);
    return 0;
}
//----------------------------------------------------------------------
// DoPaintMain - Process WM_PAINT message for window.
//
LRESULT DoPaintMain (HWND hWnd, UINT wMsg, WPARAM wParam,
                     LPARAM lParam) {
    PAINTSTRUCT ps;
    HWND hwndCB;
    RECT rect;
    HDC hdc;
    POINT ptArray[2];

    // Adjust the size of the client rect to take into account
    // the command bar or command bands height.
    GetClientRect (hWnd, &rect);
    if (hwndCB = GetDlgItem (hWnd, IDC_CMDBAND))
        rect.top += CommandBands_Height (hwndCB);
    else
        rect.top += CommandBar_Height (GetDlgItem (hWnd, IDC_CMDBAR));

    hdc = BeginPaint (hWnd, &ps);
```

(continued)

Figure 5-5. *continued*

```
    ptArray[0].x = rect.left;
    ptArray[0].y = rect.top;
    ptArray[1].x = rect.right;
    ptArray[1].y = rect.bottom;
    Polyline (hdc, ptArray, 2);

    ptArray[0].x = rect.right;
    ptArray[1].x = rect.left;
    Polyline (hdc, ptArray, 2);

    EndPaint (hWnd, &ps);
    return 0;
}
//----------------------------------------------------------------------
// DoCommandMain - Process WM_COMMAND message for window.
//
LRESULT DoCommandMain (HWND hWnd, UINT wMsg, WPARAM wParam,
                       LPARAM lParam) {
    WORD idItem, wNotifyCode;
    HWND hwndCtl;
    INT  i;

    // Parse the parameters.
    idItem = (WORD) LOWORD (wParam);
    wNotifyCode = (WORD) HIWORD (wParam);
    hwndCtl = (HWND) lParam;

    // Call routine to handle control message.
    for (i = 0; i < dim(MainCommandItems); i++) {
        if (idItem == MainCommandItems[i].Code)
            return (*MainCommandItems[i].Fxn)(hWnd, idItem, hwndCtl,
                                              wNotifyCode);
    }
    return 0;
}
//----------------------------------------------------------------------
// DoNotifyMain - Process WM_NOTIFY message for window.
//
LRESULT DoNotifyMain (HWND hWnd, UINT wMsg, WPARAM wParam,
                      LPARAM lParam) {
    LPNMHDR pnmh;

    // Parse the parameters.
    pnmh = (LPNMHDR)lParam;
```

```
    if (pnmh->code == RBN_HEIGHTCHANGE) {
        InvalidateRect (hWnd, NULL, TRUE);

    }

    return 0;
}
//----------------------------------------------------------------------
// DoDestroyMain - Process WM_DESTROY message for window.
//
LRESULT DoDestroyMain (HWND hWnd, UINT wMsg, WPARAM wParam,
                       LPARAM lParam) {
    PostQuitMessage (0);
    return 0;

}
//======================================================================
// Command handler routines
//----------------------------------------------------------------------
// DoMainCommandExit - Process Program Exit command.
//
LPARAM DoMainCommandExit (HWND hWnd, WORD idItem, HWND hwndCtl,
                          WORD wNotifyCode) {

    SendMessage (hWnd, WM_CLOSE, 0, 0);
    return 0;
}
//----------------------------------------------------------------------
// DoMainCommandVCmdBarStd - Process View | Std Command bar command.
//
LPARAM DoMainCommandViewCmdBar (HWND hWnd, WORD idItem, HWND hwndCtl,
                                WORD wNotifyCode) {
    HWND hwndCB;

    hwndCB = GetDlgItem (hWnd, IDC_CMDBAND);
    if (hwndCB)
        DestroyCommandBand (hWnd);
    else
        return 0;

    // Create a minimal command bar that has only a menu and
    // an exit button.
    hwndCB = CommandBar_Create (hInst, hWnd, IDC_CMDBAR);

    // Insert the menu.
    CommandBar_InsertMenubar (hwndCB, hInst, ID_MENU, 0);
```

(continued)

Figure 5-5. *continued*

```
    // Add exit button to command bar.
    CommandBar_AddAdornments (hwndCB, 0, 0);
    InvalidateRect (hWnd, NULL, TRUE);
    return 0;
}
//----------------------------------------------------------------------
// DoMainCommandVCmdBand - Process View | Command band command.
//
LPARAM DoMainCommandVCmdBand (HWND hWnd, WORD idItem, HWND hwndCtl,
                              WORD wNotifyCode) {
    HWND hwndCB;
    hwndCB = GetDlgItem (hWnd, IDC_CMDBAR);
    if (hwndCB)
        CommandBar_Destroy (hwndCB);
    else
        return 0;

    CreateCommandBand (hWnd, FALSE);
    InvalidateRect (hWnd, NULL, TRUE);
    return 0;
}
//----------------------------------------------------------------------
// DoMainCommandAbout - Process the Help | About menu command.
//
LPARAM DoMainCommandAbout(HWND hWnd, WORD idItem, HWND hwndCtl,
                          WORD wNotifyCode) {

    // Use DialogBox to create modal dialog box.
    DialogBox (hInst, TEXT ("aboutbox"), hWnd, AboutDlgProc);
    return 0;
}
//======================================================================
// About Dialog procedure
//
BOOL CALLBACK AboutDlgProc (HWND hWnd, UINT wMsg, WPARAM wParam,
                            LPARAM lParam) {
    switch (wMsg) {
        case WM_COMMAND:
            switch (LOWORD (wParam)) {
                case IDOK:
                case IDCANCEL:
                    EndDialog (hWnd, 0);
                    return TRUE;
            }
        break;
    }
```

```
    return FALSE;
}
//----------------------------------------------------------------------
// DestroyCommandBand - Destroy command band control after saving
// the current configuration.
//
int DestroyCommandBand (HWND hWnd) {
    HWND hwndCB;
    INT i, nBand, nMaxBand = 0;

   hwndCB = GetDlgItem (hWnd, IDC_CMDBAND);
    for (i = 0; i < NUMBANDS; i++) {

        // Get band index from ID value.
        nBand = SendMessage (hwndCB, RB_IDTOINDEX, IDB_CMDBAND+i, 0);

        // Save the band number to save order of bands.
        nBandOrder[i] = nBand;

        // Get the restore information.
        cbr[i].cbSize = sizeof (COMMANDBANDSRESTOREINFO);
        CommandBands_GetRestoreInformation (hwndCB, nBand, &cbr[i]);
    }
    DestroyWindow (hwndCB);
    return 0;
}
//----------------------------------------------------------------------
// CreateCommandBand - Create a formatted command band control.
//
int CreateCommandBand (HWND hWnd, BOOL fFirst) {
    HWND hwndCB, hwndBand, hwndChild;
    INT i, nBand, nBtnIndex, nEditIndex;
    LONG lStyle;
    HBITMAP hBmp;
    HIMAGELIST himl;
    REBARBANDINFO rbi[NUMBANDS];

    // Create image list control for bitmaps for minimized bands.
    himl = ImageList_Create (16, 16, ILC_COLOR, 3, 0);
    // Load first two images from one bitmap.
    hBmp = LoadBitmap (hInst, TEXT ("CmdBarBmps"));
    ImageList_Add (himl, hBmp, NULL);
    DeleteObject (hBmp);
    // Load third image as a single bitmap.
    hBmp = LoadBitmap (hInst, TEXT ("CmdBarEditBmp"));
    ImageList_Add (himl, hBmp, NULL);
    DeleteObject (hBmp);
```

(continued)

Figure 5-5. *continued*

```
    // Create a command band.
    hwndCB = CommandBands_Create (hInst, hWnd, IDC_CMDBAND,
                                  RBS_SMARTLABELS |
                                  RBS_AUTOSIZE | RBS_VARHEIGHT, himl);

    // Load bitmap used as background for command bar.
    hBmp = LoadBitmap (hInst, TEXT ("CmdBarBack"));
    // Initialize common REBARBANDINFO structure fields.
    for (i = 0; i < dim(rbi); i++) {
        rbi[i].cbSize = sizeof (REBARBANDINFO);
        rbi[i].fMask = RBBIM_ID | RBBIM_IMAGE | RBBIM_SIZE |
                       RBBIM_BACKGROUND | RBBIM_STYLE;
        rbi[i].wID = IDB_CMDBAND+i;
        rbi[i].hbmBack = hBmp;
    }

    // If first time, initialize the restore structure since it is
    // used to initialize the band size and style fields.
    if (fFirst) {
        nBtnIndex = 1;
        nEditIndex = 2;
        cbr[0].cxRestored = 130;
        cbr[1].cxRestored = 210;
        cbr[1].fStyle = RBBS_FIXEDBMP;
        cbr[2].cxRestored = 130;
        cbr[2].fStyle = RBBS_FIXEDBMP | RBBS_CHILDEDGE;
    } else {
        // If not first time, set order of bands depending on
        // the last order.
        if (nBandOrder[1] < nBandOrder[2]) {
            nBtnIndex = 1;
            nEditIndex = 2;
        } else {
            nBtnIndex = 2;
            nEditIndex = 1;
        }
    }
    // Initialize REBARBANDINFO structure for each band.
    // 1. Menu band
    rbi[0].fStyle = RBBS_FIXEDBMP | RBBS_NOGRIPPER;
    rbi[0].cx = cbr[0].cxRestored;
    rbi[0].iImage = 0;

    // 2. Standard button band
    rbi[nBtnIndex].fMask |= RBBIM_TEXT;
    rbi[nBtnIndex].iImage = 1;
    rbi[nBtnIndex].lpText = TEXT ("Std Btns");
```

```
// The next two parameters are initialized from saved data.
rbi[nBtnIndex].cx = cbr[1].cxRestored;
rbi[nBtnIndex].fStyle = cbr[1].fStyle;

// 3. Edit control band
hwndChild = CreateWindow (TEXT ("edit"), TEXT ("edit ctl"),
             WS_VISIBLE | WS_CHILD | ES_MULTILINE | WS_BORDER,
             0, 0, 10, 5, hWnd, (HMENU)IDC_EDITCTL, hInst, NULL);

rbi[nEditIndex].fMask |= RBBIM_TEXT | RBBIM_STYLE |
                         RBBIM_CHILDSIZE | RBBIM_CHILD;
rbi[nEditIndex].hwndChild = hwndChild;
rbi[nEditIndex].cxMinChild = 0;
rbi[nEditIndex].cyMinChild = 23;
rbi[nEditIndex].cyChild = 55;
rbi[nEditIndex].iImage = 2;
rbi[nEditIndex].lpText = TEXT ("Edit field");
// The next two parameters are initialized from saved data.
rbi[nEditIndex].cx = cbr[2].cxRestored;
rbi[nEditIndex].fStyle = cbr[2].fStyle;

// Add bands.
CommandBands_AddBands (hwndCB, hInst, 3, rbi);

// Add menu to first band.
hwndBand = CommandBands_GetCommandBar (hwndCB, 0);
CommandBar_InsertMenubar (hwndBand, hInst, ID_MENU, 0);

// Add standard buttons to second band.
hwndBand = CommandBands_GetCommandBar (hwndCB, nBtnIndex);
// Insert buttons
CommandBar_AddBitmap (hwndBand, HINST_COMMCTRL, IDB_STD_SMALL_COLOR,
                      16, 0, 0);
CommandBar_AddButtons (hwndBand, dim(tbCBStdBtns), tbCBStdBtns);

// Modify the style flags of each command bar to make transparent.
for (i = 0; i < NUMBANDS; i++) {
    hwndBand = CommandBands_GetCommandBar (hwndCB, i);
    lStyle = SendMessage (hwndBand, TB_GETSTYLE, 0, 0);
    lStyle |= TBSTYLE_TRANSPARENT;
    SendMessage (hwndBand, TB_SETSTYLE, 0, lStyle);
}

// If not the first time the command band has been created, restore
// the user's last configuration.
```

(continued)

Figure 5-5. *continued*

```
    if (!fFirst) {
        for (i = 0; i < NUMBANDS; i++) {
            if (cbr[i].fMaximized) {
                nBand = SendMessage (hwndCB, RB_IDTOINDEX,
                                     cbr[i].wID, 0);
                SendMessage (hwndCB, RB_MAXIMIZEBAND, nBand, TRUE);
            }
        }
    }
    // Add exit button to command band.
    CommandBands_AddAdornments (hwndCB, hInst, 0, NULL);
    return 0;
}
```

CmdBand creates the command band in the *CreateCommandBand* routine. This routine is initially called in *OnCreateMain* and later in the *DoMainCommandVCmdBand* menu handler. The program creates the command bands control using the RBS_SMARTLABELS style along with an image list and text labels to identify each band when it's minimized and when it's restored or maximized. An image list is created and initialized with the bitmaps that are used when the bands are minimized.

The array of REBARBANDINFO structures is initialized to define each of the three bands. If the control had previously been destroyed, data from the COMMANDBANDSRESTOREINFO structure is used to initialize the *style* and *cx* fields. The *CreateCommandBand* routine also makes a guess at the order of the button and edit bands by looking at the band indexes saved when the control was last destroyed. While this method isn't completely reliable for determining the previous order of the bands, it gives you a good estimate.

When the command bands control is created, the command bars in each band are also modified to set the TBS_TRANSPARENT style. This process, along with a background bitmap defined for each band, demonstrates how you can use a background bitmap to make the command bands control have just the right look.

When CmdBand replaces the command bands control with a command bar, the application first calls the *DestroyCommandBand* function to save the current configuration and then destroy the command bands control. This function uses the *CommandBands_GetRestoreInformation* to query the size and style of each of the bands. The function also saves the band index for each band to supply the data for the guess on the current order of the button and edit bands. The first band, the menu band, is fixed with the RBBS_NOGRIPPER style, so there's no issue as to its position.

This completes the discussion of the command bar and command bands controls. I talk about these two controls at length because you'll need one or the other for almost every Windows CE application.

For the remainder of the chapter, I'll cover the highlights of some of the other controls. These other controls aren't very different from their counterparts under Windows 98 and Windows NT. I'll spend more time on the controls I think you'll need when writing a Windows CE application. I'll start with the month calendar and the time and date picker controls. These controls are rather new to the common control set and have a direct application to the PIM-like applications that are appropriate for many Windows CE systems. I'll also spend some time covering the list view control, concentrating on features of use to Windows CE developers. The remainder of the common controls, I'll cover just briefly.

The Month Calendar Control

The month calendar control gives you a handy month-view calendar that can be manipulated by users to look up any month, week, or day as far back as the adoption of the Gregorian calendar in September 1752. The control can display as many months as will fit into the size of the control. The days of the month can be highlighted to indicate appointments. The weeks can indicate the current week into the year. Users can spin through the months by tapping on the name of the month or change years by tapping on the year displayed.

Before using the month calendar control, you must initialize the common control library either by calling *InitCommonControls* or by calling *InitCommonControlsEx* with the ICC_DATE_CLASSES flag. You create the control by calling *CreateWindow* with the MONTHCAL_CLASS flag. The style flags for the control are shown here:

- *MCS_MULTISELECT* The control allows multiple selection of days.
- *MCS_NOTODAY* The control won't display today's date under the calendar.
- *MCS_NOTODAYCIRCLE* The control won't circle today's date.
- *MCS_WEEKNUMBERS* The control displays the week number (1 through 52) to the left of each week in the calendar.
- *MCS_DAYSTATE* The control sends notification messages to the parent requesting the days of the month that should be displayed in bold. You use this style to indicate which days have appointments or events scheduled.

Initializing the control

In addition to the styles I just described, you can use a number of messages or their corresponding wrapper macros to configure the month calendar control. You can use an MCM_SETFIRSTDAYOFWEEK message to display a different starting day of the week. You can also use the MCM_SETRANGE message to display dates within a given range in the control You can configure date selection to allow the user to choose only single dates or to set a limit to the range of dates that a user can select at any one time. The single/multiple date selection ability is defined by the MCS_MULTISELECT style. If you set this style, you use the MCM_SETMAXSELCOUNT message to set the maximum number of days that can be selected at any one time.

You can set the background and text colors of the control by using the MCM_SETCOLOR message. This message can individually set colors for the different regions within the controls, including the calendar text and background, the header text and background, and the color of the days that precede and follow the days of the month being displayed. This message takes a flag indicating what part of the control to set and a COLORREF value to specify the color.

The month calendar control is designed to display months on an integral basis. That is, if the control is big enough for one and a half months, it displays only one month, centered in the control. You can use the MCM_GETMINREQRECT message to compute the minimum size necessary to display one month. Because the control must first be created before the MCM_GETMINREQRECT can be sent, properly sizing the control is a round-about process. You must create the control, send the MCM_GETMINREQRECT message, and then resize the control using the data returned from the message.

Month calendar notifications

The month calendar control has only three notification messages to send to its parent. Of these, the MCN_GETDAYSTATE notification is the most important. This notification is sent when the control needs to know what days of a month to display in bold. This is done by querying the parent for a series of bit field values encoded in a MONTHDAYSTATE variable. This value is nothing more than a 32-bit value with bits 1 through 31 representing the days 1 through 31 of the month.

When the control needs to display a month, it sends a MCN_GETDAYSTATE notification with a pointer to an NMDAYSTATE structure defined as the following:

```
typedef struct {
    NMHDR nmhdr;
    SYSTEMTIME stStart;
    int cDayState;
    LPMONTHDAYSTATE prgDayState;
} NMDAYSTATE;
```

The *nmhhdr* field is simply the NMHDR structure that's passed with every WM_NOTIFY message. The *stStart* field contains the starting date for which the control is requesting information. This date is encoded in a standard SYSTEMTIME structure used by all versions of Windows. It's detailed on the facing page.

```
typedef struct {
    WORD wYear;
    WORD wMonth;
    WORD wDayOfWeek;
    WORD wDay;
    WORD wHour;
    WORD wMinute;
    WORD wSecond;
    WORD wMilliseconds;
} SYSTEMTIME;
```

For this notification, only the *wMonth*, *wDay*, and *wYear* fields are significant.

The *cDayState* field contains the number of entries in an array of MONTHDAYSTATE values. Even if a month calendar control is displaying only one month, it could request information about the previous and following months if days of those months are needed to fill in the top or bottom lines of the calendar.

The month calendar control sends an MCN_SELCHANGE notification when the user changes the days that are selected in the control. The structure passed with this notification, NMSELCHANGE, contains the newly highlighted starting and ending days. The MCN_SELECT notification is sent when the user double-taps on a day. The same NMSELCHANGE structure is passed with this notification to indicate the days that have been selected.

The Date and Time Picker Control

The date and time picker control looks deceptively simple but is a great tool for any application that needs to ask the user to specify a date. Any programmer that has had to parse, validate, and translate a string into a valid system date or time will appreciate this control.

When used to select a date, the control resembles a combo box, which is an edit field with a down arrow button on the right side. Clicking on the arrow, however, displays a month calendar control showing the current month. Selecting a day in the month dismisses the month calendar control and fills the date and time picker control with that date. When you configure it to query for a time, the date and time picker control resembles an edit field with a spin button on the right end of the control.

The date and time picker control has three default formats: two for displaying the date and one for displaying the time. The control also allows you to provide a formatting string so that users can completely customize the fields in the control. The control even lets you insert application-defined fields in the control.

Creating a date and time picker control

Before you can create the date and time picker control, the common control library must be initialized. If *InitCommonControlsEx* is used, it must be passed a

ICC_DATE_CLASSES flag. The control is created by using *CreateWindow* with a class of DATETIMEPICK_CLASS. The control defines the following styles:

- *DTS_LONGDATEFORMAT* The control displays a date in long format, as in Saturday, September 19, 1998. The actual long date format is defined in the system registry.
- *DTS_SHORTDATEFORMAT* The control displays a date in short format, as in 9/19/98. The actual short date format is defined in the system registry.
- *DTS_TIMEFORMAT* The control displays the time in a format such as 5:50:28 PM. The actual time format is defined in the system registry.
- *DTS_SHOWNONE* The control has a check box to indicate that the date is valid.
- *DTS_UPDOWN* An up-down control replaces the drop-down button that displays a month calendar control in date view.
- *DTS_APPCANPARSE* Allows the user to directly enter text into the control. The control sends a DTN_USERSTRING notification when the user is finished.

The first three styles simply specify a default format string. These formats are based on the regional settings in the registry. Since these formats can change if the user picks different regional settings in the Control Panel, the date and time picker control needs to know when these formats change. The system informs top-level windows of these types of changes by sending a WM_SETTINGCHANGE message. An application that uses the date and time picker control and uses one of these default fonts should forward the WM_SETTINGCHANGE message to the control if one is sent. This causes the control to reconfigure the default formats for the new regional settings.

The DTS_APPCANPARSE style enables the user to directly edit the text in the control. If this isn't set, the allowable keys are limited to the cursor keys and the numbers. When a field, such as a month, is highlighted in the edit field and the user presses the 6 key, the month changes to June. With the DTS_APPCANPARSE style, the user can directly type any character into the edit field of the control. When the user has finished, the control sends a DTN_USERSTRING notification to the parent window so that the text can be verified.

Customizing the format

To customize the display format, all you need to do is create a format string and send it to the control using a DTM_SETFORMAT message. The format string can be made up of any of the following codes:

```
String        Description
fragment

"d"      One- or two-digit day.
"dd"     Two-digit day. Single digits have a leading zero.
"ddd"    The three-character weekday abbreviation. As in Sun, Mon...
"dddd"   The full weekday name.

"h"      One- or two-digit hour (12-hour format).
"hh"     Two-digit hour (12-hour format) Single digits have a leading zero.
"H"      One- or two-digit hour (24-hour format).
"HH"     Two-digit hour (24-hour format) Single digits have a leading zero.

"m"      One- or two-digit minute.
"mm"     Two-digit minute. Single digits have a leading zero.

"M"      One- or two-digit month.
"MM"     Two-digit month. Single digits have a leading zero.

"MMM"    Three-character month abbreviation.
"MMMM"   Full month name.

"t"      The one-letter AM/PM abbreviation. As in A or P.
"tt"     The two-letter AM/PM abbreviation. As in AM or PM.

"X"      Specifies a callback field that must be parsed by the application.

"y"      One-digit year. As in 8 for 1998.
"yy"     Two-digit year. As in 98 for 1998.
"yyy"    Full four-digit year. As in 1998.
```

Literal strings can be included in the format string by enclosing them in single quotes. For example, to display the string *Today is: Saturday, December 5, 1998* the format string would be

```
'Today is: 'dddd', 'MMMM' 'd', 'yyy
```

The single quotes enclose the strings that aren't parsed. That includes the *Today is:* as well as all the separator characters, such as spaces and commas.

The callback field, designated by a series of X characters, provides for the application the greatest degree of flexibility for configuring the display of the date. When the control detects an *X* field in the format string, it sends a series of notification messages to its owner asking what to display in that field. A format string can have any number of *X* fields. For example the following string has two *X* fields.

```
'Today 'XX' is: ' dddd', 'MMMM' 'd', 'yyy' and is 'XXX' birthday'
```

The number of X characters is used by the application only to differentiate the application-defined fields; it doesn't indicate the number of characters that should be displayed in the fields. When the control sends a notification asking for information about an *X* field, it includes a pointer to the *X* string so that the application can determine which field is being referenced.

When the date and time picker control needs to display an application-defined *X* field, it sends two notifications: DTN_FORMATQUERY and DTN_FORMAT. The DTN_FORMATQUERY notification is sent to get the maximum size of the text to be displayed. The DTN_FORMAT notification is then sent to get the actual text for the field. A third notification, DTN_WMKEYDOWN is sent when the user highlights an application-defined field and presses a key. The application is responsible for determining which keys are valid and modifying the date if an appropriate key is pressed.

The List View Control

The list view control is arguably the most complex of the common controls. It displays a list of items in one of four modes: large icon, small icon, list, and report. The Windows CE version of the list view control supports many, but not all, of the valuable new features recently added for Internet Explorer 4.0. Some of these new functions are a great help in the memory-constrained environment of Windows CE. These new features include the ability to manage virtual lists of almost any size, headers that can have images and be rearranged using drag and drop, the ability to indent an entry, and new styles for report mode. The list view control also supports the new custom draw interface, which allows a fairly easy way of changing the appearance of the control.

You register the list view control by calling either *InitCommonControls* or *InitCommonControls* using a ICC_LISTVIEW_CLASSES flag. You create the control by calling *CreateWindow* using the class filled with WC_LISTVIEW. Under Windows CE, the list view control supports all the styles supported by other versions of Windows, including the new LVS_OWNERDATA style that designates the control as a virtual list view control.

New styles in report mode

In addition to the standard list view styles that you can use when creating the list view, the list view control supports a number of *extended styles*. This rather unfortunate term doesn't refer to the extended styles field in the *CreateWindowsEx* function. Instead, two messages, LVM_GETEXTENDEDLISTVIEWSTYLE and LVM_SETEXTENDEDLISTVIEWSTYLE, are used to get and set these extended list view styles. The extended styles supported by Windows CE are listed below.

- *LVS_EX_CHECKBOXES* The control places check boxes next to each item in the control.
- *LVS_EX_HEADERDRAGDROP* Allows headers to be rearranged by the user using drag and drop.

- *LVS_EX_GRIDLINES* The control draws grid lines around the items in report mode.
- *LVS_EX_SUBITEMIMAGES* The control displays images in the subitem columns in report mode.
- *LVS_EX_FULLROWSELECT* The control highlights the item's entire row in report mode when that item is selected.

Aside from the LVS_EX_CHECKBOXES extended style, which works in all display modes, these new styles all affect the actions of the list view when in report mode. The effort here has clearly been to make the list view control an excellent control for displaying large lists of data.

Note that the list view control under Windows CE doesn't support other extended list view styles, such as LVS_EX_INFOTIP, LVS_EX_ONECLICKACTIVATE, LVS_EX_TWOCLICKACTIVATE, LVS_EX_TRACKSELECT, LVS_EX_REGIONAL, or LVS_EX_FLATSB, supported in some versions of the common control library.

Virtual list view

The virtual list view mode of the list view control is a huge help for Windows CE devices. In this mode, the list view control tracks only the selection and focus state of the items. The application maintains all the other data for the items in the control. This mode is handy for two reasons. First, virtual list view controls are fast. The initialization of the control is almost instantaneous because all that's required is that you set the number of items in the control. The list view control also gives you hints about what items it will be looking for in the near term. This allows applications to cache necessary data in RAM and leave the remainder of the data in a database or file. Without a virtual list view, an application would have to load an entire database or list of items in the list view when it's initialized. With the virtual list view, the application loads only what the control requires to display at any one time.

The second advantage of the virtual list view is RAM savings. Because the virtual list view control maintains little information on each item, the control doesn't keep a huge data array in RAM to support the data. The application manages what data is in RAM with some help from the virtual list view's cache hint mechanism.

The virtual list view has some limitations. The LVS_OWNERDATA style that designates a virtual list view can't be set or cleared after the control has been created. Also, virtual list views don't support drag and drop in large icon or small icon mode. A virtual list view defaults to LVS_AUTOARRANGE style and the LVM_SETITEMPOSITION message isn't supported. Also, the sort styles LVS_SORTASCENDING and LVS_SORTDESCENDING aren't supported. Even so, the ability to store large lists of items is handy.

To implement a virtual list view, an application needs to create a list view control with an LVS_OWNERDATA style and handle three notifications—LVN_GETDISPINFO, LVN_ODCACHEHINT, and LVN_ODFINDITEM. The LVN_GETDISPINFO notification should be familiar to those of you who have programmed list view controls before. It has always been sent when the list view control needed information to display an item. In the virtual list view, it's used in a similar manner but the notification is sent to gather all the information about every item in the control.

The virtual list view lets you know what data items it needs using the LVN_ODCACHEHINT notification. This notification passes the starting and ending index of items that the control expects to make use of in the near term. An application can take its cue from this set of numbers to load a cache of those items so that they can be quickly accessed. The hints tend to be requests for the items about to be displayed in the control. Because the number of items can change from view to view in the control, it's helpful that the control tracks this instead of having the application guess which items are going to be needed. Because the control often also needs information about the first and last pages of items, it also helps to cache them so that the frequent requests for those items don't clear the main cache of items that will be needed again soon.

The final notification necessary to manage a virtual list view is the LVN_ODFINDITEM notification. This is sent by the control when it needs to locate an item in response to a key press or in response to an LVM_FINDITEM message.

The LView Example Program

The LView program demonstrates a virtual list view control. The program creates a list view control that displays the contents of a fictional database. A picture of the LView window is shown in Figure 5-6 while the LView code is shown in Figure 5-7.

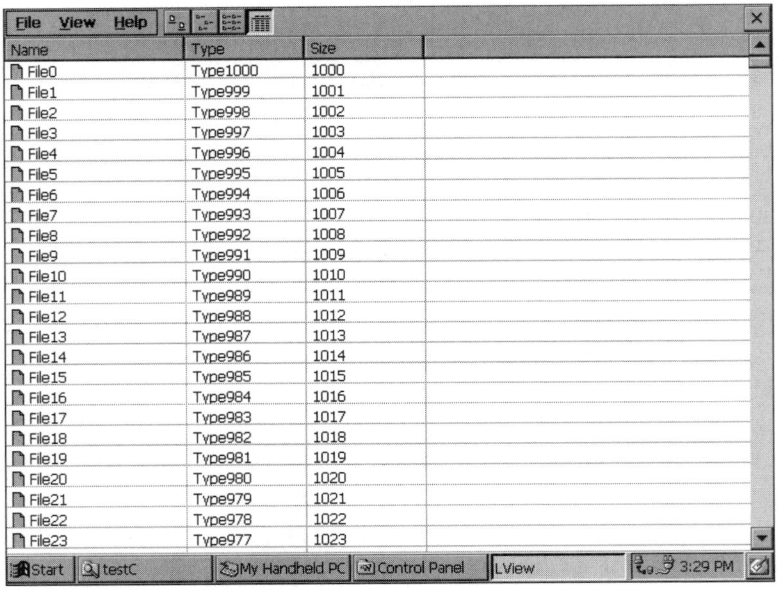

Figure 5-6. *The LView window.*

LView.rc

```
//======================================================================
// Resource file
//
// Written for the book Programming Windows CE
// Copyright (C) 1998 Douglas Boling
//======================================================================
#include "windows.h"
#include "LView.h"                          // Program-specific stuff

//----------------------------------------------------------------------
// Icons and bitmaps
//
ID_ICON        ICON   "lview.ico"          // Program icon
docicon        ICON   "docicon.ico"        // Document icon
//----------------------------------------------------------------------
// Menu
//
ID_MENU MENU DISCARDABLE
BEGIN
    POPUP "&File"
    BEGIN
        MENUITEM "E&xit",                       IDM_EXIT
    END
    POPUP "&View"
    BEGIN
        MENUITEM "&Lar&ge Icons",               IDC_LICON
        MENUITEM "&S&mall Icons",               IDC_SICON
        MENUITEM "&List",                       IDC_LIST
        MENUITEM "&Details",                    IDC_RPT
    END
    POPUP "&Help"
    BEGIN
        MENUITEM "&About",                      IDM_ABOUT
    END
END
//----------------------------------------------------------------------
// About box dialog template
//
aboutbox DIALOG discardable 10, 10, 160, 40
STYLE  WS_POPUP | WS_VISIBLE | WS_CAPTION | WS_SYSMENU | DS_CENTER |
       DS_MODALFRAME
CAPTION "About"
BEGIN
    ICON  ID_ICON,                   -1,   5,   5,  10,  10
```

Figure 5-7. *The LView program.* *(continued)*

Figure 5-7. *continued*

```
    LTEXT "LView - Written for the book Programming Windows \
            CE Copyright 1998 Douglas Boling"
                                      -1,  40,   5, 110,  30
END
```

LView.h

```
//======================================================================
// Header file
//
// Written for the book Programming Windows CE
// Copyright (C) 1998 Douglas Boling
//======================================================================
// Returns number of elements
#define dim(x) (sizeof(x) / sizeof(x[0]))

//----------------------------------------------------------------------
// Generic defines and data types
//
struct decodeUINT {                             // Structure associates
    UINT Code;                                  // messages
                                                // with a function.
    LRESULT (*Fxn)(HWND, UINT, WPARAM, LPARAM);
};
struct decodeCMD {                              // Structure associates
    UINT Code;                                  // menu IDs with a
    LRESULT (*Fxn)(HWND, WORD, HWND, WORD);     // function.
};

//----------------------------------------------------------------------
// Generic defines used by application
#define  IDC_CMDBAR   1                         // Command bar ID
#define  IDC_LISTVIEW 2                         // ID for report list box

#define  ID_ICON             10                 // Icon resource ID
#define  ID_MENU             11                 // Main menu resource ID

// Menu item and Command bar IDs
#define  IDM_EXIT            101

#define  IDC_LICON           111
#define  IDC_SICON           112
#define  IDC_LIST            113
#define  IDC_RPT             114
```

```
#define  IDM_ABOUT           120
#define  VIEW_BMPS           (VIEW_NEWFOLDER+1) // Number of BMPS in
                                                // view list
//----------------------------------------------------------------------
// Program-specific structures
//

// Defines for simulated database
typedef struct {
    TCHAR szName[32];
    TCHAR szType[32];
    INT nSize;
    INT nImage;
    INT nState;
} LVDATAITEM;
typedef LVDATAITEM *PLVDATAITEM;

//----------------------------------------------------------------------
// Function prototypes
//
// Cache functions
PLVDATAITEM GetItemData (INT nItem);
void InitDatabase (void);
void FlushMainCache (void);
void FlushEndCaches (void);
INT LoadTopCache (void);
INT LoadBotCache (void);
INT LoadMainCache (INT nStart, INT nEnd);

// Database functions
void InitDatabase (void);
PLVDATAITEM GetDatabaseItem (INT nItem);
INT SetDatabaseItem (INT nItem, PLVDATAITEM pIn);
PLVDATAITEM GetItemData (INT nItem);
INT AddItem (HWND, INT, LPTSTR, LPTSTR, INT);

int InitApp (HINSTANCE);
HWND InitInstance (HINSTANCE, LPWSTR, int);
int TermInstance (HINSTANCE, int);

// Listview compare callback
int CALLBACK CompareLV (LPARAM, LPARAM, LPARAM);

// Window procedures
LRESULT CALLBACK MainWndProc (HWND, UINT, WPARAM, LPARAM);
```

(continued)

Figure 5-7. *continued*

```
// Message handlers
LRESULT DoCreateMain (HWND, UINT, WPARAM, LPARAM);
LRESULT DoSizeMain (HWND, UINT, WPARAM, LPARAM);
LRESULT DoNotifyMain (HWND, UINT, WPARAM, LPARAM);
LRESULT DoCommandMain (HWND, UINT, WPARAM, LPARAM);
LRESULT DoDestroyMain (HWND, UINT, WPARAM, LPARAM);

// Command functions
LPARAM DoMainCommandExit (HWND, WORD, HWND, WORD);
LPARAM DoMainCommandChView (HWND, WORD, HWND, WORD);
LPARAM DoMainCommandAbout (HWND, WORD, HWND, WORD);

// Dialog procedures
BOOL CALLBACK AboutDlgProc (HWND, UINT, WPARAM, LPARAM);
```

LView.c

```
//======================================================================
// LView - ListView control demonstration
//
// Written for the book Programming Windows CE
// Copyright (C) 1998 Douglas Boling
//======================================================================
#include <windows.h>                 // For all that Windows stuff
#include <commctrl.h>                // Command bar includes
#include "LView.h"                   // Program-specific stuff
//----------------------------------------------------------------------
// Global data
//
const TCHAR szAppName[] = TEXT ("LView");
HINSTANCE hInst;                     // Program instance handle
HWND hMain;

//
// Data for simulated database
//
#define LVCNT 2000
LVDATAITEM lvdatabase[LVCNT];

// Defines and data for list view control cache
#define  CACHESIZE       100
#define  TOPCACHESIZE    100
#define  BOTCACHESIZE    100
```

```
INT nCacheItemStart = 0, nCacheSize = 0;
LVDATAITEM lvdiCache[CACHESIZE];
LVDATAITEM lvdiTopCache[TOPCACHESIZE];
LVDATAITEM lvdiBotCache[BOTCACHESIZE];

// Message dispatch table for MainWindowProc
const struct decodeUINT MainMessages[] = {
    WM_CREATE, DoCreateMain,
    WM_SIZE, DoSizeMain,
    WM_NOTIFY, DoNotifyMain,
    WM_COMMAND, DoCommandMain,
    WM_DESTROY, DoDestroyMain,
};
// Command message dispatch for MainWindowProc
const struct decodeCMD MainCommandItems[] = {
    IDM_EXIT, DoMainCommandExit,
    IDC_LICON, DoMainCommandChView,
    IDC_SICON, DoMainCommandChView,
    IDC_LIST, DoMainCommandChView,
    IDC_RPT, DoMainCommandChView,
    IDM_ABOUT, DoMainCommandAbout,
};
// Standard file bar button structure
const TBBUTTON tbCBCmboBtns[] = {
//  BitmapIndex        Command    State          Style        UserData String
    {0,                0,         0,             TBSTYLE_SEP,        0,  0},
    {VIEW_LARGEICONS, IDC_LICON, TBSTATE_ENABLED,
                                             TBSTYLE_CHECKGROUP, 0,  0},
    {VIEW_SMALLICONS, IDC_SICON, TBSTATE_ENABLED,
                                             TBSTYLE_CHECKGROUP, 0,  0},
    {VIEW_LIST,       IDC_LIST,  TBSTATE_ENABLED,
                                             TBSTYLE_CHECKGROUP, 0,  0},
    {VIEW_DETAILS,    IDC_RPT,   TBSTATE_ENABLED | TBSTATE_CHECKED,
                                             TBSTYLE_CHECKGROUP, 0,  0}
};
//======================================================================
// Program entry point
//
int WINAPI WinMain (HINSTANCE hInstance, HINSTANCE hPrevInstance,
                    LPWSTR lpCmdLine, int nCmdShow) {
    MSG msg;
    HWND hwndMain;
    int rc = 0;
```

(continued)

Figure 5-7. *continued*

```
    // Initialize application.
    rc = InitApp (hInstance);
    if (rc) return rc;

    // Initialize this instance.
    hwndMain = InitInstance (hInstance, lpCmdLine, nCmdShow);
    if (hwndMain == 0)
        return 0x10;

    hMain = hwndMain;
    // Application message loop
    while (GetMessage (&msg, NULL, 0, 0)) {
        TranslateMessage (&msg);
        DispatchMessage (&msg);
    }
    // Instance cleanup
    return TermInstance (hInstance, msg.wParam);
}
//----------------------------------------------------------------------
// InitApp - Application initialization
//
int InitApp (HINSTANCE hInstance) {
    WNDCLASS     wc;
    INITCOMMONCONTROLSEX icex;

    // Register application main window class.
    wc.style = 0;                             // Window style
    wc.lpfnWndProc = MainWndProc;             // Callback function
    wc.cbClsExtra = 0;                        // Extra class data
    wc.cbWndExtra = 0;                        // Extra window data
    wc.hInstance = hInstance;                 // Owner handle
    wc.hIcon = NULL,                          // Application icon
    wc.hCursor = NULL;                        // Default cursor
    wc.hbrBackground = (HBRUSH) GetStockObject (WHITE_BRUSH);
    wc.lpszMenuName =  NULL;                  // Menu name
    wc.lpszClassName = szAppName;             // Window class name

    if (RegisterClass (&wc) == 0) return 1;

    // Load the command bar common control class.
    icex.dwSize = sizeof (INITCOMMONCONTROLSEX);
    icex.dwICC = ICC_LISTVIEW_CLASSES;
    InitCommonControlsEx (&icex);
```

```
    // Initialize the fictional database.
    InitDatabase ();
    return 0;
}
//----------------------------------------------------------------------
// InitInstance - Instance initialization
//
HWND InitInstance (HINSTANCE hInstance, LPWSTR lpCmdLine, int nCmdShow){
    HWND hWnd;

    // Save program instance handle in global variable.
    hInst = hInstance;

    // Create main window.
    hWnd = CreateWindow (szAppName,           // Window class
                         TEXT ("LView"),      // Window title
                         WS_VISIBLE,          // Style flags
                         CW_USEDEFAULT,       // x position
                         CW_USEDEFAULT,       // y position
                         CW_USEDEFAULT,       // Initial width
                         CW_USEDEFAULT,       // Initial height
                         NULL,                // Parent
                         NULL,                // Menu, must be null
                         hInstance,           // Application instance
                         NULL);               // Pointer to create
                                              // parameters
    // Return fail code if window not created.
    if (!IsWindow (hWnd)) return 0;

    // Standard show and update calls
    ShowWindow (hWnd, nCmdShow);
    UpdateWindow (hWnd);
    return hWnd;
}
//----------------------------------------------------------------------
// TermInstance - Program cleanup
//
int TermInstance (HINSTANCE hInstance, int nDefRC) {

    // Flush caches used with list view control.
    FlushMainCache ();
    FlushEndCaches ();
    return nDefRC;
```

(continued)

Figure 5-7. *continued*

```
}
//======================================================================
// Message-handling procedures for MainWindow
//----------------------------------------------------------------------
// MainWndProc - Callback function for application window
//
LRESULT CALLBACK MainWndProc(HWND hWnd, UINT wMsg, WPARAM wParam,
                             LPARAM lParam) {
    INT i;
    //
    // Search message list to see if we need to handle this
    // message.  If in list, call procedure.
    //
    for (i = 0; i < dim(MainMessages); i++) {
        if (wMsg == MainMessages[i].Code)
            return (*MainMessages[i].Fxn)(hWnd, wMsg, wParam, lParam);
    }
    return DefWindowProc(hWnd, wMsg, wParam, lParam);
}
//----------------------------------------------------------------------
// DoCreateMain - Process WM_CREATE message for window.
//
LRESULT DoCreateMain (HWND hWnd, UINT wMsg, WPARAM wParam,
                      LPARAM lParam) {
    HWND hwndCB, hwndLV;
    INT i, nHeight;
    LPCREATESTRUCT lpcs;
    HIMAGELIST himlLarge, himlSmall;
    HICON hIcon;

    // Convert lParam into pointer to create structure.
    lpcs = (LPCREATESTRUCT) lParam;

    // Create a command bar.
    hwndCB = CommandBar_Create (hInst, hWnd, IDC_CMDBAR);

    // Insert a menu.
    CommandBar_InsertMenubar (hwndCB, hInst, ID_MENU, 0);

    // Add bitmap list followed by buttons.
    CommandBar_AddBitmap (hwndCB, HINST_COMMCTRL, IDB_VIEW_SMALL_COLOR,
                          VIEW_BMPS, 0, 0);
    CommandBar_AddButtons (hwndCB, dim(tbCBCmboBtns), tbCBCmboBtns);
```

```
// Add exit button to command bar.
CommandBar_AddAdornments (hwndCB, 0, 0);
nHeight = CommandBar_Height (hwndCB);
//
// Create the list view control.
//
hwndLV = CreateWindowEx (0, WC_LISTVIEW, TEXT (""),
                         LVS_REPORT | LVS_SINGLESEL |
                         LVS_OWNERDATA | WS_VISIBLE | WS_CHILD |
                         WS_VSCROLL, 0, nHeight, lpcs->cx,
                         lpcs->cy - nHeight, hWnd,
                         (HMENU)IDC_LISTVIEW,
                         lpcs->hInstance, NULL);
// Destroy frame if window not created.
if (!IsWindow (hwndLV)) {
    DestroyWindow (hWnd);
    return 0;
}
// Add columns.
{
    LVCOLUMN lvc;

    lvc.mask = LVCF_TEXT | LVCF_WIDTH | LVCF_FMT | LVCF_SUBITEM;
    lvc.fmt = LVCFMT_LEFT;
    lvc.cx = 150;
    lvc.pszText = TEXT ("Name");
    lvc.iSubItem = 0;
    SendMessage (hwndLV, LVM_INSERTCOLUMN, 0, (LPARAM)&lvc);

    lvc.mask |= LVCF_SUBITEM;
    lvc.pszText = TEXT ("Type");
    lvc.cx = 100;
    lvc.iSubItem = 1;
    SendMessage (hwndLV, LVM_INSERTCOLUMN, 1, (LPARAM)&lvc);

    lvc.mask |= LVCF_SUBITEM;
    lvc.pszText = TEXT ("Size");
    lvc.cx = 100;
    lvc.iSubItem = 2;
    SendMessage (hwndLV, LVM_INSERTCOLUMN, 2, (LPARAM)&lvc);
}
// Add items.
ListView_SetItemCount (hwndLV, LVCNT);
LoadTopCache ();
LoadBotCache ();
```

(continued)

Figure 5-7. *continued*

```
    // Create image list control for bitmaps for minimized bands.
    i = GetSystemMetrics (SM_CXICON);
    himlLarge = ImageList_Create(i, i, ILC_COLOR, 2, 0);
    i = GetSystemMetrics (SM_CXSMICON);
    himlSmall = ImageList_Create(i, i, ILC_COLOR, 2, 0);

    // Load large and small icons into their respective image lists.
    hIcon = LoadIcon (hInst, TEXT ("DocIcon"));
    i = ImageList_AddIcon (himlLarge, hIcon);

    hIcon = LoadImage (hInst, TEXT ("DocIcon"), IMAGE_ICON, 16, 16,
                       LR_DEFAULTCOLOR);
    ImageList_AddIcon (himlSmall, hIcon);

    ListView_SetImageList (hwndLV, himlLarge, LVSIL_NORMAL);
    ListView_SetImageList (hwndLV, himlSmall, LVSIL_SMALL);

    // Set cool new styles.
    ListView_SetExtendedListViewStyle (hwndLV, LVS_EX_GRIDLINES |
                                       LVS_EX_HEADERDRAGDROP |
                                       LVS_EX_FULLROWSELECT);
    return 0;
}
//----------------------------------------------------------------------
// DoSizeMain - Process WM_SIZE message for window.
//
LRESULT DoSizeMain (HWND hWnd, UINT wMsg, WPARAM wParam, LPARAM lParam){
    HWND hwndLV;
    RECT rect;

    hwndLV = GetDlgItem (hWnd, IDC_LISTVIEW);

    // Adjust the size of the client rect to take into account
    // the command bar height.
    GetClientRect (hWnd, &rect);
    rect.top += CommandBar_Height (GetDlgItem (hWnd, IDC_CMDBAR));

    SetWindowPos (hwndLV, NULL, rect.left, rect.top,
                  rect.right - rect.left, rect.bottom - rect.top,
                  SWP_NOZORDER);
    return 0;
}
//----------------------------------------------------------------------
// DoNotifyMain - Process WM_NOTIFY message for window.
//
```

```
LRESULT DoNotifyMain (HWND hWnd, UINT wMsg, WPARAM wParam,
                      LPARAM lParam) {
    int idItem;
    LPNMHDR    pnmh;
    LPNMLISTVIEW pnmlv;
    NMLVDISPINFO *pLVdi;
    PLVDATAITEM pdi;      // Pointer to data
    LPNMLVCACHEHINT pLVch;
    HWND hwndLV;

    // Parse the parameters.
    idItem = (int) wParam;
    pnmh = (LPNMHDR)lParam;
    hwndLV = pnmh->hwndFrom;

    if (idItem == IDC_LISTVIEW) {
        pnmlv = (LPNMLISTVIEW)lParam;

        switch (pnmh->code) {
        case LVN_GETDISPINFO:
            pLVdi = (NMLVDISPINFO *)lParam;

            // Get a pointer to the data either from the cache
            // or from the actual database.
            pdi = GetItemData (pLVdi->item.iItem);

            if (pLVdi->item.mask & LVIF_IMAGE)
                pLVdi->item.iImage = pdi->nImage;

            if (pLVdi->item.mask & LVIF_PARAM)
                pLVdi->item.lParam = 0;

            if (pLVdi->item.mask & LVIF_STATE)
                pLVdi->item.state = pdi->nState;

            if (pLVdi->item.mask & LVIF_TEXT) {
                switch (pLVdi->item.iSubItem) {
                case 0:
                    lstrcpy (pLVdi->item.pszText, pdi->szName);
                    break;
                case 1:
                    lstrcpy (pLVdi->item.pszText, pdi->szType);
                    break;
                case 2:
                    wsprintf (pLVdi->item.pszText, TEXT ("%d"),
                              pdi->nSize);
```

(continued)

Figure 5-7. *continued*

```
                    break;
                }
            }
            break;

        case LVN_ODCACHEHINT:
            pLVch = (LPNMLVCACHEHINT)lParam;
            LoadMainCache (pLVch->iFrom, pLVch->iTo);
            break;

        case LVN_ODFINDITEM:
            // We should do a reverse look up here to see if
            // an item exists for the text passed.
            return -1;
        }
    }
    return 0;
}
//----------------------------------------------------------------------
// DoCommandMain - Process WM_COMMAND message for window.
//
LRESULT DoCommandMain (HWND hWnd, UINT wMsg, WPARAM wParam,
                       LPARAM lParam) {
    WORD idItem, wNotifyCode;
    HWND hwndCtl;
    INT  i;

    // Parse the parameters.
    idItem = (WORD) LOWORD (wParam);
    wNotifyCode = (WORD) HIWORD (wParam);
    hwndCtl = (HWND) lParam;

    // Call routine to handle control message.
    for (i = 0; i < dim(MainCommandItems); i++) {
        if (idItem == MainCommandItems[i].Code)
            return (*MainCommandItems[i].Fxn)(hWnd, idItem, hwndCtl,
                                              wNotifyCode);
    }
    return 0;
}
//----------------------------------------------------------------------
// DoDestroyMain - Process WM_DESTROY message for window.
//
LRESULT DoDestroyMain (HWND hWnd, UINT wMsg, WPARAM wParam,
                       LPARAM lParam) {
    PostQuitMessage (0);
    return 0;
```

```
}
//======================================================================
// Command handler routines
//----------------------------------------------------------------------
// DoMainCommandExit - Process Program Exit command.
//
LPARAM DoMainCommandExit (HWND hWnd, WORD idItem, HWND hwndCtl,
                          WORD wNotifyCode) {

    SendMessage (hWnd, WM_CLOSE, 0, 0);
    return 0;
}
//----------------------------------------------------------------------
// DoMainCommandChView - Process View xxx command.
//
LPARAM DoMainCommandChView (HWND hWnd, WORD idItem, HWND hwndCtl,
                            WORD wNotifyCode) {
    HWND hwndLV;
    LONG lStyle;

    hwndLV = GetDlgItem (hWnd, IDC_LISTVIEW);

    lStyle = GetWindowLong (hwndLV, GWL_STYLE);
    lStyle &= ~LVS_TYPEMASK;

    switch (idItem) {
    case IDC_LICON:
        lStyle |= LVS_ICON;
        break;
    case IDC_SICON:
        lStyle |= LVS_SMALLICON;
        break;
    case IDC_LIST:
        lStyle |= LVS_LIST;
        break;
    case IDC_RPT:
        lStyle |= LVS_REPORT;
        break;
    }
    SetWindowLong (hwndLV, GWL_STYLE, lStyle);
    return 0;
}
//----------------------------------------------------------------------
// DoMainCommandAbout - Process the Help | About menu command.
//
LPARAM DoMainCommandAbout(HWND hWnd, WORD idItem, HWND hwndCtl,
                          WORD wNotifyCode) {
```

(continued)

Figure 5-7. *continued*

```
    // Use DialogBox to create modal dialog box.
    DialogBox (hInst, TEXT ("aboutbox"), hWnd, AboutDlgProc);
    return 0;
}
//======================================================================
// About Dialog procedure
//
BOOL CALLBACK AboutDlgProc(HWND hWnd, UINT wMsg, WPARAM wParam,
                           LPARAM lParam) {

    switch (wMsg) {
        case WM_COMMAND:
            switch (LOWORD (wParam)) {
                case IDOK:
                case IDCANCEL:
                    EndDialog (hWnd, 0);
                    return TRUE;
            }
        break;
    }
    return FALSE;
}
//======================================================================
// Helper routines for list view control management
//----------------------------------------------------------------------
// AddItem - Add an item to the list view control.
//
INT AddItem (HWND hwndCtl, INT nItem, LPTSTR pszName, LPTSTR pszType,
             INT nSize) {
    LVITEM lvi;
    TCHAR szTmp[40];

    lvi.mask = LVIF_TEXT | LVIF_IMAGE | LVIF_PARAM;
    lvi.iItem = nItem;
    lvi.iSubItem = 0;
    lvi.pszText = pszName;
    lvi.iImage = 0;
    lvi.lParam = nItem;
    SendMessage (hwndCtl, LVM_INSERTITEM, 0, (LPARAM)&lvi);

    lvi.mask = LVIF_TEXT;
    lvi.iItem = nItem;
    lvi.iSubItem = 1;
    lvi.pszText = pszType;
    SendMessage (hwndCtl, LVM_SETITEM, 0, (LPARAM)&lvi);
```

```
    wsprintf (szTmp, TEXT ("%d"), nSize);
    lvi.mask = LVIF_TEXT;
    lvi.iItem = nItem;
    lvi.iSubItem = 2;
    lvi.pszText = szTmp;
    SendMessage (hwndCtl, LVM_SETITEM, 0, (LPARAM)&lvi);

    return 0;
}
//----------------------------------------------------------------------
// GetItemData - This routine returns a pointer to the data.  It
// first checks the caches before calling directly to the database.
//
PLVDATAITEM GetItemData (INT nItem) {
    INT nCacheIndex;
    PLVDATAITEM pdi;

    // See if it's in the top cache.
    if (nItem < TOPCACHESIZE) {

        nCacheIndex = nItem;
        pdi = &lvdiTopCache[nCacheIndex];
    }

    // See if it's in the bottom cache.
    else if (nItem > LVCNT - BOTCACHESIZE) {

        nCacheIndex = nItem - (LVCNT - BOTCACHESIZE);
        pdi = &lvdiBotCache[nCacheIndex];
    }
    // See if item's in the main cache.
    else if ((nItem >= nCacheItemStart) &&
             (nItem < nCacheItemStart + nCacheSize)) {

        nCacheIndex = nItem - nCacheItemStart;
        pdi = &lvdiCache[nCacheIndex];
    }

    // Otherwise it's not in any cache.
    else
        pdi = GetDatabaseItem (nItem);

    return pdi;
}
```

(continued)

Figure 5-7. *continued*

```
//----------------------------------------------------------------------
INT LoadACache (PLVDATAITEM pCache, INT nStart, INT nSize) {
    PLVDATAITEM pdi;
    INT i;

    for (i = 0; i < nSize; i++) {
        // Get a pointer to the data.
        pdi = GetDatabaseItem (nStart+i);

        // Save the data in the cache.
        lstrcpy (pCache[i].szName, pdi->szName);
        lstrcpy (pCache[i].szType, pdi->szType);
        pCache[i].nSize = pdi->nSize;
        pCache[i].nImage = pdi->nImage;
        pCache[i].nState = pdi->nState;
    }
    return 0;
}
//----------------------------------------------------------------------
// LoadMainCache - This routine loads the hint cache.  If the
// recommended range is already in the top or bottom caches, the range
// is adjusted to grab items outside the end caches.
//
// The logic expects the total number of items to be greater than the
// size of the start and end caches.
//
INT LoadMainCache (INT nStart, INT nEnd) {
    INT nOverlap;

    // Size the hint range to fit the cache.
    if (nEnd - nStart > CACHESIZE)
        nEnd = nStart + CACHESIZE;

    // See if end of hint in bottom cache.
    if (nEnd > LVCNT - BOTCACHESIZE) {

        // If completely in bottom cache, keep old data.
        if (nStart > LVCNT - BOTCACHESIZE)
            return 0;

        // If partial overlap, adjust end points to get data just
        // above the bottom cache.
        nOverlap = nEnd - (LVCNT - BOTCACHESIZE);
        nEnd = LVCNT - BOTCACHESIZE - 1;
        if (nStart - nOverlap < TOPCACHESIZE)
            nStart = TOPCACHESIZE;
```

```
        else
            nStart -= nOverlap;
    }
    // See if start of hint in top cache.
    if (nStart < TOPCACHESIZE) {

        // If completely in top cache, keep old data.
        if (nEnd < TOPCACHESIZE)
            return 0;

        // Adjust the starting value to just beyond top cache end.
        nOverlap = TOPCACHESIZE - nStart;
        nStart = TOPCACHESIZE;
        if (nOverlap + nEnd > (LVCNT - BOTCACHESIZE))
            nEnd = LVCNT - BOTCACHESIZE;
        else
            nEnd += nOverlap;
    }
    // If hint already completely contained in the cache, exit.
    if ((nStart >= nCacheItemStart) &&
        (nEnd < nCacheItemStart + nCacheSize))
        return 0;

    // Flush old data in cache.  We should really be smart here to
    // see whether part of the data is already in the cache.
    FlushMainCache ();

    // Load the new data.
    nCacheSize = nEnd - nStart;
    nCacheItemStart = nStart;
    LoadACache (lvdiCache, nStart, nCacheSize);
    return 0;
}
//----------------------------------------------------------------------
INT LoadTopCache (void) {

    LoadACache (lvdiTopCache, 0, TOPCACHESIZE);
    return 0;
}
//----------------------------------------------------------------------
INT LoadBotCache (void) {

    LoadACache (lvdiBotCache, LVCNT - BOTCACHESIZE, BOTCACHESIZE);
    return 0;
}
```

(continued)

Figure 5-7. *continued*

```
//----------------------------------------------------------------------
void FlushMainCache (void) {
    INT i;

    // Send the data back to the database.
    for (i = 0; i < nCacheSize; i++) {
        SetDatabaseItem (nCacheItemStart+i, &lvdiCache[i]);
    }
    return;
}
//----------------------------------------------------------------------
void FlushEndCaches (void) {
    INT i;

    // Flush the top cache.
    for (i = 0; i < TOPCACHESIZE; i++) {
        SetDatabaseItem (i, &lvdiCache[i]);
    }
    // Flush the bottom cache.
    for (i = 0; i < BOTCACHESIZE; i++) {
        SetDatabaseItem (LVCNT - BOTCACHESIZE + i, &lvdiBotCache[i]);
    }
    return;
}
//======================================================================
// Code for fictional database to be displayed in the list view control
//
//----------------------------------------------------------------------
// InitDatabaseItem - Copy an item into the database.
//
INT InitDatabaseItem (INT nItem, LPTSTR pszName, LPTSTR pszType,
                      INT nSize) {

    lstrcpy (lvdatabase[nItem].szName, pszName);
    lstrcpy (lvdatabase[nItem].szType, pszType);
    lvdatabase[nItem].nSize = nSize;
    lvdatabase[nItem].nImage = 0;
    lvdatabase[nItem].nState = 0;
    return 0;
}
//----------------------------------------------------------------------
// InitDatabase - Create fictional data for fictional database.
//
```

```
void InitDatabase (void) {
    TCHAR szName[64];
    TCHAR szType[64];
    HCURSOR hOldCur;
    INT i;

    hOldCur = SetCursor (LoadCursor (NULL, IDC_WAIT));

    for (i = 0; i < LVCNT; i++) {
        wsprintf (szName, TEXT ("File%d"), i);
        wsprintf (szType, TEXT ("Type%d"), 1000 - i);
        InitDatabaseItem (i, szName, szType, i+1000);
    }
    SetCursor (hOldCur);
    return;
}
//----------------------------------------------------------------------
// GetDatabaseItem - Return a pointer to data in the database.
//
PLVDATAITEM GetDatabaseItem (INT nItem) {

    // Normally, this would be more work. But since
    // we have only a simulated data store, the
    // code is trivial.
    return &lvdatabase[nItem];
}
//----------------------------------------------------------------------
// SetDatabaseItem - Copy data from list view control back into database.
//
INT SetDatabaseItem (INT nItem, PLVDATAITEM pIn) {

    lstrcpy (lvdatabase[nItem].szName, pIn->szName);
    lstrcpy (lvdatabase[nItem].szType, pIn->szType);
    lvdatabase[nItem].nSize = pIn->nSize;
    lvdatabase[nItem].nImage = pIn->nImage;
    lvdatabase[nItem].nState = pIn->nState;
    return 0;
}
```

Notice that the size for the database is set to 2000 items by default. Even with this large number, the performance of the list view control is quite acceptable. Most of the brief application startup time is taken up not by initializing the list view control, but just by filling in the dummy database. Support for the virtual list view is centered on the *OnNotifyMain* routine.

Data for each item is supplied to the list view control through responses to the LVN_GETDISPINFO notification. The flags in the mask field of the LVDISPINFO determine exactly what element of the item is being requested. The code that handles the notification simply requests the item data from the cache and fills in the requested fields.

The cache implemented by LView uses three separate buffers. Two of the buffers are initialized with the first and last 100 items from the database. The third 100-item cache, referred to as the main cache, is loaded using the hints passed by the list view control.

The routine that reads the data from the cache is located in the *GetItemData* routine. That routine uses the index value of the requested item to see whether the data is in the top or bottom caches, and if not, whether it's in the main cache. If the data isn't in one of the caches, a call to *GetDatabaseItem* is made to read the data directly from the dummy database.

The routine that handles the cache hints from the list view control is *LoadMainCache*. This routine is called when the program receives a LVN_ODCACHEHINT notification. The routine takes two parameters, the starting and ending values of the hint passed by the notification. The routine first checks to see if the range of items in the hint lies in the two end caches that store data from the top and bottom of the database. If the range does lie in one of the end caches, the hint is ignored and the main cache is left unchanged. If the hint range isn't in either end cache and isn't already in the current main cache, the main cache is flushed to send any updated information back into the database. The cache is then loaded with data from the database from the range of items indicated by the hint.

The cache hint notifications sent by the list view control aren't necessarily intelligent. The control sends a request for a range of one item if that item is double-clicked by the user. The cache management code should always check to see whether the requested data is already in the cache before flushing and reloading the cache based on a single hint. The cache strategy you use, and the effort you must make to optimize it, of course depends on the access speed of the real data.

OTHER COMMON CONTROLS

Windows CE supports a number of other common controls available under Windows 98 and Windows NT. Most of these controls are supported completely within the limits of the capability of Windows CE. For example, while the tab control supports vertical tabs, Windows CE supports vertical text only on systems that support TrueType fonts. For other systems, including the Palm-size PC, the text in the tabs must be manually generated by the Windows CE application by rotating bitmap images of each letter. Frankly, it's probably much easier to devise a dialog box that doesn't need vertical tabs. Short descriptions of the other supported common controls follow.

The status bar control

The status bar is carried over unchanged from the desktop versions of Windows. The only difference is that under Windows CE, the SBARS_SIZEGRIP style that created a gripper area on the right end of the status bar has no meaning because users can't size Windows CE windows.

The tab control

The tab control is fully supported, the above-mentioned vertical text limitation not withstanding. But because the stylus can't hover over a tab, the TCS_HOTTRACK style that highlighted tabs under the cursor isn't supported. The TCS_EX_REGISTERDROP extended style is also not supported.

The trackbar control

The trackbar control gains the capacity for two "buddy" controls that are automatically updated with the trackbar value. The trackbar also supports the custom draw service, providing separate item drawing indications for the channel, the thumb, and the tic marks.

The progress bar control

The progress bar includes the latest support for vertical progress bars and 32-bit ranges. This control also supports the new smooth progression instead of moving the progress indicator in discrete chunks.

The up-down control

The up-down control under Windows CE only supports edit controls for its buddy control.

The toolbar control

The Windows CE toolbar supports tooltips differently from the way tool tips are supported by the desktop versions of this control. You add toolbar support for tool tips in Windows CE the same way you do for the command bar, by passing a pointer to a permanently allocated array of strings. The toolbar also supports the transparent and flat styles that are supported by the command bar.

The tree view control

The tree view control supports two new styles recently added to the tree view common control: TVS_CHECKBOXES and TVS_SINGLESEL. The TVS_CHECKBOXES style places a check box adjacent to each item in the control. The TVS_SINGLESEL style causes a previously expanded item to close up when a new item is selected. The tree view control also supports the custom draw service. The tree view control doesn't support the TVS_TRACKSELECT style, which allows you to highlight an item when the cursor hovers over it.

UNSUPPORTED COMMON CONTROLS

Windows CE doesn't support four common controls seen under other versions of Windows. The animation control, the drag list control, the hot key control, and, sadly, the rich edit control are all unsupported. Animation would be hard to support given the slower processors often seen running Windows CE. The hot key control is problematic in that keyboard layouts and key labels, standardized on the PC, vary dramatically on the different hardware that runs Windows CE. And the drag list control isn't that big a loss, given the improved power of the report style of the list view control.

The rich edit control is another story. The lack of an edit control that can contain multiple fonts and paragraph formatting is a noticeable gap in the Windows CE shell. Applications needing this functionality are forced to implement independent, and mutually incompatible, solutions. Let's hope the rich edit control is supported under future versions of Windows CE.

Windows CE supports fairly completely the common control library seen under other versions of Windows. The date and time picker, month calendar, and command bar are a great help given the target audience of Windows CE devices.

I've spent a fair amount of time in the past few chapters looking at the building blocks of applications. Now it's time to turn to the operating system itself. Over the next three chapters, I'll cover memory management, files and databases, and processes and threads. These chapters are aimed at the core of the Windows CE operating system.

Chapter 6

Memory Management

If you have an overriding concern when you're writing a Microsoft Windows CE program, it should be dealing with memory. A Windows CE machine might have only 1 or 2 MB of RAM. This is a tiny amount compared to that of a standard personal computer, which can range somewhere between 16 and 64 MB of RAM. In fact, memory on a Windows CE machine is so scarce that it's often necessary to write programs that conserve memory even to the point of sacrificing the overall performance of the application.

Fortunately, although the amount of memory is small in a Windows CE system, the functions available for managing that memory are fairly complete. Windows CE implements almost the full Win32 memory management API available under Microsoft Windows NT and Microsoft Windows 98. Windows CE supports virtual memory allocations, local and separate heaps, and even memory-mapped files.

Like Windows NT, Windows CE supports a 32-bit flat address space with memory protection between applications. But because Windows CE was designed for different environments, its underlying memory architecture is different from that for Windows NT. These differences can affect how you design a Windows CE application. In this chapter, I'll cover the basic memory architecture of Windows CE. I'll also cover the different types of memory allocation available to Windows CE programs and how to use each memory type to minimize your application's memory footprint.

Memory Basics

As with all computers, systems running Windows CE have both ROM (read only memory) and RAM (random access memory). Under Windows CE, however, both ROM and RAM are used somewhat differently than they are in a standard personal computer.

About RAM

The RAM in a Windows CE system is divided into two areas: *program memory* and *object store*. The object store can be considered something like a permanent virtual RAM disk. Unlike the old virtual RAM disks on a PC, the object store retains the files stored in it even if the system is turned off.[1] This is the reason Windows CE systems such as the Handheld PC and the Palm-size PC each have a battery and a backup battery. When the user replaces the main batteries, the backup battery's job is to provide power to the RAM to retain the files in the object store. Even when the user hits the reset button, the Windows CE kernel starts up looking for a previously created object store in RAM and uses that store if it finds one.

The other area of the RAM is devoted to the program memory. Program memory is used like the RAM in personal computers. It stores the heaps and stacks for the applications that are running. The boundary between the object store and the program RAM is movable. The user can move the dividing line between object store and program RAM using the System control panel applet. Under low-memory conditions, the system will ask the user for permission to take some object store RAM to use as program RAM to satisfy an application's demand for more RAM.

About ROM

In a personal computer, the ROM is used to store the BIOS (basic input output system) and is typically 64–128 KB. In a Windows CE system, the ROM can range from 4 to 16 MB and stores the entire operating system, as well as the applications that are bundled with the system. In this sense, the ROM in a Windows CE system is like a small, read-only hard disk.

In a Windows CE system, ROM-based programs can be designated as Execute in Place (XIP). That is, they're executed directly from the ROM instead of being loaded into program RAM and then executed. This is a huge advantage for small systems in two ways. The fact that the code is executed directly from ROM means that the program code doesn't take up valuable program RAM. Also, since the program doesn't

1. On mobile systems like the H/PC and the Palm-size PC, the system is never really off. When the user presses the Off button, the system enters a very low power suspended state.

have to be copied into RAM before it's launched, it takes less time to start an application. Programs that aren't in ROM but are contained in the object store or on a Flash memory storage card aren't executed in place; they're copied into the RAM and executed.

About Virtual Memory

Windows CE implements a virtual memory management system. In a virtual memory system, applications deal with virtual memory, which is a separate, imaginary address space that might not relate to the physical memory address space that's implemented by the hardware. The operating system uses the memory management unit of the microprocessor to translate virtual addresses to physical addresses in real time.

The key advantage of a virtual memory system can be seen in the complexity of the MS-DOS address space. Once demand for RAM exceeded the 640-KB limit of the original PC design, programmers had to deal with schemes such as *expanded* and *extended* memory to increase the available RAM. OS/2 1.*x* and Windows 3.0 replaced these schemes with a segment-based virtual memory system. Applications using virtual memory have no idea (nor should they care) where the actual physical memory resides, only that the memory is available. In these systems, the virtual memory was implemented in segments, resizable blocks of memory that ranged from 16 bytes to 64 KB in size. The 64-KB limit wasn't due to the segments themselves, but to the 16-bit nature of the Intel 80286 that was the basis for the segmented virtual memory system in Windows 3.*x* and OS/2 1.*x*.

Paged memory

The Intel 80386 supported segments larger than 64 KB, but when Microsoft and IBM began the design for OS/2 2.0, they chose to use a different virtual memory system, also supported by the 386, known as a *paged virtual memory system*. In a paged memory system, the smallest unit of memory the microprocessor manages is the *page*. For Windows NT and OS/2 2.0, the pages were set to 386's default page size of 4096 bytes. When an application accesses a page, the microprocessor translates the virtual address of the page to a physical page in ROM or RAM. A page can also be tagged so that accessing the page causes an exception. The operating system then determines whether the virtual page is valid and, if so, maps a physical page of memory to the virtual page.

Windows CE implements a paged virtual memory management system similar to the other Win32 operating systems, Windows NT and Windows 98. Under Windows CE, a page is either 1024 or 4096 bytes, depending on the microprocessor, with the 1-KB page size preferred by the Windows CE architects. This is a change from Windows NT, where page sizes are 4096 bytes for Intel microprocessors and 8192 bytes for the DEC Alpha. For the CPUs currently supported by Windows CE, the NEC 4100 series and the Hitachi SH3 use 1024-byte pages and the 486, the Phillips 3910, and Power PC 821 use 4096-byte pages.

Virtual pages can be in one of three states: *free*, *reserved*, or *committed*. A free page is, as it sounds, free and available to be allocated. A reserved page is a page that has been reserved so that its virtual address can't be allocated by the operating system or another thread in the process. A reserved page can't be used elsewhere, but it also can't be used by the application because it isn't mapped to physical memory. To be mapped, a page must be committed. A committed page has been reserved by an application and has been directly mapped to a physical address.

All that I've just explained is old hat to experienced Win32 programmers. The important thing for the Windows CE programmer is to learn how Windows CE changes the equation. While Windows CE implements most of the same memory API set of its bigger Win32 cousins, the underlying architecture of Windows CE does impact programs. To better understand how the API is affected, it helps to look at how Windows CE uses memory under the covers.

The Windows CE Address Space

In OS circles, much is made of the extent to which the operating system goes to protect one application's memory from other applications. Microsoft Windows 95 used a single address space that provided minimal protection between applications and the Windows operating system code. Windows NT, on the other hand, implements completely separate address spaces for each Win32 application, although old 16-bit applications under Windows NT do share a single address space.

Windows CE implements a single, 2-GB virtual address space for all applications, but the memory space of an application is protected so that it can't be accessed by another application. A diagram of the Windows CE virtual address space is shown in Figure 6-1. A little over half of the virtual address space is divided into thirty-three 32-MB *slots*. Each slot is assigned to a currently running process, with the lowest slot, slot 0, assigned to the active process. As Windows CE switches between processes, it remaps the address space to move the old process out of slot 0 and the new process into slot 0. This task is quickly accomplished by the OS by manipulating the page translation tables of the microprocessor.

The region of the address space above the 33 slots is reserved for the operating system and for mapping memory-mapped files. Like Windows NT, Windows CE also reserves the lowest 64-KB block of the address space from access by any process.

Address	*Comments*	*Slot*
7FFF FFFF	End of virtual address space	
•	•	•
•	•	•
•	•	•
	Used for memory-mapped files	
•	•	•
•	•	•
•	•	•
4200 0000		
4000 0000		Slot 32
3E00 0000		Slot 31
3C00 0000		Slot 30
3A00 0000		
⋮	⋮	⋮
0C00 0000		Slot 6
0A00 0000		Slot 5
0800 0000		Slot 4
0600 0000		Slot 3
0400 0000		Slot 2
0200 0000	Process 1: Each slot from 1 to 32 contains one process. When a process is active, it's also mapped into slot 0.	Slot 1
0000 0000	Slot for the currently active process. First 64 KB reserved by the OS.	Slot 0

Figure 6-1. *A diagram of the Windows CE memory map.*

Querying the system memory

If an application knows the current memory state of the system, it can better manage the available resources. Windows CE implements both the Win32 *GetSystemInfo* and *GlobalMemoryStatus* functions. The *GetSystemInfo* function is prototyped below:

```
VOID GetSystemInfo (LPSYSTEM_INFO lpSystemInfo);
```

It's passed a pointer to a SYSTEM_INFO structure defined as

```
typedef struct {
    WORD wProcessorArchitecture;
    WORD wReserved;
    DWORD  dwPageSize;
    LPVOID lpMinimumApplicationAddress;
    LPVOID lpMaximumApplicationAddress;
    DWORD  dwActiveProcessorMask;
    DWORD  dwNumberOfProcessors;
    DWORD  dwProcessorType;
    DWORD  dwAllocationGranularity;
    WORD   wProcessorLevel;
    WORD   wProcessorRevision;
} SYSTEM_INFO;
```

The *wProcessorArchitecture* field identifies the type of microprocessor in the system. The value should be compared to the known constants defined in Winnt.h, such as PROCESSOR_ARCHITECTURE_INTEL. Windows CE has extended these constants to include PROCESSOR_ARCHITECTURE_ARM, PROCESSOR_ARCHITECTURE_SHx and others. Additional processor constants are added as net CPUs are supported by any of the Win32 operating systems. Skipping a few fields, the *dwProcessorType* field further narrows the microprocessor from a family to a specific microprocessor. Constants for the Hitachi SHx architecture include PROCESSOR_HITACHI_SH3 and PROCESSOR_HITACHI_SH4. The last two fields, *wProcessorLevel* and *wProcessorRevision*, further refine the CPU type. The *wProcessorLevel* field is similar to the *dwProcessorType* field in that it defines the specific microprocessor within a family. The *dwProcessorRevision* field tells you the model and the stepping level of the chip.

The *dwPageSize* field specifies the page size, in bytes, of the microprocessor. Knowing this value comes in handy when you're dealing directly with the virtual memory API, which I talk about shortly. The *lpMinimumApplicationAddress* and *lpMaximumApplicationAddress* fields specify the minimum and maximum virtual address available to the application. The *dwActiveProcessorMask* and *dwNumberOfProcessors* fields are used in Windows NT for systems that support more than one microprocessor. Since Windows CE supports only one microprocessor, you can ignore these fields. The *dwAllocationGranularity* field specifies the boundaries to which virtual memory regions are rounded. Like Windows NT, Windows CE rounds virtual regions to 64-KB boundaries.

A second handy function for determining the system memory state is this:

```
void GlobalMemoryStatus(LPMEMORYSTATUS lpmst);
```

which returns a MEMORYSTATUS structure defined as

```
typedef struct {
    DWORD dwLength;
    DWORD dwMemoryLoad;
    DWORD dwTotalPhys;
    DWORD dwAvailPhys;
    DWORD dwTotalPageFile;
    DWORD dwAvailPageFile;
    DWORD dwTotalVirtual;
    DWORD dwAvailVirtual;
} MEMORYSTATUS;
```

The *dwLength* field must be initialized by the application before the call is made to *GlobalMemoryStatus*. The *dwMemoryLoad* field is of dubious value; it makes available a general loading parameter that's supposed to indicate the current memory use in the system. The *dwTotalPhys* and *dwAvailPhys* fields indicate how many pages of RAM are assigned to the program RAM and how many are available. These values don't include RAM assigned to the object store.

The *dwTotalPageFile* and *dwAvailPageFile* fields are used under Windows NT and Windows 98 to indicate the current status of the paging file. Because paging files aren't supported under Windows CE, these fields are always 0. The *dwTotalVirtual* and *dwAvailVirtual* fields indicate the total and available number of virtual memory pages accessible to the application.

The information returned by *GlobalMemoryStatus* provides confirmation of the memory architecture of Windows CE. Making this call on an HP 360 H/PC with 8 MB of RAM returned the following values:

```
dwMemoryLoad        0x18          (24)
dwTotalPhys         0x00555400    (5,592,064)
dwAvailPhys         0x00415C00    (4,283,392)
dwTotalPageFile     0
dwAvailPageFile     0
dwTotalVirtual      0x02000000    (33,554,432)
dwAvailVirtual      0x01EF0000    (32,440,320)
```

The *dwTotalPhys* field indicates that of the 8 MB of RAM in the system, I have dedicated 5.5 MB to the program RAM, of which 4.2 MB is still free. Note that there's no way for an application, using this call, to know that another 3 MB of RAM has been dedicated to the object store. To determine the amount of RAM dedicated to the object store, use the function *GetStoreInformation*.

The *dwTotalPageFile* and *dwAvailPageFile* fields are 0, indicating no support for a paging file under Windows CE. The *dwTotalVirtual* field is interesting because it shows the 32-MB limit on virtual memory that Windows CE enforces on an application. Meanwhile, the *dwAvailVirtual* field indicates that in this application little of that 32 MB of virtual memory is being used.

An Application's Address Space

Although it's always interesting to look at the global memory map for an operating system, the fact is an application should be interested only in its own memory space, not the global address space. Nevertheless, the design of the Windows CE address space does have an impact on applications. Under Windows CE, an application is limited to the virtual memory space available in its 32-MB slot. While 32 MB might seem like a fair amount of space available to an application that might run on a system with only 4 MB of RAM, Win32 application programmers, used to a 2-GB virtual address space, need to keep in mind the limited virtual address space available to a Windows CE application.

Figure 6-2 shows the layout of an application's 32-MB virtual address space. Each line of the figure represents a block of virtual memory made up of one or more pages. The address of the blocks are offsets into the application's slot in the system address space. The Page status is free, reserved, private, or image. While I've just explained the terms *free* and *reserved*, *private* and *image* merit an explanation. *Image* indicates pages that have been committed and mapped to the image of an executable file in ROM or RAM. *Private* simply means the pages have been committed for use by the application. The size field indicates the size of the block, which is always a multiple of the page size. The access rights field displays the access rights for the block.

This memory map was captured on a Casio H/PC that has a SH3 processor with a 1024-byte page size. The application used in this example was stored in the object store and then launched. This allowed Windows CE to demand page only parts of the EXE image into RAM, as they're needed. If the application had been launched from an external storage device that didn't support demand paging, Windows CE would have loaded the entire application into memory when it was launched.

Address	*Page Status*	*Size*	*Access Rights*	*Comments*
0000 0000	Reserved	65,536		**EXE image**
0001 0000	Reserved	4,096		**Code**
0001 1000	Image	2,048	Execute, Read only	**Code**
0001 1800	Reserved	1,024		**Code**
0001 1C00	Image	1,024	Execute, Read only	**Code**
0001 2000	Reserved	2,048		**Code**
0001 2800	Image	8,192	Execute, Read only	**Code**
0001 4800	Reserved	2,048		**Code**
0001 5000	Image	1,024	Execute, Read only	**Code**

Figure 6-2. *Memory map of a Windows CE Application.*

Address	*Page Status*	*Size*	*Access Rights*	*Comments*
0001 5400	Reserved	11,264		
0001 8000	Image	3,072	Read only	**Read only static data**
0001 8C00	Reserved	1,024		
0001 9000	Image	1,024	Read/Write	**Read/Write static data**
0001 9400	Reserved	1,024		**Read/Write static data**
0001 9800	Image	7,168	Read/Write	**Read/Write static data**
0001 B400	Reserved	7,168		
0001 D000	Image	2,048	Read only	**Resource data segment**
0001 D800	Reserved	2,048		**Resource data segment**
0001 E000	Free	8,192		
0002 0000	Reserved	54,272		**Stack**
0002 D400	Private	7,168	Read/Write	
0002 F000	Free	4,096		
0003 0000	Private	1,024	Read/Write	**Local heap**
0003 0400	Reserved	92,192		
0009 0000	Free	30,408,704		**Free**
01D9 0000	Reserved	1,024		**COMMCTRL image**
01D9 0400	Image	237,568	Execute, Read only	
01DC A400	Image	2,048	Read/Write	
01DC AC00	Reserved	7,168		
01DC C800	Image	7,168	Read only	
01DC E400	Reserved	13,312		
01DD 1800	Free	2,091,008		**Free**
01FD 0000	Reserved	1,024		**COREDLL image**
01FD 0400	Image	119,808	Execute, Read only	
01FE D800	Image	1,024	Read/Write	
01FE DC00	Reserved	8,192		
01FE FC00	Image	1,024	Read only	
01FF 0000	Reserved	5,120		
01FF 1400	Free	60,416		

Notice that the application is mapped as a 64-KB region starting at 0x10000. Remember, the lowest 64 KB of the address space for any application is reserved by Windows CE. The image of the file contains the code along with the static data segments and the resource segments. Although it appears that the program code is broken into a number of disjointed pages from 0x10000 to 0x15400, this is actually the result of demand paging. What's happening is that only the pages containing executed code are mapped into the address space. The reserved pages within the code segment will be mapped into the space only when they're executed.

The read-only static data segment is mapped at 0x18000 and takes three pages. The read/write static data is mapped from 0x19000 to 0x1B3FF. Like the code, the read/write data segment is committed to RAM only as it's written to by the application. Any static data that was initialized by the loader is already committed, as is the static variables written before this capture of the address space was made. The resources for the application are mapped starting at 0x1D000. The resources are read only and are paged into the RAM only as they're accessed by the application.

Starting at 0x20000, the application's stack is mapped. The stack segment is easily recognized because the committed pages are at the end of the reserved section, indicative of a stack that grows from higher addresses down. If this application had more than one thread, more than one stack segment would be reserved in the application's address space.

Following the stack is the local heap. The heap has only a few blocks currently allocated, requiring only one page of RAM. The loader reserves another 392,192 bytes, or 383 pages, for the heap to grow. The over-30 MB of address space from the end of the reserved pages for the local heap to the start of the DLLs mapped into the address space is free to be reserved and, if RAM permits, committed by the application.

This application accesses two dynamic-link libraries. Coredll.dll is the DLL that contains the entry points to the Windows CE operating system. In Windows CE, the function entry points are combined into one DLL, unlike in Windows NT or Windows 98, where the core functions are distributed across Kernel, User, and GDI. The other DLL is the common control DLL, commctrl.dll. As with the executable image, these DLLs are mapped into the address space as linear images. However, unlike the EXE, these DLLs are in ROM and directly mapped into the virtual address space of the application; therefore, they don't take up any RAM.

THE DIFFERENT KINDS OF MEMORY ALLOCATION

A Windows CE application has a number of different methods for allocating memory. At the bottom of the memory-management food chain are the *Virtual*xxx functions that directly reserve, commit, and free virtual memory pages. Next comes the heap API.

Heaps are regions of reserved memory space managed by the system for the application. Heaps come in two flavors: the default local heap automatically allocated when an application is started, and separate heaps that can be manually created by the application. After the heap API is static data—data blocks defined by the compiler and that are allocated automatically by the loader. Finally, we come to the stack, where an application stores variables local to a function.

The one area of the Win32 memory API that Windows CE doesn't support is the global heap. The global heap API, which includes calls such as *GlobalAlloc*, *GlobalFree*, and *GlobalRealloc*, are therefore not present in Windows CE. The global heap is really just a holdover from the Win16 days of Windows 3.*x*. In Win32, the global and local heaps are quite similar. One unique use of global memory, allocating memory for data in the clipboard, is handled by using the local heap under Windows CE.

The key to minimizing memory use in Windows CE is choosing the proper memory-allocation strategy that matches the memory-use patterns for a given block of memory. I'll review each of these memory types and then describe strategies for minimizing memory use in Windows CE applications.

Virtual Memory

Virtual memory is the most basic of the memory types. The system uses calls to the virtual memory API to allocate memory for the other types of memory, including heaps and stacks. The virtual memory API, including the *VirtualAlloc*, *VirtualFree*, and *VirtualReSize* functions directly manipulate virtual memory pages in the application's virtual memory space. Pages can be reserved, committed to physical memory, and freed using these functions.

Allocating virtual memory

Allocating and reserving virtual memory is accomplished using this function:

```
LPVOID VirtualAlloc (LPVOID lpAddress, DWORD dwSize,
                     DWORD flAllocationType,
                     DWORD flProtect);
```

The first parameter to *VirtualAlloc* is the virtual address of the region of memory to allocate. The lpAddress parameter is used to identify the previously reserved memory block when you use VirtualAlloc to commit a block of memory previously reserved. If this parameter is NULL, the system determines where to allocate the memory region, rounded to a 64-KB boundary. The second parameter is *dwSize*, the size of the region to allocate or reserve. While this parameter is specified in bytes, not pages, the system rounds the requested size up to the next page boundary.

The *flAllocationType* parameter specifies the type of allocation. You can specify a combination of the following flags: MEM_COMMIT, MEM_AUTO_COMMIT, MEM_RESERVE, and MEM_TOP_DOWN. The MEM_COMMIT flag allocates the memory to be used by the program. MEM_RESERVE reserves the virtual address space to be later committed. Reserved pages can't be accessed until another call is made to *VirtualAlloc* specifying the region and using the MEM_COMMIT flag. The third flag, MEM_TOP_DOWN, tells the system to map the memory at the highest permissible virtual address for the application.

The MEM_AUTO_COMMIT flag is unique to Windows CE and is quite handy. When this flag is specified the block of memory is reserved immediately, but each page in the block will automatically be committed by the system when it's accessed for the first time. This allows you to allocate large blocks of virtual memory without burdening the system with the actual RAM allocation until the instant each page is first used. The drawback to auto-commit memory is that the physical RAM needed to back up a page might not be available when the page is first accessed. In this case, the system will generate an exception.

VirtualAlloc can be used to reserve a large region of memory with subsequent calls committing parts of the region or the entire region. Multiple calls to commit the same region won't fail. This allows an application to reserve memory and then blindly commit a page before it's written to. While this method isn't particularly efficient, it does free the application from having to check the state of a reserved page to see whether it's already committed before making the call to commit the page.

The *flProtect* parameter specifies the access protection for the region being allocated. The different flags available for this parameter are summarized in the following list.

- *PAGE_READONLY* The region can be read. If an application attempts to write to the pages in the region, an access violation will occur.
- *PAGE_READWRITE* The region can be read from or written to by the application.
- *PAGE_EXECUTE* The region contains code that can be executed by the system. Attempts to read from or write to the region will result in an access violation.
- *PAGE_EXECUTE_READ* The region can contain executable code and applications can also read from the region.
- *PAGE_EXECUTE_READWRITE* The region can contain executable code and applications can read from and write to the region.

- *PAGE_GUARD* The first access to this region results in a STATUS_GUARD_PAGE exception. This flag should be combined with the other protection flags to indicate the access rights of the region after the first access.
- *PAGE_NOACCESS* Any access to the region results in an access violation.
- *PAGE_NOCACHE* The RAM pages mapped to this region won't be cached by the microprocessor.

The PAGE_GUARD and PAGE_NOCHACHE flags can be combined with the other flags to further define the characteristics of a page. The PAGE_GUARD flag specifies a guard page, a page that generates a one-shot exception when it's first accessed and then takes on the access rights that were specified when the page was committed. The PAGE_NOCACHE flag prevents the memory that's mapped to the virtual page from being cached by the microprocessor. This flag is handy for device drivers that share memory blocks with devices using direct memory access (DMA).

Regions vs. pages

Before I go on to talk about the virtual memory API, I need to make a somewhat subtle distinction. Virtual memory is reserved in regions that must align on 64-KB boundaries. Pages within a region can then be committed page by page. You can directly commit a page or a series of pages without first reserving a region of pages, but the page, or series of pages, directly committed will be aligned on a 64-KB boundary. For this reason, it's best to reserve blocks of virtual memory in 64-KB chunks and then commit that page within the region as needed.

With the limit of a 32-MB virtual memory space per process, this leaves a maximum of 32 MB / 64 KB – 1= 511 virtual memory regions that can be reserved before the system reports that it's out of memory. Take, for example, the following code fragment:

```
#define PAGESIZE 1024    // Assume we're on a 1-KB page machine
for (i = 0; i < 512; i++)
    pMem[i] = VirtualAlloc (NULL, PAGESIZE, MEM_RESERVE | MEM_COMMIT,
                            PAGE_READWRITE);
```

This code attempts to allocate 512 one-page blocks of virtual memory. Even if you have half a megabyte of RAM available in the system, *VirtualAlloc* will fail before the loop completes because it will run out of virtual address space for the application. This happens because each 1-KB block is allocated on a 64-KB boundary. Since the code, stack, and local heap for an application must also be mapped into the same, 32-MB virtual address space, available virtual allocation regions usually top out at about 490.

A better way to make 512 distinct virtual allocations is to do something like this:

```
#define PAGESIZE 1024   // Assume we're on a 1-KB page machine.

// Reserve a region first.
pMemBase = VirtualAlloc (NULL, PAGESIZE * 512, MEM_RESERVE,
                         PAGE_NOACCESS);

for (i = 0; i < 512; i++)
    pMem[i] = VirtualAlloc (pMemBase + (i*PAGESIZE), PAGESIZE,
                            MEM_COMMIT, PAGE_READWRITE);
```

This code first reserves a region; the pages are committed later. Because the region was first reserved, the committed pages aren't rounded to 64-KB boundaries, and so, if you have 512 KB of available memory in the system, the allocations will succeed.

Although the code I just showed you is a contrived example (there are better ways to allocate 1-KB blocks than directly allocating virtual memory), it does demonstrate a major difference (from other Windows systems) in the way memory allocation works in Windows CE. In Windows NT, applications have a full 2-GB virtual address space with which to work. In Windows CE however, a programmer should remain aware of the relatively small 32-MB virtual address per application.

Freeing virtual memory

You can decommit or free virtual memory by calling *VirtualFree*. Decommitting a page unmaps the page from a physical page of RAM but keeps the page or pages reserved. The function is prototyped as

```
BOOL VirtualFree (LPVOID lpAddress, DWORD dwSize,
                  DWORD dwFreeType);
```

The *lpAddress* parameter should contain a pointer to the virtual memory region that's to be freed or decommitted. The *dwSize* parameter contains the size, in bytes, of the region if the region is to be decommitted. If the region is to be freed, this value must be 0. The *dwFreeType* parameter contains the flags that specify the type of operation. The MEM_DECOMMIT flag specifies that the region will be decommited but will remain reserved. The MEM_RELEASE flag both decommits the region if the pages are committed and also frees the region.

All the pages in a region being freed by means of *VirtualFree* must be in the same state. That is, all the pages in the region to be freed must either be committed or reserved. *VirtualFree* fails if some of the pages in the region are reserved while some are committed. To free a region with pages that are both reserved and committed, the committed pages should be decommitted first, and then the entire region can be freed.

Changing and querying access rights

You can modify the access rights of a region of virtual memory, initially specified in VirtualAlloc, by calling *VirtualProtect*. This function can change the access rights only on committed pages. The function is prototyped as

```
BOOL VirtualProtect (LPVOID lpAddress, DWORD dwSize,
                     DWORD flNewProtect, PDWORD lpflOldProtect);
```

The first two parameters, *lpAddress* and *dwSize,* specify the block and the size of the region that the function acts on. The *flNewProtect* parameter contains the new protection flags for the region. These flags are the same ones I mentioned when I explained the *VirtualAlloc* function. The *lpflOldProtect* parameter should point to a DWORD that will receive the old protection flags of the first page in the region.

The current protection rights of a region can be queried with a call to

```
DWORD VirtualQuery (LPCVOID lpAddress,
                    PMEMORY_BASIC_INFORMATION lpBuffer,
                    DWORD dwLength);
```

The *lpAddress* parameter contains the starting address of the region being queried. The *lpBuffer* pointer points to a PMEMORY_BASIC_INFORMATION structure that I'll talk about soon. The third parameter, *dwLength*, must contain the size of the PMEMORY_BASIC_INFORMATION structure.

The PMEMORY_BASIC_INFORMATION structure is defined as

```
typedef struct _MEMORY_BASIC_INFORMATION {
    PVOID BaseAddress;
    PVOID AllocationBase;
    DWORD AllocationProtect;
    DWORD RegionSize;
    DWORD State;
    DWORD Protect;
    DWORD Type;
} MEMORY_BASIC_INFORMATION;
```

The first field of MEMORY_BASIC_INFORMATION, *BaseAddress*, is the address passed to the *VirtualQuery* function. The *AllocationBase* field contains the base address of the region when it was allocated using a *VirtualAlloc* function. The *AllocationProtect* field contains the protection attributes for the region when it was originally allocated. The *RegionSize* field contains the number of bytes from the pointer passed to *VirtualQuery* to the end of series of pages that have the same attributes. The *State* field contains the state—free, reserved, or committed—of the pages in the region. The *Protect* field contains the current protection flags for the region. Finally, the *Type* field contains the type of memory in the region. This field can contain the flags MEM_PRIVATE, indicating that the region contains private data for the application; MEM_MAPPED, indicating that the region is mapped to a memory-mapped file; or MEM_IMAGE, indicating that the region is mapped to an EXE or DLL module.

The best way to understand the values returned by *VirtualQuery* is to look at an example. Say an application uses *VirtualAlloc* to reserve 16,384 bytes (16 pages on a 1-KB page-size machine). The system reserves this 16-KB block at address 0xA0000. Later, the application commits 9216 bytes (9 pages) starting 2048 bytes (2 pages) into the initial region. Figure 6-3 shows a diagram of this scenario.

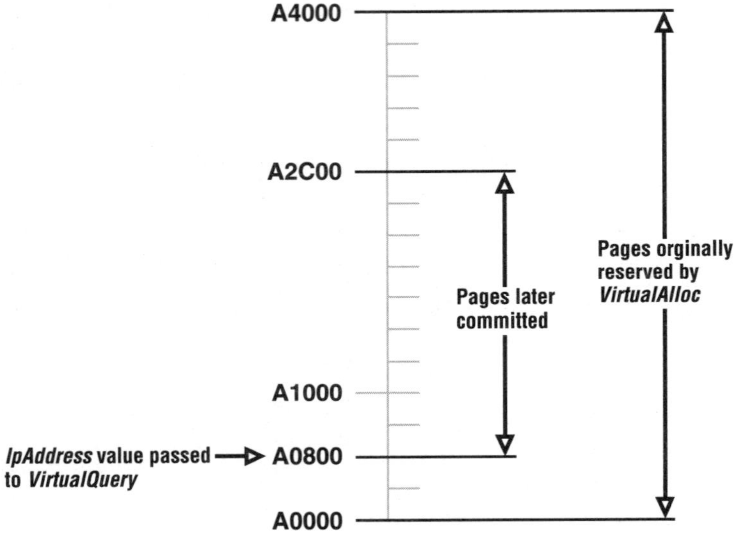

Figure 6-3. *A region of reserved virtual memory that has nine pages committed.*

If a call is made to *VirtualQuery* with the *lpAddress* pointer pointing 4 pages into the initial region (address 0xA1000), the returned values would be the following:

```
BaseAddress         0xA1000
AllocationBase      0xA0000
AllocationProtect   PAGE_NOACCESS
RegionSize          0x1C00    (7,168 bytes or 7 pages)
State               MEM_COMMIT
Protect             PAGE_READWRITE
Type                MEM_PRIVATE
```

The *BaseAddress* field contains the address passed to *VirtualQuery*, 0xA1000, 4096 bytes into the initial region. The *AllocationBase* field contains the base address of the original region while *AllocationProtect* contains PAGE_NOACCESS, indicating that the region was originally reserved, not directly committed. The *RegionSize* field contains the number of bytes from the pointer passed to *VirtualQuery*, 0xA1000 to the end of the committed pages at 0xA2C00. The *State* and *Protect* fields contain the flags indicating the current state of the pages. The *Type* field indicates that the region was allocated by the application for its own use.

Heaps

Clearly, allocating memory on a page basis is inefficient for most applications. To optimize memory use, an application needs to be able to allocate and free memory on a per byte, or at least a per 4-byte, basis. The system enables allocations of this size through heaps. Using heaps also protects an application from having to deal with the differing page sizes of the microprocessors that support Windows CE. An application can simply allocate a block in a heap and the system deals with the number of pages necessary for the allocation.

As I mentioned before, heaps are regions of reserved virtual memory space managed by the system for the application. The system gives you a number of functions that allow you to allocate and free blocks within the heap with a granularity much smaller than a page. As memory is allocated by the application within a heap, the system automatically grows the size of the heap to fill the request. As blocks in the heap are freed, the system looks to see if an entire page is freed. If so, that page is decommitted.

Unlike Windows NT or Windows 98, Windows CE supports the allocation of only fixed blocks in the heap. This simplifies the handling of blocks in the heap, but it can lead to the heaps becoming fragmented over time as blocks are allocated and freed. The result can be a heap being fairly empty but still requiring a large number of virtual pages because the system can't reclaim a page from the heap unless it's completely free.

Each application has a default, or local, heap created by the system when the application is launched. Blocks of memory in the local heap can be allocated, freed, and resized using the *LocalAlloc*, *LocalFree*, and *LocalRealloc* functions. An application can also create any number of separate heaps. These heaps have the same properties as the local heap but are managed through a separate set of *Heap*xxxx functions.

The Local Heap

By default, Windows CE initially reserves 384 pages, or 393,216 bytes, for the local heap but only commits the pages as they are allocated. If the application allocates more than the 384 KB in the local heap, the system allocates more space for the local heap. Growing the heap might require a separate, disjointed address space reserved for the additional space on the heap. Applications shouldn't assume that the local heap is contained in one block of virtual address space. Because Windows CE heaps support only fixed blocks, Windows CE implements only the subset of the Win32 local heap functions necessary to allocate, resize, and free fixed blocks on the local heap.

Allocating memory on the local heap

You allocate a block of memory on the local heap by calling

```
HLOCAL LocalAlloc (UINT uFlags, UINT uBytes);
```

The call returns a value cast as an HLOCAL, which is a handle to a local memory block, but since the block allocated is always fixed, the return value can simply be recast as a pointer to the block.

The *uFlags* parameter describes the characteristics of the block. The flags supported under Windows CE are limited to those that apply to fixed allocations. They are the following:

- *LMEM_FIXED* Allocates a fixed block in the local heap. Since all local heap allocations are fixed, this flag is redundant.
- *LMEM_ZEROINIT* Initializes memory contents to 0.
- *LPTR* Combines the LMEM_FIXED and LMEM_ZEROINIT flags.

The *uBytes* parameter specifies the size of the block to allocate in bytes. The size of the block is rounded up, but only to the next DWORD (4 byte) boundary.

Freeing memory on the local heap

You can free a block by calling

```
HLOCAL LocalFree (HLOCAL hMem);
```

The function takes the handle to the local memory block and returns NULL if successful. If the function fails, it returns the original handle to the block.

Resizing and querying the size of local heap memory

You can resize blocks on the local heap by calling

```
HLOCAL LocalReAlloc (HLOCAL hMem, UINT uBytes, UINT uFlag);
```

The *hMem* parameter is the pointer (handle) returned by *LocalAlloc*. The *uBytes* parameter is the new size of the block. The *uFlag* parameter contains the flags for the new block. Under Windows CE, two flags are relevant, LMEM_ZEROINIT and LMEM_MOVEABLE. LMEM_ZEROINIT causes the contents of the new area of the block to be set to 0 if the block is grown as a result of this call. The LMEM_MOVEABLE flag tells Windows that it can move the block if the block is being grown and there's not enough room immediately above the current block. Without this flag, if you don't have enough space immediately above the block to satisfy the request, *LocalRealloc* will fail with an out-of-memory error. If you specify the LMEM_MOVEABLE flag, the handle (really the pointer to the block of memory) might change as a result of the call.

The size of the block can be queried by calling

```
UINT LocalSize (HLOCAL hMem);
```

The size returned will be at least as great as the requested size for the block. As I mentioned earlier, Windows CE rounds the size of a local heap allocation up to the next 4-byte boundary.

Separate Heaps

To avoid fragmenting the local heap, it's better to create a separate heap if you need a series of blocks of memory that will be used for a set amount of time. An example of this would be a text editor that might manage a file by creating a separate heap for each file it's editing. As files are opened and closed, the heaps would be created and destroyed.

Heaps under Windows CE have the same API as those under Windows NT or Windows 98. The only noticeable difference is the lack of support for the HEAP_GENERATE_EXCEPTIONS flag. Under Windows NT, this flag causes the system to generate an exception if an allocation request can't be accommodated.

A subtle, but more important difference to the programmer is how Windows CE manages heaps. While the heap API looks like the standard Win32 heap API, Windows CE doesn't implement the functions as you might expect. For example, the *HeapCreate* function has parameters that allow a program to specify how much memory to allocate and reserve for a heap. Windows CE ignores these values. In fact, simply creating a heap doesn't allocate or reserve any memory. Memory is reserved and committed only when the first block of the heap is allocated.

Under most conditions, going through the details about when heap memory is reserved and committed would seem like nitpicking. But if you've used up the 32-MB virtual address space for other uses, a heap might not have the virtual address space available for the allocation even if you thought you had reserved enough using the *HeapCreate* call. On the other hand, Windows CE doesn't use the reserved parameter in the *HeapCreate* call as a hard-coded limit on the size of the heap. Windows CE accommodates almost any heap allocation request if the memory is available. Well, enough editorializing: on to the heap API.

Creating a separate heap

You create heaps by calling

```
HANDLE HeapCreate (DWORD flOptions, DWORD dwInitialSize,
                   DWORD dwMaximumSize);
```

Under Windows CE, the first parameter, *flOptions*, can be NULL, or it can contain the HEAP_NO_SERIALIZE flag. By default, Windows heap management routines prevent two threads in a process from accessing the heap at the same time. This serialization prevents the heap pointers that the system uses to track the allocated blocks in the heap from being corrupted. In other versions of Windows the HEAP_NO_SERIALIZE flag can be used if you don't want this type of protection. Under Windows CE however, this flag is only provided for compatibility and all heap accesses are serialized.

The other two parameters, *dwInitialSize* and *dwMaximumSize*, specify the initial size and expected maximum size of the heap. Windows NT and Windows 98 use the *dwMaximumSize* value to determine how many pages in the virtual address space to reserve for the heap. You can set this parameter to 0 if you want to defer to Windows' determination of how many pages to reserve. The *dwInitialSize* parameter is then used to determine how many of those initially reserved pages will be immediately committed. As I mentioned, while these two size parameters are documented exactly the same way as their counterparts under Windows NT and 98, the current version of Windows CE doesn't actually use them. You should, however, use valid numbers to retain compatibility with future versions of Windows CE that might use these parameters.

Allocating memory in a separate heap

You allocate memory on the heap using

```
LPVOID HeapAlloc (HANDLE hHeap, DWORD dwFlags, DWORD dwBytes);
```

Notice that the return value is a pointer, not a handle as in the *LocalAlloc* function. Separate heaps always allocate fixed blocks, even under Windows NT and Windows 98. The first parameter is the handle to the heap returned by the *HeapCreate* call. The *dwFlags* parameter can be one of two self-explanatory values, HEAP_NO_SERIALIZE and HEAP_ZERO_MEMORY. The final parameter, *dwBytes*, specifies the number of bytes in the block to allocate. The size is rounded up to the next DWORD.

Freeing memory in a separate heap

You can free a block in a heap by calling

```
BOOL HeapFree (HANDLE hHeap, DWORD dwFlags, LPVOID lpMem);
```

The only flag allowable in the *dwFlags* parameter is HEAP_NO_SERIALIZE. The *lpMem* parameter points to the block to free, while *hHeap* contains the handle to the heap.

Resizing and querying the size of memory in a separate heap

You can resize heap allocations by calling

```
LPVOID HeapReAlloc (HANDLE hHeap, DWORD dwFlags, LPVOID lpMem,
                    DWORD dwBytes);
```

The *dwFlags* parameter can be any combination of three flags: HEAP_NO_SERIALIZE, HEAP_REALLOC_IN_PLACE_ONLY, and HEAP_ZERO_MEMORY. The only new flag here is HEAP_REALLOC_IN_PLACE_ONLY, which tells the heap manager to fail the reallocation if the space can't be found for the block without relocating it. This flag is handy if you already have a number of pointers pointing to data in the block and you aren't interested in updating them. The *lpMem* parameter is the pointer to the block being resized, and the *dwBytes* parameter is the requested new size of the block. Notice that the function of the HEAP_REALLOC_IN_PLACE_ONLY flag in *HeapReAlloc* provides the opposite function from the one that the LMEM_MOVEABLE flag provides for *LocalReAlloc*. HEAP_REALLOC_IN_PLACE_ONLY prevents a block that would be moved by default in a separate heap while LMEM_MOVEABLE enables a block to be moved that by default would not be moved in the local heap. *HeapReAlloc* returns a pointer to the block if the reallocation was successful, and returns NULL otherwise. Unless you specified that the block not be relocated, the returned pointer might be different from the pointer passed in if the block had to be relocated to find enough space in the heap.

To determine the actual size of a block, you can call

```
DWORD HeapSize (HANDLE hHeap, DWORD dwFlags, LPCVOID lpMem);
```

The parameters are as you expect: the handle of the heap, the single, optional flag, HEAP_NO_SERIALIZE, and the pointer to the block of memory being checked.

Destroying a separate heap

You can completely free a heap by calling

```
BOOL HeapDestroy (HANDLE hHeap);
```

Individual blocks within the heap don't have to be freed before you destroy the heap.

One final heap function is valuable when writing DLLs. The function

```
HANDLE GetProcessHeap (VOID);
```

returns the handle to the local heap of the process calling the DLL. This allows a DLL to allocate memory within the calling process's local heap. All the other heap calls, with the exception of *HeapDestroy*, can be used with the handle returned by *GetProcessHeap*.

The Stack

The stack is the easiest to use (the most self-managing) of the different types of memory under Windows CE. The stack under Windows CE, as in any operating system, is the storage place for temporary variables that are referenced within a function. The operating system also uses the stack to store return addresses for functions and the state of the microprocessor registers during exception handling.

Windows CE manages a separate stack for every thread in the system. Under all versions of the operating system before Windows CE 2.1, each stack in the system is limited to fewer than 58 KB. Separate threads within one process can each grow its stack up to the 58-KB limit. This limit has to do with how Windows CE manages the stack. When a thread is created, Windows CE reserves a 60-KB region for the thread's stack. It then commits virtual pages from the top down as the stack grows. As the stack shrinks, the system will, under low-memory conditions, reclaim the unused but still committed pages below the stack. The limit of 58 KB comes from the size of the 64-KB region dedicated to the stack minus the number of pages necessary to guard the stack against overflow and underflow.

Starting with Windows CE 2.1, the size of the stack can be specified by a linker switch when an application is linked. The same guard pages are applied, but the stack size can be specified up to 1 MB. Note that the size defined for the default stack is also the size used for all the separate thread stacks. That is, if you specify the main stack to be 128 KB, all other threads in the application have a stack size limit of 128 KB.

One other consideration must be made when you're planning how to use the stack in an application. When an application calls a function that needs stack space, Windows CE attempts to commit the pages immediately below the current stack pointer to satisfy the request. If no physical RAM is available, the thread needing the stack space is briefly suspended. If the request can't be granted within a short period of time, an exception is raised. Windows CE goes to great lengths to free the required pages, but if this can't happen the system raises an exception. I'll cover low-memory situations shortly, but for now just remember that you shouldn't try to use large amounts of stack space in low-memory situations.

Static Data

C and C++ applications have predefined blocks of memory that are automatically allocated when the application is loaded. These blocks hold statically allocated strings, buffers, and global variables as well as buffers necessary for the library functions that were statically linked with the application. None of this is new to the C programmer, but under Windows CE, these spaces are handy for squeezing the last useful bytes out of RAM.

Windows CE allocates two blocks of RAM for the static data of an application, one for the read/write data and one for the read-only data. Because these areas are allocated on a per-page basis, you can typically find some space left over from the static data up to the next page boundary. The finely tuned Windows CE application should be written to ensure that it has little or no extra space left over. If you have space in the static data area, sometimes it's better to move a buffer or two into the static data area instead of allocating those buffers dynamically.

Another consideration is that if you're writing a ROM-based application, you should move as much data as possible to the read-only static data area. Windows CE doesn't allocate RAM to the read-only area for ROM-based applications. Instead, the ROM pages are mapped directly into the virtual address space. This essentially gives you unlimited read-only space with no impact on the RAM requirements of the application.

The best place to determine the size of the static data areas is to look in the map file that's optionally generated by the linker. The map file is chiefly used to determine the locations of functions and data for debugging purposes, but it also shows the size of the static data, if you know where to look. Figure 6-4 shows a portion of an example map file generated by Visual C++.

```
memtest

Timestamp is 34ce4088 (Tue Jan 27 12:16:08 1998)

Preferred load address is 00010000

Start         Length     Name                   Class
0001:00000000 00006100H .text                   CODE
0002:00000000 00000310H .rdata                  DATA
0002:00000310 00000014H .xdata                  DATA
0002:00000324 00000028H .idata$2                DATA
0002:0000034c 00000014H .idata$3                DATA
0002:00000360 000000f4H .idata$4                DATA
0002:00000454 000003eeH .idata$6                DATA
0002:00000842 00000000H .edata                  DATA
0003:00000000 000000f4H .idata$5                DATA
0003:000000f4 00000004H .CRT$XCA                DATA
0003:000000f8 00000004H .CRT$XCZ                DATA
0003:000000fc 00000004H .CRT$XIA                DATA
0003:00000100 00000004H .CRT$XIZ                DATA
0003:00000104 00000004H .CRT$XPA                DATA
0003:00000108 00000004H .CRT$XPZ                DATA
0003:0000010c 00000004H .CRT$XTA                DATA
```

(continued)

```
0003:00000110 00000004H .CRT$XTZ                  DATA
0003:00000114 000011e8H .data                     DATA
0003:000012fc 0000108cH .bss                      DATA
0004:00000000 000003e8H .pdata                    DATA
0005:00000000 000000f0H .rsrc$01                  DATA
0005:000000f0 00000334H .rsrc$02                  DATA

 Address          Publics by Value              Rva+Base      Lib:Object

0001:00000000       _WinMain                    00011000 f    memtest.obj
0001:0000007c       _InitApp                    0001107c f    memtest.obj
0001:000000d4       _InitInstance               000110d4 f    memtest.obj
0001:00000164       _TermInstance               00011164 f    memtest.obj
0001:00000248       _MainWndProc                00011248 f    memtest.obj
0001:000002b0       _GetFixedEquiv              000112b0 f    memtest.obj
0001:00000350       _DoCreateMain               00011350 f    memtest.obj.
:
```

Figure 6-4. *The top portion of a map file showing the size of the data segments in an application.*

The map file in Figure 6-4 indicates that the EXE has five sections. Section *0001* is the text segment containing the executable code of the program. Section *0002* contains the read-only static data. Section *0003* contains the read/write static data. Section *0004* contains the fix-up table to support calls to other DLLs. Finally, section *0005* is the resource section containing the application's resources, such as menu and dialog box templates.

Let's examine the *.data*, *.bss*, and *.rdata* lines. The *.data* section contains the initialized read/write data. If you initialized a global variable as in

```
static HINST g_hLoadlib = NULL;
```

the *g_loadlib* variable would end up in the *.data* segment. The *.bss* segment contains the uninitialized read/write data. A buffer defined as

```
static BYTE g_ucItems[256];
```

would end up in the *.bss* segment. The final segment, *.rdata*, contains the read-only data. Static data that you've defined using the *const* keyword ends up in the *.rdata* segment. An example of this would be the structures I use for my message look-up tables, as in the following:

```
// Message dispatch table for MainWindowProc
const struct decodeUINT MainMessages[] = {
    WM_CREATE, DoCreateMain,
    WM_SIZE, DoSizeMain,
    WM_COMMAND, DoCommandMain,
    WM_DESTROY, DoDestroyMain,
};
```

The *.data* and *.bss* blocks are folded into the *0003* section which, if you add the size of all blocks in the third section, has a total size of 0x2274, or 8820, bytes. Rounded up to the next page size, the read/write section ends up taking nine pages, with 396 bytes not used. So, in this example, placing a buffer or two in the static data section of the application would be essentially free. The read-only segment, section *0002*, including *.rdata*, ends up being 0x0842, or 2114, bytes, which takes up three pages with 958 bytes, almost an entire page, wasted. In this case, moving 75 bytes of constant data from the read-only segment to the read /write segment saves a page of RAM when the application is loaded.

String Resources

One often forgotten area for read-only data is the resource segment of your application. While I mentioned a new, Windows CE–specific feature of the *LoadString* function in Chapter 3, it's worth repeating here. If you call *LoadString* with 0 in place of the pointer to the buffer, the function returns a pointer to the string in the resource segment. An example would be

```
LPCTSTR pString;

pString  = (LPCTSTR)LoadString (hInst, ID_STRING, NULL, 0)
```

The string returned is read only, but it does allow you to reference the string without having to allocate a buffer to hold the string.

Selecting the Proper Memory Type

Now that we've looked at the different types of memory, it's time to consider the best use of each. For large blocks of memory, directly allocating virtual memory is best. An application can reserve as much address space (up to the 32-MB limit of the application) but can commit only the pages necessary at any one time. While directly allocated virtual memory is the most flexible memory allocation type, it shifts to us the burden of worrying about page granularity as well as keeping track of the reserved versus committed pages.

The local heap is always handy. It doesn't need to be created and will grow as necessary to satisfy a request. Fragmentation is the issue here. Consider that applications on an H/PC might run for weeks or even months at a time. There's no Off button on an H/PC or a Palm-size PC—just a Suspend command. So, when you're thinking about memory fragmentation, don't assume that a user will open the application, change one item, and then close it. A user is likely to start an application and keep it running so that the application is just a quick click away.

The advantage of separate heaps is that you can destroy them when their time is up, nipping the fragmentation problem in the bud. A minor disadvantage of separate heaps is the need to manually create and destroy them. Another thing to remember about separate heaps is that Windows CE doesn't reserve virtual address space when a heap is created, which can become an issue if your application uses much of the virtual address space available to the application.

The static data area is a great place to slip in a buffer or two essentially for free because the page is going to be allocated anyway. The key to managing the static data is to make the size of the static data segments close to, but over the page size of, your target processor. For applications written for the H/PC or Palm-size PC, consider the 1024-byte page size of the NEC MIPS 4100 and Hitachi SH3 processors as the default. Sometimes it's better to move constant data from the read-only segment to the read/write segment if it saves a page in the read-only segment. The only time you wouldn't do this is if the application is to be burned into ROM. Then, the more constant data, the better, because it doesn't take up RAM.

The stack is, well, the stack—simple to use and always around. The only considerations are the maximum size of the stack and the problems of enlarging the stack in a low memory condition. Make sure your application doesn't require large amounts of stack space to shut down. If the system suspends a thread in your application while it's being shut down, the user will more than likely lose data. That won't help customer satisfaction.

Managing Low-Memory Conditions

Even for applications that have been fine-tuned to minimize their memory use, there are going to be times when the system runs very low on RAM. Windows CE applications operate in an almost perpetual low-memory environment. The Palm-size PC is designed intentionally to run in a low-memory situation Applications on the Palm-size PC don't have a Close button—the shell automatically closes them when the system needs additional memory. Because of this, Windows CE offers a number of methods to distribute the scarce memory in the system among the running applications.

The WM_HIBERNATE message

The first and most obvious addition to Windows CE is the WM_HIBERNATE message. Windows CE sends this message to all top-level windows that have the WS_OVERLAPPED style (that is, have neither the WS_POPUP nor the WS_CHILD style) and have the WS_VISIBLE style. These qualifications should allow most applications to have at least one window that receives a WM_HIBERNATE message. An exception to this would be an application that doesn't really terminate, but simply hides all its windows. This arrangement allows an application a quick start because it only has to show its window, but this situation also means that the application is taking up RAM even when the user thinks it's closed. While this is exactly the kind of application design that should *not* be used under Windows CE, those that are designed this way must act as if they're always in hibernate mode when hidden because they'll never receive a WM_HIBERNATE message.

Windows CE sends WM_HIBERNATE messages to the top-level windows in reverse Z-order until enough memory is freed to push the available memory above a preset threshold. When an application receives a WM_HIBERNATE message, it should reduce its memory footprint as much as possible. This can involve releasing cached data; freeing any GDI objects such as fonts, bitmaps, and brushes; and destroying any window controls. In essence, the application should reduce its memory use to the smallest possible footprint that's necessary to retain its internal state.

If sending WM_HIBERNATE messages to the applications in the background doesn't free enough memory to move the system out of a limited-memory state, a WM_HIBERNATE message is sent to the application in the foreground. If part of your hibernation routine is to destroy controls on your window, you should be sure that you aren't the foreground application. Disappearing controls don't give the user a warm and fuzzy feeling.

Memory thresholds

Windows CE monitors the free RAM in the system and responds differently as less and less RAM is available. As less memory is available, Windows CE first sends WM_HIBERNATE messages and then begins limiting the size of allocations possible. The two figures below show the free-memory levels used by the Handheld PC and the Palm-size PC to trigger low-memory events in the system. Windows CE defines four memory states: normal, limited, low, and critical. The memory state of the system depends on how much free memory is available to the system as a whole. These limits are higher for 4-KB page systems because those systems have less granularity in allocations.

Event	*Free Memory 1024-Page Size*	*Free Memory 4096-Page Size*	*Comments*
Limited-memory state	128 KB	160 KB	Send MWM_HIBERNATE messages to applications in reverse Z-order. Free stack space reclaimed as needed.
Low-memory state	64 KB	96 KB	Limit virtual allocs to 16 KB. Low-memory dialog displayed.
Critical-memory state	16 KB	48 KB	Limit virtual allocs to 8 KB.

Figure 6-5. *Memory thresholds for the Handheld PC.*

Event	*Free Memory 1024-Page Size*	*Free Memory 4096-Page Size*	*Comments*
Hibernate threshold	200 KB	224 KB	Send WM_HIBERNATE messages to applications in reverse Z-order.
Limited-memory state	128 KB	160 KB	Begin to close applications in reverse Z-order. Free stack space reclaimed as needed.
Low-memory state	64 KB	96 KB	Limit virtual allocs to 16 KB.
Critical-memory state	16 KB	48 KB	Limit virtual allocs to 8 KB.

Figure 6-6. *Memory thresholds for the Palm-size PC.*

The effect of these memory states is to share the remaining wealth. First, WM_HIBERNATE messages are sent to the applications to ask them to reduce their memory footprint. After an application is sent a WM_HIBERNATE message, the system memory levels are checked to see whether the available memory is now above the threshold that caused the WM_HIBERNATE messages to be sent. If not, a WM_HIBERNATE message is sent to the next application. This continues until all applications have been sent a WM_HIBERNATE message.

The low-memory strategies of the Handheld PC and the Palm-size PC diverge at this point. If the memory level drops below the next threshold, limited for the Palm-size PC and Low for the H/PC, the system starts shutting down applications. On the H/PC, the system displays the OOM, the out-of-memory dialog, and requests that the user either select an application to close or reallocate some RAM dedicated to the object store to the program memory. If, after the selected application has been shut down or memory has been moved into program RAM, you still don't have enough memory, the out-of-memory dialog is displayed again. This process is repeated until there's enough memory to lift the H/PC above the threshold.

For the Palm-size PC, the actions are somewhat different. The Palm-size PC shell automatically starts shutting down applications in least recently used order without asking the user. If there still isn't enough memory after all applications except the foreground application and the shell are closed, the system uses its other techniques of scavenging free pages from stacks and limiting any allocations of virtual memory.

If, on either system, an application is requested to shut down and it doesn't, the system will purge the application after waiting approximately 8 seconds. This is the reason an application shouldn't allocate large amounts of stack space. If the application is shutting down due to low-memory conditions, it's quite possible that the stack space can't be allocated and the application will be suspended. If this happens after the system has requested that the application close, it could be purged from memory without properly saving its state.

In the low- and critical-memory states, applications are limited in the amount of memory they can allocate. In these states, a request for virtual memory larger than what's allowed is refused even if there's memory available to satisfy the request. Remember that it isn't just virtual memory allocations that are limited; allocations on the heap and stack are rejected if, to satisfy the request, those allocations require virtual memory allocations above the allowable limits.

I should point out that sending WM_HIBERNATE messages and automatically closing down applications is performed by the shell of the H/PC and Palm-size PC. The embedded version of Windows CE uses a much simpler shell that doesn't support these memory management techniques. On these embedded systems, you'll have to devise your own strategy for managing low-memory situations.

It should go without saying that applications should check the return codes of any memory allocation call, but since some still don't, I'll say it. *Check the return codes from calls that allocate memory*. There's a much better chance of a memory allocation failing under Windows CE than under Windows NT or Windows 98. Applications must be written to react gracefully to rejected memory allocations.

The Win32 memory management API isn't fully supported by Windows CE, but there's clearly enough support for you to use the limited memory of a Windows CE device to the fullest. A great source for learning about the intricacies of the Win32 memory management API is Jeff Richter's *Advanced Windows* (Microsoft Press, 1997). Jeff spends five chapters on memory management while I have summarized the same topic in one.

We've looked at the program RAM, the part of RAM that is available to applications. Now it's time, in the next chapter, to look at the other part of the RAM, the object store. The object store supports more than a file system. It also supports the registry API as well as a database API unique to Windows CE.

Chapter 7

Files, Databases, and the Registry

One of the areas where Windows CE diverges the farthest from its larger cousins, Windows NT and Windows 98, is in the area of file storage. Instead of relying on ferromagnetic storage media such as floppy disks or hard disk drives, Windows CE implements a unique, RAM-based file system known as the *object store*. In implementation, the object store more closely resembles a database than it does a file allocation system for a disk. In the object store resides the files as well as the registry for the system and any Windows CE databases. Fortunately for the programmer, most of the unique implementation of the object store is hidden behind standard Win32 functions.

The Windows CE file API is taken directly from Win32. Aside from the lack of functions that directly reference volumes, the API is fairly complete. Windows CE implements the standard registry API, albeit without the vast levels of security found in Windows NT. The database API, however, is unique to Windows CE. The database functions provide a simple tool for managing and organizing data. They aren't to be confused with the powerful, multilevel SQL databases found on other computers. Even with its modest functionality, the database API is convenient for storing and organizing simple groups of data, such as address lists or mail folders.

Some differences in the object store do expose themselves to the programmer. Execute-in-place files, stored in ROM, appear as files in the object store but these functions can't be opened and read as standard files. Some of the ROM-based applications are also statically linked to other ROM-based dynamic-link libraries (DLLs).

This means that some ROM-based DLLs can't be replaced by copying an identically named file into the object store.

The concept of the *current directory*, so important in other versions of Windows, isn't present in Windows CE. Files are specified by their complete path. DLLs must be in the Windows directory, the root directory of the object store, or in the root directory of an attached file storage device, such as a PC Card.

As a general rule, Windows CE doesn't support the deep application-level security available under Windows NT. However, because the generic Win32 API was originally based on Windows NT, a number of the functions for file and registry operations have one or more parameters that deal with security rights. Under Windows CE, these values should be set to their default, not security state. This means you should almost always pass NULL in the security parameters for functions that request security information.

In this rather long chapter, I'll first explain the file system and the file API. Then I'll give you an overview of the database API. Finally, we'll do a tour of the registry API. The database API is one of the areas that has experienced a fair amount of change as Windows CE has evolved. Essentially, functionality has been added to later versions of Windows CE. Where appropriate, I'll cover the differences between the different versions and present workarounds, where possible, for maintaining a common code base.

THE WINDOWS CE FILE SYSTEM

The default file system, supported on all Windows CE platforms, is the object store. The object store is equivalent to the hard disk on a Windows CE device. It's a subtly complex file storage system incorporating compressed RAM storage for read/write files and seamless integration with ROM-based files. A user sees no difference between a file in RAM in the object store and those files based in ROM. Files in RAM and ROM can reside in the same directory, and document files in ROM can be opened (although not modified) by the user. In short, the object store integrates the default files provided in ROM with the user-generated files stored in RAM.

In addition to the object store, Windows CE supports multiple, installable file systems that can support up to 256 different storage devices or partitions on storage devices. (The limit is 10 storage devices for WIndows CE 2.0 and earlier.) The interface to these devices is the installable file system (IFS) API. Most Windows CE platforms include an IFS driver for the FAT file system for files stored on ATA flash cards or hard disks. In addition, under Windows CE 2.1 and later, third party manufacturers can write an IFS driver to support other file systems.

Windows CE doesn't use drive letters as is the practice on PCs. Instead, every storage device is simply a directory off the root directory. Under Windows CE 1.0, an application can count on the name of the directory of the external drive being *PC Card*. If more than one PC Card was inserted, the additional ones are numbered, as in *PC Card 1* and *PC Card 2*, up to *PC Card 99* for the 100th card.[1] Under Windows CE 2.0, the default name was changed from *PC Card* to *Storage Card*, but the numbering concept stayed the same. For Windows CE 2.1, Windows CE doesn't assume a name. Instead it asks the driver what it wants to call the directory.[2] Later in this chapter, I'll demonstrate a method for determining which directories in the root are directories and which are actually storage devices.

As should be expected for a Win32-compatible operating system, the filename format for Windows CE is the same as its larger counterparts. Windows CE supports long filenames. Filenames and their complete path can be up to MAX_PATH in length, which is currently defined at 260 bytes. Filenames have the same *name.ext* format as they do in other Windows operating systems. The extension is the three characters following the last period in the filename and defines the type of file. The file type is used by the shell when determining the difference between executable files and different documents. Allowable characters in filenames are the same as for Windows NT and Windows 98.

Windows CE files support most of the same attribute flags as Windows 98 with a few additions. Attribute flags include the standard read-only, system, hidden, compressed, and archive flags. A few additional flags have been included to support the special RAM/ROM mix of files in the object store.

The Object Store vs. Other Storage Media

To the programmer, the difference between files in the RAM part of the object store and the files based in ROM are subtle. The files in ROM can be detected by a special, in-ROM file attribute flag. However, files in the RAM part of the object store that are always compressed don't have the compressed file attribute as might be expected. The reason is that the compressed attribute is used to indicate when a file or directory is in a compressed state relative to the other files on the drive. In the object store, all files are compressed, which makes the compressed attribute redundant.

The object store in Windows CE has some basic limitations. First, the size of the object store is currently limited to 16 MB of RAM. Given the compression features of the object store, this means that the amount of data that the object store can contain is somewhere around 32 MB. Individual files in the object store are limited to 4 MB under Windows CE 2.0 and earlier. Files under Windows CE 2.1 and later are limited only by the size of the object store's 16-MB limit. These file size limits don't apply to files on secondary storage such as hard disks, PC Cards, or Compact Flash Cards.

---

1. This limit is 10 cards for Windows CE 2.0 and earlier.

2. The Handheld PC Pro uses Storage Card as its default name.

Standard File I/O

Windows CE supports the most of the same file I/O functions found on Windows NT and Windows 98. The same Win32 API calls, such as *CreateFile*, *ReadFile*, *WriteFile* and *CloseFile*, are all supported. A Windows CE programmer must be aware of a few differences, however. First of all, the standard C file I/O functions, such as *fopen*, *fread*, and *fprintf*, aren't supported under Windows CE. Likewise, the old Win16 standards, *_lread*, *_lwrite*, and *_llseek*, aren't supported. This isn't really a huge problem because all of these functions can easily be implemented by wrapping the Windows CE file functions with a small amount of code. Windows CE 2.1 does support basic console library functions such as *printf* for console applications.

Windows CE doesn't support the overlapped I/O that's supported under Windows NT. Files or devices can't be opened with the FILE_FLAG_OVERLAPPED flag nor can reads or writes use the overlapped mode of asynchronous calls and returns.

File operations in Windows CE follow the traditional handle-based methodology used since the days of MS-DOS. Files are opened by means of a function that returns a handle. Read and write functions are passed the handle to indicate the file to act on. Data is read from or written to the offset in the file indicated by a system-maintained file pointer. Finally, when the reading and writing have been completed, the application indicates this by closing the file handle. Now on to the specifics.

Creating and Opening Files

Creating a file or opening an existing file or device is accomplished by means of the standard Win32 function:

```
HANDLE CreateFile (LPCTSTR lpFileName, DWORD dwDesiredAccess,
                   DWORD dwShareMode,
                   LPSECURITY_ATTRIBUTES lpSecurityAttributes,
                   DWORD dwCreationDistribution,
                   DWORD dwFlagsAndAttributes, HANDLE hTemplateFile);
```

The first parameter is the filename of the file to be opened or created. The name of the file should have a fully specified path. Filenames with no path information are assumed to be in the root directory of the object store.

The *dwDesiredAccess* parameter indicate the requested access rights. The allowable flags are GENERIC_READ to request read access to the file and GENERIC_WRITE for write access. Both flags must be passed to get read/write access. You can open a file with neither read nor write permissions. This is handy if you just want to get the attributes of a device. The *dwShareMode* parameter specifies the access rights that can be granted to other processes. This parameter can be FILE_SHARE_READ and/or FILE_SHARE_WRITE. The *lpSecurityAttributes* parameter is ignored by Windows CE and should be set to NULL.

The *dwCreationDistribution* parameter tells *CreateFile* how to open or create the file. The following flags are allowed:

- *CREATE_NEW* Creates a new file. If the file already exists, the function fails.
- *CREATE_ALWAYS* Creates a new file or truncates an existing file.
- *OPEN_EXISTING* Opens a file only if it already exists.
- *OPEN_ALWAYS* Opens a file or creates a file if it doesn't exist. This differs from CREATE_ALWAYS because it doesn't truncate the file to 0 bytes if the file exists.
- *TRUNCATE_EXISTING* Opens a file and truncates it to 0 bytes. The function fails if the file doesn't already exist.

The *dwFlagsAndAttributes* parameter defines the attribute flags for the file if it's being created in addition to flags in order to tailor the operations on the file. The following flags are allowed under Windows CE:

- *FILE_ATTRIBUTE_NORMAL* This is the default attribute. It's overridden by any of the other file attribute flags.
- *FILE_ATTRIBUTE_READONLY* Sets the read-only attribute bit for the file. Subsequent attempts to open the file with write access will fail.
- *FILE_ATTRIBUTE_ARCHIVE* Sets the archive bit for the file.
- *FILE_ATTRIBUTE_SYSTEM* Sets the system bit for the file indicating that the file is critical to the operation of the system.
- *FILE_ATTRIBUTE_HIDDEN* Sets the hidden bit. The file will be visible only to users who have the View All Files option set in the Explorer.
- *FILE_FLAG_WRITE_THROUGH* Write operations to the file won't be lazily cached in memory.
- *FILE_FLAG_RANDOM_ACCESS* Indicates to the system that the file will be randomly accessed instead of sequentially accessed. This flag can help the system determine the proper caching strategy for the file.

Windows CE doesn't support a number of file attributes and file flags that are supported under Windows 98 and Windows NT. The unsupported flags include but aren't limited to the following: FILE_ATTRIBUTE_OFFLINE, FILE_FLAG_OVERLAPPED, FILE_FLAG_NO_BUFFERING, FILE_FLAG_SEQUENTIAL_SCAN, FILE_FLAG_DELETE_ON_CLOSE, FILE_FLAG_BACKUP_SEMANTICS, and FILE_FLAG_POSIX_SEMANTICS.

Under Windows NT and Windows 98, the flag FILE_ATTRIBUTE_TEMPORARY is used to indicate a temporary file, but as we'll see below, it's used by Windows CE to indicate a directory that is in reality a separate drive or network share.

The final parameter in *CreateFile*, *hTemplate*, is ignored by Windows CE and should be set to 0. *CreateFile* returns a handle to the opened file if the function was successful. If the function fails, it returns INVALID_HANDLE_VALUE. To determine why the function failed, call *GetLastError*. If the *dwCreationDistribution* flags included CREATE_ALWAYS or OPEN_ALWAYS, you can determine whether the file previously existed by calling *GetLastError* to see if it returns ERROR_ALREADY_EXISTS. *CreateFile* will set this error code even though the function succeeded.

Reading and Writing

Windows CE supports the standard Win32 functions *ReadFile* and *WriteFile*. Reading a file is as simple as calling the following:

```
BOOL ReadFile (HANDLE hFile, LPVOID lpBuffer,
               DWORD nNumberOfBytesToRead,
               LPDWORD lpNumberOfBytesRead, LPOVERLAPPED lpOverlapped);
```

The parameters are fairly self-explanatory. The first parameter is the handle of the opened file to read followed by a pointer to the buffer that will receive the data and the number of bytes to read. The fourth parameter is a pointer to a DWORD that will receive the number of bytes that was actually read. Finally, the *lpOverlapped* parameter must be set to NULL because Windows CE doesn't support overlapped file operations. As an aside, Windows CE does support multiple reads and writes pending on a device; it just doesn't support the ability to return from the function before the operation completes.

Data is read from the file starting at the file offset indicated by the file pointer. After the read has completed, the file pointer is adjusted by the number of bytes read.

ReadFile won't read beyond the end of a file. If a call to *ReadFile* asks for more bytes than remains in the file, the read will succeed, but only the number of bytes remaining in the file will be returned. This is why you must check the variable pointed to by *lpNumberOfBytesRead* after a read completes to learn how many bytes were actually read. A call to *ReadFile* with the file pointer pointing to the end of the file results in the read being successful, but the number of read bytes is set to 0.

Writing to a file is accomplished with this:

```
BOOL WriteFile (HANDLE hFile, LPCVOID lpBuffer,
                DWORD nNumberOfBytesToWrite,
                LPDWORD lpNumberOfBytesWritten,
                LPOVERLAPPED lpOverlapped);
```

The parameters are similar to *ReadFile* with the obvious exception that *lpBuffer* now points to the data that will be written to the file. As in *ReadFile*, the *lpOverlapped* parameter must be NULL. The data is written to the file offset indicated by the file pointer, which is updated after the write so that it points to the byte immediately beyond the data written.

Moving the file pointer

The file pointer can be adjusted manually with a call to the following:

```
DWORD SetFilePointer (HANDLE hFile, LONG lDistanceToMove,
                      PLONG lpDistanceToMoveHigh, DWORD dwMoveMethod);
```

The parameters for *SetFilePointer* are the handle of the file; a signed offset distance to move the file pointer; a second, upper 32-bit offset parameter; and *dwMoveMethod*, a parameter indicating how to interpret the offset. While *lDistanceToMove* is a signed 32-bit value, *lpDistanceToMoveHigh* is a *pointer* to a signed 32-bit value. For file pointer moves of greater than 4 GB, *lpDistanceToMoveHigh* should point to a LONG that contains the upper 32-bit offset of the move. This variable will receive the high 32 bits of the resulting file pointer. For moves of less than 4 GB, simply set *lpDistance-ToMoveHigh* to NULL. Clearly, under Windows CE, the *lpDistanceToMoveHigh* parameter is a bit excessive, but having the function the same format as its Windows NT counterpart aids in portability across platforms.

The offset value is interpreted as being from the start of the file if *dwMoveMethod* contains the flag FILE_BEGIN. To base the offset on the current position of the file pointer, use FILE_CURRENT. To base the offset from the end of the file, use FILE_END in *dwMoveMethod*.

SetFilePointer returns the file pointer at its new position after the move has been accomplished. To query the current file position without changing the file pointer, simply call *SetFilePointer* with a zero offset and relative to the current position in the file, as shown here:

```
nCurrFilePtr = SetFilePointer (hFile, 0, NULL, FILE_CURRENT);
```

Closing a file

Closing a file handle is a simple as calling

```
BOOL CloseHandle (HANDLE hObject);
```

This generic call, used to close a number of handles, is also used to close file handles. The function returns TRUE if it succeeds. If the function fails, a call to *GetLastError* will return the reason for the failure.

Truncating a file

When you have finished writing the data to a file, you can close it with a call to *CloseHandle* and you're done. Sometimes, however, you must truncate a file to make it smaller than it currently is. In the days of MS-DOS, the way to set the end of a file was to make a call to write zero bytes to a file. The file was then truncated at the current file pointer. This won't work in Windows CE. To set the end of a file, move the file pointer to the location in the file where you want the file to end and call:

```
BOOL SetEndOfFile (HANDLE hFile);
```

Of course, for this call to succeed, you need write access to the file. The function returns TRUE if it succeeds.

To insure that all the data has been written to a storage device and isn't just sitting around in a cache, you can call this function:

```
WINBASEAPI BOOL WINAPI FlushFileBuffers (HANDLE hFile);
```

The only parameter is the handle to the file you want to flush to the disk, or more likely in Windows CE a PC Card.

Getting file information

A number of calls allow you to query information about a file or directory. To quickly get the attributes knowing only the file or directory name, you can use this function:

```
DWORD GetFileAttributes (LPCTSTR lpFileName);
```

In general, the attributes returned by this function are the same ones that I covered for *CreateFile*, with the addition of the attributes listed below:

- *FILE_ATTRIBUTE_COMPRESSED* The file is compressed.
- *FILE_ATTRIBUTE_INROM* The file is in ROM.
- *FILE_ATTRIBUTE_ROMMODULE* The file is an executable module in ROM formatted for execute-in-place loading. These files can't be opened with *CreateFile*.
- *FILE_ATTRIBUTE_DIRECTORY* The name specifies a directory, not a file.
- *FILE_ATTRIBUTE_TEMPORARY* When this flag is set in combination with FILE_ATTRIBUTE_DIRECTORY, the directory is the root of a secondary storage device, such as a PC Card or a hard disk.

The attribute FILE_ATTRIBUTE_COMPRESSED is somewhat misleading on a Windows CE device. Files in the RAM-based object store are always compressed, but this flag isn't set for those files. On the other hand, the flag does accurately reflect whether a file in ROM is compressed. Compressed ROM files have the advantage of taking up less space but the disadvantage of not being execute-in-place files.

An application can change the basic file attributes, such as read only, hidden, system, and attribute by calling this function:

```
BOOL SetFileAttributes (LPCTSTR lpFileName, DWORD dwFileAttributes);
```

This function simply takes the name of the file and the new attributes. Note that you can't compress a file by attempting to set its compressed attribute. Under other Windows systems that do support selective compression of files, the way to compress a file is to make a call directly to the file system driver.

A number of other informational functions are supported by Windows CE. All of these functions, however, require a file handle instead of a filename, so the file must have been previously opened by means of a call to *CreateFile*.

File times

The standard Win32 API supports three file times: the time the file was created, the time the file was last accessed (that is, the time it was last read, written, or executed), and the last time the file was written to. That being said, the Windows CE object store keeps track of only one time, the time the file was last written to. One of the ways to query the file times for a file is to call this function:

```
BOOL GetFileTime (HANDLE hFile, LPFILETIME lpCreationTime,
                  LPFILETIME lpLastAccessTime,
                  LPFILETIME lpLastWriteTime);
```

The function takes a handle to the file being queried and pointers to three FILETIME values that will receive the file times. If you're interested in only one of the three values, the other pointers can be set to NULL.

When the file times are queried for a file in the object store, Windows CE copies the last write time into all FILETIME structures. This goes against Win32 documentation, which states that any unsupported time fields should be set to 0. For the FAT file system used on storage cards, two times are maintained: the file creation time and the last write time. When *GetFileTime* is called on a file on a storage card, the file creation and last write times are returned and the last access time is set to 0.

The FILETIME structures returned by *GetFileTime* and other functions can be converted to something readable by calling

```
BOOL FileTimeToSystemTime (const FILETIME *lpFileTime,
                           LPSYSTEMTIME lpSystemTime);
```

This function translates the FILETIME structure into a SYSTEMTIME structure that has documented day, date, and time fields that can be used. One large caveat is that file times are stored in coordinated universal time format (UTC), also known as Greenwich

Mean Time. This doesn't make much difference as long as you're using unreadable FILETIME structures but when you're translating a file time into something readable, a call to

```
BOOL FileTimeToLocalFileTime (const FILETIME *lpFileTime,
                              LPFILETIME lpLocalFileTime);
```

before translating the file time into system time provides the proper time zone translation to the user.

You can manually set the file times of a file by calling

```
BOOL SetFileTime (HANDLE hFile, const FILETIME *lpCreationTime,
                  const FILETIME *lpLastAccessTime,
                  const FILETIME *lpLastWriteTime);
```

The function takes a handle to a file and three times each in FILETIME format. If you want to set only one or two of the times, the remaining parameters can be set to NULL. Remember that file times must be in UTC time, not local time.

For files in the Windows CE object store, setting any one of the time fields results in all three being updated to that time. If you set multiple fields to different times and attempt to set the times for an object store file, the *lpLastWriteTime* takes precedence. Files on storage cards maintain separate creation and last-write times. You must open the file with write access for *SetFileTime* to work.

File size and other information

You can query a file's size by calling

```
DWORD GetFileSize (HANDLE hFile, LPDWORD lpFileSizeHigh);
```

The function takes the handle to the file and an optional pointer to a DWORD that's set to the high 32 bits of the file size. This second parameter can be set to NULL if you don't expect to be dealing with files over 4 GB. *GetFileSize* returns the low 32 bits of the file size.

I've been talking about these last few functions separately, but an additional function, *GetFileInformationByHandle*, returns all this information and more. The function prototyped as

```
BOOL GetFileInformationByHandle (HANDLE hFile,
                       LPBY_HANDLE_FILE_INFORMATION lpFileInformation);
```

takes the handle of an opened file and a pointer to a BY_HANDLE_FILE_INFORMATION structure. The function returns TRUE if it was successful.

The BY_HANDLE_FILE_INFORMATION structure is defined this way:

```
typedef struct _BY_HANDLE_FILE_INFORMATION {
    DWORD dwFileAttributes;
    FILETIME ftCreationTime;
    FILETIME ftLastAccessTime;
```

```
    FILETIME ftLastWriteTime;
    DWORD dwVolumeSerialNumber;
    DWORD nFileSizeHigh;
    DWORD nFileSizeLow;
    DWORD nNumberOfLinks;
    DWORD nFileIndexHigh;
    DWORD nFileIndexLow;
    DWORD dwOID;
} BY_HANDLE_FILE_INFORMATION;
```

As you can see, the structure returns data in a number of fields that separate functions return. I'll talk about only the new fields here.

The *dwVolumeSerialNumber* field is filled with the serial number of the volume in which the file resides. The *volume* is what's considered a disk or partition under Windows 98 or Windows NT. Under Windows CE, the volume refers to the object store, a storage card, or a disk on a local area network. For files in the object store, the volume serial number is 0.

The *nNumberOfLinks* field is used by Windows NT's NTFS file system and can be ignored under Windows CE. The *nFileIndexHigh* and *nFileIndexLow* fields contain a systemwide unique identifier number for the file. This number can be checked to see whether two different file handles point to the same file. The File Index value is used under Windows NT and Windows 98, but Windows CE has a more useful value, the *object ID* of the file, which is returned in the *dwOID* field. I'll explain the object ID later in the chapter; for now I'll just mention that it's a universal identifier that can be used to reference directories, files, databases, and individual database records. Handy stuff.

The FileView Sample Program

FileView is an example program that displays the contents of a file in a window. It displays the data in hexadecimal format instead of text, which makes it different from simply opening the file in Microsoft Pocket Word or another editor. FileView is simply a file *viewer*; it doesn't allow you to modify the file. The code for FileView is shown in Figure 7-1.

FileView.rc

```
//======================================================================
// Resource file
//
// Written for the book Programming Windows CE
// Copyright (C) 1998 Douglas Boling
//======================================================================
```

Figure 7-1. *The Viewer program.* *(continued)*

Figure 7-1. *continued*

```
#include "windows.h"
#include "FileView.h"                    // Program-specific stuff

//----------------------------------------------------------------------
// Icons and bitmaps
ID_ICON ICON   "fileview.ico"            // Program icon

//----------------------------------------------------------------------
// Menu
ID_MENU MENU DISCARDABLE
BEGIN
    POPUP "&File"
    BEGIN
        MENUITEM "&Open...",                    IDM_OPEN
        MENUITEM SEPARATOR
        MENUITEM "E&xit",                       IDM_EXIT
    END
    POPUP "&Help"
    BEGIN
        MENUITEM "&About...",                   IDM_ABOUT
    END
END
//----------------------------------------------------------------------
// About box dialog template
aboutbox DIALOG discardable 10, 10, 160, 40
STYLE  WS_POPUP | WS_VISIBLE | WS_CAPTION | WS_SYSMENU | DS_CENTER |
       DS_MODALFRAME
CAPTION "About"
BEGIN
    ICON  ID_ICON,                   -1,   5,   5,  10,  10
    LTEXT "FileView - Written for the book Programming Windows \
           CE Copyright 1998 Douglas Boling"
                                     -1,  40,   5, 110,  30
END
```

FileView.h

```
//======================================================================
// Header file
//
// Written for the book Programming Windows CE
// Copyright (C) 1998 Douglas Boling
//======================================================================
// Returns number of elements.
```

```
#define dim(x) (sizeof(x) / sizeof(x[0]))

//----------------------------------------------------------------------
// Generic defines and data types
//
struct decodeUINT {                             // Structure associates
    UINT Code;                                  // messages
                                                // with a function.
    LRESULT (*Fxn)(HWND, UINT, WPARAM, LPARAM);
};
struct decodeCMD {                              // Structure associates
    UINT Code;                                  // menu IDs with a
    LRESULT (*Fxn)(HWND, WORD, HWND, WORD);     // function.
};

//----------------------------------------------------------------------
// Generic defines used by application
#define  ID_ICON            1                   // Application icon
                                                // Resource ID
#define  IDC_CMDBAR         2                   // Command band ID
#define  ID_MENU            3                   // Main menu resource ID
#define  ID_VIEWER          4                   // View control ID

// Menu item IDs
#define  IDM_OPEN           101                 // File menu
#define  IDM_EXIT           102
#define  IDM_ABOUT          120                 // Help menu

//----------------------------------------------------------------------
// Function prototypes
//
INT MyGetFileName (HWND hWnd, LPTSTR szFileName, INT nMax);

int InitApp (HINSTANCE);
HWND InitInstance (HINSTANCE, LPWSTR, int);
int TermInstance (HINSTANCE, int);

// Window procedures
LRESULT CALLBACK MainWndProc (HWND, UINT, WPARAM, LPARAM);

// Message handlers
LRESULT DoCreateMain (HWND, UINT, WPARAM, LPARAM);
LRESULT DoSizeMain (HWND, UINT, WPARAM, LPARAM);
LRESULT DoCommandMain (HWND, UINT, WPARAM, LPARAM);
LRESULT DoDestroyMain (HWND, UINT, WPARAM, LPARAM);
```

(continued)

Figure 7-1. *continued*

```
// Command functions
LPARAM DoMainCommandOpen (HWND, WORD, HWND, WORD);
LPARAM DoMainCommandExit (HWND, WORD, HWND, WORD);
LPARAM DoMainCommandAbout (HWND, WORD, HWND, WORD);

// Dialog procedures
BOOL CALLBACK AboutDlgProc (HWND, UINT, WPARAM, LPARAM);
```

FileView.c

```
//======================================================================
// FileView - A Windows CE file viewer
//
// Written for the book Programming Windows CE
// Copyright (C) 1998 Douglas Boling
//======================================================================
#include <windows.h>                 // For all that Windows stuff
#include <commctrl.h>                // Command bar includes
#include <commdlg.h>                 // Common dialog includes

#include "FileView.h"                // Program-specific stuff
#include "Viewer.h"                  // Program-specific stuff
//----------------------------------------------------------------------
// Global data
//
const TCHAR szAppName[] = TEXT ("FileView");
extern TCHAR szViewerCls[];
HINSTANCE hInst;                     // Program instance handle

// Message dispatch table for MainWindowProc
const struct decodeUINT MainMessages[] = {
    WM_CREATE, DoCreateMain,
    WM_SIZE, DoSizeMain,
    WM_COMMAND, DoCommandMain,
    WM_DESTROY, DoDestroyMain,
};

// Command message dispatch for MainWindowProc
const struct decodeCMD MainCommandItems[] = {
    IDM_OPEN, DoMainCommandOpen,
    IDM_EXIT, DoMainCommandExit,
    IDM_ABOUT, DoMainCommandAbout,
};
```

```
//======================================================================
//
// Program entry point
//
int WINAPI WinMain (HINSTANCE hInstance, HINSTANCE hPrevInstance,
                    LPWSTR lpCmdLine, int nCmdShow) {
    HWND hwndMain;
    MSG msg;
    int rc = 0;

    // Initialize application.
    rc = InitApp (hInstance);
    if (rc) return rc;

    // Initialize this instance.
    hwndMain = InitInstance (hInstance, lpCmdLine, nCmdShow);
    if (hwndMain == 0)
        return 0x10;

    // Application message loop
    while (GetMessage (&msg, NULL, 0, 0)) {
        TranslateMessage (&msg);
        DispatchMessage (&msg);
    }
    // Instance cleanup
    return TermInstance (hInstance, msg.wParam);
}
//----------------------------------------------------------------------
// InitApp - Application initialization
//
int InitApp (HINSTANCE hInstance) {
    WNDCLASS wc;
    INITCOMMONCONTROLSEX icex;

    // Register application main window class.
    wc.style = 0;                             // Window style
    wc.lpfnWndProc = MainWndProc;             // Callback function
    wc.cbClsExtra = 0;                        // Extra class data
    wc.cbWndExtra = 0;                        // Extra window data
    wc.hInstance = hInstance;                 // Owner handle
    wc.hIcon = NULL,                          // Application icon
    wc.hCursor = NULL;                        // Default cursor
    wc.hbrBackground = (HBRUSH) GetStockObject (WHITE_BRUSH);
    wc.lpszMenuName =  NULL;                  // Menu name
    wc.lpszClassName = szAppName;             // Window class name
```

(continued)

Figure 7-1. *continued*

```
    if (RegisterClass (&wc) == 0) return 1;

    RegisterCtl (hInstance);                  // Register viewer window.

    // Load the command bar common control class.
    icex.dwSize = sizeof (INITCOMMONCONTROLSEX);
    icex.dwICC = ICC_BAR_CLASSES;
    InitCommonControlsEx (&icex);
    return 0;
}
//----------------------------------------------------------------------
// InitInstance - Instance initialization
//
HWND InitInstance (HINSTANCE hInstance, LPWSTR lpCmdLine, int nCmdShow){
    HWND hWnd;

    // Save program instance handle in global variable.
    hInst = hInstance;
    // Create main window.
    hWnd = CreateWindow (szAppName, TEXT ("FileView"),
                         WS_VISIBLE, CW_USEDEFAULT, CW_USEDEFAULT,
                         CW_USEDEFAULT, CW_USEDEFAULT, NULL, NULL,
                         hInstance, NULL);

    // Return fail code if window not created.
    if (!IsWindow (hWnd)) return 0;

    // Standard show and update calls
    ShowWindow (hWnd, nCmdShow);
    UpdateWindow (hWnd);
    return hWnd;
}
//----------------------------------------------------------------------
// TermInstance - Program cleanup
//
int TermInstance (HINSTANCE hInstance, int nDefRC) {
    TermViewer (hInstance, nDefRC);
    return nDefRC;
}
//======================================================================
// Message handling procedures for MainWindow
//----------------------------------------------------------------------
// MainWndProc - Callback function for application window.
//
```

```
LRESULT CALLBACK MainWndProc (HWND hWnd, UINT wMsg, WPARAM wParam,
                              LPARAM lParam) {
    INT i;
    //
    // Search message list to see if we need to handle this
    // message.  If in list, call function.
    //
    for (i = 0; i < dim(MainMessages); i++) {
        if (wMsg == MainMessages[i].Code)
            return (*MainMessages[i].Fxn)(hWnd, wMsg, wParam, lParam);
    }
    return DefWindowProc (hWnd, wMsg, wParam, lParam);
}
//----------------------------------------------------------------------
// DoCreateMain - Process WM_CREATE message for window.
//
LRESULT DoCreateMain (HWND hWnd, UINT wMsg, WPARAM wParam,
                      LPARAM lParam) {
    HWND hwndCB, hwndChild;
    INT nHeight, nCnt;
    RECT rect;
    LPCREATESTRUCT lpcs;

    // Convert lParam into pointer to create structure.
    lpcs = (LPCREATESTRUCT) lParam;

    // Create a minimal command bar that only has a menu and an
    // exit button.
    hwndCB = CommandBar_Create (hInst, hWnd, IDC_CMDBAR);
    // Insert the menu.
    CommandBar_InsertMenubar (hwndCB, hInst, ID_MENU, 0);
    // Add exit button to command bar.
    CommandBar_AddAdornments (hwndCB, 0, 0);
    nHeight = CommandBar_Height (hwndCB);

    SetRect (&rect, 0, nHeight, lpcs->cx, lpcs->cy - nHeight);
    hwndChild = CreateViewer (hWnd, &rect, ID_VIEWER);

    // Destroy frame if window not created.
    if (!IsWindow (hwndChild)) {
        DestroyWindow (hWnd);
        return 0;
    }
    ListView_SetItemCount (hwndChild, nCnt);
    return 0;
}
```

(continued)

Figure 7-1. *continued*

```
//----------------------------------------------------------------------
// DoSizeMain - Process WM_SIZE message for window.
//
LRESULT DoSizeMain (HWND hWnd, UINT wMsg, WPARAM wParam, LPARAM lParam){
    HWND hwndViewer;
    RECT rect;

    hwndViewer = GetDlgItem (hWnd, ID_VIEWER);

    // Adjust the size of the client rect to take into account
    // the command bar height.
    GetClientRect (hWnd, &rect);
    rect.top += CommandBar_Height (GetDlgItem (hWnd, IDC_CMDBAR));

    SetWindowPos (hwndViewer, NULL, rect.left, rect.top,
                  (rect.right - rect.left), rect.bottom - rect.top,
                  SWP_NOZORDER);
    return 0;
}
//----------------------------------------------------------------------
// DoCommandMain - Process WM_COMMAND message for window.
//
LRESULT DoCommandMain (HWND hWnd, UINT wMsg, WPARAM wParam,
                       LPARAM lParam) {
    WORD idItem, wNotifyCode;
    HWND hwndCtl;
    INT i;

    // Parse the parameters.
    idItem = (WORD) LOWORD (wParam);
    wNotifyCode = (WORD) HIWORD (wParam);
    hwndCtl = (HWND) lParam;

    // Call routine to handle control message.
    for (i = 0; i < dim(MainCommandItems); i++) {
        if (idItem == MainCommandItems[i].Code)
            return (*MainCommandItems[i].Fxn)(hWnd, idItem, hwndCtl,
                                              wNotifyCode);
    }
    return 0;
}
//----------------------------------------------------------------------
// DoDestroyMain - Process WM_DESTROY message for window.
//
```

```
LRESULT DoDestroyMain (HWND hWnd, UINT wMsg, WPARAM wParam,
                       LPARAM lParam) {
    PostQuitMessage (0);
    return 0;
}
//======================================================================
// Command handler routines
//----------------------------------------------------------------------
// DoMainCommandOpen - Process File Open command.
//
LPARAM DoMainCommandOpen (HWND hWnd, WORD idItem, HWND hwndCtl,
                          WORD wNotifyCode) {
    TCHAR szFileName[MAX_PATH], szText[64];
    HWND hwndViewer;
    INT rc;

    hwndViewer = GetDlgItem (hWnd, ID_VIEWER);

    if (MyGetFileName (hWnd, szFileName, dim(szFileName)) == 0)
        return 0;
    // Tell the viewer control to open the file.
    rc = SendMessage (hwndViewer, VM_OPEN, 0, (LPARAM)szFileName);

    if (rc) {
        wsprintf (szText, TEXT ("File open failed.  rc: %d ") ,rc);
        MessageBox (hWnd, szText, szAppName, MB_OK);
        return 0;
    }
    return 0;
}
//----------------------------------------------------------------------
// DoMainCommandExit - Process Program Exit command.
//
LPARAM DoMainCommandExit (HWND hWnd, WORD idItem, HWND hwndCtl,
                          WORD wNotifyCode) {

    SendMessage (hWnd, WM_CLOSE, 0, 0);
    return 0;
}
//----------------------------------------------------------------------
// DoMainCommandVText - Process the View Text command.
//
LPARAM DoMainCommandVText (HWND hWnd, WORD idItem, HWND hwndCtl,
                           WORD wNotifyCode) {
    return 0;
}
```

(continued)

Figure 7-1. *continued*

```
//----------------------------------------------------------------------
// DoMainCommandVHex - Process the View Hex command.
//
LPARAM DoMainCommandVHex (HWND hWnd, WORD idItem, HWND hwndCtl,
                          WORD wNotifyCode) {
    return 0;
}
//----------------------------------------------------------------------
// DoMainCommandAbout - Process the Help | About menu command.
//
LPARAM DoMainCommandAbout(HWND hWnd, WORD idItem, HWND hwndCtl,
                          WORD wNotifyCode) {

    // Use DialogBox to create a modal dialog.
    DialogBox (hInst, TEXT ("aboutbox"), hWnd, AboutDlgProc);
    return 0;
}
//======================================================================
// About Dialog procedure
//
BOOL CALLBACK AboutDlgProc (HWND hWnd, UINT wMsg, WPARAM wParam,
                            LPARAM lParam) {
    switch (wMsg) {
        case WM_COMMAND:
            switch (LOWORD (wParam)) {
                case IDOK:
                case IDCANCEL:
                    EndDialog (hWnd, 0);
                    return TRUE;
            }
        break;
    }
    return FALSE;
}

//----------------------------------------------------------------------
// MyGetFileName - Returns a filename using the common dialog.
//
INT MyGetFileName (HWND hWnd, LPTSTR szFileName, INT nMax) {
    OPENFILENAME of;
    const LPTSTR pszOpenFilter = TEXT ("All Documents (*.*)\0*.*\0\0");

    szFileName[0] = '\0';                // Initial filename
    memset (&of, 0, sizeof (of));        // Initial file open structure
```

```
    of.lStructSize = sizeof (of);
    of.hwndOwner = hWnd;
    of.lpstrFile = szFileName;
    of.nMaxFile = nMax;
    of.lpstrFilter = pszOpenFilter;
    of.Flags = 0;

    if (GetOpenFileName (&of))
        return lstrlen (szFileName);
    else
        return 0;
}
```

Viewer.h

```
//======================================================================
// Header file
//
// Written for the book Programming Windows CE
// Copyright (C) 1998 Douglas Boling
//======================================================================

#define  VM_OPEN              (WM_USER+100)

//----------------------------------------------------------------------
// Function prototypes
//
int RegisterCtl (HINSTANCE hInstance);
HWND CreateViewer (HWND hParent, RECT *prect, int nID);
int TermViewer (HINSTANCE hInstance, int nDefRC);
```

Viewer.c

```
//======================================================================
// Viewer - A file view control
//
// Written for the book Programming Windows CE
// Copyright (C) 1998 Douglas Boling
//======================================================================
#include <windows.h>                    // For all that Windows stuff

#include "fileview.h"                   // Program-specific stuff
#include "viewer.h"                     // Control-specific stuff
```

(continued)

Figure 7-1. *continued*

```
//----------------------------------------------------------------------
// Internal function prototypes
LRESULT CALLBACK ViewerWndProc (HWND, UINT, WPARAM, LPARAM);

// Message handlers
LRESULT DoCreateViewer (HWND, UINT, WPARAM, LPARAM);
LRESULT DoSizeViewer (HWND, UINT, WPARAM, LPARAM);
LRESULT DoPaintViewer (HWND, UINT, WPARAM, LPARAM);
LRESULT DoVScrollViewer (HWND, UINT, WPARAM, LPARAM);
LRESULT DoDestroyViewer (HWND, UINT, WPARAM, LPARAM);
LRESULT DoOpenViewer (HWND, UINT, WPARAM, LPARAM);

HFONT GetFixedEquiv (HWND hWnd, HFONT hFontIn);

#define BUFFSIZE   4096
//----------------------------------------------------------------------
// Global data
extern HINSTANCE hInst;             // Program instance handle
HANDLE g_hFile = 0;                 // Handle to the opened file
LONG g_lFileSize;                   // Size of the file
PBYTE g_pBuff = 0;                  // Pointer to file data buffer
LONG g_lFilePtr = 0;                // Pointer to current offset
                                    // into file

LONG g_lBuffBase = 0;               // Offset into file of buffer data
INT g_nBuffLen = 0;                 // Size of data in file buffer
HFONT g_hFont = 0;                  // Fixed pitch font used for text
INT g_nPageLen = 0;                 // Number of bytes displayed / page

const TCHAR szViewerCls[] = TEXT ("Viewer");

// Message dispatch table for ViewerWindowProc
const struct decodeUINT ViewerMessages[] = {
    WM_CREATE, DoCreateViewer,
    WM_PAINT, DoPaintViewer,
    WM_SIZE, DoSizeViewer,
    WM_VSCROLL, DoVScrollViewer,
    WM_DESTROY, DoDestroyViewer,
    VM_OPEN, DoOpenViewer,
};

//----------------------------------------------------------------------
// RegisterCtl - Register the viewer control.
//
int RegisterCtl (HINSTANCE hInstance) {
    WNDCLASS     wc;
```

```
    // Register application viewer window class.
    wc.style = 0;                               // Window style
    wc.lpfnWndProc = ViewerWndProc;             // Callback function
    wc.cbClsExtra = 0;                          // Extra class data
    wc.cbWndExtra = 0;                          // Extra window data
    wc.hInstance = hInstance;                   // Owner handle
    wc.hIcon = NULL,                            // Application icon
    wc.hCursor = NULL;                          // Default cursor
    wc.hbrBackground = (HBRUSH) GetStockObject (WHITE_BRUSH);
    wc.lpszMenuName =  NULL;                    // Menu name
    wc.lpszClassName = szViewerCls;             // Window class name

    if (RegisterClass (&wc) == 0) return 1;

    return 0;
}
//----------------------------------------------------------------------
// CreateViewer - Create a viewer control.
//
HWND CreateViewer (HWND hParent, RECT *prect, int nID) {
    HWND hwndCtl;

    // Create viewer control.
    hwndCtl = CreateWindowEx (0, szViewerCls, TEXT (""),
                              WS_VISIBLE | WS_CHILD | WS_VSCROLL |
                              WS_BORDER, prect->left, prect->top,
                              prect->right - prect->left,
                              prect->bottom - prect->top,
                              hParent, (HMENU)nID, hInst, NULL);
    return hwndCtl;
}
//----------------------------------------------------------------------
// TermInstance - Program cleanup
//
int TermViewer (HINSTANCE hInstance, int nDefRC) {

    if (g_hFile)
        CloseHandle (g_hFile);                  // Close the opened file.

    if (g_pBuff)
        LocalFree (g_pBuff);                    // Free buffer.
    if (g_hFont)
        DeleteObject (g_hFont);
    return nDefRC;
}
```

(continued)

Figure 7-1. *continued*

```
//======================================================================
// Message handling procedures for ViewerWindow
//----------------------------------------------------------------------
// ViewerWndProc - Callback function for viewer window
//
LRESULT CALLBACK ViewerWndProc (HWND hWnd, UINT wMsg, WPARAM wParam,
                                LPARAM lParam) {
    INT i;
    //
    // Search message list to see if we need to handle this
    // message.  If in list, call procedure.
    //
    for (i = 0; i < dim(ViewerMessages); i++) {
        if (wMsg == ViewerMessages[i].Code)
            return (*ViewerMessages[i].Fxn)(hWnd, wMsg, wParam, lParam);
    }
    return DefWindowProc (hWnd, wMsg, wParam, lParam);
}
//----------------------------------------------------------------------
// DoCreateViewer - Process WM_CREATE message for window.
//
LRESULT DoCreateViewer (HWND hWnd, UINT wMsg, WPARAM wParam,
                        LPARAM lParam) {
    LPCREATESTRUCT lpcs;

    // Convert lParam into pointer to create struct.
    lpcs = (LPCREATESTRUCT) lParam;

    // Allocate a buffer.
    g_pBuff = LocalAlloc (LMEM_FIXED, BUFFSIZE);
    if (!g_pBuff) {
        MessageBox (NULL, TEXT ("Not enough memory"),
                    TEXT ("Error"), MB_OK);
        return 0;
    }
    // Create a fixed-pitch font.
    g_hFont = GetFixedEquiv (hWnd, 0);
    return 0;
}
//----------------------------------------------------------------------
// DoSizeViewer - Process WM_SIZE message for window.
//
LRESULT DoSizeViewer (HWND hWnd, UINT wMsg, WPARAM wParam,
                      LPARAM lParam){
    return 0;
}
```

```
//----------------------------------------------------------------------
// ComposeLine - Converts hex buff to unicode string
//
int ComposeLine (INT nOffset, LPTSTR szOut) {
    INT i, nLen, nBuffOffset;
    TCHAR szTmp[16];
    LPBYTE pPtr;
    DWORD cBytes;

    szOut[0] = TEXT ('\0');
    if (g_hFile == 0)                   // If no file open, no text
        return 0;
    // Make sure we have enough bytes in buffer for dump.
    if ((nOffset + 16 > g_lBuffBase + g_nBuffLen) ||
        (nOffset < g_lBuffBase)) {

        // Move file pointer to new place and read data.
        SetFilePointer (g_hFile, nOffset, NULL, FILE_BEGIN);
        if (!ReadFile (g_hFile, g_pBuff, BUFFSIZE, &cBytes, NULL))
            return 0;
        g_lBuffBase = nOffset;
        g_nBuffLen = cBytes;
    }
    nBuffOffset = nOffset - g_lBuffBase;
    if (nBuffOffset > g_nBuffLen)
        return 0;

    // Now create the text for the line.
    wsprintf (szOut, TEXT ("%08X   "), nOffset);

    pPtr = g_pBuff + nBuffOffset;
    nLen = g_nBuffLen - nBuffOffset;
    if (nLen > 16)
        nLen = 16;
    for (i = 0; i < nLen; i++) {
        wsprintf (szTmp, TEXT ("%02X"), *pPtr++);
        lstrcat (szOut, szTmp);
        if (i == 7)
            lstrcat (szOut, TEXT ("-"));
        else
            lstrcat (szOut, TEXT (" "));
    }
    return nLen;
}
```

(continued)

Figure 7-1. *continued*

```
//----------------------------------------------------------------------
// DoPaintViewer - Process WM_PAINT message for window.
//
LRESULT DoPaintViewer (HWND hWnd, UINT wMsg, WPARAM wParam,
                       LPARAM lParam) {
    TCHAR szOut[128];
    INT nFontHeight;
    INT i, yCurrent;
    TEXTMETRIC tm;
    PAINTSTRUCT ps;
    HFONT hOldFont;
    RECT rect;
    HDC hdc;

    hdc = BeginPaint (hWnd, &ps);
    GetClientRect (hWnd, &rect);

    hOldFont = SelectObject (hdc, g_hFont);

    // Get the height of the default font.
    GetTextMetrics (hdc, &tm);
    nFontHeight = tm.tmHeight + tm.tmExternalLeading;

    i = 0;
    yCurrent = rect.top;
    while (yCurrent < rect.bottom) {
        i += ComposeLine (g_lFilePtr+i, szOut);
        ExtTextOut (hdc, 5, yCurrent, 0, NULL,
                    szOut, lstrlen (szOut),    NULL);

        // Update new draw point.
        yCurrent += nFontHeight;
    }
    SelectObject (hdc, hOldFont);
    EndPaint (hWnd, &ps);
    g_nPageLen = i;
    return 0;
}
//----------------------------------------------------------------------
// DoVScrollViewer - Process WM_VSCROLL message for window.
//
LRESULT DoVScrollViewer (HWND hWnd, UINT wMsg, WPARAM wParam,
                         LPARAM lParam) {
    RECT rect;
    SCROLLINFO si;
    INT sOldPos = g_lFilePtr;
```

```
    GetClientRect (hWnd, &rect);

    switch (LOWORD (wParam)) {
    case SB_LINEUP:
        g_lFilePtr -= 16;
        break;

    case SB_LINEDOWN:
        g_lFilePtr += 16;
        break;

    case SB_PAGEUP:
        g_lFilePtr -= g_nPageLen;
        break;

    case SB_PAGEDOWN:
        g_lFilePtr += g_nPageLen;
        break;

    case SB_THUMBPOSITION:
        g_lFilePtr = HIWORD (wParam);
        break;
    }
    // Check range.
    if (g_lFilePtr < 0)
        g_lFilePtr = 0;
    if (g_lFilePtr > g_lFileSize-16)
        g_lFilePtr = (g_lFileSize - 16) & 0xfffffff0;

    // If scroll position changed, update scrollbar and
    // force redraw of window.
    if (g_lFilePtr != sOldPos) {
        si.cbSize = sizeof (si);
        si.nPos = g_lFilePtr;
        si.fMask = SIF_POS;
        SetScrollInfo (hWnd, SB_VERT, &si, TRUE);

        InvalidateRect (hWnd, NULL, TRUE);
    }
    return 0;
}
//----------------------------------------------------------------------
// DoDestroyViewer - Process WM_DESTROY message for window.
//
```

(continued)

Figure 7-1. *continued*

```
LRESULT DoDestroyViewer (HWND hWnd, UINT wMsg, WPARAM wParam,
                          LPARAM lParam) {
    if (g_hFile)
        CloseHandle (g_hFile);
    g_hFile = 0;
    return 0;
}
//----------------------------------------------------------------------
// DoOpenViewer - Process VM_OPEN message for window.
//
LRESULT DoOpenViewer (HWND hWnd, UINT wMsg, WPARAM wParam,
                      LPARAM lParam){
    SCROLLINFO si;

    if (g_hFile)
        CloseHandle (g_hFile);

    // Open the file.
    g_hFile = CreateFile ((LPTSTR)lParam, GENERIC_READ | GENERIC_WRITE,
                          FILE_SHARE_READ, NULL, OPEN_EXISTING,
                          FILE_ATTRIBUTE_NORMAL, NULL);

    if (g_hFile == INVALID_HANDLE_VALUE) {
        g_hFile = 0;
        return GetLastError();
    }
    g_lFilePtr = wParam;
    g_lFileSize = GetFileSize (g_hFile, NULL);

    si.cbSize = sizeof (si);
    si.nMin = 0;
    si.nMax = g_lFileSize;
    si.nPos = g_lFilePtr;
    si.fMask = SIF_POS | SIF_RANGE;
    SetScrollInfo (hWnd, SB_VERT, &si, TRUE);

    InvalidateRect (hWnd, NULL, TRUE);
    return 0;
}
//----------------------------------------------------------------------
HFONT GetFixedEquiv (HWND hWnd, HFONT hFontIn) {
    HDC hdc;
    TEXTMETRIC tm;
    LOGFONT lf;
    HFONT hOldFont;
```

```
    hdc = GetDC (hWnd);
    if (hFontIn == 0)
        hFontIn = GetStockObject (SYSTEM_FONT);
    hOldFont = SelectObject (hdc, hFontIn);
    GetTextMetrics (hdc, &tm);
    SelectObject (hdc, hOldFont);
    ReleaseDC (hWnd, hdc);

    memset (&lf, 0, sizeof (lf));

    lf.lfHeight = -(tm.tmHeight);
    lf.lfWeight    = tm.tmWeight;
    lf.lfItalic    = tm.tmItalic;
    lf.lfUnderline = tm.tmUnderlined;
    lf.lfStrikeOut = tm.tmStruckOut;
    lf.lfCharSet   = tm.tmCharSet;
    lf.lfOutPrecision = OUT_DEFAULT_PRECIS;
    lf.lfClipPrecision = CLIP_DEFAULT_PRECIS;
    lf.lfQuality = DEFAULT_QUALITY;
    lf.lfPitchAndFamily = (tm.tmPitchAndFamily & 0xf0) | TMPF_FIXED_PITCH;
    lf.lfFaceName[0] = TEXT ('\0');

    // Create the font from the LOGFONT structure passed.
    return CreateFontIndirect (&lf);
}
```

The C source code is divided into two files, FileView.c and Viewer.c. FileView.c contains the standard windows functions and the menu command handlers. In Viewer.c, you find the source code for a child window that opens the file and displays its contents. The routines of interest are *DoOpenViewer*, where the file is opened, and *ComposeLine*, where the file data is read. Both of these routines are in Viewer.c. *DoOpenViewer* uses *CreateFile* to open the file with read only access. If the function succeeds, it calls *GetFileSize* to query the size of the file being viewed. This is used to initialize the range of the view window scrollbar. The window is then invalidated to force a WM_PAINT message to be sent.

In the WM_PAINT handler, *OnPaintViewer*, a fixed pitch font is selected into the device context, and data from the file, starting at the current scroll location, is displayed in the window after the application calls the *ComposeLine* function. This routine is responsible for reading the file data into a 4096-byte buffer. The data is then read out of the buffer 16 bytes at a time as each line is displayed. If the data for the line isn't in the file buffer, *ComposeLine* refills the buffer with the proper data from the file by calling *SetFilePointer* and then *ReadFile*.

Memory-Mapped Files and Objects

Memory-mapped files give you a completely different method for reading and writing files. With the standard file I/O functions, files are read as streams of data. To access bytes in different parts of a file, the file pointer must be moved to the first byte, the data read, the file pointer moved to the other byte, and then the file read again.

With memory-mapped files, the file is mapped to a region of memory. Then, instead of using *FileRead* and *FileWrite*, you simply read and write the region of memory that's mapped to the file. Updates of the memory are automatically reflected back to the file itself. Setting up a memory-mapped file is a somewhat more complex process than making a simple call to *CreateFile*, but once a file is mapped, reading and writing the file is trivial.

Memory-mapped files

Windows CE uses a slightly different procedure from Windows NT or Windows 98 to access a memory-mapped file. To open a file for memory-mapped access, a new function, unique to Windows CE, is used; it's named *CreateFileForMapping*. The prototype for this function is the following:

```
HANDLE CreateFileForMapping (LPCTSTR lpFileName, DWORD dwDesiredAccess,
                             DWORD dwShareMode,
                             LPSECURITY_ATTRIBUTES lpSecurityAttributes,
                             DWORD dwCreationDisposition,
                             DWORD dwFlagsAndAttributes,
                             HANDLE hTemplateFile);
```

The parameters for this function are similar to those for *CreateFile*. The filename is the name of the file to read. The *dwDesiredAccess* parameter, specifying the access rights to the file, must be a combination of GENERIC_READ and GENERIC_WRITE, or it must be 0. The security attributes must be NULL, while the *hTemplateFile* parameter is ignored by Windows CE. Note that Windows CE 2.1 is the first version of Windows CE to support write access to memory-mapped files. If you try to use this function in versions earlier than 2.1, it will fail if the *dwDesiredAccess* parameter contains the GENERIC_WRITE flag.

The handle returned by *CreateFileForMapping* can then be passed to

```
HANDLE CreateFileMapping (HANDLE hFile,
                          LPSECURITY_ATTRIBUTES lpFileMappingAttributes,
                          DWORD flProtect, DWORD dwMaximumSizeHigh,
                          DWORD dwMaximumSizeLow, LPCTSTR lpName);
```

This function creates a file mapping object and ties the opened file to it. The first parameter for this function is the handle to the opened file. The security attributes parameter must be set to NULL under Windows CE. The *flProtect* parameter should be loaded with the protection flags for the virtual pages that will contain the file data.

The maximum size parameters should be set to the expected maximum size of the object, or they can be set to 0 if the object should be the same size as the file being mapped. The *lpName* parameter allows you to specify a name for the object. This is handy when you're using a memory-mapped file to share information across different processes. Calling *CreateFileMapping* with the name of an already-opened file-mapping object returns a handle to the object already opened instead of creating a new one.

Once a mapping object has been created, a view into the object is created by calling

```
LPVOID MapViewOfFile (HANDLE hFileMappingObject, DWORD dwDesiredAccess,
                      DWORD dwFileOffsetHigh, DWORD dwFileOffsetLow,
                      DWORD dwNumberOfBytesToMap);
```

MapViewOfFile returns a pointer to memory that's mapped to the file. The function takes as its parameters the handle of the mapping object just opened as well as the access rights, which can be FILE_MAP_READ, FILE_MAP_WRITE, or FILE_MAP_ALL_ACCESS. The offset parameters let you specify the starting point within the file that the view starts, while the *dwNumberOfBytesToMap* parameter specifies the size of the view window.

These last three parameters are useful when you're mapping large objects. Instead of attempting to map the file as one large object, you can specify a smaller view that starts at the point of interest in the file. This reduces the memory required because only the view of the object, not the object itself, is backed up by physical RAM.

When you're finished with the memory-mapped file, a little cleanup is required. First a call to

```
BOOL UnmapViewOfFile (LPCVOID lpBaseAddress);
```

unmaps the view to the object. The only parameter is the pointer to the base address of the view.

Next, a call should be made to close the mapping object and the file itself. Both these actions are accomplished by means of calls to *CloseHandle*. The first call should be to close the memory-mapped object, and then *CloseHandle* should be called to close the file.

The code fragment that follows shows the entire process of opening a file for memory mapping, creating the file-mapping object, mapping the view, then cleaning up. The routine is written to open the file in read-only mode. This allows the code to run under all versions of Windows CE.

```
HANDLE hFile, hFileMap;
PBYTE pFileMem;
TCHAR szFileName[MAX_PATH];
```

(continued)

```
// Get the filename.

hFile = CreateFileForMapping (szFileName, GENERIC_READ,
                              FILE_SHARE_READ, NULL,
                              OPEN_EXISTING, FILE_ATTRIBUTE_NORMAL |
                              FILE_FLAG_RANDOM_ACCESS,0);

if (hFile != INVALID_HANDLE_VALUE) {

    hFileMap = CreateFileMapping (hFile, NULL, PAGE_READONLY, 0, 0, 0);
    if (hFileMap) {
        pFileMem = MapViewOfFile (hFileMap, FILE_MAP_READ, 0, 0, 0);
        if (pFileMem) {
            //
            // Use the data in the file.
            //

            // Start cleanup by unmapping view.
            UnmapViewOfFile (pFileMem);
        }
        CloseHandle (hFileMap);
    }
    CloseHandle (hFile);
}
```

Memory-mapped objects

One of the more popular uses for memory-mapped objects is for interprocess communication. For this purpose, you don't need to have an actual file; it's the shared memory that's important. Windows CE supports entities referred to as *unnamed memory-mapped objects*. These objects are memory-mapped objects that, under Windows NT and Windows 98, are backed up by the paging file but under Windows CE are simply areas of virtual memory with only program RAM to back up the object. Without the paging file, these objects can't be as big as they would be under Windows NT or Windows 98 but Windows CE does have a way of minimizing the RAM required to back up the memory-mapped object.

You create such a memory-mapped object by eliminating the call to *CreateFileForMapping* and passing a –1 in the handle field of *CreateFileMapping*. Since no file is specified, you must specify the size of the memory-mapped region in the maximum size fields of *CreateFileMapping*. The following routine creates a 16-MB region using a memory-mapped file:

```
// Create a 16-MB memory mapped object.
hNFileMap = CreateFileMapping ((HANDLE)-1, NULL, PAGE_READWRITE,
                               0, 0x1000000, NULL);
```

```
if (hNFileMap)
    // Map in the object.
    pNFileMem = MapViewOfFile (hNFileMap,
                               FILE_MAP_WRITE, 0, 0, 0);
```

The memory object created by the code above doesn't actually commit 16 MB of RAM. Instead, only the address space is reserved. Pages are autocommitted as they're accessed. This process allows an application to create a huge, sparse array of pages that takes up only as much physical RAM as is needed to hold the data. At some point, however, if you start reading or writing to a greater number of pages, you'll run out of memory. When this happens, the system generates an exception. I'll talk about how to deal with exceptions in the next chapter. The important thing to remember is that if you really need RAM to be committed to a memory-mapped object, you need to read each of the pages so that the system will commit physical RAM to that object. Of course, don't be too greedy with RAM; commit only the pages you absolutely require.

Naming a memory-mapped object

A memory-mapped object can be named by passing a string to *CreateFileMapping*. This isn't the name of a file being mapped. Instead the name identifies the mapping object being created. In the previous example, the region was unnamed. The following code creates a named memory-mapped object named *Bob*. This name is global so that if another process opens a mapping object with the same name, the two processes will share the same memory mapped object.

```
// Create a 16-MB memory mapped object.
hNFileMap = CreateFileMapping ((HANDLE)-1, NULL, PAGE_READWRITE,
                               0, 0x1000000, TEXT ("Bob"));
if (hNFileMap)
    // Map in the object.
    pNFileMem = MapViewOfFile (hNFileMap,
                               FILE_MAP_WRITE, 0, 0, 0);
```

The difference between named and unnamed file mapping objects is that a named object is allocated only once in the system. Subsequent calls to *CreateFileMapping* that attempt to create a region with the same name will succeed, but the function will return a handle to the original mapping object instead of creating a new one. For unnamed objects, the system creates a new object each time *CreateFileMapping* is called.

When using a memory-mapped object for interprocess communication, processes should create a named object and pass the name of the region to the second process, not a pointer. While the first process can simply pass a pointer to the mapping region to the other process, this isn't advisable. If the first process frees the memory-mapped file region while the second process is still accessing the file, an exception will occur. Instead, the second process should create a memory-mapped object with the same name as the initial process. Windows knows to pass a pointer to the same region that was opened by the first process. The system also increments a use count to track the number of opens. A named memory-mapped object won't be destroyed until all processes have closed the object. This assures a process that the object will remain at least until it closes the object itself. The XTALK example in Chapter 8 provides an example of how to use a named memory mapped object for interprocess communication.

Navigating the File System

Now that we've seen how files are read and written, let's take a look at how the files themselves are managed in the file system. Windows CE supports most of the convenient file and directory management APIs, such as *CopyFile*, *MoveFile*, and *CreateDirectory*.

File and directory management

Windows CE supports a number of functions useful in file and directory management. You can move files using *MoveFile*, copy them using *CopyFile*, and delete them using *DeleteFile*. You can create directories using *CreateDirectory* and delete them using *RemoveDirectory*. While most of these functions are straightforward, I should cover a few intricacies here.

To copy a file, call

```
BOOL CopyFile (LPCTSTR lpExistingFileName, LPCTSTR lpNewFileName,
               BOOL bFailIfExists);
```

The parameters are the name of the file to copy and the name of the destination directory. The third parameter indicates whether the function should overwrite the destination file if one already exists before the copy is made.

Files and directories can be moved and renamed using

```
BOOL MoveFile (LPCTSTR lpExistingFileName, LPCTSTR lpNewFileNam);
```

To move a file, simply indicate the source and destination names for the file. The destination file must not already exist. File moves can be made within the object store, from the object store to an external drive, or from an external drive to the object store. *MoveFile* can also be used to rename a file. In this case, the source and target directories remain the same; only the name of the file changes.

MoveFile can also be used in the same manner to move or rename directories. The only exception is that *MoveFile* can't move a directory from one volume to another. Under Windows CE, *MoveFile* moves a directory and all its subdirectories and files to a different location within the object store or different locations within another volume.

Deleting a file is as simple as calling

```
BOOL DeleteFile (LPCTSTR lpFileName);
```

You pass the name of the file to delete. For the delete to be successful, the file must not be currently open.

You can create and destroy directories using the following two functions:

```
BOOL CreateDirectory (LPCTSTR lpPathName,
                      LPSECURITY_ATTRIBUTES lpSecurityAttributes);
```

and

```
BOOL RemoveDirectory (LPCTSTR lpPathName);
```

CreateDirectory takes the name of the directory to create and a security parameter that should be NULL under Windows CE. *RemoveDirectory* deletes a directory. The directory must be empty for the function to be successful.

Finding files

Windows CE supports the basic *FindFirstFile*, *FindNextFile*, *FindClose* procedure for enumerating files as is supported under Windows NT or Windows 98. Searching is accomplished on a per-directory basis using template filenames with wild card characters in the template.

Searching a directory involves first passing a filename template to *FindFirstFile*, which is prototyped in this way:

```
HANDLE FindFirstFile (LPCTSTR lpFileName,
                      LPWIN32_FIND_DATA lpFindFileData);
```

The first parameter is the template filename used in the search. This filename can contain a fully specified path if you want to search a directory other than the root. Windows CE has no concept of *Current Directory* built into it; if no path is specified in the search string, the root directory of the object store is searched.

As would be expected, the wildcards for the filename template are ? and *. The question mark (?) indicates that any single character can replace the question mark. The asterisk (*) indicates that any number of characters can replace the asterisk. For example, the search string *\windows\alarm?.wav* would return the files \windows\alarm1.wav, \windows\alarm2.wav, and \windows\alarm3.wav. On the other hand, a search string of *\windows*.wav* would return all files in the windows directory that have a wav extension.

The second parameter of *FindFirstFile* is a pointer to a WIN32_FIND_DATA structure as defined at the top of the following page.

```
typedef struct _WIN32_FIND_DATA {
    DWORD dwFileAttributes;
    FILETIME ftCreationTime;
    FILETIME ftLastAccessTime;
    FILETIME ftLastWriteTime;
    DWORD nFileSizeHigh;
    DWORD nFileSizeLow;
    DWORD dwOID;
    WCHAR cFileName[ MAX_PATH ];
} WIN32_FIND_DATA;
```

This structure is filled with the file data for the first file found in the search. The fields shown are similar to what we've seen.

If *FindFirstFile* finds no files or directories that match the template filename, it returns INVALID_HANDLE_VALUE. If at least one file is found, *FindFirstFile* fills in the WIN32_FIND_DATA structure with the specific data for the found file and returns a handle value that you use to track the current search.

To find the next file in the search, call this function:

```
BOOL FindNextFile (HANDLE hFindFile,
                   LPWIN32_FIND_DATA lpFindFileData);
```

The two parameters are the handle returned by *FindFirstFile* and a pointer to a find data structure. *FindNextFile* returns TRUE if a file matching the template passed to *FindFirstFile* is found and fills in the appropriate file data in the WIN32_FIND_DATA structure. If no file is found, *FindNextFile* returns FALSE.

When you've finished searching either because *FindNextFile* returned FALSE or because you simply don't want to continue searching, you must call this function:

```
BOOL FindClose (HANDLE hFindFile);
```

This function accepts the handle returned by *FindFirstFile*. If *FindFirstFile* returned INVALID_ HANDLE_VALUE, you shouldn't call *FindClose*.

The following short code fragment encompasses the entire file search process. This code computes the total size of all files in the Windows directory.

```
WIN32_FIND_DATA fd;
HANDLE hFind;
INT nTotalSize = 0;

// Start search for all files in the windows directory.
hFind = FindFirstFile (TEXT ("\\windows\\*.*"), &fd);

// If a file was found, hFind will be valid.
if (hFind != INVALID_HANDLE_VALUE) {
```

```
    // Loop through found files.  Be sure to process file
    // found with FindFirstFile before calling FindNextFile.
    do {
        // If found file is not a directory, add its size to
        // the total.  (Assume that the total size of all files
        // is less than 2 GB.)
        if (!(fd.dwFileAttributes & FILE_ATTRIBUTE_DIRECTORY))
            nTotalSize += fd.nFileSizeLow;

    // See if another file exists.
    } while (FindNextFile (hFind, &fd));

    // Clean up by closing file search handle.
    FindClose (hFind);
}
```

In this example, the windows directory is searched for all files. If the found "file" isn't a directory, that is, if it's a true file, its size is added to the total. Notice that the return handle from *FindFirstFile* must be checked, not only so that you know whether a file was found but also to prevent *FindClose* from being called if the handle is invalid.

Determining drives from directories

As I mentioned at the beginning of this chapter, Windows CE doesn't support the concept of drive letters so familiar to MS-DOS and Windows users. Instead, file storage devices such as PC Cards or even hard disks are shown as directories in the root directory. That leads to the question, "How can you tell a directory from a drive?" The newer versions of Windows CE, starting with version 2.1, don't have a predefined name for these other storage devices. Using a predefined name is shaky at best, anyway, given that the name was originally *PC Card* and then changed to *Storage Card*. Instead, you need to look at the file attributes for the directory. Directories that are actually secondary storage devices—that is, they store files in a place other than the object store—have the file attribute flag FILE_ATTRIBUTE_TEMPORARY set. So, finding storage devices on any version of Windows CE is fairly easy as is shown in the following code fragment:

```
WIN32_FIND_DATA fd;
HANDLE hFind;
TCHAR szPath[MAX_PATH];
ULARGE_INTEGER lnTotal, lnFree;

lstrcpy (szPath, TEXT ("\\*.*"));
hFind = FindFirstFile (szPath, &fd);

if (hFind != INVALID_HANDLE_VALUE) {
```

(continued)

```
        do {
            if ((fd.dwFileAttributes & FILE_ATTRIBUTE_DIRECTORY) &&
                (fd.dwFileAttributes & FILE_ATTRIBUTE_TEMPORARY)) {

                // Get the disk space statistics for drive.
                GetDiskFreeSpaceEx (fd.cFileName, NULL, &lnTotal,
                                    &lnFree);
            }
        } while (FindNextFile (hFind, &fd));
        FindClose (hFind);
    }
```

This code uses the find first/find next functions to search the root directory for all directories with the FILE_ATTRIBUTE_TEMPORARY attribute set.

Notice in the code I just showed you, the call to this function:

```
BOOL GetDiskFreeSpaceEx (LPCWSTR lpDirectoryName,
                         PULARGE_INTEGER lpFreeBytesAvailableToCaller,
                         PULARGE_INTEGER lpTotalNumberOfBytes,
                         PULARGE_INTEGER lpTotalNumberOfFreeBytes);
```

This function provides information about the total size of the drive, and amount of free space it contains. The first parameter is the name of any directory on the drive in question. This doesn't have to be the root directory of the drive. *GetDiskFreeSpaceEx* returns three values: the free bytes available to the caller, the total size of the drive, and the total free space on the drive. These values are returned in three ULARGE_INTEGER structures. These structures contain two DWORD fields named *LowPart* and *HighPart*. This allows *GetDiskFreeSpaceEx* to return 64-bit values. Those 64-bit values can come in handy on Windows NT and Windows 98, where the drives can be large. If you aren't interested in one or more of the fields, you can pass a NULL in place of the pointer for that parameter. You can also use *GetDiskFreeSpaceEx* to determine the size of the object store.

Another function that can be used to determine the size of the object store is

```
BOOL GetStoreInformation (LPSTORE_INFORMATION lpsi);
```

GetStoreInformation takes one parameter a pointer to a STORE_INFORMATION structure defined as

```
typedef struct STORE_INFORMATION {
    DWORD dwStoreSize;
    DWORD dwFreeSize;
} STORE_INFORMATION, *LPSTORE_INFORMATION;
```

As you can see, this structure simply returns the total size and amount of free space in the object store. Why would you use *GetStoreInformation* when *GetDiskFreeSpaceEx* is available and more general? Because *GetDiskFreeSpaceEx* wasn't available under Windows CE 1.0 but *GetStoreInformation* was.

That covers the Windows CE file API. As you can see, very little Windows CE–unique code is necessary when you're working with the object store. Now let's look at an entirely new set of functions, the database API.

DATABASES

Windows CE gives you an entirely unique set of database APIs not available under the other versions of Windows. The database implemented by Windows CE is simple, with only one level and a maximum of four sort indexes, but it serves as an effective tool for organizing uncomplicated data, such as address lists or to-do lists.

Under the first two versions of Windows CE, databases could reside only in the object store, not on external media such as PC Cards. Starting with the release of Windows CE 2.1 however, Windows CE can now work with databases on PC Cards or other storage devices. This new feature required changes to the database API, effectively doubling the number of functions with xxx*Ex* database functions now shadowing the original database API. While the newer versions of Windows CE still support the original database functions, those functions can be used only with databases stored in the object store.

Basic Definitions

A Windows CE database is composed of a series of records. Records can contain any number of properties. These properties can be one of the data types shown in Figure 7-2.

Data Type	*Description*
iVal	2-byte signed integer
uiVal	2-byte unsigned integer
lVal	4-byte signed integer
ulVal	4-byte unsigned integer
FILETIME	A time and date structure
LPWSTR	0-terminated Unicode string
CEBLOB	A collection of bytes
BOOL*	Boolean
Double*	8-byte signed value

* This data type supported only under Windows CE 2.1 and later

Figure 7-2. *Database data types supported by Windows CE.*

Records can't contain other records. Also, records can reside on only one database. Windows CE databases can't be locked. However, Windows CE does provide a method of notifying a process that another thread has modified a database.

A Windows CE database can have up to four sort indices. These indices are defined when the database is created but can be redefined later, although the restructuring of a database takes a large amount of time. Each sort index by itself results in a fair amount of overhead, so you should limit the number of sort indices to what you really need.

In short, Windows CE gives you a basic database functionality that helps applications organize simple data structures. The pocket series of Windows CE applications provided by Microsoft with the H/PC, H/PC Pro, and the Palm-size PC use the database API to manage the address book, the task list, and e-mail messages. So, if you have a collection of data, this database API might just be the best method of managing that data.

Designing a database

Before you can jump in with a call to *CeCreateDatabase*, you need to think carefully about how the database will be used. While the basic limitations of the Windows CE database structure rule out complex databases, the structure is quite handy for managing collections of related data on a small personal device, which, after all, is one of the target markets for Windows CE.

Each record in a database can have as many properties as you need as long as they don't exceed the basic limits of the database structure. The limits are fairly loose. An individual property can't exceed the constant CEDB_MAXPROPDATASIZE, which is set to 65,471. A single record can't exceed CEDB_MAXRECORDSIZE, currently defined as 131,072.

Database volumes

Starting with Windows CE 2.1, database files can now be stored in volumes instead of directly in the object store. A database volume is nothing more than a specially formatted file where Windows CE databases can be located. Because database volumes can be stored on file systems other than the object store, database information can be stored on PC Cards or similar external storage devices. The most immediate disadvantage of working with database volumes is that they must be first *mounted* and then *unmounted* after you close the databases within the volume. Essentially, mounting the database creates or opens the file that contains one or more databases along with the transaction data for those databases.

There are disadvantages to database volumes aside from the overhead of mounting and unmounting the volumes. Database volumes are actual files and therefore can be deleted by means of standard file operations. The volumes are, by default, marked as hidden, but that wouldn't deter the intrepid user from finding and deleting a volume in a desperate search for more space on the device. Databases created directly within the object store aren't files and therefore are much more difficult for the user to accidentally delete.

The Database API

Once you have planned your database, given the restrictions and considerations necessary to it, the programming can begin.

Mounting a database volume

To mount a database volume, call

```
BOOL CeMountDBVol (PCEGUID pguid, LPWSTR lpszVol, DWORD dwFlags);
```

This function performs a dual purpose: it can create a new volume or open an existing volume. The first parameter is a pointer to a guid. *CeMountDBVol* returns a guid that's used by many of the *Ex* database functions to identify the location of the database file. You shouldn't confuse the CEGUID-type guid parameter in the database functions with the GUID type that is used by OLE and parts of the Windows shell. A CEGUID is simply a handle that tracks the opened database volume.

The second parameter in *CeMountDBVol* is the name of the volume to mount. This isn't a database name, but the name of a file that will contain one or more databases. Since the parameter is a filename, you should define it in \path\name.ext format. The standard extension should be cdb.

The last parameter, *dwFlags*, should be loaded with flags that define how this function acts. The possible flags are the following:

- *CREATE_NEW* Creates a new database volume. If the volume already exists, the function fails.
- *CREATE_ALWAYS* Creates a new database volume. If the volume already exists, it overwrites the old volume.
- *OPEN_EXISTING* Opens a database volume. If the volume doesn't exist, the function fails.
- *OPEN_ALWAYS* Opens a database volume. If the volume doesn't exist, a new database volume is created.
- *TRUNCATE_EXISTING* Opens a database volume and truncates it to 0 bytes. If the volume already exists, the function fails.

If the flags resemble the action flags for *CreateFile*, they should. The actions of *CeMountDBVol* essentially mirror *CreateFile* except that instead of creating or opening a generic file, *CeMountDBVol* creates or opens a file especially designed to hold databases.

If the function succeeds, it returns TRUE and the guid is set to a value that is then passed to the other database functions. If the function fails, a call to *GetLastError* returns an error code indicating the reason for the failure.

Database volumes can be open by more than one process at a time. The system maintains a reference count for the volume. As the last process unmounts a database volume, the system unmounts the volume.

Enumerated mounted database volumes

You can determine what database volumes are currently mounted by repeatedly calling this function:

```
BOOL CeEnumDBVolumes (PCEGUID pguid, LPWSTR lpBuf, DWORD dwSize);
```

The first time you call *CeEnumDBVolumes*, set the guid pointed to by *pguid* to be invalid. You use the CREATE_INVALIDGUID macro to accomplish this. *CeEnumDBVolumes* returns TRUE if a mounted volume is found and returns the guid and name of that volume in the variables pointed to by *pguid* and *lpBuff*. The *dwSize* parameter should be loaded with the size of the buffer pointed to by *lpBuff*. To enumerate the next volume, pass the guid returned by the previous call to the function. Repeat this process until *CeEnumDBVolumes* returns FALSE. The code below demonstrates this process:

```
CEGUID guid;
TCHAR szVolume[MAX_PATH];
INT nCnt = 0;

CREATE_INVALIDGUID (&guid);
while (CeEnumDBVolumes (&guid, szVolume, sizeof (szVolume))) {
    // guid contains the guid of the mounted volume,
    // szVolume contains the name of the volume.
    nCnt++;   // Count the number of mounted volumes.
}
```

Unmounting a database volume

When you have completed using the volume, you should unmount it by calling this function:

```
BOOL CeUnmountDBVol (PCEGUID pguid);
```

The function's only parameter is the guid of a mounted database volume. Calling this function is necessary when you no longer need a database volume and you want to free system resources. Database volumes are only unmounted when all applications that have mounted the volume have called *CeUnmountDBVol*.

Using the object store as a database volume

If you're writing an application for Windows CE 2.1 or later, you still might want to use the new *Ex* database functions but not want to use a separate database volume. Because most of the new *Ex* functions require a CEGUID that identifies a database volume, you need a CEGUID that references the system object store. Fortunately, one can be created using this macro:

```
CREATE_SYSTEMGUID (PCEGUID pguid);
```

The parameter is, of course, a pointer to a CEGUID. The value set in the CEGUID by this macro can then be passed to any of the *Ex* database functions as a placeholder for a separate volume CEGUID. Databases created within this system CEGUID are actually created directly in the object store as if you were using the old non-*Ex* database functions.

Creating a database

Creating a database is accomplished by calling one of two functions, *CeCreateDatabase* or *CeCreateDatabaseEx*. The newer function is *CeCreateDatabaseEx* and works only for Windows CE 2.1 and later. *CeCreateDatabase* is the proper function to use on Windows CE 2.0. First, I'm going to talk about *CeCreateDatabase*, then I'll talk about the expanded functionality of *CeCreateDatabaseEx*.

CeCreateDatabase is prototyped as

```
CEOID CeCreateDatabase (LPWSTR lpszName, DWORD dwDbaseType,
                        WORD wNumSortOrder,
                        SORTORDERSPEC * rgSortSpecs);
```

The first parameter of the function is the name of the new database. Unlike filenames, the database name is limited to 32 characters, including the terminating zero. The *deDbaseType* parameter is a user-defined parameter that can be employed to differentiate families of databases. For example, you might want to use a common type value for all databases that your application creates. This allows them to be easily enumerated. At this point, there are no rules for what type values to use. Some example type values used by the Microsoft Pocket suite are listed in Figure 7-3.

Database	*Value*
Contacts	24 (18 hex)
Appointments	25 (19 hex)
Tasks	26 (1A hex)
Categories	27 (1B hex)

Figure 7-3. *Predefined database types.*

The values listed in Figure 7-3 aren't guaranteed to remain constant; I simply wanted to show some typical values. If you use a 4-byte value, it shouldn't be too hard to find a unique database type for your application although there's no reason another application couldn't use the same type.

The final two parameters specify the sort specification for the database. The parameter *wNumSortOrder* specifies the number of sort specifications, up to a maximum of 4, while the *rgSortSpecs* parameter points to an array of SORTORDERSPEC structures defined as

```
typedef struct _SORTORDERSPEC {
    PEGPROPID propid;
    DWORD dwFlags;
} SORTORDERSPEC;
```

The first field in the SORTORDERSPEC structure is a property ID or PEGPROPID. A property ID is nothing more than a unique identifier for a property in the database. Remember that a property is one field within a database record. The property ID is a DWORD value with the low 16 bits containing the data type and the upper 16 bits containing an application-defined value. These values are defined as constants and are used by various database functions to identify a property. For example, a property that contained the name of a contact might be defined as

```
#define PID_NAME       MAKELONG (CEVT_LPWSTR, 1)
```

The MAKELONG macro simply combines two 16-bit values into a DWORD or LONG. The first parameter is the low word or the result, while the second parameter becomes the high word. In this case, the CEVT_LPWSTR constant indicates that the property contains a string while the second parameter is simply a value that uniquely identifies the *Name* property, distinguishing it from other string properties in the record.

The second field in the SORTORDERSPEC, *dwFlags*, contains flags that define how the sort is to be accomplished. The following flags are defined for this field:

- *CEDB_SORT_DESCENDING* The sort is to be in descending order. By default, properties are sorted in ascending order.
- *CEDB_SORT_CASEINSENSITIVE* The sort should ignore the case of the letters in the string.
- *CEDB_SORT_UNKNOWNFIRST* Records without this property are to be placed at the start of the sort order. By default, these records are placed last.

A typical database might have three or four sort orders defined. After a database is created, these sort orders can be changed by calling *CeSetDatabaseInfo*. However, this function is quite resource intensive and can take from seconds up to minutes to execute on large databases.

If you want to open a database outside of the object store, you can use the following function:

```
CEOID CeCreateDatabaseEx (PCEGUID pguid, CEDBASEINFO *pInfo);
```

This function takes a *pguid* parameter that identifies the mounted database volume where the database is located. The second parameter is a pointer to a CEDBASEINFO structure defined as

```
typedef struct _CEDBASEINFO {
    DWORD   dwFlags;
    WCHAR   szDbaseName[CEDB_MAXDBASENAMELEN];
    DWORD   dwDbaseType;
    WORD    wNumRecords;
    WORD    wNumSortOrder;
    DWORD   dwSize;
    FILETIME ftLastModified;
    SORTORDERSPEC rgSortSpecs[CEDB_MAXSORTORDER];
} CEDBASEINFO;
```

As you can see, this structure contains a number of the same parameters passed individually to *CeCreateDatabase*. The *szDatabaseName*, *dwDbaseType*, *wNumSortOrder*, and *rgSortSpecs* fields must be initialized in the same manner as they are when you call *CeCreateDatabase*.

The *dwFlags* parameter has two uses. First, it contains flags indicating which fields in the structure are valid. The possible values for the *dwFlags* field are: CEDB_VALIDNAME, CEDB_VALIDTYPE, CEDB_VALIDSORTSPEC, and CEDB_VALIDDBFLAGS. When you're creating a database, it's easier to simply set the *dwFlags* field to CEDB_VALIDCREATE, which is a combination of the flags I just listed. An additional flag, CEDB_VALIDMODTIME, is used when this structure is used by *CeOidGetInfo*.

The other use for the *dwFlags* parameter is to specify the properties of the database. The only flag currently defined is CEDB_NOCOMPRESS. This flag can be specified if you don't want the database you're creating to be compressed. By default, all databases are compressed, which saves storage space at the expense of speed. By specifing the CEDB_NOCOMPRESS flag, the database will be larger but you will be able to read and write the database faster.

You can use *CeCreateDatabaseEx* but create a database within the object store instead of within a separate database volume. The advantage of this strategy is that the database itself isn't created within a file and is therefore safer from a user who might delete the database volume.

The value returned by either *CeCreateDatabase* or *CeCreateDatabaseEx* is a CEOID. We have seen this kind of value a couple of times so far in this chapter. It's an ID value that uniquely identifies the newly created database, not just among other databases, but also among all files, directories, and even database records in the file system. If the value is 0, an error occurred while you were trying to create the database. You can call *GetLastError* to diagnose the reason the database creation failed.

Opening a database

In contrast to what happens when you create a file, creating a database doesn't also open the database. To do that, you must make an additional call to

```
HANDLE CeOpenDatabase(PCEOID poid, LPWSTR lpszName, CEPROPID propid,
                      DWORD dwFlags, HWND hwndNotify);
```

A database can be opened either by referencing its CEOID value or by referencing its name. To open the database by using its name, set the value pointed to by the *poid* parameter to 0 and specify the name of the database using the *lpszName* parameter. If you already know the CEOID of the database, simply put that value in the parameter pointed to by *poid*. If the CEOID value isn't 0, the functions ignore the *lpszName* parameter.

The *propid* parameter specifies which of the sort order specifications should be used to sort the database while it's opened. A Windows CE database can have only one active sort order. To use a different sort order, you can open a database again, specifying a different sort order.

The *dwFlags* parameter can contain either 0 or CEDB_AUTOINCREMENT. If CEDB_AUTOINCREMENT is specified, each read of a record in the database results in the database pointer being moved to the next record in the sort order. Opening a database without this flag means that the record pointer must be manually moved to the next record to be read. This flag is helpful if you plan to read the database records in sequential order.

The final parameter is the handle of a window that's to be notified when another process or thread modifies the database. This message-based notification allows you to monitor changes to the database while you have it opened. When a database is opened with *CeOpenDatabase*, Windows CE sends the following three messages to notify you of changes.

- *DB_CEOID_CREATED* A record has been created in the database.
- *DB_CEOID_CHANGED* A record has been changed.
- *DB_CEOID_RECORD_DELETED* A record has been deleted.

These messages are encoded as WM_USER+1, WM_USER+3, and WM_USER+6 respectively, so be careful not to use these low WM_USER messages for your own purposes if you want to have that window monitor database changes.

If the function is successful, it returns a handle to the opened database. This handle is then used by the other database functions to reference this opened database. If the handle returned is 0, the function failed for some reason and you can use *GetLastError* to identify the problem.

If you're running under Windows CE 2.1 or later you can use the function:

```
HANDLE CeOpenDatabaseEx (PCEGUID pguid,
                         PCEOID poid, LPWSTR lpszName, CEPROPID propid,
                         DWORD dwFlags, CENOTIFYREQUEST *pRequest);
```

With a couple of exceptions, the parameters for *CeOpenDatabaseEx* are the same as for *CeOpenDatabase*. The first difference between the two functions is the extra pointer to a guid that identifies the volume in which the database resides.

The other difference is the method Windows CE uses to notify you of a change to the database. Instead of passing a handle to a window that will receive one of three WM_USER based messages, you pass a pointer to a CENOTIFYREQUEST structure that you have previously filled in. This structure is defined as

```
typedef struct _CENOTIFYREQUEST {
    DWORD dwSize;
    HWND hWnd;
    DWORD dwFlags;
    HANDLE hHeap;
    DWORD dwParam;
} CENOTIFYREQUEST;
```

The first field must be initialized to the size of the structure. The *hWnd* field should be set to the window that will receive the change notifications. The *dwFlags* field specifies how you want to be notified. If you put 0 in this field, you'll receive the same DB_CEIOD_*xxx* messages that are sent if you'd opened the database with *CeOpenDatabase*. If you put CEDB_EXNOTIFICATION in the *dwFlags* field, your window will receive an entirely new and more detailed notification method.

Instead of receiving the three DB_CEIOD_ messages, your window receives a WM_ DBNOTIFICATION message. When your window receives this message, the *lParam* parameter points to a CENOTIFICATION structure defined as

```
typedef struct _CENOTIFICATION {
    DWORD dwSize
    DWORD dwParam;
    UINT uType;
    CEGUID guid;
    CEOID oid;
    CEOID oidParent;
} CENOTIFICATION;
```

As expected, the *dwSize* field fills with the size of the structure. The *dwParam* field contains the value passed in the *dwParam* field in the CENOTIFYREQUEST structure. This is an application-defined value that can be used for any purpose.

The *uType* field indicates why the WM_DBNOTIFICATION message was sent. It will be set to one of the following values:

- *DB_CEOID_CREATED* A new file system object was created.
- *DB_CEOID_DATABASE_DELETED* The database was deleted from a volume.
- *DB_CEOID_RECORD_DELETED* A record was deleted in a database.
- *DB_CEOID_CHANGED* An object was modified.

The *guid* field contains the guid for the database volume that the message relates to while the *oid* field contains the relevant database record oid. Finally, the *oidParent* field contains the oid of the parent of the oid that the message references.

When you receive a WM_DBNOTIFICATION message, the CENOTIFICATION structure is placed in a memory block that you must free. If you specified a handle to a heap in the *hHeap* field of CENOTIFYREQUEST, the notification structure will be placed in that heap; otherwise, the system defined where the structure is placed. Regardless of its location, you are responsible for freeing the memory that contains the CENOTIFICATION structure. You do this with a call to

```
BOOL CeFreeNotification(PCENOTIFYREQUEST pRequest,
                        PCENOTIFICATION pNotify);
```

The function's two parameters are a pointer to the original CENOTIFYREQUEST structure and a pointer to the CENOTIFICATION structure to free. You must free the CENOTIFICATION structure each time you receive a WM_DBNOTIFICATION message.

Seeking (or searching for) a record

Now that the database is opened, you can read and write the records. But before you can read or write a record, you must *seek* to that record. That is, you must move the database pointer to the record you want to read or write. You accomplish this using

```
CEOID CeSeekDatabase (HANDLE hDatabase, DWORD dwSeekType, DWORD dwValue,
                      LPDWORD lpdwIndex);
```

The first parameter for this function is the handle to the opened database. The *dwSeekType* parameter describes how the seek is to be accomplished. The parameter can have one of the following values:

- *CEDB_SEEK_CEOID* Seek a specific record identified by its object ID. The object ID is specified in the *dwValue* parameter. This type of seek is particularly efficient in Windows CE databases.
- *CEDB_SEEK_BEGINNING* Seek the nth record in the database. The index is contained in the *dwValue* parameter.
- *CEDB_SEEK_CURRENT* Seek from the current position *n* records forward or backward in the database. The offset is contained in the *dwValue* parameter. Even though *dwValue* is typed as a unsigned value, for this seek it's interpreted as a signed value.
- *CEDB_SEEK_END* Seek backward from the end of the database *n* records. The number of records to seek backward from the end is specified in the *dwValue* parameter.
- *CEDB_SEEK_VALUESMALLER* Seek from the current location until a record is found that contains a property that is the closest to, but not equal to or over the value specified. The value is specified by a CEPROPVAL structure pointed to by *dwValue*.
- *CEDB_SEEK_VALUEFIRSTEQUAL* Starting with the current location, seek until a record is found that contains the property that's equal to the value specified. The value is specified by a CEPROPVAL structure pointed to by *dwValue*. The location returned can be the current record.
- *CEDB_SEEK_VALUENEXTEQUAL* Starting with the next location, seek until a record is found that contains a property that's equal to the value specified. The value is specified by a CEPROPVAL structure pointed to by *dwValue*.
- *CEDB_SEEK_VALUEGREATER* Seek from the current location until a record is found that contains a property that is equal to, or the closest to, the value specified. The value is specified by a CEPROPVAL structure pointed to by *dwValue*.

As you can see from the available flags, seeking in the database is more than just moving a pointer; it also allows you to search the database for a particular record.

As I just mentioned in the descriptions of the seek flags, the *dwValue* parameter can either be loaded with an offset value for the seeks or point to a property value for the searches. The property value is described in a CEPROPVAL structure defined as

```
typedef struct _CEPROPVAL {
    CEPROPID propid;
```

(continued)

```
    WORD wLenData;
    WORD wFlags;
    CEVALUNION val;
} CEPROPVAL;
```

The *propid* field should contain one of the property ID values you defined for the properties in your database. Remember that the property ID is a combination of a data type identifier along with an application specific ID value that uniquely identifies a property in the database. This field identifies the property to examine when seeking. The *wLenData* field is ignored. None of the defined flags for the *wFlags* field is used by *CeSeekDatabase*, so this field should be set to 0. The *val* field is actually a union of the different data types supported in the database.

Following is a short code fragment that demonstrates seeking to the third record in the database.

```
DWORD dwIndex;
CEOID oid;

// Seek to the third record.
oid = CeSeekDatabase (g_hDB, CEDB_SEEK_BEGINNING, 3, &dwIndex);
if (oid == 0) {
    // There is no third item in the database.
}
```

Now say we want to find the first record in the database that has a height property of greater than 100. For this example, assume the size property type is a signed long value.

```
// Define pid for height property as a signed long with ID of one.
#define PID_HEIGHT     MAKELONG (CEVT_I4, 1)

CEOID oid;
DWORD dwIndex;
CEPROPVAL Property;

// First seek to the start of the database.
oid = CeSeekDatabase (g_hDB, CEDB_SEEK_BEGINNING, 0, &dwIndex);

// Seek the record with height > 100.
Property.propid = PID_HEIGHT;           // Set property to search.
Property.wLenData = 0;                  // Not used but clear anyway.
Property.wFlags = 0;                    // No flags to set
Property.val.lVal = 100;                // Data for property

oid = CeSeekDatabase (g_hDB, CEDB_SEEK_VALUEGREATER, &Property,
                      &dwIndex);
```

```
if (oid == 0) {
    // No matching property found, db pointer now points to end of db.
} else {
    // oid contains the object ID for the record,
    // dwIndex contains the offset from the start of the database
    // of the matching record.
}
```

Because the search for the property starts at the current location of the database pointer, you first need to seek to the start of the database if you want to find the first record in the database that has the matching property.

Changing the sort order

I talked earlier about how *CeDatabaseSeek* depends on the sort order of the opened database. If you want to choose one of the predefined sort orders instead, you must close the database and then reopen it specifying the predefined sort order. But what if you need a sort order that isn't one of the four sort orders that were defined when the database was created? You can redefine the sort orders using this function:

```
BOOL CeSetDatabaseInfo (CEOID oidDbase, CEDBASEINFO *pNewInfo);
```

or, under Windows CE 2.1 or later, this function:

```
BOOL CeSetDatabaseInfoEx (PCEGUID pguid,
                          CEOID oidDbase, CEDBASEINFO *pNewInfo);
```

Both these functions take the object ID of the database you want to redefine and a pointer to a CEDBASEINFO structure. This structure is the same one used by *CeCreateDatabaseEx*. You can use these functions to rename the database, change its type, or redefine the four sort orders. You shouldn't redefine the sort orders casually. When the database sort orders are redefined, the system has to iterate through every record in the database to rebuild the sort indexes. This can take minutes for large databases. If you must redefine the sort order of a database, you should inform the user of the massive amount of time it might take to perform the operation.

Reading a record

Once you have the database pointer at the record you're interested in, you can read or write that record. You can read a record in a database by calling the following function:

```
CEOID CeReadRecordProps (HANDLE hDbase, DWORD dwFlags, LPWORD lpcPropID,
                         CEPROPID *rgPropID, LPBYTE *lplpBuffer,
                         LPDWORD lpcbBuffer);
```

or, if you're running under Windows CE 2.1 or later, by calling the function you see at the top of the next page.

```
CEOID CeReadRecordPropsEx (HANDLE hDbase, DWORD dwFlags,
                           LPWORD lpcPropID,
                           CEPROPID *rgPropID, LPBYTE *lplpBuffer,
                           LPDWORD lpcbBuffer,
                           HANDLE hHeap);
```

The differences between these two functions is the addition of the *hHeap* parameter in *CeReadRecordPropsEx*. I'll explain the significance of this parameter shortly.

The first parameter in these functions is the handle to the opened database. The *lpcPropID* parameter points to a variable that contains the number of CEPROPID structures pointed to by the next parameter *rgPropID*. These two parameters combine to tell the function which properties of the record you want to read. There are two ways to utilize the *lpcPropID* and *rgPropID* parameters. If you want only to read a selected few of the properties of a record, you can initialize the array of CEPROPID structures with the ID values of the properties you want and set the variable pointed to by *lpcPropID* with the number of these structures. When you call the function, the returned data will be inserted into the CEPROPID structures for data types such as integers. For strings and blobs, where the length of the data is variable, the data is returned in the buffer indirectly pointed to by *lplpBuffer*.

Since *CeReadRecordProps* and *CeReadRecordPropsEx* have a significant overhead to read a record, it is always best to read all the properties necessary for a record in one call. To do this, simply set *rgPropID* to NULL. When the function returns, the variable pointed to by *lpcPropID* will contain the count of properties returned and the function will return all the properties for that record in the buffer. The buffer will contain an array of CEPROPID structures created by the function immediately followed by the data for those properties such as blobs and strings where the data isn't stored directly in the CEPROPID array.

One very handy feature of *CeReadRecordProps* and *CeReadRecordPropsEx* is that if you set CEDB_ALLOWREALLOC in the *dwFlags* parameter, the function will enlarge, if necessary, the results buffer to fit the data being returned. Of course, for this to work, the buffer being passed to the function must not be on the stack or in the static data area. Instead, it must be an allocated buffer, in the local heap for *CeReadRecordProps* or in the case of *CeReadRecordPropsEx*, in the local heap or a separate heap. In fact, if you use the CEDB_ALLOWREALLOC flag, you don't even need to pass a buffer to the function, instead you can set the buffer pointer to 0. In this case, the function will allocate the buffer for you.

Notice that the buffer parameter isn't a pointer to a buffer but a pointer to a pointer to a buffer. There actually is a method to this pointer madness. Since the resulting buffer can be reallocated by the function, it might be moved if the buffer needs to be reallocated. So the pointer to the buffer must be modified by the function. You must always use the pointer the buffer returned by the function because it might have changed. Also, you're responsible for freeing the buffer after you have used it. Even if the function failed for some reason, the buffer might have moved or even have been freed by the function. You must clean up after the read by freeing the buffer if the pointer returned isn't 0.

Now to the difference between *CeReadRecordProps* and *CeReadRecordPropsEx*. As you might have guessed by the above discussion, the extra *hHeap* parameter allows *CeReadRecordPropsEx* to use a heap different from the local heap when reallocating the buffer. When you use *CeReadRecordPropsEx* and you want to use the local heap, simply pass a 0 in the *hHeap* parameter.

The routine below reads all the properties for a record, then copies the data into a structure.

```
int ReadDBRecord (HANDLE hDB, DATASTRUCT *pData) {
    WORD wProps;
    CEOID oid;
    PCEPROPVAL pRecord;
    PBYTE pBuff;
    DWORD dwRecSize;
    int i;

    // Read all properties for the record.
    pBuff = 0;    // Let the function allocate the buffer.
    oid = CeReadRecordProps (hDB, CEDB_ALLOWREALLOC, &wProps, NULL,
                             &(LPBYTE)pBuff, &dwRecSize);
    // Failure on read.
    if (oid == 0)
        return 0;

    // Copy the data from the record to the structure.  The order
    // of the array is not defined.
    memset (pData, 0 , sizeof (DATASTRUCT));  // Zero return struct
    pRecord = (PCEPROPVAL)pBuff;              // Point to CEPROPVAL
                                              // array.
    for (i = 0; i < wProps; i++) {
        switch (pRecord->propid) {
        case PID_NAME:
            lstrcpy (pData->szName, pRecord->val.lpwstr);
            break;
        case PID_TYPE:
            lstrcpy (pData->szType, pRecord->val.lpwstr);
            break;
```

(continued)

```
            case PID_SIZE:
                pData->nSize = pRecord->val.iVal;
                break;
            }
            pRecord++;
        }
        LocalFree (pBuff);
        return i;
}
```

Since the function above reads all the properties for the record, *CeReadRecordProps* creates the array of CEPROPVAL structures. The order of these structures isn't defined so the function cycles through each one to look for the data to fill in the structure. After all the data has been read, a call to *LocalFree* is made to free the buffer that was returned by *CeReadRecordProps*.

There is no requirement for every record to contain all the same properties. You might encounter a situation where you request a specific property from a record by defining the CEPROPID array and that property doesn't exist in the record. When this happens, *CeReadRecordProps* will set the CEDB_PROPNOTFOUND flag in the *wFlags* field of the CEPROPID structure for that property. You should always check for this flag if you call *CeReadRecordProps* and you specify the properties to be read. In the example above, all properties were requested, so if a property didn't exist, no CEPROPID structure for that property would have been returned.

Writing a record

You can write a record to the database using this function:

```
CEOID CeWriteRecordProps (HANDLE hDbase, CEOID oidRecord, WORD cPropID,
                          CEPROPVAL * rgPropVal);
```

The first parameter is the obligatory handle to the opened database. The *oidRecord* parameter is the object ID of the record to be written. To create a new record instead of modifying a record in the database, set *oidRecord* to 0. The *cPropID* parameter should contain the number of items in the array of property ID structures pointed to by *rgPropVal*. The *rcPropVal* array specifies which of the properties in the record to modify and the data to write.

Deleting properties, records, and entire databases

You can delete individual properties in a record using *CeWriteRecordProps*. To do this, create a CEPROPVAL structure that identifies the property to delete and set CEDB_PROPDELETE in the *wFlags* field.

To delete an entire record in a database, call

```
BOOL CeDeleteRecord (HANDLE hDatabase, CEOID oidRecord);
```

The parameters are the handle to the database and the object ID of the record to delete.

You can delete an entire database using this function:

```
BOOL CeDeleteDatabase (CEOID oidDbase);
```

or, under Windows CE 2.1 or later, this function:

```
BOOL CeDeleteDatabaseEx (PCEGUID pguid, CEOID oid);
```

The database being deleted can't be currently open. The difference between the two functions is that *CeDeleteDatabaseEx* can delete databases outside the object store.

Enumerating databases

Sometimes you must search the system to determine what databases are on the system. Windows CE provides two sets of functions to enumerate the databases in a volume. The first set of these functions works only for databases directly within the object store. These functions are

```
HANDLE CeFindFirstDatabase (DWORD dwDbaseType);
```

and

```
CEOID CeFindNextDatabase (HANDLE hEnum);
```

These functions act like *FindFirstFile* and *FindNextFile* with the exception that *CeFindFirstDatabase* only opens the search, it doesn't return the first database found. With these functions the only way to limit the search is to specify the ID of a specific database type in the *dwDbaseType* parameter. If this parameter is set to 0, all databases are enumerated. *CeFindFirstDatabase* returns a handle that is then passed to *CeFindNextDatabase* to actually enumerate the databases.

Below is an example of how to enumerate the databases in the object store.

```
HANDLE hDBList;
CEOID oidDB;

SendDlgItemMessage (hWnd, IDC_RPTLIST, WM_SETREDRAW, FALSE, 0);

hDBList = CeFindFirstDatabase (0);
if (hDBList != INVALID_HANDLE_VALUE) {

    oidDB = CeFindNextDatabase (hDBList);
    while (oidDB) {
        // Enumerated database identified by object ID.
        MyDisplayDatabaseInfo (hCeDB);

        hCeDB = CeFindNextDatabase (hDBList);
    }
    CloseHandle (hDBList);
}
```

To enumerate databases within a separate database volume, use

```
HANDLE CeFindFirstDatabaseEx (PCEGUID pguid, DWORD dwClassID);
```

and

```
HANDLE CeFindFirstDatabaseEx (PCEGUID pguid, DWORD dwClassID);
```

For the most past, these two functions work identically to their non-*Ex* predecessors with the exception that they enumerate the different databases within a single database volume. The additional parameter in these functions is the *CEOID* of the mounted volume to search.

Querying object information

To query information about a database, use this function:

```
BOOL CeOidGetInfo (CEOID oid, CEOIDINFO *poidInfo);
```

or, if under Windows CE 2.1 or later, use this function:

```
BOOL CeOidGetInfoEx (PCEGUID pguid, CEOID oid, CEOIDINFO *oidInfo);
```

These functions return information about not just databases, but any object in the file system. This includes files and directories as well as databases and database records. The functions are passed the object ID of the item of interest and a pointer to an CEOIDINFO structure. Here is the definition of the CEIOIDINFO structure:

```
typedef struct _CEOIDINFO {
    WORD wObjType;
    WORD wPad;
    union {
        CEFILEINFO infFile;
        CEDIRINFO infDirectory;
        CEDBASEINFO infDatabase;
        CERECORDINFO infRecord;
    };
} CEOIDINFO;
```

This structure contains a word indicating the type of the item and a union of four different structures each detailing information on that type of object. The currently supported flags are: OBJTYPE_FILE, indicating that the object is a file, OBJTYPE_DIRECTORY for directory objects, OBJTYPE_DATABASE for database objects, and OBJTYPE_RECORD indicating that the object is a record inside a database. The structures in the union are specific to each object type.

The CEFILEINFO structure is defined as

```
typedef struct _CEFILEINFO {
    DWORD dwAttributes;
```

```
    CEOID oidParent;
    WCHAR szFileName[MAX_PATH];
    FILETIME ftLastChanged;
    DWORD dwLength;
} CEFILEINFO;
```

the CEDIRINFO structure is defined as

```
typedef struct _CEDIRINFO {
    DWORD dwAttributes;
    CEOID oidParent;
    WCHAR szDirName[MAX_PATH];
} CEDIRINFO;
```

and the CERECORDINFO structure is defined as

```
typedef struct _CERECORDINFO {
    CEOID oidParent;
} CERECORDINFO;
```

You have already seen the CEDBASEINFO structure used in *CeCreateDatabaseEx* and *CeSetDatabaseInfo*. As you can see from the above structures, *CeGetOidInfo* returns a wealth of information about each object. One of the more powerful bits of information is the object's parent oid, which will allow you to trace the chain of files and directories back to the root. These functions also allow you to convert an object ID into a name of a database, directory, or file.

The object ID method of tracking a file object should not be confused with the PID scheme used by the shell. Object IDs are maintained by the file system, and are independent of whatever shell is being used. This would be a minor point under other versions of Windows, but with the ability of Windows CE to be built as components and customized for different targets, it's important to know what parts of the operating system support which functions.

The AlbumDB Example Program

It's great to talk about the database functions; it's another experience to use them in an application. The example program that follows, AlbumDB, is a simple database that tracks record albums, the artist that recorded them, and the individual tracks on the albums. It has a simple interface because the goal of the program is to demonstrate the database functions, not the user interface. Figure 7-4 on the next page shows the AlbumDB window with a few albums entered in the database.

Figure 7-5 contains the code for the AlbumDB program. When the program is first launched, it attempts to open a database called AlbumDB. If one isn't found, a new one is created. This is accomplished in the *OpenCreateDB* function.

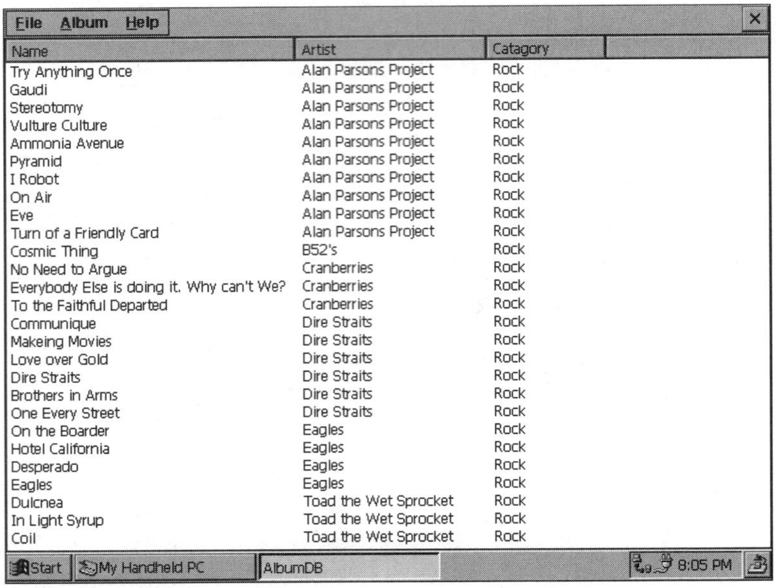

Figure 7-4. *The AlbumDB window.*

AlbumDB.rc

```
//======================================================================
// Resource file
//
// Written for the book Programming Windows CE
// Copyright (C) 1998 Douglas Boling
//======================================================================

#include "windows.h"
#include "albumdb.h"                          // Program-specific stuff
//----------------------------------------------------------------------
// Icons and bitmaps
//
ID_ICON ICON   "albumdb.ico"                  // Program icon

//----------------------------------------------------------------------
// Menu
//
ID_MENU MENU DISCARDABLE
BEGIN
    POPUP "&File"
    BEGIN
```

Figure 7-5. *The AlbumDB program.*

```
        MENUITEM "&Delete Database",              IDM_DELDB
        MENUITEM SEPARATOR
        MENUITEM "E&xit",                         IDM_EXIT
    END
    POPUP "&Album"
    BEGIN
        MENUITEM "&New",                          IDM_NEW
        MENUITEM "&Edit",                         IDM_EDIT
        MENUITEM "&Delete",                       IDM_DELETE
        MENUITEM SEPARATOR
        MENUITEM "&Sort Name",                    IDM_SORTNAME
        MENUITEM "Sort &Artist",                  IDM_SORTARTIST
        MENUITEM "Sort &Category",                IDM_SORTCATEGORY
    END
    POPUP "&Help"
    BEGIN
        MENUITEM "&About...",                     IDM_ABOUT
    END
END
//----------------------------------------------------------------------
// New/Edit Track dialog template
//
EditTrackDlg DIALOG discardable 10, 10, 165, 40
STYLE  WS_POPUP | WS_VISIBLE | WS_CAPTION | WS_SYSMENU | DS_CENTER |
       DS_MODALFRAME
EXSTYLE WS_EX_CAPTIONOKBTN
CAPTION "Edit Track"
BEGIN
    LTEXT "Track Name"                   -1,   5,   5,  50,  12
    EDITTEXT                   IDD_TRACK,  60,   5, 100,  12, WS_TABSTOP

    LTEXT "Time"                         -1,   5,  20,  50,  12
    EDITTEXT                   IDD_TIME,  60,  20,  50,  12, WS_TABSTOP
END
//----------------------------------------------------------------------
// New/Edit Album data dialog template
//
EditAlbumDlg DIALOG discardable 10, 10, 200, 100
STYLE  WS_POPUP | WS_VISIBLE | WS_CAPTION | WS_SYSMENU | DS_CENTER |
       DS_MODALFRAME
EXSTYLE WS_EX_CAPTIONOKBTN
CAPTION "Edit Album"
BEGIN
    LTEXT "Album Name"                   -1,   5,   5,  50,  12
    EDITTEXT                   IDD_NAME,  60,   5, 135,  12, WS_TABSTOP
```

(continued)

Figure 7-5. *continued*

```
    LTEXT "Artist"                          -1,   5,  20,  50,  12
    EDITTEXT                    IDD_ARTIST,  60,  20, 135,  12,
                                    WS_TABSTOP

    LTEXT "Category"                        -1,   5,  35,  50,  12
    COMBOBOX                    IDD_CATEGORY,  60,  35, 135,  60,
                                    WS_TABSTOP | CBS_DROPDOWN
    LISTBOX                     IDD_TRACKS,  60,  50, 135,  45,
                                    LBS_USETABSTOPS

    PUSHBUTTON "&New Track...",
                                IDD_NEWTRACK,   5,  50,  50,  12,
                                    WS_TABSTOP
    PUSHBUTTON "&Edit Track...",
                                IDD_EDITTRACK,   5,  65,  50,  12,
                                    WS_TABSTOP
    PUSHBUTTON "&Del Track",
                                IDD_DELTRACK,   5,  80,  50,  12,
                                    WS_TABSTOP
END
//----------------------------------------------------------------------
// About box dialog template
//
aboutbox DIALOG discardable 10, 10, 160, 40
STYLE  WS_POPUP | WS_VISIBLE | WS_CAPTION | WS_SYSMENU | DS_CENTER |
       DS_MODALFRAME
CAPTION "About"
BEGIN
    ICON  ID_ICON,                          -1,   5,   5,  10,  10
    LTEXT "AlbumDB - Written for the book Programming Windows \
           CE Copyright 1998 Douglas Boling"
                                            -1,  40,   5, 110,  30
END
```

AlbumDB.h

```
//======================================================================
// Header file
//
// Written for the book Programming Windows CE
// Copyright (C) 1998 Douglas Boling
//======================================================================
// Returns number of elements
#define dim(x) (sizeof(x) / sizeof(x[0]))
```

```
//----------------------------------------------------------------------
// Generic defines and data types
//
struct decodeUINT {                             // Structure associates
    UINT Code;                                  // messages
                                                // with a function.
    LRESULT (*Fxn)(HWND, UINT, WPARAM, LPARAM);
};
struct decodeCMD {                              // Structure associates
    UINT Code;                                  // menu IDs with a
    LRESULT (*Fxn)(HWND, WORD, HWND, WORD);     // function.
};

//----------------------------------------------------------------------
// Generic defines used by application
#define  ID_ICON            1                   // App icon resource ID
#define  IDC_CMDBAR         2                   // Command band ID
#define  ID_MENU            3                   // Main menu resource ID
#define  ID_LISTV           5                   // List view control ID

// Menu item IDs
#define  IDM_DELDB          101                 // File menu
#define  IDM_EXIT           102

#define  IDM_NEW            110                 // Album menu
#define  IDM_EDIT           111
#define  IDM_DELETE         112

#define  IDM_SORTNAME       120                 // Sort IDs must be
#define  IDM_SORTARTIST     121                 // consecutive.
#define  IDM_SORTCATEGORY   122

#define  IDM_ABOUT          150                 // Help menu

// IDs for dialog box controls
#define  IDD_NAME           100                 // Edit album dialog.
#define  IDD_ARTIST         101
#define  IDD_NUMTRACKS      102
#define  IDD_CATEGORY       103
#define  IDD_TRACKS         104
#define  IDD_NEWTRACK       105
#define  IDD_EDITTRACK      106
#define  IDD_DELTRACK       107

#define  IDD_TRACK          200                 // Edit track dialog.
#define  IDD_TIME           201
```

(continued)

Figure 7-5. *continued*

```
//----------------------------------------------------------------------
// Program-specific structures
//
// Structure used by New/Edit Album dlg proc
#define MAX_NAMELEN          64
#define MAX_ARTISTLEN        64
#define MAX_TRACKNAMELEN     512
typedef struct {
    TCHAR szName[MAX_NAMELEN];
    TCHAR szArtist[MAX_ARTISTLEN];
    INT nDateRel;
    SHORT sCategory;
    SHORT sNumTracks;
    INT nTrackDataLen;
    TCHAR szTracks[MAX_TRACKNAMELEN];
} ALBUMINFO, *LPALBUMINFO;

// Structure used by Add/Edit album track
typedef struct {
    TCHAR szTrack[64];
    TCHAR szTime[16];
} TRACKINFO, *LPTRACKINFO;

// Structure used by GetItemData
typedef struct {
    int nItem;
    ALBUMINFO Album;
} LVCACHEDATA, *PLVCACHEDATA;

// Database property identifiers
#define PID_NAME        MAKELONG (CEVT_LPWSTR, 1)
#define PID_ARTIST      MAKELONG (CEVT_LPWSTR, 2)
#define PID_RELDATE     MAKELONG (CEVT_I2, 3)
#define PID_CATEGORY    MAKELONG (CEVT_I2, 4)
#define PID_NUMTRACKS   MAKELONG (CEVT_I2, 5)
#define PID_TRACKS      MAKELONG (CEVT_BLOB, 6)
#define NUM_DB_PROPS    6

//----------------------------------------------------------------------
// Function prototypes
//
int InitApp (HINSTANCE);
HWND InitInstance (HINSTANCE, LPWSTR, int);
int TermInstance (HINSTANCE, int);

HANDLE OpenCreateDB (HWND, int *);
void ReopenDatabase (HWND, INT);
```

```
int GetItemData (int, PLVCACHEDATA);
HWND CreateLV (HWND, RECT *);
void ClearCache (void);

// Window procedures
LRESULT CALLBACK MainWndProc (HWND, UINT, WPARAM, LPARAM);

// Message handlers
LRESULT DoCreateMain (HWND, UINT, WPARAM, LPARAM);
LRESULT DoSizeMain (HWND, UINT, WPARAM, LPARAM);
LRESULT DoCommandMain (HWND, UINT, WPARAM, LPARAM);
LRESULT DoNotifyMain (HWND, UINT, WPARAM, LPARAM);
LRESULT DoDbNotifyMain (HWND, UINT, WPARAM, LPARAM);
LRESULT DoDestroyMain (HWND, UINT, WPARAM, LPARAM);

// Command functions
LPARAM DoMainCommandDelDB (HWND, WORD, HWND, WORD);
LPARAM DoMainCommandExit (HWND, WORD, HWND, WORD);
LPARAM DoMainCommandNew (HWND, WORD, HWND, WORD);
LPARAM DoMainCommandEdit (HWND, WORD, HWND, WORD);
LPARAM DoMainCommandDelete (HWND, WORD, HWND, WORD);
LPARAM DoMainCommandSort (HWND, WORD, HWND, WORD);
LPARAM DoMainCommandAbout (HWND, WORD, HWND, WORD);

// Dialog procedures
BOOL CALLBACK AboutDlgProc (HWND, UINT, WPARAM, LPARAM);
BOOL CALLBACK EditAlbumDlgProc (HWND, UINT, WPARAM, LPARAM);
```

AlbumDB.c

```
//======================================================================
// AlbumDB - A Windows CE database
//
// Written for the book Programming Windows CE
// Copyright (C) 1998 Douglas Boling
//======================================================================
#include <windows.h>                 // For all that Windows stuff
#include <windowsx.h>                // For Window Controls macros
#include <commctrl.h>                // Command bar includes

#include "AlbumDB.h"                 // Program-specific stuff

//----------------------------------------------------------------------
// Global data
//
```

(continued)

Figure 7-5. *continued*

```
const TCHAR szAppName[] = TEXT ("AlbumDB");
HINSTANCE hInst;                      // Program instance handle
HANDLE g_hDB = 0;                     // Handle to album database
CEOID g_oidDB = 0;                    // Handle to album database
INT g_nLastSort = PID_NAME;           // Last sort order used

// These two variables represent a one item cache for
// the list view control.
int g_nLastItem = -1;
LPBYTE g_pLastRecord = 0;

// Message dispatch table for MainWindowProc
const struct decodeUINT MainMessages[] = {
    WM_CREATE, DoCreateMain,
    WM_SIZE, DoSizeMain,
    WM_COMMAND, DoCommandMain,
    WM_NOTIFY, DoNotifyMain,
    WM_DESTROY, DoDestroyMain,
    DB_CEOID_CHANGED, DoDbNotifyMain,
    DB_CEOID_CREATED, DoDbNotifyMain,
    DB_CEOID_RECORD_DELETED, DoDbNotifyMain,
};

// Command message dispatch for MainWindowProc
const struct decodeCMD MainCommandItems[] = {
    IDM_DELDB, DoMainCommandDelDB,
    IDM_EXIT, DoMainCommandExit,
    IDM_NEW, DoMainCommandNew,
    IDM_EDIT, DoMainCommandEdit,
    IDM_DELETE, DoMainCommandDelete,
    IDM_SORTNAME, DoMainCommandSort,
    IDM_SORTARTIST, DoMainCommandSort,
    IDM_SORTCATEGORY, DoMainCommandSort,
    IDM_ABOUT, DoMainCommandAbout,
};
// Album category strings; must be alphabetical.
const TCHAR *pszCategories[] = {TEXT ("Classical"), TEXT ("Country"),
                                TEXT ("New Age"), TEXT ("Rock")};
//======================================================================
// Program entry point
//
int WINAPI WinMain (HINSTANCE hInstance, HINSTANCE hPrevInstance,
                    LPWSTR lpCmdLine, int nCmdShow) {
    HWND hwndMain;
    MSG msg;
    int rc = 0;
```

```
    // Initialize application.
    rc = InitApp (hInstance);
    if (rc) return rc;

    // Initialize this instance.
    hwndMain = InitInstance (hInstance, lpCmdLine, nCmdShow);
    if (hwndMain == 0)
        return 0x10;

    // Application message loop
    while (GetMessage (&msg, NULL, 0, 0)) {
        TranslateMessage (&msg);
        DispatchMessage (&msg);
    }
    // Instance cleanup
    return TermInstance (hInstance, msg.wParam);
}
//----------------------------------------------------------------------
// InitApp - Application initialization
//
int InitApp (HINSTANCE hInstance) {
    WNDCLASS wc;
    INITCOMMONCONTROLSEX icex;

    // Register application main window class.
    wc.style = 0;                             // Window style
    wc.lpfnWndProc = MainWndProc;             // Callback function
    wc.cbClsExtra = 0;                        // Extra class data
    wc.cbWndExtra = 0;                        // Extra window data
    wc.hInstance = hInstance;                 // Owner handle
    wc.hIcon = NULL,                          // Application icon
    wc.hCursor = NULL;                        // Default cursor
    wc.hbrBackground = (HBRUSH) GetStockObject (WHITE_BRUSH);
    wc.lpszMenuName =  NULL;                  // Menu name
    wc.lpszClassName = szAppName;             // Window class name

    if (RegisterClass (&wc) == 0) return 1;

    // Load the command bar common control class.
    icex.dwSize = sizeof (INITCOMMONCONTROLSEX);
    icex.dwICC = ICC_BAR_CLASSES | ICC_TREEVIEW_CLASSES |
                 ICC_LISTVIEW_CLASSES;
    InitCommonControlsEx (&icex);
    return 0;
}
```

(continued)

Figure 7-5. *continued*

```
//----------------------------------------------------------------------
// InitInstance - Instance initialization
//
HWND InitInstance (HINSTANCE hInstance, LPWSTR lpCmdLine, int nCmdShow){
    HWND hWnd;

    // Save program instance handle in global variable.
    hInst = hInstance;

    // Create main window.
    hWnd = CreateWindow (szAppName, TEXT ("AlbumDB"), WS_VISIBLE,
                         CW_USEDEFAULT, CW_USEDEFAULT, CW_USEDEFAULT,
                         CW_USEDEFAULT, NULL, NULL, hInstance, NULL);

    // Return fail code if window not created.
    if (!IsWindow (hWnd)) return 0;

    // Standard show and update calls
    ShowWindow (hWnd, nCmdShow);
    UpdateWindow (hWnd);
    return hWnd;
}
//----------------------------------------------------------------------
// TermInstance - Program cleanup
//
int TermInstance (HINSTANCE hInstance, int nDefRC) {
    // Close the opened database.
    if (g_hDB)
        CloseHandle (g_hDB);
    // Free the last db query if saved.
    ClearCache ();

    return nDefRC;
}
//======================================================================
// Message handling procedures for MainWindow
//----------------------------------------------------------------------
// MainWndProc - Callback function for application window
//
LRESULT CALLBACK MainWndProc (HWND hWnd, UINT wMsg, WPARAM wParam,
                              LPARAM lParam) {
    INT i;
    //
    // Search message list to see if we need to handle this
    // message.  If in list, call procedure.
    //
```

```
    for (i = 0; i < dim(MainMessages); i++) {
        if (wMsg == MainMessages[i].Code)
            return (*MainMessages[i].Fxn)(hWnd, wMsg, wParam, lParam);
    }
    return DefWindowProc (hWnd, wMsg, wParam, lParam);
}
//----------------------------------------------------------------------
// DoCreateMain - Process WM_CREATE message for window.
//
LRESULT DoCreateMain (HWND hWnd, UINT wMsg, WPARAM wParam,
                      LPARAM lParam) {
    HWND hwndCB, hwndChild;
    INT  nHeight, nCnt;
    RECT rect;
    LPCREATESTRUCT lpcs;

    // Convert lParam into pointer to create structure.
    lpcs = (LPCREATESTRUCT) lParam;

    // Create a minimal command bar that only has a menu and an
    // exit button.
    hwndCB = CommandBar_Create (hInst, hWnd, IDC_CMDBAR);
    // Insert the menu.
    CommandBar_InsertMenubar (hwndCB, hInst, ID_MENU, 0);
    // Add exit button to command bar.
    CommandBar_AddAdornments (hwndCB, 0, 0);
    nHeight = CommandBar_Height (hwndCB);

    // Open the album database.  If one doesn't exist, create it.
    g_hDB = OpenCreateDB (hWnd, &nCnt);
    if (g_hDB == INVALID_HANDLE_VALUE) {
        MessageBox (hWnd, TEXT ("Could not open database."), szAppName,
                    MB_OK);
        DestroyWindow (hWnd);
        return 0;
    }
    // Create the list view control in right pane.
    SetRect (&rect, 0, nHeight, lpcs->cx, lpcs->cy - nHeight);
    hwndChild = CreateLV (hWnd, &rect);

    // Destroy frame if window not created.
    if (!IsWindow (hwndChild)) {
        DestroyWindow (hWnd);
        return 0;
    }
```

(continued)

Figure 7-5. *continued*

```
    ListView_SetItemCount (hwndChild, nCnt);
    return 0;
}
//----------------------------------------------------------------------
// DoSizeMain - Process WM_SIZE message for window.
//
LRESULT DoSizeMain (HWND hWnd, UINT wMsg, WPARAM wParam, LPARAM lParam){
    HWND hwndLV;
    RECT rect;

    hwndLV = GetDlgItem (hWnd, ID_LISTV);

    // Adjust the size of the client rect to take into account
    // the command bar height.
    GetClientRect (hWnd, &rect);
    rect.top += CommandBar_Height (GetDlgItem (hWnd, IDC_CMDBAR));

    SetWindowPos (hwndLV, NULL, rect.left, rect.top,
                  (rect.right - rect.left), rect.bottom - rect.top,
                  SWP_NOZORDER);
    return 0;
}
//----------------------------------------------------------------------
// DoCommandMain - Process WM_COMMAND message for window.
//
LRESULT DoCommandMain (HWND hWnd, UINT wMsg, WPARAM wParam,
                       LPARAM lParam) {
    WORD idItem, wNotifyCode;
    HWND hwndCtl;
    INT  i;

    // Parse the parameters.
    idItem = (WORD) LOWORD (wParam);
    wNotifyCode = (WORD) HIWORD (wParam);
    hwndCtl = (HWND) lParam;

    // Call routine to handle control message.
    for (i = 0; i < dim(MainCommandItems); i++) {
        if (idItem == MainCommandItems[i].Code)
            return (*MainCommandItems[i].Fxn)(hWnd, idItem, hwndCtl,
                                              wNotifyCode);
    }
    return 0;
}
//----------------------------------------------------------------------
// DoNotifyMain - Process DB_CEOID_xxx messages for window.
```

```
//
LRESULT DoDbNotifyMain (HWND hWnd, UINT wMsg, WPARAM wParam,
                        LPARAM lParam) {
    switch (wMsg) {
    case DB_CEOID_CHANGED:
        InvalidateRect (GetDlgItem (hWnd, ID_LISTV), NULL, TRUE);
        break;
    case DB_CEOID_CREATED:
        ReopenDatabase (hWnd, -1);
        break;
    case DB_CEOID_RECORD_DELETED:
        ReopenDatabase (hWnd, -1);
        break;
    }
    return 0;
}
//----------------------------------------------------------------------
// DoNotifyMain - Process WM_NOTIFY message for window.
//
LRESULT DoNotifyMain (HWND hWnd, UINT wMsg, WPARAM wParam,
                      LPARAM lParam) {
    int idItem, i;
    LPNMHDR pnmh;
    LPNMLISTVIEW pnmlv;
    NMLVDISPINFO *pLVdi;
    LVCACHEDATA data;
    HWND hwndLV;

    // Parse the parameters.
    idItem = (int) wParam;
    pnmh = (LPNMHDR)lParam;
    hwndLV = pnmh->hwndFrom;

    if (idItem == ID_LISTV) {
        pnmlv = (LPNMLISTVIEW)lParam;

        switch (pnmh->code) {
        case LVN_GETDISPINFO:
            pLVdi = (NMLVDISPINFO *)lParam;

            // Get a pointer to the data either from the cache
            // or from the actual database.
            GetItemData (pLVdi->item.iItem, &data);

            if (pLVdi->item.mask & LVIF_IMAGE)
                pLVdi->item.iImage = 0;
```

(continued)

Figure 7-5. *continued*

```
            if (pLVdi->item.mask & LVIF_PARAM)
                pLVdi->item.lParam = 0;

            if (pLVdi->item.mask & LVIF_STATE)
                pLVdi->item.state = 0;

            if (pLVdi->item.mask & LVIF_TEXT) {
                switch (pLVdi->item.iSubItem) {
                case 0:
                    lstrcpy (pLVdi->item.pszText, data.Album.szName);
                    break;
                case 1:
                    lstrcpy (pLVdi->item.pszText, data.Album.szArtist);
                    break;
                case 2:
                    lstrcpy (pLVdi->item.pszText,
                             pszCategories[data.Album.sCategory]);
                    break;
                }
            }
            break;

        // Ignore cache hinting for db example.
        case LVN_COLUMNCLICK:
            i = ((NM_LISTVIEW *)lParam)->iSubItem + IDM_SORTNAME;
            PostMessage (hWnd, WM_COMMAND, MAKELPARAM (i, 0), 0);
            break;

        // Ignore cache hinting for db example.
        case NM_DBLCLK:
            PostMessage (hWnd, WM_COMMAND, MAKELPARAM (IDM_EDIT, 0), 0);
            break;

        // Ignore cache hinting for db example.
        case LVN_ODCACHEHINT:
            break;

        case LVN_ODFINDITEM:
            // We should do a reverse look up here to see if
            // an item exists for the text passed.
            return -1;
        }
    }
    return 0;
}
```

```
//----------------------------------------------------------------------
// DoDestroyMain - Process WM_DESTROY message for window.
//
LRESULT DoDestroyMain (HWND hWnd, UINT wMsg, WPARAM wParam,
                       LPARAM lParam) {
    PostQuitMessage (0);
    return 0;
}
//======================================================================
// Command handler routines
//----------------------------------------------------------------------
// DoMainCommandDelDB - Process Program Delete command.
//
LPARAM DoMainCommandDelDB (HWND hWnd, WORD idItem, HWND hwndCtl,
                           WORD wNotifyCode) {
    int i, rc;

    i = MessageBox (hWnd, TEXT ("Delete the entire database?"),
                    TEXT ("Delete"), MB_YESNO);
    if (i != IDYES)
        return 0;
    if (g_oidDB) {
        CloseHandle (g_hDB);
        rc = CeDeleteDatabase (g_oidDB);
        if (rc == 0) {
            TCHAR szDbg[128];
            rc = GetLastError();
            wsprintf (szDbg, TEXT ("Couldn\'t delete db. rc=%d"), rc);
            MessageBox (hWnd, szDbg, szAppName, MB_OK);
            g_hDB = CeOpenDatabase (&g_oidDB, NULL, g_nLastSort,
                                    0, hWnd);
            return 0;
        }
        g_hDB = 0;
        g_oidDB = 0;
    }
    ListView_SetItemCount (GetDlgItem (hWnd, ID_LISTV), 0);
    return 0;
}
//----------------------------------------------------------------------
// DoMainCommandExit - Process Program Exit command.
//
LPARAM DoMainCommandExit (HWND hWnd, WORD idItem, HWND hwndCtl,
                          WORD wNotifyCode) {
```

(continued)

Figure 7-5. *continued*

```
    SendMessage (hWnd, WM_CLOSE, 0, 0);
    return 0;
}
//----------------------------------------------------------------------
// DoMainCommandNew - Process Program New command.
//
LPARAM DoMainCommandNew (HWND hWnd, WORD idItem, HWND hwndCtl,
                         WORD wNotifyCode) {
    PCEPROPVAL pcepv;
    INT i, rc;
    CEOID oid;
    HWND hwndLV = GetDlgItem (hWnd, ID_LISTV);

    // Display the new/edit dialog.
    pcepv = 0;
    rc = DialogBoxParam (hInst, TEXT ("EditAlbumDlg"), hWnd,
                         EditAlbumDlgProc, (LPARAM)&pcepv);
    if (rc == 0)
        return 0;

    // Write the record.
    oid = CeWriteRecordProps(g_hDB, 0, NUM_DB_PROPS, pcepv);
    if (!oid) {
        TCHAR szText[64];
        rc = GetLastError ();
        wsprintf (szText, TEXT ("Write Rec fail. Error %d (%x)"),
                  rc, rc);
        MessageBox (hWnd, szText, TEXT ("Error"), MB_OK);
    }
    ClearCache ();                               // Clear the lv cache.

    i = ListView_GetItemCount (hwndLV) + 1;      // Increment list view
                                                 // count.
    ListView_SetItemCount (hwndLV, i);
    InvalidateRect (hwndLV, NULL, TRUE);         // Force list view
                                                 // redraw.
    return 0;
}
//----------------------------------------------------------------------
// DoMainCommandEdit - Process Program Edit command.
//
LPARAM DoMainCommandEdit (HWND hWnd, WORD idItem, HWND hwndCtl,
                          WORD wNotifyCode) {
    PCEPROPVAL pcepv = 0;
    INT nSel, rc;
    WORD wProps = 0;
```

```
DWORD dwRecSize, dwIndex;
CEOID oid;
HWND hwndLV = GetDlgItem (hWnd, ID_LISTV);

nSel = ListView_GetSelectionMark (hwndLV);
if (nSel == -1)
    return 0;

// Seek to the necessary record.
oid = CeSeekDatabase (g_hDB, CEDB_SEEK_BEGINNING, nSel, &dwIndex);
if (oid == 0) {
    TCHAR szTxt[64];
    INT rc = GetLastError();
    wsprintf (szTxt, TEXT ("Db item not found. rc = %d (%x)"),
              rc, rc);
    MessageBox (NULL, szTxt, TEXT ("err"), MB_OK);
    return 0;
}
// Read all properties for the record.  Have the system
// allocate the buffer containing the data.
oid = CeReadRecordProps (g_hDB, CEDB_ALLOWREALLOC, &wProps, NULL,
                         &(LPBYTE)pcepv, &dwRecSize);
if (oid == 0) {
    TCHAR szTxt[64];
    INT rc = GetLastError();
    wsprintf (szTxt, TEXT ("Db item not read. rc = %d (%x)"),
              rc, rc);
    MessageBox (NULL, szTxt, TEXT ("err"), MB_OK);
    return 0;
}
// Display the edit dialog.
rc = DialogBoxParam (hInst, TEXT ("EditAlbumDlg"), hWnd,
                     EditAlbumDlgProc, (LPARAM)&pcepv);
if (rc == 0)
    return 0;

// Write the record.
oid = CeWriteRecordProps(g_hDB, oid, NUM_DB_PROPS, pcepv);
if (!oid) {
    TCHAR szText[64];
    rc = GetLastError ();
    wsprintf (szText, TEXT ("Write Rec fail. Error %d (%x)"),
              rc, rc);
    MessageBox (hWnd, szText, TEXT ("Error"), MB_OK);
}
```

(continued)

Figure 7-5. *continued*

```
    LocalFree ((LPBYTE)pcepv);
    ClearCache ();                              // Clear the lv cache.

    InvalidateRect (hwndLV, NULL, TRUE);        // Force list view
                                                // redraw.
    return 0;
}
//----------------------------------------------------------------------
// DoMainCommandDelete - Process Program Delete command.
//
LPARAM DoMainCommandDelete (HWND hWnd, WORD idItem, HWND hwndCtl,
                            WORD wNotifyCode) {
    HWND hwndLV;
    TCHAR szText[64];
    DWORD dwIndex;
    int i;
    CEOID oid;
    int nSel;

    hwndLV = GetDlgItem (hWnd, ID_LISTV);
    nSel = ListView_GetSelectionMark (hwndLV);
    if (nSel != -1) {

        wsprintf (szText, TEXT ("Delete this item?"));
        i = MessageBox (hWnd, szText, TEXT ("Delete"), MB_YESNO);
        if (i != IDYES)
            return 0;

        // Seek to the necessary record.
        oid = CeSeekDatabase (g_hDB, CEDB_SEEK_BEGINNING, nSel, &dwIndex);
        CeDeleteRecord (g_hDB, oid);

        // Reduce the list view count by one and force redraw.
        i = ListView_GetItemCount (hwndLV) - 1;
        ListView_SetItemCount (hwndLV, i);
        ClearCache ();                          // Clear the lv cache.
        InvalidateRect (hwndLV, NULL, TRUE);
    }
    return 0;
}
//----------------------------------------------------------------------
// DoMainCommandSort - Process the Sort commands.
//
LPARAM DoMainCommandSort(HWND hWnd, WORD idItem, HWND hwndCtl,
                         WORD wNotifyCode) {
    int nSort;
```

```
    switch (idItem) {
    case IDM_SORTNAME:
        nSort = PID_NAME;
        break;
    case IDM_SORTARTIST:
        nSort = PID_ARTIST;
        break;
    case IDM_SORTCATEGORY:
        nSort = PID_CATEGORY;
        break;
    }
    if (nSort == g_nLastSort)
        return 0;

    ReopenDatabase (hWnd, nSort);      // Close and reopen the database.
    return 0;
}
//----------------------------------------------------------------------
// DoMainCommandAbout - Process the Help | About menu command.
//
LPARAM DoMainCommandAbout(HWND hWnd, WORD idItem, HWND hwndCtl,
                          WORD wNotifyCode) {
    // Use DialogBox to create modal dialog.
    DialogBox (hInst, TEXT ("aboutbox"), hWnd, AboutDlgProc);
    return 0;
}
//----------------------------------------------------------------------
// CreateLV - Creates the list view control
//
HWND CreateLV (HWND hWnd, RECT *prect) {
    HWND hwndLV;
    LVCOLUMN lvc;

    // Create album list window.
    hwndLV = CreateWindowEx (0, WC_LISTVIEW, TEXT (""),
                          WS_VISIBLE | WS_CHILD | WS_VSCROLL |
                          LVS_OWNERDATA | WS_BORDER | LVS_REPORT,
                          prect->left, prect->top,
                          prect->right - prect->left,
                          prect->bottom - prect->top,
                          hWnd, (HMENU)ID_LISTV,
                          hInst, NULL);

    // Add columns.
    if (hwndLV) {
        lvc.mask = LVCF_TEXT | LVCF_WIDTH | LVCF_FMT | LVCF_SUBITEM;
```

(continued)

Figure 7-5. *continued*

```
        lvc.fmt = LVCFMT_LEFT;
        lvc.cx = 150;
        lvc.pszText = TEXT ("Name");
        lvc.iSubItem = 0;
        SendMessage (hwndLV, LVM_INSERTCOLUMN, 0, (LPARAM)&lvc);

        lvc.mask |= LVCF_SUBITEM;
        lvc.pszText = TEXT ("Artist");
        lvc.cx = 100;
        lvc.iSubItem = 1;
        SendMessage (hwndLV, LVM_INSERTCOLUMN, 1, (LPARAM)&lvc);

        lvc.mask |= LVCF_SUBITEM;
        lvc.pszText = TEXT ("Category");
        lvc.cx = 100;
        lvc.iSubItem = 2;
        SendMessage (hwndLV, LVM_INSERTCOLUMN, 2, (LPARAM)&lvc);
    }

    return hwndLV;
}
//----------------------------------------------------------------------
// OpenCreateDB - Open database, create if necessary.
//
HANDLE OpenCreateDB (HWND hWnd, int *pnRecords) {
    INT i, rc;
    CEOIDINFO oidinfo;
    SORTORDERSPEC sos[4];

    g_oidDB = 0;
    g_hDB = CeOpenDatabase (&g_oidDB, TEXT ("\\Albums"),
                            g_nLastSort, 0, hWnd);
    if (g_hDB == INVALID_HANDLE_VALUE) {
        rc = GetLastError();
        if (rc == ERROR_FILE_NOT_FOUND) {
            i = 0;
            sos[i].propid = PID_NAME;
            sos[i++].dwFlags = 0;

            sos[i].propid = PID_ARTIST;
            sos[i++].dwFlags = 0;

            sos[i].propid = PID_CATEGORY;
            sos[i++].dwFlags = 0;
```

```
            g_oidDB = CeCreateDatabase (TEXT ("\\Albums"), 0, 3,
                                        sos);
            if (g_oidDB == 0) {
                TCHAR szErr[128];
                wsprintf (szErr, TEXT ("Database create failed. \
                          rc %d"), GetLastError());
                MessageBox (hWnd, szErr, szAppName, MB_OK);
                return 0;
            }
            g_hDB = CeOpenDatabase(&g_oidDB,NULL, g_nLastSort, 0, hWnd);
        }
    }
    CeOidGetInfo (g_oidDB, &oidinfo);
    *pnRecords = oidinfo.infDatabase.wNumRecords;
    return g_hDB;
}
//----------------------------------------------------------------------
// ClearCache - Clears the one item cache for the list view control
//
void ClearCache (void) {

    if (g_pLastRecord)
        LocalFree (g_pLastRecord);
    g_pLastRecord = 0;
    g_nLastItem = -1;
    return;
}
//----------------------------------------------------------------------
// ReopenDatabase - Closes and reopens the database
//
void ReopenDatabase (HWND hWnd, INT nNewSort) {
    INT nCnt;

    if (nNewSort != -1)
        g_nLastSort = nNewSort;

    if (g_hDB)
        CloseHandle (g_hDB);
    ClearCache ();                          // Clear the lv cache.

    g_hDB = OpenCreateDB (hWnd, &nCnt);

    ListView_SetItemCount (GetDlgItem (hWnd, ID_LISTV), nCnt);
    InvalidateRect (GetDlgItem (hWnd, ID_LISTV), NULL, 0);
    return;
}
```

(continued)

Figure 7-5. *continued*

```
//----------------------------------------------------------------------
// Get the album data from the database for the requested lv item.
//
int GetItemData (int nItem, PLVCACHEDATA pcd) {
    static WORD wProps;
    DWORD dwIndex;
    CEOID oid;
    PCEPROPVAL pRecord = NULL;
    DWORD dwRecSize;
    int i;

    // See if the item requested was the previous one.  If so,
    // just use the old data.
    if ((nItem == g_nLastItem) && (g_pLastRecord))
        pRecord = (PCEPROPVAL)g_pLastRecord;
    else {
        // Seek to the necessary record.
        oid = CeSeekDatabase (g_hDB, CEDB_SEEK_BEGINNING, nItem, &dwIndex);
        if (oid == 0) {
            TCHAR szTxt[64];
            INT rc = GetLastError();
            wsprintf (szTxt, TEXT ("Db item not found. rc = %d (%x)"),
                      rc, rc);
            MessageBox (NULL, szTxt, TEXT ("err"), MB_OK);
            return 0;
        }
        // Read all properties for the record.  Have the system
        // allocate the buffer containing the data.
        oid = CeReadRecordProps (g_hDB, CEDB_ALLOWREALLOC, &wProps, NULL,
                                 &(LPBYTE)pRecord, &dwRecSize);
        if (oid == 0) {
            TCHAR szTxt[64];
            INT rc = GetLastError();
            wsprintf (szTxt, TEXT ("Db item not read. rc = %d (%x)"),
                      rc, rc);
            MessageBox (NULL, szTxt, TEXT ("err"), MB_OK);
            return 0;
        }
        // Free old record and save the newly read one.
        if (g_pLastRecord)
            LocalFree (g_pLastRecord);
        g_nLastItem = nItem;
        g_pLastRecord = (LPBYTE)pRecord;

    }
```

```
    // Copy the data from the record to the album structure.
    for (i = 0; i < wProps; i++) {
        switch (pRecord->propid) {
        case PID_NAME:
            lstrcpy (pcd->Album.szName, pRecord->val.lpwstr);
            break;
        case PID_ARTIST:
            lstrcpy (pcd->Album.szArtist, pRecord->val.lpwstr);
            break;
        case PID_CATEGORY:
            pcd->Album.sCategory = pRecord->val.iVal;
            break;
        case PID_NUMTRACKS:
            pcd->Album.sNumTracks = pRecord->val.iVal;
            break;
        }
        pRecord++;
    }
    return 1;
}
//----------------------------------------------------------------------
// InsertLV - Add an item to the list view control.
//
INT InsertLV (HWND hWnd, INT nItem, LPTSTR pszName, LPTSTR pszType,
              INT nSize) {
    LVITEM lvi;
    HWND hwndLV = GetDlgItem (hWnd, ID_LISTV);

    lvi.mask = LVIF_TEXT | LVIF_IMAGE | LVIF_PARAM;
    lvi.iItem = nItem;
    lvi.iSubItem = 0;
    lvi.pszText = pszName;
    lvi.iImage = 0;
    lvi.lParam = nItem;
    SendMessage (hwndLV, LVM_INSERTITEM, 0, (LPARAM)&lvi);

    lvi.mask = LVIF_TEXT;
    lvi.iItem = nItem;
    lvi.iSubItem = 1;
    lvi.pszText = pszType;
    SendMessage (hwndLV, LVM_SETITEM, 0, (LPARAM)&lvi);

    return 0;
}
//----------------------------------------------------------------------
```

(continued)

Figure 7-5. *continued*

```
// ValidateTime - Trival error checking of time field
//
BOOL ValidateTime (TCHAR *pStr) {
    BOOL fSep = FALSE;
    TCHAR *pPtr;

    pPtr = pStr;
    // See if field contains only numbers and up to one colon.
    while (*pPtr) {
        if (*pPtr == TEXT (':')) {
            if (fSep)
                return FALSE;
            fSep = TRUE;
        } else if ((*pPtr < TEXT ('0')) || (*pPtr > TEXT ('9')))
            return FALSE;
        pPtr++;
    }
    // Reject empty field.
    if (pPtr > pStr)
        return TRUE;
    return FALSE;
}
//======================================================================
// EditTrack dialog procedure
//
BOOL CALLBACK EditTrackDlgProc (HWND hWnd, UINT wMsg, WPARAM wParam,
                                LPARAM lParam) {
    static LPTRACKINFO lpti;

    switch (wMsg) {
        case WM_INITDIALOG:
            lpti = (LPTRACKINFO)lParam;
            SendDlgItemMessage (hWnd, IDD_TRACK, EM_SETLIMITTEXT,
                                sizeof (lpti->szTrack), 0);
            SendDlgItemMessage (hWnd, IDD_TIME, EM_SETLIMITTEXT,
                                sizeof (lpti->szTime), 0);
            // See if new album or edit of old one.
            if (lstrlen (lpti->szTrack) == 0) {
                SetWindowText (hWnd, TEXT ("New Track"));
            } else {
                SetDlgItemText (hWnd, IDD_TRACK, lpti->szTrack);
                SetDlgItemText (hWnd, IDD_TIME, lpti->szTime);
            }
            return TRUE;
```

```
        case WM_COMMAND:
            switch (LOWORD (wParam)) {
                case IDOK:
                    Edit_GetText (GetDlgItem (hWnd, IDD_TRACK),
                                  lpti->szTrack, sizeof (lpti->szTrack));
                    Edit_GetText (GetDlgItem (hWnd, IDD_TIME),
                                   lpti->szTime, sizeof (lpti->szTime));
                    if (ValidateTime (lpti->szTime))
                        EndDialog (hWnd, 1);
                    else
                        MessageBox (hWnd, TEXT ("Track time must \
be entered in mm:ss format"),
                                    TEXT ("Error"), MB_OK);
                    return TRUE;
                case IDCANCEL:
                    EndDialog (hWnd, 0);
                    return TRUE;
            }
        break;
    }
    return FALSE;
}
//======================================================================
// EditAlbum dialog procedure
//
BOOL CALLBACK EditAlbumDlgProc (HWND hWnd, UINT wMsg, WPARAM wParam,
                                LPARAM lParam) {
    static PCEPROPVAL *ppRecord;
    static int nTracks;
    PCEPROPVAL pRecord, pRecPtr;
    TCHAR *pPtr, szTmp[128];
    HWND hwndTList, hwndCombo;
    TRACKINFO ti;
    BOOL fEnable;
    INT i, nLen, rc;

    switch (wMsg) {
        case WM_INITDIALOG:
            ppRecord = (PCEPROPVAL *)lParam;
            pRecord = *ppRecord;

            hwndCombo = GetDlgItem (hWnd, IDD_CATEGORY);
            hwndTList = GetDlgItem (hWnd, IDD_TRACKS);

            Edit_LimitText (GetDlgItem (hWnd, IDD_NAME), MAX_NAMELEN);
```

(continued)

Figure 7-5. *continued*

```
        Edit_LimitText (GetDlgItem (hWnd, IDD_ARTIST),
                        MAX_ARTISTLEN);
        // Set tabstops on track list box.
        i = 110;
        ListBox_SetTabStops (hwndTList, 1, &i);
        // Initialize category combo box.
        for (i = 0; i < dim(pszCategories); i++)
            ComboBox_AddString (hwndCombo, pszCategories[i]);
        ComboBox_SetCurSel (hwndCombo, 3);
        nTracks = 0;

        // See if new album or edit of old one.
        if (pRecord == 0) {
            SetWindowText (hWnd, TEXT ("New Album"));
        } else {
            // Copy the data from the record to album structure.
            for (i = 0; i < NUM_DB_PROPS; i++) {
                switch (pRecord->propid) {
                case PID_NAME:
                    SetDlgItemText (hWnd, IDD_NAME,
                                    pRecord->val.lpwstr);
                    break;
                case PID_ARTIST:
                    SetDlgItemText (hWnd, IDD_ARTIST,
                                    pRecord->val.lpwstr);
                    break;
                case PID_CATEGORY:
                    ComboBox_SetCurSel (hwndCombo,
                                        pRecord->val.iVal);
                    break;
                case PID_TRACKS:
                    pPtr = (TCHAR *)pRecord->val.blob.lpb;
                    for (i = 0; *pPtr; i++){
                      ListBox_InsertString (hwndTList,i,pPtr);
                        pPtr += lstrlen (pPtr) + 1;
                        nTracks++;
                    }
                    break;
                }
                pRecord++;
            }
        }
        // Select first track or disable buttons if no tracks.
        if (nTracks)
            ListBox_SetCurSel (GetDlgItem (hWnd, IDD_TRACKS), 3);
```

```
        else {
            EnableWindow (GetDlgItem (hWnd, IDD_DELTRACK),
                          FALSE);
            EnableWindow (GetDlgItem (hWnd, IDD_EDITTRACK),
                          FALSE);
        }
        return TRUE;

    case WM_COMMAND:
        hwndTList = GetDlgItem (hWnd, IDD_TRACKS);
        hwndCombo = GetDlgItem (hWnd, IDD_CATEGORY);
        pRecord = *ppRecord;
        switch (LOWORD (wParam)) {
            case IDD_TRACKS:
                switch (HIWORD (wParam)) {
                case LBN_DBLCLK:
                    PostMessage (hWnd, WM_COMMAND,
                                 MAKELONG(IDD_EDITTRACK, 0), 0);
                    break;
                case LBN_SELCHANGE:
                    i = ListBox_GetCurSel (hwndTList);
                    if (i == LB_ERR)
                        fEnable = FALSE;
                    else
                        fEnable = TRUE;
                    EnableWindow (GetDlgItem (hWnd,
                                  IDD_DELTRACK), fEnable);
                    EnableWindow (GetDlgItem (hWnd,
                                  IDD_EDITTRACK), fEnable);
                    break;
                }
                return TRUE;

            case IDD_NEWTRACK:
                memset (&ti, 0, sizeof (ti));
                rc = DialogBoxParam (hInst,
                    TEXT ("EditTrackDlg"), hWnd,
                    EditTrackDlgProc, (LPARAM)&ti);
                if (rc) {
                    wsprintf (szTmp, TEXT ("%s\t%s"),
                              ti.szTrack, ti.szTime);
                    i = ListBox_GetCurSel (hwndTList);
                    if (i != LB_ERR)
                        i++;
                    i = ListBox_InsertString (hwndTList, i,
                                              szTmp);
```

(continued)

Figure 7-5. *continued*

```
                ListBox_SetCurSel (hwndTList, i);
            }
            return TRUE;

        case IDD_EDITTRACK:
            i = ListBox_GetCurSel (hwndTList);
            if (i != LB_ERR) {
                ListBox_GetText (hwndTList, i, szTmp);
                pPtr = szTmp;
                while ((*pPtr != TEXT ('\t')) &&
                       (*pPtr != TEXT ('\0')))
                    pPtr++;
                if (*pPtr == TEXT ('\t'))
                    *pPtr++ = TEXT ('\0');

                lstrcpy (ti.szTime, pPtr);
                lstrcpy (ti.szTrack, szTmp);
                rc = DialogBoxParam (hInst,
                                     TEXT ("EditTrackDlg"),
                                     hWnd, EditTrackDlgProc,
                                     (LPARAM)&ti);
                if (rc) {
                    wsprintf (szTmp, TEXT ("%s\t%s"),
                              ti.szTrack, ti.szTime);
                    i = ListBox_GetCurSel (hwndTList);
                    ListBox_DeleteString (hwndTList, i);
                    ListBox_InsertString (hwndTList, i,
                                          szTmp);
                    ListBox_SetCurSel (hwndTList, i);
                }
            }
            return TRUE;

        case IDD_DELTRACK:
            // Grab the current selection and remove
            // it from list box.
            i = ListBox_GetCurSel (hwndTList);
            if (i != LB_ERR) {
                rc = MessageBox (hWnd,
                                 TEXT ("Delete this item?"),
                                 TEXT ("Track"), MB_YESNO);
                if (rc == IDYES) {
                    i=ListBox_DeleteString (hwndTList,i);
                    if (i > 0)
                        i--;
```

```
                ListBox_SetCurSel (hwndTList, i);
            }
        }
        return TRUE;

    case IDOK:
        // Be lazy and assume worst case size values.
        nLen = sizeof (CEPROPVAL) * NUM_DB_PROPS +
               MAX_NAMELEN + MAX_ARTISTLEN +
               MAX_TRACKNAMELEN;
        // See if prev record, alloc if not.
        if (pRecord) {
            // Resize record if necessary.
            if (nLen > (int)LocalSize (pRecord))
                pRecPtr =
                   (PCEPROPVAL)LocalReAlloc (pRecord,
                   nLen, LMEM_MOVEABLE);
            else
                pRecPtr = pRecord;
        } else
            pRecPtr = LocalAlloc (LMEM_FIXED, nLen);
        if (!pRecPtr)
            return 0;
        // Copy the data from the controls to a
        // marshaled data block with the structure
        // at the front and the data in the back.
        pRecord = pRecPtr;
        nTracks = ListBox_GetCount (hwndTList);
        pPtr = (TCHAR *)((LPBYTE)pRecPtr +
                 (sizeof (CEPROPVAL) * NUM_DB_PROPS));
        // Zero structure to start over.
        memset (pRecPtr, 0, LocalSize (pRecPtr));

        pRecPtr->propid = PID_NAME;
        pRecPtr->val.lpwstr = pPtr;
        GetDlgItemText (hWnd, IDD_NAME, pPtr,
                        MAX_NAMELEN);
        pPtr += lstrlen (pPtr) + 1;
        pRecPtr++;

        pRecPtr->propid = PID_ARTIST;
        pRecPtr->val.lpwstr = pPtr;
        GetDlgItemText (hWnd, IDD_ARTIST, pPtr,
                        MAX_ARTISTLEN);
        pPtr += lstrlen (pPtr) + 1;
        pRecPtr++;
```

(continued)

Figure 7-5. *continued*

```
                    pRecPtr->propid = PID_RELDATE;
                    pRecPtr->val.iVal = 0;
                    pRecPtr++;

                    pRecPtr->propid = PID_CATEGORY;
                    pRecPtr->val.iVal =
                                    ComboBox_GetCurSel (hwndCombo);
                    pRecPtr++;

                    pRecPtr->propid = PID_NUMTRACKS;
                    pRecPtr->val.iVal = nTracks;
                    pRecPtr++;

                    pRecPtr->propid = PID_TRACKS;
                    pRecPtr->val.blob.lpb = (LPBYTE)pPtr;

                    // Get the track titles from the list box.
                    rc = MAX_TRACKNAMELEN;
                    for (i = 0; i < nTracks; i++) {
                        // Make sure we have the room in the buff.
                        rc -= ListBox_GetTextLen(hwndTList, i);
                        if (rc)
                            ListBox_GetText (hwndTList, i, pPtr);
                        else {
                            nTracks = i;
                            break;
                        }
                        pPtr += lstrlen (pPtr) + 1;
                    }
                    *pPtr++ = TEXT ('\0');
                    pRecPtr->val.blob.dwCount =
                              (LPBYTE)pPtr - pRecPtr->val.blob.lpb;
                    *ppRecord = pRecord;
                    EndDialog (hWnd, 1);
                    return TRUE;

                case IDCANCEL:
                    EndDialog (hWnd, 0);
                    return TRUE;
            }
        break;
    }
    return FALSE;
}
```

```
//======================================================================
// About dialog procedure
//
BOOL CALLBACK AboutDlgProc (HWND hWnd, UINT wMsg, WPARAM wParam,
                           LPARAM lParam) {
    switch (wMsg) {
        case WM_COMMAND:
            switch (LOWORD (wParam)) {
                case IDOK:
                case IDCANCEL:
                    EndDialog (hWnd, 0);
                    return TRUE;
            }
        break;
    }
    return FALSE;
}
```

The program uses a virtual list view control to display the records in the database. As I explained in Chapter 5, virtual list views don't store any data internally. Instead, the control makes calls back to the owning window using notification messages to query the information for each item in the list view control. The WM_NOTIFY handler *OnNotifyMain* calls *GetItemData* to query the database in response to the list view control sending LVN_GETDISPINFO notifications. The *GetItemInfo* function first seeks the record to read then reads all the properties of a database record with one call to *CeReadRecordProps*. Since the list view control typically uses the LVN_GETDISPINFO notification multiple times for one item, *GetItemInfo* saves the data from the last record read. If the next read is of the same record, the program uses the cached data instead of rereading the database.

As I've explained before, you can change the way you sort by simply closing the database and reopening it in one of the other sort modes. The list view control is then invalidated, causing it to again request the data for each record being displayed. With a new sort order defined, the seek that happens with each database record read automatically sorts the data by the sort order defined when the database was opened.

AlbumDB doesn't use the new *Ex* database functions provided by Windows CE 2.1 based systems. This allows the program to run under earlier versions of the operating system. To modify the example to use separate database volumes, only minor changes would be necessary. First a global variable *g_guidDB* of type CEOID would be added. In the *DoCreateMain* routine, code such as the following, which mounts the volume, would be added.

```
if (!CeMountDBVol (&g_guidDB, TEXT ("\\Albums.cdb"), OPEN_ALWAYS)) {
    wsprintf (szErr, TEXT ("Database mount failed. rc %d"),
              GetLastError());
    MessageBox (NULL, szErr, szAppName, MB_OK);
}
```

The following code would be added to the *OnDestroyMain* routine to unmount the volume:

```
if (!CHECK_INVALIDGUID (&g_guidDB))
    CeUnmountDBVol (&g_guidDB);
```

Finally, the *OpenCreateDB* routine would be replaced by this version:

```
HANDLE OpenCreateDB (HWND hWnd, int *pnRecords) {
    INT i, rc;
    CEOIDINFO oidinfo;
    CEDBASEINFO dbi;
    TCHAR szErr[128];
    CENOTIFYREQUEST cenr;

    g_oidDB = 0;
    cenr.dwSize = sizeof (cenr);
    cenr.hWnd = hWnd;
    cenr.dwFlags = 0;                    // Use old style notifications.
    cenr.hHeap = 0;
    cenr.dwParam = 0;

    g_hDB = CeOpenDatabaseEx (&g_guidDB, &g_oidDB, TEXT ("\\Albums"),
                              g_nLastSort, 0, &cenr);
    if (g_hDB == INVALID_HANDLE_VALUE) {
        rc = GetLastError();
        if (rc == ERROR_FILE_NOT_FOUND) {
            i = 0;
            dbi.rgSortSpecs[i].propid = PID_NAME;
            dbi.rgSortSpecs[i++].dwFlags = 0;

            dbi.rgSortSpecs[i].propid = PID_ARTIST;
            dbi.rgSortSpecs[i++].dwFlags = 0;

            dbi.rgSortSpecs[i].propid = PID_CATEGORY;
            dbi.rgSortSpecs[i++].dwFlags = 0;

            dbi.dwFlags = CEDB_VALIDCREATE;
            lstrcpy (dbi.szDbaseName, TEXT ("\\Albums"));
            dbi.dwDbaseType = 0;
            dbi.wNumSortOrder = 3;

            g_oidDB = CeCreateDatabaseEx (&g_guidDB, &dbi);
```

```
            if (g_oidDB == 0) {
                wsprintf (szErr,
                          TEXT ("Database create failed. rc %d"),
                          GetLastError());
                MessageBox (hWnd, szErr, szAppName, MB_OK);
                return 0;
            }
            g_hDB = CeOpenDatabaseEx (&g_guidDB, &g_oidDB, NULL,
                                      g_nLastSort, 0,  &cenr);
        }
    } else if (g_hDB == 0){
        wsprintf (szErr,
                  TEXT ("Database open failed. rc %X  ext err:%d"),
                  g_hDB, GetLastError());
        MessageBox (hWnd, szErr, szAppName, MB_OK);
    }
    CeOidGetInfoEx (&g_guidDB, g_oidDB, &oidinfo);
    *pnRecords = oidinfo.infDatabase.wNumRecords;
    return g_hDB;
}
```

THE REGISTRY

The registry is a system database used to store configuration information in applications and in Windows itself. The registry as defined by Windows CE is similar but not identical in function and format to the registries under Windows 98 and Windows NT. In other words, for an application, most of the same registry access functions exist, but the layout of the Windows CE registry doesn't exactly follow either Windows 98 or Windows NT.

As in all versions of Windows, the registry is made up of keys and values. Keys can contain keys or values or both. Values contain data in one of a number of predefined formats. Since keys can contain keys, the registry is distinctly hierarchical. The highest level keys, the root keys, are specified by their predefined numeric constants. Keys below the root keys and values are identified by their text name. Multiple levels of keys can be specified in one text string by separating the keys with a backslash (\).

To query or modify a value, the key containing the value must first be opened, the value queried and or written, then the key closed. Keys and values can also be enumerated so that an application can determine what a specific key contains. Data in the registry can be stored in a number of different predefined data types. Among the available data types are strings, 32-bit numbers, and free form binary data.

Registry Organization

The Windows CE registry supports three of the high-level, root keys seen on other Windows platforms, HKEY_LOCAL_MACHINE, HKEY_CURRENT_USER, and HKEY_CLASSES_ROOT. As with other Windows platforms, Windows CE uses the HKEY_LOCAL_MACHINE key to store hardware and driver configuration data, the HKEY_CURRENT_USER to store user-specific configuration data, and the HKEY_CLASSES_ROOT key to store file type matching and OLE configuration data.

As a practical matter, the registry is used by applications and drivers to store state information that needs to be saved across invocations. Applications typically store their current state when they are requested to close and then restore this state when they are launched again. The traditional location for storing data in the registry by an application is obtained by means of the following structure:

{ROOT_KEY}\Software\{Company Name}\{Company Product}

In this template, the ROOT_KEY is either HKEY_LOCAL_MACHINE for machine-specific data such as what optional components of an application may be installed on the machine or HKEY_CURRENT_USER for user-specific information, such as the list of the user's last-opened files. Under the Software key, the company's name that wrote the application is used followed by the name of the specific application. For example, Microsoft saves the configuration information for Pocket Word under the key

HKEY_LOCAL_MACHINE\Software\Microsoft\Pocket Word

While this hierarchy is great for segregating registry values from different applications from one another, it's best not to create too deep a set of keys. Because of the way the registry is designed, it takes less memory to store a value than it does a key. Because of this, you should design you registry storage so that it uses fewer keys and more values. To optimize even further, it's more efficient to store more information in one value than to have the same information stored across a number of values.

The window in Figure 7-6 shows the hierarchy of keys used to store data for Pocket Word. The left pane shows the hierarchy of keys down to the Settings key under the Pocket Word key. In the Settings key, three values are stored: Wrap To Window, Vertical Scrollbar Visibility, and Horizontal Scrollbar Visibility. In this case, these values are DWORDs, but they could have been strings or other data types.

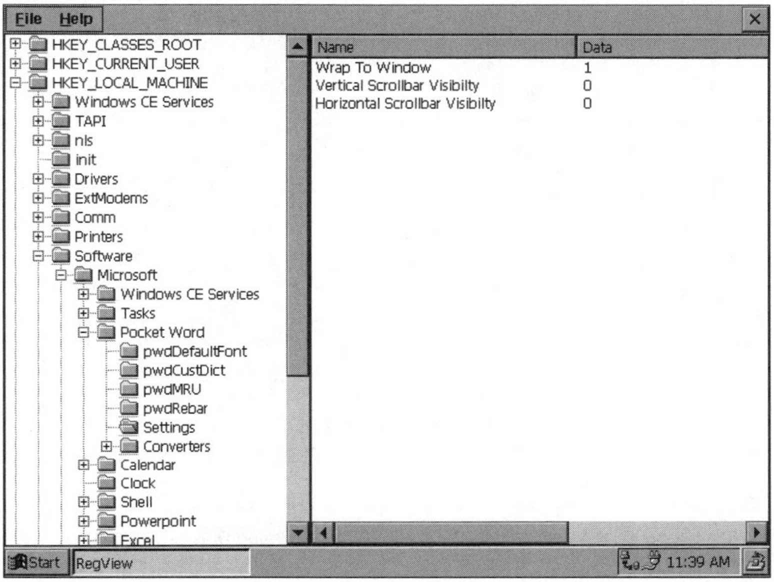

Figure 7-6. *You can see the hierarchy of the registry by looking at the values stored by Pocket Word.*

The Registry API

Now let's turn toward the Windows CE registry API. In general, the registry API provides all the functions necessary to read and write data in the registry as well as enumerate the keys and data store within. Windows CE doesn't support the security features of the registry that are supported under Windows NT.

Opening and creating keys

A registry key is opened with a call to this function:

```
LONG RegOpenKeyEx (HKEY hKey, LPCWSTR lpszSubKey, DWORD ulOptions,
                   REGSAM samDesired, PHKEY phkResult);
```

The first parameter is the key that contains the second parameter, the subkey. This first key must be either one of the root key constants or a previously opened key. The subkey to open is specified as a text string that contains the key to open. This subkey string can contain multiple levels of subkeys as long as each subkey is separated by a backslash. For example, to open the subkey HKEY_LOCAL_MACHINE\Software\Microsoft\Pocket Word, an application could either call *RegOpenKeyEx* with HKEY_LOCAL_MACHINE as the key and Software\Microsoft\Pocket Word as the subkey or it could open the Software\Microsoft key and then make a call with that opened handle to *RegOpenKeyEx* specifying the subkey Pocket Word. Key and value names aren't case specific.

Windows CE ignores the *ulOptions* and *samDesired* parameters. To remain compatible with future versions of the operating system that might use security features, these parameters should be set to 0 for *ulOptions* and NULL for *samDesired*. The *phkResult* parameter should point to a variable that will receive the handle to the opened key. The function, if successful, returns a value of ERROR_SUCCESS and an error code if it fails.

Another method for opening a key is

```
LONG RegCreateKeyEx (HKEY hKey, LPCWSTR lpszSubKey, DWORD Reserved,
                     LPWSTR lpszClass, DWORD dwOptions,
                     REGSAM samDesired,
                     LPSECURITY_ATTRIBUTES lpSecurityAttributes,
                     PHKEY phkResult, LPDWORD lpdwDisposition);
```

The difference between *RegCreateKeyEx* and *RegOpenKeyEx*, aside from the extra parameters, is that *RegCreateKeyEx* creates the key if it didn't exist before the call. The first two parameters, the key handle and the subkey name, are the same as in *RegOpenKeyEx*. The *Reserved* parameter should be set to 0. The *lpClass* parameter points to a string that contains the class name of the key if it's to be created. This parameter can be set to NULL if no class name needs to be specified. The *dwOptions* and *samDesired* and *lpSecurityAttributes* parameters should be set to 0, NULL, and NULL respectively. The *phkResult* parameter points to the variable that receives the handle to the opened or newly created key. The *lpdwDisposition* parameter points to a variable that's set to indicate whether the key was opened or created by the call.

Reading registry values

You can query registry values by first opening the key containing the values of interest and calling this function:

```
LONG RegQueryValueEx (HKEY hKey, LPCWSTR lpszValueName,
                      LPDWORD lpReserved, LPDWORD lpType,
                      LPBYTE lpData, LPDWORD lpcbData);
```

The *hKey* parameter is the handle of the key opened by *RegCreateKeyEx* or *RegOpenKeyEx*. The *lpszValueName* is the name of the value that's being queried. The *lpType* parameter is a pointer to a variable that receives the variable type. This variable is filled with The *lpData* parameter points to the buffer to receive the data, while the *lpcbData* parameter points to a variable that receives the size of the data. If *RegQueryValueEx* is called with the *lpData* parameter equal to NULL, Windows returns the size of the data but doesn't return the data itself. This allows applications to first query the size and type of the data before actually receiving it.

Writing registry values

You set a registry value by calling

```
LONG RegSetValueEx (HKEY hKey, LPCWSTR lpszValueName, DWORD Reserved,
                    DWORD dwType, const BYTE *lpData, DWORD cbData);
```

The parameters here are fairly obvious: the handle to the open key followed by the name of the value to set. The function also requires that you pass the type of data, the data itself, and the size of the data. The data type parameter is simply a labeling aid for the application that eventually reads the data. Data in the registry is stored in a binary format and returned in that same format. Specifying a different type has no effect on how the data is stored in the registry or how it's returned to the application. However, given the availability of third-party registry editors, you should make every effort to specify the appropriate data type in the registry.

The data types can be one of the following:

- *REG_SZ* A zero-terminated Unicode string
- *REG_EXPAND_SZ* A zero-terminated Unicode string with embedded environment variables
- *REG_MULTI_SZ* A series of zero-terminated Unicode strings terminated by two zero characters
- *REG_DWORD* A 4-byte binary value
- *REG_BINARY* Free-form binary data
- *REG_DWORD_BIG_ENDIAN* A DWORD value stored in big-endian format
- *REG_DWORD_LITTLE_ENDIAN* Equivalent to REG_DWORD
- *REG_LINK*
- *REG_NONE*
- *REG_RESOURCE_LIST*

Deleting keys and values

You delete a registry key by calling

```
LONG RegDeleteKey (HKEY hKey, LPCWSTR lpszSubKey);
```

The parameters are the handle to the open key and the name of the subkey you plan to delete. For the deletion to be successful, the key must not be currently open. You can delete a value by calling

```
LONG RegDeleteValue (HKEY hKey, LPCWSTR lpszValueName);
```

A wealth of information can be gleaned about a key by calling this function:

```
LONG RegQueryInfoKey (HKEY hKey, LPWSTR lpszClass, LPDWORD lpcchClass,
                      LPDWORD lpReserved, LPDWORD lpcSubKeys,
                      LPDWORD lpcchMaxSubKeyLen,
                      LPDWORD lpcchMaxClassLen,
                      LPDWORD lpcValues, LPDWORD lpcchMaxValueNameLen,
                      LPDWORD lpcbMaxValueData,
                      LPDWORD lpcbSecurityDescriptor,
                      PFILETIME lpftLastWriteTime);
```

The only input parameter to this function is the handle to a key. The function returns the class of the key, if any, as well as the maximum lengths of the subkeys and values under the key. The last two parameters, the security attributes and the last write time, are unsupported under Windows CE and should be set to NULL.

Closing keys

You close a registry key by calling

```
LONG RegCloseKey (HKEY hKey);
```

When a registry key is closed, Windows CE flushes any unwritten key data to the registry before returning from the call.

Enumerating registry keys

In some instances, you'll find it helpful to be able to query a key to see what subkeys and values it contains. You accomplish this with two different functions: one to query the subkeys, another to query the values. The first function

```
LONG RegEnumKeyEx (HKEY hKey, DWORD dwIndex, LPWSTR lpszName,
                   LPDWORD lpcchName, LPDWORD lpReserved,
                   LPWSTR lpszClass,
                   LPDWORD lpcchClass, PFILETIME lpftLastWriteTime);
```

enumerates the subkeys of a registry key through repeated calls. The parameters to pass the function are the handle of the opened key and an index value. To enumerate the first subkey, the *dwIndex* parameter should be 0. For each subsequent call to *RegEnumKeyEx*, *dwIndex* should be incremented to get the next subkey. When there are no more subkeys to be enumerated, *RegEnumKeyEx* returns ERROR_NO_MORE_ITEMS.

For each call to *RegEnumKeyEx*, the function returns the name of the subkey, and its classname. The last write time parameter isn't supported under Windows CE.

Values within a key can be enumerated with a call to this function:

```
LONG RegEnumValue (HKEY hKey, DWORD dwIndex, LPWSTR lpszValueName,
                   LPDWORD lpcchValueName, LPDWORD lpReserved,
                   LPDWORD lpType, LPBYTE lpData, LPDWORD lpcbData);
```

Like *RegEnumKey*, this function is called repeatedly, passing index values to enumerate the different values stored under the key. When the function returns ERROR_NO_MORE_ITEMS, there are no more values under the key. *RegEnumValue* returns the name of the values, the data stored in the value, as well as its data type and the size of the data.

The RegView Example Program

The following program is a registry viewer application. It allows a user to navigate the trees in the registry and examine the contents of the data stored. Unlike RegEdit, which is provided by Windows NT and Windows 98, RegView doesn't let you edit the registry. However, such an extension wouldn't be difficult to make. Figure 7-7 contains the code for the RegView program.

RegView.rc

```
//======================================================================
// Resource file
//
// Copyright (C) 1998 Douglas Boling
//======================================================================
#include "windows.h"
#include "regview.h"                    // Program-specific stuff

//----------------------------------------------------------------------
// Icons and bitmaps
//
ID_ICON ICON   "regview.ico"            // Program icon
ID_BMPS BITMAP "TVBmps.bmp"

//----------------------------------------------------------------------
// Menu
//
ID_MENU MENU DISCARDABLE
BEGIN
    POPUP "&File"
    BEGIN
        MENUITEM "E&xit",                       IDM_EXIT
    END
```

Figure 7-7. *The RegView program.* *(continued)*

Figure 7-7. *continued*

```
    POPUP "&Help"
    BEGIN
        MENUITEM "&About...",                          IDM_ABOUT
    END
END
//----------------------------------------------------------------------
// About box dialog template
//
aboutbox DIALOG discardable 10, 10, 160, 40
STYLE  WS_POPUP | WS_VISIBLE | WS_CAPTION | WS_SYSMENU | DS_CENTER |
       DS_MODALFRAME
CAPTION "About"
BEGIN
    ICON  ID_ICON,                    -1,   5,   5,  10,  10
    LTEXT "RegView - Written for the book Programming Windows CE \
           Copyright 1998 Douglas Boling"
                                      -1,  40,   5, 110,  30
END
```

RegView.h

```
//======================================================================
// Header file
//
// Written for the book Programming Windows CE
// Copyright (C) 1998 Douglas Boling
//======================================================================
// Returns number of elements
#define dim(x) (sizeof(x) / sizeof(x[0]))

//----------------------------------------------------------------------
// Generic defines and data types
//
struct decodeUINT {                            // Structure associates
    UINT Code;                                 // messages
                                               // with a function.
    LRESULT (*Fxn)(HWND, UINT, WPARAM, LPARAM);
};
struct decodeCMD {                             // Structure associates
    UINT Code;                                 // control IDs with a
    LRESULT (*Fxn)(HWND, WORD, HWND, WORD);    // function.
};
```

```
struct decodeNotify {                              // Structure associates
    UINT Code;                                     // control IDs with a
    LRESULT (*Fxn)(HWND, WORD, HWND, LPNMHDR);     // notify handler.
};

//----------------------------------------------------------------------
// Generic defines used by application
#define  ID_ICON            1                      // App icon resource ID
#define  ID_BMPS            2                      // Bitmap resource ID

#define  IDC_CMDBAR         10                     // Command band ID
#define  ID_MENU            11                     // Main menu resource ID
#define  ID_TREEV           12                     // Tree view control ID
#define  ID_LISTV           13                     // List view control ID

// Menu item IDs
#define  IDM_EXIT           101                    // File menu
#define  IDM_ABOUT          150                    // Help menu

//----------------------------------------------------------------------
// Function prototypes
//
int InitApp (HINSTANCE);
HWND InitInstance (HINSTANCE, LPWSTR, int);
int TermInstance (HINSTANCE, int);

INT EnumChildren (HWND, HTREEITEM, HKEY, LPTSTR);
DWORD CountChildren (HKEY, LPTSTR, LPTSTR);
INT EnumValues (HWND, HKEY, LPTSTR);
INT DisplayValue (HWND, INT, LPTSTR, PBYTE, DWORD, DWORD);
INT GetTree (HWND, HTREEITEM, HKEY *, TCHAR *, INT);
HTREEITEM InsertTV (HWND, HTREEITEM, TCHAR *, LPARAM, DWORD);
INT InsertLV (HWND, INT, LPTSTR, LPTSTR);
HWND CreateLV (HWND, RECT *);
HWND CreateTV (HWND, RECT *);

// Window procedures
LRESULT CALLBACK MainWndProc (HWND, UINT, WPARAM, LPARAM);

// Message handlers
LRESULT DoCreateMain (HWND, UINT, WPARAM, LPARAM);
LRESULT DoSizeMain (HWND, UINT, WPARAM, LPARAM);
LRESULT DoNotifyMain (HWND, UINT, WPARAM, LPARAM);
LRESULT DoCommandMain (HWND, UINT, WPARAM, LPARAM);
LRESULT DoDestroyMain (HWND, UINT, WPARAM, LPARAM);
```

(continued)

Figure 7-7. *continued*

```
// Command functions
LPARAM DoMainCommandExit (HWND, WORD, HWND, WORD);
LPARAM DoMainCommandAbout (HWND, WORD, HWND, WORD);

// Notify functions
LPARAM DoMainNotifyListV (HWND, WORD, HWND, LPNMHDR);
LPARAM DoMainNotifyTreeV (HWND, WORD, HWND, LPNMHDR);

// Dialog procedures
BOOL CALLBACK AboutDlgProc (HWND, UINT, WPARAM, LPARAM);
```

RegView.c

```
//======================================================================
// RegView - WinCE registry viewer
//
// Written for the book Programming Windows CE
// Copyright (C) 1998 Douglas Boling
//======================================================================
#include <windows.h>                 // For all that Windows stuff
#include <commctrl.h>                // Command bar includes
#include <commdlg.h>                 // Common dialog includes

#include "RegView.h"                 // Program-specific stuff

//----------------------------------------------------------------------
// Global data
//
const TCHAR szAppName[] = TEXT ("RegView");
HINSTANCE hInst;                     // Program instance handle

INT nDivPct = 40;                    // Divider setting between windows

// Message dispatch table for MainWindowProc
const struct decodeUINT MainMessages[] = {
    WM_CREATE, DoCreateMain,
    WM_SIZE, DoSizeMain,
    WM_COMMAND, DoCommandMain,
    WM_NOTIFY, DoNotifyMain,
    WM_DESTROY, DoDestroyMain,
};
// Command message dispatch for MainWindowProc
const struct decodeCMD MainCommandItems[] = {
    IDM_EXIT, DoMainCommandExit,
    IDM_ABOUT, DoMainCommandAbout,
```

```
};
// Notification message dispatch for MainWindowProc
const struct decodeNotify MainNotifyItems[] = {
    ID_LISTV, DoMainNotifyListV,
    ID_TREEV, DoMainNotifyTreeV,
};
//======================================================================
//
// Program entry point
//
int WINAPI WinMain (HINSTANCE hInstance, HINSTANCE hPrevInstance,
                    LPWSTR lpCmdLine, int nCmdShow) {
    HWND hwndMain;
    MSG msg;
    int rc = 0;

    // Initialize application.
    rc = InitApp (hInstance);
    if (rc) return rc;

    // Initialize this instance.
    hwndMain = InitInstance (hInstance, lpCmdLine, nCmdShow);
    if (hwndMain == 0)
        return 0x10;

    // Application message loop
    while (GetMessage (&msg, NULL, 0, 0)) {
        TranslateMessage (&msg);
        DispatchMessage (&msg);
    }
    // Instance cleanup
    return TermInstance (hInstance, msg.wParam);
}
//----------------------------------------------------------------------
// InitApp - Application initialization
//
int InitApp (HINSTANCE hInstance) {
    WNDCLASS wc;
    INITCOMMONCONTROLSEX icex;

    // Register application main window class.
    wc.style = 0;                             // Window style
    wc.lpfnWndProc = MainWndProc;             // Callback function
    wc.cbClsExtra = 0;                        // Extra class data
    wc.cbWndExtra = 0;                        // Extra window data
    wc.hInstance = hInstance;                 // Owner handle
```

(continued)

Figure 7-7. *continued*

```
    wc.hIcon = NULL,                            // Application icon
    wc.hCursor = NULL;                          // Default cursor
    wc.hbrBackground = (HBRUSH) GetStockObject (WHITE_BRUSH);
    wc.lpszMenuName =  NULL;                    // Menu name
    wc.lpszClassName = szAppName;               // Window class name

    if (RegisterClass (&wc) == 0) return 1;

    // Load the command bar common control class.
    icex.dwSize = sizeof (INITCOMMONCONTROLSEX);
    icex.dwICC = ICC_BAR_CLASSES | ICC_TREEVIEW_CLASSES |
                 ICC_LISTVIEW_CLASSES;
    InitCommonControlsEx (&icex);
    return 0;
}
//----------------------------------------------------------------------
// InitInstance - Instance initialization
//
HWND InitInstance (HINSTANCE hInstance, LPWSTR lpCmdLine, int nCmdShow){
    HWND hWnd;

    // Save program instance handle in global variable.
    hInst = hInstance;

    // Create main window.
    hWnd = CreateWindow (szAppName,             // Window class
                         TEXT ("RegView"),      // Window title
                         WS_VISIBLE,            // Style flags
                         CW_USEDEFAULT,         // x position
                         CW_USEDEFAULT,         // y position
                         CW_USEDEFAULT,         // Initial width
                         CW_USEDEFAULT,         // Initial height
                         NULL,                  // Parent
                         NULL,                  // Menu, must be null
                         hInstance,             // Application instance
                         NULL);                 // Pointer to create
                                                // parameters
    // Return fail code if window not created.
    if (!IsWindow (hWnd)) return 0;

    // Standard show and update calls
    ShowWindow (hWnd, nCmdShow);
    UpdateWindow (hWnd);
    return hWnd;
}
```

```
//----------------------------------------------------------------------
// TermInstance - Program cleanup
//
int TermInstance (HINSTANCE hInstance, int nDefRC) {
    return nDefRC;
}
//======================================================================
// Message handling procedures for MainWindow
//----------------------------------------------------------------------
// MainWndProc - Callback function for application window
//
LRESULT CALLBACK MainWndProc (HWND hWnd, UINT wMsg, WPARAM wParam,
                              LPARAM lParam) {
    INT i;
    //
    // Search message list to see if we need to handle this
    // message.  If in list, call procedure.
    //
    for (i = 0; i < dim(MainMessages); i++) {
        if (wMsg == MainMessages[i].Code)
            return (*MainMessages[i].Fxn)(hWnd, wMsg, wParam, lParam);
    }
    return DefWindowProc (hWnd, wMsg, wParam, lParam);
}
//----------------------------------------------------------------------
// DoCreateMain - Process WM_CREATE message for window.
//
LRESULT DoCreateMain (HWND hWnd, UINT wMsg, WPARAM wParam,
                      LPARAM lParam) {
    HWND hwndCB, hwndChild;
    INT  nHeight;
    RECT rect;
    LPCREATESTRUCT lpcs;

    // Convert lParam into pointer to create structure.
    lpcs = (LPCREATESTRUCT) lParam;

    // Create a minimal command bar that only has a menu and an
    // exit button.
    hwndCB = CommandBar_Create (hInst, hWnd, IDC_CMDBAR);
    // Insert the menu.
    CommandBar_InsertMenubar (hwndCB, hInst, ID_MENU, 0);
    // Add exit button to command bar.
    CommandBar_AddAdornments (hwndCB, 0, 0);
    nHeight = CommandBar_Height (hwndCB);
```

(continued)

Figure 7-7. *continued*

```
    // Create the tree view control in the left pane.
    SetRect (&rect, 0, nHeight, lpcs->cx/3, lpcs->cy - nHeight);
    hwndChild = CreateTV (hWnd, &rect);

    // Destroy frame if window not created.
    if (!IsWindow (hwndChild)) {
        DestroyWindow (hWnd);
        return 0;
    }

    // Create the list view control in right pane.
    SetRect (&rect, lpcs->cx/3, nHeight, (lpcs->cx*2)/3,
             lpcs->cy - nHeight);
    hwndChild = CreateLV (hWnd, &rect);

    // Destroy frame if window not created.
    if (!IsWindow (hwndChild)) {
        DestroyWindow (hWnd);
        return 0;
    }
    // Insert the base keys.
    InsertTV (hWnd, NULL, TEXT ("HKEY_CLASSES_ROOT"),
                         (LPARAM)HKEY_CLASSES_ROOT, 1);
    InsertTV (hWnd, NULL, TEXT ("HKEY_CURRENT_USER"),
              (LPARAM)HKEY_CURRENT_USER, 1);
    InsertTV (hWnd, NULL, TEXT ("HKEY_LOCAL_MACHINE"),
              (LPARAM)HKEY_LOCAL_MACHINE, 1);
    InsertTV (hWnd, NULL, TEXT ("HKEY_USERS"),
              (LPARAM)HKEY_USERS, 1);
    return 0;
}
//----------------------------------------------------------------------
// DoSizeMain - Process WM_SIZE message for window.
//
LRESULT DoSizeMain (HWND hWnd, UINT wMsg, WPARAM wParam, LPARAM lParam){
    HWND hwndLV, hwndTV;
    RECT rect;
    INT nDivPos;

    hwndTV = GetDlgItem (hWnd, ID_TREEV);
    hwndLV = GetDlgItem (hWnd, ID_LISTV);

    // Adjust the size of the client rect to take into account
    // the command bar height.
    GetClientRect (hWnd, &rect);
    rect.top += CommandBar_Height (GetDlgItem (hWnd, IDC_CMDBAR));
```

```
    nDivPos = ((rect.right - rect.left) * nDivPct)/100;

    SetWindowPos (hwndTV, NULL, rect.left, rect.top,
                  nDivPos, rect.bottom - rect.top,
                  SWP_NOZORDER);

    SetWindowPos (hwndLV, NULL, nDivPos, rect.top,
                  (rect.right - rect.left) - nDivPos,
                  rect.bottom - rect.top, SWP_NOZORDER);
    return 0;
}
//----------------------------------------------------------------------
// DoCommandMain - Process WM_COMMAND message for window.
//
LRESULT DoCommandMain (HWND hWnd, UINT wMsg, WPARAM wParam,
                       LPARAM lParam) {
    WORD idItem, wNotifyCode;
    HWND hwndCtl;
    INT  i;

    // Parse the parameters.
    idItem = (WORD) LOWORD (wParam);
    wNotifyCode = (WORD) HIWORD (wParam);
    hwndCtl = (HWND) lParam;

    // Call routine to handle control message.
    for (i = 0; i < dim(MainCommandItems); i++) {
        if (idItem == MainCommandItems[i].Code)
            return (*MainCommandItems[i].Fxn)(hWnd, idItem, hwndCtl,
                                              wNotifyCode);
    }
    return 0;
}
//----------------------------------------------------------------------
// DoNotifyMain - Process WM_NOTIFY message for window.
//
LRESULT DoNotifyMain (HWND hWnd, UINT wMsg, WPARAM wParam,
                      LPARAM lParam) {
    UINT    idItem;
    HWND    hCtl;
    LPNMHDR pHdr;
    INT     i;

    // Parse the parameters.
    idItem = wParam;
    pHdr = (LPNMHDR) lParam;
    hCtl = pHdr->hwndFrom;
```

(continued)

Figure 7-7. *continued*

```
    // Call routine to handle control message.
    for (i = 0; i < dim(MainNotifyItems); i++) {
        if (idItem == MainNotifyItems[i].Code)
            return (*MainNotifyItems[i].Fxn)(hWnd, idItem, hCtl, pHdr);
    }
    return 0;
}
//----------------------------------------------------------------------
// DoDestroyMain - Process WM_DESTROY message for window.
//
LRESULT DoDestroyMain (HWND hWnd, UINT wMsg, WPARAM wParam,
                       LPARAM lParam) {
    PostQuitMessage (0);
    return 0;
}
//======================================================================
// Command handler routines
//----------------------------------------------------------------------
// DoMainCommandExit - Process Program Exit command.
//
LPARAM DoMainCommandExit (HWND hWnd, WORD idItem, HWND hwndCtl,
                          WORD wNotifyCode) {

    SendMessage (hWnd, WM_CLOSE, 0, 0);
    return 0;
}
//----------------------------------------------------------------------
// DoMainCommandAbout - Process the Help | About menu command.
//
LPARAM DoMainCommandAbout(HWND hWnd, WORD idItem, HWND hwndCtl,
                          WORD wNotifyCode) {

    // Use DialogBox to create modal dialog box.
    DialogBox (hInst, TEXT ("aboutbox"), hWnd, AboutDlgProc);
    return 0;
}
//======================================================================
// Notify handler routines
//----------------------------------------------------------------------
// DoMainNotifyListV - Process notify message for list view.
//
LPARAM DoMainNotifyListV (HWND hWnd, WORD idItem, HWND hwndCtl,
                          LPNMHDR pnmh) {
    return 0;
}
```

```
//----------------------------------------------------------------------
// DoMainNotifyTreeV - Process notify message for list view.
//
LPARAM DoMainNotifyTreeV (HWND hWnd, WORD idItem, HWND hwndCtl,
                          LPNMHDR pnmh) {

    LPNM_TREEVIEW pNotifyTV;
    TCHAR szKey[256];
    HKEY hRoot;
    HTREEITEM hChild, hNext;
    INT i;

    pNotifyTV = (LPNM_TREEVIEW) pnmh;

    switch (pnmh->code) {
        case TVN_ITEMEXPANDED:
            if (pNotifyTV->action == TVE_COLLAPSE) {
                // Delete the children so that on next open, they will
                // be reenumerated.
                hChild = TreeView_GetChild (hwndCtl,
                                     pNotifyTV->itemNew.hItem);
                while (hChild) {
                    hNext = TreeView_GetNextItem (hwndCtl, hChild,
                                                  TVGN_NEXT);
                    TreeView_DeleteItem (hwndCtl, hChild);
                    hChild = hNext;
                }
            }
            break;

        case TVN_SELCHANGED:
            GetTree (hWnd, pNotifyTV->itemNew.hItem, &hRoot,
                     szKey, dim(szKey));
            EnumValues (hWnd, hRoot, szKey);
            break;

        case TVN_ITEMEXPANDING:
            if (pNotifyTV->action == TVE_EXPAND) {
                GetTree (hWnd, pNotifyTV->itemNew.hItem, &hRoot,
                         szKey, dim(szKey));
                i = EnumChildren (hWnd, pNotifyTV->itemNew.hItem,
                                  hRoot, szKey);
            }
            break;
    }
    return 0;
}
```

(continued)

Figure 7-7. *continued*

```
//----------------------------------------------------------------------
// CreateLV - Create list view control.
//
HWND CreateLV (HWND hWnd, RECT *prect) {
    HWND hwndLV;
    LVCOLUMN lvc;

    //
    // Create report window.  Size it so that it fits under
    // the command bar and fills the remaining client area.
    //
    hwndLV = CreateWindowEx (0, WC_LISTVIEW, TEXT (""),
                             WS_VISIBLE | WS_CHILD | WS_VSCROLL |
                             WS_BORDER | LVS_REPORT,
                             prect->left, prect->top,
                             prect->right - prect->left,
                             prect->bottom - prect->top,
                             hWnd, (HMENU)ID_LISTV,
                             hInst, NULL);
    // Add columns.
    if (hwndLV) {
        lvc.mask = LVCF_TEXT | LVCF_WIDTH | LVCF_FMT | LVCF_SUBITEM |
                   LVCF_ORDER;
        lvc.fmt = LVCFMT_LEFT;
        lvc.cx = 120;
        lvc.pszText = TEXT ("Name");
        lvc.iOrder = 0;
        lvc.iSubItem = 0;
        SendMessage (hwndLV, LVM_INSERTCOLUMN, 0, (LPARAM)&lvc);

        lvc.mask |= LVCF_SUBITEM;
        lvc.pszText = TEXT ("Data");
        lvc.cx = 250;
        lvc.iOrder = 1;
        lvc.iSubItem = 1;
        SendMessage (hwndLV, LVM_INSERTCOLUMN, 1, (LPARAM)&lvc);
    }
    return hwndLV;
}
//----------------------------------------------------------------------
// InitTreeView - Initialize tree view control.
//
HWND CreateTV (HWND hWnd, RECT *prect) {
    HBITMAP hBmp;
    HIMAGELIST himl;
    HWND hwndTV;
```

```
    //
    // Create tree view.  Size it so that it fits under
    // the command bar and fills the left part of the client area.
    //
    hwndTV = CreateWindowEx (0, WC_TREEVIEW,
                         TEXT (""), WS_VISIBLE | WS_CHILD | WS_VSCROLL |
                         WS_BORDER | TVS_HASLINES | TVS_HASBUTTONS |
                         TVS_LINESATROOT, prect->left, prect->top,
                         prect->right, prect->bottom,
                         hWnd, (HMENU)ID_TREEV, hInst, NULL);

    // Destroy frame if window not created.
    if (!IsWindow (hwndTV))
        return 0;

    // Create image list control for tree view icons.
    himl = ImageList_Create (16, 16, ILC_COLOR, 2, 0);
    // Load first two images from one bitmap.
    hBmp = LoadBitmap (hInst, MAKEINTRESOURCE (ID_BMPS));
    ImageList_Add (himl, hBmp, NULL);
    DeleteObject (hBmp);

    TreeView_SetImageList(hwndTV, himl, TVSIL_NORMAL);
    return hwndTV;
}
//----------------------------------------------------------------------
// InsertLV - Add an item to the list view control.
//
INT InsertLV (HWND hWnd, INT nItem, LPTSTR pszName, LPTSTR pszData) {

    HWND hwndLV = GetDlgItem (hWnd, ID_LISTV);
    LVITEM lvi;
    INT rc;

    lvi.mask = LVIF_TEXT | LVIF_IMAGE | LVIF_PARAM;
    lvi.iItem = nItem;
    lvi.iSubItem = 0;
    lvi.pszText = pszName;
    lvi.iImage = 0;
    lvi.lParam = nItem;
    rc = SendMessage (hwndLV, LVM_INSERTITEM, 0, (LPARAM)&lvi);

    lvi.mask = LVIF_TEXT;
    lvi.iItem = nItem;
    lvi.iSubItem = 1;
    lvi.pszText = pszData;
```

(continued)

Figure 7-7. *continued*

```
    rc = SendMessage (hwndLV, LVM_SETITEM, 0, (LPARAM)&lvi);
    return 0;
}
//----------------------------------------------------------------------
// InsertTV - Insert item into tree view control.
//
HTREEITEM InsertTV (HWND hWnd, HTREEITEM hParent, TCHAR *pszName,
                    LPARAM lParam, DWORD nChildren) {
    TV_INSERTSTRUCT tvis;

    HWND hwndTV = GetDlgItem (hWnd, ID_TREEV);
    // Initialize the insertstruct.
    memset (&tvis, 0, sizeof (tvis));
    tvis.hParent = hParent;
    tvis.hInsertAfter = TVI_LAST;
    tvis.item.mask = TVIF_TEXT | TVIF_PARAM | TVIF_CHILDREN |
                     TVIF_IMAGE;
    tvis.item.pszText = pszName;
    tvis.item.cchTextMax = lstrlen (pszName);
    tvis.item.iImage = 1;
    tvis.item.iSelectedImage = 1;
    tvis.item.lParam = lParam;
    if (nChildren)
        tvis.item.cChildren = 1;
    else
        tvis.item.cChildren = 0;

    return TreeView_InsertItem (hwndTV, &tvis);
}
//----------------------------------------------------------------------
// GetTree - Compute the full path of the tree view item.
//
INT GetTree (HWND hWnd, HTREEITEM hItem, HKEY *pRoot, TCHAR *pszKey,
             INT nMax) {
    TV_ITEM tvi;
    TCHAR szName[256];
    HTREEITEM hParent;
    HWND hwndTV = GetDlgItem (hWnd, ID_TREEV);

    memset (&tvi, 0, sizeof (tvi));

    hParent = TreeView_GetParent (hwndTV, hItem);
    if (hParent) {
        // Get the parent of the parent of the...
        GetTree (hWnd, hParent, pRoot, pszKey, nMax);
```

```
        // Get the name of the item.
        tvi.mask = TVIF_TEXT;
        tvi.hItem = hItem;
        tvi.pszText = szName;
        tvi.cchTextMax = dim(szName);
        TreeView_GetItem (hwndTV, &tvi);

        lstrcat (pszKey, TEXT ("\\"));
        lstrcat (pszKey, szName);
    } else {
        *pszKey = TEXT ('\0');
        szName[0] = TEXT ('\0');
        // Get the name of the item.
        tvi.mask = TVIF_TEXT | TVIF_PARAM;
        tvi.hItem = hItem;
        tvi.pszText = szName;
        tvi.cchTextMax = dim(szName);
        if (TreeView_GetItem (hwndTV, &tvi))
            *pRoot = (HTREEITEM)tvi.lParam;
        else {
            INT rc = GetLastError();
        }
    }
    return 0;
}
//----------------------------------------------------------------------
// DisplayValue - Display the data depending on the type.
//
INT DisplayValue (HWND hWnd, INT nCnt, LPTSTR pszName, PBYTE pbData,
                  DWORD dwDSize, DWORD dwType) {
    TCHAR szData[512];
    INT i, len;

    switch (dwType) {
    case REG_MULTI_SZ:
    case REG_EXPAND_SZ:
    case REG_SZ:
        lstrcpy (szData, (LPTSTR)pbData);
        break;

    case REG_DWORD:
        wsprintf (szData, TEXT ("%X"), *(int *)pbData);
        break;
```

(continued)

Figure 7-7. *continued*

```
    case REG_BINARY:
        szData[0] = TEXT ('\0');
        for (i = 0; i < (int)dwDSize; i++) {
            len = lstrlen (szData);
            wsprintf (&szData[len], TEXT ("%02X "), pbData[i]);
            if (len > dim(szData) - 6)
                break;
        }
        break;
    default:
        wsprintf (szData, TEXT ("Unknown type: %x"), dwType);
    }
    InsertLV (hWnd, nCnt, pszName, szData);
    return 0;
}
//----------------------------------------------------------------------
// EnumValues - Enumerate each of the values of a key.
//
INT EnumValues (HWND hWnd, HKEY hRoot, LPTSTR pszKey) {
    INT nCnt = 0, rc;
    DWORD dwNSize, dwDSize, dwType;
    TCHAR szName[MAX_PATH];
    BYTE bData[1024];
    HKEY hKey;

    if (lstrlen (pszKey)) {
        if (RegOpenKeyEx (hRoot, pszKey, 0, 0, &hKey) != ERROR_SUCCESS)
            return 0;
    } else
        hKey = hRoot;

    // Clean out list view.
    ListView_DeleteAllItems (GetDlgItem (hWnd, ID_LISTV));

    // Enumerate the values in the list view control.
    nCnt = 0;
    dwNSize = dim(szName);
    dwDSize = dim(bData);
    rc = RegEnumValue (hKey, nCnt, szName, &dwNSize,
                       NULL, &dwType, bData, &dwDSize);

    while (rc == ERROR_SUCCESS) {
        // Display the value in the list view control.
        DisplayValue (hWnd, nCnt, szName, bData, dwDSize, dwType);
```

```
        dwNSize = dim(szName);
        dwDSize = dim(bData);
        nCnt++;
        rc = RegEnumValue (hKey, nCnt, szName, &dwNSize,
                           NULL, &dwType, bData, &dwDSize);
    }
    if (hKey != hRoot)
        RegCloseKey (hKey);
    return 1;
}
//----------------------------------------------------------------------
// CountChildren - Count the number of children of a key.
//
DWORD CountChildren (HKEY hRoot, LPTSTR pszKeyPath, LPTSTR pszKey) {
    TCHAR *pEnd;
    DWORD dwCnt;
    HKEY hKey;

    pEnd = pszKeyPath + lstrlen (pszKeyPath);
    lstrcpy (pEnd, TEXT ("\\"));
    lstrcat (pEnd, pszKey);

    if (RegOpenKeyEx(hRoot, pszKeyPath, 0, 0, &hKey) == ERROR_SUCCESS){
        RegQueryInfoKey (hKey, NULL, NULL, 0, &dwCnt, NULL, NULL, NULL,
                         NULL, NULL, NULL, NULL);
        RegCloseKey (hKey);
    }
    *pEnd = TEXT ('\0');
    return dwCnt;
}
//----------------------------------------------------------------------
// EnumChildren - Enumerate the child keys of a key.
//
INT EnumChildren (HWND hWnd, HTREEITEM hParent, HKEY hRoot,
                  LPTSTR pszKey) {
    INT i = 0, rc;
    DWORD dwNSize;
    DWORD dwCSize;
    TCHAR szName[MAX_PATH];
    TCHAR szClass[256];
    FILETIME ft;
    DWORD nChild;
    HKEY hKey;
    TVITEM tvi;
```

(continued)

Figure 7-7. *continued*

```
    // All keys but root need to be opened.
    if (lstrlen (pszKey)) {
        if (RegOpenKeyEx (hRoot, pszKey, 0, 0, &hKey) != ERROR_SUCCESS) {
            rc = GetLastError();
            return 0;
        }
    } else
        hKey = hRoot;

    dwNSize = dim(szName);
    dwCSize = dim(szClass);
    rc = RegEnumKeyEx (hKey, i, szName, &dwNSize, NULL,
                       szClass, &dwCSize, &ft);
    while (rc == ERROR_SUCCESS) {

        nChild = CountChildren (hRoot, pszKey, szName);
        // Add key to tree view.
        InsertTV (hWnd, hParent, szName, 0, nChild);
        dwNSize = dim(szName);
        rc = RegEnumKeyEx (hKey, ++i, szName, &dwNSize,
                           NULL, NULL, 0, &ft);
    }
    // If this wasn't the a root key, close it.
    if (hKey != hRoot)
        RegCloseKey (hKey);

    // If no children, remove expand button.
    if (i == 0) {
        tvi.hItem = hParent;
        tvi.mask = TVIF_CHILDREN;
        tvi.cChildren = 0;
        TreeView_SetItem (GetDlgItem (hWnd, ID_TREEV), &tvi);
    }
    return i;
}
//======================================================================
// About Dialog procedure
//
BOOL CALLBACK AboutDlgProc (HWND hWnd, UINT wMsg, WPARAM wParam,
                            LPARAM lParam) {
    switch (wMsg) {
        case WM_COMMAND:
            switch (LOWORD (wParam)) {
                case IDOK:
                case IDCANCEL:
```

```
                        EndDialog (hWnd, 0);
                        return TRUE;
                }
            break;
    }
    return FALSE;
}
```

The workhorses of this program are the enumeration functions that query what keys and values are under each key. As a key is opened in the tree view control, the control sends a WM_NOTIFY message. In response, RegView enumerates the items below that key and fills the tree view with the child keys and the list view control with the values.

CONCLUSION

We have covered a huge amount of ground in this chapter. The file system, while radically different under the covers, presents a standard Win32 interface to the programmer and a familiar directory structure to the user. The database API is unique to Windows CE and provides a valuable function for the information-centric devices that Windows CE supports. The registry structure and interface are quite familiar to Windows programmers and should present no surprises.

The last two chapters have covered memory and the file system. Now it's time to look at the third part of the kernel triumvirate, processes and threads. As with the other parts of Windows CE, the API will be familiar if perhaps a bit smaller. However, the underlying architecture of Windows CE does make itself known.

Chapter 8

Processes and Threads

Like Windows NT, Windows CE is a fully multitasking and multithreaded operating system. What does that mean? In this chapter I'll present a few definitions and then some explanations to answer that question.

A *process* is a single instance of an application. If two copies of Microsoft Pocket Word are running, two unique processes are running. Every process has its own, protected, 32-MB address space as described in Chapter 6. Windows CE enforces a limit of 32 separate processes that can run at any time.

Each process has at least one *thread*. A thread executes code within a process. A process can have multiple threads running "at the same time." I put the phrase *at the same time* in quotes because, in fact, only one thread executes at any instant in time. The operating system simulates the concurrent execution of threads by rapidly switching between the threads, alternatively stopping one thread and switching to another.

PROCESSES

Windows CE treats processes differently than does Windows 98 or Windows NT. First and foremost, Windows CE has the aforementioned system limit of 32 processes being run at any one time. When the system starts, at least four processes are created: NK.EXE, which provides the kernel services; FILESYS.EXE, which provides file system services; GWES.EXE, which provides the GUI support; and DEVICE.EXE, which loads and maintains the device drivers for the system. On most systems, other processes are also started, such as the shell, EXPLORER.EXE, and, if the system is connected to a PC, REPLLOG.EXE and RAPISRV.EXE, which service the link between the PC and the Windows CE system. This leaves room for about 24 processes that the user or other applications that are running can start. While this sounds like a harsh limit, most systems don't need that many processes. A typical H/PC that's being used heavily might have 15 processes running at any one time.

Windows CE diverges from its desktop counterparts in other ways. Compared with processes under Windows 98 or Windows NT, Windows CE processes contain much less state information. Since Windows CE supports neither drives nor the concept of a current directory, the individual processes don't need to store that information. Windows CE also doesn't maintain a set of environment variables, so processes don't need to keep an environment block. Windows CE doesn't support handle inheritance, so there's no need to tell a process to enable handle inheritance. Because of all this, the parameter-heavy *CreateProcess* function is passed mainly NULLs and zeros, with just a few parameters actually used by Windows CE.

Many of the process and thread-related functions are simply not supported by Windows CE because the system doesn't support certain features supported by Windows 98 or Windows NT. Since Windows CE doesn't support an environment, all the Win32 functions dealing with the environment don't exist in Windows CE. While Windows CE supports threads, it doesn't support fibers, a lightweight version of a thread supported by Windows NT. So, the fiber API doesn't exist under Windows CE. Some functions aren't supported because there's an easy way to work around the lack of the function. For example, *GetCommandLine* doesn't exist in Windows CE, so an application needs to save a pointer to the command line passed to WinMain if it needs to access it later. Finally, *ExitProcess* doesn't exist under Windows CE. But, as you might expect, there's a workaround that allows a process to close.

Enough of what Windows CE doesn't do; let's look at what you can do with Windows CE.

Creating a Process

The function for creating another process is

```
BOOL CreateProcess (LPCTSTR lpApplicationName,
                    LPTSTR lpCommandLine,
                    LPSECURITY_ATTRIBUTES lpProcessAttributes,
                    LPSECURITY_ATTRIBUTES lpThreadAttributes,
                    BOOL bInheritHandles, DWORD dwCreationFlags,
                    LPVOID lpEnvironment,
                    LPCTSTR lpCurrentDirectory,
                    LPSTARTUPINFO lpStartupInfo,
                    LPPROCESS_INFORMATION lpProcessInformation);
```

While the list of parameters looks daunting, most of the parameters must be set to NULL or 0 because Windows CE doesn't support security or current directories, nor does it handle inheritance. This results in a function prototype that looks more like this:

```
BOOL CreateProcess (LPCTSTR lpApplicationName,
                    LPTSTR lpCommandLine,  NULL, NULL, FALSE,
                    DWORD dwCreationFlags, NULL, NULL, NULL,
                    LPPROCESS_INFORMATION lpProcessInformation);
```

The parameters that remain start with a pointer to the name of the application to launch. Windows CE looks for the application in the following directories, in this order:

1. The path, if any, specified in the *lpApplicationName*.
2. For Windows CE 2.1 or later, the path specified in the *SystemPath* value in [HKEY_LOCAL_MACHINE]\Loader. For earlier versions, the root of any external storage devices, such as PC Cards.
3. The windows directory, (\Windows).
4. The root directory in the object store, (\).

This action is different from Windows NT, where *CreateProcess* searches for the executable only if *lpApplicationName* is set to NULL and the executable name is passed through the *lpCcommnadLine* parameter. In the case of Windows CE, the application name must be passed in the *lpApplicaitonName* parameter because Windows CE doesn't support the technique of passing a NULL in *lpApplicationName* with the application name as the first token in the *lpCommandLine* parameter.

The *lpCommandLine* parameter specifies the command line that will be passed to the new process. The only difference between Windows CE and Windows NT in this parameter is that under Windows CE the command line is always passed as a Unicode string. And, as I mentioned previously, you can't pass the name of the executable as the first token in *lpCommandLine*.

The *dwCreationFlags* parameter specifies the initial state of the process after it has been loaded. Windows CE limits the allowable flags to the following:

- *0* Creates a standard process.
- *CREATE_SUSPENDED* Creates the process, then suspends the primary thread.
- *DEBUG_PROCESS* The process being created is treated as a process being debugged by the caller. The calling process receives debug information from the process being launched.
- *DEBUG_ONLY_THIS_PROCESS* When combined with DEBUG_PROCESS, debugs a process but doesn't debug any child processes that are launched by the process being debugged.

- *CREATE_NEW_CONSOLE* Forces a new console to be created. This is supported only in Windows CE 2.1 and later.

The only other parameter of *CreateProcess* used by Windows CE is *lpProcessInformation*. This parameter can be set to NULL, or it can point to a PROCESS_INFORMATION structure that's filled by *CreateProcess* with information about the new process. The PROCESS_INFORMATION structure is defined this way:

```
typedef struct _PROCESS_INFORMATION {
    HANDLE hProcess;
    HANDLE hThread;
    DWORD dwProcessId;
    DWORD dwThreadId;
} PROCESS_INFORMATION;
```

The first two fields in this structure are filled with the handles of the new process and the handle of the primary thread of the new process. These handles are useful for monitoring the newly created process, but with them comes some responsibility. When the system copies the handles for use in the PROCESS_INFORMATION structure, it increments the use count for the handles. This means that, if you don't have any use for the handles, the calling process must close them. Ideally, they should be closed immediately following a successful call to *CreateProcess*. I'll describe some good uses for these handles later in this chapter in the section, "Synchronization."

The other two fields in the PROCESS_INFORMATION structure are filled with the process ID and primary thread ID of the new process. These ID values aren't handles but simply unique identifiers that can be passed to Windows functions to identify the target of the function. Be careful when using these IDs. If the new process terminates and another new one is created, the system can reuse the old ID values. You must take measures to assure that ID values for other processes are still identifying the process you're interested in before using them. For example, you can, by using synchronization objects, be notified when a process terminates. When the process terminated, you would then know not to use the ID values for that process.

Using the create process is simple, as you can see in the following code fragment:

```
TCHAR szFileName[MAX_PATH];
TCHAR szCmdLine[64];
DWORD dwCreationFlags;
PROCESS_INFORMATION pi;
INT rc;

lstrcpy (szFileName, TEXT ("calc"));
lstrcpy (szCmdLine, TEXT (""));
dwCreationFlags = 0;
```

```
rc = CreateProcess (szFileName, szCmdLine, NULL, NULL, FALSE,
                    dwCreationFlags, NULL, NULL, NULL, &pi);
if (rc) {
    CloseHandle (pi.hThread);
    CloseHandle (pi.hProcess);
}
```

This code launches the standard Calculator applet found on Handheld PCs and Palm-size PCs. Since the file name doesn't specify a path, *CreateProcess* will, using the standard Windows CE search path, find calc.exe in the \Windows directory. Because I didn't pass a command line to *Calc*, I could have simply passed a NULL value in the *lpCmdLine* parameter. But I passed a null string in *szCmdLine* to differentiate the *lpCmdLine* parameter from the many other parameters in *CreateProcess* that aren't used. I used the same technique for *dwCreationFlags*. If the call to *CreateProcess* is successful, it returns a nonzero value. The code above checks for this, and if the call was successful, closes the process and thread handles returned in the PROCESS_INFORMATION structure. Remember that this must be done by all Win32 applications to prevent memory leaks.

Terminating a Process

A process can terminate itself by simply returning from the *WinMain* procedure. For console applications, a simple return from *main* suffices. Windows CE doesn't support the *ExitProcess* function found in Windows 98 and Windows NT. Instead, you can have the primary thread of the process call *ExitThread*. Under Windows CE, if the primary thread terminates, the process is terminated as well, regardless of what other threads are currently active in the process. The exit code of the process will be the exit code provided by *ExitThread*. You can determine the exit code of a process by calling

```
BOOL GetExitCodeProcess (HANDLE hProcess, LPDWORD lpExitCode);
```

The parameters are the handle to the process and a pointer to a DWORD that receives the exit code that was returned by the terminating process. If the process is still running, the return code is the constant STILL_ACTIVE.

You can terminate another process. But while it's possible to do that, you shouldn't be in the business of closing other processes. The user might not be expecting that process to be closed without his or her consent. If you need to terminate a process (or close a process, which is the same thing but much nicer a word), the following methods can be used.

If the process to be closed is one that you created, you can use some sort of interprocess communication to tell the process to terminate itself. This is the most advisable method because you've designed the target process to be closed by another party. Another method of closing a process is to send the main window of the process a WM_CLOSE message. This is especially effective on the Palm-size PC, where applications are designed to respond to WM_CLOSE messages by quietly saving their state and closing. Finally, if all else fails and you absolutely must close another process, you can use *TerminateProcess*.

TerminateProcess is prototyped as

```
BOOL TerminateProcess (HANDLE hProcess, DWORD uExitCode);
```

The two parameters are the handle of the process to terminate and the exit code the terminating process will return.

Other Processes

Of course, to terminate another process, you've got to know the handle to that process. You might want to know the handle for a process for other reasons, as well. For example, you might want to know *when* the process terminates. Windows CE supports two additional functions that come in handy here (both of which are seldom discussed). The first function is *OpenProcess*, which returns the handle of an already running process. *OpenProcess* is prototyped as

```
HANDLE OpenProcess (DWORD dwDesiredAccess, BOOL bInheritHandle,
                    DWORD dwProcessId);
```

Under Windows CE, the first parameter isn't used and should be set to 0. The *bInheritHandle* parameter must be set to FALSE because Windows CE doesn't support handle inheritance. The final parameter is the process ID value of the process you want to open.

The other function useful in this circumstance is

```
DWORD GetWindowThreadProcessId (HWND hWnd, LPDWORD lpdwProcessId);
```

This function takes a handle to a window and returns the process ID for the process that created the window. So, using these two functions, you can trace a window back to the process that created it.

Two other functions allow you to directly read from and write to the memory space of another process. These functions are

```
BOOL ReadProcessMemory (HANDLE hProcess, LPCVOID lpBaseAddress,
                        LPVOID lpBuffer, DWORD nSize,
                        LPDWORD lpNumberOfBytesRead);
```

and

```
BOOL WriteProcessMemory (HANDLE hProcess, LPVOID lpBaseAddress,
                         LPVOID lpBuffer, DWORD nSize,
                         LPDWORD lpNumberOfBytesWritten);
```

The parameters for these functions are fairly self-explanatory. The first parameter is the handle of the remote process. The second parameter is the base address in the other process's address space of the area to be read or written. The third and fourth parameters specify the name and the size of the local buffer in which the data is to be read from or written to. Finally, the last parameter specifies the bytes actually read or written. Both functions require that the entire area being read to or written from must be accessible. Typically, you use these functions for debugging but there's no requirement that this be their only use.

THREADS

A thread is, fundamentally, a unit of execution. That is, it has a stack and a processor context, which is a set of values in the CPU internal registers. When a thread is suspended, the registers are pushed onto the thread's stack, the active stack is changed to the next thread to be run, that thread's CPU state is pulled off its stack, and the new thread starts executing instructions.

Threads under Windows CE are similar to threads under Windows NT or Windows 98. Each process has a primary thread. Using the functions that I describe below, a process can create any number of additional threads within the process. The only limit to the number of threads in a Windows CE process is the memory and process address space available for the thread's stack.

Threads within a process share the address space of the process. Memory allocated by one thread is accessible to all threads in the process. Threads share the same access rights for handles whether they be file handles, memory objects handles, or handles to synchronization objects.

Before Windows CE 2.1, the size of all thread stacks was set at around 58 KB. Starting with Windows CE 2.1, the stack size of all threads created within a process is set by the linker. (The linker switch for setting the stack size in Microsoft Visual C++ is */stack*.) Secondary threads under Windows CE 2.1 are created with the same stack size as the primary thread.

The System Scheduler

Windows CE schedules threads in a preemptive manner. Threads run for a *quantum* or time slice, which is usually 25 milliseconds on H/PCs and Palm-size PCs. (OEMs developing custom hardware can specify a different quantum.) After that time, if the thread hasn't already relinquished its time slice and if the thread isn't a time-critical thread, it's suspended and another thread is scheduled to run. Windows CE chooses which thread to run based on a priority scheme. Threads of a higher priority are scheduled before threads of lower priority.

The rules for how Windows CE allocates time among the threads are quite different from Windows NT and from Windows 98. Unlike Windows NT, Windows CE processes don't have a *priority class*. Under Windows NT, a process is created with a priority class. Threads derive their priority based on the priority class of their parent processes. A process with a higher-priority class has threads that run at a higher priority than threads in a lower-priority class process. Threads within a process can then refine their priority within that process by setting their relative thread priority.

Because Windows CE has no priority classes, all processes are treated as peers. Individual threads can have different priorities, but the process that the thread runs within doesn't influence those priorities. Also, unlike Windows NT, the foreground thread in Windows CE doesn't get a boost in priority.

In Windows CE, a thread can have one of eight priority levels. Those priorities are listed below:

- *THREAD_PRIORITY_TIME_CRITICAL* Indicates 3 points above normal priority. Threads of this priority aren't preempted.
- *THREAD_PRIORITY_HIGHEST* Indicates 2 points above normal priority.
- *THREAD_PRIORITY_ABOVE_NORMAL* Indicates 1 point above normal priority.
- *THREAD_PRIORITY_NORMAL* Indicates normal priority. All threads are created with this priority.
- *THREAD_PRIORITY_BELOW_NORMAL* Indicates 1 point below normal priority.
- *THREAD_PRIORITY_LOWEST* Indicates 2 points below normal priority.
- *THREAD_PRIORITY_ABOVE_IDLE* Indicates 3 points below normal priority.
- *THREAD_PRIORITY_IDLE* Indicates 4 points below normal priority.

All higher-priority threads run before lower-priority threads. This means that before a thread set to run at particular priority can be scheduled, all threads that have a higher priority must be *blocked*. A blocked thread is one that's waiting on some system resource or synchronization object before it can continue. Threads of equal priority are scheduled in a round-robin fashion. Once a thread has voluntarily given up its time slice, is blocked, or has completed its time slice, all other threads of the same priority are allowed to run before the original thread is allowed to continue. If a thread of higher priority is unblocked and a thread of lower priority is currently running, the lower-priority thread is immediately suspended and the higher-priority thread is scheduled. Lower-priority threads can never preempt a higher-priority thread.

There are two exceptions to the rules I just stated. If a thread has a priority of THREAD_PRIORITY_TIME_CRITICAL, it's never preempted, even by another THREAD_PRIORITY_TIME_CRITICAL thread. As you can see, a THREAD_PRIORITY_TIME_CRITICAL thread can and will starve everyone else in the system unless written carefully. This priority is reserved by convention for interrupt service threads in device drivers, which are written so that each thread quickly performs its task and releases its time slice.

The other exception to the scheduling rules happens if a low-priority thread owns a resource that a higher-priority thread is waiting on. In this case, the low-priority thread is temporarily given the higher-priority thread's priority in a scheme known as *priority inversion*, so that it can quickly accomplish its task and free the needed resource.

While it might seem that lower-priority threads never get a chance to run in this scheme, it works out that threads are almost always blocked, waiting on something to free up before they can be scheduled. Threads are always created at THREAD_PRIORITY_NORMAL, so, unless they proactively change their priority level, a thread is usually at an equal priority to most of the other threads in the system. Even at the normal priority level, threads are almost always blocked. For example, an application's primary thread is typically blocked waiting on messages. Other threads should be designed to block on one of the many synchronization objects available to a Windows CE application.

Never Do This!

What's not supported by the arrangement I just described, or by any other thread-based scheme, is code like the following:

```
while (bFlag == FALSE) {
    // Do nothing, and spin
}
// Now do something.
```

This kind of code isn't just bad manners, since it wastes CPU power, it's a death sentence to a battery-powered Windows CE device. To understand why this is important, I need to digress into a quick lesson on Windows CE power management.

Windows CE is designed so that when all threads are blocked, which happens over 90 percent of the time, it calls down to the OEM Abstraction Layer (the equivalent to the BIOS on an MS-DOS machine) to enter a low-power waiting state. Typically, this low-power state means that the CPU is halted; that is, it simply stops executing instructions. Because the CPU isn't executing any instructions, no power-consuming reads and writes of memory are performed by the CPU. At this point, the only power necessary for the system is to maintain the contents of the RAM and light the display. This low-power mode can reduce power consumption by up to 99 percent of what is required when a thread is running in a well-designed system.

Doing a quick back-of-the-envelope calculation, say a Palm-size PC is designed to run for 15 hours on a couple of AAA batteries. Given that the system turns itself off after a few minutes of non-use, this 15 hours translates into a month or two of battery life in the device for the user. (I'm basing this calculation on the assumption that the system indeed spends 90 percent or more of its time in its low-power idle state.) Say a poorly written application thread spins on a variable instead of blocking. While this application is running, the system will never enter its low-power state. So, instead of

900 minutes of battery time (15 hours × 60 minutes/hour), the system spends 100 percent of its time at full power, resulting in a battery life of slightly over 98 minutes, or right at 1.5 hours. So, as you can see, it's good to have the system in its low-power state.

Fortunately, since Windows applications usually spend their time blocked in a call to *GetMessage,* the system power management works by default. However, if you plan on using multiple threads in your application, you must use synchronization objects to block threads while they're waiting. First, let's look at how to create a thread, and then I'll dive into the synchronization tools available to Windows CE programs.

Creating a Thread

You create a thread by calling this function:

```
HANDLE CreateThread (LPSECURITY_ATTRIBUTES lpThreadAttributes,
                     DWORD dwStackSize,
                     LPTHREAD_START_ROUTINE lpStartAddress,
                     LPVOID lpParameter, DWORD dwCreationFlags,
                     LPDWORD lpThreadId);
```

As with *CreateProcess*, Windows CE doesn't support a number of the parameters in *CreateThread*, and so they are set to NULL or 0 as appropriate. For *CreateThread*, the *lpThreadAttributes*, and *dwStackSize* parameters aren't supported. The parameter *lpThreadAttributes* must be set to NULL and *dwStackSize* is ignored by the system and should be set to 0. The third parameter, *lpStartAddress*, must point to the start of the thread routine. The *lpParameter* parameter in *CreateThread* is an application-defined value that's passed to the thread function as its one and only parameter. The *dwCreationFlags* parameter can be set to either 0 or CREATE_SUSPENDED. If CREATE_SUSPENDED is passed, the thread is created in a suspended state and must be resumed with a call to *ResumeThread.* The final parameter is a pointer to a DWORD that receives the newly created thread's ID value.

The thread routine should be prototyped this way:

```
DWORD WINAPI ThreadFunc (LPVOID lpArg);
```

The only parameter is the *lpParameter* value, passed unaltered from the call to *CreateThread*. The parameter can be an integer or a pointer. Make sure, however, that you don't pass a pointer to a stack-based structure that will disappear when the routine that called *CreateThread* returns.

If *CreateThread* is successful, it creates the thread and returns the handle to the newly created thread. As with *CreateProcess*, the handle returned should be closed when you no longer need the handle. Following is a short code fragment that contains a call to start a thread and the thread routine.

```
//----------------------------------------------------------------------
//
//
HANDLE hThread1;
DWORD dwThread1ID = 0;
INT nParameter = 5;

hThread1 = CreateThread (NULL, 0, Thread2, nParameter, 0,
                         &dwThread1ID);
CloseHandle (hThread1);

//----------------------------------------------------------------------
// Second thread routine
//
DWORD WINAPI Thread2 (PVOID pArg) {

    INT nParam = (INT) pArg;

    //
    // Do something here.
    // .
    // .
    // .
    return 0x15;
}
```

In this code, the second thread is started with a call to *CreateThread*. The *nParameter* value is passed to the second thread as the single parameter to the thread routine. The second thread executes until it terminates, in this case simply by returning from the routine.

A thread can also terminate itself by calling this function:

```
VOID ExitThread (DWORD dwExitCode);
```

The only parameter is the exit code that's set for the thread. That thread exit code can be queried by another thread using this function:

```
BOOL GetExitCodeThread (HANDLE hThread, LPDWORD lpExitCode);
```

The function takes the handle to the thread (not the thread ID) and returns the exit code of the thread. If the thread is still running, the exit code is STILL_ACTIVE, a constant defined as 0x0103. The exit code is set by a thread using *ExitThread* or the value returned by the thread procedure. In the preceding code, the thread sets its exit code to 0x15 when it returns.

All threads within a process are terminated when the process terminates. As I said earlier, a process is terminated when its primary thread terminates.

Setting and querying thread priority

Threads are always created at a priority level of THREAD_PRIORITY_NORMAL. The thread priority can be changed either by the thread itself or by another thread calling this function:

```
BOOL SetThreadPriority (HANDLE hThread, int nPriority);
```

The two parameters are the thread handle and the new priority level. The level passed can be one of the constants described previously, ranging from THREAD_PRIORITY_IDLE up to THREAD_PRIORITY_TIME_CRITICAL. You must be extremely careful when you're changing a thread's priority. Remember that threads of a lower priority almost never preempt threads of higher priority. So, a simple bumping up of a thread one notch above normal can harm the responsiveness of the rest of the system unless that thread is carefully written.

To query the priority level of a thread, call this function:

```
int GetThreadPriority (HANDLE hThread);
```

This function returns the priority level of the thread. You shouldn't use the hard-coded priority levels. Instead, use constants, such as THREAD_PRIORITY_NORMAL, defined by the system. This ensures that any change to the priority scheme in future versions of Windows CE doesn't affect your program.

Suspending and resuming a thread

You can suspend a thread at any time by calling this function:

```
DWORD SuspendThread (HANDLE hThread);
```

The only parameter is the handle to the thread to suspend. The value returned is the *suspend count* for the thread. Windows maintains a suspend count for each thread. Any thread with a suspend count greater than 0 is suspended. Since *SuspendThread* increments the suspend count, multiple calls to *SuspendThread* must be matched with an equal number of calls to *ResumeThread* before a thread is actually scheduled to run. *ResumeCount* is prototyped as

```
DWORD ResumeThread (HANDLE hThread);
```

Here again, the parameter is the handle to the thread and the return value is the previous suspend count. So, if *ResumeThread* returns 1, the thread is no longer suspended.

At times, a thread simply wants to kill some time. Since I've already explained why simply spinning in a *while* loop is a very bad thing to do, you need another way to kill time. The best way to do this is to use this function:

```
void Sleep (DWORD dwMilliseconds);
```

Sleep suspends the thread for at least the number of milliseconds specified in the *dwMilliseconds* parameter. Since the quantum, or time slice, on a Windows CE system is usually 25 milliseconds, specifying very small numbers of milliseconds results in sleeps of at least 25 milliseconds. This strategy is entirely valid, and sometimes it's equally valid to pass a 0 to *Sleep*. When a thread passes a 0 to *Sleep*, it gives up its time slice but is rescheduled immediately according to the scheduling rules I described previously.

Thread Local Storage

Thread local storage is a mechanism that allows a routine to maintain separate instances of data for each thread calling the routine. This capability might not seem like much, but it has some very handy uses. Take the following thread routine:

```
INT g_nGlobal;              // System global variable

int ThreadProc (pStartData) {
    INT nValue1;
    INT nValue2;

    while (unblocked) {
        //
        // Do some work.
        //
    }
    // We're done now, terminate the thread by returning.
    return 0;
}
```

For this example, imagine that multiple threads are created to execute the same routine, *ThreadProc*. Each thread has its own copy of *nValue1* and *nValue2* because these are stack-based variables and each thread has its own stack. All threads, though, share the same static variable, *g_nGlobal*.

Now, imagine that the *ThreadProc* routine calls another routine, *WorkerBee*. As in

```
int g_nGlobal;              // System global variable

int ThreadProc (pStartData) {
    int nValue1;
    int nValue2;
    while (unblocked) {
        WorkerBee();        // Let someone else do the work.
    }
    // We're done now, terminate the thread by returning.
    return 0;
}
```

(continued)

```
int WorkerBee (void) {
    int nLocal1;
    static int nLocal2;
    //
    // Do work here.
    //
    return nLocal1;
}
```

Now *WorkerBee* doesn't have access to any persistent memory that's local to a thread. *nLocal1* is persistent only for the life of a single call to *WorkerBee*. *nLocal2* is persistent across calls to *WorkerBee* but is static and therefore shared among all threads calling *WorkerBee*. One solution would be to have *ThreadProc* pass a pointer to a stack-based variable to *WorkerBee*. This strategy works, but only if you have control over the routines calling *WorkerBee*. What if you're writing a DLL and you need to have a routine in the DLL maintain a different state for each thread calling the routine? You can't define static variables in the DLL because they would be shared across the different threads. You can't define local variables because they aren't persistent across calls to your routine. The answer is to use thread local storage.

Thread local storage allows a process to have its own cache of values that are guaranteed to be unique for each thread in a process. This cache of values is small because an array must be created for every thread created in the process, but it's large enough, if used intelligently. To be specific, the system constant, TLS_MINIMUM_AVAILABLE, is defined to be the number of slots in the TLS array that's available for each process. For Windows CE, like Windows NT, this value is defined as 64. So, each process can have 64 4-byte values that are unique for each thread in that process. For the best results, of course, you must manage those 64 slots well.

To reserve one of the TLS slots, a process calls

```
DWORD TlsAlloc (void);
```

TlsAlloc looks through the array to find a free slot in the TLS array, marks it as *in use*, and then returns an index value to the newly assigned slot. If no slots are available, the function returns -1. It's important to understand that the individual threads don't call *TlsAlloc*. Instead, the process or DLL calls it before creating the threads that will use the TLS slot.

Once a slot has been assigned, each thread can access its unique data in the slot by calling this function:

```
BOOL TlsSetValue (DWORD dwTlsIndex, LPVOID lpTlsValue);
```

and

```
LPVOID TlsGetValue (DWORD dwTlsIndex);
```

For both of these functions, the TLS index value returned by *TlsAlloc* specifies the slot that contains the data. Both *TlsGetValue* and *TlsSetValue* type the data as a PVOID, but the value can be used for any purpose. The advantage of thinking of the TLS value as a pointer is that a thread can allocate a block of memory on the heap, and then keep the pointer to that data in the TLS value. This allows each thread to maintain a block of thread-unique data of almost any size.

One other matter is important to thread local storage. When *TlsAlloc* reserves a slot, it zeros the value in that slot for all currently running threads. All new threads are created with their TLS array initialized to 0 as well. This means that a thread can safely assume that the value in its slot will be initialized to 0. This is helpful for determining whether a thread needs to allocate a memory block the first time the routine is called.

When a process no longer needs the TLS slot, it should call this function:

```
BOOL TlsFree (DWORD dwTlsIndex);
```

The function is passed the index value of the slot to be freed. The function returns TRUE if successful. This function frees only the TLS slot. If threads have allocated storage in the heap and stored pointers to those blocks in their TLS slots, that storage isn't freed by this function. Threads are responsible for freeing their own memory blocks.

SYNCHRONIZATION

With multiple threads running around the system, you need to coordinate the activities. Fortunately, Windows CE supports almost the entire extensive set of standard Win32 synchronization objects. The concept of synchronization objects is fairly simple. A thread *waits* on a synchronization object. When the object is signaled, the waiting thread is unblocked and is scheduled (according to the rules governing the thread's priority) to run.

Windows CE doesn't support some of the synchronization primitives supported by Windows NT. These unsupported elements include semaphores, file change notifications, and waitable timers. Support for semaphores is planed for Windows CE in the near future. The lack of waitable timer support can easily be worked around using the more flexible Notification API, unique to Windows CE.

One aspect of Windows CE unique to it is that the different synchronization objects don't share the same namespace. This means that if you have an event named Bob, you can also have a *mutex* named Bob. (I'll talk about mutexes later in this chapter.) This naming convention is different from Windows NT's rule, where all kernel objects (of which synchronization objects are a part) share the same namespace. While having the same names in Windows CE is possible, it's not advisable. Not only does the practice make your code incompatible with Windows NT, there's no telling whether a redesign of the internals of Windows CE might just enforce this restriction in the future.

Events

The first synchronization primitive I'll describe is the *event object*. An event object is a synchronization object that can be in a *signaled* or *nonsignaled* state. Events are useful to a thread to let it be known that, well, an event has occurred. Event objects can either be created to automatically reset from a signaled state to a nonsignaled state or require a manual reset to return the object to its nonsignaled state. Starting with Windows CE 2.0, events can be named and therefore shared across different processes allowing interprocess synchronization.

An event is created by means of this function:

```
HANDLE CreateEvent (LPSECURITY_ATTRIBUTES lpEventAttributes,
                    BOOL bManualReset, BOOL bInitialState,
                    LPTSTR lpName);
```

As with all calls in Windows CE, the security attributes parameter, *lpEventAttributes*, should be set to NULL. The second parameter indicates whether the event being created requires a manual reset or will automatically reset to a nonsignaled state immediately after being signaled. Setting *bManualReset* to TRUE creates an event that must be manually reset. The *bInitialState* parameter specifies whether the event object is initially created in the signaled or nonsignaled state. Finally, the *lpName* parameter points to an optional string that names the event. Events that are named can be shared across processes. If two processes create event objects of the same name, the processes actually share the same object. This allows one process to signal the other process using event objects. If you don't want a named event, the *lpname* parameter can be set to NULL.

To share an event object across processes, each process must individually create the event object. You can't simply create the event in one process and send the handle of that event to another process. To determine whether a call to *CreateEvent* created a new event object or opened an already created object, you can call *GetLastError* immediately following the call to *CreateEvent*. If *GetLastError* returns ERROR_ALREADY_EXISTS, the call opened an existing event.

Once you have an event object, you'll need to be able to signal the event. You accomplish this using either of the following two functions:

```
BOOL SetEvent (HANDLE hEvent);
```

or

```
BOOL PulseEvent (HANDLE hEvent);
```

The difference between these two functions is that *SetEvent* doesn't automatically reset the event object to a nonsignaled state. For autoreset events, *SetEvent* is all you need because the event is automatically reset once a thread unblocks on the event. For manual reset events, you must manually reset the event with this function:

```
BOOL ResetEvent (HANDLE hEvent);
```

These event functions sound like they overlap, so let's review. An event object can be created to reset itself or require a manual reset. If it can reset itself, a call to *SetEvent* signals the event object. The event is then automatically reset to the nonsignaled state when *one* thread is unblocked after waiting on that event. An event that resets itself doesn't need *PulseEvent* or *ResetEvent*. If, however, the event object was created requiring a manual reset, the need for *ResetEvent* is obvious.

PulseEvent signals the event and then resets the event, which allows *all* threads waiting on that event to be unblocked. So, the difference between *PulseEvent* on a manually resetting event and *SetEvent* on an automatic resetting event is that using *SetEvent* on an automatic resetting event frees only one thread to run even if many threads are waiting on that event. *PulseEvent* frees all threads waiting on that event.

You destroy event objects by calling *CloseHandle*. If the event object is named, Windows maintains a use count on the object so one call to *CloseHandle* must be made for every call to *CreateEvent*.

Waiting...

It's all well and good to have event objects; the question is how to use them. Threads wait on events, as well as on the soon to be described mutex, using one of the following functions: *WaitForSingleObject*, *WaitForMultipleObjects*, *MsgWaitForMultipleObjects*, or *MsgWaitForMultipleObjectsEx*. Under Windows CE, the *WaitForMultiple* functions are limited in that they can't wait for all objects of a set of objects to be signaled. These functions support waiting for *one* object in a set of objects being signaled. Whatever the limitations of waiting, I can't emphasize enough that waiting is good. While a thread is blocked with one of these functions, the thread enters an extremely efficient state that takes very little CPU processing power and battery power.

Another point to remember is that the thread responsible for handling a message loop in your application (usually the application's primary thread) shouldn't be blocked by *WaitForSingleObject* or *WaitForMultipleObjects* because the thread can't be retrieving and dispatching messages in the message loop if it's blocked waiting on an object. The function *MsgWaitForMultipleObjects* gives you a way around this problem, but in a multithreaded environment, it's usually easier to let the primary thread handle the message loop and secondary threads handle the shared resources that require blocking on events.

Waiting on a single object

A thread can wait on a synchronization object with the function:

```
DWORD WaitForSingleObject (HANDLE hHandle, DWORD dwMilliseconds);
```

The function takes two parameters: the handle to the object being waited on and a timeout value. If you don't want the wait to time out, you can pass the value INFINITE in the *dwMilliseconds* parameter. The function returns a value that indicates why the function returned. Calling *WaitForSingleObject* blocks the thread until the event is signaled, the synchronization object is abandoned, or the timeout value is reached.

WaitForSingleObject returns one of the following values:

- *WAIT_OBJECT_0* The specified object was signaled.
- *WAIT_TIMEOUT* The timeout interval elapsed, and the object's state remains nonsignaled.
- *WAIT_ABANDONED* The thread that owned a mutex object being waited on ended without freeing the object.
- *WAIT_FAILED* The handle of the synchronization object was invalid.

You must check the return code from *WaitForSingleObject* to determine whether the event was signaled or simply that the time out had expired. (The WAIT_ABANDONED return value will be relevant when I talk about mutexes soon.)

Waiting on processes and threads

I've talked about waiting on events, but you can also wait on handles to processes and threads. These handles are signaled when their processes or threads terminate. This allows a process to monitor another process (or thread) and perform some action when the process terminates. One common use for this feature is for one process to launch another, and then by blocking on the handle to the newly created process, wait until that process terminates.

The rather irritating routine below is a thread that demonstrates this technique by launching an application, blocking until that application closes, and then relaunching the application:

```
DWORD WINAPI KeepRunning (PVOID pArg) {
    PROCESS_INFORMATION pi;
    TCHAR szFileName[MAX_PATH];
    INT rc = 0;

    // Copy the filename.
    Lstrcpy (szFileName, (LPTSTR)pArg);
    while (1) {
        // Launch the application.
        rc = CreateProcess (szFileName, NULL, NULL, NULL, FALSE,
                            0, NULL, NULL, NULL, &pi);
        // If the application didn't start, terminate thread.
        if (!rc)
            return -1;
        // Close the new process's primary thread handle.
        CloseHandle (pi.hThread);
```

```
        // Wait for user to close the application.
        rc = WaitForSingleObject (pi.hProcess, INFINITE);

        // Close the old process handle.
        CloseHandle (pi.hProcess);

        // Make sure we returned from the wait correctly.
        if (rc != WAIT_OBJECT_0)
            return -2;
    }
    return 0;  //This should never get executed.
}
```

This code simply launches the application using *CreateProcess* and waits on the process handle returned in the PROCESS_INFORMATION structure. Notice that the thread closes the child process's primary thread handle and, after the wait, the handle to the child process itself.

Waiting on multiple objects

A thread can also wait on a number of events. The wait can end when any one of the events is signaled. The function that enables a thread to wait on multiple objects is this one:

```
DWORD WaitForMultipleObjects (DWORD nCount, CONST HANDLE *lpHandles,
                              BOOL bWaitAll, DWORD dwMilliseconds);
```

The first two parameters are a count of the number of events or mutexes to wait on and a pointer to an array of handles to these events. The *bWaitAll* parameter must be set to FALSE to indicate the function should return if any of the events are signaled. The final parameter is a timeout value, in milliseconds. As with *WaitForSingleObject*, passing INFINITE in the timeout parameter disables the time out. Windows CE doesn't support the use of *WaitForMultipleObjects* to enable waiting for all events in the array to be signaled before returning.

Like *WaitForSingleObject*, *WaitForMultipleObjects* returns a code that indicates why the function returned. If the function returned due to a synchronization object being signaled, the return value will be WAIT_OBJECT_0 plus an index into the handle array that was passed in the *lpHandles* parameter. For example, if the first handle in the array unblocked the thread, the return code would be WAIT_OBJECT_0; if the second handle was the cause, the return code would be WAIT_OBJECT_0 + 1. The other return codes used by *WaitForSingleObject*—WAIT_TIMEOUT, WAIT_ABANDONED, and WAIT_FAILED—are also returned by *WaitForMultipleObjects* for the same reasons.

Waiting while dealing with messages

The Win32 API provides other functions that allow you to wait on a set of objects as well as messages: these are *MsgWaitForMultipleObjects* and *MsgWaitForMultipleObjectsEx*. Under Windows CE, these functions act identically, so I'll describe only *MsgWaitForMultipleObjects*. This function essentially combines the wait function, *MsgWaitForMultipleObjects*, with an additional check into the message queue so that the function returns if any of the selected categories of messages are received during the wait. The prototype for this function is the following:

```
DWORD MsgWaitForMultipleObjectsEx (DWORD nCount, LPHANDLE pHandles,
                                   BOOL fWaitAll, DWORD dwMilliseconds,
                                   DWORD dwWakeMasks);
```

This function has a number of limitations under Windows CE. As with *WaitForMultipleObjects*, *MsgWaitForMultipleObjectsEx* can't wait for all objects to be signaled. Nor are all the *dwWakeMask* flags supported by Windows CE. Windows CE supports the following flags in *dwWakeMask*. Each flag indicates a category of messages that, when received in the message queue of the thread, causes the function to return.

- *QS_ALLINPUT* Any message has been received.
- *QS_INPUT* An input message has been received.
- *QS_KEY* A key up, key down, or syskey up or down message has been received.
- *QS_MOUSE* A mouse move or mouse click message has been received.
- *QS_MOUSEBUTTON* A mouse click message has been received.
- *QS_MOUSEMOVE* A mouse move message has been received.
- *QS_PAINT* A WM_PAINT message has been received.
- *QS_POSTMESSAGE* A posted message, other than those in this list, has been received.
- *QS_SENDMESSAGE* A sent message, other than those in this list, has been received.
- *QS_TIMER* A WM_TIMER message has been received.

The function is used inside the message loop, so that an action or actions can take place in response to the signaling of a synchronization object while your program is still processing messages.

The return value is WAIT_OBJECT_0 up to WAIT_OBJECT_0 + *nCount* - 1 for the objects in the handle array. If a message causes the function to return, the return value is WAIT_OBJECT_0 + *nCount*. An example of how this function might be used follows. In this code, the handle array has only one entry, *hSyncHandle*.

```
fContinue = TRUE;
while (fContinue) {
    rc = MsgWaitForMultipleObjects (1, &hSyncHandle, FALSE,
                                    INFINITE, QS_ALLINPUT);
    if (rc == WAIT_OBJECT_0) {
        //
        // Do work as a result of sync object.
        //
    } else if (rc == WAIT_OBJECT_0 + 1) {
        // It's a message, process it.
        PeekMessage (&msg, hWnd, 0, 0, PM_REMOVE);
        if (msg.message == WM_QUIT)
            fContinue = FALSE;
        else {
            TranslateMessage (&msg);
            DispatchMessage (&msg);
        }
    }
}
```

Mutexes

Earlier I described the event object. That object resides in either a signaled or nonsignaled state. Another synchronization object is the *mutex*. A mutex is a synchronization object that's signaled when it's not owned by a thread and nonsignaled when it *is* owned. Mutexes are extremely useful for coordinating exclusive access to a resource such as a block of memory across multiple threads.

A thread gains ownership by waiting on that mutex with one of the wait functions. When no other threads own the mutex, the thread waiting on the mutex is unblocked, and implicitly gains ownership of the mutex. After the thread has completed the work that requires ownership of the mutex, the thread must explicitly release the mutex with a call to *ReleaseMutex*.

To create a mutex, call this function:

```
HANDLE CreateMutex (LPSECURITY_ATTRIBUTES lpMutexAttributes,
                    BOOL bInitialOwner, LPCTSTR lpName);
```

The *lpMutexAttributes* parameter should be set to NULL. The *bInitialOwner* parameter lets you specify that the calling thread should immediately own the mutex being created. Finally, the *lpName* parameter lets you specify a name for the object so that it can be shared across other processes. When calling *CreateMutex* with a name specified in the *lpName* parameter, Windows CE checks whether a mutex with the same name has already been created. If so, a handle to the previously created mutex is returned. To determine whether the mutex already exists, call *GetLastError*. It returns ERROR_ALREADY_EXISTS if the mutex has been previously created.

Gaining immediate ownership of a mutex using the *bInitialOwner* parameter works only if the mutex is being created. Ownership isn't granted if you're opening a previously created mutex. If you need ownership of a mutex, be sure to call *GetLast-Error* to determine whether the mutex had been previously committed. If so, call *WaitForSingleObject* to gain ownership of the mutex.

You release the mutex with this function:

```
BOOL ReleaseMutex (HANDLE hMutex);
```

The only parameter is the handle to the mutex.

If a thread owns a mutex and calls one of the wait functions to wait on that same mutex, the wait call immediately returns because the thread already owns the mutex. Since mutexes retain an ownership count for the number of times the wait functions are called, a call to *ReleaseMutex* must be made for each nested call to the wait function.

Critical Sections

Using *critical sections* is another method of thread synchronization. Critical sections are good for protecting sections of code from being executed by two different threads at the same time. Critical sections work by having a thread call *EnterCriticalSection* to indicate that it has entered a critical section of code. If another thread calls *EnterCriticalSection* referencing the same critical section object, it's blocked until the first thread makes a call to *LeaveCriticalSection*. Critical sections can protect more than one linear section of code. All that's required is that all sections of code that need to be protected use the same critical section object. The one limitation of critical sections is that they can be used to coordinate threads only within a process.

To use a critical section, you first create a critical section handle with this function:

```
void InitializeCriticalSection (LPCRITICAL_SECTION lpCriticalSection);
```

The only parameter is a pointer to a CRITICAL_SECTION structure that you define somewhere in your application. Be sure not to allocate this structure on the stack of a function that will be deallocated as soon the function returns. You should also not move or copy the critical section structure. Since the other critical section functions require a pointer to this structure, you'll need to allocate it within the scope of all functions using the critical section. While the CRITICAL_SECTION structure is defined in WINBASE.H, an application doesn't need to manipulate any of the fields in that structure. So, for all practical purposes, think of a pointer to a CRITICAL_SECTION structure as a handle, instead of as a pointer to a structure of a known format.

When a thread needs to enter a protected section of code, it should call this function:

```
void EnterCriticalSection (LPCRITICAL_SECTION lpCriticalSection);
```

The function takes as its only parameter a pointer to the critical section structure initialized with *InitializeCriticalSection*. If the critical section is already owned by another thread, this function blocks the new thread and doesn't return until the other thread releases the critical section. If the thread calling *EnterCriticalSection* already owns the critical section, then a use count is incremented and the function returns immediately.

When a thread leaves a critical section, it should call this function:

```
void LeaveCriticalSection (LPCRITICAL_SECTION lpCriticalSection);
```

As with all the critical section functions, the only parameter is the pointer to the critical section structure. Since critical sections track a use count, one call to *LeaveCriticalSection* must be made for each call to *EnterCriticalSection* by the thread that owns the section.

Finally, when you're finished with the critical section, you should call

```
void DeleteCriticalSection (LPCRITICAL_SECTION lpCriticalSection);
```

This cleans up any system resources used to manage the critical section.

Interlocked Variable Access

Here's one more low-level method for synchronizing threads—using the functions for interlocked access to variables. While programmers with multithread experience already know this, I need to warn you that Murphy's Law[1] seems to come into its own when you're using multiple threads in a program. One of the sometimes overlooked issues in a preemptive multitasking system is that a thread can be preempted in the middle of incrementing or checking a variable. For example, a simple code fragment such as

```
if (!i++) {
    // Do something because i was zero.
}
```

can cause a great deal of trouble. To understand why, let's look into how that statement might be compiled. The assembly code for that if statement might look something like this:

```
load     reg1, [addr of i]          ;Read variable
add      reg2, reg1, 1              ;reg2 = reg1 + 1
store    reg2, [addr of i]          ;Save incremented var
bne      reg1, zero, skipblk        ;Branch reg1 != zero
```

There's no reason that the thread executing this section of code couldn't be preempted by another thread after the load instruction and before the store instruction. If this

1. Murphy's Law: Anything that can go wrong will go wrong. Murphy's first corollary: When something goes wrong, it happens at the worst possible moment.

happened, two threads could enter the block of code when that isn't the way the code is supposed to work. Of course, I've already described a number of methods (such as critical sections and the like) that you can use to prevent such incidents from occurring. But for something like this, a critical section is overkill. What you need is something lighter.

Windows CE supports three of the *interlocked* functions from the Win32 API; *InterlockedIncriment*, *InterlockedDecriment*, and *InterlockedExchange*. Each of these allows a thread to increment, decrement, and exchange a variable without your having to worry about the thread being preempted in the middle of the operation. The functions are prototyped here:

```
LONG InterlockedIncrement(LPLONG lpAddend);

LONG InterlockedDecrement(LPLONG lpAddend);

LONG InterlockedExchange(LPLONG Target, LONG Value);
```

For the interlocked increment and decrement, the one parameter is a pointer to the variable to increment or decrement. The returned value is the new value of the variable after it has been incremented or decremented. The *InterlockedExchange* function takes a pointer to the target variable and the new value for the variable. It returns the previous value of the variable. Rewriting the previous code fragment so that it's thread safe produces this code:

```
if (!InterlockedIncrement(&i)) {
    // Do something because i was zero.
}
```

INTERPROCESS COMMUNICATION

There are many cases where two Windows CE processes need to communicate. The walls between processes that protect processes from one another prevent casual exchanging of data. The memory space of one process isn't exposed to another process. Handles to files or other objects can't be passed from one process to another. Windows CE doesn't support the *DuplicateHandle* function available under Windows NT, which allows one process to open a handle used by another process. Nor, as I mentioned before, does Windows CE support handle inheritance. Some of the other more common methods of interprocess communication, such as named pipes, are also not supported under Windows CE. However, you can choose from plenty of ways to enable two or more processes to exchange data.

Finding Other Processes

Before you can communicate with another process, you have to determine whether it's running on the system. Strategies for finding whether another process is running depend mainly on whether you have control of the other process. If the process to be found is a third-party application in which you have no control over the design of the other process, the best method might be to use *FindWindow* to locate the other process's main window. *FindWindow* can search either by window class or by window title. You can also enumerate the top-level windows in the system using *EnumWindows*. You can also use the ToolHelp debugging functions to enumerate the processes running, but this works only when the ToolHelp DLL is loaded on the system and unfortunately, it generally isn't included, by default, on most systems.

If you're writing both processes, however, it's much easier to enumerate them. In this case, the best methods include using the tools you'll later use in one process to communicate with the other process, such as named mutexes, events, or memory-mapped objects. When you create one of these objects, you can determine whether you're the first to create the object or you're simply opening another object by calling *GetLastError* after another call created the object. And the simplest method might be the best; call *FindWindow* and send a WM_USER message to the main window of the other process.

WM_COPYDATA

Once you've found your target process, the talking can begin. If you're staying at the window level, a simple method of communicating is to send a WM_COPYDATA message. WM_COPYDATA is unique in that it's designed to send blocks of data from one process to another. You can't use a standard, user-defined message to pass pointers to data from one process to another because a pointer isn't valid across processes. WM_COPYDATA gets around this problem by having the system translate the pointer to a block of data from one process's address space to another's. The recipient process is required to copy the data immediately into its own memory space, but this message does provide a quick and dirty method of sending blocks of data from one process to another.

Named memory-mapped objects

The problem with WM_COPYDATA is that it can be used only to copy fixed blocks of data at a specific time. Using a named memory-mapped object, two processes can allocate a shared block of memory that's equally accessible to both processes at the same time. You should use named memory-mapped objects so that the system can maintain a proper use count on the object. This procedure prevents one process from freeing the block when it terminates while the other process is still using the block.

Of course, this level of interaction comes with a price. You need some synchronization between the processes when they're reading and writing data in the shared memory block. The use of named mutexes and named events allows processes to coordinate their actions. Using these synchronization objects requires the use of secondary threads so that the message loop can be serviced, but this isn't an exceptional burden.

I described how to create memory-mapped objects in Chapter 6. The example program that shortly follows uses memory-mapped objects and synchronization objects to coordinate access to the shared block of memory.

Communicating with files and databases

A more basic method of interprocess communication is the use of files or a custom database. These methods provide a robust, if slower, communication path. Slow is relative. Files and databases in the Windows CE object store are slow in the sense that the system calls to access these objects must find the data in the object store, uncompress the data, and deliver it to the process. However, since the object store is based in RAM, you see none of the extreme slowness of a mechanical hard disk that you'd see under Windows NT or Windows 98.

The XTalk Example Program

The following example program, XTalk, uses events, mutexes, and a shared memory-mapped block of memory to communicate among different copies of itself. The example demonstrates the rather common problem of one-to-many communication. In this case, the XTalk window has an edit box with a Send button next to it. When a user taps the Send button, the text in the edit box is communicated to every copy of XTalk running on the system. Each copy of XTalk receives the text from the sending copy and places it in a list box also in the XTalk window. Figure 8-1 shows two XTalk programs communicating.

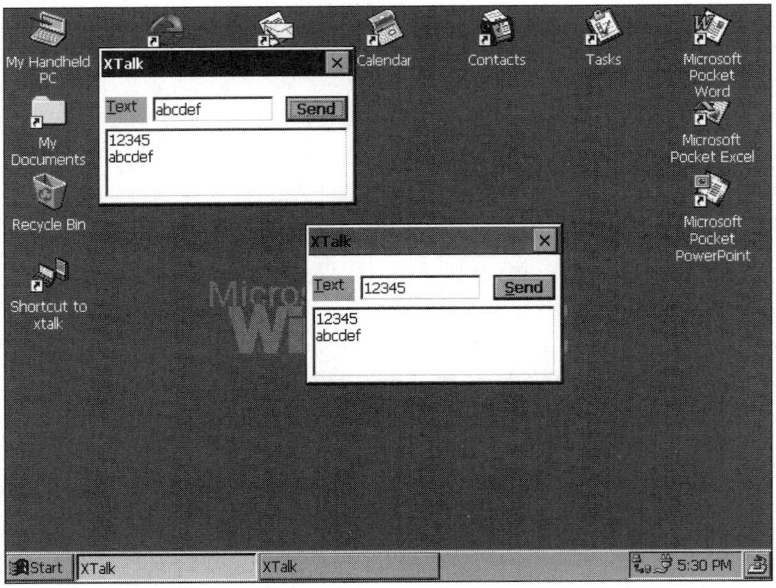

Figure 8-1.
The desktop showing two XTalk windows.

To perform this feat of communication, XTalk uses a named memory-mapped object as a transfer buffer, a mutex to coordinate access to the buffer, and two event objects to indicate the start and end of communication. A third event is used to tell the sender thread to read the text from the edit control and write the contents to the shared memory block. Figure 8-2 shows the source code for XTalk.

XTalk.rc

```
//======================================================================
// Resource file
//
// Written for the book Programming Windows CE
// Copyright (C) 1998 Douglas Boling
//======================================================================
#include "windows.h"
#include "xtalk.h"                          // Program-specific stuff

//----------------------------------------------------------------------
// Icons and bitmaps
//
ID_ICON ICON   "xtalk.ico"                  // Program icon

//----------------------------------------------------------------------
xtalk DIALOG discardable 10, 10, 120, 60
STYLE  WS_OVERLAPPED | WS_VISIBLE | WS_CAPTION | WS_SYSMENU |
       DS_CENTER | DS_MODALFRAME
CAPTION "XTalk"
CLASS "xtalk"
BEGIN
    LTEXT "&Text"                         -1,  2,  10,  20,  12
    EDITTEXT                    IDD_OUTTEXT, 25,  10,  58,  12,
                                                WS_TABSTOP | ES_AUTOHSCROLL
    PUSHBUTTON "&Send",        IDD_SENDTEXT, 88,  10,  30,  12, WS_TABSTOP

    LISTBOX                      IDD_INTEXT,  2,  25, 116,  40,
                                                WS_TABSTOP | WS_VSCROLL
END
```

XTalk.h

```
//======================================================================
// Header file
//
// Written for the book Programming Windows CE
```

Figure 8-2. *The source code for XTalk.* *(continued)*

Figure 8-2. *continued*

```
// Copyright (C) 1998 Douglas Boling
//======================================================================
// Returns number of elements
#define dim(x) (sizeof(x) / sizeof(x[0]))
//----------------------------------------------------------------------
// Generic defines and data types
//
struct decodeUINT {                             // Structure associates
    UINT Code;                                  // messages
                                                // with a function.
    LRESULT (*Fxn)(HWND, UINT, WPARAM, LPARAM);
};
struct decodeCMD {                              // Structure associates
    UINT Code;                                  // menu IDs with a
    LRESULT (*Fxn)(HWND, WORD, HWND, WORD);     // function.
};

//----------------------------------------------------------------------
// Generic defines used by application
#define  ID_ICON             1

#define  IDD_INTEXT          10                 // Control IDs
#define  IDD_SENDTEXT        11
#define  IDD_OUTTEXT         12

#define  MMBUFFSIZE          1024               // Size of shared buffer
#define  TEXTSIZE            256

// Interprocess communication structure mapped in shared memory
typedef struct {
    int nAppCnt;
    int nReadCnt;
    TCHAR szText[TEXTSIZE];
} SHAREBUFF;
typedef SHAREBUFF *PSHAREBUFF;

//----------------------------------------------------------------------
// Function prototypes
//
int InitApp (HINSTANCE);
HWND InitInstance (HINSTANCE, LPWSTR, int);
int TermInstance (HINSTANCE, int);

// Window procedures
LRESULT CALLBACK MainWndProc (HWND, UINT, WPARAM, LPARAM);
```

```
// Message handlers
LRESULT DoCommandMain (HWND, UINT, WPARAM, LPARAM);
LRESULT DoDestroyMain (HWND, UINT, WPARAM, LPARAM);

// Command functions
LPARAM DoMainCommandSend (HWND, WORD, HWND, WORD);
LPARAM DoMainCommandExit (HWND, WORD, HWND, WORD);

// Thread functions
int SenderThread (PVOID pArg);
int ReaderThread (PVOID pArg);
```

XTalk.c

```
//======================================================================
// XTalk - A simple application for Windows CE
//
// Written for the book Programming Windows CE
// Copyright (C) 1998 Douglas Boling
//======================================================================
#include <windows.h>                 // For all that Windows stuff
#include <commctrl.h>                // Command bar includes
#include "xtalk.h"                   // Program-specific stuff

//----------------------------------------------------------------------
// Global data
//
const TCHAR szAppName[] = TEXT ("xtalk");
HINSTANCE hInst;                     // Program instance handle

HANDLE g_hMMObj = 0;                 // Memory-mapped object
PSHAREBUFF g_pBuff = 0;              // Pointer to mm object
HANDLE g_hmWriteOkay = 0;            // Write mutex
HANDLE g_hSendEvent = 0;             // Local send event
HANDLE g_hReadEvent = 0;             // Shared read data event
HANDLE g_hReadDoneEvent = 0;         // Shared data read event

// Message dispatch table for MainWindowProc
const struct decodeUINT MainMessages[] = {
    WM_COMMAND, DoCommandMain,
    WM_DESTROY, DoDestroyMain,
};
// Command Message dispatch for MainWindowProc
const struct decodeCMD MainCommandItems[] = {
    IDOK, DoMainCommandExit,
```

(continued)

Figure 8-2. *continued*

```
    IDCANCEL, DoMainCommandExit,
    IDD_SENDTEXT, DoMainCommandSend,
};
//======================================================================
// Program entry point
//
int WINAPI WinMain (HINSTANCE hInstance, HINSTANCE hPrevInstance,
                    LPWSTR lpCmdLine, int nCmdShow) {
    MSG msg;
    int rc = 0;
    HWND hwndMain;

    // Initialize application.
    rc = InitApp (hInstance);
    if (rc) return rc;

    // Initialize this instance.
    hwndMain = InitInstance (hInstance, lpCmdLine, nCmdShow);
    if (hwndMain == 0)
        return TermInstance (hInstance, 0x10);

    // Application message loop
    while (GetMessage (&msg, NULL, 0, 0)) {
        if ((hwndMain == 0) || !IsDialogMessage (hwndMain, &msg)) {
            TranslateMessage (&msg);
            DispatchMessage (&msg);
        }
    }
    // Instance cleanup
    return TermInstance (hInstance, msg.wParam);
}
//----------------------------------------------------------------------
// InitApp - Application initialization
//
int InitApp (HINSTANCE hInstance) {
    WNDCLASS wc;

    // Register application main window class.
    wc.style = 0;                             // Window style
    wc.lpfnWndProc = MainWndProc;             // Callback function
    wc.cbClsExtra = 0;                        // Extra class data
    wc.cbWndExtra = DLGWINDOWEXTRA;           // Extra window data
    wc.hInstance = hInstance;                 // Owner handle
    wc.hIcon = NULL,                          // Application icon
    wc.hCursor = NULL;                        // Default cursor
    wc.hbrBackground = (HBRUSH) GetStockObject (WHITE_BRUSH);
```

```
    wc.lpszMenuName =  NULL;                        // Menu name
    wc.lpszClassName = szAppName;                   // Window class name

    if (RegisterClass (&wc) == 0) return 1;
    return 0;
}
//----------------------------------------------------------------------
// InitInstance - Instance initialization
//
HWND InitInstance (HINSTANCE hInstance, LPWSTR lpCmdLine, int nCmdShow){
    HWND hWnd;
    HANDLE hThread;
    INT rc;
    BOOL fFirstApp = TRUE;

    // Save program instance handle in global variable.
    hInst = hInstance;

    // Create mutex used to share memory-mapped structure.
    g_hmWriteOkay = CreateMutex (NULL, TRUE, TEXT ("XTALKWRT"));
    rc = GetLastError();
    if (rc == ERROR_ALREADY_EXISTS)
        fFirstApp = FALSE;
    else if (rc) return 0;

    // Wait here for ownership to ensure the initialization is done.
    // This is necessary since CreateMutex doesn't wait.
    rc = WaitForSingleObject (g_hmWriteOkay, 2000);
    if (rc != WAIT_OBJECT_0)
        return 0;

    // Create a file-mapping object.
    g_hMMObj = CreateFileMapping ((HANDLE)-1, NULL, PAGE_READWRITE, 0,
                                  MMBUFFSIZE, TEXT ("XTALKBLK"));
    if (g_hMMObj == 0) return 0;

    // Map into memory the file-mapping object.
    g_pBuff = (PSHAREBUFF)MapViewOfFile (g_hMMObj, FILE_MAP_WRITE,
                                         0, 0, 0);
    if (!g_pBuff)
        CloseHandle (g_hMMObj);

    // Initialize structure if first application started.
    if (fFirstApp)
        memset (g_pBuff, 0, sizeof (SHAREBUFF));
```

(continued)

Figure 8-2. *continued*

```
    // Increment app running count. Interlock not needed due to mutex.
    g_pBuff->nAppCnt++;

    // Release the mutex.  We need to release the mutext twice
    // if we owned it when we entered the wait above.
    ReleaseMutex (g_hmWriteOkay);
    if (fFirstApp)
        ReleaseMutex (g_hmWriteOkay);

    // Now create events for read and send notification.
    g_hSendEvent = CreateEvent (NULL, FALSE, FALSE, NULL);
    g_hReadEvent = CreateEvent (NULL, TRUE, FALSE, TEXT ("XTALKREAD"));
    g_hReadDoneEvent = CreateEvent (NULL, FALSE, FALSE,
                                    TEXT ("XTALKDONE"));
    if (!g_hReadEvent || !g_hSendEvent || !g_hReadDoneEvent)
        return 0;

    // Create main window.
    hWnd = CreateDialog (hInst, szAppName, NULL, NULL);
    rc = GetLastError();

    // Create secondary threads for interprocess communication.
    hThread = CreateThread (NULL, 0, SenderThread, hWnd, 0, &rc);
    if (hThread)
        CloseHandle (hThread);
    else {
        DestroyWindow (hWnd);
        return 0;
    }
    hThread = CreateThread (NULL, 0, ReaderThread, hWnd, 0, &rc);
    if (hThread)
        CloseHandle (hThread);
    else {
        DestroyWindow (hWnd);
        return 0;
    }

    // Return fail code if window not created.
    if (!IsWindow (hWnd)) return 0;

    // Standard show and update calls
    ShowWindow (hWnd, nCmdShow);
    UpdateWindow (hWnd);
    return hWnd;
}
```

```
//----------------------------------------------------------------------
// TermInstance - Program cleanup
//
int TermInstance (HINSTANCE hInstance, int nDefRC) {

    // Free memory-mapped object.
    if (g_pBuff) {
        // Decrement app running count.
        InterlockedDecrement (&g_pBuff->nAppCnt);
        UnmapViewOfFile (g_pBuff);
    }
    if (g_hMMObj)
        CloseHandle (g_hMMObj);

    // Free mutex.
    if (g_hmWriteOkay)
        CloseHandle (g_hmWriteOkay);

    // Close event handles.
    if (g_hReadEvent)
        CloseHandle (g_hReadEvent);

    if (g_hReadDoneEvent)
        CloseHandle (g_hReadDoneEvent);

    if (g_hSendEvent)
        CloseHandle (g_hSendEvent);
    return nDefRC;
}
//======================================================================
// Message handling procedures for main window
//----------------------------------------------------------------------
// MainWndProc - Callback function for application window
//
LRESULT CALLBACK MainWndProc (HWND hWnd, UINT wMsg, WPARAM wParam,
                              LPARAM lParam) {
    INT i;
    //
    // Search message list to see if we need to handle this
    // message.  If in list, call procedure.
    //
    for (i = 0; i < dim(MainMessages); i++) {
        if (wMsg == MainMessages[i].Code)
            return (*MainMessages[i].Fxn)(hWnd, wMsg, wParam, lParam);
    }
    return DefWindowProc (hWnd, wMsg, wParam, lParam);
```

(continued)

Figure 8-2. *continued*

```
}
//----------------------------------------------------------------------
// DoCommandMain - Process WM_COMMAND message for window.
//
LRESULT DoCommandMain (HWND hWnd, UINT wMsg, WPARAM wParam,
                       LPARAM lParam) {
    WORD    idItem, wNotifyCode;
    HWND    hwndCtl;
    INT    i;

    // Parse the parameters.
    idItem = (WORD) LOWORD (wParam);
    wNotifyCode = (WORD) HIWORD (wParam);
    hwndCtl = (HWND) lParam;

    // Call routine to handle control message.
    for(i = 0; i < dim(MainCommandItems); i++) {
        if(idItem == MainCommandItems[i].Code)
            return (*MainCommandItems[i].Fxn)(hWnd, idItem, hwndCtl,
                                               wNotifyCode);
    }
    return 0;
}
//----------------------------------------------------------------------
// DoDestroyMain - Process WM_DESTROY message for window.
//
LRESULT DoDestroyMain (HWND hWnd, UINT wMsg, WPARAM wParam,
                       LPARAM lParam) {
    PostQuitMessage (0);
    return 0;
}
//======================================================================
// Command handler routines
//----------------------------------------------------------------------
// DoMainCommandExit - Process Program Exit command
//
LPARAM DoMainCommandExit (HWND hWnd, WORD idItem, HWND hwndCtl,
                          WORD wNotifyCode) {

    SendMessage (hWnd, WM_CLOSE, 0, 0);
    return 0;
}
//----------------------------------------------------------------------
// DoMainCommandSend - Process Program Send command.
//
LPARAM DoMainCommandSend (HWND hWnd, WORD idItem, HWND hwndCtl,
```

```
                               WORD wNotifyCode) {

    SetEvent (g_hSendEvent);
    return 0;
}
//======================================================================
// SenderThread - Performs the interprocess communication
//
int SenderThread (PVOID pArg) {
    HWND hWnd;
    INT nGoCode, rc;
    TCHAR szText[TEXTSIZE];

    hWnd = (HWND)pArg;
    while (1) {
        nGoCode = WaitForSingleObject (g_hSendEvent, INFINITE);
        if (nGoCode == WAIT_OBJECT_0) {
            SendDlgItemMessage (hWnd, IDD_OUTTEXT, WM_GETTEXT,
                                sizeof (szText), (LPARAM)szText);

            rc = WaitForSingleObject (g_hmWriteOkay, 2000);
            if (rc == WAIT_OBJECT_0) {
                lstrcpy (g_pBuff->szText, szText);
                g_pBuff->nReadCnt = g_pBuff->nAppCnt;
                PulseEvent (g_hReadEvent);

                // Wait while reader threads get data.
                while (g_pBuff->nReadCnt)
                    rc = WaitForSingleObject (g_hReadDoneEvent,
                                              INFINITE);
                ReleaseMutex (g_hmWriteOkay);
            }
        } else
            return -1;
    }
    return 0;
}
//======================================================================
// ReaderThread - Performs the interprocess communication
//
int ReaderThread (PVOID pArg) {
    HWND hWnd;
    INT nGoCode, rc, i;
    TCHAR szText[TEXTSIZE];

    hWnd = (HWND)pArg;
```

(continued)

Figure 8-2. *continued*

```
    while (1) {
        nGoCode = WaitForSingleObject (g_hReadEvent, INFINITE);
        if (nGoCode == WAIT_OBJECT_0) {
            i = SendDlgItemMessage (hWnd, IDD_INTEXT, LB_ADDSTRING, 0,
                                    (LPARAM)g_pBuff->szText);
            SendDlgItemMessage (hWnd, IDD_INTEXT, LB_SETTOPINDEX, i, 0);

            InterlockedDecrement (&g_pBuff->nReadCnt);
            SetEvent (g_hReadDoneEvent);
        } else {
            rc = GetLastError();
            wsprintf (szText, TEXT ("rc:%d"), rc);
            MessageBox (hWnd, szText, TEXT ("ReadThread Err"), MB_OK);
        }
    }
    return 0;
}
```

The interesting routines in the XTalk example are the *InitInstance* procedure and the two thread procedures *SenderThread* and *ReaderThread*. The relevant part of *InitInstance* is shown below with the error checking code removed for brevity.

```
// Create mutex used to share memory-mapped structure.
g_hmWriteOkay = CreateMutex (NULL, TRUE, TEXT ("XTALKWRT"));
rc = GetLastError();
if (rc == ERROR_ALREADY_EXISTS)
    fFirstApp = FALSE;

// Wait here for ownership to insure the initialization is done.
// This is necessary since CreateMutex doesn't wait.
rc = WaitForSingleObject (g_hmWriteOkay, 2000);
if (rc != WAIT_OBJECT_0)
    return 0;

// Create a file-mapping object.
g_hMMObj = CreateFileMapping ((HANDLE)-1, NULL, PAGE_READWRITE, 0,
                              MMBUFFSIZE, TEXT ("XTALKBLK"));

// Map into memory the file-mapping object.
g_pBuff = (PSHAREBUFF)MapViewOfFile (g_hMMObj, FILE_MAP_WRITE,
                                     0, 0, 0);

// Initialize structure if first application started.
if (fFirstApp)
    memset (g_pBuff, 0, sizeof (SHAREBUFF));
```

```
// Increment app running count. Interlock not needed due to mutex.
g_pBuff->nAppCnt++;

// Release the mutex.  We need to release the mutex twice
// if we owned it when we entered the wait above.
ReleaseMutex (g_hmWriteOkay);
if (fFirstApp)
    ReleaseMutex (g_hmWriteOkay);

// Now create events for read and send notification.
g_hSendEvent = CreateEvent (NULL, FALSE, FALSE, NULL);
g_hReadEvent = CreateEvent (NULL, TRUE, FALSE, TEXT ("XTALKREAD"));
g_hReadDoneEvent = CreateEvent (NULL, FALSE, FALSE,
                                TEXT ("XTALKDONE"));
```

This code is responsible for creating the necessary synchronization objects as well as creating and initializing the shared memory block. The mutex object is created first with the parameters set to request initial ownership of the mutex object. A call is then made to *GetLastError* to determine whether the mutex object has already been created. If not, the application assumes the first instance of XTalk is running and later will initialize the shared memory block. Once the mutex is created, an additional call is made to *WaitForSingleObject* to wait until the mutex is released. This call is necessary to prevent a late starting instance of XTalk from disturbing communication in progress. Once the mutex is owned, calls are made to *CreateFileMapping* and *MapViewOfFile* to create a named memory-mapped object. Since the object is named, each process that opens the object opens the same object and is returned a pointer to the same block of memory.

Once the shared memory block is created, the first instance of XTalk zeros out the block. This procedure also forces the block of RAM to be committed because memory-mapped objects by default are autocommit blocks. Then *nAppCnt*, which keeps a count of the running instances of XTalk, is incremented. Finally the mutex protecting the shared memory is released. If this is the first instance of XTalk, *ReleaseMutex* must be called twice because it gains ownership of the mutex twice—once when the mutex is created and again when the call to *WaitForSingleObject* is made.

Finally, three event objects are created. *SendEvent* is an unnamed event, local to each instance of XTalk. The primary thread uses this event to signal the sender thread that the user has pressed the Send button and wants the text in the edit box transmitted. The *ReadEvent* is a named event that tells the other instances of XTalk that there's data to be read in the transfer buffer. The *ReadDoneEvent* is a named event signaled by each of the receiving copies of XTalk to indicate that they have read the data.

The two threads, *ReaderThread* and *SenderThread* are created immediately after the main window of XTalk is created. The code for *SenderThread* is shown here:

```
int SenderThread (PVOID pArg) {
    HWND hWnd;
    INT nGoCode, rc;
    TCHAR szText[TEXTSIZE];

    hWnd = (HWND)pArg;
    while (1) {
        nGoCode = WaitForSingleObject (g_hSendEvent, INFINITE);
        if (nGoCode == WAIT_OBJECT_0) {
            SendDlgItemMessage (hWnd, IDD_OUTTEXT, WM_GETTEXT,
                                sizeof (szText), (LPARAM)szText);

            rc = WaitForSingleObject (g_hmWriteOkay, 2000);
            if (rc == WAIT_OBJECT_0) {
                lstrcpy (g_pBuff->szText, szText);
                g_pBuff->nReadCnt = g_pBuff->nAppCnt;
                PulseEvent (g_hReadEvent);

                // Wait while reader threads get data.
                while (g_pBuff->nReadCnt)
                    rc = WaitForSingleObject (g_hReadDoneEvent,
                                              INFINITE);
                ReleaseMutex (g_hmWriteOkay);
            }
        }
    }
    return 0;
}
```

The routine waits on the primary thread of XTalk to signal *SendEvent*. The primary thread of XTalk makes the signal in response to a WM_COMMAND message from the Send button. The thread is then unblocked, reads the text from the edit control, and waits to gain ownership of the *WriteOkay* mutex. This mutex protects two copies of XTalk from writing to the shared block at the same time. When the thread owns the mutex, it writes the string read from the edit control into the shared buffer. It then copies the number of active copies of XTalk into the *nReadCnt* variable in the same shared buffer, and pulses the *ReadEvent* to tell the other copies of XTalk to read the newly written data. A manual resetting event is used so that all threads waiting on the event will be unblocked when the event is signaled.

The thread then waits for the *nReadCnt* variable to return to 0. Each time a reader thread reads the data, the *nReadCnt* variable is decremented and the *ReadDone* event signaled. Note that the thread doesn't spin on this variable but uses an event to tell it when to check the variable again. This would actually be a great place to use

WaitForMultipleObjects and have all reader threads signal when they've read the data, but Windows CE doesn't support the *WaitAll* flag in *WaitForMultipleObjects*.

Finally, when all the reader threads have read the data, the sender thread releases the mutex protecting the shared segment and the thread returns to wait for another send event.

The *ReaderThread* routine is even simpler. Here it is:

```
int ReaderThread (PVOID pArg) {
    HWND hWnd;
    INT nGoCode, rc, i;
    TCHAR szText[TEXTSIZE];

    hWnd = (HWND)pArg;
    while (1) {
        nGoCode = WaitForSingleObject (g_hReadEvent, INFINITE);
        if (nGoCode == WAIT_OBJECT_0) {
            i = SendDlgItemMessage (hWnd, IDD_INTEXT, LB_ADDSTRING, 0,
                                    (LPARAM)g_pBuff->szText);
            SendDlgItemMessage (hWnd, IDD_INTEXT, LB_SETTOPINDEX, i, 0);

            InterlockedDecrement (&g_pBuff->nReadCnt);
            SetEvent (g_hReadDoneEvent);
        }
    }
    return 0;
}
```

The reader thread starts up and immediately blocks on *ReadEvent*. When it's unblocked, it adds the text from the shared buffer into the list box in its window. The list box is then scrolled to show the new line. After this is accomplished, the *nReadCnt* variable is decremented using *InterlockedDecrement* to be thread safe, and the *ReadDone* event is signaled to tell the *SenderThread* to check the read count. After that's accomplished, the routine loops around and waits for another read event to occur.

EXCEPTION HANDLING

Windows CE, along with Visual C++ for Windows CE, supports Microsoft's standard, structured exception handling extensions to the C language, the *__try*, *__except* and *__try*, *__finally* blocks. Note that Visual C++ for Windows CE doesn't support the full C++ exception handling framework with keywords such as *catch* and *throw*.

Windows exception handling is complex and if I were to cover it completely, I could easily write another entire chapter. The following review introduces the concepts to non-Win32 programmers and conveys enough information about the subject for you to get your feet wet. If you want to wade all the way in, the best source for a complete explanation of Win32 exception handling is Jeffrey Richter's *Advanced Windows* third edition (Microsoft Press, 1997).

The *__try, __except* Block

The first construct I'll talk about is the *__try*, *__except* block which looks like this:

```
__try {

    // Try some code here that might cause an exception.

}
__except (exception filter) {

    // This code is depending on the filter on the except line.

}
```

Essentially, the *try-except* pair allows you the ability to anticipate exceptions and handle them locally instead of having Windows terminate the thread or the process because of an unhandled exception.

The exception filter is essentially a return code that tells Windows how to handle the exception. You can hard code one of the three possible values or call a function that dynamically decides how to respond to the exception.

If the filter returns EXCEPTION_EXECUTE_HANDLER, Windows aborts the execution in the *try* block and jumps to the first statement in the *except* block. This is helpful if you're expecting the exception and you know how to handle it. In the code that follows, the access to memory is protected by a *__try*, *__except* block.

```
BYTE ReadByteFromMemory (LPBYTE pPtr, BOOL *bDataValid) {
    BYTE ucData = 0;

    *bDataValid = TRUE;
    __try {
        ucData = *pPtr;
    }
    __except (DecideHowToHandleException ()) {
        // The pointer isn't valid, clean up.
        ucData = 0;
        *bDataValid = FALSE;
    }
    return ucData;
}
int DecideHowToHandleException (void) {
    return EXCEPTION_EXECUTE_HANDLER;
}
```

If the memory read line above wasn't protected by a *__try*, *__except* block and an invalid pointer was passed to the routine, the exception generated would have been passed up to the system, causing the thread and perhaps the process to be terminated. If you use the *__try*, *__except* block, the exception is handled locally and the process continues with the error handled locally.

Another possibility is to have the system retry the instruction that caused the exception. You can do this by having the filter return EXCEPTION_CONTINUE_EXECUTION. On the surface, this sounds like a great option—simply fix the problem and retry the operation your program was performing. The problem with this approach is that what will be retried isn't the *line* that caused the exception, but *the machine instruction* that caused the exception. The difference is illustrated by the following code fragment that looks okay but probably won't work:

```
// An example that doesn't work...
int DivideIt (int aVal, int bVal) {
    int cVal;
    __try {
        cVal = aVal / bVal;
    }
    __except (EXCEPTION_CONTINUE_EXECUTION) {
        bVal = 1;
    }
    return cVal;
}
```

The idea in this code is noble; protect the program from a divide-by-zero error by ensuring that if the error occurs, the error is corrected by replacing *bVal* with 1. The problem is that the line

```
cVal = aVal / bVal;
```

is probably compiled to something like the following on a MIPS-compatible CPU:

```
lw    t6,aVal(sp)        ;Load aVal
lw    t7,bVal(sp)        ;Load bVal
div   t6,t7              ;Perform the divide
sw    t6,cVal(sp)        ;Save result into cVal
```

In this case, the third instruction, the *div*, causes the exception. Restarting the code after the exception results in the restart beginning with the *div* instruction. The problem is that the execution needs to start at least one instruction earlier to load the new value from *bVal* into the register. The moral of the story is that attempting to restart code at the point of an exception is risky at best and at worst, unpredictable.

The third option for the exception filter is to not even attempt to solve the problem and to pass the exception up to the next, higher *__try*, *__except* block in code.

This is accomplished by the exception filter returning EXCEPTION_CONTINUE_SEARCH. Since *__try*, *__except* blocks can be nested, it's good practice to handle specific problems in a lower, nested *__try*, *__except* block and more global errors at a higher level.

Determining the problem

With these three options available, it would be nice if Windows let you in on why the exception occurred. Fortunately, Windows provides the function

```
DWORD GetExceptionCode (void);
```

This function returns a code that indicates why the exception occurred in the first place. The codes are defined in WINBASE.H and range from EXCEPTION_ACCESS_VIOLATION to CONTROL_C_EXIT, with a number of codes in between. Another function allows even more information:

```
LPEXCEPTION_POINTERS GetExceptionInformation (void);
```

GetExceptionInformation returns a pointer to a structure that contains pointers to two structures: EXCEPTION_RECORD and CONTEXT. EXCEPTION_RECORD is defined as

```
typedef struct _EXCEPTION_RECORD {
    DWORD ExceptionCode;
    DWORD ExceptionFlags;
    struct _EXCEPTION_RECORD *ExceptionRecord;
    PVOID ExceptionAddress;
    DWORD NumberParameters;
    DWORD ExceptionInformation[EXCEPTION_MAXIMUM_PARAMETERS];
} EXCEPTION_RECORD;
```

The fields in this structure go into explicit detail about why an exception occurred. To narrow the problem down even further, you can use the CONTEXT structure. The CONTEXT structure is different for each CPU and essentially defines the exact state of the CPU when the exception occurred.

There are limitations on when these two exception information functions can be called. *GetExecptionCode* can only be called from inside an *except* block or from within the exception filter function. The *GetExceptionInformation* function can be called only from within the exception filter function.

The *__try, __finally* Block

Another tool of the structured exception handling features of the Win32 API is the *__try*, *__finally* block. It looks like this:

```
__try {

    // Do something here.

}
__finally {

    // This code is executed regardless of what happens in the try block.

}
```

The goal of the *__try*, *__finally* block is to provide a block of code, the *finally* block, that always executes regardless of how the other code in the *try* block attempts to leave the block. If there's no *return*, *break* or *goto* in the *try* block, the code in the *finally* block executes immediately following the last statement in the *try* block. If the *try* block has a *return* or a *goto* or some other statement that transfers execution out of the *try* block, the compiler insures that the code in the *finally* block will get executed before execution leaves the *try* block. Take, for example, the following code:

```
int ClintSimFunc (int TodaysTask) {

    __try {
        switch (TodaysTask) {
        case THEGOOD:
            //Do the good stuff.
            return 1;
        case THEBAD:
            //Do the bad stuff.
            return 2;
        case THEUGLY:
            //Do the ugly stuff.
            break;
        }
        // Climb the Eiger.
        return 0;
    }
    __finally {
        // Reload the .44.
    }
}
```

In this example, the *try* block can be left three ways: returning after executing the Good case or the Bad case or after executing the Ugly case, which breaks and executes the Eiger code. However the code exits the *try* block, Clint's gun is always reloaded because the *finally* block is always executed.

It works out that having the compiler build the code to protect the *try* block exits tends to create a fair amount of extra code. To help, you can use another statement, *__leave*, which makes it easier for the compiler to recognize what's happening and make a code-efficient path to the *finally* block. Using the *__leave* statement, the code above becomes

```
int ClintSimFunc (int TodaysTask) {
    int nFistfull;

    __try {
        switch (TodaysTask) {
        case THEGOOD:

            //Do the good stuff.
            nFistfull = 1;
            __leave;
        case THEBAD:
            //Do the bad stuff.
            nFistfull = 2;
            __leave;
        case THEUGLY:
            //Do the ugly stuff.
            break;
        }
        // Climb the Eiger.
        nFistFull = 0;
    }
    // The code falls into the __finally block.
    __finally {
        // Reload the .44.
    }
    return nFistfull;
}
```

The *__try*, *__finally* block is helpful for writing clean code because you can use the *__leave* statement to jump out of a sequence of statements that build upon one another and put all the cleanup code in the *finally* block. The *finally* block also has a place in structured exception handling since the *finally* code is executed if an exception in the *try* block causes a premature exit of the block.

In the past three chapters, I've covered the basics of the Windows CE kernel from memory to files to processes and threads. Now it's time to break from this low-level stuff and starting looking outward. The next section covers the different communication aspects of Windows CE. I start at the low level, with explanations of basic serial and I/R communication and TAPI. Chapter 10 covers networking from a Windows CE perspective. Finally, Chapter 11 covers Windows CE to PC communications. That's a fair amount of ground to cover. Let's get started.

Part III

COMMUNICATIONS

Chapter 9

Serial Communications

If there's one area of the Win32 API that Windows CE doesn't skimp, it's in communication. It makes sense. Systems running Windows CE are either mobile, requiring extensive communication functionality, or they're devices generally employed to communicate with remote servers. In this chapter, I introduce the low-level serial and infrared communication APIs. You use the infrared port at this level in almost the same manner as a serial port. The only functional difference is that infrared transmission is *half duplex*, that is, transmission can occur in only one direction at a time.

BASIC DRIVERS

Before I can delve into the serial drivers, we must take a brief look at how Windows CE handles drivers in general. Windows CE separates device drivers into two main groups: native and stream interface. Native drivers, sometimes called *built-in drivers*, are those device drivers that are required for the hardware and were created by the OEM when the Windows CE hardware was designed. Among the devices that have native drivers are the keyboard, the touch panel, audio, and the PCMCIA controller. These drivers might not support the generic device driver interface I describe below. Instead, they might extend the interface or have a totally custom interface to the operating system. Native drivers frequently require minor changes when a new version of the operation system is released. These drivers are designed using the OEM adaptation kit supplied by Microsoft. A more general adaptation kit, the

Embedded Toolkit (ETK), also enables you to develop built-in drivers. However these drivers are developed, they're tightly bound to the Windows CE operating system and aren't usually replaced after the device has been sold.

On the other hand, stream interface device drivers (which used to be referred to as installable drivers) can be supplied by third-party manufacturers to support hardware added to the system. Since Windows CE systems generally don't have a bus such as an ISA bus or a PCI bus for extra cards, the additional hardware is usually installed via a PCMCIA or a Compact Flash slot. In this case, the device driver would use functions provided by the low-level PCMCIA driver to access the card in the PCMCIA or the Compact Flash slot.

In addition, a device driver might be written to extend the functionality of an existing driver. For example, you might write a driver to provide a compressed or encrypted data stream over a serial link. In this case, an application would access the encryption driver, which would then in turn use the serial driver to access the serial hardware.

Device drivers under Windows CE operate at the same protection level as applications. They differ from applications in that they're DLLs. Most drivers are loaded by the device manager process (DEVICE.EXE) when the system boots. All these drivers, therefore, share the same process address space. Some of the built-in drivers, on the other hand, are loaded by GWE (GWES.EXE). (GWE stands for Graphics Windowing and Event Manager.) These drivers include the display driver (DDI.DLL) as well as the keyboard and touch panel (or mouse) drivers.

Driver Names

Stream interface device drivers are identified by a three-character name followed by a single digit. This scheme allows for 10 device drivers of one name to be installed on a Windows CE device at any one time. Here are a few examples of some three-character names currently in use:

COM	Serial driver
ACM	Audio compression manager
WAV	Audio wave driver
CON	Console driver

When referencing a stream interface driver, an application uses the three-character name, followed by the single digit, followed by a colon (:). The colon is required under Windows CE for the system to recognize the driver name.

Enumerating the Active Drivers

The documented method for determining what drivers are loaded onto a Windows CE system is to look in the registry under the key \Drivers\Active under HKEY_LOCAL_MACHINE. The device manager dynamically updates the subkeys contained here as drivers are loaded and unloaded from the system. Contained in this key is a list of subkeys, one for each active driver. The name of the key is simply a placeholder; it's the values inside the keys that indicate the active drivers. Figure 9-1 shows the registry key for the COM1 serial driver on an HP 620.

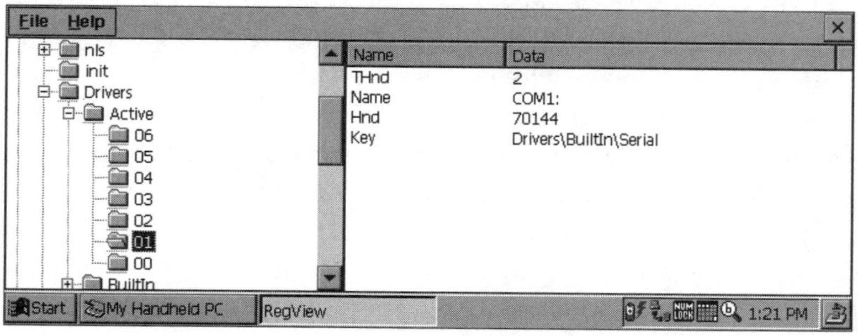

Figure 9-1. *The registry's active list values for the serial device driver for COM1.*

In Figure 9-1, the *Name* value contains the official five-character name (four characters plus a colon) of the device. The *THnd* and *Hnd* values are handles that are used internally by Windows CE. The interesting entry is the *Key* value. This value points to the registry key where the device driver stores its configuration information. This second key is necessary because the active list is dynamic, changing whenever a device is installed. In the case of the serial driver, its configuration data is generally stored in Drivers\BuiltIn\Serial although you shouldn't hard code this value. Instead, you can look at the *Key* value in the active list to determine the location of a driver's permanent configuration data. The configuration data for the serial driver is shown in Figure 9-2.

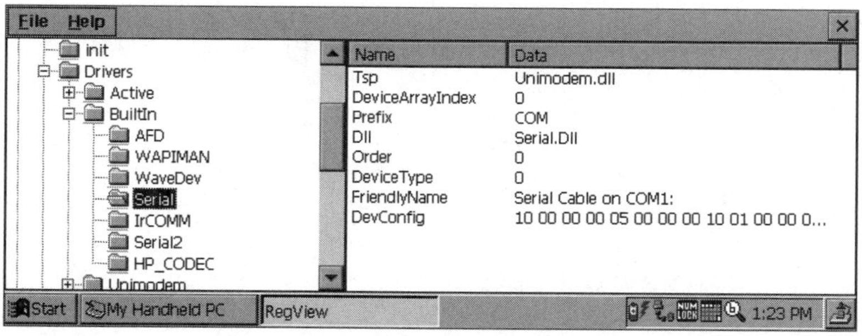

Figure 9-2. *The registry entry for the serial driver.*

You can look in the serial driver registry key for such information as the name of the DLL that actually implements the driver, the three-letter prefix defining the driver name, the order in which the driver wants to be loaded, and something handy for user interfaces, the *friendly name* of the driver. Not all drivers have this friendly name, but when they do, it's a much more user-friendly name than COM2 or NDS1.

Drivers for PCMCIA or Compact Flash Cards have an additional value in their active list key. The *PnpId* value contains the Plug and Play ID string for the card. While this string is more descriptive than the five-character driver name, some PCMCIA and Compact Flash Cards have their *PnpId* strings registered in the system. If so, a registry key for the *PnpId* is located in the *Drivers\PCMCIA* key under HKEY_LOCAL_MACHINE. For example, a PCMCIA Card that had a *PnpId* string *This_is_a_pc_card* would be registered under the key *\Drivers\PCMCIA\This_is_a_pc_card*. That key may contain a *FriendlyName* string for the driver.

Following is a routine (and a small helper routine) that creates a list of active drivers and, if specified, their friendly names. The routine produces a series of Unicode strings, two for each active driver. The first string is the driver name, followed by its friendly name. If a driver doesn't have a friendly name, a zero-length string is inserted in the list. The list ends with a zero-length string for the driver name.

```
//----------------------------------------------------------------------
// AddToList - Helper routine
int AddToList (LPTSTR *pPtr, INT *pnListSize, LPTSTR pszStr) {
    INT nLen = lstrlen (pszStr) + 1;

    if (*pnListSize < nLen)
        return -1;
    lstrcpy (*pPtr, pszStr);
    *pPtr += nLen;
    *pnListSize -= nLen;
    return 0;
}
//----------------------------------------------------------------------
// EnumActiveDrivers - Produces a list of active drivers
//
int EnumActiveDrivers (LPTSTR pszDrvrList, int nListSize) {
    INT i = 0, rc;
    HKEY hKey, hSubKey, hDrvrKey;
    TCHAR szKey[128], szValue[128];
    LPTSTR pPtr = pszDrvrList;
    DWORD dwType, dwSize;

    *pPtr = TEXT ('\0');
    if (RegOpenKeyEx (HKEY_LOCAL_MACHINE, TEXT ("drivers\\active"), 0,
                      0, &hKey) != ERROR_SUCCESS)
        return 0;

    while (1) {
        // Enumerate active driver list.
        dwSize = sizeof (szKey);
        if (RegEnumKeyEx (hKey, i++, szKey, &dwSize, NULL, NULL,
                          NULL, NULL) != ERROR_SUCCESS)
            break;
```

```
        // Open active driver key.
        rc = RegOpenKeyEx (hKey, szKey, 0, 0, &hSubKey);
        if (rc != ERROR_SUCCESS)
            continue;

        // Get name of device.
        dwSize = sizeof (szValue);
        rc = RegQueryValueEx (hSubKey, TEXT ("Name"), 0, &dwType,
                              (PBYTE)szValue, &dwSize);
        if (rc != ERROR_SUCCESS)
            szValue[0] = TEXT ('\0');

        if (AddToList (&pPtr, &nListSize, szValue)) {
            rc = -1;
            RegCloseKey (hSubKey);
            break;
        }

        // Get friendly name of device.
        szValue[0] = TEXT ( '\0');
        dwSize = sizeof (szKey);
        rc = RegQueryValueEx (hSubKey, TEXT ("Key"), 0, &dwType,
                              (PBYTE)szKey, &dwSize);
        if (rc == ERROR_SUCCESS) {
            // Get driver friendly name.
            if (RegOpenKeyEx (HKEY_LOCAL_MACHINE, szKey, 0, 0,
                              &hDrvrKey) == ERROR_SUCCESS) {

                dwSize = sizeof (szValue);
                RegQueryValueEx (hDrvrKey, TEXT ("FriendlyName"), 0,
                                 &dwType, (PBYTE)szValue, &dwSize);
                RegCloseKey (hDrvrKey);
            }
        }
        RegCloseKey (hSubKey);
        if (AddToList (&pPtr, &nListSize, szValue)) {
            rc = -1;
            break;
        }
    }
    RegCloseKey (hKey);
    // Add terminating zero.
    if (!rc)
        rc = AddToList (&pPtr, &nListSize, TEXT (""));
    return rc;
}
```

Reading and Writing Device Drivers

Your application accesses device drivers under Windows CE through the file I/O functions, *CreateFile*, *ReadFile*, *WriteFile*, and *CloseHandle*. You open the device using *CreateFile*, with the name of the device being the five-character (three characters plus digit plus colon) name of the driver. Drivers can be opened with all the varied access rights: read only, write only, read/write, or neither read nor write access.

Once a device is open, you can send data to it using *WriteFile* and can read from the device using *ReadFile*. As is the case with file operations, overlapped I/O isn't supported for devices under Windows CE. The driver can be sent control characters using the function (not described in Chapter 7) *DeviceIoControl*. The function is prototyped this way:

```
BOOL DeviceIoControl (HANDLE hDevice, DWORD dwIoControlCode,
                      LPVOID lpInBuffer, DWORD nInBufferSize,
                      LPVOID lpOutBuffer, DWORD nOutBufferSize,
                      LPDWORD lpBytesReturned,
                      LPOVERLAPPED lpOverlapped);
```

The first parameter is the handle to the opened device. The second parameter, *dwIoControlCode*, is the *IoCtl* (pronounced eye-OC-tal) code. This value defines the operation of the call to the driver. The next series of parameters are generic input and output buffers and their sizes. The use of these buffers is dependent on the *IoCtl* code passed in *dwIoControlCode*. The *lpBytesReturned* parameter must point to a DWORD value that will receive the number of bytes returned by the driver in the buffer pointed to by *lpOutBuffer*.

Each driver has its own set of *IoCtl* codes. If you look in the source code for the example serial driver provided in the ETK, you'll see that the following *IoCtl* codes are defined for the COM driver. Note that these codes aren't defined in the Windows CE SDK because an application doesn't need to directly call *DeviceIoControl* using these codes.

IOCTL_SERIAL_SET_BREAK_ON	IOCTL_SERIAL_SET_BREAK_OFF
IOCTL_SERIAL_SET_DTR	IOCTL_SERIAL_CLR_DTR
IOCTL_SERIAL_SET_RTS	IOCTL_SERIAL_CLR_RTS
IOCTL_SERIAL_SET_XOFF	IOCTL_SERIAL_SET_XON
IOCTL_SERIAL_GET_WAIT_MASK	IOCTL_SERIAL_SET_WAIT_MASK
IOCTL_SERIAL_WAIT_ON_MASK	IOCTL_SERIAL_GET_COMMSTATUS
IOCTL_SERIAL_GET_MODEMSTATUS	IOCTL_SERIAL_GET_PROPERTIES
IOCTL_SERIAL_SET_TIMEOUTS	IOCTL_SERIAL_GET_TIMEOUTS
IOCTL_SERIAL_PURGE	IOCTL_SERIAL_SET_QUEUE_SIZE
IOCTL_SERIAL_IMMEDIATE_CHAR	IOCTL_SERIAL_GET_DCB
IOCTL_SERIAL_SET_DCB	IOCTL_SERIAL_ENABLE_IR
IOCTL_SERIAL_DISABLE_IR	

As you can see from the fairly self-descriptive names, the serial driver *IoCtl* functions expose significant function to the calling process. Windows uses these *IoCtl* codes to control some of the specific features of a serial port, such as the handshaking lines and time outs. Each driver has its own set of *IoCtl* codes. I've shown the ones above simply as an example of how the *DeviceIoControl* function is typically used. Under most circumstances, there's no reason for an application to use the *DeviceIoControl* function with the serial driver. Windows provides its own set of functions that then call down to the serial driver using *DeviceIoControl.*

Okay, we've talked enough about generic drivers. It's time to sit down to the meat of the chapter—serial communication. I'll talk first about basic serial connections, and then venture into infrared communication. Windows CE provides excellent support for serial communications, but the API is a subset of the API for Windows NT or Windows 98. Fortunately, the basics are quite similar, and the differences mainly inconsequential.

BASIC SERIAL COMMUNICATION

The interface for a serial device is a combination of generic driver I/O calls and specific communication-related functions. The serial device is treated as a generic, installable, stream device for opening, closing, reading, and writing the serial port. For configuring the port, the Win32 API supports a set of Comm functions. Windows CE supports most of the Comm functions supported by Windows NT and Windows 98.

A word of warning: programming a serial port under Windows CE isn't like programming one under MS-DOS. You can't simply find the base address of the serial port and program the registers directly. While there are ways for a program to gain access to the physical memory space, every Windows CE device has a different physical memory map. Even if you solved the access problem by knowing exactly where the serial hardware resided in the memory map, there's no guarantee the serial hardware is going to be compatible with the 8250 (or, these days, a 16550) serial interface we've all come to know and love in the PC world. In fact, the implementation of the serial port on some Windows CE devices looks nothing like an 8250.

But even if you know where to go in the memory map and the implementation of the serial hardware, you still don't need to "hack down to the hardware." The serial port drivers in Windows CE are efficient, interrupt-driven designs and are written to support its specific serial hardware. If you have any special needs not provided by the base serial driver, you can purchase the Embedded Toolkit and write a serial driver yourself. Aside from that extreme case, there's just no reason not to use the published Win32 serial interface under Windows CE.

Opening and Closing a Serial Port

As with all stream device drivers, a serial port device is opened using *CreateFile*. The name used needs to follow the standards I described previously, with the three letters COM followed by the number of the COM port to open and then a colon. The colon is required under Windows CE and is a departure from the naming convention used for device driver names used in Windows NT and Windows 98. The following line opens COM port 1 for reading and writing:

```
hSer = CreateFile (TEXT ("COM1:"), GENERIC_READ | GENERIC_WRITE,
                   0, NULL, OPEN_EXISTING, 0, NULL);
```

You must pass a 0 in the sharing parameter as well as in the security attributes and the template file parameters of *CreateFile*. Windows CE doesn't support overlapped I/O for devices, so you can't pass the FILE_FLAG_OVERLAPPED flag in the *dwFlagsAndAttributes* parameter. The handle returned is either the handle to the opened serial port or INVALID_HANDLE_VALUE. Remember that, unlike many of the Windows functions, *CreateFile* doesn't return a 0 for a failed open.

You close a serial port by calling *CloseHandle*, as in the following:

```
CloseHandle (hSer);
```

You don't do anything differently when using *CloseHandle* to close a serial device than when you use it to close a file handle.

Reading and Writing to a Serial Port

Just as you use the *CreateFile* function to open a serial port, you use the functions *ReadFile* and *WriteFile* to write to that serial port. Reading data from a serial port is as simple as making this call to *ReadFile*:

```
INT rc;
DWORD cBytes;
BYTE ch;

rc = ReadFile(hSer, &ch, 1, &cBytes, NULL);
```

This call assumes the serial port has been successfully opened with a call to *CreateFile*. If the call is successful, one byte is read into the variable *ch*, and *cBytes* is set to the number of bytes read.

Writing to a serial port is just as simple. The call would look something like the following:

```
INT rc;
DWORD cBytes;
BYTE ch;

ch = TEXT ('a');
rc = WriteFile(hSer, &ch, 1, &cBytes, NULL);
```

This code writes the character *a* to the serial port previously opened. As you may remember from Chapter 7, both *ReadFile* and *WriteFile* return TRUE if successful.

Since overlapped I/O isn't supported under Windows CE, you should be careful not to attempt to read or write a large amount of serial data from your primary thread or from any thread that has created a window. Because those threads are also responsible for handling the message queues for their windows, they can't be blocked waiting on a relatively slow serial read or write. Instead, you should use separate threads for reading and writing the serial port.

You can also transmit a single character using this function:

```
BOOL TransmitCommChar (HANDLE hFile, char cChar);
```

The difference between *TransmitCommChar* and *WriteFile* is that *TransmitCommChar* puts the character to be transmitted at the front of the transmit queue. When you call *WriteFile*, the characters are queued up after any characters that haven't yet been transmitted by the serial driver. *TransmitCommChar* allows you to insert control characters quickly in the stream without having to wait for the queue to empty.

Asynchronous Serial I/O

While Windows CE doesn't support overlapped I/O, there's no reason why you can't use multiple threads to implement the same type of overlapped operation. All that's required is that you launch separate threads to handle the synchronous I/O operations while your primary thread goes about its business. In addition to using separate threads for reading and writing, Windows CE supports the Win32 *WaitCommEvent* function that blocks a thread until one of a group of preselected serial events occurs. I'll demonstrate how to use separate threads for reading and writing a serial port in the CeChat example program later in this chapter.

You can make a thread wait on serial driver events by means of the following three functions:

```
BOOL SetCommMask (HANDLE hFile, DWORD dwEvtMask);
BOOL GetCommMask (HANDLE hFile, LPDWORD lpEvtMask);
```

and

```
BOOL WaitCommEvent (HANDLE hFile, LPDWORD lpEvtMask,
                    LPOVERLAPPED lpOverlapped);
```

To wait on an event, you first set the event mask using *SetCommMask*. The parameters for this function are the handle to the serial device and a combination of the following event flags:

- *EV_BREAK* A break was detected.
- *EV_CTS* The Clear to Send (CTS) signal changed state.

- *EV_DSR* The Data Set Ready (DSR) signal changed state.
- *EV_ERR* An error was detected by the serial driver.
- *EV_RLSD* The Receive Line Signal Detect (RLSD) line changed state.
- *EV_RXCHAR* A character was received.
- *EV_RXFLAG* An event character was received.
- *EV_TXEMPTY* The transmit buffer is empty.

You can set any or all of the flags in this list at the same time using *SetCommMask*. You can query the current event mask using *GetCommMask*.

To wait on the events specified by *SetCommMask*, you call *WaitCommEvent*. The parameters for this call are the handle to the device, a pointer to a DWORD that will receive the reason the call returned, and *lpOverlapped*, which under Windows CE must be set to NULL. The code fragment that follows waits on a character being received or an error. The code assumes that the serial port has already been opened and the handle is contained in *hComPort*.

```
DWORD dwMask;
// Set mask and wait.
SetCommMask (hComPort, EV_RXCHAR | EV_ERR);
if (WaitCommEvent (hComPort, &dwMask, 0) {

    // Use the flags returned in dwMask to determine the reason
    // for returning.
    Switch (dwMask) {
    case EV_RXCHAR:
        //Read character.
        break;
    case EV_ERR:
        // Process error.
        break;
    }
}
```

Configuring the Serial Port

Reading and writing to a serial port is fairly straightforward, but you also must configure the port for the proper baud rate, character size, and so forth. The masochist could configure the serial driver through device I/O control (IOCTL) calls but the *IoCtl* codes necessary for this are exposed only in the Embedded Toolkit, not the Software Development Kit. Besides, here's a simpler method.

You can go a long way in configuring the serial port using two functions, *GetCommState* and *SetCommState*, prototyped here:

```
BOOL SetCommState (HANDLE hFile, LPDCB lpDCB);
BOOL GetCommState (HANDLE hFile, LPDCB lpDCB);
```

Both these functions take two parameters, the handle to the opened serial port and a pointer to a DCB structure. The extensive DCB structure is defined as follows:

```
typedef struct _DCB {
    DWORD DCBlength;
    DWORD BaudRate;
    DWORD fBinary: 1;
    DWORD fParity: 1;
    DWORD fOutxCtsFlow:1;
    DWORD fOutxDsrFlow:1;
    DWORD fDtrControl:2;
    DWORD fDsrSensitivity:1;
    DWORD fTXContinueOnXoff:1;
    DWORD fOutX: 1;
    DWORD fInX: 1;
    DWORD fErrorChar: 1;
    DWORD fNull: 1;
    DWORD fRtsControl:2;
    DWORD fAbortOnError:1;
    DWORD fDummy2:17;
    WORD wReserved;
    WORD XonLim;
    WORD XoffLim;
    BYTE ByteSize;
    BYTE Parity;
    BYTE StopBits;
    char XonChar;
    char XoffChar;
    char ErrorChar;
    char EofChar;
    char EvtChar;
    WORD wReserved1;
} DCB;
```

As you can see from the structure, the *SetCommState* can set a fair number of states. Instead of attempting to fill out the entire structure from scratch, you should use the best method of modifying a serial port, which is to call *GetCommState* to fill in a DCB structure, modify the fields necessary, and then call *SetCommState* to configure the serial port.

The first field in the DCB structure, *DCBlength*, should be set to the size of the structure. The *BaudRate* field should be set to one of the baud rate constants defined in WINBASE.H. The baud rate constants range from CBR_110 for 110 bits per second to CBR_256000 for 256 kilobits per second (Kbps). Just because constants are defined for speeds up to 256 Kbps doesn't mean that all serial ports support that speed. To determine what baud rates a serial port supports, you can call *GetCommProperties*, which I'll describe shortly. Windows CE devices generally support speeds up to 115 Kbps, although some support faster speeds. The *fBinary* field must be set to TRUE because no Win32 operating system currently supports a nonbinary serial transmit mode familiar to MS-DOS programmers. The *fParity* field can be set to TRUE to enable parity checking.

The *fOutxCtsFlow* field should be set to TRUE if the output of the serial port should be controlled by the port CTS line. The *fOutxDsrFlow* field should be set to TRUE if the output of the serial port should be controlled by the DSR line of the serial port. The *fDtrControl* field can be set to one of three values: DTR_CONTROL_DISABLE, which disables the DTR (Data Terminal Ready) line and leaves it disabled; DTR_CONTROL_ENABLE, which enables the DTR line; or DTR_CONTROL_HANDSHAKE, which tells the serial driver to toggle the DTR line in response to how much data is in the receive buffer.

The *fDsrSensitivity* field is set to TRUE, and the serial port ignores any incoming bytes unless the port DSR line is enabled. Setting the *fTXContinueOnXoff* field to TRUE tells the driver to stop transmitting characters if its receive buffer has reached its limit and the driver has transmitted an XOFF character. Setting the *fOutX* field to TRUE specifies that the XON/XOFF control is used to control the serial output. Setting the *fInX* field to TRUE specifies that the XON/XOFF control is used for the input serial stream.

The *fErrorChar* and *ErrorChar* fields are ignored by the default implementation of the Windows CE serial driver although some drivers might support these fields. Likewise, the *fAbortOnError* fields is also ignored. Setting the *fNull* field to TRUE tells the serial driver to discard null bytes received.

The *fRtsControl* field specifies the operation of the RTS (Request to Send) line. The field can be set to one of the following: RTS_CONTROL_DISABLE, indicating that the RTS line is set to the disabled state while the port is open; RTS_CONTROL_ENABLE, indicating that the RTS line is set to the enabled state while the port is open; or RTS_CONTROL_HANDSHAKE, indicating that the RTS line is controlled by the driver. In this mode, if the serial input buffer is less than half full, the RTS line is enabled and disabled otherwise. Finally, RTS_CONTROL_TOGGLE indicates the driver enables the RTS line if there are bytes in the output buffer ready to be transmitted and disables the line otherwise.

The *XonLim* field specifies the minimum number of bytes in the input buffer before an XON character is automatically sent. The *XoffLim* field specifies the maximum number of bytes in the input buffer before the XOFF character is sent. This limit value is computed by taking the size of the input buffer and subtracting the value in *XoffLim*. In the sample Windows CE implementation of the serial driver provided in the ETK, the *XonLim* field is ignored and XON and XOFF characters are sent based on the value in *XoffLim*. However, this behavior might differ in some systems.

The next three fields, *ByteSize*, *Parity*, and *StopBits*, define the format of the serial data word transmitted. The *ByteSize* field specifies the number of bits per byte, usually a value of 7 or 8, but in some older modes the number of bits per byte can be as small as 5. The parity field can be set to the self-explanatory constants EVENPARITY, MARKPARITY, NOPARITY, ODDPARITY, or SPACEPARITY. The *StopBits* field should be set to ONESTOPBIT, ONE5STOPBITS, or TWOSTOPBITS depending on whether you want one, one and a half, or two stop bits per byte.

The next two fields, *XonChar* and *XoffChar*, let you specify the XON and XOFF characters. Likewise, the *EvtChar* field lets you specify the character used to signal an event. If an event character is received, an EV_RXFLAG event is signaled by the driver. This "event" is what triggers the *WaitCommEvent* function to return if the EV_RXFLAG bit is set in the event mask.

Setting the Port Timeout Values

As you can see, *SetCommState* can fine-tune, to almost the smallest detail, the operation of the serial driver. However, one more step is necessary—setting the timeout values for the port. The time out is the length of time Windows CE waits on a read or write operation before *ReadFile* or *WriteFile* automatically returns. The functions that control the serial time outs are the following:

```
BOOL GetCommTimeouts (HANDLE hFile, LPCOMMTIMEOUTS lpCommTimeouts);
```

and

```
BOOL SetCommTimeouts (HANDLE hFile, LPCOMMTIMEOUTS lpCommTimeouts);
```

Both functions take the handle to the open serial device and a pointer to a COMMTIMEOUTS structure, defined as the following:

```
typedef struct _COMMTIMEOUTS {
    DWORD ReadIntervalTimeout;
    DWORD ReadTotalTimeoutMultiplier;
    DWORD ReadTotalTimeoutConstant;
    DWORD WriteTotalTimeoutMultiplier;
    DWORD WriteTotalTimeoutConstant;
} COMMTIMEOUTS;
```

The COMMTIMEOUTS structure provides for a set of timeout parameters that time both the interval between characters and the total time to read and write a block of characters. Time outs are computed in two ways. First *ReadIntervalTimeout* specifies the maximum interval between characters received. If this time is exceeded, the *ReadFile* call returns immediately. The other time out is based on the number of characters you're waiting to receive. The value in *ReadTotalTimeoutMultiplier* is multiplied by the number of characters requested in the call to *ReadFile*, and is added to *ReadTotalTimeoutConstant* to compute a total time out for a call to *ReadFile*.

The write time out can be specified only for the total time spent during the *WriteFile* call. This time out is computed the same way as the total read time out, by specifying a multiplier value, the time in *WriteTotalTimeoutMultiplier*, and a constant value in *WriteTotalTimeoutConstant*. All of the times in this structure are specified in milliseconds.

In addition to the basic time outs that I just described, you can set values in the COMMTIMEOUTS structure to control whether and exactly how time outs are used in calls to *ReadFile* and *WriteFile*. You can configure the time outs in the following ways:

- Time outs for reading and writing as well as an interval time out. Set the fields in the COMMTIMEOUTS structure for the appropriate timeout values.
- Time outs for reading and writing with no interval time out. Set *ReadIntervalTimeout* to 0. Set the other fields for the appropriate timeout values.
- *ReadFile* returns immediately regardless of whether there is data to be read. Set *ReadIntervalTimeout* to MAXDWORD. Set *ReadTotalTimeoutMultiplier* and *ReadTotalTimeoutConstant* to 0.
- *ReadFile* doesn't have a time out. The function doesn't return until the proper number of bytes is returned or an error occurs. Set *ReadIntervalTimeout*, *ReadTotalTimeoutMultiplier*, and *ReadTotalTimeoutConstant* to 0.
- WriteFile doesn't have a time out. Set *WriteTotalTimeoutMultiplier* and *WriteTotalTimeoutConstant* to 0.

The timeout values are important because the worst thing you can do is to spin in a loop waiting on characters from the serial port. While the calls to *ReadFile* and *WriteFile* are waiting on the serial port, the calling threads are efficiently blocked on an event object internal to the driver. This saves precious CPU and battery power during the serial transmit and receive operations. Of course, to block on the *ReadFile* and *WriteFile*, you'll have to create secondary threads because you can't have your primary thread blocked waiting on the serial port.

Another call isn't quite as useful—*SetupComm,* prototyped this way:

```
BOOL SetupComm (HANDLE hFile, DWORD dwInQueue, DWORD dwOutQueue);
```

This function lets you specify the size of the input and output buffers for the driver. However, the sizes passed in *SetupComm* are only recommendations, not requirements to the serial driver. For example, the example implementation of the serial driver in the ETK ignores these recommended buffer sizes.

Querying the Capabilities of the Serial Driver

The configuration functions enable you to configure the serial driver, but with varied implementations of serial ports you need to know just what features a serial port supports before you configure it. The function *GetCommProperties* provides just this service. The function is prototyped this way:

```
BOOL GetCommProperties (HANDLE hFile, LPCOMMPROP lpCommProp);
```

GetCommProperties takes two parameters: the handle to the opened serial driver, and a pointer to a COMMPROP structure defined as

```
typedef struct _COMMPROP {
    WORD wPacketLength;
    WORD wPacketVersion;
    DWORD dwServiceMask;
    DWORD dwReserved1;
    DWORD dwMaxTxQueue;
    DWORD dwMaxRxQueue;
    DWORD dwMaxBaud;
    DWORD dwProvSubType;
    DWORD dwProvCapabilities;
    DWORD dwSettableParams;
    DWORD dwSettableBaud;
    WORD wSettableData;
    WORD wSettableStopParity;
    DWORD dwCurrentTxQueue;
    DWORD dwCurrentRxQueue;
    DWORD dwProvSpec1;
    DWORD dwProvSpec2;
    WCHAR wcProvChar[1];
} COMMPROP;
```

As you can see from the fields of the COMMPROP structure, *GetCommProperties* returns generally enough information to determine the capabilities of the device. Of immediate interest to speed demons is the *dwMaxBaud* field that indicates the maximum baud rate of the serial port. The *dwSettableBaud* field contains bit flags that indicate the allowable baud rates for the port. Both these fields use bit flags that are defined in WINBASE.H. These constants are expressed as BAUD_*xxxx*, as in BAUD_19200, which indicates the port is capable of a speed of 19.2 kbps. Note that these constants are *not* the constants used to set the speed of the serial port in the DCB structure. Those constants are numbers, not bit flags. To set the speed of a COM port in the DCB structure to 19.2 kbps, you would use the constant CBR_19200 in the *BaudRate* field of the DCB structure.

Starting back at the top of the structure are the *wPacketLength* and *wPacketVersion* fields. These fields allow you to request more information from the driver than is supported by the generic call. The *dwServiceMask* field indicates what services the port supports. The only service currently supported is SP_SERIALCOMM, indicating that the port is a serial communication port.

The *dwMaxTxQueue* and *dwMaxRxQueue* fields indicate the maximum size of the output and input buffers internal to the driver. A value of 0 in these fields indicates that you'll encounter no limit in the size of the internal queues. The *dwCurrentTxQueue* and *dwCurrentRxQueue* fields indicate the current size for the queues. These fields are 0 if the queue size can't be determined.

The *dwProvSubType* field contains flags that indicate the type of serial port supported by the driver. Values here include PST_RS232, PST_RS422, and PST_RS423, indicating the physical layer protocol of the port. PST_MODEM indicates a modem device, and PST_FAX tells you the port is a fax device. This field reports what the driver thinks the port is, not what device is attached to the port. For example, if an external modem is attached to a standard, RS-232 serial port, the driver returns the PST_RS232 flag, not the PST_MODEM flag.

The *dwProvCapabilities* field contains flags indicating the handshaking the port supports, such as XON/XOFF, RTS/CTS, and DTR/DSR. This field also shows you whether the port supports setting the characters used for XON/XOFF, parity checking, and so forth. The *dwSettableParams*, *dwSettableData*, and *dwSettableStopParity* fields give you information about how the serial data stream can be configured. Finally, the fields *dwProvSpec1*, *dwProvSpec2*, and *wcProvChar* are used by the driver to return driver-specific data.

Controlling the Serial Port

You can stop and start a serial stream using the following functions:

```
BOOL SetCommBreak (HANDLE hFile);
```

and

```
BOOL ClearCommBreak (HANDLE hFile);
```

The only parameter for both these functions is the handle to the opened COM port. When *SetCommBreak* is called, the COM port stops transmitting characters and places the port in a break state. Communication is resumed with the *ClearCommBreak* function.

You can clear out any characters in either the transmit or receive queues internal to the serial driver using this function:

```
BOOL PurgeComm (HANDLE hFile, DWORD dwFlags);
```

The *dwFlags* parameter can be a combination of the flags PURGE_TXCLEAR and PURGE_RXCLEAR. These flags terminate any pending writes and reads and reset the queues. In the case of PURGE_RXCLEAR, the driver also clears any receive holds due to any flow control states, transmitting an XON character if necessary, and setting RTS and DTR if those flow control methods are enabled. Since Windows CE doesn't support overlapped I/O, the flags PURGE_TXABORT and PURGE_RXABORT, used under Windows NT and Windows 98, are ignored.

The *EscapeCommFunction* provides a more general method of controlling the serial driver. It allows you to set and clear the state of specific signals on the port. On Windows CE devices, it's also used to control serial hardware that's shared between the serial port and the IrDA port. (I'll talk more about infrared data transmission and the Infrared Data Association (IrDA) standard later in this chapter.) The function is prototyped as

```
BOOL EscapeCommFunction (HANDLE hFile, DWORD dwFunc);
```

The function takes two parameters, the handle to the device and a set of flags in *dwFunc*. The flags can be one of the following values:

- *SETDTR* Sets the DTR signal.
- *CLRDTR* Clears the DTR signal.
- *SETRTS* Sets the RTS signal
- *CLRRTS* Clears the RTS) ignal.
- *SETXOFF* Tells the driver to act as if an XOFF character has been received.
- *SETXON* Tells the driver to act as if an XON character has been received.
- *SETBREAK* Suspends serial transmission and sets the port in a break state.
- *CLRBREAK* Resumes serial transmission from a break state.
- *SETIR* Tells the serial port to transmit and receive through the infrared transceiver.
- *CLRIR* Tells the serial port to transmit and receive through the standard serial transceiver.

The SETBREAK and CLRBREAK commands act identically to *SetCommBreak* and *ClearCommBreak* and can be used interchangeably. For example, you can use *EscapeCommFunction* to put the port in a break state and *ClearCommBreak* to restore communication.

Clearing Errors and Querying Status

The function

```
BOOL ClearCommError (HANDLE hFile, LPDWORD lpErrors, LPCOMSTAT lpStat);
```

performs two functions. As you might expect from the name, it clears any error states within the driver so that I/O can continue. The serial device driver is responsible for reporting the errors. The default serial driver returns the following flags in the variable pointed to by *lpErrors*: CE_OVERRUN, CE_RXPARITY, CE_FRAME, and CE_TXFULL. *ClearCommError* also returns the status of the port. The third parameter of *ClearCommError* is a pointer to a COMSTAT structure defined as

```
typedef struct _COMSTAT {
    DWORD fCtsHold : 1;
    DWORD fDsrHold : 1;
    DWORD fRlsdHold : 1;
    DWORD fXoffHold : 1;
    DWORD fXoffSent : 1;
    DWORD fEof : 1;
    DWORD fTxim : 1;
    DWORD fReserved : 25;
    DWORD cbInQue;
    DWORD cbOutQue;
} COMSTAT;
```

The first five fields indicate that serial transmission is waiting for one of the following reasons. It's waiting for a CTS signal, waiting for a DSR signal, waiting for a Receive Line Signal Detect (also known as a Carrier Detect), waiting for an XON character, or it's waiting because an XOFF character was sent by the driver. The *fEor* field indicates that an end-of-file character has been received. The *fTxim* field is TRUE if a character placed in the queue by the *TransmitCommChar* function instead of a call to *WriteFile* is queued for transmission. The final two fields, *cbInQue* and *cbOutQue*, return the number of characters in the input and output queues of the serial driver.

The function

```
BOOL GetCommModemStatus (HANDLE hFile, LPDWORD lpModemStat);
```

returns the status of the modem control signals in the variable pointed to by *lpModemStat*. The flags returned can be any of the following:

- *MS_CTS_ON* Clear to Send (CTS) is active.
- *MS_DSR_ON* Data Set Ready (DSR) is active.
- *MS_RING_ON* Ring Indicate (RI) is active.
- *MS_RLSD_ON* Receive Line Signal Detect (RLSD) is active.

Stay'n Alive

One of the issues with serial communication is preventing the system from powering down while a serial link is active. A Windows CE system determines activity by the number of key presses and screen taps. It doesn't take into account such tasks as a serial port transmitting data. To prevent a Windows CE device from powering off, you can simulate a keystroke using either of the following functions:

```
VOID keybd_event (BYTE bVk, BYTE bScan, DWORD dwFlags,
                  DWORD dwExtraInfo);
```

or

```
UINT SendInput (UINT nInputs, LPINPUT pInputs, int cbSize);
```

These functions can be used to simulate a keystroke that resets the activity timer used by Windows CE to determine when the system should automatically power down. Windows CE supports an additional constant for both these functions—KEYEVENTF_SILENT, which prevents the default keyboard click sound from being played.

THE INFRARED PORT

Windows CE devices almost always have an infrared, IrDA-compatible serial port. In fact, all H/PC and Palm-size PC systems are guaranteed to have one. The IR ports on Windows CE devices are IrDA (Infrared Data Association) compliant. The IrDA standard specifies everything from the physical implementation, such as the frequency of light used, to the handshaking between devices and how remote systems find each other and converse.

The IR port can be used in a variety of ways. At the most basic level, the port can be accessed as a serial port with an IR transmitter and receiver attached. This method is known as *raw IR*. When you're using raw IR, the port isn't IrDA compliant because the IrDA standard requires the proper handshaking for the link. However, raw IR gives you the most control over the IR link. A word of warning: While all Windows CE devices I know currently support raw IR, some might not in the future.

You can also use the IR port in IrComm mode. In this mode, the IR link looks like a serial port. However, under the covers, Windows CE works to hide the differences between a standard serial port and the IR link. This is perhaps the easiest way to link two custom applications because the applications can use the rather simple Comm API while Windows CE uses the IrDA stack to handle the IR link.

The most robust and complex method of using the IR port is to use IrSock. In this mode, the IR link appears to be just another socket. IrSock is an extension to WinSock, the Windows version of the socket interface used by applications communicating with TCP/IP. I'll cover WinSock in Chapter 10, so I'll defer any talk of IrSock until then.

Raw IR

As I mentioned previously, when you use raw IR you're mainly on your own. You essentially have a serial port with an IR transceiver attached to it. Since both the transmitter and receiver use the same ether (the air), collisions occur if you transmit at the same time that you're receiving a stream of data from another device. This doesn't happen when a serial cable connects two serial ports because the cable gives you separate transmit and receive wires that can be used at the same time.

Finding the raw IR port

To use raw IR, you must first find the serial port attached to the IR transceiver. On some Windows CE units, the serial port and the IR port use the same serial hardware. This means you can't use the serial port at the same time you use the IR port. Other Windows CE devices have separate serial hardware for the IR port. Regardless of how a device is configured, Windows CE gives you a separate instance of a COM driver for the IR port that's used for raw IR mode.

There is no official method of determining the COM port used for raw IR. However, the following technique works for current devices. To find the COM port used for raw IR, look in the registry in the \Comm\IrDA key under HKEY_LOCAL_MACHINE. There, you should find the Port key that contains the COM port number for the raw IR device. Below is a short routine that returns the device name of the raw IR port.

```
//----------------------------------------------------------------------
// GetRawIrDeviceName - Returns the device name for the RawIR com port
//
INT GetRawIrDeviceName (LPTSTR pDevName) {
    DWORD dwSize, dwType, dwData;
    HKEY hKey;
    INT rc;

    *pDevName = TEXT ('\0');
    // Open the IrDA key.
    if (RegOpenKeyEx (HKEY_LOCAL_MACHINE, TEXT ("Comm\\IrDA"), 0,
                      0, &hKey) == ERROR_SUCCESS) {

        // Query the device number.
        dwSize = sizeof (dwData);
        if (RegQueryValueEx (hKey, TEXT ("Port"), 0, &dwType,
                             (PBYTE)&dwData, &dwSize) == ERROR_SUCCESS)

            // Check for valid port number. Assume buffer > 5 chars.
            if (dwData < 10)
                wsprintf (pDevName, TEXT ("COM%d:"), dwData);

        RegCloseKey (hKey);
    }
    return lstrlen (pDevName);
}
```

Using raw IR

Once you have the port name, you must perform one more task before you can use the port. If the COM port hardware is being shared by the serial port and the IR port, you must tell the driver to direct the serial stream through the IR transceiver. You do this by first opening the device and calling *EscapeCommFunction*. The command passed to the device is SETIR. When you've finished using the IR port, you should call *EscapeCommFunction* again with the command CLRIR to return the port back to its original serial function.

Once the port is set up, there's one main difference between raw IR and standard serial communication. You have to be careful when using raw IR not to transmit while another device is also transmitting. The two transmissions will collide, corrupting both data streams. With raw IR, you're also responsible for detecting the other device and handling the dropped bytes that will occur as the infrared beam between the two devices is occasionally broken.

IrComm

Using IrComm is much easier than using raw IR. IrComm takes care of remote device detection, collision detection, and data buffering while communication with the other device is temporally interrupted. The disadvantage of IrComm is that it's a point-to-point protocol—only two devices can be connected. In most instances, however, this is sufficient.

Finding the IrComm port

Here again, there's no official method for determining the IrComm port. But you should be able to find the IrComm port by looking in the registry under the Drivers\builtin \IrCOMM key under HKEY_LOCAL_MACHINE. The item to query is the *Index* value, which is the COM device number for the IrComm port. Following is a routine that returns the device name of the IrComm port.

```
//----------------------------------------------------------------------
// GetIrCommDeviceName - Returns the device name for the IrComm port
//
INT GetIrCommDeviceName (LPTSTR pDevName) {
    DWORD dwSize, dwType, dwData;
    HKEY hKey;

    *pDevName = TEXT ('\0');
    // Open the IrDA key.
    if (RegOpenKeyEx (HKEY_LOCAL_MACHINE,
                      TEXT ("Drivers\\BuiltIn\\IrCOMM"), 0,
                      0, &hKey) == ERROR_SUCCESS) {
```

(continued)

```
        // Query the device number.
        dwSize = sizeof (dwData);
        if (RegQueryValueEx (hKey, TEXT ("Index"), 0, &dwType,
                             (PBYTE)&dwData, &dwSize) == ERROR_SUCCESS)

            // Check for valid port number. Assume buffer > 5 chars.
            if (dwData < 10)
                wsprintf (pDevName, TEXT ("COM%d:"), dwData);

        RegCloseKey (hKey);
    }
    return lstrlen (pDevName);
}
```

The IrComm port is different in a number of ways from the serial port and the raw IR port. These differences arise from the fact that the IrComm port is a simulated port, not a real device. The IrComm driver uses IrSock to manage the IR link. The driver is then responsible only for reflecting the data stream and a few control characters to simulate the serial connection. If you try to query the communication settings for the IrComm port using *GetCommState*, the DCB returned is all zeros. If you try to set a baud rate or some of the other parameters, and later call *GetCommState* again, the DCB will still be 0. IrSock manages the speed and the handshaking protocol, so IrComm simply ignores your configuration requests.

On the other hand, the IrComm driver happily queues up pending writes waiting on another IrComm device to come within range. After the IrComm driver automatically establishes a link, it transmits the pending bytes to the other device. This assistance is a far cry from raw IR and is what makes using IrComm so easy.

The best way to learn about the characteristics of the two methods of IR communication I've described is to use them. Which brings us to this chapter's example program.

THE CECHAT EXAMPLE PROGRAM

The CeChat program is a simple point-to-point chat program that connects two Windows CE devices using one of the three methods of serial communication covered in this chapter. The CeChat window is shown in Figure 9-3. Most of the window is taken up by the receive text window. Text received from the other device is displayed here. Along the bottom of the screen is the send text window. If you type characters here and either hit the Enter key or tap on the Send button, the text is sent to the other device. The combo box on the command bar selects the serial medium to use: standard serial, raw IR, or IrComm.

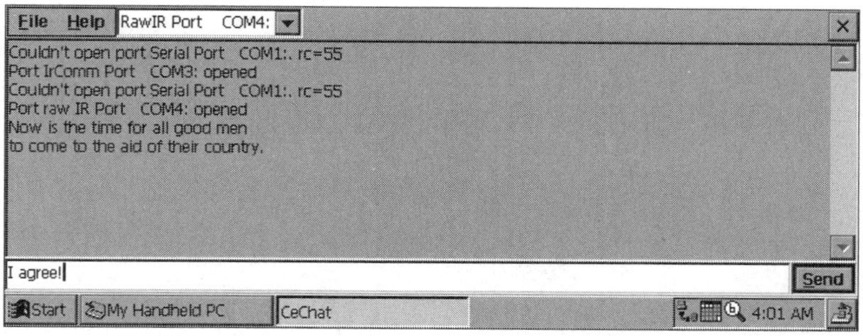

Figure 9-3. *The CeChat window.*

The source code for CeChat is shown in Figure 9-4. CeChat uses three threads to accomplish its work. The primary thread manages the window and the message loop. The two secondary threads handle reading from and writing to the appropriate serial port.

CeChat.rc

```
//======================================================================
// Resource file
//
// Written for the book Programming Windows CE
// Copyright (C) 1998 Douglas Boling
//======================================================================
#include "windows.h"
#include "CeChat.h"                         // Program-specific stuff
//----------------------------------------------------------------------
// Icons and bitmaps
//
ID_ICON ICON   "CeChat.ico"                 // Program icon

//----------------------------------------------------------------------
// Menu
//
ID_MENU MENU DISCARDABLE
BEGIN
    POPUP "&File"
    BEGIN
        MENUITEM "E&xit",                          IDM_EXIT
    END
    POPUP "&Help"
    BEGIN
        MENUITEM "&About...",                      IDM_ABOUT
    END
END
```

Figure 9-4. *The CeChat source code.* *(continued)*

Figure 9-4. *continued*

```
//----------------------------------------------------------------------
// Accelerator table
//
ID_ACCEL ACCELERATORS DISCARDABLE
BEGIN
    "S", ID_SENDBTN, VIRTKEY, ALT
    VK_RETURN, ID_SENDBTN, VIRTKEY
END

//----------------------------------------------------------------------
// About box dialog template
//
aboutbox DIALOG discardable 10, 10, 160, 40
STYLE  WS_POPUP | WS_VISIBLE | WS_CAPTION | WS_SYSMENU | DS_CENTER |
       DS_MODALFRAME
CAPTION "About"
BEGIN
    ICON  ID_ICON,                    -1,   5,   5,  10,  10
    LTEXT "CeChat - Written for the book Programming Windows \
           CE Copyright 1998 Douglas Boling"
                                      -1,  40,   5, 110,  30
END
```

CeChat.h

```
//======================================================================
// Header file
//
// Written for the book Programming Windows CE
// Copyright (C) 1998 Douglas Boling
//======================================================================
// Returns number of elements
#define dim(x) (sizeof(x) / sizeof(x[0]))

//----------------------------------------------------------------------
// Generic defines and data types
//
struct decodeUINT {                             // Structure associates
    UINT Code;                                  // messages
                                                // with a function.
    LRESULT (*Fxn)(HWND, UINT, WPARAM, LPARAM);
};
struct decodeCMD {                              // Structure associates
    UINT Code;                                  // menu IDs with a
    LRESULT (*Fxn)(HWND, WORD, HWND, WORD);     // function.
```

```
};
//----------------------------------------------------------------------
// Generic defines used by application
#define  ID_ICON            1                  // App icon resource ID
#define  ID_MENU            2                  // Menu resource ID
#define  ID_ACCEL           3                  // Accel table ID
#define  IDC_CMDBAR         4                  // Command band ID
#define  ID_RCVTEXT         5                  // Receive text box
#define  ID_SENDTEXT        6                  // Send text box
#define  ID_SENDBTN         7                  // Send button

// Menu item IDs
#define  IDM_EXIT           101

#define  IDM_USECOM         110                // Use COM.
#define  IDM_ABOUT          120                // Help menu

// Command bar IDs
#define  IDC_COMPORT        150                // COM port combo box
#define  IDC_BAUDRATE       151                // Baud rate combo box

#define TEXTSIZE 256
//----------------------------------------------------------------------
// Function prototypes
//
int ReadThread (PVOID pArg);
int SendThread (PVOID pArg);
HANDLE InitCommunication (HWND, LPTSTR);
INT GetIrCommDeviceName (LPTSTR);
INT GetRawIrDeviceName (LPTSTR);
int FillComComboBox (HWND);

int InitApp (HINSTANCE);
HWND InitInstance (HINSTANCE, LPWSTR, int);
int TermInstance (HINSTANCE, int);

// Window procedures
LRESULT CALLBACK MainWndProc (HWND, UINT, WPARAM, LPARAM);

// Message handlers
LRESULT DoCreateMain (HWND, UINT, WPARAM, LPARAM);
LRESULT DoSizeMain (HWND, UINT, WPARAM, LPARAM);
LRESULT DoSetFocusMain (HWND, UINT, WPARAM, LPARAM);
LRESULT DoCommandMain (HWND, UINT, WPARAM, LPARAM);
LRESULT DoDestroyMain (HWND, UINT, WPARAM, LPARAM);
```

(continued)

Figure 9-4. *continued*

```
// Command functions
LPARAM DoMainCommandExit (HWND, WORD, HWND, WORD);
LPARAM DoMainCommandComPort (HWND, WORD, HWND, WORD);
LPARAM DoMainCommandSendText (HWND, WORD, HWND, WORD);
LPARAM DoMainCommandAbout (HWND, WORD, HWND, WORD);

// Dialog procedures
BOOL CALLBACK AboutDlgProc (HWND, UINT, WPARAM, LPARAM);
BOOL CALLBACK EditAlbumDlgProc (HWND, UINT, WPARAM, LPARAM);
```

CeChat.c

```
//======================================================================
// CeChat - A Windows CE communication demo
//
// Written for the book Programming Windows CE
// Copyright (C) 1998 Douglas Boling
//======================================================================
#include <windows.h>                 // For all that Windows stuff
#include <commctrl.h>                // Command bar includes
#include "CeChat.h"                  // Program-specific stuff

//----------------------------------------------------------------------
// Global data
//
const TCHAR szAppName[] = TEXT ("CeChat");
HINSTANCE hInst;                     // Program instance handle.

BOOL fContinue = TRUE;
HANDLE hComPort = INVALID_HANDLE_VALUE;
INT nSpeed = CBR_19200;
int nLastDev = -1;

HANDLE g_hSendEvent = INVALID_HANDLE_VALUE;
HANDLE hReadThread = INVALID_HANDLE_VALUE;

// Message dispatch table for MainWindowProc
const struct decodeUINT MainMessages[] = {
    WM_CREATE, DoCreateMain,
    WM_SIZE, DoSizeMain,
    WM_COMMAND, DoCommandMain,
    WM_SETFOCUS, DoSetFocusMain,
    WM_DESTROY, DoDestroyMain,
};
// Command Message dispatch for MainWindowProc
```

```
const struct decodeCMD MainCommandItems[] = {
    IDC_COMPORT, DoMainCommandComPort,
    ID_SENDBTN, DoMainCommandSendText,
    IDM_EXIT, DoMainCommandExit,
    IDM_ABOUT, DoMainCommandAbout,
};
//======================================================================
// Program entry point
//
int WINAPI WinMain (HINSTANCE hInstance, HINSTANCE hPrevInstance,
                    LPWSTR lpCmdLine, int nCmdShow) {
    HWND hwndMain;
    HACCEL hAccel;
    MSG msg;
    int rc = 0;

    // Initialize application.
    rc = InitApp (hInstance);
    if (rc) return rc;

    // Initialize this instance.
    hwndMain = InitInstance (hInstance, lpCmdLine, nCmdShow);
    if (hwndMain == 0)
        return 0x10;

    // Load accelerator table.
    hAccel = LoadAccelerators (hInst, MAKEINTRESOURCE (ID_ACCEL));

    // Application message loop
    while (GetMessage (&msg, NULL, 0, 0)) {
        if (!TranslateAccelerator (hwndMain, hAccel, &msg)) {
            TranslateMessage (&msg);
            DispatchMessage (&msg);
        }
    }
    // Instance cleanup
    return TermInstance (hInstance, msg.wParam);
}
//----------------------------------------------------------------------
// InitApp - Application initialization
//
int InitApp (HINSTANCE hInstance) {
    WNDCLASS wc;
    INITCOMMONCONTROLSEX icex;

    // Register application main window class.
```

(continued)

Figure 9-4. *continued*

```
    wc.style = 0;                                    // Window style
    wc.lpfnWndProc = MainWndProc;                    // Callback function
    wc.cbClsExtra = 0;                               // Extra class data
    wc.cbWndExtra = 0;                               // Extra window data
    wc.hInstance = hInstance;                        // Owner handle
    wc.hIcon = NULL,                                 // Application icon
    wc.hCursor = NULL;                               // Default cursor
    wc.hbrBackground = (HBRUSH) GetStockObject (WHITE_BRUSH);
    wc.lpszMenuName =  NULL;                         // Menu name
    wc.lpszClassName = szAppName;                    // Window class name

    if (RegisterClass (&wc) == 0) return 1;

    // Load the command bar common control class.
    icex.dwSize = sizeof (INITCOMMONCONTROLSEX);
    icex.dwICC = ICC_BAR_CLASSES;
    InitCommonControlsEx (&icex);
    return 0;
}
//----------------------------------------------------------------------
// InitInstance - Instance initialization
//
HWND InitInstance (HINSTANCE hInstance, LPWSTR lpCmdLine, int nCmdShow){
    HWND hWnd;
    INT rc;
    HANDLE hThread;

    // Save program instance handle in global variable.
    hInst = hInstance;

    // Create unnamed auto-reset event initially false.
    g_hSendEvent = CreateEvent (NULL, FALSE, FALSE, NULL);

    // Create main window.
    hWnd = CreateWindow (szAppName, TEXT ("CeChat"),
                         WS_VISIBLE, CW_USEDEFAULT, CW_USEDEFAULT,
                         CW_USEDEFAULT, CW_USEDEFAULT, NULL,
                         NULL, hInstance, NULL);
    // Return fail code if window not created.
    if (!IsWindow (hWnd)) return 0;

    // Create write thread. Read thread created when port opened.
    hThread = CreateThread (NULL, 0, SendThread, hWnd, 0, &rc);
    if (hThread)
        CloseHandle (hThread);
    else {
```

```
        DestroyWindow (hWnd);
        return 0;
    }
    // Standard show and update calls
    ShowWindow (hWnd, nCmdShow);
    UpdateWindow (hWnd);
    return hWnd;
}
//----------------------------------------------------------------------
// TermInstance - Program cleanup
//
int TermInstance (HINSTANCE hInstance, int nDefRC) {
    HANDLE hPort = hComPort;

    fContinue = FALSE;

    hComPort = INVALID_HANDLE_VALUE;
    if (hPort != INVALID_HANDLE_VALUE)
        CloseHandle (hPort);

    if (g_hSendEvent != INVALID_HANDLE_VALUE) {
        PulseEvent (g_hSendEvent);
        Sleep(100);
        CloseHandle (g_hSendEvent);
    }
    return nDefRC;
}
//======================================================================
// Message handling procedures for MainWindow
//----------------------------------------------------------------------
// MainWndProc - Callback function for application window
//
LRESULT CALLBACK MainWndProc (HWND hWnd, UINT wMsg, WPARAM wParam,
                              LPARAM lParam) {
    INT i;
    //
    // Search message list to see if we need to handle this
    // message.  If in list, call procedure.
    //
    for (i = 0; i < dim(MainMessages); i++) {
        if (wMsg == MainMessages[i].Code)
             return (*MainMessages[i].Fxn)(hWnd, wMsg, wParam, lParam);
    }
    return DefWindowProc (hWnd, wMsg, wParam, lParam);
}
//----------------------------------------------------------------------
```

(continued)

Figure 9-4. *continued*

```
// DoCreateMain - Process WM_CREATE message for window.
//
LRESULT DoCreateMain (HWND hWnd, UINT wMsg, WPARAM wParam,
                      LPARAM lParam) {
    HWND hwndCB, hC1, hC2, hC3;
    INT  i, j, nHeight;
    TCHAR szFirstDev[32];
    LPCREATESTRUCT lpcs;

    // Convert lParam into pointer to create structure.
    lpcs = (LPCREATESTRUCT) lParam;

    // Create a command bar.
    hwndCB = CommandBar_Create (hInst, hWnd, IDC_CMDBAR);
    CommandBar_InsertMenubar (hwndCB, hInst, ID_MENU, 0);

    // Insert the com port combo box.
    CommandBar_InsertComboBox (hwndCB, hInst, 140, CBS_DROPDOWNLIST,
                               IDC_COMPORT, 1);
    FillComComboBox (hWnd);

    // Add exit button to command bar.
    CommandBar_AddAdornments (hwndCB, 0, 0);
    nHeight = CommandBar_Height (hwndCB);

    // Create receive text window.
    hC1 = CreateWindowEx (WS_EX_CLIENTEDGE, TEXT ("edit"),
                          TEXT (""), WS_VISIBLE | WS_CHILD |
                          WS_VSCROLL | ES_MULTILINE | ES_AUTOHSCROLL |
                          ES_READONLY, 0, nHeight, lpcs->cx,
                          lpcs->cy - nHeight - 25, hWnd,
                          (HMENU)ID_RCVTEXT, hInst, NULL);
    // Create send text window.
    hC2 = CreateWindowEx (WS_EX_CLIENTEDGE, TEXT ("edit"),
                          TEXT (""), WS_VISIBLE | WS_CHILD,
                          0, lpcs->cy - 25, lpcs->cx-50, 25,
                          hWnd, (HMENU)ID_SENDTEXT, hInst, NULL);
    // Create send text window.
    hC3 = CreateWindowEx (WS_EX_CLIENTEDGE, TEXT ("button"),
                          TEXT ("&Send"), WS_VISIBLE | WS_CHILD |
                          BS_DEFPUSHBUTTON,
                          lpcs->cx-50, lpcs->cy - 25, 50, 25,
                          hWnd, (HMENU)ID_SENDBTN, hInst, NULL);
    // Destroy frame if window not created.
    if (!IsWindow (hC1) || !IsWindow (hC2) || !IsWindow (hC3)) {
        DestroyWindow (hWnd);
```

```
        return 0;
    }
    // Open a com port.
    for (i = 0; i < 3; i++) {
        SendDlgItemMessage (hwndCB, IDC_COMPORT, CB_GETLBTEXT, i,
                            (LPARAM)szFirstDev);
        j = lstrlen (szFirstDev);
        // Really bad hack to determine which is the RAW IR port
        if (InitCommunication (hWnd, szFirstDev) !=
            INVALID_HANDLE_VALUE) {
            SendDlgItemMessage (hwndCB, IDC_COMPORT, CB_SETCURSEL, i,
                                (LPARAM)szFirstDev);
            break;
        }
    }
    return 0;
}
//----------------------------------------------------------------------
// DoSizeMain - Process WM_SIZE message for window.
//
LRESULT DoSizeMain (HWND hWnd, UINT wMsg, WPARAM wParam, LPARAM lParam){
    RECT rect;

    // Adjust the size of the client rect to take into account
    // the command bar height.
    GetClientRect (hWnd, &rect);
    rect.top += CommandBar_Height (GetDlgItem (hWnd, IDC_CMDBAR));

    SetWindowPos (GetDlgItem (hWnd, ID_RCVTEXT), NULL, rect.left,
                  rect.top, (rect.right - rect.left),
                  rect.bottom - rect.top - 25, SWP_NOZORDER);
    SetWindowPos (GetDlgItem (hWnd, ID_SENDTEXT), NULL, rect.left,
                  rect.bottom - 25, (rect.right - rect.left) - 50,
                  25, SWP_NOZORDER);
    SetWindowPos (GetDlgItem (hWnd, ID_SENDBTN), NULL,
                  (rect.right - rect.left) - 50, rect.bottom - 25,
                  50, 25, SWP_NOZORDER);
    return 0;
}
//----------------------------------------------------------------------
// DoFocusMain - Process WM_SETFOCUS message for window.
//
LRESULT DoSetFocusMain (HWND hWnd, UINT wMsg, WPARAM wParam,
                        LPARAM lParam) {
    SetFocus (GetDlgItem (hWnd, ID_SENDTEXT));
    return 0;
```

(continued)

Figure 9-4. *continued*

```
}
//----------------------------------------------------------------------
// DoCommandMain - Process WM_COMMAND message for window.
//
LRESULT DoCommandMain (HWND hWnd, UINT wMsg, WPARAM wParam,
                       LPARAM lParam) {
    WORD    idItem, wNotifyCode;
    HWND hwndCtl;
    INT  i;

    // Parse the parameters.
    idItem = (WORD) LOWORD (wParam);
    wNotifyCode = (WORD) HIWORD (wParam);
    hwndCtl = (HWND) lParam;

    // Call routine to handle control message.
    for (i = 0; i < dim(MainCommandItems); i++) {
        if (idItem == MainCommandItems[i].Code)
            return (*MainCommandItems[i].Fxn)(hWnd, idItem, hwndCtl,
                                              wNotifyCode);
    }
    return 0;
}
//----------------------------------------------------------------------
// DoDestroyMain - Process WM_DESTROY message for window.
//
LRESULT DoDestroyMain (HWND hWnd, UINT wMsg, WPARAM wParam,
                       LPARAM lParam) {
    PostQuitMessage (0);
    return 0;
}
//======================================================================
// Command handler routines
//----------------------------------------------------------------------
// DoMainCommandExit - Process Program Exit command.
//
LPARAM DoMainCommandExit (HWND hWnd, WORD idItem, HWND hwndCtl,
                          WORD wNotifyCode) {
    SendMessage (hWnd, WM_CLOSE, 0, 0);
    return 0;
}
//----------------------------------------------------------------------
// DoMainCommandComPort - Process the COM port combo box commands.
//
LPARAM DoMainCommandComPort (HWND hWnd, WORD idItem, HWND hwndCtl,
                             WORD wNotifyCode) {
```

```
    INT i;
    TCHAR szDev[32];

    if (wNotifyCode == CBN_SELCHANGE) {
        i = SendMessage (hwndCtl, CB_GETCURSEL, 0, 0);
        if (i != nLastDev) {
            nLastDev = i;
            SendMessage (hwndCtl, CB_GETLBTEXT, i, (LPARAM)szDev);
            InitCommunication (hWnd, szDev);
            SetFocus (GetDlgItem (hWnd, ID_SENDTEXT));
        }
    }
    return 0;
}
//----------------------------------------------------------------------
// DoMainCommandSendText - Process the Send text button.
//
LPARAM DoMainCommandSendText (HWND hWnd, WORD idItem, HWND hwndCtl,
                              WORD wNotifyCode) {

    // Set event so that sender thread will send the text.
    SetEvent (g_hSendEvent);
    SetFocus (GetDlgItem (hWnd, ID_SENDTEXT));
    return 0;
}
//----------------------------------------------------------------------
// DoMainCommandAbout - Process the Help | About menu command.
//
LPARAM DoMainCommandAbout(HWND hWnd, WORD idItem, HWND hwndCtl,
                          WORD wNotifyCode) {
    // Use DialogBox to create modal dialog.
    DialogBox (hInst, TEXT ("aboutbox"), hWnd, AboutDlgProc);
    return 0;
}
//======================================================================
// About Dialog procedure
//
BOOL CALLBACK AboutDlgProc (HWND hWnd, UINT wMsg, WPARAM wParam,
                            LPARAM lParam) {
    switch (wMsg) {
        case WM_COMMAND:
            switch (LOWORD (wParam)) {
                case IDOK:
                case IDCANCEL:
                    EndDialog (hWnd, 0);
                    return TRUE;
```

(continued)

Figure 9-4. *continued*

```
            }
        break;
    }
    return FALSE;
}
//----------------------------------------------------------------------
// GetRawIrDeviceName - Returns the device name for the RawIR com port
//
INT GetRawIrDeviceName (LPTSTR pDevName) {
    DWORD dwSize, dwType, dwData;
    HKEY hKey;

    *pDevName = TEXT ('\0');
    // Open the IrDA key.
    if (RegOpenKeyEx (HKEY_LOCAL_MACHINE, TEXT ("Comm\\IrDA"), 0,
                      0, &hKey) == ERROR_SUCCESS) {

        // Query the device number.
        dwSize = sizeof (dwData);
        if (RegQueryValueEx (hKey, TEXT ("Port"), 0, &dwType,
                             (PBYTE)&dwData, &dwSize) == ERROR_SUCCESS)

            // Check for valid port number. Assume buffer > 5 chars.
            if (dwData < 10)
                wsprintf (pDevName, TEXT ("COM%d:"), dwData);

        RegCloseKey (hKey);
    }
    return lstrlen (pDevName);
}
//----------------------------------------------------------------------
// GetIrCommDeviceName - Returns the device name for the IrComm port
//
INT GetIrCommDeviceName (LPTSTR pDevName) {
    DWORD dwSize, dwType, dwData;
    HKEY hKey;

    *pDevName = TEXT ('\0');
    // Open the IrDA key.
    if (RegOpenKeyEx (HKEY_LOCAL_MACHINE,
                      TEXT ("Drivers\\BuiltIn\\IrCOMM"), 0,
                      0, &hKey) == ERROR_SUCCESS) {

        // Query the device number.
        dwSize = sizeof (dwData);
        if (RegQueryValueEx (hKey, TEXT ("Index"), 0, &dwType,
```

```
                           (PBYTE)&dwData, &dwSize) == ERROR_SUCCESS)

            // Check for valid port number. Assume buffer > 5 chars.
            if (dwData < 10)
                wsprintf (pDevName, TEXT ("COM%d:"), dwData);

        RegCloseKey (hKey);
    }
    return lstrlen (pDevName);
}
//----------------------------------------------------------------------
// FillComComboBox - Fills the com port combo box
//
int FillComComboBox (HWND hWnd) {
    TCHAR szDev[64];

    lstrcpy (szDev, TEXT ("Serial Port   COM1:"));
    SendDlgItemMessage (GetDlgItem (hWnd, IDC_CMDBAR),
                        IDC_COMPORT, CB_INSERTSTRING,
                        -1, (LPARAM)szDev);

    lstrcpy (szDev, TEXT ("IrComm Port   "));
    GetIrCommDeviceName (&szDev[lstrlen (szDev)]);
    SendDlgItemMessage (GetDlgItem (hWnd, IDC_CMDBAR),
                        IDC_COMPORT, CB_INSERTSTRING,
                        -1, (LPARAM)szDev);

    lstrcpy (szDev, TEXT ("Raw IR Port   "));
    GetRawIrDeviceName (&szDev[lstrlen (szDev)]);
    SendDlgItemMessage (GetDlgItem (hWnd, IDC_CMDBAR),
                        IDC_COMPORT, CB_INSERTSTRING,
                        -1, (LPARAM)szDev);
    SendDlgItemMessage (GetDlgItem (hWnd, IDC_CMDBAR), IDC_COMPORT,
                        CB_SETCURSEL, 0, 0);
    return 0;
}
//----------------------------------------------------------------------
// InitCommunication - Open and initialize selected COM port.
//
HANDLE InitCommunication (HWND hWnd, LPTSTR pszDevName) {
    DCB dcb;
    INT i;
    TCHAR szDbg[128];
    COMMTIMEOUTS cto;
    HANDLE hLocal;
    DWORD dwTStat;
```

(continued)

Figure 9-4. *continued*

```
    hLocal = hComPort;
    hComPort = INVALID_HANDLE_VALUE;

    if (hLocal != INVALID_HANDLE_VALUE)
        CloseHandle (hLocal);  // This causes WaitCommEvent to return.

    // The com port name is the last 5 characters of the string.
    i = lstrlen (pszDevName);
    hLocal = CreateFile (&pszDevName[i-5], GENERIC_READ | GENERIC_WRITE,
                         0, NULL, OPEN_EXISTING, 0, NULL);

    if (hLocal != INVALID_HANDLE_VALUE) {
        // Configure port.
        GetCommState (hLocal, &dcb);
        dcb.BaudRate = nSpeed;
        dcb.fParity = FALSE;
        dcb.fNull = FALSE;
        dcb.StopBits = ONESTOPBIT;
        dcb.Parity = NOPARITY;
        dcb.ByteSize = 8;
        SetCommState (hLocal, &dcb);

        // Set the timeouts.  Set infinite read timeout.
        cto.ReadIntervalTimeout = 0;
        cto.ReadTotalTimeoutMultiplier = 0;
        cto.ReadTotalTimeoutConstant = 0;
        cto.WriteTotalTimeoutMultiplier = 0;
        cto.WriteTotalTimeoutConstant = 0;
        SetCommTimeouts (hLocal, &cto);

        wsprintf (szDbg, TEXT ("Port %s opened\r\n"), pszDevName);
        SendDlgItemMessage (hWnd, ID_RCVTEXT, EM_REPLACESEL, 0,
                            (LPARAM)szDbg);
        // Really bad hack to determine which is the raw IR selection.
        // We need to enable IR on the raw IR port in case port is
        // shared with the standard serial port.
        if (*pszDevName == TEXT ('R')) {
            if (!EscapeCommFunction (hLocal, SETIR)) {
                wsprintf (szDbg, TEXT ("Set IR failed. rc %d\r\n"),
                          GetLastError());
                SendDlgItemMessage (hWnd, ID_RCVTEXT, EM_REPLACESEL,
                                    0, (LPARAM)szDbg);
            }
        }
        // Start read thread if not already started.
        hComPort = hLocal;
```

```
        if (!GetExitCodeThread (hReadThread, &dwTStat) ||
            (dwTStat != STILL_ACTIVE)) {
            hReadThread = CreateThread (NULL, 0, ReadThread, hWnd,
                                        0, &dwTStat);
            if (hReadThread)
                CloseHandle (hReadThread);
        }
    } else {
        wsprintf (szDbg, TEXT ("Couldn\'t open port %s. rc=%d\r\n"),
                  pszDevName, GetLastError());
        SendDlgItemMessage (hWnd, ID_RCVTEXT, EM_REPLACESEL,
                            0, (LPARAM)szDbg);
    }
    return hComPort;
}
//======================================================================
// SendThread - Sends characters to the serial port
//
int SendThread (PVOID pArg) {
    HWND hWnd, hwndSText;
    INT cBytes, nGoCode;
    TCHAR szText[TEXTSIZE];

    hWnd = (HWND)pArg;
    hwndSText = GetDlgItem (hWnd, ID_SENDTEXT);
    while (1) {
        nGoCode = WaitForSingleObject (g_hSendEvent, INFINITE);
        if (nGoCode == WAIT_OBJECT_0) {
            if (!fContinue)
                break;
            GetWindowText (hwndSText, szText, dim(szText));
            lstrcat (szText, TEXT ("\r\n"));
            WriteFile (hComPort, szText, lstrlen (szText)*sizeof (TCHAR),
                       &cBytes, 0);
            SetWindowText (hwndSText, TEXT (""));  // Clear out text box
        } else
            break;
    }
    return 0;
}
//======================================================================
// ReadThread - Receives characters from the serial port
//
int ReadThread (PVOID pArg) {
    HWND hWnd;
    INT cBytes, i;
```

(continued)

Figure 9-4. *continued*

```
    BYTE szText[TEXTSIZE], *pPtr;
    TCHAR tch;

    hWnd = (HWND)pArg;
    while (fContinue) {
        tch = 0;
        pPtr = szText;
        for (i = 0; i < sizeof (szText)-sizeof (TCHAR); i++) {

            while (!ReadFile (hComPort, pPtr, 1, &cBytes, 0))
                if (hComPort == INVALID_HANDLE_VALUE)
                    return 0;

            // This syncs the proper byte order for Unicode.
            tch = (tch << 8) & 0xff00;
            tch |= *pPtr++;
            if (tch == TEXT ('\n'))
                break;
        }
        *pPtr++ = 0;  // Avoid alignment probs by addressing as bytes.
        *pPtr++ = 0;

        // If out of byte sync, move bytes down one.
        if (i % 2) {
            pPtr = szText;
            while (*pPtr || *(pPtr+1)) {
                *pPtr = *(pPtr+1);
                pPtr++;
            }
            *pPtr = 0;
        }
        SendDlgItemMessage (hWnd, ID_RCVTEXT, EM_REPLACESEL, 0,
                            (LPARAM)szText);
    }
    return 0;
}
```

When the CeChat window is created, it sniffs out the three port names using the methods I described earlier in the chapter. The combo box is then filled and an attempt is made to open one of the COM ports. Once a port is opened, the read thread is created to wait on characters. The read thread isn't as simple as it should be because it must deal with 2-byte Unicode characters. Because it's quite possible to drop a byte or two in a serial IR link, the receive thread must attempt to resync the proper high bytes with their low byte pair to form a correct Unicode character.

The send thread is actually quite simple. All it does is block on an event that was created when CeChat was started. When the event is signaled, it reads the text from the send text edit control and calls *WriteFile*. Once that has completed, the send thread clears the text from the edit control and loops back to where it blocks again.

In the CeChat window shown in Figure 9-3 on page 561, the program reports that it can't open COM1; this is because COM1 was being used by PC Link to connect to my PC. One of the problems with debugging serial programs on the H/PC or Palm-size PC is that you're generally using the one port that attaches to the PC. In these situations, it helps to have a secondary communication path from the PC to the Windows CE device. While you could put an additional serial PCMCIA Card into the H/PC to add ports, a faster link can be made with a PCMCIA Ethernet Card. Which brings us right to the next chapter, "Windows Networking and IrSock."

Chapter 10

Windows Networking and IrSock

Networks are at the heart of modern computer systems. Over the years, Microsoft Windows has supported a variety of networks and networking APIs. The evolving nature of networking APIs along with the need to keep systems backward compatible has resulted in a huge array of overlapping functions and parallel APIs. As in many places in Windows CE, the networking API is a subset of the vast array of networking functions supported under Windows NT and Windows 98.

Windows CE supports a variety of networking APIs. This chapter covers two. First is the Windows Networking API, WNet. This API supports basic network connections so that a Windows CE device can access disks and printers on a network.

Windows CE also supports a subset of the WinSock 1.1 API. I'm not going to cover the complete WinSock API because plenty of other books do that. I'll spend some time covering what is directly relevant to Windows CE developers. Of particular interest is the fact that that WinSock is the high-level API to the IrDA infrared communication stack. I'll also cover another extension to WinSock, the Internet control message protocol (ICMP) functions that allow Windows CE applications to ping other machines on a TCP/IP network.

WINDOWS NETWORKING SUPPORT

The WNet API is a provider-independent interface that allows Windows applications to access network resources without regard for the network implementation. The Windows CE version of the WNet API has fewer functions but provides the basics so that a Windows CE application can gain access to shared network resources, such as disks and printers. The WNet API is implemented by a "redirector" DLL that translates the WNet functions into network commands for a specific network protocol.

By default, the only network supported by the WNet API is Windows Networking. Support for even this network is limited by the fact that redirector files that implement Windows Networking aren't bundled with most H/PCs or Palm-size PCs. The two files that implement this support, REDIR.DLL and NETBIOS.DLL, are available from Microsoft. As a convenience, I've also included them on the book's companion disc as well. As an aside, the NetBIOS DLL doesn't export a NetBIOS-like interface to applications or drivers.

WNet Functions

Windows CE's support for the WNet functions started with Windows CE 2.0. As with other areas in Windows CE, the WNet implementation under Windows CE is a subset of the same API on the desktop, but support is provided for the critical functions while eliminating the overlapping and obsolete functions. For example, the standard WNet API contains four different and overlapping *WNetAddConnection* functions while Windows CE supports only one, *WNetAddConnection3*.

For the WNet API to work, the redirector DLLs must be installed in the \windows directory. In addition, the network control panel, also a supplementary component on most systems, must be used to configure the network card so that it can access the network. If the redirector DLLs aren't installed, or an error occurs configuring or initializing the network adapter, the WNet functions return the error code ERROR_NO_NETWORK.

Conventions of UNC

Network drives can be accessed in one of two ways. The first method is to explicitly name the resource using the *Universal Naming Convention* (UNC) naming syntax, which is a combination of the name of the server and the shared resource. An example of this is *\\BIGSRVR\DRVC*, where the server name is BIGSERV and the resource on the server is named DRVC. The leading double backslashes immediately indicate that the name is a UNC name. Directories and filenames can be included in the UNC name, as in *\\bigservr\drvc\dir2\file1.ext*. Notice that I changed case in the two names. That doesn't matter because UNC paths are case insensitive.

As long as the WNet redirector is installed, you can use UNC names wherever you use standard filenames in the Windows CE API. You'll have problems, though, with some programs, including, in places, the Windows CE shell, where the application doesn't understand UNC syntax. For example, the Explorer in a Windows CE 2.0 H/PC device understands UNC names, but the File Open dialog box on the same system doesn't.

Mapping a remote drive

To get around applications that don't understand UNC names, you can map a network drive to a local name. When a network drive is mapped on a Windows CE system, the remote drive appears as a folder in the \network folder in the object store. The \network folder isn't a standard folder; in fact, before Windows CE 2.1, it didn't even show up in the Explorer. (For systems based on Windows CE 2.1, the visibility of the \network folder depends on a registry setting.) Instead it's a placeholder name by which the local names of the mapped network drives can be addressed. For example, the network drive *\\BigSrvr\DrvC* could be mapped to the local name JoeBob. Files and directories on *\\BigSrvr\DrvC* would appear under the folder \network\joebob. Since Windows CE doesn't support drive letters, the local name can't be specified in the form of a drive, as in G:.

I mentioned that the \network folder is a virtual folder; this needs further explanation. Before Windows CE 2.1, the network folder wasn't visible to the standard file system functions. If you use the *FindFirstFile/FindNextFile* process to enumerate the directories in the root directory, the \network directory won't be enumerated. However, *FindFirstFile/FindNextFile* enumerates the mapped resources contained in the \network folder. So if the search string is **.** to enumerate the root directory, the network isn't enumerated, but if you use *\network*.** as the search string, any mapped drives will be enumerated.

Starting with Windows CE 2.1, the \network folder can be enumerated by *FindFirstFile* and *FindNextFile* if the proper registry settings are made. However, even though the folder can be enumerated, you still can't place files or create folders within the \network folder. To make the \network folder visible, the DWORD value *RegisterFSRoot* under the key [HKEY_LOCAL_MACHINE]\comm\redir, must be set to a nonzero value.

The most direct way to map a remote resource is to call this function:

```
DWORD WNetAddConnection3 (HWND hwndOwner, LPNETRESOURCE lpNetResource,
                          LPTSTR lpPassword, LPTSTR lpUserName,
                          DWORD dwFlags);
```

The first parameter is a handle to a window that owns any network support dialogs that might need to be displayed to complete the connection. The window handle can be NULL if you don't want to specify an owner window. This effectively turns the *WNetAddConnection3* function into the *WNetAddConnection2* function supported under other versions of Windows.

The second parameter, *lpNetResource*, should point to a NETRESOURCE structure that defines the remote resource being connected. The structure is defined as

```
typedef struct _NETRESOURCE {
    DWORD  dwScope;
    DWORD  dwType;
    DWORD  dwDisplayType;
    DWORD  dwUsage;
    LPTSTR lpLocalName;
    LPTSTR lpRemoteName;
    LPTSTR lpComment;
    LPTSTR lpProvider;
} NETRESOURCE;
```

Most of these fields aren't used for the *WNetAddConnection3* function and should be set to 0. All you need to do is to specify the UNC name of the remote resource in a string pointed to by *lpRemoteName* and the local name in a string pointed to by *lpLocalName*. The local name is limited to 64 characters in length. The other fields in this structure are used by the WNet enumeration functions that I'll describe shortly.

You use the next two parameters in *WNetAddConnection3*, *lpPassword* and *lpUserName*, when requesting access from the server to the remote device. If you don't specify a user name and Windows CE can't find user information for network access already defined in the registry, the system displays a dialog box requesting the user name and password. Finally, the *dwFlags* parameter can be either 0 or the flag CONNECT_UPDATE_PROFILE. When this flag is set, the connection is dubbed *persistent*. Windows CE stores the connection data for persistent connections in the registry. Unlike other versions of Windows, Windows CE doesn't restore persistent connections when the user logs on. Instead, the local name to remote name mapping is tracked only in the registry. If the local folder is later accessed after the original connection was dropped, a reconnection is automatically attempted when the local folder is accessed.

If the call to *WNetAddConnection3* is successful, it returns NO_ERROR. Unlike most Win32 functions, *WNetAddConnection3* returns an error code in the return value if an error occurs. This is a nod to compatibility that stretches back to the Windows 3.1 days. You can also call *GetLastError* to return the error information. As an aside, the function *WNetGetLastError* is supported under Windows CE in that it's redefined as *GetLastError*, so you can call that function if compatibility with other platforms is important.

The other function you can use under Windows CE to connect a remote resource is *WNetConnectionDialog1*. This function presents a dialog box to the user requesting the remote and local names for the connection. The function is prototyped as

```
DWORD WNetConnectionDialog1 (LPCONNECTDLGSTRUCT lpConnectDlgStruc);
```

The one parameter is a pointer to a CONNECTDLGSTRUCT structure defined as the following:

```
typedef struct {
    DWORD cbStructure;
    HWND hwndOwner;
    LPNETRESOURCE lpConnRes;
    DWORD dwFlags;
    DWORD dwDevNum;
} CONNECTDLGSTRUCT;
```

The first field in the structure is the size field and must be set with the size of the CONNECTDLGSTRUCT structure before you call *WNetConnectionDialog1*. The *hwndOwner* field should be filled with the handle of the owner window for the dialog box. The *lpConnRes* field should point to a NETRESOURCE structure. This structure should be filled with zeros except for the *lpRemoteName* field, which may be filled to specify the default remote name in the dialog. You can leave the *lpRemoteName* field 0 if you don't want to specify a suggested remote path.

The *dwFlags* field can either be 0 or set to the flag CONNDLG_RO_PATH. When this flag is specified, the user can't change the remote name field in the dialog box. Of course, this means that the *lpRemoteName* field in the NETRESOURCE structure must contain a valid remote name. Windows CE ignores the *dwDevNum* field in the CONNECTDLGSTRUCT structure.

When the function is called, it displays a dialog box that allows the user to specify a local and, if not invoked with the CONNDLG_RO_PATH flag, the remote name as well. If the user taps on the OK button, Windows attempts to make the connection specified. The connection, if successful, is recorded as a persistent connection in the registry.

If the connection is successful, the function returns NO_ERROR. If the user presses the Cancel button in the dialog box, the function returns –1. Other return codes indicate errors processing the function.

Disconnecting a remote resource

You can choose from three ways to disconnect a connected resource. The first method is to delete the connection with this function:

```
DWORD WNetCancelConnection2 (LPTSTR lpName, DWORD dwFlags,
                             BOOL fForce);
```

The *lpName* parameter points to either the local name or the remote network name of the connection you want to remove. The *dwFlags* parameter should be set to 0 or CONNECT_UPDATE_PROFILE. If CONNECT_UPDATE_PROFILE is set, the entry in the registry that references the connection is removed; otherwise the call won't change that information. Finally, the *fForce* parameter indicates whether the system should continue with the disconnect, even if there are open files or print jobs on the remote device. If the function is successful, it returns NO_ERROR.

You can prompt the user to specify a network resource to delete using this function:

```
DWORD WNetDisconnectDialog (HWND hwnd, DWORD dwType);
```

This function brings up a system provided dialog box that lists all connections currently defined. The user can select one from the list and tap on the OK button to disconnect that resource. The two parameters for this function are a handle to the window that owns the dialog box and *dwType*, which is supposed to define the type of resources—printer (RESOURCETYPE_PRINT) or disk (RESOURCETYPE_DISK)—enumerated in the dialog box. However, some systems ignore this parameter and enumerate both disk and print devices. This dialog, displayed by *WnetDisconnectDialog*, is actually implemented by the network driver. So it's up to each OEM to get this dialog to work correctly.

A more specific method to disconnect a network resource is to call

```
DWORD WNetDisconnectDialog1 (LPDISCDLGSTRUCT lpDiscDlgStruc);
```

This function is misleadingly named in that it won't display a dialog box if all the parameters in DISCDLGSTRUCT are correct and point to a resource not currently being used. The dialog part of this function appears when the resource is being used.

The DISCDLGSTRUCT is defined as

```
typedef struct {
    DWORD cbStructure;
    HWND hwndOwner;
    LPTSTR lpLocalName;
    LPTSTR lpRemoteName;
    DWORD dwFlags;
} DISCDLGSTRUCT;
```

As usual, the *cbStructure* field should be set to the size of the structure. The *hwndOwner* field should be set to the window that owns any dialog box displayed. The *lpLocalName* and *lpRemoteName* fields should be set to the local and remote names of the resource that's to be disconnected. Under current implementations, the *lpLocalName* is optional while the *lpRemoteName* field must be set for the function to work correctly. The *dwFlags* parameter can be either 0 or DISC_NO_FORCE. If this flag is set and the network resource is currently being used, the system simply fails the function. Otherwise, a dialog appears asking the user if he or she wants to disconnect the resource even though the resource is being used. Under the current implementations, the DISC_NO_FORCE flag is ignored.

Enumerating network resources

It's all very well and good to connect to a network resource, but it helps if you know what resources are available to connect to. Windows CE supports three WNet functions used to enumerate network resources: *WNetOpenEnum*, *WNetEnumResource*, and *WNetCloseEnum*. The process is similar to enumerating files with *FileFindFirst*, *FileFindNext*, and *FileFindClose*.

To start the process of numerating network resources, first call the function

```
DWORD WNetOpenEnum (DWORD dwScope, DWORD dwType, DWORD dwUsage,
                    LPNETRESOURCE lpNetResource,
                    LPHANDLE lphEnum);
```

The first parameter *dwScope* specifies the scope of the enumeration. It can be one of the following flags:

- *RESOURCE_CONNECTED* Enumerate the connected resources.
- *RESOURCE_REMEMBERED* Enumerate the persistent network connections.
- *RESOURCE_GLOBALNET* Enumerate all resources on the network.

The first two flags, RESOURCE_CONNECTED and RESOURCE_REMEMBERED, simply enumerate the resources already connected on your machine. The difference is that RESOURCE_CONNECTED returns the network resources that are connected at the time of the call, while RESOURCE_REMEMBERED returns those that are persistent regardless of whether they're currently connected. When using either of these flags, the *dwUsage* parameter is ignored and the *lpNetResource* parameters must be NULL.

The third flag, RESOURCE_GLOBALNET, allows you to enumerate resources—such as servers, shared drives, or printers out on the network—that aren't connected. The *dwType* parameter specifies what you're attempting to enumerate—shared disks (RESOURCETYPE_DISK), shared printers (RESOURCETYPE_PRINT), or both (RESOURCETYPE_ANY).

You use the third and fourth parameters only if the *dwScope* parameter is set to RESOURCE_GLOBALNET. The *dwUsage* parameter specifies the usage of the resource and can be 0 to enumerate any resource, RESOURCEUSAGE_CONNECTABLE to enumerate only connectable resources, or RESOURCEUSAGE_CONTAINER to enumerate only containers such as servers.

If the *dwScope* parameter is set to RESOURCE_GLOBALNET, the fourth parameter, *lpNetResource* must point to a NETRESOURCE structure; otherwise the parameter must be NULL. The NETRESOURCE structure should be initialized to specify the starting point on the network for the enumeration. The starting point is specified by a UNC name in the *lpRemoteName* field of NETRESOURCE. The *dwUsage* field of the NETRESOURCE structure must be set to RESOURCETYPE_CONTAINER. For example, to enumerate the shared resources on the server BIGSERV the *lpRemoteName* field would point to the string *\\BIGSERV*. To enumerate all servers in a domain, the *lpRemoteName* should simply specify the domain name. For the domain EntireNet, the *lpRemoteName* field should point to the string *EntireNet*. Because Windows CE doesn't allow you to pass a NULL into *lpRemoteName* when you use the RESOURCE_GLOBALNET flag, you can't enumerate all resources in the network namespace as you can under Windows 98 or Windows NT. This restriction exists because Windows CE doesn't support the concept of a Windows CE device belonging to a specific network context.

The final parameter of *WNetOpenEnum*, *lphEnum*, is a pointer to an enumeration handle that will be passed to the other functions in the enumeration process. *WNetOpenEnum* returns a value of NO_ERROR if successful. If the function isn't successful, you can call *GetLastError* to query the extended error information.

Once you have successfully started the enumeration process, you actually query data by calling this function:

```
DWORD WNetEnumResource (HANDLE hEnum, LPDWORD lpcCount,
                        LPVOID lpBuffer,
                        LPDWORD lpBufferSize);
```

The function takes the handle returned by *WNetOpenEnum* as its first parameter. The second parameter is a pointer to a variable that should be initialized with the number of resources you want to enumerate in each call to *WNetEnumResource*. You can specify a –1 in this variable if you want *WNetEnumResource* to return the data for as many resources as will fit in the return buffer specified by the *lpBuffer* parameter. The final parameter is a pointer to a DWORD that should be initialized with the size of the buffer pointed to by *lpBuffer*. If the buffer is too small to hold the data for even one resource, *WNetEnumResource* sets this variable to the required size for the buffer.

The information about the shared resources returned by data is returned in the form of an array of NETRESOURCE structures. While this is the same structure I described when I talked about the *WNetAddConnection3* function, I'll list the elements of the structure here again for convenience:

```
typedef struct _NETRESOURCE {
    DWORD  dwScope;
    DWORD  dwType;
    DWORD  dwDisplayType;
    DWORD  dwUsage;
    LPTSTR lpLocalName;
    LPTSTR lpRemoteName;
    LPTSTR lpComment;
    LPTSTR lpProvider;
} NETRESOURCE;
```

The interesting fields in the context of enumeration start with the *dwType* field, which indicates the type of resource that was enumerated. The value can be RESOURCETYPE_DISK or RESOURCETYPE_PRINT. The *dwDisplayType* field provides even more information about the resource, demarcating domains (RESOURCE-DISPLAYTYPE_DOMAIN) from servers (RESOURCEDISPLAYTYPE_SERVER) and from shared disks and printers (RESOURCEDISPLAYTYPE_SHARE). A fourth flag, RESOURCEDISPLAYTYPE_GENERIC, is returned if the display type doesn't matter.

The *lpLocalName* field points to a string containing the local name of the resource if the resource is currently connected or is a persistent connection. The *lpRemoteName* field points to the UNC name of the resource. The *lpComment* field contains the comment line describing the resource that's provided by some servers.

WNetEnumResource either returns NO_ERROR, indicating the function passed (but you need to call it again to enumerate more resources), or ERROR_NO_MORE_ITEMS, indicating that you have enumerated all resources matching the specification passed in *WNetOpenEnum*. With any other return code, you should call *GetLastError* to further diagnose the problem.

You have few strategies when enumerating the network resources. You can specify a huge buffer and pass a –1 in the variable pointed to by *lpcCount*, telling *WNetEnumResource* to return as much information as possible in one shot. Or you can specify a smaller buffer and ask for only one or two resources for each call to *WNetEnumResource*. The one caveat on the small buffer approach is that the strings that contain the local and remote names are also placed in the specified buffer. The name pointers inside the NETRESOURCE structure then point to those strings. This means that you can't specify the size of the buffer to be exactly the size of the NETRESOURCE structure and expect to get any data back. A third possibility is to call *WNetEnumResource* twice, the first time with the *lpBuffer* parameter 0, and have Windows CE tell you the size necessary for the buffer. Then you allocate the buffer and call *WNetEnumResource* again to actually query the data. However you use *WnetEnumResource*, you'll need to check the return code to see whether it needs to be called again to enumerate more resources.

When you have enumerated all the resources, you must make one final call to the function:

```
DWORD WNetCloseEnum (HANDLE hEnum);
```

The only parameter to this function is the enumeration handle first returned by *WNetOpenEnum*. This function cleans up the system resources used by the enumeration process.

Following is a short routine that uses the enumeration functions to query the network for available resources. You pass to a function a UNC name to use as the root of the search. The function returns a buffer of zero-delimited strings that designate the local name, if any, and the UNC name of each shared resource found.

```
// Helper routine
int AddToList (LPTSTR *pPtr, INT *pnListSize, LPTSTR pszStr) {
    INT nLen = lstrlen (pszStr) + 1;

    if (*pnListSize < nLen) return -1;
    lstrcpy (*pPtr, pszStr);
    *pPtr += nLen;
    *pnListSize -= nLen;
    return 0;
}
//----------------------------------------------------------------------
// EnumNetDisks - Produces a list of shared disks on a network
//
int EnumNetDisks (LPTSTR pszRoot, LPTSTR pszNetList, int nNetSize){
    INT i = 0, rc, nBuffSize = 1024;
    DWORD dwCnt, dwSize;
    HANDLE hEnum;
    NETRESOURCE nr;
    LPNETRESOURCE pnr;
    PBYTE pPtr, pNew;

    // Allocate buffer for enumeration data.
    pPtr = (PBYTE) LocalAlloc (LPTR, nBuffSize);
    if (!pPtr)
        return -1;

    // Initialize specification for search root.
    memset (&nr, 0, sizeof (nr));
    nr.lpRemoteName = pszRoot;
    nr.dwUsage = RESOURCEUSAGE_CONTAINER;

    // Start enumeration.
    rc = WNetOpenEnum (RESOURCE_GLOBALNET, RESOURCETYPE_DISK, 0, &nr,
                       &hEnum);
    if (rc != NO_ERROR)
        return -1;

    // Enumerate one item per loop.
    do {
        dwCnt = 1;
        dwSize = nBuffSize;
        rc = WNetEnumResource (hEnum, &dwCnt, pPtr, &dwSize);

        // Process returned data.
        if (rc == NO_ERROR) {
            pnr = (NETRESOURCE *)pPtr;
            if (pnr->lpRemoteName)
                rc = AddToList (&pszNetList, &nNetSize,
                                pnr->lpRemoteName);
```

```
        // If our buffer was too small, try again.
        } else if (rc == ERROR_MORE_DATA) {
            pNew = LocalReAlloc (pPtr, dwSize, LMEM_MOVEABLE);
            if (pNew) {
                pPtr = pNew;
                nBuffSize = LocalSize (pPtr);
                rc = 0;
            }
        }
    } while (rc == 0);

    // If the loop was successful, add extra zero to list.
    if (rc == ERROR_NO_MORE_ITEMS) {
        rc = AddToList (&pszNetList, &nNetSize, TEXT (""));
        rc = 0;
    }

    // Clean up.
    WNetCloseEnum (hEnum);
    LocalFree (pPtr);
    return rc;
}
```

While the enumeration functions work well to query what's available on the net, you can use another strategy for determining the current connected resources. At the simplest level, you can use *FileFindFirst* and *FileFindNext* to enumerate the locally connected network disks by searching the folders in the \network directory. Once you have the local name, a few functions are available to you for querying just what that local name is connected to.

Querying connections and resources

The folders in the \network directory represent the local names of network shared disks that are persistently connected to network resources. To determine which of the folders are currently connected, you can use the function

```
DWORD WNetGetConnection (LPCTSTR lpLocalName,
                         LPTSTR lpRemoteName,
                         LPDWORD lpnLength);
```

WNetGetConnection returns the UNC name of the network resource associated with a local device or folder. The *lpLocalName* parameter is filled with the local name of a shared folder or printer. The *lpRemoteName* parameter should point to a buffer that can receive the UNC name for the device. The *lpnLength* parameter points to a DWORD value that initially contains the length in characters of the remote name buffer. If the buffer is too small to receive the name, the length value is loaded with the number of characters required to hold the UNC name.

One feature (or problem, depending on how you look at it) of *WNetGetConnection* is that it fails unless the local folder or device has a current connection to the remote shared device. This allows us an easy way to determine which local folders are currently connected and which are just placeholders for persistent connections that aren't currently connected.

Sometimes you need to transfer a filename from one system to another and you need a common format for the filename that would be understood by both systems. The *WNetGetUniversalName* function translates a filename that contains a local network name into one using the UNC name of the connected resource. The prototype for *WNetGetUniversalName* is the following:

```
DWORD WNetGetUniversalName (LPCTSTR lpLocalPath, DWORD dwInfoLevel,
                            LPVOID lpBuffer, LPDWORD lpBufferSize);
```

Like *WNetGetConnection*, this function returns a UNC name for a local name. There are two main differences between *WNetGetConnection* and *WNetGetUniversalName*. First, *WNetGetUniversalName* works even if the remote resource isn't currently connected. Second, you can pass a complete filename to *WNetGetUniversalName* instead of simply the local name of the shared resource, which is all that is accepted by *WNetGetConnection*.

WNetGetUniversalName returns the remote information in two different formats. If the *dwInfoLevel* parameter is set to UNIVERSAL_NAME_INFO_LEVEL, the buffer pointed to by *lpBuffer* is loaded with the following structure:

```
typedef struct _UNIVERSAL_NAME_INFO {
    LPTSTR  lpUniversalName;
} UNIVERSAL_NAME_INFO;
```

The only field in the structure is a pointer to the UNC name for the shared resource. The string is returned in the buffer immediately following the structure. So, if a server *\\BigServ\DriveC* was attached as LocC and you pass *WnetGetUniversalName* the filename \network\LocC\win32\filename.ext, it returns the UNC name *\\BigServ\DriveC\win32\filename.ext*.

If the *dwInfoLevel* parameter is set to REMOTE_NAME_INFO_LEVEL, the buffer is filled with the following structure:

```
typedef struct _REMOTE_NAME_INFO
    LPTSTR  lpUniversalName;
    LPTSTR  lpConnectionName;
    LPTSTR  lpRemainingPath;
} REMOTE_NAME_INFO;
```

This structure returns not just the UNC name, but also parses the UNC name into the share name and the remaining path. So, using the same filename as in the previous example, \network\LocC\win32\filename.ext, the REMOTE_NAME_INFO fields would point to the following strings:

lpUniveralName: *\\BigServ\DriveC\win32\filename.ext*
lpConnectionName: *\\BigServ\DriveC*
lpRemainingPath: *\win32\filename.ext*

One more thing: you don't have to prefix the local share name with \network. In the preceding example, the filename \LocC\Win32\filename.ext would have produced the same results.

One final WNet function supported by Windows CE is

```
DWORD WnetGetUser (LPCTSTR lpName, LPTSTR lpUserName,
                   LPDWORD lpnLength);
```

This function returns the name the system used to connect to the remote resource. *WnetGetUser* is passed the local name of the shared resource and returns the user name the system used when connecting to the remote resource in the buffer pointed to by *lpUserName*. The *lpnLengh* parameter should point to a variable that contains the size of the buffer. If the buffer isn't big enough to contain the user name, the variable pointed to by *lpnLength* is filled with the required size for the buffer.

The ListNet Example Program

ListNet is a short program that lists the persistent network connections on a Windows CE machine. The program's window is a dialog box with three controls: a list box that displays the network connections, a Connect button that lets you add a new persistent connection, and a Disconnect button that lets you delete one of the connections. Double-clicking on a connection in the list box opens an Explorer window to display the contents of that network resource. Figure 10-1 shows the ListNet window while Figure 10-2 on the next page shows the ListNet source code.

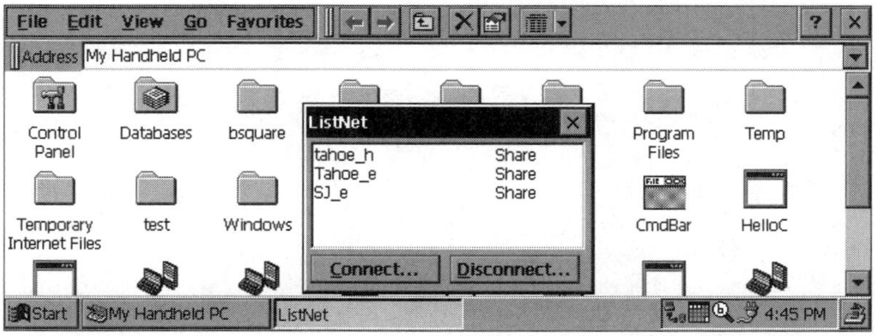

Figure 10-1. *The ListNet window containing a few network folders.*

ListNet.rc

```
//======================================================================
// Resource file
//
// Written for the book Programming Windows CE
// Copyright (C) 1998 Douglas Boling
//======================================================================
#include "windows.h"
#include "ListNet.h"                     // Program-specific stuff

//----------------------------------------------------------------------
// Icons and bitmaps
//
ID_ICON ICON   "ListNet.ico"             // Program icon

//----------------------------------------------------------------------
// Main window dialog template
//
ListNet DIALOG discardable 10, 10, 120, 65
STYLE  WS_OVERLAPPED | WS_VISIBLE | WS_CAPTION | WS_SYSMENU |
       DS_CENTER | DS_MODALFRAME
CAPTION "ListNet"
BEGIN
    LISTBOX                  IDD_NETLIST,   2,   2, 116,  46,
                          WS_TABSTOP | WS_VSCROLL |
                          LBS_NOINTEGRALHEIGHT | LBS_USETABSTOPS
    PUSHBUTTON "&Connect...",   IDD_CNCT,   2,  50,  55,  12, WS_TABSTOP
    PUSHBUTTON "&Disconnect...",
                               IDD_DCNCT,  61,  50,  55,  12, WS_TABSTOP
END
```

ListNet.h

```
//======================================================================
// Header file
//
// Written for the book Programming Windows CE
// Copyright (C) 1998 Douglas Boling
//======================================================================
// Returns number of elements
#define dim(x) (sizeof(x) / sizeof(x[0]))

//----------------------------------------------------------------------
// Generic defines and data types
```

Figure 10-2. *The ListNet source.*

```
//
struct decodeUINT {                             // Structure associates
    UINT Code;                                  // messages
                                                // with a function.
    LRESULT (*Fxn)(HWND, UINT, WPARAM, LPARAM);
};
struct decodeCMD {                              // Structure associates
    UINT Code;                                  // menu IDs with a
    LRESULT (*Fxn)(HWND, WORD, HWND, WORD);     // function.
};
//----------------------------------------------------------------------
// Generic defines used by application

#define  ID_ICON            1

#define  IDD_NETLIST        100                 // Control IDs
#define  IDD_CNCT           101
#define  IDD_DCNCT          102

//----------------------------------------------------------------------
// Function prototypes
//
int InitApp (HINSTANCE);
HWND InitInstance (HINSTANCE, LPWSTR, int);
int TermInstance (HINSTANCE, int);
INT RefreshLocalNetDrives (HWND hWnd);

// Dialog window procedure
BOOL CALLBACK MainWndProc (HWND, UINT, WPARAM, LPARAM);

// Dialog window Message handlers
BOOL DoCommandMain (HWND, UINT, WPARAM, LPARAM);

// Command functions
LPARAM DoMainCommandExit (HWND, WORD, HWND, WORD);
LPARAM DoMainCommandViewDrive (HWND, WORD, HWND, WORD);
LPARAM DoMainCommandMapDrive (HWND, WORD, HWND, WORD);
LPARAM DoMainCommandFreeDrive  (HWND, WORD, HWND, WORD);
```

ListNet.c

```
//======================================================================
// ListNet - A network demo application for Windows CE
//
// Written for the book Programming Windows CE
```

(continued)

Figure 10-2. *continued*

```
// Copyright (C) 1998 Douglas Boling
//======================================================================
#include <windows.h>                    // For all that Windows stuff
#include <winnetwk.h>                   // Network includes
#include "ListNet.h"                    // Program-specific stuff

//----------------------------------------------------------------------
// Global data
//
const TCHAR szAppName[] = TEXT ("ListNet");
HINSTANCE hInst;                        // Program instance handle
BOOL fFirst = TRUE;

// Command Message dispatch for MainWindowProc
const struct decodeCMD MainCommandItems[] = {
    IDOK, DoMainCommandExit,
    IDCANCEL, DoMainCommandExit,
    IDD_NETLIST, DoMainCommandViewDrive,
    IDD_CNCT, DoMainCommandMapDrive,
    IDD_DCNCT, DoMainCommandFreeDrive,
};
//======================================================================
//
// Program entry point
//
int WINAPI WinMain (HINSTANCE hInstance, HINSTANCE hPrevInstance,
                    LPWSTR lpCmdLine, int nCmdShow) {
    // Save program instance handle in global variable.
    hInst = hInstance;

    // Create main window.
    DialogBox (hInst, szAppName, NULL, MainWndProc);
    return 0;
}
//======================================================================
// Message handling procedures for main window
//----------------------------------------------------------------------
// MainWndProc - Callback function for application window
//
BOOL CALLBACK MainWndProc (HWND hWnd, UINT wMsg, WPARAM wParam,
                           LPARAM lParam) {
    INT i;
    // With only two messages, do it the old-fashioned way.
    switch (wMsg) {
    case WM_INITDIALOG:
        i = 75;
```

```
        SendDlgItemMessage (hWnd, IDD_NETLIST, LB_SETTABSTOPS, 1,
                            (LPARAM)&i);
        RefreshLocalNetDrives (hWnd);
        break;

    case WM_COMMAND:
    return DoCommandMain (hWnd, wMsg, wParam, lParam);
    }
    return FALSE;
}
//----------------------------------------------------------------------
// DoCommandMain - Process WM_COMMAND message for window.
//
BOOL DoCommandMain (HWND hWnd, UINT wMsg, WPARAM wParam, LPARAM lParam){
    WORD idItem, wNotifyCode;
    HWND hwndCtl;
    INT  i;

    // Parse the parameters.
    idItem = (WORD) LOWORD (wParam);
    wNotifyCode = (WORD) HIWORD (wParam);
    hwndCtl = (HWND) lParam;

    // Call routine to handle control message.
    for (i = 0; i < dim(MainCommandItems); i++) {
        if (idItem == MainCommandItems[i].Code) {
            (*MainCommandItems[i].Fxn)(hWnd, idItem, hwndCtl,
                                       wNotifyCode);
            return TRUE;
        }
    }
    return FALSE;
}
//======================================================================
// Command handler routines
//----------------------------------------------------------------------
// DoMainCommandExit - Process Program Exit command
//
LPARAM DoMainCommandExit (HWND hWnd, WORD idItem, HWND hwndCtl,
                          WORD wNotifyCode) {
    EndDialog (hWnd, 0);
    return 0;
}
//----------------------------------------------------------------------
// DoMainCommandViewDrive - Process list box double clicks
//
```

(continued)

Figure 10-2. *continued*

```
LPARAM DoMainCommandViewDrive (HWND hWnd, WORD idItem, HWND hwndCtl,
                               WORD wNotifyCode) {
    TCHAR szCmdLine[128], szFolder[MAX_PATH];
    PROCESS_INFORMATION pi;
    HCURSOR hOld;
    INT i, rc;

    // We're only interested in list box double-clicks.
    if (wNotifyCode != LBN_DBLCLK)
        return 0;

    i = SendMessage (hwndCtl, LB_GETCURSEL, 0, 0);
    if (i == LB_ERR) return 0;
    i = SendMessage (hwndCtl, LB_GETTEXT, i, (LPARAM)szFolder);

    hOld = SetCursor (LoadCursor (NULL, IDC_WAIT));
    lstrcpy (szCmdLine, TEXT ("\\network\\"));
    lstrcat (szCmdLine, szFolder);

    rc = CreateProcess (TEXT ("Explorer"), szCmdLine, NULL, NULL,
                        FALSE, 0, NULL, NULL, NULL, &pi);
    if (rc) {
        CloseHandle (pi.hProcess);
        CloseHandle (pi.hThread);
    }
    SetCursor (hOld);
    return TRUE;
}
//----------------------------------------------------------------------
// DoMainCommandMapDrive - Process map network drive command.
//
LPARAM DoMainCommandMapDrive (HWND hWnd, WORD idItem, HWND hwndCtl,
                              WORD wNotifyCode) {
    DWORD rc;
    CONNECTDLGSTRUCT cds;
    NETRESOURCE nr;
    TCHAR szRmt[256];

    memset (&nr, 0, sizeof (nr));
    nr.dwType = RESOURCETYPE_DISK;
    memset (szRmt, 0, sizeof (szRmt));

    cds.cbStructure = sizeof (cds);
    cds.hwndOwner = hWnd;
    cds.lpConnRes = &nr;
    cds.dwFlags = CONNDLG_PERSIST;
```

```
    // Display dialog box.
    rc = WNetConnectionDialog1 (&cds);

    if (rc == NO_ERROR)
        RefreshLocalNetDrives (hWnd);
    return 0;
}
//----------------------------------------------------------------------
// DoMainCommandFreeDrive - Process disconnect network drive command.
//
LPARAM DoMainCommandFreeDrive (HWND hWnd, WORD idItem, HWND hwndCtl,
                               WORD wNotifyCode) {
    WNetDisconnectDialog (hWnd, RESOURCETYPE_DISK);
    RefreshLocalNetDrives (hWnd);
    return 0;
}
//======================================================================
// Network browsing functions
//----------------------------------------------------------------------
// EnumerateLocalNetDrives - Add an item to the list view control.
//
INT RefreshLocalNetDrives (HWND hWnd) {
    HWND hwndCtl = GetDlgItem (hWnd, IDD_NETLIST);
    INT rc, nBuffSize = 1024;
    DWORD dwCnt, dwSize;
    HANDLE hEnum;
    LPNETRESOURCE pnr;
    NETRESOURCE nr;
    PBYTE pPtr, pNew;
    TCHAR szText[256];

    SendMessage (hwndCtl, LB_RESETCONTENT, 0, 0);

    // Allocate buffer for enumeration data.
    pPtr = (PBYTE) LocalAlloc (LPTR, nBuffSize);
    if (!pPtr)
        return -1;

    // Initialize specification for search root.
    memset (&nr, 0, sizeof (nr));
    lstrcpy (szText, TEXT ("\\sjdev"));
    nr.lpRemoteName = szText;
    nr.dwUsage = RESOURCEUSAGE_CONTAINER;

    // Start enumeration.
    rc = WNetOpenEnum (RESOURCE_REMEMBERED, RESOURCETYPE_ANY, 0, 0,
                       &hEnum);
```

(continued)

Figure 10-2. *continued*

```
    if (rc != NO_ERROR) return -1;

    // Enumerate one item per loop.
    do {
        dwCnt = 1;
        dwSize = nBuffSize;
        rc = WNetEnumResource (hEnum, &dwCnt, pPtr, &dwSize);
        pnr = (NETRESOURCE *)pPtr;
        lstrcpy (szText, pnr->lpLocalName);
        // Process returned data.
        if (rc == NO_ERROR) {
            switch (pnr->dwType) {
            case RESOURCETYPE_ANY:
                lstrcat (szText, TEXT ("\t Share"));
                break;
            case RESOURCETYPE_PRINT:
                lstrcat (szText, TEXT ("\t Printer"));
                break;
            case RESOURCETYPE_DISK:
                lstrcat (szText, TEXT ("\t Disk"));
                break;
            }
            SendMessage (hwndCtl, LB_ADDSTRING, 0, (LPARAM)szText);

        // If our buffer was too small, try again.
        } else if (rc == ERROR_MORE_DATA) {
            pNew = LocalReAlloc (pPtr, dwSize, LMEM_MOVEABLE);
            if (pNew) {
                pPtr = pNew;
                nBuffSize = LocalSize (pPtr);
                rc = 0;
            } else
                break;
        }
    } while (rc == 0);
    // Clean up.
    WNetCloseEnum (hEnum);
    LocalFree (pPtr);
    return 0;
}
```

The heart of the networking code is at the end of ListNet, in the routine *RefreshLocalNetDrives*. This routine uses the WNet enumerate functions to determine the persistent network resources mapped to the system. Network connections and disconnections are accomplished with calls to *WNetConnectionDialog1* and

WnetDisconnectDialog respectively. You open an Explorer window containing the shared network disk by launching EXPLORER.EXE with a command line that's the path of the folder to open.

BASIC SOCKETS

WinSock is the name for the Windows socket API. WinSock is the API for Windows CE TCP/IP networking stack as well as the IrDA infrared communication stack. Windows CE implements a subset of WinSock version 1.1. What's left out of the Windows CE implementation of WinSock is the ever-so-handy *WSAAsyncSelect* function that enables (under other Windows systems) an application to be informed when a WinSock event occurred. Actually, most of the *WSAxxx* calls that provide asynchronous actions are missing from Windows CE. Instead, the Windows CE implementation is more like the original "Berkeley" socket API. Windows CE's developers decided not to support these functions to reduce the size of the WinSock implementation. These functions were handy, but not required because Windows CE is multithreaded.

The lack of asynchronous functions doesn't mean that you're left with calling socket functions that block on every call. You can put a socket in nonblocking mode so that any function that can't accomplish its task without waiting on an event will return with a return code indicating that the task isn't yet completed.

Windows CE has extended WinSock in one area. As I mentioned in Chapter 9, WinSock is also the primary interface for IrDA communication. To do this, Windows CE extends the socket addressing scheme, actually providing an entirely different addressing mode designed for the transitory nature of IrDA communication.

In this section, I'm not going to dive into a complete explanation of socket-based communication. Instead, I'll present an introduction that will get you started communicating with sockets. In addition, I'll spend time with the IrSock side because this interface is so significant for Windows CE devices.

Initializing the WinSock DLL

Like other versions of WinSock, the Windows CE version should be initialized before you use it. You accomplish this by calling *WSAStartup*, which initializes the WinSock DLL. It's prototyped as

```
int WSAStartup (WORD wVersionRequested, LPWSADATA lpWSAData );
```

The first parameter is the version of WinSock you're requesting to open. For all current versions of Windows CE, you must indicate version 1.1. An easy way to do this is to use the MAKEWORD macro as in MAKEWORD (1,1). The second parameter must point to a WSAData structure, shown in the code on the next page.

```
struct WSAData {
    WORD wVersion;
    WORD wHighVersion;
    char szDescription[WSADESCRIPTION_LEN+1];
    char szSystemStatus[WSASYSSTATUS_LEN+1];
    unsigned short iMaxSockets;
    unsigned short iMaxUdpDg;
    char FAR * lpVendorInfo;
};
```

This structure is filled in by *WSAStartup*, providing information about the specific implementation of this version of WinSock. Currently, the first two fields return *0x0101*, indicating support for version 1.1. The *szDescription* and *szSystemStatus* fields can be used by WinSock to return information about itself. In the current Windows CE version of WinSock, these fields aren't used. The *iMaxSockets* parameter suggests a maximum number of sockets that an application should be able to open. This number isn't a hard maximum but more a suggested maximum. Finally, the *iMaxUdpDg* field indicates the maximum size of a datagram packet. A 0 indicates no maximum size for this version of WinSock.

WSAStartup returns 0 if successful; otherwise the return value is the error code for the function. Don't call *WSAGetLastError* in this situation because the failure of this function indicates that WinSock, which provides *WSAGetLastError*, wasn't initialized correctly.

Windows CE also supports *WSACleanup*, which is traditionally called when an application has finished using the WinSock DLL. For Windows CE, this function performs no action but is provided for compatibility. Its prototype is

```
int WSACleanup ();
```

ASCII vs. Unicode

One issue that you'll have to be careful of is that almost all the string fields used in the socket structures are char fields, not Unicode. Because of this, you'll find yourself using the functions

```
int WideCharToMultiByte(UINT CodePage, DWORD dwFlags,
                        LPCWSTR lpWideCharStr, int cchWideChar,
                        LPSTR lpMultiByteStr, int cchMultiByte,
                        LPCSTR lpDefaultChar, LPBOOL lpUsedDefaultChar);
```

to convert Unicode strings into multibyte strings and

```
int MultiByteToWideChar (UINT CodePage, DWORD dwFlags,
                        LPCSTR lpMultiByteStr, int cchMultiByte,
                        LPWSTR lpWideCharStr, int cchWideChar);
```

to convert multibyte characters into Unicode. The functions refer to multibyte characters instead of ASCII because on double-byte coded systems, they convert double-byte characters into Unicode.

Stream Sockets

Like all socket implementations, WinSock under Windows CE supports both stream and datagram connections. In a stream connection, a socket is basically a data pipe. Once two points are connected, data is sent back and forth without the need for additional addressing. In a datagram connection, the socket is more like a mailslot, with discrete packets of data being sent to specific addresses. In describing the WinSock functions, I'm going to cover the process of a creating a *stream* connection (sometimes called a *connection-oriented* connection) between a client and server application. I'll leave explanation of the datagram connection to other, more network-specific books.

The life of a stream socket is fairly straightforward: it's created, bound, or connected to an address; read from or written to; and finally closed. A few extra steps along the way, however, complicate the story slightly. Sockets work in a client/server model. A client initiates a conversation with a known server. The server, on the other hand, waits around until a client requests data. When setting up a socket, you have to approach the process from either the client side or the server side. This decision determines which functions you call to configure a socket. Figure 10-3 illustrates the process from both the client and the server side. For each step in the process, the corresponding WinSock function is shown.

Server	*Function*	*Client*	*Function*
Create socket	*socket*	Create socket	*socket*
Bind socket to an address	*bind*	Find desired server	(many functions)
Listen for client connections	*listen*	Connect to server	*connect*
Accept client's connection	*accept*		
Receive data from client	*recv*	Send data to server	*send*
Send data to client	*send*	Receive data from server	*recv*

Figure 10-3. *The process for producing a connection-oriented socket connection.*

Both the client and the server must first create a socket. After that, the process diverges. The server must attach, or to use the function name, *bind*, the socket to an address so that another computer or even a local process, can connect to the socket. Once an address has been bound, the server configures the socket to listen for a connection from a client. The server then waits to accept a connection from a client. Finally, after all this, the server is ready to converse.

The client's job is simpler: the client creates the socket, connects the socket to a remote address, and then sends and receives data. This procedure, of course, ignores the sometimes not-so-simple process of determining the address to connect to. I'll leave that problem for a few moments while I talk about the functions behind this process.

Creating a socket

You create a socket with the function

```
SOCKET socket (int af, int type, int protocol);
```

The first parameter, *af*, specifies the addressing family for the socket. Windows CE supports two addressing formats; AF_INET and AF_IRDA. You use the AF_IRDA constant when you're creating a socket for IrDA use, and you use AF_INET for TCP/IP communication. The type parameter specifies the type of socket being created. For a TCP/IP socket, this can be either SOCK_STREAM for a stream socket or SOCK_DGRAM for a datagram socket. For IrDA sockets, the type parameter must be SOCK_STREAM. Windows CE doesn't currently expose a method to create a raw socket, which is a socket that allows you to interact with the IP layer of the TCP/IP protocol. Among other uses, raw sockets are used to send an echo request to other servers, in the process known as pinging. However, Windows CE does provide a method of sending an ICMP echo request. I'll talk about that shortly.

The protocol parameter specifies the protocol used by the address family specified by the *af* parameter. The function returns a handle to the newly created socket. If an error occurs, the socket returns INVALID_SOCKET. You can call *WSAGetLastError* to query the extended error code.

Server side: binding a socket to an address

For the server, the next step is to bind the socket to an address. You accomplish this with the function

```
int bind (SOCKET s, const struct sockaddr FAR *addr, int namelen);
```

The first parameter is the handle to the newly created socket. The second parameter is dependent on whether you're dealing with a TCP/IP socket or an IrDa socket. For a standard TCP/IP socket, the structure pointed to by *addr* should be SOCKADDR_IN, which is defined as

```
struct sockaddr_in {
    short sin_family;
    unsigned short sin_port;
    IN_ADDR sin_addr;
    char sin_zero[8];
};
```

The first field, *sin_family* must be set to AF_INET. The second field is the IP port while the third field specifies the IP address. The last field is simply padding to fit the standard SOCKADDR structure. The last parameter of bind, *namelen*, should be set to the size of the SOCKADDR_IN structure.

When you're using IrSock, the address structure pointed to by *sockaddr* is SOCKADDR_IRDA, which is defined as

```
struct sockaddr_irda {
    u_short irdaAddressFamily;
    u_char irdaDeviceID[4];
    char irdaServiceName[25];
};
```

The first field, *irdaAddressFamily*, should be set to AF_IRDA to identify the structure. The second field, *irdaDeviceID*, is a 4-byte array that defines the address for this IR socket. This can be set to 0 for an IrSock server. The last field should be set to a string to identify the server.

You can also use a special, predefined name in the *irdaServiceName* field to bypass the IrDA address resolution features. If you specify the name LSAP-SEL*xxx* where *xxx* is a value from 001 through 127, the socket will be bound directly to the LSAP (Logical Service Assess Point) selector defined by the value. Applications should not, unless absolutely required, bind directly to a specific LSAP selector. Instead, by specifying a generic string, the IrDA Address resolution code determines a free LSAP selector and uses it.

Listening for a connection

Once a socket has been bound to an address, the server places the socket in listen mode so that it will accept incoming communication attempts. You place the socket in listen mode by using the aptly named function

```
int listen (SOCKET s, int backlog);
```

The two parameters are the handle to the socket and the size of the queue that you're creating to hold the pending connection attempts. This value can be set to SOMAXCONN to set the queue to the maximum supported by the socket implementation. For Windows CE, the only supported queue sizes are 1 and 2. Values outside this range are rounded to the closest valid value.

Accepting a connection

When a server is ready to accept a connection to a socket in listen mode, it calls this function:

```
SOCKET accept (SOCKET s, struct sockaddr FAR *addr,
               int FAR *addrlen);
```

The first parameter is the socket that has already been placed in listen mode. The next parameter should point to a buffer that receives the address of the client socket that has initiated a connection. The format of this address is dependent on the protocol used by the socket. For Windows CE, this is either a SOCKADDR_IN or a SOCKADDR_IRDA structure. The final parameter is a pointer to a variable that contains the size of the buffer. This variable is updated with the size of the structure returned in the address buffer when the function returns.

The *accept* function returns the handle to a new socket that's used to communicate with the client. The socket that was originally created by the call to *socket* will remain in listen mode, and can potentially accept other connections. If *accept* detects an error, it returns INVALID_SOCKET. In this case, you can call *WSAGetLastError* to get the error code.

The *accept* function is the first function I've talked about so far that blocks. That is, it won't return until a remote client requests a connection. You can set the socket in nonblocking mode so that, if no request for connection is queued, *accept* will return INVALID_SOCKET with an extended error code of WSAEWOULDBLOCK. I'll talk about blocking vs. nonblocking sockets shortly.

Client side: connecting a socket to a server

On the client side, things are different. Instead of calling the *bind* and *accept* functions, the client simply connects to a known server. I said simply, but as with most things, we must note a few complications. The primary one is addressing—knowing the address of the server you want to connect to. I'll put that topic aside for a moment and assume the client knows the address of the server.

To connect a newly created socket to a server, the client uses the function

```
int connect (SOCKET s, const struct sockaddr FAR *name,
             int namelen);
```

The first parameter is the socket handle that the client created with a call to *socket*. The other two parameters are the address and address length values we've seen in the *bind* and *accept* functions. Here again, Windows CE supports two addressing formats: SOCKADDR_IN for TCP/IP–based communication and SOCKADDR_IRDA for IrDA communication.

If connect is successful, it returns 0. Otherwise it returns SOCKET_ERROR, and you should call *WSAGetLastError* to get the reason for the failure.

Sending and receiving data

At this point, both the server and client have socket handles they can use to communicate with one another. The client uses the socket originally created with the call to *socket*, while the server uses the socket handle returned by the *accept* function.

All that remains is data transfer. You write data to a socket this way:

```
int send (SOCKET s, const char FAR *buf, int len, int flags);
```

The first parameter is the socket handle to send the data. You specify the data you want to send in the buffer pointed to by the *buf* parameter while the length of that data is specified in *len*. The *flags* parameter must be 0.

You receive data by using the function

```
int recv (SOCKET s, char FAR *buf, int len, int flags);
```

The first parameter is the socket handle. The second parameter points to the buffer that receives the data, while the third parameter should be set to the size of the buffer. The flags parameter can be 0, or it can be MSG_PEEK if you want to have the current data copied into the receive buffer but not removed from the input queue or if this is a TCP/IP socket (MSG_OOB) for receiving any out-of-band data that has been sent.

Two other functions can send and receive data; they are the following:

```
int sendto (SOCKET s, const char FAR *buf, int len, int flags,
            const struct sockaddr FAR *to, int token);
```

and

```
int recvfrom (SOCKET s, char FAR *buf, int len, int flags,
              struct sockaddr FAR *from, int FAR *fromlen);
```

These functions enable you to direct individual packets of data using the address parameters provided in the functions. They're used for connectionless sockets, but I mention them now for completeness. When used with connection-oriented sockets such as those I've just described, the addresses in *sendto* and *recvfrom* are ignored and the functions act like their simpler counterparts, *send* and *recv*.

Closing a socket

When you have finished using the sockets, call this function:

```
int shutdown (SOCKET s, int how);
```

The *shutdown* function takes the handle to the socket and a flag indicating what part of the connection you wish to shut down. The *how* parameter can be SD_RECEIVE to prevent any further *recv* calls from being processed, SD_SEND to prevent any further *send* calls from being processed, or SD_BOTH to prevent either *send* or *recv* calls from being processed. The *shutdown* function affects the higher level functions *send* and *recv* but doesn't prevent data previously queued from being processed. Once you have shut down a socket, it can't be used again. It should be closed and a new socket created to restart a session.

Once a connection has been shut down, you should close the socket with a call to this function:

```
int closesocket (SOCKET s);
```

The action of *closesocket* depends on how the socket is configured. If you've properly shut down the socket with a call to *shutdown*, no more events will be pending and *closesocket* should return without blocking. If the socket has been configured into "linger" mode and configured with a timeout value, *closesocket* will block until any data in the send queue has been sent or the timeout expires.

IrSock

I've alluded to IrSock a number of times as I've described functions. IrSock is essentially a socketlike API built over the top of the IrDA stack used for infrared communication. IrSock is the only high-level interface to the IrDA stack. Even the IrComm virtual comm port described in Chapter 9 uses the IrSock API underneath the covers.

The major differences between IrSock and WinSock are that IrSock doesn't support datagrams, it doesn't support security, and the method used for addressing it is completely different from that used for WinSock. What IrSock does provide is a method to query the devices ready to talk across the infrared port, as well as arbitration and collision detection and control.

From a programmer's perspective, the main difference in programming IrSock and WinSock is that the client side needs a method of detecting what infrared capable devices are within range and are ready to accept a socket connection. This is accomplished by calling *getsockopt* with the level parameter set to SOL_IRLMP and the *optname* parameter set to IRLMP_ENUMDEVICES, as in the following:

```
dwBuffSize = sizeof (buffer);
rc = getsockopt (hIrSock, SOL_IRLMP, IRLMP_ENUMDEVICES,
                 buffer, &dwBuffSize);
```

When called with IRLMP_ENUMDEVICES, *getsockopt* returns a DEVICELIST structure in the buffer. DEVICELIST is defined as

```
typedef struct _DEVICELIST {
    ULONG numDevice;
    IRDA_DEVICE_INFO Device[1];
} DEVICELIST;
```

The DEVICELIST structure is simply a count followed by an array of IRDA_DEVICE_INFO structures, one for each device found. The IRDA_DEVICE_INFO structure is defined as

```
typedef struct _IRDA_DEVICE_INFO {
    u_char irdaDeviceID[4];
    char irdaDeviceName[22];
    u_char Reserved[2];
} IRDA_DEVICE_INFO;
```

The two fields in the IRDA_DEVICE_INFO structure are a device ID and a string that can be used to identify the remote device.

Following is a routine that opens an IR socket and uses *getsockopt* to query the remote devices that are in range. If any devices are found, their names and IDs are printed to the debug port.

```
//
// Poll for IR devices.
//
DWORD WINAPI IrPoll (HWND hWnd) {
    INT rc, nSize, i, j;
    char cDevice[256];
    TCHAR szName[32], szOut[256];
    DEVICELIST *pDL;
    SOCKET irsock;

    // Open an infrared socket.
    irsock = socket (AF_IRDA, SOCK_STREAM, 0);
    if (irsock == INVALID_SOCKET)
        return -1;

    // Search for someone to talk to, try 10 times over 5 seconds.
    for (i = 0; i < 10; i++) {

        // Call getsockopt to query devices.
        memset (cDevice, 0, sizeof (cDevice));
        nSize = sizeof (cDevice);
        rc = getsockopt (irsock, SOL_IRLMP, IRLMP_ENUMDEVICES,
                         cDevice, &nSize);
        if (rc)
            break;

        pDL = (DEVICELIST *) cDevice;
        if (pDL->numDevice) {
            Add2List (hWnd, TEXT ("%d devices found."), pDL->numDevice);

            for (j = 0; j < (int)pDL->numDevice; j++) {
                // Convert device ID.
                wsprintf (szOut,
                          TEXT ("DeviceID \t%02X.%02X.%02X.%02X"),
                          pDL->Device[j].irdaDeviceID[0],
                          pDL->Device[j].irdaDeviceID[1],
                          pDL->Device[j].irdaDeviceID[2],
                          pDL->Device[j].irdaDeviceID[3]);
                OutputDebugString (szOut);

                // Convert device name to Unicode.
                mbstowcs (szName, pDL->Device[j].irdaDeviceName,
                          sizeof (pDL->Device[j].irdaDeviceName));

                wsprintf (szOut, TEXT ("irdaDeviceName \t%s"),
                          szName);
                OutputDebugString (szOut);
            }
```

(continued)

```
        }
        Sleep(500);
    }
    closesocket (irsock);
    return 0;
}
```

Just having a device with an IR port in range isn't enough; the remote device must have an application running that has opened an IR socket, bound it, and placed it into listen mode. This requirement is appropriate because these are the steps any server using the socket API would perform to configure a socket to accept communication.

Querying and setting IR socket options

IrSock supports the *getsockopt* and *setsockopt* functions for getting and setting the socket options, but the options supported have little overlap with the socket options supported for a standard TCP/IP socket. To query socket options, use this function:

```
int getsockopt (SOCKET s, int level, int optname,
                char FAR *optval, int FAR *optlen);
```

The first parameter is the handle to the socket while the second parameter is the level in the communications stack for the specific option. The level can be at the socket level SO_SOCKET or a level unique to IrSock, SOL_IRLMP. The options supported for IrSock are shown in the lists below.

For the SOL_SOCKET level, your option is

- *SO_LINGER* It queries the linger mode.

For the SOL_IRLMP level, your options are

- *IRLMP_ENUMDEVICES* which enumerate remote IrDA devices
- *IRLMP_IAS_QUERY* which queries IAS attributes
- *IRLMP_SEND_PDU_LEN* which queries the maximum size of send packet for IrLPT mode.

The corresponding function with which to set the options is

```
int setsockopt (SOCKET s, int level, int optname,
                const char FAR *optval, int optlen);
```

The parameters are similar to *getsockopt*. The allowable options are shown below.

For the SOL_SOCKET level, your option is

- *SO_LINGER* which delays the close of a socket if unsent data remains in the outgoing queue

For the SOL_IRLMP level, your options are

- *IRLMP_IAS_SET* which sets IAS attributes
- *IRLMP_IRLPT_MODE* which sets the IrDA protocol to IrLPT
- *IRLMP_9WIRE_MODE* which sets the IrDA protocol to 9-wire serial mode
- *IRLMP_SHARP_MODE* which sets the IrDA protocol to Sharp mode

Blocking vs. nonblocking sockets

One issue I briefly touched on as I was introducing sockets is blocking. Windows programmers are used to the quite handy asynchronous socket calls that are an extension of the standard Berkeley socket API. By default, a socket is in blocking mode so that, for example, if you call *recv* to read data from a socket and no data is available, the call blocks until some data can be read. This isn't the type of call you want to be making with a thread that's servicing the message loop for your application.

Although Windows CE doesn't support the *WSAAsync* calls available to desktop versions of Windows, you can switch a socket from its default blocking mode to nonblocking mode. In nonblocking mode, any socket call that might need to wait to successfully perform its function instead returns immediately with an error code of WSAEWOULDBLOCK. You are then responsible for calling the would-have-blocked function again at a later time to complete the task.

To set a socket into blocking mode, use this function:

```
int ioctlsocket (SOCKET s, long cmd, u_long *argp);
```

The parameters are the socket handle, a command, and a pointer to a variable that either contains data or receives data depending on the value in *cmd*. The allowable commands for Windows CE IrSock sockets are the following:

- *FIONBIO* Set or clear a socket's blocking mode. If the value pointed to by *argp* is nonzero, the socket is placed in blocking mode. If the value is zero, the socket is placed in nonblocking mode.
- *FIONREAD* Returns the number of bytes that can be read from the socket with one call to the *recv* function.

So to set a socket in blocking mode, you should make a call like this one:

```
fBlocking = FALSE;
rc = ioctlsocket (sock, FIONBIO, &fBlocking);
```

Of course, once you have a socket in nonblocking mode, the worst thing you can do is continually poll the socket to see if the nonblocked event occurred. On a battery-powered system, this can dramatically lower battery life. Instead of polling, you can use the *select* function to inform you when a socket or set of sockets is in a nonblocking state. The prototype for this function is

```
int select (int nfds, fd_set FAR *readfds, fd_set FAR *writefds,
            fd_set FAR *exceptfds,
            const struct timeval FAR *timeout);
```

The parameters for the *select* function look somewhat complex, which, in fact, they are. Just to throw a curve, the function ignores the first parameter. The reason it exists at all is for compatibility with the Berkeley version of the *select* function. The next three parameters are pointers to sets of socket handles. The first set should contain the sockets that you want to be notified when one or more of the sockets is in a nonblocking read state. The second set contains socket handles of sockets that you want informed when a write function can be called without blocking. Finally, the third set, pointed to by *exceptfds*, contains the handles of sockets that you want notified when an error condition exists in that socket.

The final parameter is a timeout value. In keeping with the rather interesting parameter formats for the *select* function, the timeout value isn't a simple millisecond count. Rather, it's a pointer to a TIMEVAL structure defined as

```
struct timeval {
    long    tv_sec;
    long    tv_usec;
};
```

If the two fields in TIMEVAL are 0, the *select* call returns immediately even if none of the sockets has had an event occur. If the pointer, *timeout*, is NULL instead of pointing to a TIMEVAL structure, the select call won't time out and returns only when an event occurs in one of the sockets. Otherwise, the timeout value is specified in seconds and microseconds in the two fields provided.

The function returns the total number of sockets for which the appropriate events occur, 0 if the function times out, or SOCKET_ERROR if an error occurred while processing the call. If an error does occur, you can call *WSAGetLastError* to get the error code. The function modifies the contents of the sets so that, on returning from the function, the sets contain only the socket handles of sockets for which events occur.

The sets that contain the events should be considered opaque. The format of the sets doesn't match their Berkeley socket counterparts. Each of the sets is manipulated by four macros defined in WINSOCK.H. These are the four macros:

- *FD_CLR* Removes the specified socket handle from the set
- *FD_ISSET* Returns true if the socket handle is part of the set

- *FD_SET* Adds the specified socket handle to the set
- *FD_ZERO* Initializes the set to 0

To use a set, you have to declare a set of type *fd_set*. Then initialize the set with a call to FD_ZERO and add the socket handles you want with FD_SET. An example would be

```
fd_set fdReadSocks;

FD_ZERO (&fdReadSocks);
FD_SET (hSock1, &fdReadSocks);
FD_SET (hSock2, &fdReadSocks);

rc = select (0, &fdReadSocks, NULL, NULL, NULL);
if (rc != SOCKET_ERROR) {
    if (FD_ISSET (hSock1, &fdReadSocks))
        // A read event occurred in socket 1.
    if (FD_ISSET (hSock2, &fdReadSocks))
        // A read event occurred in socket 2.
}
```

In this example, the *select* call waits on read events from two sockets with handles of *hSock1* and *hSock2*. The write and error sets are NULL as is the pointer to the *timeout* structure, so the call to *select* won't return until a read event occurs in one of the two sockets. When the function returns, the code checks to see if the socket handles are in the returned set. If so, that socket has a nonblocking read condition.

The last little subtlety concerning the *select* function is just what qualifies as a read, write, and error condition. A socket in the read set is signaled when one of the following events occur:

- There is data in the input queue so that *recv* can be called without blocking.
- The socket is in listen mode and a connection has been attempted so that a call to *accept* won't block.
- The connection has been closed, reset, or terminated. If the connection was gracefully closed, *recv* returns with 0 bytes read; otherwise the *recv* call returns SOCKET_ERROR. If the socket has been reset, the *recv* function returns the error WSACONNRESET.

A socket in the write set is signaled under the following conditions:

- Data can be written to the socket. A call to send still might block if you attempt to write more data than can be held in the outgoing queue.

- A socket is processing a *connect* and the connect has been accepted by the server.

A socket in the exception set is signaled under the following condition:

- A socket is processing a *connect* and the connect failed.

The MySqurt Example Program

To demonstrate IrSock, the following program, MySqurt, shows how to transfer files from one Windows CE device to another. It's similar to the IrSquirt program provided with the H/PC and Palm-size PC. The difference is that instead of sending a file across the infrared link and having the receiving side accept whatever file is sent, MySqurt has the receiving side specify the file that's sent from the serving side of the application. In addition, MySqurt has a window that displays a list of status messages as the handshaking takes place between the two Windows CE systems. To use MySqurt, you'll need to have it running on both the Windows CE systems. To transfer a file, enter the name of the file you want from the other system and tap on the Get File button. The system transmits the request to the system and, if the file exists, it will be sent back to the requesting system. The MySqurt window is shown in Figure 10-4. The source code for the example is shown in Figure 10-5.

Figure 10-4. *The MySqurt window after a file has been transferred.*

MySqurt.rc

```
//======================================================================
// Resource file
//
// Written for the book Programming Windows CE
// Copyright (C) 1998 Douglas Boling
//======================================================================
```

Figure 10-5. *The MySqurt source.*

```
#include "windows.h"
#include "MySqurt.h"                           // Program-specific stuff

//----------------------------------------------------------------------
// Icons and bitmaps
//
ID_ICON ICON   "MySqurt.ico"                   // Program icon

//----------------------------------------------------------------------
// Main window dialog template
//
MySqurt DIALOG discardable 10, 10, 130, 110
STYLE  WS_OVERLAPPED | WS_VISIBLE | WS_CAPTION | WS_SYSMENU |
       DS_CENTER | DS_MODALFRAME
CAPTION "MySqurt"
CLASS "MySqurt"
BEGIN
    LTEXT "&File:"                    -1,   2,  11,  15,  12
    EDITTEXT                IDD_OUTTEXT,  17,  10,  71,  12,
                                        WS_TABSTOP | ES_AUTOHSCROLL
    PUSHBUTTON "&Get File"  IDD_GETFILE,  92,  10,  34,  12, WS_TABSTOP

    LISTBOX                 IDD_INTEXT,   2,  25, 124,  80,
                                        WS_TABSTOP | WS_VSCROLL
END
```

MySqurt.h

```
//======================================================================
// Header file
//
// Written for the book Programming Windows CE
// Copyright (C) 1998 Douglas Boling
//======================================================================
// Returns number of elements
#define dim(x) (sizeof(x) / sizeof(x[0]))

//----------------------------------------------------------------------
// Generic defines and data types
//
struct decodeUINT {                             // Structure associates
    UINT Code;                                  // messages
                                                // with a function.
    LRESULT (*Fxn)(HWND, UINT, WPARAM, LPARAM);
};
```

(continued)

Figure 10-5. *continued*

```
struct decodeCMD {                                  // Structure associates
    UINT Code;                                      // menu IDs with a
    LRESULT (*Fxn)(HWND, WORD, HWND, WORD);         // function.
};

//----------------------------------------------------------------------
// Generic defines used by application

#define  ID_ICON             1

#define  IDD_INTEXT          10                     // Control IDs
#define  IDD_GETFILE         11
#define  IDD_OUTTEXT         12

// Error codes used by transfer protocol
#define GOOD_XFER        0
#define BAD_FILEOPEN     -1
#define BAD_FILEMEM      -2
#define BAD_FILEREAD     -3
#define BAD_FILEWRITE    -3
#define BAD_SOCKET       -4
#define BAD_SOCKETRECV   -5
#define BAD_FILESIZE     -6
#define BAD_MEMORY       -7

#define BLKSIZE          2048                        // Transfer block size

//----------------------------------------------------------------------
// Function prototypes
//
int ServerThread (PVOID pArg);
int SenderThread (PVOID pArg);
int GetFile (HWND hWnd, TCHAR *szFileName);

int InitApp (HINSTANCE);
HWND InitInstance (HINSTANCE, LPWSTR, int);
int TermInstance (HINSTANCE, int);

// Window procedures
LRESULT CALLBACK MainWndProc (HWND, UINT, WPARAM, LPARAM);

// Message handlers
LRESULT DoCommandMain (HWND, UINT, WPARAM, LPARAM);
LRESULT DoDestroyMain (HWND, UINT, WPARAM, LPARAM);
```

```
// Command functions
LPARAM DoMainCommandGet (HWND, WORD, HWND, WORD);
LPARAM DoMainCommandExit (HWND, WORD, HWND, WORD);

// Thread functions
int SenderThread (PVOID pArg);
int ReaderThread (PVOID pArg);
```

MySqurt.c

```
//======================================================================
// MySqurt - A simple IrSock application for Windows CE
//
// Written for the book Programming Windows CE
// Copyright (C) 1998 Douglas Boling
//======================================================================
#include <windows.h>                    // For all that Windows stuff
#include <winsock.h>                    // socket includes
#include <af_irda.h>                    // IrDA includes

#include "MySqurt.h"                    // Program-specific stuff
//----------------------------------------------------------------------
// Global data
//
const TCHAR szAppName[] = TEXT ("MySqurt");
const char chzAppName[] = "MySqurt";
HINSTANCE hInst;                        // Program instance handle
HWND hMain;                             // Main window handle
BOOL fContinue = TRUE;                  // Server thread cont. flag

// Message dispatch table for MainWindowProc
const struct decodeUINT MainMessages[] = {
    WM_COMMAND, DoCommandMain,
    WM_DESTROY, DoDestroyMain,
};
// Command Message dispatch for MainWindowProc
const struct decodeCMD MainCommandItems[] = {
    IDOK, DoMainCommandGet,
    IDCANCEL, DoMainCommandExit,
    IDD_GETFILE, DoMainCommandGet,
};
//======================================================================
// Program entry point
//
int WINAPI WinMain (HINSTANCE hInstance, HINSTANCE hPrevInstance,
```

(continued)

Figure 10-5. *continued*

```
                    LPWSTR lpCmdLine, int nCmdShow) {
    MSG msg;
    int rc = 0;

    // Initialize application.
    rc = InitApp (hInstance);
    if (rc) return rc;

    // Initialize this instance.
    hMain = InitInstance (hInstance, lpCmdLine, nCmdShow);
    if (hMain == 0)
        return TermInstance (hInstance, 0x10);

    // Application message loop
    while (GetMessage (&msg, NULL, 0, 0)) {
        if ((hMain == 0) || !IsDialogMessage (hMain, &msg)) {
            TranslateMessage (&msg);
            DispatchMessage (&msg);
        }
    }
    // Instance cleanup
    return TermInstance (hInstance, msg.wParam);
}
//----------------------------------------------------------------------
// InitApp - Application initialization
//
int InitApp (HINSTANCE hInstance) {
    WNDCLASS wc;
    HWND hWnd;

    // If previous instance, activate it instead of us.
    hWnd = FindWindow (szAppName, NULL);
    if (hWnd) {
        SetForegroundWindow (hWnd);
        return -1;
    }
    // Register application main window class.
    wc.style = 0;                             // Window style
    wc.lpfnWndProc = MainWndProc;             // Callback function
    wc.cbClsExtra = 0;                        // Extra class data
    wc.cbWndExtra = DLGWINDOWEXTRA;           // Extra window data
    wc.hInstance = hInstance;                 // Owner handle
    wc.hIcon = NULL,                          // Application icon
    wc.hCursor = NULL;                        // Default cursor
    wc.hbrBackground = (HBRUSH) GetStockObject (LTGRAY_BRUSH);
    wc.lpszMenuName =  NULL;                  // Menu name
```

```
    wc.lpszClassName = szAppName;              // Window class name

    if (RegisterClass (&wc) == 0) return 1;
    return 0;
}
//----------------------------------------------------------------------
// InitInstance - Instance initialization
//
HWND InitInstance (HINSTANCE hInstance, LPWSTR lpCmdLine, int nCmdShow){
    HWND hWnd;
    HANDLE hThread;
    INT rc;

    hInst = hInstance;                  // Save program instance handle.

    // Create main window.
    hWnd = CreateDialog (hInst, szAppName, NULL, NULL);
    // Return fail code if window not created.
    if (!IsWindow (hWnd)) return 0;

    // Create secondary threads for interprocess comm.
    hThread = CreateThread (NULL, 0, ServerThread, hWnd, 0, &rc);
    if (hThread == 0) {
        DestroyWindow (hWnd);
        return 0;
    }
    CloseHandle (hThread);

    ShowWindow (hWnd, nCmdShow);        // Standard show and update calls
    UpdateWindow (hWnd);
    SetFocus (GetDlgItem (hWnd, IDD_OUTTEXT));
    return hWnd;
}
//----------------------------------------------------------------------
// TermInstance - Program cleanup
//
int TermInstance (HINSTANCE hInstance, int nDefRC) {
    return nDefRC;
}
//======================================================================
// Message handling procedures for main window
//----------------------------------------------------------------------
// MainWndProc - Callback function for application window
//
LRESULT CALLBACK MainWndProc (HWND hWnd, UINT wMsg, WPARAM wParam,
                              LPARAM lParam) {
```

(continued)

Figure 10-5. *continued*

```
    INT i;
    //
    // Search message list to see if we need to handle this
    // message.  If in list, call procedure.
    //
    for (i = 0; i < dim(MainMessages); i++) {
        if (wMsg == MainMessages[i].Code)
            return (*MainMessages[i].Fxn)(hWnd, wMsg, wParam, lParam);
    }
    return DefWindowProc (hWnd, wMsg, wParam, lParam);
}
//----------------------------------------------------------------------
// DoCommandMain - Process WM_COMMAND message for window.
//
LRESULT DoCommandMain (HWND hWnd, UINT wMsg, WPARAM wParam,
                       LPARAM lParam) {
    WORD idItem, wNotifyCode;
    HWND hwndCtl;
    INT i;

    // Parse the parameters.
    idItem = (WORD) LOWORD (wParam);
    wNotifyCode = (WORD) HIWORD (wParam);
    hwndCtl = (HWND) lParam;

    // Call routine to handle control message.
    for (i = 0; i < dim(MainCommandItems); i++) {
        if (idItem == MainCommandItems[i].Code)
            return (*MainCommandItems[i].Fxn)(hWnd, idItem, hwndCtl,
                                              wNotifyCode);
    }
    return 0;
}
//----------------------------------------------------------------------
// DoDestroyMain - Process WM_DESTROY message for window.
//
LRESULT DoDestroyMain (HWND hWnd, UINT wMsg, WPARAM wParam,
                       LPARAM lParam) {
    fContinue = FALSE;                      // Shut down server thread.
    Sleep (0);                              // Pass on timeslice.
    PostQuitMessage (0);
    return 0;
}
//======================================================================
// Command handler routines
//----------------------------------------------------------------------
```

```
// DoMainCommandExit - Process Program Exit command.
//
LPARAM DoMainCommandExit (HWND hWnd, WORD idItem, HWND hwndCtl,
                          WORD wNotifyCode) {

    SendMessage (hWnd, WM_CLOSE, 0, 0);
    return 0;
}
//----------------------------------------------------------------------
// DoMainCommandGet - Process Program Get File command.
//
LPARAM DoMainCommandGet (HWND hWnd, WORD idItem, HWND hwndCtl,
                         WORD wNotifyCode) {
    TCHAR szName[MAX_PATH];
    INT rc;

    GetDlgItemText (hWnd, IDD_OUTTEXT, szName, dim(szName));
    rc = GetFile (hWnd, szName);            //Receive file
    return 0;
}
//----------------------------------------------------------------------
// Add2List - Add string to the report list box.
//
void Add2List (HWND hWnd, LPTSTR lpszFormat, ...) {
    int i, nBuf;
    TCHAR szBuffer[512];

    va_list args;
    va_start(args, lpszFormat);

    nBuf = _vstprintf(szBuffer, lpszFormat, args);

    i = SendDlgItemMessage (hWnd, IDD_INTEXT, LB_ADDSTRING, 0,
                            (LPARAM)(LPCTSTR)szBuffer);
    if (i != LB_ERR)
        SendDlgItemMessage (hWnd, IDD_INTEXT, LB_SETTOPINDEX, i,
                            (LPARAM)(LPCTSTR)szBuffer);
    va_end(args);
}
//======================================================================
// ServerThread - Monitors for connections, connnects and notifies
// window when a connection occurs
//
int ServerThread (PVOID pArg) {
    HWND hWnd = (HWND)pArg;
    INT rc, nSize, i;
    SOCKADDR_IRDA iraddr, t_iraddr;
```

(continued)

Figure 10-5. *continued*

```
    SOCKET t_sock, s_sock;
    HANDLE hThread;

    Add2List (hWnd, TEXT ("server thread entered"));

    // Open an infrared socket.
    s_sock = socket (AF_IRDA, SOCK_STREAM, 0);
    if (s_sock == INVALID_SOCKET) {
        Add2List (hWnd, TEXT ("socket failed. rc %d"),
                  WSAGetLastError());
        return 0;
    }
    // Fill in irda socket address structure.
    iraddr.irdaAddressFamily = AF_IRDA;
    for (i = 0; i < dim(iraddr.irdaDeviceID); i++)
        iraddr.irdaDeviceID[i] = 0;
    memcpy (iraddr.irdaServiceName, chzAppName, sizeof (chzAppName)+1);

    // Bind address to socket.
    rc = bind (s_sock, (struct sockaddr *)&iraddr, sizeof (iraddr));
    if (rc) {
        Add2List (hWnd, TEXT (" bind failed"));
        closesocket (s_sock);
        return -2;
    }
    // Set socket into listen mode.
    rc = listen (s_sock, SOMAXCONN);
    if (rc == SOCKET_ERROR) {
        Add2List (hWnd, TEXT (" listen failed %d"), GetLastError());
        closesocket (s_sock);
        return -3;
    }
    // Wait for remote requests.
    while (fContinue) {
        // Block on accept.
        nSize = sizeof (t_iraddr);
        t_sock = accept (s_sock, (struct sockaddr *)&t_iraddr, &nSize);
        if (t_sock == INVALID_SOCKET) {
            Add2List (hWnd, TEXT (" accept failed %d"),
                      GetLastError());
            break;
        }
        Add2List (hWnd, TEXT ("sock accept..."));
        hThread = CreateThread (NULL, 0, SenderThread,
                                (PVOID)t_sock, 0, &rc);
        if (hThread)
```

```
            CloseHandle (hThread);
        }
        closesocket (s_sock);
        return rc;
}
//======================================================================
// SenderThread - Sends the file requested by the remote device
//
int SenderThread (PVOID pArg) {
    SOCKET t_sock = (SOCKET)pArg;
    int nCnt, nFileSize, rc;
    TCHAR szFileName[MAX_PATH];
    PBYTE pBuff, pPtr;
    HWND hWnd = hMain;
    HANDLE hFile;

    Add2List (hWnd, TEXT ("sender thread entered"));

    // Read the number of bytes in the filename.
    rc = recv (t_sock, (PBYTE)&nCnt, sizeof (nCnt), 0);
    if ((rc == SOCKET_ERROR) || (nCnt > MAX_PATH)) {
        Add2List (hWnd, TEXT ("failed receiving name size"));
        closesocket (t_sock);
        return -1;
    }

    // Read the filename.
    rc = recv (t_sock, (PBYTE)&szFileName, nCnt, 0);
    if (rc == SOCKET_ERROR) {
        Add2List (hWnd, TEXT ("failed receiving name"));
        closesocket (t_sock);
        return -2;
    }
    Add2List (hWnd, TEXT ("name: %s"), szFileName);
    hFile = CreateFile (szFileName, GENERIC_READ, FILE_SHARE_READ,
                        NULL, OPEN_EXISTING, 0, NULL);
    if (hFile == INVALID_HANDLE_VALUE) {
        Add2List (hWnd, TEXT ("file opened failed. rc %d"),
                  GetLastError());
        rc = BAD_FILEOPEN;
    } else {
        rc = 0;
        nFileSize = GetFileSize (hFile, NULL);

        // Allocate buffer and read file.
        pBuff = LocalAlloc (LPTR, nFileSize);
```

(continued)

Figure 10-5. *continued*

```
        if (pBuff) {
            ReadFile (hFile, pBuff, nFileSize, &nCnt, NULL);
            if (nCnt != nFileSize)
                rc = BAD_FILEREAD;
        } else
            rc = BAD_MEMORY;
    }
    // Start transfer. First send size and get acknowledgment.
    if (!rc) {
        // Send file size. Size will always be < 2 GB.
        rc = send (t_sock, (PBYTE)&nFileSize, sizeof (nFileSize), 0);
        if (rc == SOCKET_ERROR)
            rc = BAD_SOCKET;
        else
            // Receive acknowledgment of file size.
            recv (t_sock, (PBYTE)&rc, sizeof (rc), 0);
    }
    // Send the file.
    pPtr = pBuff;
    while ((!rc) && nFileSize) {
        // Send up to the block size.
        nCnt = min (BLKSIZE, nFileSize);
        rc = send (t_sock, pPtr, nCnt, 0);
        if (rc == SOCKET_ERROR) {
            Add2List (hWnd, TEXT ("send error %d "), GetLastError());
            rc = BAD_SOCKET;
        } else
            Add2List (hWnd, TEXT ("sent %d bytes"), rc);
        pPtr += rc;
        nFileSize -= rc;

        // Receive acknowledgment.
        recv (t_sock, (PBYTE)&rc, sizeof (rc), 0);
    }
    // Send close code.
    if (rc != BAD_SOCKET)
        send (t_sock, (PBYTE)&rc, sizeof (rc), 0);

    closesocket (t_sock);
    // Clean up.
    if (hFile != INVALID_HANDLE_VALUE)
        CloseHandle (hFile);
    LocalFree (pBuff);
    Add2List (hWnd, TEXT ("sender thread exit"));
    return 0;
}
```

```
//----------------------------------------------------------------------
// GetFile - Reads a file from the remote device
//
int GetFile (HWND hWnd, TCHAR *szFileName) {
    SOCKET c_sock;
    HANDLE hFile;
    INT rc, nSize, i, nFileSize, nCnt;
    char cDevice[256];
    SOCKADDR_IRDA iraddr;
    DEVICELIST *pDL;
    STORE_INFORMATION si;
    PBYTE pBuff;

    // Open an infrared socket.
    c_sock = socket (AF_IRDA, SOCK_STREAM, 0);
    if (c_sock == INVALID_SOCKET) {
        Add2List (hWnd, TEXT ("sock failed. rc %d"), WSAGetLastError());
        return 0;
    }
    // Search for someone to talk to.
    for (i = 0; i < 5; i++) {
        memset (cDevice, 0, sizeof (cDevice));
        nSize = sizeof (cDevice);
        rc = getsockopt (c_sock, SOL_IRLMP, IRLMP_ENUMDEVICES,
                         cDevice, &nSize);
        if (rc)
            Add2List (hWnd, TEXT ("getsockopt failed. rc %d"),
                      WSAGetLastError());

        pDL = (DEVICELIST *) cDevice;
        if (pDL->numDevice)
            break;
        Sleep(500);
    }
    // If no device found, exit.
    if (pDL->numDevice == 0) {
        closesocket (c_sock);
        return -1;
    }

    // Copy address of found device.
    memset (&iraddr, 0, sizeof (iraddr));
    iraddr.irdaAddressFamily = AF_IRDA;
    memcpy (iraddr.irdaDeviceID, pDL->Device[0].irdaDeviceID, 4);
    // Now initialize the specific socket we're interested in.
    memcpy (iraddr.irdaServiceName, chzAppName, sizeof (chzAppName)+1);
```

(continued)

Figure 10-5. *continued*

```
    Add2List (hWnd, TEXT ("Found: %hs"), pDL->Device[0].irdaDeviceName);
    // Connect to remote socket.
    rc = connect (c_sock, (struct sockaddr *)&iraddr, sizeof (iraddr));
    if (rc) {
        Add2List (hWnd, TEXT ("connect failed. rc %d"),
                  WSAGetLastError());
        closesocket (c_sock);
        return -4;
    }
    Add2List (hWnd, TEXT ("connected..."));

    // Send name size.
    nCnt = (lstrlen (szFileName) + 1) * sizeof (TCHAR);
    rc = send (c_sock, (PBYTE)&nCnt, sizeof (nCnt), 0);
    if (rc != SOCKET_ERROR) {
        // Send filename.
        rc = send (c_sock, (PBYTE)szFileName, nCnt, 0);
    }
    pBuff = LocalAlloc (LPTR, BLKSIZE);        // Create buffer for file.
    // Receive file size.
    rc = recv (c_sock, (PBYTE)&nFileSize, sizeof (nFileSize), 0);
    Add2List (hWnd, TEXT ("received file size of %d bytes"), nFileSize);
    if ((rc != SOCKET_ERROR) && (nFileSize > 0)) {

        GetStoreInformation (&si);
        Add2List (hWnd, TEXT ("free space of %d bytes"), si.dwFreeSize);
        if ((INT)si.dwFreeSize < nFileSize + 1000)
            rc = BAD_FILESIZE;
        else
            rc = GOOD_XFER;

        if (rc == GOOD_XFER) {
            // Create the file.  Overwrite if user says so.
            hFile = CreateFile (szFileName, GENERIC_WRITE, 0, NULL,
                               CREATE_NEW, FILE_ATTRIBUTE_NORMAL, NULL);
            if (hFile == INVALID_HANDLE_VALUE) {
                if (GetLastError() == ERROR_FILE_EXISTS) {
                    i = MessageBox (hWnd,
                               TEXT ("File already exists. Replace?"),
                               szAppName, MB_YESNO);
                    if (i == IDYES)
                        hFile = CreateFile (szFileName,
                                GENERIC_WRITE, 0, NULL,
                                CREATE_ALWAYS,
                                FILE_ATTRIBUTE_NORMAL, NULL);
                }
```

```
            }
        }
        if (hFile == INVALID_HANDLE_VALUE) {
            Add2List (hWnd, TEXT ("File Open failed. rc %d"),
                      GetLastError());
            rc = BAD_FILEWRITE;
        }
        // Send acknowledgment code.
        Add2List (hWnd, TEXT ("Sending size ack."));
        send (c_sock, (PBYTE)&rc, sizeof (rc), 0);
        //
        // Receive file.
        //
        while ((!rc) && (nFileSize > 0)) {

            nCnt = min (BLKSIZE, nFileSize);
            for (nSize = 0; nSize < nCnt;) {
                i = recv (c_sock, pBuff+nSize, nCnt-nSize, 0);
                if (i == SOCKET_ERROR) {
                    Add2List (hWnd, TEXT ("recv socket err %d"),
                              GetLastError());
                    rc = BAD_SOCKETRECV;
                    break;
                }
                nSize += i;
            }
            Add2List (hWnd, TEXT ("recv'd %d bytes."), nSize);
            if (i) {
                if (!WriteFile (hFile, pBuff, nSize, &i, 0))
                    rc = BAD_FILEWRITE;
                nFileSize -= i;
            } else
                Sleep(50);
            // Send acknowledgment of packet.
            send (c_sock, (PBYTE)&rc, sizeof (rc), 0);
        }
    } else if (rc == BAD_FILEOPEN)
        Add2List (hWnd, TEXT ("File not found."));
    Add2List (hWnd, TEXT ("receive finished"));

    CloseHandle (hFile);
    closesocket (c_sock);
    LocalFree (pBuff);
    return 0;
}
```

From a Windows standpoint, MySqurt is a simple program. It uses a dialog box as its main window. When the program is first launched, it creates the server thread that creates an infrared socket, binds it to a service name, puts the socket into listen mode, and blocks on a call to *accept*. When a remote device connects, the server thread creates another thread to handle the actual sending of the file while it loops back and waits for another connection.

The sender thread reads the filename from the client, opens the file, and attempts to send the file to the client device. Once the file is sent, the sender thread closes its socket and terminates. To support the transfer, a minimal amount of handshaking takes place. The sender thread sends the size of the file or an error code if the file can't be opened. The client then responds with an acknowledgment that the file size is acceptable and that the send can take place. The actual sending of the data is broken down into blocks arbitrarily set at 2048 bytes. After each block is sent, the sender thread waits for an acknowledgment from the client before it sends the next block.

On the client side, a transmission is initiated when the user taps the Get File button. If text exists in the edit box, it is read and the *GetFile* routine is called. In this routine, a socket is created and any remote devices are enumerated using repeated calls to *getsockopt*. If a device is found, a connection is attempted with a call to *connect*. *Connect* succeeds only if the remote device has bound an IR socket using the same service name, which happens to be defined as the string contained in *chzAppName*, an ASCII representation of the program name. This addressing scheme ensures that if a connection is made, the remote device is running MySqurt. Once a connection is made, the client sends over the filename it wants. This is actually done in two steps: first the byte length of the filename is sent, followed by the name itself. This process allows the server to know how many characters to receive before continuing. If the file sent by the server device fits in the object store, the routine creates the file on the client side, notifying the user if the file already exists. If all has gone well to this point, the data is received and written to the file. The socket is closed, and the buffer created to read the data into is freed.

While I've spent most of the explanation of sockets focused on IrSock, one area of the TCP/IP WinSock is unique to Windows CE—the ICMP functions. These functions allow a "back door" that allows raw socketlike functions on a stack that doesn't support raw sockets. Let's look now at why that's useful.

TCP/IP PINGING

On a TCP/IP network, there's no more basic diagnostic than to *ping* a site. Pinging is the process of sending a request to a TCP/IP server to respond with an acknowledgment back to the sender. If you look at the source code for a ping utility, you'll see that pinging is simply the process of sending a specific type of IP packet to the requested server and waiting for a reply.

The format of these packets is defined by *ICMP*. ICMP stands for *Internet Control Message Protocol*. This a protocol used by routers and servers on TCP/IP networks to report errors and status information. While most of this work goes unseen by applications because it's handled at the IP layer of the network stack, ping requests take place at this level.

Under most systems, an application would have to open a raw socket. While Windows CE's version of WinSock doesn't expose a way of opening raw sockets, Windows CE gives you a few functions that encapsulate the process of pinging another server.

Windows CE supports three functions that allow Windows CE applications to ping Internet addresses. Essentially, a Windows CE application opens a handle, sends the ICMP request as many times as you want, and closes the handle. While the functions are documented in the Windows CE SDK, the *include* files that define these prototypes aren't in all versions of the Windows CE SDK. The file ICMPAPI.H contains the function prototypes while IPEXPORTS.H contains the definitions for the packet structures and constants used at the IP layer. These two include files are on the CD-ROM included with this book.

To start the process, you must open an ICMP handle using this function:

```
HANDLE IcmpCreateFile (VOID);
```

The function takes no arguments and returns a handle that will be used in the other ICMP functions. If the function fails, the return value will be INVALID_HANDLE_VALUE.

To actually send a ping request, you use this function:

```
DWORD WINAPI IcmpSendEcho (HANDLE IcmpHandle, IPAddr DestinationAddress,
                           LPVOID RequestData, WORD RequestSize,
                           PIP_OPTION_INFORMATION RequestOptions,
                           LPVOID ReplyBuffer, DWORD ReplySize,
                           DWORD Timeout);
```

The first parameter is the handle returned by the *ICMPCreateFile* function. The second parameter is the destination address that will be sent to the IP packet. The data type for this address, *IPAddr*, is essentially an unsigned long value with the four bytes of the IP address packed inside. The *RequestData* parameter is a pointer to a buffer containing the data to be sent while the *RequestSize* parameter should specify the size of the data. You can define any data you want in the buffer pointed to by *RequestData* although you generally don't want to exceed the 8-KB packet size limit found on some TCP/IP systems. What you do *not* get to do is directly define the ICMP packet that's sent. That packet is automatically formed by *IcmpSendEcho* and sent along with the data specified in the *RequestData* buffer.

The *RequestOptions* parameter should point to an IP_OPTION_INFORMATION structure that's defined as

```
Typedef struct ip_option_information {
    unsigned char      Ttl;
    unsigned char      Tos;
    unsigned char      Flags;
    unsigned char      OptionsSize;
    unsigned char FAR *OptionsData;
} IP_OPTION_INFORMATION;
```

The data in this structure will be used by the function to fill in some of the IP packet header that you use when sending an ICMP packet. The structure is a subset of the IP packet structure since Windows CE takes care of things like computing checksums and the like. The formal definitions of these fields are best left to texts that explain the IP protocol in detail. What follows is a quick overview.

The first field, *Ttl*, is the "Time to Live" for the packet. If the packet isn't received in this amount of time, it will be dropped. The *Tos* field defines the type of service for the IP packet. The *Flags* field contains the flags for the IP header. Finally, the *OptionsData* and *OptionsSize* fields specify the IP packet options. The options are defined as bytes in the buffer pointed to by *OptionsData*. The *OptionsSize* field should contain the number of bytes in the *OptionsData* buffer. The format of the options buffer is defined by the IP protocol.

The next two parameters in *IcmpSendEcho* are the pointer to the buffer that receives the reply and the size of that buffer. The receiving buffer must be large enough to hold an ICMP_ECHO_REPLY structure plus the size of the data you specified in the *RequestData* buffer. At a minimum, you must specify the buffer to be the size of ICMP_ECHO_REPLY plus 8 bytes. The 8-byte allowance is the size of an ICMP error message.

The final parameter is *Timeout*, which is the time, in milliseconds, that *IcmpSendEcho* waits for returning packets before giving up.

IcmpSendEcho returns the number of reply packets received in response to the ping request. If the return value is 0, an error occurred. In this case, you should call *GetLastError* to receive the error code.

The data received by *IcmpSendEcho* is in the form of an array of ICMP_ECHO_REPLY structures, one from each router or server that replied to the original packet. Following the array will be the data sent out by *IcmpSendEcho* that returns with each of the packets. The ICMP_ECHO_REPLY structure is defined as

```
struct icmp_echo_reply {
    IPAddr          Address;          // Replying address
    unsigned long   Status;           // Reply IP_STATUS
    unsigned long   RoundTripTime;    // RTT in milliseconds
    unsigned short  DataSize;         // Reply data size in bytes
```

```
    unsigned short  Reserved;          // Reserved for system use
    void FAR        Data;              // Pointer to the reply data
    struct IP_OPTION_INFORMATION Options;          // Reply options
}; /* icmp_echo_reply */
```

The *Address* field is the TCP/IP address of the responding router or server. The address is in *IPAddr* format. The *Status* field contains the status returned by the responding server. If the ping was successful, this field will contain IP_SUCCESS. Other values indicate errors and are defined in IPEXPORT.H. The *RoundTripTime* field contains the elapsed time, in milliseconds, from when the original packet was sent until the packet from this server was received. The *DataSize* field contains the size of the data returned by the server. This value should match the size of the data originally sent. The *Data* field contains a pointer to the data returned by the server. This data should match the data originally sent. Finally, the *Options* field is an IP_OPTION_INFORMATION structure that defines the details of the responding packet.

Generally, you'll call *IcmpSendEcho* a number of times to ping a site and then clean up with a call to *IcmpCloseHandle*. This function is prototyped as

```
BOOL WINAPI IcmpCloseHandle (HANDLE IcmpHandle);
```

The only parameter is the handle that was received with *IcmpCreateFile*.

The routine below implements a very basic ping. The routine calls *IcmpOpen* and then fills in the IP packet data and calls *IcmpSendEcho* five times. The address passed to *PingAddress* is a Unicode string in Internet *dot* format, as in 123.45.56.78. The *inet_addr* function translates this into a DWORD value used by *IcmpSendEcho*. Notice that the address string passed to *PingAddress* is first translated into ASCII before the call is made to *inet_addr*.

```
//----------------------------------------------------------------------
// PingAddress - Ping a TCP/IP address.
//
INT PingAddress (HWND hWnd, LPTSTR lpszPingAddr, LPTSTR lpszOut) {
    HANDLE hPing;
    BYTE bOut[32];
    BYTE bIn[1024];
    char cOptions[12];
    char szdbAddr[32];
    IP_OPTION_INFORMATION ipoi;
    PICMP_ECHO_REPLY pEr;
    struct in_addr Address;
    INT i, j, rc;
    DWORD adr;

    // Convert xx.xx.xx.xx string to a DWORD. First, convert the string
    // to ascii.
```

(continued)

```
wcstombs (szdbAddr, lpszPingAddr, 31);
if ((adr = inet_addr(szdbAddr)) == -1L)
    return -1;

// Open icmp handle.
hPing = IcmpCreateFile ();
if (hPing == INVALID_HANDLE_VALUE)
    return -2;

wsprintf (lpszOut, TEXT ("Pinging: %s\n\n"), lpszPingAddr);
lpszOut += lstrlen (lpszOut) + 1;

// Ping loop
for (j = 0; j < 5; j++) {

    // Initialize the send data buffer.
    memset (&bOut, 0, sizeof (bOut));

    // Initialize the IP structure.
    memset (&ipoi, 0, sizeof (ipoi));
    ipoi.Ttl = 32;
    ipoi.Tos = 0;
    ipoi.Flags = IP_FLAG_DF;
    memset (cOptions, 0, sizeof (cOptions));

    // Ping!
    rc = IcmpSendEcho (hPing, adr, bOut, sizeof (bOut), &ipoi,
                       bIn, sizeof (bIn), 1000);
    if (rc) {
        // Loop through replies.
        pEr = (PICMP_ECHO_REPLY)bIn;
        for (i = 0; i < rc; i++) {

            Address.S_un.S_addr = (IPAddr)pEr->Address;
            // Format output string
            wsprintf (lpszOut,
                      TEXT ("Reply from %hs: bytes:%d time"),
                      inet_ntoa (Address), pEr->DataSize);

            // Append round-trip time.
            if (pEr->RoundTripTime < 10)
                lstrcat (lpszOut, TEXT ("<10mS\n"));
            else
                wsprintf (&lpszOut[lstrlen(lpszOut)],
                          TEXT ("%dmS\n"), pEr->RoundTripTime);

            lpszOut += lstrlen (lpszOut) + 1;
            pEr++;
```

```
            }
        } else {
            lstrcpy (lpszOut, TEXT ("Request timed out."));
            lpszOut += lstrlen (lpszOut) + 1;
        }
    }
    IcmpCloseHandle (hPing);

    *lpszOut = TEXT ('\0');                  // Add final terminating zero.
    return 0;
}
```

The response packet from *IcmpSendEcho* is interpreted by looping through the array of ICMP_ECHO_REPLY structures. Within each of these structures is enough data to provide the very basic ping information. The routine could be extended in a number of ways. For example, the reply packets could be dissected to determine the route of the packets.

This chapter has given you a basic introduction to some of the networking features of Windows CE. Next on our plate is networking from a different angle. In Chapter 11, we look at the Windows CE device from the perspective of its companion PC. The link between the Windows CE device and a PC is based on some of the same networking infrastructure that we touched upon here. Let's take a look.

Chapter 11

Connecting to the Desktop

One of the major market segments that Windows CE is designed for is desktop companions. In answer to the requirements of this market, the first two product categories created using Windows CE are desktop companions: the Handheld PC and the Palm-size PC. Both these products require a strong and highly functional link between the Windows CE device and the desktop PC running Windows 98 or Windows NT.

Given this absolute necessity for good desktop connectivity, it's not surprising that Windows CE has a vast array of functions that enable applications on the desktop and the remote Windows CE device to communicate with one another. In general, most of this desktop-to-device processing takes place on the desktop. This is logical because the desktop PC has much greater processing power and more storage space than the less powerful and much smaller Windows CE system.

The total of helper DLLs, communications support, and viewer programs is collected in a package named Windows CE Services. When a user buys any of the horizontal platforms, such as the Palm-size PC or the Handheld PC, a CD loaded with Windows CE Services comes with the device. The user becomes accustomed to seeing the Mobile Devices folder that, once Windows CE Services is installed, appears on his desktop. But there's much more to Windows CE Services than Mobile Devices. A number of DLLs are included, for example, to help the Windows CE application developer write PC-based applications that can work with the remote Windows CE device.

In this chapter, I'll cover the various APIs that provide the desktop–to–Windows CE link. These include the Remote API, or RAPI, that allows applications running on the desktop to directly invoke functions on the remote Windows CE system. I'll tell you how to write a file filter that converts files as they're transferred from the PC to the Windows CE device and back. I'll also look at methods a PC application can use to notified itself when a connection exists between a PC and a Windows CE device.

In a departure from the other chapters in this book, almost all the examples in this chapter are PC-based Windows programs. They're written to work both for Windows 95/98 and Windows NT. I take the same approach with the PC-based examples as I do for the CE-based examples, writing to the API instead of using a class library such as MFC. The principles shown here could easily be used by MFC-based applications.

THE WINDOWS CE REMOTE API

The remote API (RAPI) allows applications on one machine to call functions on another machine. Windows CE supports essentially a one-way RAPI; applications on the PC can call functions on a connected Windows CE system. In the language of RAPI, the Windows CE device is the RAPI server while the PC is the RAPI client. The application runs on the client, the PC, which in turn calls functions that are executed on the server, the Windows CE device.

RAPI Overview

RAPI under Windows CE is designed so that PC applications can manage the Windows CE device remotely. The exported functions deal with the file system, registry, and databases, as well as functions for querying the system configuration. While most RAPI functions are duplicates of functions in the Windows CE API, a few functions extend the API. You use these functions mainly for initializing the RAPI subsystem and enhancing performance of the communication link by compressing iterative operations into one RAPI call.

The RAPI functions are listed in the Windows CE API reference but are called by PC applications—not by Windows CE applications. The RAPI functions are prefixed with a *Ce* in the function name to differentiate them from their Windows CE–side counterparts; for example, the function *GetStoreInformation* in Windows CE is called *CeGetStoreInformation* in the RAPI version of the function. Unfortunately, some APIs in Windows CE, such as the database API, also have functions prefixed with *Ce*. In these cases, both the CE function (for example, *CeCreateDatabase*) and the RAPI function (again, *CeCreateDatabase*) have the same name. The linker isn't confused in this case because a Windows CE application won't be calling the RAPI function and a PC based program can't call the database function except through the RAPI interface.

As I said, these Windows CE RAPI functions work for Windows 95/98 as well as Windows NT, but because they're Win32 functions applications developed for the

Win16 API can't use the Windows CE RAPI functions. The RAPI functions can be called from either a Windows-based application or a Win32-console application. All you have to do to use the RAPI functions is to include the RAPI.h header file and link with the RAPI.lib library.

Essentially, RAPI is a remote procedure call. It communicates a PC application's request to invoke a function and returns the results of that function. Because the RAPI layer is simple on the Windows CE side, all strings used in RAPI functions must be in Unicode regardless of whether the PC-based application calling the RAPI function uses the Unicode format.

Dealing with different versions of RAPI

The problem of versioning has always been an issue with redistributable DLLs under Windows. RAPI.DLL, the DLL on the PC that handles the RAPI API, is distributed with the Mobile Devices software that comes with an H/PC, Palm-size PC, or other PC companion Windows CE devices. Trouble arises because the RAPI API has been extended over time as the Windows CE functions have expanded; you have to be aware that the RAPI DLL you load on a machine might not be the most up-to-date RAPI DLL. Older RAPI DLLs don't have all the exported functions that the newest RAPI DLL has.

For example, any RAPI DLL distributed with a device running Windows CE 2.1 or later will export the newer database *Ex* functions so that you can manipulate databases that aren't in the object store of the remote device. However, if you assume that those functions are there and you run your RAPI application on a PC with an older RAPI DLL, the application won't load because the extended database functions aren't exported by the older DLL.

On the other hand, just because *you're* using the latest RAPI DLL doesn't mean that the Windows CE system on the other end of the RAPI connection supports all the functions that the RAPI DLL supports. An H/PC running Windows CE 2.0 won't support the extended database API of Windows CE 2.1 no matter what RAPI DLL you're using on the PC.

The best way to solve the problem of multiple versions of RAPI.DLL is to program defensively. Instead of loading the RAPI DLL implicitly by specifying an import library and directly calling the RAPI functions, you might want to load the RAPI DLL explicitly with a call to *LoadLibrary*. You can then access the exported functions by calling *GetProcAddress* for each function and then by calling the pointer to that function.

The problem of different versions of Windows CE has a much easier solution. Just be sure to call *CeGetVersionEx* to query the version of Windows CE on the remote device. This gives you a good idea of what the device capabilities of that device are. If the remote device has a newer version of Windows CE than RAPI.DLL, you might want to inform the user of the version issue and suggest an upgrade of the synchronization software on the PC.

Initializing RAPI

Before you can call any of the RAPI functions, you must first initialize the RAPI library with a call to either *CeRapiInit* or *CeRapiInitEx*. The difference between the two functions is that *CeRapiInit* blocks, waiting on a successful connection with a Windows CE device, while *CeRapiInitEx* doesn't block. Contrary to what you might expect, neither of these functions creates a connection between a PC and a device physically hooked up to one another but unconnected.

The first initialization function is prototyped as

```
HRESULT CeRapiInit (void);
```

This function has no parameters. When the function is called, Windows looks for an established link to a Windows CE device. If one doesn't exist, the function blocks until one is established or another thread in your application calls *CeRapiUninit*, which is generally called to clean up after a RAPI session. The return value is either 0, indicating that a RAPI session has been established, or the constant E_FAIL, indicating an error. In this case, you can call *GetLastError* to diagnose the problem.

Unfortunately *CeRapiInit* blocks, sometimes, for an extended period of time. To avoid this, you can use the other initialization function,

```
HRESULT CeRapiInitEx (RAPIINIT* pRapiInit);
```

The only parameter is a pointer to a RAPIINIT structure defined as

```
typedef struct _RAPIINIT {
    DWORD cbSize;
    HANDLE heRapiInit;
    HANDLE hrRapiInit;
} RAPIINIT;
```

The *cbSize* field must be filled in before the call is made to *CeRapiInitEx*. After the size field has been initialized, you call *CeRapiInitEx* and the function returns without blocking. It fills in the second of the two fields, *heRapiInit*, with the handle to an event object that will be signaled when the RAPI connection is initialized. You can use *WaitForSingleObject* to have a thread block on this event to determine when the connection is finally established. When the event is signaled, the final field in the structure, *hrRapiInit*, is filled with the return code from the initialization. This value can be 0 if the connection was successful or E_FAIL if the connection wasn't made for some reason.

Handling RAPI errors

When you're dealing with the extra RAPI layer between the caller and the execution of the function, a problem arises when an error occurs: did the error occur because the function failed or because of an error in the RAPI connection? RAPI functions return error codes indicating success or failure of the function. If a function fails, you can use the following two functions to isolate the cause of the error:

```
HRESULT CeRapiGetError (void);
```

and

```
DWORD CeGetLastError (void);
```

The difference between these two functions is that *CeRapiGetError* returns an error code for failures due to the network or other RAPI-layer reasons. On the other hand, *CeGetLastError* is the RAPI counterpart to *GetLastError*; it returns the extended error for a failed function on the Windows CE device. So, if a function fails, call *CeRapiGetError* to determine whether an error occurred in the RAPI layer. If *CeRapiGetError* returns 0, the error occurred in the original function on the CE device. In this case, a call to *CeGetLastError* returns the extended error for the failure on the device.

Here's one last general function, used to free buffers that are returned by some of the RAPI functions. This function is

```
HRESULT CeRapiFreeBuffer (LPVOID Buffer);
```

The only parameter is the pointer to the buffer you want to free. The function returns SOK when successful and E_FAIL if not. Throughout the explanation of RAPI functions, I'll mention those places where you need to use *CeRapiFreeBuffer*. In general, though, you use this function anywhere a RAPI function returns a buffer that it allocated for you.

Ending a RAPI session

When you have finished making all the RAPI calls necessary, you should clean up by calling

```
HRESULT CeRapiUninit (void);
```

This function gracefully closes down the RAPI communication with the remote device. *CeRapiUninit* returns E_FAIL if a RAPI session hasn't been initialized.

Predefined RAPI Functions

As I mentioned in the beginning of this chapter, the RAPI services include a number of predefined RAPI functions that duplicate Windows CE functions on the PC side of the connection. So, for example, just as *GetStoreInformation* returns the size and free space of the object store to a Windows CE program, *CeGetStoreInformation* returns that same information about a connected Windows CE device to a PC-based application. The functions are divided into a number of groups that I'll talk about in the following pages. Since the actions of the functions are identical to their Windows CE–based counterparts,

I won't go into the details of each function. Instead, although I'll list every RAPI function, I'll explain at length only the functions that are unique to RAPI.

RAPI system information functions

The RAPI database functions are shown in the following list. I've previously described most of the counterpart Windows CE functions shown, with the exception of *CeGetPassword* and *CeRapiInvoke*. The *CeGetPassword* function, as well as its Windows CE counterpart *GetPassword*, compares a string to the current system password. If the strings match, the function returns TRUE. The comparison is case specific. Another function you might not recognize is *CeGetDesktopDeviceCaps*. This is the RAPI equivalent of *GetDeviceCaps* on the Windows CE side.

System information functions

CeGetVersionEx

CeGlobalMemoryStatus

CeGetSystemPowerStatusEx

CeGetStoreInformation

CeGetSystemMetrics

CeGetDesktopDeviceCaps

CeGetSystemInfo

CeCheckPassword

CeCreateProcess

RAPI file and directory management functions

The following list shows the RAPI file management functions, illustrating that almost any file function available to a Windows CE application is also available to a PC-based program.

File and directory management functions

CeFindAllFiles

CeFindFirstFile

CeFindNextFile

CeFindClose

CeGetFileAttributes

CeSetFileAttributes

CeCreateFile

CeReadFile

CeWriteFile

CeCloseHandle

CeSetFilePointer

CeSetEndOfFile

CeCreateDirectory

CeRemoveDirectory

CeMoveFile

CeCopyFile

CeDeleteFile

CeGetFileSize

CeGetFileTime

CeSetFileTime

Here's a new function, *CeFindAllFiles*, that's not even available to a Windows CE application. This function is prototyped as

```
BOOL CeFindAllFiles (LPCWSTR szPath, DWORD dwFlags,
                     LPDWORD lpdwFoundCount,
                     LPLPCE_FIND_DATA ppFindDataArray);
```

CeFindAllFiles is designed to enhance performance by returning all the files of a given directory with one call rather than having to make repeated RAPI calls using *CeFindFirstFile* and *CeFindNextFile*. The first parameter is the search string. This string must be specified in Unicode, so if you're not creating a Unicode application, the TEXT macro won't work because the TEXT macro produces char strings for non-Unicode applications. In Microsoft Visual C++, prefixing the string with an *L* before the quoted string as in *L"*.*"* produces a proper Unicode for the function even in a non-Unicode application. For string conversion, you can use the *WideCharToMultiByte* and *MultiByteToWideChar* library functions to convert Unicode and ANSI strings into one another.

The second parameter of the *CeFindAllFiles* function, *dwFlags*, defines the scope of the search and what data is returned. The first set of flags can be one or more of the following:

- *FAF_ATTRIB_CHILDREN* Return only directories that have child items.
- *FAF_ATTRIB_NO_HIDDEN* Don't report hidden files or directories.
- *FAF_FOLDERS_ONLY* Return only folders in the directory.
- *FAF_NO_HIDDEN_SYS_ROMMODULES* Don't report ROM-based system files.

The second set of flags defines what data is returned by the *CeFindAllFiles* function. These flags can be one or more of the following:

- *FAF_ATTRIBUTES* Return file attributes.
- *FAF_CREATION_TIME* Return file creation time.
- *FAF_LASTACCESS_TIME* Return file last access time.

- *FAF_LASTWRITE_TIME* Return file last write time.
- *FAF_SIZE_HIGH* Return upper 32 bits of file size.
- *FAF_SIZE_LOW* Return lower 32 bits of file size.
- *FAF_OID* Return the OID for the file.
- *FAF_NAME* Return the filename.

Just because the flags are listed above doesn't mean you can find a good use for them. For example, the FAF_SIZE_HIGH flag is overkill, considering that few files on a Windows CE device are going to be larger than 4 GB. The file time flags are also limited by the support of the underlying file system. For example, the Windows CE object store tracks only the last access time and reports it in all file time fields.

There also appears to be a bug with the FAF_ATTRIB_CHILDREN flag. This valuable flag allows you to know when a directory contains subdirectories without your having to make an explicit call to that directory to find out. The flag seems to work only if the filename specification—the string to the right of the last directory separator backslash (\)—contains only one character. For example, the file specification

```
\\windows\*
```

works with FAF_ATTRIB_CHILDREN, while

```
\\windows\*.*
```

returns the same file list but the flag FILE_ATTRIBUTE_HAS_CHILDREN isn't set for directories that have subdirectories.

The third parameter of *CeFindAllFiles* should point to a DWORD value that will receive the number of files and directories found by the call. The final parameter, *ppFindDataArray*, should point to a variable of type LPCE_FIND_DATA, which is a pointer to an array of CE_FIND_DATA structures. When *CeFindAllFiles* returns, this variable will point to an array of CE_FIND_DATA structures that contain the requested data for each of the files found by the function. The CE_FIND_DATA structure is defined as

```
typedef struct _CE_FIND_DATA {
    DWORD dwFileAttributes;
    FILETIME ftCreationTime;
    FILETIME ftLastAccessTime;
    FILETIME ftLastWriteTime;
    DWORD nFileSizeHigh;
    DWORD nFileSizeLow;
    DWORD dwOID;
    WCHAR cFileName[MAX_PATH];
} CE_FIND_DATA;
```

The fields of CE_FIND_DATA look familiar to us by now. The only interesting field is the *dwOID* field that allows a PC-based application to receive the OID of a Windows CE file. This can be used with *CeGetOidGetInfo* to query more information about the file or directory. The flags in the *dwFileAttributes* field relate to Windows CE file attributes even though your application is running on a PC. This means, for example, that the FILE_ATTRIBUTE_TEMPORARY flag indicates an external storage device like a PC Card. Also, attribute flags are defined for execute in place ROM files. The additional attribute flag, FILE_ATTRIBUTE_HAS_CHILDREN, is defined to indicate that the directory contains child directories.

The buffer returned by *CeFindAllFiles* is originally allocated by the RAPI.DLL. Once you have finished with the buffer, you must call *CeRapiFreeBuffer* to free the buffer.

RAPI database functions

The RAPI database functions are shown in the following list. As you can see, these functions mimic the extensive database API found in Windows CE. Here's a case in which explicitly loading the RAPI DLL can come in handy. The many RAPI functions that support the extended database API of Windows CE 2.1 aren't exported by older RAPI DLLs. If your application attempts implicitly to load one of these functions, it won't load if the PC has an older version of RAPI.DLL.

Database management functions	***Support in***
CeCreateDatabase	
CeCreateDatabaseEx	Windows CE 2.1 or later
CeDeleteDatabase	
CeDeleteDatabaseEx	Windows CE 2.1 or later
CeDeleteRecord	
CeFindFirstDatabase	
CeFindFirstDatabaseEx	Windows CE 2.1 or later
CeFindNextDatabase	
CeFindNextDatabaseEx	Windows CE 2.1 or later
CeOidGetInfo	
CeOidGetInfoEx	Windows CE 2.1 or later
CeOpenDatabase	
CeOpenDatabaseEx	Windows CE 2.1 or later
CeReadRecordProps	
CeReadRecordPropsEx	Windows CE 2.1 or later
CeSeekDatabase	
CeSetDatabaseInfo	
CeSetDatabaseInfoEx	Windows CE 2.1 or later
CeWriteRecordProps	

(continued)

continued

Database management functions	***Support in***
CeMountDBVol	Windows CE 2.1 or later
CeUnmountDBVol	Windows CE 2.1 or later
CeEnumDBVolumes	Windows CE 2.1 or later
CeFindAllDatabases	

All but one of the database functions has a Windows CE counterpart. The only new function is *CeFindAllDatabases*. Like *CeFindAllFiles*, this function is designed as a performance enhancement so that applications can query all the databases on the system without having to iterate using the *FindFirstDatabase* and *FindNextDatabase* functions. The function is prototyped as

```
BOOL CeFindAllDatabases (DWORD dwDbaseType, WORD wFlags,
                         LPWORD cFindData,
                         LPLPCEDB_FIND_DATA ppFindData);
```

The first parameter is the database type value, or 0, if you want to return all databases. The *wFlags* parameter can contain one or more of the following flags, which define what data is returned by the function.

- *FAD_OID* Returns the database OID
- *FAD_FLAGS* Returns the *dwFlags* field of the DbInfo structure
- *FAD_NAME* Returns the name of the database
- *FAD_TYPE* Returns the type of the database
- *FAD_NUM_RECORDS* Returns the number of records in the database
- *FAD_NUM_SORT_ORDER* Returns the number of sort orders
- *FAD_SORT_SPECS* Returns the sort order specs for the database

The *cFindData* parameter should point to a WORD variable that receives the number of databases found. The last parameter should be the address of a pointer to an array of CEDB_FIND_DATA structures. As with the *CeFindAllFiles* function, *CeFindAllDatabases* returns the information about the databases found in an array and sets the *ppFindData* parameter to point to this array. The CEDB_FIND_DATA structure is defined as

```
struct CEDB_FIND_DATA {
    CEOID OidDb;
    CEDBASEINFO DbInfo;
};
```

The structure contains the OID for a database followed by a CEDBASEINFO structure. I described this structure in Chapter 7, but I'll repeat it here so that you can see what information can be queried by *FindAllDatabases*.

```
typedef struct _CEDBASEINFO {
    DWORD dwFlags;
    WCHAR szDbaseName[CEDB_MAXDBASENAMELEN];
    DWORD dwDbaseType;
    WORD wNumRecords;
    WORD wNumSortOrder;
    DWORD dwSize;
    FILETIME ftLastModified;
    SORTORDERSPEC rgSortSpecs[CEDB_MAXSORTORDER];
} CEDBASEINFO;
```

As with *CeFindAllFiles*, you must free the buffer returned by *CeFindAllDatabases* with a call to *CeRapiFreeBuffer*.

One other function in this section requires a call to *CeRapiFreeBuffer*. The function *CeReadRecordProps*, which returns properties for a database record, allocates the buffer where the data is returned. If you call the RAPI version function, you need to call *CeRapiFreeBuffer* to free the returned buffer.

RAPI registry management functions

The RAPI functions for managing the registry are shown in the following list. The functions work identically to their Windows CE counterparts. But remember that all strings, whether they are specifying keys and values or strings returned by the functions, are in Unicode.

Registry management functions

CeRegOpenKeyEx

CeRegEnumKeyEx

CeRegCreateKeyEx

CeRegCloseKey

CeRegDeleteKey

CeRegEnumValue

CeRegDeleteValue

CeRegQueryInfoKey

CeRegQueryValueEx

CeRegSetValueEx

RAPI shell management functions

The RAPI shell management functions are shown in the first list on the following page. While I'll cover the Windows CE–equivalent functions in the next chapter, you can see that the self-describing names of the functions pretty well document themselves. The *CeSHCreateShortcut* and *CeSHGetShortcutTarget* functions allow you to create and query shortcuts. The other two functions, *CeGetTempPath* and *CeGetSpecialFolderPath*, let you query the locations of some of the special-purpose directories on the Windows CE system, such as the programs directory and the recycle bin.

Shell management functions

CeSHCreateShortcut

CeSHGetShortcutTarget

CeGetTempPath

CeGetSpecialFolderPath

RAPI window management functions

The final set of predefined RAPI functions allow a desktop application to manage the windows on the Windows CE desktop. These functions are shown in the following list. The functions work similarly to their Windows CE functions. The *CeGetWindow* function allows a PC-based program to query the windows and child windows on the desktop while the other functions allow you to query the values in the window structures.

Window management functions

CeGetWindow

CeGetWindowLong

CeGetWindowText

CeGetClassName

The RapiDir Example Program

The RapiDir example is a PC-console application that displays the contents of a directory on an attached Windows CE device. The output of RapiDir, shown in Figure 11-1, resembles the output of the standard DIR command from a PC command line. RapiDir is passed one argument, the directory specification of the directory on the Windows CE machine. The directory specification can take wildcard arguments such as **.exe* if you want, but the program isn't completely robust in parsing the directory specification. Perfect parsing of a directory string isn't the goal of RapiDir—demonstrating RAPI is.

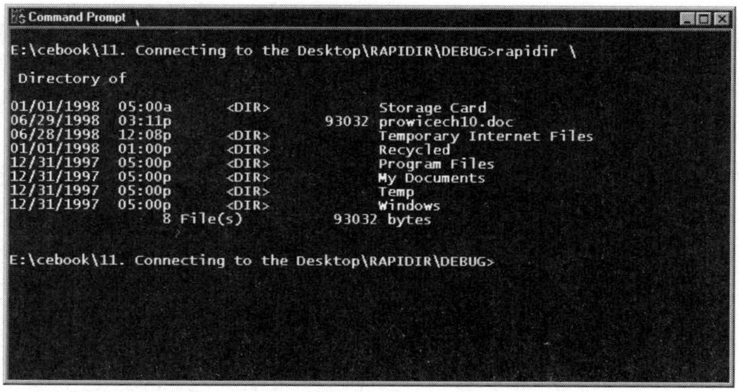

Figure 11-1. *The output of RapiDir.*

The source code for RapiDir is shown in Figure 11-2. The program is a command line application and therefore doesn't need the message loop or any of the other structure seen in a Windows-based application. Instead the *WinMain* function is replaced by our old C friend, *main*.

Remember that RapiDir is a standard Win32 desktop application. It won't even compile for Windows CE. On the other hand, you have the freedom to use the copious amounts of RAM and disk space provided by the comparatively huge desktop PC. When you build RapiDir, you'll need to add *rapi.lib* to the libraries that the linker uses. Otherwise, you'll get unresolved external errors for all the RAPI functions you call in your application.

```
//======================================================================
// RapiDir - Returns the contents of a directory on a Windows CE system
//
// Written for the book Programming Windows CE
// Copyright (C) 1998 Douglas Boling
//======================================================================
#include <windows.h>                 // For all that Windows stuff
#include <stdio.h>
#include <rapi.h>                    // RAS includes

//======================================================================
// main - Program entry point
//
int main (int argc, char **argv) {
    RAPIINIT ri;
    char szSrch[MAX_PATH], *pPtr;
    WCHAR szwDir[MAX_PATH];
    CE_FIND_DATA *pfd;
    DWORD i, cItems, dwTotal = 0;
    FILETIME ft;
    SYSTEMTIME st;
    char ampm = 'a';
    INT rc;

    // Call RapiInitEx to asynchronously start RAPI session.
    ri.cbSize = sizeof (ri);
    rc = CeRapiInitEx (&ri);

    if (rc != NOERROR) {
        printf (TEXT ("Rapi Initialization failed\r\n"));
        return 0;
    }
    // Wait 5 seconds for connect.
    rc = WaitForSingleObject (ri.heRapiInit, 5000);
```

Figure 11-2. *The RapiDir source code.* *(continued)*

Figure 11-2. *continued*

```
    if (rc == WAIT_OBJECT_0) {
        if (ri.hrRapiInit != NOERROR) {
            printf (TEXT ("Rapi Initialization failed.\r\n"));
            return 0;
        }
    } else if (rc == WAIT_TIMEOUT) {
        printf (TEXT ("Rapi Initialization timed out.\r\n"));
        return 0;
    }
    // If no argument, assume root directory.
    if (argc > 1)
        lstrcpy (szSrch, argv[1]);
    else
        lstrcpy (szSrch, "\\");

    // Point to end of name.
    pPtr = szSrch + lstrlen (szSrch) - 1;

    // Strip any trailing backslash.
    if (*pPtr == '\\')
        *pPtr = '\0';

    // Look for wildcards in filename. pPtr points to string end.
    for (i = 0; (pPtr >= szSrch) && (*pPtr != '\\'); pPtr--) {
        if ((*pPtr == '*') || (*pPtr == '?'))
            i++;
    }
    // Display dir name first so that on long calls we show we're alive.
    if (pPtr >= szSrch) {
        char ch;
        ch = *pPtr;
        *pPtr = '\0';
        printf (TEXT ("\r\n Directory of %s\r\n\r\n"), szSrch);
        *pPtr = ch;
    } else if (i)
        printf (TEXT ("\r\n Directory of \\\r\n\r\n"));
    else
        printf (TEXT ("\r\n Directory of %s\r\n\r\n"), szSrch);

    // No wildcards, append *.*
    if (i == 0)
        lstrcat (szSrch, "\\*.*");

    // Convert ANSI string to Unicode.
    mbstowcs (szwDir, szSrch, lstrlen (szSrch));
    // RAPI call
```

```
    rc = CeFindAllFiles (szwDir, FAF_SIZE_LOW | FAF_NAME |
                         FAF_ATTRIBUTES | FAF_LASTACCESS_TIME,
                         &cItems, &pfd);

    // Display the results.
    if (cItems) {
        for (i = 0; i < cItems; i++) {
            // Convert file time.
            FileTimeToLocalFileTime (&pfd->ftLastAccessTime, &ft);
            FileTimeToSystemTime (&ft, &st);
            // Adjust for AM/PM.
            if (st.wHour == 0)
                st.wHour = 12;
            else if (st.wHour > 11) {
                ampm = 'p';
                if (st.wHour > 12)
                    st.wHour -= 12;
            }
            printf (TEXT ("%02d/%02d/%02d  %02d:%02d%c\t"),
                    st.wMonth, st.wDay, st.wYear,
                    st.wHour, st.wMinute, ampm);

            // Display dir marker or file size.
            if (pfd->dwFileAttributes & FILE_ATTRIBUTE_DIRECTORY)
                printf (TEXT ("<DIR>\t\t "));
            else {
                printf (TEXT ("\t%8d "), pfd->nFileSizeLow);
                dwTotal += pfd->nFileSizeLow;
            }

            // Display name, use Cap %S to indicate Unicode.
            printf (TEXT ("%S\r\n"), pfd->cFileName);
            pfd++;
        }
        printf (TEXT ("\t%10d File(s)\t%9d bytes\r\n\r\n"),
                cItems, dwTotal);
    } else
        printf (TEXT ("File not Found\r\n\r\n"));

    // Clean up by uninitializing RAPI.
    CeRapiUninit ();
    return 0;
}
```

This single procedure application first calls *CeRapiInitEx* to initialize the RAPI session. I used the *Ex* version of the initialization function so that RapiDir can time out and terminate if a connection isn't made within 5 seconds of starting the program.

If I'd used *CeRapiInit* instead, the only way to terminate RapiDir if a remote CE device weren't connected would be a user-unfriendly Control-C key combination.

Once the RAPI session is initialized, a minimal amount of work is done on the single command line argument that's the search string for the directory. Once that work is complete, the string is converted into Unicode and passed to *CeFindAllFiles*. This RAPI function then returns with an array of CE_FIND_DATA structures that contain the names and requested data of the files and directories found. The data from that array is then displayed using *printf* statements. Finally, the RAPI session is terminated with a call to *CeRapiUninit*.

If you compare the output of RapiDir with the output of the standard DIR command, you notice that RapiDir doesn't display the total bytes free on the disk after the listing of files. While I could have displayed the total free space for the object store using *CeGetStorageInformation*, this wouldn't work if the user displayed a directory on a PCMCIA card or other external media. Windows CE supports the *GetDiskFreeSpaceEx* function, but the Windows CE RAPI DLL doesn't expose this function. To get this information, we'll use RAPI's ability to call user defined functions on a Windows CE system.

Custom RAPI Functions

No matter how many functions the RAPI interface supports, you can always think of functions that an application needs but the RAPI interface doesn't give you. Because of this, RAPI provides a method for a PC application to call a user-defined function on the Windows CE device.

You can invoke a user-defined RAPI function in one of two ways. The first way is called *block mode*. In block mode, you make a call to the RAPI remote invocation function, the function makes the call to a specified function in a specified DLL, the DLL function does its thing and returns, and the RAPI function then returns to the calling PC program with the output. The second method is called stream mode. In this mode, the RAPI call to the function returns immediately, but a connection is maintained between the calling PC application and the Windows CE DLL–based function. This method allows information to be fed back to the PC on an ongoing basis.

Using RAPI to call a custom function

The RAPI function that lets you call a generic function on the Windows CE device is *CeRapiInvoke*, which is prototyped as

```
HRESULT CeRapiInvoke (LPCWSTR pDllPath, LPCWSTR pFunctionName,
                      DWORD cbInput, BYTE *pInput, DWORD *pcbOutput,
                      BYTE **ppOutput, IRAPIStream **ppIRAPIStream,
                      DWORD dwReserved);
```

The first parameter to *CeRapiInvoke* is the name of the DLL on the Windows CE device that contains the function you want to call. The name must be in Unicode but can include a path. If no path is specified, the DLL is assumed to be in the \windows directory on the device. The second parameter is the name of the function to be called. The function name must be in Unicode and is case specific.

The next two parameters, *cbInput* and *pInput*, should be set to the buffer containing the data and the size of that data to be sent to the Windows CE–based function. The *pcbOutput* and *ppOutput* parameters are both pointers—the first a pointer to a DWORD that receives the size of the data returned and the second a pointer to a PBYTE variable that receives the pointer to the buffer containing the data returned by the Windows CE function. I'll describe the next-to-last parameter, *ppIRAPIStream*, later.

To use *CeRapiInvoke* in block mode, all you do is specify the DLL containing the function you want to call, the name of the function, and the data and make the call. When *CeRapiInvoke* returns, the data from the CE-based function will be sitting in the buffer pointed to by your output pointer variable.

Writing a RAPI server function

You can't just call any function in a Windows CE DLL. The structure of the Windows CE function must conform to the following function prototype:

```
STDAPI INT FuncName (DWORD cbInput, BYTE *pInput, DWORD *pcbOutput,
                     BYTE **ppOutput, IRAPIStream *pIRAPIStream);
```

As you can see, the parameters closely match those of *CeRapiInvoke*. As with *CeRapiInvoke*, I'll talk about the parameter *pIRAPIStream*, later.

Figure 11-3 contains the source code for a very simple block-mode RAPI server. This is a DLL and therefore has a different structure from the application files previously used in the book. The primary difference is that the DLL contains a *LibMain* routine instead of *WinMain*. The *LibMain* routine is called by Windows whenever a DLL is loaded or freed by a process or thread. In our case, we don't need to take any action other that to return TRUE indicating all is well.

You should be careful to make the name of your RAPI server DLL eight characters or less. Current implementations of the RAPI DLL will fail to find server DLLs with names not in the old 8.3 format.

```
//======================================================================
// RapiServ - A RAPI block mode server DLL
//
// Written for the book Programming Windows CE
// Copyright (C) 1998 Douglas Boling
//======================================================================
#include <windows.h>                 // For all that Windows stuff
```

Figure 11-3. *RapiServ.c, a simple block-mode RAPI server DLL.* *(continued)*

Figure 11-3. *continued*

```
// This ensures that the function will be exported by the DLL.
__declspec(dllexport) INT RAPIGetDiskSize (DWORD, BYTE *, DWORD *,
                                           BYTE **, PVOID);

//======================================================================
// DllMain - DLL initialization entry point
//
BOOL WINAPI DllMain (HINSTANCE hinstDLL, DWORD dwReason,
                     LPVOID lpvReserved) {
    return TRUE;
}
//======================================================================
// RAPIGetDiskSize - Returns the disk size and free space.  Called from
// PC application using RAPI.
//
INT RAPIGetDiskSize (DWORD cbInput, BYTE *pInput, DWORD *pcbOutput,
                     BYTE **ppOutput, PVOID reserved) {
    PDWORD pdwLocal;
    LPTSTR pPtr;
    DWORD i;
    ULARGE_INTEGER lnFree, lnTotal;

    *pcbOutput = 0;            // Zero output bytes for now.

    // See if proper zero-terminated string.
    pPtr = (LPTSTR)pInput;
    for (i = 0; i < cbInput / 2; i++)
        if (!*pPtr++)
            break;

    // If not zero terminated or if zero length, return error.
    if ((i >= cbInput / 2) || (i == 0))
        return -2;

    // Call the function.
    if (GetDiskFreeSpaceEx ((LPTSTR)pInput, NULL, &lnTotal, &lnFree)) {

        // Allocate memory for the return buffer.
        pdwLocal = (PDWORD) LocalAlloc (LPTR, 2 * sizeof (DWORD));
        if (pdwLocal) {
            // Copy data from function to output buffer.
            pdwLocal[0] = lnTotal.LowPart;
            pdwLocal[1] = lnFree.LowPart;
```

```
            // Specify size and buffer.
            *pcbOutput = 2 * sizeof (DWORD);
            *ppOutput = (PBYTE)pdwLocal;
        } else
            return GetLastError();
    } else
        return GetLastError();
    return 0;
}
```

The unusual prefix before the function prototype for *RAPIGetDiskSize*,

```
__declspec (dllexport) INT RAPIGetDiskSize…
```

tells the linker to export the function listed so that external modules can call the function directly. This declaration is a shortcut for the old way of defining exports in a separate function definition (DEF) file used in Win16 programming. While this shortcut is convenient, sometimes you still need to fall back on a DEF file.

The function of RapiServ is to make available that *GetDiskFreeSpaceEx* function we needed in the RapiDir example application. The server function, *RAPIGetDiskSize*, has the same prototype I described earlier. The input buffer is used to pass a directory name to the DLL while the output buffer returns the total disk space and the free disk space for the directory passed. The format of the input and output buffers is totally up to you. However, the output buffer should be allocated using *LocalAlloc* so that the RAPI library can free it after it has been used. The value returned by *RAPIGetDiskSize* is the value that's returned by the *CeRapiInvoke* function to the PC-based application.

On the PC side, a call to a block mode RAPI server function looks like the following.

```
//----------------------------------------------------------------------
// MyCeGetDiskFreeSpaceEx - Homegrown implementation of a RAPI
// GetDiskFreeSpace function
//
BOOL MyCeGetDiskFreeSpaceEx (LPWSTR pszDir, PDWORD pdwTotal,
                             PDWORD pdwFree) {
    HRESULT hr;
    DWORD dwIn, dwOut;
    LPBYTE pInput;
    LPWSTR pPtr;
    PDWORD pOut;

    // Get length of Unicode string.
    for (dwIn = 2, pPtr = pszDir; *pPtr++; dwIn+=2);
```

(continued)

```
    // Allocate buffer for input.
    pInput = LocalAlloc (LPTR, dwIn);
    if (!pInput)
        return FALSE;
    // Copy directory name into input buffer.
    memcpy (pInput, pszDir, dwIn);

    // Call function on Windows CE device.
    hr = CeRapiInvoke (L"\\RapiServ", L"RAPIGetDiskSize", dwIn,
                       pInput, &dwOut, (PBYTE *)&pOut, NULL, 0);

    // If successful, return total and free values.
    if (hr == 0) {
        *pdwTotal = pOut[0];
        *pdwFree = pOut[1];
        CeRapiFreeBuffer (pOut);
        return TRUE;
    }
    return FALSE;
}
```

This routine encapsulates the call to *CeRapiInvoke* so that the call looks just like another CE RAPI call. The code in this routine simply computes the length of the Unicode string that contains the directory specification, allocates a buffer and copies the string into it, and passes it to the *CeRapiInvoke* function. When the routine returns, the return code indicates success or failure of the call. *CeRapiInvoke* frees the input buffer passed to it. The data is then copied from the output buffer and that buffer is freed with a call to *CeRapiFreeBuffer*.

Throughout this section, I've put off any explanation of the parameters referring to *IRAPIStream*. In fact, in the example code above, the prototype for the server call, *RAPIGetDiskSize*, simply typed the *pIRAPIStream* pointer as a PVOID and ignored it. In the client code, the *CeRapiInvoke* call passed a NULL to the *ppIRAPIStream* pointer. This treatment of the *IRAPIStream* interface is what differentiates a block-mode call from a stream-mode call. Now let's look at the *IRAPIStream* interface.

Stream mode

Stream-mode RAPI calls are different from block mode in that the initial RAPI call creates a link between the PC application and the server routine on the Windows CE device. When you call *CeRapiInvoke* in stream mode, the call returns immediately. You communicate with the server DLL using an *IRAPIStream* interface. You access this interface using a pointer returned by the *CeRapiInvoke* call in the variable pointed to by *ppIRAPIStream*.

The *IRAPIStream* interface is derived from the standard COM *IStream* interface. The only methods added to *IStream* to create *IRAPIStream* are *SetRapiStat* and *GetRapiStat*, which let you set a timeout value for the RAPI communication. Fortunately, we don't have to implement an *IRAPIStream* interface either on the client side or in the server DLL. This interface is provided for us by the RAPI services as a way to communicate.

Following is a call to *CeRapiInvoke* that establishes a stream connection and then writes and reads back 10 bytes from the remote server DLL.

```
DWORD dwIn, dwOut, cbBytes;
IRAPIStream *pIRAPIStream;
BYTE bBuff[BUFF_SIZE];
PBYTE pOut;
HRESULT hr;

// RAPI call
hr = CeRapiInvoke (L"ServDLL", L"RAPIRmtFunc", dwIn, bBuff,
                   &dwOut, &pOut, &pIRAPIStream, 0);
if (hr == S_OK) {
    // Write 10 bytes.
    pIRAPIStream->Write (bBuff, 10, &cbBytes);
    // Read data from server.
    pIRAPIStream->Read (bBuff, 10, &cbBytes);
}
```

When establishing a stream connection, you can still use the input buffer to pass initial data down to the remote server. From then on, you should use the *Read* and *Write* methods of *IRAPIStream* to communicate with the server.

The RapiFind Example Program

The RapiFind example program searches the entire directory tree of a Windows CE device for files matching a search specification. The program is in two parts: a RAPI server DLL, FindSrv.DLL, and a console-based, Win32 application, RapiFind. The program works by passing a search string on the command line. RapiFind returns any files on the attached Windows CE device that match the search string. If the search specification includes a directory, only that directory and any of its subdirectories are searched for matching files. Figure 11-4 on the following page shows the output of RapiFind.

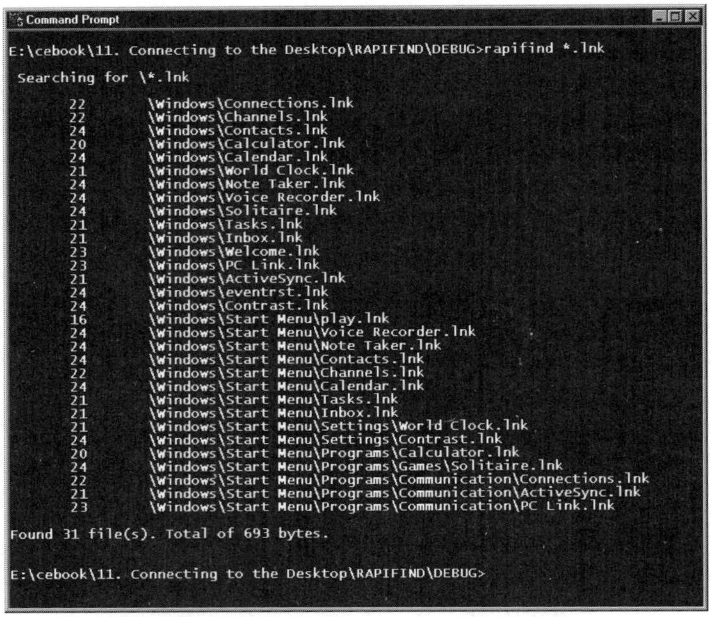

Figure 11-4. *The output of RapiFind.*

You'll notice that the following example is written in C++, and so are the rest of the examples in this chapter. Actually, almost all the code in both files is standard C, but the C++ extensions are used to reference the *IRAPIStream* interface. I could have written a C-equivalent structure to access the interface, but I could see little reason to avoid using C++ in this case. (As an aside, most COM interfaces defined in Win32 have C-interface equivalents for those of us who still like C.) First, let's look at the server DLL, FindSrv, shown in Figure 11-5.

```
//======================================================================
// FindSrv - A RAPI stream server DLL
//
// Written for the book Programming Windows CE
// Copyright (C) 1998 Douglas Boling
//======================================================================
#include <windows.h>                    // For all that Windows stuff

// Returns number of elements
#define dim(x) (sizeof(x) / sizeof(x[0]))

//----------------------------------------------------------------------
// Not included in a server-side include file
```

Figure 11-5. *FindSrv.cpp, a stream-mode RAPI server DLL.*

```
typedef enum tagRAPISTREAMFLAG {
    STREAM_TIMEOUT_READ
} RAPISTREAMFLAG;

DECLARE_INTERFACE_ (IRAPIStream,  IStream)
{
    STDMETHOD(SetRapiStat)(THIS_ RAPISTREAMFLAG Flag,
                           DWORD dwValue) PURE;
    STDMETHOD(GetRapiStat)(THIS_ RAPISTREAMFLAG Flag,
                           DWORD *pdwValue) PURE;
};
//----------------------------------------------------------------------
// Function prototypes declared as exports from the DLL.
// Bracket so that function name won't be mangled by C++.
extern "C" {
__declspec(dllexport) INT RAPIFindFile (DWORD cbInput, BYTE *pInput,
                              DWORD *pcbOutput, BYTE **ppOutput,
                              IRAPIStream *pIRAPIStream);
}

//======================================================================
// DllMain - DLL initialization entry point
//
BOOL WINAPI DllMain (HINSTANCE hinstDLL, DWORD dwReason,
                     LPVOID lpvReserved) {
    return TRUE;
}
//----------------------------------------------------------------------
// WriteToClient - Writes a command and optional string to the client
//
int WriteToClient (INT nCmd, INT nSize, LPTSTR pszStr,
                   IRAPIStream *pIRAPIStream) {
    INT nBuff;
    DWORD cbBytes;
    HRESULT hr;

    // Write command code.
    hr = pIRAPIStream->Write (&nCmd, sizeof (nCmd), &cbBytes);

    // Write size value.
    hr = pIRAPIStream->Write (&nSize, sizeof (nSize), &cbBytes);

    // Write length of string.
    nBuff = (lstrlen (pszStr) + 1) * sizeof (TCHAR);
    hr = pIRAPIStream->Write (&nBuff, sizeof (nBuff), &cbBytes);
```

(continued)

Figure 11-5. *continued*

```
    // Write string.
    hr = pIRAPIStream->Write (pszStr, nBuff, &cbBytes);
    return 0;
}
int nFlag;
//----------------------------------------------------------------------
// SrchDirectory - Recursive routine that searches a directory and all
// child dirs for matching files
//
int SrchDirectory (LPTSTR pszDir, IRAPIStream *pIRAPIStream) {
    WIN32_FIND_DATA fd;
    TCHAR szNew[MAX_PATH];
    INT i, rc, nErr = 0;
    HANDLE hFind;
    TCHAR *pPtr, *pSrcSpec;

    // Separate subdirectory from search specification.
    for (pSrcSpec = pszDir + lstrlen (pszDir); pSrcSpec >= pszDir;
         pSrcSpec--)
        if (*pSrcSpec == TEXT ('\\'))
            break;

    // Copy the search specification up to the last directory sep char.
    if (pSrcSpec <= pszDir)
        lstrcpy (szNew, TEXT ("\\"));
    else {
        for (i = 0; (i < dim(szNew)-10) &&
                    ((pszDir+i) <= pSrcSpec); i++)
            szNew[i] = *(pszDir+i);
        szNew[i] = TEXT ('\0');
    }
    pPtr = szNew + lstrlen (szNew);

    // Report directory we're searching.
    WriteToClient (2, 0, szNew, pIRAPIStream);

    // Find matching files.
    hFind = FindFirstFile (pszDir, &fd);
    if (hFind != INVALID_HANDLE_VALUE) {

        do {
            // Report all matching files.
            if (!(fd.dwFileAttributes & FILE_ATTRIBUTE_DIRECTORY))
                WriteToClient (1, fd.nFileSizeLow, fd.cFileName,
                               pIRAPIStream);
```

```
            rc = FindNextFile (hFind, &fd);
        } while (rc);

        FindClose (hFind);
    } else {
        rc = GetLastError();
        if ((rc != ERROR_FILE_NOT_FOUND)  &&
            (rc != ERROR_NO_MORE_FILES)) {
            TCHAR szDbg[64];
            wsprintf (szDbg, TEXT ("1Find Error:%d"), rc);
            WriteToClient (99, 0, szDbg, pIRAPIStream);
            return -1;
        }
    }

    // Create generic search string for all directories.
    lstrcat (szNew, TEXT ("*.*"));

    hFind = FindFirstFile (szNew, &fd);
    if (hFind != INVALID_HANDLE_VALUE) {
        do {
            if (fd.dwFileAttributes & FILE_ATTRIBUTE_DIRECTORY) {
                // Recurse to the lower directory.
                lstrcpy (pPtr, fd.cFileName);
                lstrcat (pPtr, pSrcSpec);
                nErr = SrchDirectory (szNew, pIRAPIStream);
                if (nErr) break;
                *pPtr = TEXT ('\0');
            }
            rc = FindNextFile (hFind, &fd);
        } while (rc);

        FindClose (hFind);
    } else {
        rc = GetLastError();
        if ((rc != ERROR_FILE_NOT_FOUND) &&
            (rc != ERROR_NO_MORE_FILES)) {
            TCHAR szDbg[64];
            wsprintf (szDbg, TEXT ("2Find Error:%d"), rc);
            WriteToClient (99, 0, szDbg, pIRAPIStream);
            return -1;
        }
    }
    return nErr;
}
```

(continued)

Figure 11-5. *continued*

```
//======================================================================
// RAPIFindFile - Searches the device for matching files.  Called from
// PC application using RAPI.
//
INT RAPIFindFile (DWORD cbInput, BYTE *pInput, DWORD *pcbOutput,
                  BYTE **ppOutput, IRAPIStream *pIRAPIStream) {

    INT nBuff;
    DWORD i, cbBytes;
    TCHAR *pPtr;
    HRESULT hr;

    *pcbOutput = 0;
    // See if proper zero-terminated string.
    pPtr = (LPTSTR)pInput;
    for (i = 0; i < cbInput / 2; i++)
        if (!*pPtr++)
            break;

    // If not zero terminated or if zero length, return error.
    if ((i >= cbInput / 2) || (i == 0))
        return -2;
    nFlag = 0;
    // Search for files
    SrchDirectory ((LPTSTR) pInput, pIRAPIStream);

    // Write end code.  Cmd 0 -> end of search
    nBuff = 0;
    hr = pIRAPIStream->Write (&nBuff, sizeof (nBuff), &cbBytes);
    return 0;
}
```

As with the earlier RAPI server DLL, FindSrv is short and to the point. The differences between this server and the block server can be seen early in the file. The *IRAPIStream* interface isn't defined in any of the include files used by Windows CE applications, so this interface is derived at the top of the file from *IStream*. Immediately following the interface declaration is the exported function prototype. Notice that the prototype is enclosed in an extern C bracket. This prevents the default mangling of the function name that the C++ precompiler would normally perform. We need the name of the function unmangled so that it's a known name to the client.

The exported RAPI function is *RAPIFindFile*, which you can see at the end of the source code. This routine does little more than check to see that the search string is valid before it calls *SrchDirectory*, a function internal to the DLL. *SrchDirectory* is a recursive function that searches the directory defined in the search specification and all subdirectories underneath. When a file is found that matches the search specification, the name and size of the file is sent back to the client caller using the *Write* method of *IRAPIStream*. The format of the data transmitted between the client and server is up to the programmer. In this case, I send a command word, followed by the file size, the length of the name, and finally the filename itself. The command word gives you a minimal protocol for communication with the client. A command value of 1 indicates a found file, a value of 2 indicates the server is looking in a new directory, and a value of 0 indicates that the search is complete.

The source code for the client application, RapiFind, is shown in Figure 11-6.

```
//======================================================================
// RapiFind - Searches for a file or files on a Windows CE system
//
// Written for the book Programming Windows CE
// Copyright (C) 1998 Douglas Boling
//======================================================================
#include <windows.h>                    // For all that Windows stuff
#include <stdio.h>
#include <rapi.h>                       // RAS includes

//======================================================================
// main - Program entry point
//
int main (int argc, char **argv) {
    RAPIINIT ri;
    char szSrch[MAX_PATH], *pPtr;
    WCHAR szwDir[MAX_PATH];
    WCHAR szName[MAX_PATH];
    DWORD i, dwTotal = 0, dwFiles = 0, dwIn, dwOut, cbBytes;
    IRAPIStream *pIRAPIStream;
    PBYTE pInput, pOut;
    HRESULT hr;
    INT rc, nCmd, nSize;

    // If no argument, fail.
    if (argc < 2) {
        printf ("\r\nUSAGE: %s <search spec>\r\n\r\n", argv[0]);
        return -1;
    }
    lstrcpy (szSrch, argv[1]);

    // Call RapiInitEx to asynchronously start RAPI session.
    ri.cbSize = sizeof (ri);
    rc = CeRapiInitEx (&ri);
```

Figure 11-6. *RapiFind.cpp, a stream-mode RAPI client application.* *(continued)*

Figure 11-6. *continued*

```
    if (rc != NOERROR) {
        printf (TEXT ("Rapi Initialization failed\r\n"));
        return 0;
    }
    // Wait 5 seconds for connect.
    rc = WaitForSingleObject (ri.heRapiInit, 5000);
    if (rc == WAIT_OBJECT_0) {
        if (ri.hrRapiInit != NOERROR) {
            printf (TEXT ("Rapi Initialization failed\r\n"));
            return 0;
        }
    } else if (rc == WAIT_TIMEOUT) {
        printf (TEXT ("Rapi Initialization timed out.\r\n"));
        return 0;
    }
    // Point to end of name.
    pPtr = szSrch + lstrlen (szSrch) - 1;

    // Strip any trailing backslash.
    if (*pPtr == '\\')
        *pPtr = '\0';

    // Look for wildcards in filename. pPtr points to string end.
    for (i = 0; (pPtr >= szSrch) && (*pPtr != '\\'); pPtr--) {
        if ((*pPtr == '*') || (*pPtr == '?'))
            i++;
    }
    if (pPtr <= szSrch) {
        lstrcpy (szSrch, TEXT ("\\"));
        lstrcat (szSrch, argv[1]);
    }

    if (i) {
        printf (TEXT ("\r\n Searching for %s\r\n\r\n"), pPtr+1);
    } else
        printf (TEXT ("\r\n Searching in %s\r\n\r\n"), szSrch);

    // No wildcards, append *.*
    if (i == 0)
        lstrcat (szSrch, "\\*.*");

    // Convert ANSI string to Unicode.  At the same time, copy it
    // into a discardable buffer for CeRapiInvoke.
    dwIn = lstrlen (szSrch)+1;
```

```
    pInput = (PBYTE)LocalAlloc (LPTR, dwIn * sizeof (WCHAR));
    if (!pInput) {
        printf (TEXT ("\r\nOut of memory\r\n"));
        return -1;
    }
    mbstowcs ((LPWSTR)pInput, szSrch, dwIn);
    dwIn *= sizeof (WCHAR);

    // RAPI call
    hr = CeRapiInvoke (L"\\FindSrv", L"RAPIFindFile", dwIn,
                       pInput, &dwOut, &pOut, &pIRAPIStream, 0);
    if (hr == S_OK) {
        // Read command.
        pIRAPIStream->Read (&nCmd, sizeof (nCmd), &cbBytes);
        while (nCmd) {
            switch (nCmd) {
            // Display found file.
            case 1:
                // Read length of file.
                pIRAPIStream->Read (&i, sizeof (i), &cbBytes);
                dwTotal += i;
                dwFiles++;

                // Read length of filename.
                pIRAPIStream->Read (&nSize, sizeof (nSize), &cbBytes);
                // Read name itself.
                pIRAPIStream->Read (szName, nSize, &cbBytes);

                // Print directory and name.
                printf (TEXT ("%9d\t%S%S\r\n"), i, szwDir, szName);
                break;

            // Display name of directory we're currently searching.
            case 2:
                // Read and discard dummy length value.
                pIRAPIStream->Read (&nSize, sizeof (nSize), &cbBytes);
                // Read length of directory.
                pIRAPIStream->Read (&nSize, sizeof (nSize), &cbBytes);
                // Read directory name itself.
                pIRAPIStream->Read (szwDir, nSize, &cbBytes);
                break;
            }
            // Read next command.
            pIRAPIStream->Read (&nCmd, sizeof (nCmd), &cbBytes);
        }
```

(continued)

Figure 11-6. *continued*

```
    } else if (hr == ERROR_FILE_NOT_FOUND)
        printf (TEXT ("The RAPI server DLL FindSrv could not be found \
on the CE target device.\r\n"));
    else
        printf (TEXT ("CeRapiInvoke returned %d"), hr);

    printf (TEXT ("\r\nFound %d file(s). Total of %d bytes.\r\n\r\n"),
                dwFiles, dwTotal);

    // Clean up by uninitializing RAPI.
    CeRapiUninit ();
    return 0;
}
```

The call to *CeRapiInvoke* returns a pointer to an *IRAPIStream* interface that's then used to read data from the server. The client reads one integer value to determine whether the following data is a found file, a report of the current search directory, or a report that the search has ended. With each command, the appropriate data is read using the *Read* method. The result of the search is then reported using *printf* statements.

While you could implement the same file find function of RapiFind using a block-mode connection, the stream format has a definite advantage in this case. By reporting back results as files are found, the program lets the user known that the program is executing correctly. If the program were designed to use a block-mode call, RapiFind would appear to go dead while the server DLL completed its entire search, which could take 10 or 20 seconds.

As I mentioned in the explanation of *CeRapiInit*, a call to this function doesn't initiate a connection to a device. You can, however, be notified when a connection to a Windows CE device is established. There are ways, both on the PC and on the Windows CE device, to know when a connection is made between the two systems. After a brief look at CeUtil, which provides some handy helper functions for PC applications dealing with Windows CE devices, I'll talk about connection notifiers in the next section.

THE CEUTIL FUNCTIONS

Windows CE Services uses the PC registry to store voluminous amounts of information about the Windows CE devices that have partnered with the PC. Windows CE Services also uses the registry to store extensive configuration information. While most of these registry keys are documented, if you access them by name you're assuming that those key names will always remain the same. This might not be the case, especially in international versions of Windows where registry keys are sometimes in a different language.

The CeUtil DLL exports functions that provide an abstraction layer over the registry keys used by Windows CE Services. Using this DLL allows a PC application to query the devices that are currently registered and to add or delete registry values underneath the keys that hold data for specific devices. The CeUtil DLL doesn't communicate with a remote Windows CE device; it only looks in the PC registry for information that has already been put there by Windows CE Services.

The keys in the registry related to Windows CE Services are separated into either HKEY_LOCAL_MACHINE, for generic configurations such as the initial configuration for a newly registered device, or HKEY_CURRENT_USER, where the configuration information for the already registered devices is located. When a new device is registered, CE Services copies the template in HKEY_LOCAL_MACHINE to a new subkey under HKEY_CURRENT_USER that identifies the specific device.

In general, you register a new filter in the keys under HKEY_LOCAL_MACHINE to ensure that all devices that are registered in the future also use your filter. You use the registry entries under HKEY_CURRENT_USER to register that filter for a specific device that was already registered before you installed that same filter.

Accessing Windows CE Services registry entries

To open one of the many registry keys that hold connection information, you can use this function:

```
HRESULT CeSvcOpen (UINT uSvc, LPTSTR pszPath, BOOL fCreate,
                   PHCESVC phSvc);
```

The first parameter of this function is a flag that indicates which predefined key you want to open. The available flags are listed below.

Keys under HKEY_LOCAL_MACHINE that apply to generic Windows CE Services configuration information

- *CESVC_ROOT_MACHINE* Windows CE Services root key under HKEY_LOCAL_MACHINE
- *CESVC_FILTERS* Root key for filter registration
- *CESVC_CUSTOM_MENUS* Root key for custom menu registration
- *CESVC_SERVICES_COMMON* Root key for services
- *CESVC_SYNC_COMMON* Root key for synchronization services registration

Keys under HKEY_CURRENT_USER that apply to specific Windows CE devices that are partnered with the PC

- *CESVC_ROOT_USER* Windows CE Services root key under HKEY_LOCAL_USER
- *CESVC_DEVICES* Root key for individual device registration

- *CESVC_DEVICEX* Root key for a specific device
- *CESVC_DEVICE_SELECTED* Root key for the device currently selected in the Windows CE Services window
- *CESVC_SERVICES_USER* Root services subkey for a specific device
- *CESVC_SYNC* Synchronization subkey for a specific device

Of the many registry keys that can be returned by *CeSvcOpen*, the ones I'll be using throughout the chapter are CESVC_FILTERS, the key in which a filter is registered for all future devices; CESVC_DEVICES, the key in which information for all registered devices is located; and CESVC_DEVICEX, which is used to open keys for a specific registered devices. The other flags are useful for registering synchronization objects as well as for registering general Windows CE Services configuration information.

The second parameter to *CeSvcOpen* is *pszPath*. This parameter points either to the name of a subkey to open underneath the key specified by the *uSvc* flag or to a DWORD value that specifies the registered Windows CE device that you want to open if the *uSvc* flag requires that a device be specified. The *fCreate* parameter should be set to TRUE if you want to create the key being opened because it currently doesn't exist. If this parameter is set to FALSE, *CeSvcOpen* fails if the key doesn't already exist in the registry. Finally, the *phSvc* parameter points to a *CESVC* handle that receives the handle of the newly opened key. While this isn't typed as a handle to a registry key (an HKEY), the key can be used in both the CeUtil registry functions as well as the standard registry functions.

CeSvcOpen returns a standard Win32 error code if the function fails. Otherwise, the key to the opened registry key is placed in the variable pointed to by *phSvc*.

You can open registry keys below those opened by *CeSvcOpen* by calling *CeSvcOpenEx*. This function is prototyped as

```
HRESULT CeSvcOpenEx (HCESVC hSvcRoot, LPTSTR pszPath, BOOL fCreate,
                     PHCESVC phSvc);
```

The parameters for this closely mirror those of *RegOpenKey*. The first parameter is a handle to a previously opened key. Typically, this key would have been opened by *CeSvcOpen*. The second parameter is the string that specifies the name of the subkey to be opened. Notice that since we're running on the PC, this string might not be a Unicode value. The *fCreate* parameter should be set to TRUE if you want the key to be created if it doesn't already exist. Finally, the *phSvc* parameter points to a *CESVC* handle that receives the handle to the opened key.

When you have finished with a key, you should close it with a call to this function:

```
HRESULT CeSvcClose (HCESVC hSvc);
```

The only parameter is the handle you want to close.

Enumerating registered devices

Of course, the requirement to specify the device ID value in *CeSvcOpen* begs the question of how you determine what devices have already been partnered with the PC. To determine this, you can use the function

```
HRESULT CeSvcEnumProfiles (PHCESVC phSvc, DWORD lProfileIndex,
                           PDWORD plProfile);
```

The first parameter to *CeSvcEnumProfiles* is a pointer to a CESVC handle. The handle this parameter points to is uninitiated the first time the function is called. The function returns a handle that must be passed in subsequent calls to *CeSvcEnumProfiles*. The second parameter is an index value. This value should be set to 0 the first time the function is called and incremented for each subsequent call. The final parameter is a pointer to a DWORD that receives the device ID for the registered device. This value can be used when calling *CeSvcOpen* to open a registry key for that device.

Each time the function is called, it returns NOERROR if a new device ID is returned. When all devices have been enumerated, *CeSvcEnumProfiles* returns ERROR_NO_MORE_ITEMS. You should be careful to continue calling *CeSvcEnumProfiles* until the function returns ERROR_NO_MORE_ITEMS so that the enumeration process will close the handle parameter pointed to by *phSvc*. If you want to stop enumerating after you've found a particular device ID, you'll need to call *CeSvcClose* to close the *hSvc* handle manually.

The following routine enumerates the Windows CE devices that have been registered on the PC. The program enumerates all the registered Windows CE devices and prints out the name and device type of each of the devices. The program uses the function *CeSvcGetString*, which I'll describe shortly.

```
int PrintCeDevices (void) {
    HCESVC hSvc, hDevKey;
    TCHAR szName[128], szType[64];
    DWORD dwPro;
    INT i;

    // Enumerate each registered device.
    i = 0;
    while (CeSvcEnumProfiles (&hSvc, i++, &dwPro) == 0) {

        // Open the registry key for the device enumerated.
        CeSvcOpen (CESVC_DEVICEX, (LPTSTR)dwPro, FALSE, &hDevKey);

        // Get the name and device type strings.
        CeSvcGetString (hDevKey, TEXT ("DisplayName"),
            szName, dim(szName));
```

(continued)

```
        CeSvcGetString (hDevKey, TEXT ("DeviceType"),
            szType, dim(szType));

        // Print to the console.
        printf (TEXT ("Name: %s\t\tType: %s"), szName, szType);

        // Close the key opened by CeSvcOpen.
        CeSvcClose (hDevKey);
    }
    return i-1;         // Return the number of devices found.
}
```

Reading and writing values

The remainder of the CeUtil library functions concern reading and writing values in the registry. In fact, you can skip these functions and use the registry functions directly, but the *CeSvc*xxx functions are a bit simpler to use. These functions allow you to read and write three of the data types used in the registry, DWORD, string, and binary data. These just happen to be the only data types used in the values under the Windows CE Services keys. The functions are all listed here:

```
HRESULT CeSvcGetDword (HCESVC hSvc, LPCTSTR pszValName,
                       LPDWORD pdwVal);
HRESULT CeSvcSetDword (HCESVC hSvc, LPCTSTR pszValName,
                       DWORD dwVal);

HRESULT CeSvcGetString (HCESVC hSvc, LPCTSTR pszValName,
                        LPTSTR pszVal, DWORD cbVal);

HRESULT CeSvcSetString (HCESVC hSvc, LPCTSTR pszValName,
                        LPCTSTR pszVal);

HRESULT CeSvcGetBinary (HCESVC hSvc, LPCTSTR pszValName,
                        LPBYTE pszVal, LPDWORD pcbVal);

HRESULT CeSvcSetBinary (HCESVC hSvc, LPCTSTR pszValName,
                        LPBYTE pszVal, DWORD cbVal);
```

The parameters for these functions are fairly self-explanatory. The first parameter is the handle to an open key. The second parameter is the name of the value being read or written. The third parameter specifies the data or a pointer to where the data will be written. The fourth parameter on some of the functions specifies the size of the buffer for the data being read or, in the case of *CeSvcSetBinary*, the length of the data being written.

One final function in the CeUtil library is

```
HRESULT CeSvcDeleteVal (HCESVC hSvc, LPCTSTR pszValName);
```

This function, as you might expect, lets you delete a value from the registry. The parameters are the handle to an open key and the name of the value to be deleted.

The CeUtil library doesn't provide any function that you couldn't do yourself with a bit of work and the standard registry functions. However, using these functions frees you from having to depend on hard-coded registry key names that could change in the future. I strongly advise using these functions whenever possible when you're accessing registry entries that deal with Windows CE Services.

CONNECTION NOTIFICATION

Windows CE Services gives you two ways of notifying PC-based applications when a connection is made with a Windows CE device. The first method is to simply launch all the applications listed under a given registry key. When the connection is broken, all applications listed under another key are launched. This method has the advantage of simplicity at the cost of having the application not know why it was launched.

The second method of notification is a COM-interface method. This notification method involves two interfaces: *IDccMan*, provided by RAPI.DLL, and *IDccManSink,* which must be implemented by the application that wants to be notified. This method has the advantage of providing much more information to the application as to what is actually happening at the cost of having to implement a COM-style interface.

Registry Method

To have your PC application launched when a connection is made to a Windows CE device, simply add a value to the PC registry under the following key:

```
[HKEY_LOCAL_MACHINE]
\Software\Microsoft\Windows CE Services\AutoStartOnConnect
```

I'll show you shortly how to access this key using *CeSvcOpen* so that the precise name of the key can be abstracted. The name of the value under *AutoStartOnConnect* can be anything, but it must be something unique. The best way to ensure this is to include your company name and product name plus its version in the value name. The actual data for the value should be a string that contains the fully specified path for the application you want to launch. The string can only be the filename; appending a command line string causes an error when the program is launched. For example, to launch a myapp program that's loaded in the directory *c:\windowsce\tools\syncstuff*, the value and data might be

```
MyCorpThisApp  c:\windowsce\tools\syncstuff\myapp.exe
```

To have a command line passed to your application, you can have the entry in the registery point to a shortcut that will launch your application. The entry in the registry can't pass a command line, but shortcuts don't have that limitation.

You can have an application launched when the connection is broken between the PC and the Windows CE device by placing a value under the following key:

```
[HKEY_LOCAL_MACHINE]
\Software\Microsoft\Windows CE Services\AutoStartOnDisconnect
```

The format for the value name and the data is the same as the format used in the *AutoStartOnConnect* key.

A routine to set these values is simple to write. The example routine below uses the *CeSvcOpen* and *CeSvcSetString* functions to write the name of the module to the registry. Remember that since this routine runs on a PC, and therefore perhaps under Windows NT, you'll need administrator access for this routine to have write access to the registry.

```
//
// RegStartOnConnect - Have module started when connect occurs.
//
LPARAM RegStartOnConnect (HINSTANCE hInst) {
    TCHAR szName[MAX_PATH];
    HCESVC hSvc;
    HRESULT rc;

    // Get the name of the module.
    GetModuleFileName (hInst, szName, dim(szName));

    // Open the AutoStartOnConnect key.
    rc = CeSvcOpen (CESVC_ROOT_MACHINE, "AutoStartOnConnect",
        TRUE, &hSvc);
    if (rc == NOERROR) {
        // Write the module name into the registry.
        CeSvcSetString (hSvc, TEXT ("MyCompanyMyApp"), szName);
        CeSvcClose (hSvc);
    }
    return rc;
}
```

The routine above doesn't have to know the absolute location of the Windows CE Services keys in the registry, only that the AutoStart key is under CESVC_ROOT_MACHINE. You can modify this routine to have your application started when a connection is broken by substituting *AutoStartOnConnect* with *AutoStartOnDisconnect* in the call to *CeSvcOpen*.

COM Method

As I mentioned before, the COM method of connection notification is implemented using two COM interfaces—*IDccMan* and *IDccManSink*. The system implements *IDccMan*, while you are responsible for implementing *IDccManSink*. The *IDccMan* interface gives you a set of methods that allow you to control the link between the PC and the Windows CE device. Unfortunately, most of the methods in *IDccMan* aren't currently implemented. The *IDccManSink* interface is a series of methods that are called by the connection manager to notify you that a connection event has occurred. Implementing each of the methods in *IDccManSink* is trivial because you don't need to take any action to acknowledge the notification.

The process of connection notification is simple. You request an *IDccMan* interface. You call a method in *IDccMan* to pass a pointer to your *IDccManSink* interface. Windows CE Services calls the methods in *IDccManSink* to notify you of events as they occur. In this section, I'll talk about the unique methods in *IDccManSink* and *IDccMan*, but I'll skip over the *IUnknown* methods that are part of every COM interface. For a very brief introduction to COM, read the sidebar, "COM Isn't a Four-Letter Word" at the end of this chapter and the Appendix, "COM Basics."

The *IDccMan* interface

To gain access to the *IDccMan* interface, you need to call the COM library function *CoInitialize* to initialize the COM library. Then you make a call to *CoCreateInstance* to retrieve a pointer to the *IDccMan* interface. Once you have this interface pointer, you call the method *IDccMan::Advise* to notify the connection manager that you want to be notified about connection events. This method is prototyped as

```
HRESULT IDccMan::Advise (IDccManSink *pDccSink,
                         DWORD *pdwContext);
```

The first parameter is a pointer to an *IDccManSink* interface that you must have previously created. I'll talk about *IDccManSink* shortly. The second parameter is a pointer to a DWORD that receives a context value that you pass to another *IDccMan* method when you request that you no longer be advised of events.

You can display the communications configuration dialog of Windows CE Services by calling this method:

```
HRESULT IDccMan::ShowCommSettings (void);
```

There are no parameters. This method simply displays the communications dialog box. The user is responsible for making any changes to the configuration and for dismissing the dialog box.

When you no longer need connection notifications, you call the *Unadvise* method, prototyped as

```
HRESULT IDccMan::Unadvise (DWORD dwContext);
```

The only parameter is the context value that was returned by the *Advise* method. After you have called *Unadvise*, you no longer need to maintain the *IDccManSink* interface.

The *IDccManSink* interface

You are responsible for creating and maintaining the *IDccManSink* interface for as long as you want notifications from the connection manager. The interface methods are simple to implement—you simply provide a set of methods that are called by the connection manager when a set of events occurs. Following are the prototypes for the methods of *IDccManSink*:

```
HRESULT IDccManSink::OnLogListen (void);

HRESULT IDccManSink::OnLogAnswered (void);

HRESULT IDccManSink::OnLogIpAddr (DWORD dwIpAddr);

HRESULT IDccManSink::OnLogActive (void);

HRESULT IDccManSink::OnLogTerminated (void);

HRESULT IDccManSink::OnLogInactive (void);

HRESULT IDccManSink::OnLogDisconnection (void);

HRESULT IDccManSink::OnLogError (void);
```

While the documentation describes a step-by-step notification by the connection manager, calling each of the methods of *IDccManSink* as the events occur, I've found that only a few of the methods are actually called with any consistency.

When you call *CoCreateInstance* to get a pointer to the *IDccManSink* interface, the connection manager is loaded into memory. When you call *Advise*, the connection manager responds with a call to *OnLogListen*, indicating that the connection manager is listening for a connection. When a connection is established, the connection manager calls *OnLogIpAddr* to notify you of the IP address of the connected device. *OnLogIpAddr* is the only method in *IDccManSink* that has a parameter. This parameter is the IP address of the device being connected. This address is handy if you want to establish a socket connection to the device, bypassing the extensive support of the connection manager and RAPI. This IP address can change between different devices and even when connecting the same device if one connection is made using the serial link and a later connection is made across a LAN. The connection manager then calls *OnLogActive* to indicate that the connection between the PC and the device is up and fully operational.

When the connection between the PC and the Windows CE devices is dropped, the connection manager calls the *OnLogDisconnection* method. This disconnection notification can take up to a few seconds before it's sent after the connection has actually been dropped. The connection manager then calls the *OnLogListen* method to indicate that it is in the listen state, ready to initiate another connection.

Some of the other methods are called under Windows 98. Those methods simply refine the state of the connection even further. Since your application has to operate as well under Windows NT as it does under Windows 98, you'll need to be able to operate properly using only the notifications I've just described.

The CnctNote Example Program

The CnctNote program is a simple dialog box–based application that uses the COM-based method for monitoring the PC–to–Windows CE device connection state. The example doesn't act on the notifications—it simply displays them in a list box. The source code for CnctNote is shown in Figure 11-7.

CnctNote.rc

```
//======================================================================
// Resource file
//
// Written for the book Programming Windows CE
// Copyright (C) 1998 Douglas Boling
//======================================================================

#include "windows.h"
#include "CnctNote.h"                    // Program-specific stuff

//----------------------------------------------------------------------
// Icons and bitmaps
//
ID_ICON ICON   "CnctNote.ico"            // Program icon

//----------------------------------------------------------------------
CnctNote DIALOG discardable 10, 10, 220, 160
STYLE  WS_OVERLAPPED | WS_VISIBLE | WS_CAPTION | WS_SYSMENU |
       DS_CENTER | DS_MODALFRAME
CAPTION "CnctNote"
CLASS "CnctNote"
```

Figure 11-7. *CnctNote source code.* *(continued)*

Figure 11-7. *continued*

```
BEGIN
    LISTBOX                  IDC_RPTLIST,   2,  10, 216, 140,
                                                 WS_TABSTOP | WS_VSCROLL
END
```

CnctNote.h

```
//======================================================================
// Header file
//
// Written for the book Programming Windows CE
// Copyright (C) 1998 Douglas Boling
//======================================================================
// Returns number of elements
#define dim(x) (sizeof(x) / sizeof(x[0]))
//----------------------------------------------------------------------
// Generic defines and data types
//
struct decodeUINT {                              // Structure associates
    UINT Code;                                   // messages
                                                 // with a function.
    LRESULT (*Fxn)(HWND, UINT, WPARAM, LPARAM);
};
struct decodeCMD {                               // Structure associates
    UINT Code;                                   // menu IDs with a
    LRESULT (*Fxn)(HWND, WORD, HWND, WORD);      // function.
};

//----------------------------------------------------------------------
// Generic defines used by application

#define  ID_ICON             1
#define  IDC_RPTLIST         10                  // Control IDs

//----------------------------------------------------------------------
// Function prototypes
//
int InitApp (HINSTANCE);
HWND InitInstance (HINSTANCE, LPSTR, int);
int TermInstance (HINSTANCE, int);
void Add2List (HWND hWnd, LPTSTR lpszFormat, ...);

// Window procedures
LRESULT CALLBACK MainWndProc (HWND, UINT, WPARAM, LPARAM);
```

```
//**********************************************************************
// MyDccSink
//
class MyDccSink : public IDccManSink {
public:
    MyDccSink (HWND hWnd, IDccMan *pDccMan);
    ~MyDccSink ();

    // *** IUnknown methods ***
    STDMETHODIMP QueryInterface (THIS_ REFIID riid, LPVOID * ppvObj);
    // Note: No reference counting is actually maintained on this object.
    STDMETHODIMP_(ULONG) AddRef (THIS);
    STDMETHODIMP_(ULONG) Release (THIS);

    // These methods correspond to GW_LOG messages generated by the Win95
    // DccMan application. (On NT, the GW_LOG messages are simulated.)
    STDMETHODIMP OnLogIpAddr (THIS_ DWORD dwIpAddr);
    STDMETHODIMP OnLogTerminated (THIS);
    STDMETHODIMP OnLogActive (THIS);
    STDMETHODIMP OnLogInactive (THIS);
    STDMETHODIMP OnLogAnswered (THIS);
    STDMETHODIMP OnLogListen (THIS);
    STDMETHODIMP OnLogDisconnection (THIS);
    STDMETHODIMP OnLogError (THIS);

private:
    long m_lRef;
    HWND hWnd;
    IDccMan *m_pDccMan;
};
```

CnctNote.cpp

```
//======================================================================
// CnctNote - A simple application for Windows CE
//
// Written for the book Programming Windows CE
// Copyright (C) 1998 Douglas Boling
//======================================================================
#include <windows.h>                    // For all that Windows stuff
#include <stdio.h>
#include <initguid.h>
#include <dccole.h>
#include "CnctNote.h"                   // Program-specific stuff
```

(continued)

Figure 11-7. *continued*

```
//----------------------------------------------------------------------
// Global data
//
const TCHAR szAppName[] = TEXT ("CnctNote");
HINSTANCE hInst;                      // Program instance handle
BOOL fFirst = TRUE;

IDccMan *pDccMan;
MyDccSink *pMySink;                   // Notification interface
DWORD g_Context;                      // Context variable

//======================================================================
// Program entry point
//
int WINAPI WinMain (HINSTANCE hInstance, HINSTANCE hPrevInstance,
                    LPSTR lpCmdLine, int nCmdShow) {
    MSG msg;
    int rc = 0;
    HWND hwndMain;
    // Initialize application.
    rc = InitApp (hInstance);
    if (rc) return rc;

    // Initialize this instance.
    hwndMain = InitInstance (hInstance, lpCmdLine, nCmdShow);
    if (hwndMain == 0)
        return TermInstance (hInstance, 0x10);

    // Application message loop
    while (GetMessage (&msg, NULL, 0, 0)) {
        if ((hwndMain == 0) || !IsDialogMessage (hwndMain, &msg)) {
            TranslateMessage (&msg);
            DispatchMessage (&msg);
        }
    }
    // Instance cleanup
    return TermInstance (hInstance, msg.wParam);
}
//----------------------------------------------------------------------
// InitApp - Application initialization
//
int InitApp (HINSTANCE hInstance) {
    WNDCLASS wc;
```

```
    // Register application main window class.
    wc.style = 0;                               // Window style
    wc.lpfnWndProc = MainWndProc;               // Callback function
    wc.cbClsExtra = 0;                          // Extra class data
    wc.cbWndExtra = DLGWINDOWEXTRA;             // Extra window data
    wc.hInstance = hInstance;                   // Owner handle
    wc.hIcon = NULL,                            // Application icon
    wc.hCursor = NULL;                          // Default cursor
    wc.hbrBackground = (HBRUSH) (COLOR_WINDOW + 1);
    wc.lpszMenuName =  NULL;                    // Menu name
    wc.lpszClassName = szAppName;               // Window class name

    if (RegisterClass (&wc) == 0) return 1;
    return 0;
}
//----------------------------------------------------------------------
// InitInstance - Instance initialization
//
HWND InitInstance (HINSTANCE hInstance, LPSTR lpCmdLine, int nCmdShow){
    HWND hWnd;
    HRESULT hr;
    INT rc;
    // Save program instance handle in global variable.
    hInst = hInstance;

    // Initialize COM.
    hr = CoInitialize(NULL);
    if (FAILED(hr)) {
        MessageBox (NULL, "CoInitialize failed", szAppName, MB_OK);
        return 0;
    }
    // Create main window.
    hWnd = CreateDialog (hInst, szAppName, NULL, NULL);
    rc = GetLastError();

    // Return fail code if window not created.
    if (!IsWindow (hWnd)) return 0;

    // Standard show and update calls
    ShowWindow (hWnd, nCmdShow);
    UpdateWindow (hWnd);
    return hWnd;
}
```

(continued)

Figure 11-7. *continued*

```
//----------------------------------------------------------------------
// TermInstance - Program cleanup
//
int TermInstance (HINSTANCE hInstance, int nDefRC) {

    // Release COM.
    CoUninitialize();

    return nDefRC;
}
//======================================================================
// MainWndProc - Callback function for application window
//
LRESULT CALLBACK MainWndProc (HWND hWnd, UINT wMsg, WPARAM wParam,
                              LPARAM lParam) {

    switch (wMsg) {

    case WM_SIZE:
        if (fFirst) {
            HRESULT hr;
            IDccManSink *pdms;
            fFirst = FALSE;

            // Get a pointer to the IDccMan COM interface.
            hr = CoCreateInstance (CLSID_DccMan, NULL, CLSCTX_SERVER,
                                   IID_IDccMan, (LPVOID*)&pDccMan);
            if (FAILED(hr)) {
                Add2List (hWnd, "CoCreateInstance failed");
                break;
            }

            // Create new notification object.
            pMySink = new MyDccSink(hWnd, pDccMan);
            pMySink->QueryInterface (IID_IDccManSink, (void **)&pdms);
            // Ask to be advised of connect state changes.
            pDccMan->Advise (pdms, &g_Context);
        }
        break;
    case WM_COMMAND:

        switch (LOWORD (wParam)) {
        case IDOK:
        case IDCANCEL:
            SendMessage (hWnd, WM_CLOSE, 0, 0);
            break;
        }
```

```
        break;
    case WM_DESTROY:
        // Stop receiving notifications.
        pDccMan->Unadvise (g_Context);

        // Release the DccMan object.
        pDccMan->Release();

        PostQuitMessage (0);
        break;
    }
    return DefWindowProc (hWnd, wMsg, wParam, lParam);
}
//----------------------------------------------------------------------
// Add2List - Add string to the report list box.
//
void Add2List (HWND hWnd, LPTSTR lpszFormat, ...) {
    int nBuf, i;
    TCHAR szBuffer[512];

    va_list args;
    va_start(args, lpszFormat);

    nBuf = vsprintf(szBuffer, lpszFormat, args);

    i = SendDlgItemMessage (hWnd, IDC_RPTLIST, LB_ADDSTRING, 0,
                            (LPARAM)(LPCTSTR)szBuffer);
    if (i != LB_ERR)
        SendDlgItemMessage (hWnd, IDC_RPTLIST, LB_SETTOPINDEX, i,
                            (LPARAM)(LPCTSTR)szBuffer);
    va_end(args);
}
//**********************************************************************
// Constructor
MyDccSink::MyDccSink (HWND hwndMain, IDccMan *pDccMan) {

    m_pDccMan = pDccMan;
    hWnd = hwndMain;

    m_pDccMan->AddRef();
    return;
}
//----------------------------------------------------------------------
// Destructor
```

(continued)

Figure 11-7. *continued*

```
MyDccSink::~MyDccSink () {

    m_pDccMan->Release();
    return;
}
//----------------------------------------------------------------------
// AddRef - Increment object ref count.
STDMETHODIMP_(ULONG) MyDccSink::AddRef (THIS) {

    return (ULONG)InterlockedIncrement (&m_lRef);
}
//----------------------------------------------------------------------
// Release - Decrement object ref count.
STDMETHODIMP_(ULONG) MyDccSink::Release (THIS) {
    ULONG cnt;

    cnt = (ULONG)InterlockedDecrement (&m_lRef);
    if (cnt == 0) {
        delete this;
        return 0;
    }
    return cnt;
}
//----------------------------------------------------------------------
// QueryInterface - Return a pointer to interface.
STDMETHODIMP MyDccSink::QueryInterface (REFIID riid, LPVOID * ppvObj) {

    if (IID_IUnknown==riid || IID_IDccManSink==riid)
        *ppvObj = (IDccManSink*)this;
    else {
        *ppvObj = NULL;
        return E_NOINTERFACE;
    }
    AddRef();
    return NO_ERROR;
}
//----------------------------------------------------------------------
//
STDMETHODIMP MyDccSink::OnLogIpAddr (DWORD dwIpAddr) {
    Add2List (hWnd, TEXT ("OnLogIpAddr %08x"), dwIpAddr);
    return NO_ERROR;
}
//----------------------------------------------------------------------
//
```

```
STDMETHODIMP MyDccSink::OnLogTerminated () {
    Add2List (hWnd, TEXT ("OnLogTerminated "));
    return NO_ERROR;
}
//----------------------------------------------------------------------
//
STDMETHODIMP MyDccSink::OnLogActive () {
    Add2List (hWnd, TEXT ("OnLogActive "));
    return NO_ERROR;
}
//----------------------------------------------------------------------
//
STDMETHODIMP MyDccSink::OnLogInactive () {
    Add2List (hWnd, TEXT ("OnLogInactive "));
    return NO_ERROR;
}
//----------------------------------------------------------------------
//
STDMETHODIMP MyDccSink::OnLogAnswered () {
    Add2List (hWnd, TEXT ("OnLogAnswered"));
    return NO_ERROR;
}
//----------------------------------------------------------------------
//
STDMETHODIMP MyDccSink::OnLogListen () {
    Add2List (hWnd, TEXT ("OnLogListen "));
    return NO_ERROR;
}
//----------------------------------------------------------------------
//
STDMETHODIMP MyDccSink::OnLogDisconnection () {
    Add2List (hWnd, TEXT ("OnLogDisconnection "));
    return NO_ERROR;
}
//----------------------------------------------------------------------
//
STDMETHODIMP MyDccSink::OnLogError () {
    Add2List (hWnd, TEXT ("OnLogError "));
    return NO_ERROR;
}
```

The meat of CnctNote is in the WM_SIZE handler of the window procedure. Here, *CoCreateInstance* is called to get a pointer to the *IDccMan* interface. If this is successful, an object is created that implements an *IDccManSink* interface. The

Advise method is then called to register the *IDccManSink* object. The sole job of the methods in *IDccManSink* is to report when they're called by posting a message in the list box, which is the only control on the dialog box.

Connection Detection on the Windows CE Side

As you know, this chapter describes the PC-side applications that work with remote Windows CE devices. However, while reading the previous section, you probably wondered how a Windows CE application can know when a connection is made between the Windows CE device and a PC.

Windows CE supports a unique API known as the Notification API. While I'll describe this API fully in the next chapter, a quick mention of one function, *CeRunAppAtEvent*, which provides Windows CE applications the ability to be notified when a connection is made, wouldn't hurt. *CeRunAppAtEvent* registers an application with the system so that it can be launched when a specified event occurs in the system. Such events include when the system time is changed, when a system is restored from a backup, and yes, when a connection is made to a PC. This function is prototyped as

```
BOOL CeRunAppAtEvent (TCHAR *pwszAppName, LONG lWhichEvent);
```

The first parameter is the name of the application to be launched when the event occurs. The second parameter is a set of bit flags that indicate which events you want to monitor. A number of flags are related to various events in the system. For the moment, I'll mention two: APP_RUN_AT_RS232_DETECT and APP_RUN_AFTER_SYNC. These flags launch the specified program after a connection is detected and after the synchronization process has completed.

When the application is launched by the notification system, a predefined string is passed to the application on the command line. For an application launched due to an RS232 detection, the command line string is *AppRunAtRs232Detect*. For an application launched at the end of synchronization, the command line is *AppRunAfterSync*. For a complete description of this function and the other notification functions, refer to Chapter 12.

FILE FILTERS

Windows CE file filters are COM objects that exist on the PC. They're loaded and called by Windows CE Services. When a file is copied to or from the Windows CE device to the PC using Windows CE Services, it checks to see whether a file converter is registered for the file type being transferred. If so, the file filter is loaded and requested to convert the file. All this takes place on the PC side of the link. If a file is being moved from the Windows CE system to the PC—exported, in Windows CE–speak—it's copied in its original form to the PC, then converted by the file filter, and finally stored on the PC. Likewise, if a file is being imported to the Windows CE device, it's first converted and then copied to the Windows CE device.

Windows CE file filters are tied closely to the Mobile Devices folder. Only files moved to and from a Windows CE device by users dragging and dropping them in the Mobile Devices folder are converted. If a file is transferred to a Windows CE system by any other method, accessing a file through the Windows CE LAN redirector, for example, the file filter isn't loaded and file won't be converted. Likewise, if a file is downloaded from the Internet using Pocket Inbox, the file won't be converted.

Registering a File Filter

Windows CE Services knows about file filters by looking in the registry. File filters need to be registered in two places. First, file filters should be among the Windows CE Services entries for each registered device under HKEY_CURRENT_USER. Second, they should be registered under the Windows CE Services entries under HKEY_LOCAL_MACHINE so that each filter will be automatically registered for any new devices that link to the PC. The CeUtil functions are helpful when you're registering a file filter because they handle opening the proper subkeys in which you register the file filter.

In addition to registering the file filter itself, you must make a few other new entries in the registry. The COM server that implements the file filter must be registered under [HKEY_CLASSES_ROOT]\CLSID. This registration follows the standard format for a COM object with a few extensions I'll describe in a moment. In addition to registering the COM object, you must also register the file extensions for both the PC file type and the file type for the Windows CE version of the file.

To sum up, a file filter needs to make a number of changes in the registry to properly function. For example, the program that installed the Pocket Word converter, which changes DOC format files used by Microsoft Word to the Pocket Word format PWD used by Pocket Word, must first register the PWD file type under [HKEY_CLASSES_ROOT]. You do this with two entries: one to associate the file extension with a file type and another entry to associate the file type with its name and the default shell actions. For the Pocket Word files, the entries look like this:

```
[HKEY_CLASSES_ROOT]\.pwd                pwdfile
```

and

```
[HKEY_CLASSES_ROOT]\pwdfile            Pocket Word File
   DefaultIcon      c:\Program Files\Windows CE Services\minshell.dll,-204
   Shell
      Open          c:\Program Files\Microsoft Office\Office\WinWord.exe
```

The Windows CE file type must be registered on the PC even though this file type generally exists only on a Windows CE system.

The DOC file type, which is the PC-side file type of the Pocket Word file filter, is already registered on Windows-based PCs, but if you introduce a new file type for the PC side of your converter it, too, must be registered.

The COM object that implements the Pocket Word file filter is registered in an entry under the [HKEY_CLASSES_ROOT]\CLSID key. The key name is the CLSID for the COM server that provides the file filter. Underneath this key are entries for the object's icon and the location of the DLL that provides this class ID. For Pocket Word, the entry looks like this:

```
[HKEY_CLASSES_ROOT]\CLSID\{4D3E2CF2-9B22-11D0-82A3-00AA00C267C1}
      DefaultIcon       c:\Program Files\Windows CE Services\pwdcnv.dll,0
      InProcServer32    c:\Program Files\Windows CE Services\pwdcnv.dll
                        ThreadingModel    Apartment
      PegasusFilter
                        Description       Pocket Word 2.0 Document
                        Import
                        NewExtension      .pwd
```

The long series of numbers in the key name is the GUID for the PWD file filter. Each object will have a unique GUID that matches the GUID the object checks for when the *DllGetClassObject* call is made. The *DefaultIcon* and *InProcServer32* keys are standard for all COM object servers. The *PegasusFilter* key is unique to Windows CE file filters. This key contains the *Description* and *NewExtension* values that give you the extension and description of the resulting file type of the converter. The *Import* value indicates that this file filter will be converting files copied from the PC to the Windows CE device. If this filter converted Windows CE format files to PC format files it would have a value named Export under the *PegasusFilter* key.

Now that the file types and the filter DLL itself have been registered, all that remains is to register the filter with Windows CE Services so that it will be called when a file is copied to or from the Windows CE device. To register the filter so that it will be used on guest devices and all future devices, you add a key with the name of the destination file extension under the key [HKEY_LOCAL_MACHINE]\Software \Microsoft\Windows CE Services\Filters. Under this key, you add entries that associate the import and export action with the CLSID of the COM server that implements the filter.

The file extension that you register is the extension of the source file, whether it's being imported to the Windows CE device or exported to the PC. So a Word document file with the extension DOC wouldn't require any conversion when copied up to a PC, but would need to be converted to the pocket word (PWD) format when it's copied from the PC to the Windows CE. The entry that registers a filter to convert DOC files to PWD format looks like this:

```
[HKEY_LOCAL_MACHINE]\Software\Microsoft\Windows CE Services\Filters\.DOC
            DefaultExport      Binary Copy
            DefaultImport      {4D3E2CF2-9B22-11D0-82A3-00AA00C267C1}
        InstalledFilters
            {4D3E2CEC-9B22-11D0-82A3-00AA00C267C1}
            {4D3E2CED-9B22-11D0-82A3-00AA00C267C1}
            {4D3E2CF2-9B22-11D0-82A3-00AA00C267C1}
                 .
                 .
                 .
            {4D3E3068-9B22-11D0-82A3-00AA00C267C1}
```

This entry registers filters for all files with the DOC file extension. When the file is imported to the Windows CE device, the filter used is contained in the COM server with the CLSID of 4D3E2CF2-9B22-11D0-82A3-00AA00C267C1. When a DOC file is exported from the Windows CE device to the PC, no conversion is needed, so the placeholder *Binary Copy* is used in place of a CLSID. When Windows CE Services sees this, it simply copies the file without modification. If this entry isn't in the registry, Windows CE Services thinks no filter is registered for this file type and displays a warning to the user when the file is copied. In this case, we don't want to convert a DOC file when it's being exported from the Windows CE device, so the registry has a Binary Copy flag entry for this entry.

Under the *InstalledFilters* key, you place one or more CLSIDs for different filters. Pocket Word for example, has a number of filters to convert PWD files into Word 97 documents, Word 95 documents, Word Perfect documents, and such. All these selections are presented to the user in the File Conversion dialog box that can be displayed from the Mobile Devices window on the PC.

One limitation of the current registry setup for file filters is that the same CLSID can't be defined to perform both the import and export conversions on a file. This is because the destination file extension is taken from the registry entries under the CLSID key. You can, however, have one COM server that supports two CLSIDs that, in turn, create the appropriate filters for each CLSID.

In addition to registering the file filter generically, you need to register the filter for any devices that already have a partnership with the PC. Otherwise, these devices won't use your filter. To do this, you need to repeat the registration procedures just described in this section under the key [HKEY_CURRENT_USER]\Software\Microsoft\Windows CE Services\Partners\<<Device ID>>\filters.

You register the file filter for a specific device the same way you register the filter generically: by specifying the filter under its file extension.

In the key on the preceding page, the <<Device ID>> placeholder should be replaced with the device ID of each of the devices for which you want to register the filter. This is where the CeUtil functions come in handy. Using *CeSvcEnumDevices*, you can specify each device and then open the proper key using *CeSvcOpen*. So for the remainder of this section, I'll use the *CeSvc* functions provided by the CeUtil library to abstract the keys instead of talking about the proper registry keys in terms of their absolute key names.

To open the registry key where filters are located, you would use the *CeSvcOpen* function and pass the constant CESVC_FILTERS. In the subkey name parameter, you would pass the extension of the file filter, as in

```
hr = CeSvcOpen (CESVC_FILTERS, [[your file extension]],
                TRUE, &hSvc);
```

To carry on our example, the key for the Pocket Word converter would be opened this way:

```
hr = CeSvcOpen (CESVC_FILTERS, TEXT (".pwd"), TRUE, &hSvc);
```

Once the key is opened, you can use *CeSvcSetString* to write the specific entries in the registry.

In the routine below, a file filter is registered both generically and under each currently registered device. The routines below use the *CeSvc*xxx functions, although you could use standard registry functions if you feel the need.

```
//----------------------------------------------------------------------
// RegExtensionforDevice - Helper routine that registers the filter for
// one device
//
HRESULT RegExtensionforDevice (HCESVC hSvc, LPTSTR pszGUID,
                               LPTSTR pszExt, BOOL bImport) {
    TCHAR szTag[32];
    HCESVC hKey;
    HRESULT hr;

    if (bImport)
        lstrcpy (szTag, TEXT ("DefaultImport"));
    else
        lstrcpy (szTag, TEXT ("DefaultExport"));
    CeSvcSetString (hSvc, szTag, pszGUID);
    hr = CeSvcOpenEx (hSvc, TEXT ("InstalledFilters"), TRUE, &hKey);
    if (hr) return hr;
    CeSvcSetString (hKey, pszGUID, TEXT (""));

    return hr;
}
```

```
//----------------------------------------------------------------------
// RegFileExtension - This routine registers a file extension for all
// currently partnered devices as well as for guest devices.
//
HRESULT RegFileExtension (LPTSTR pszGUID, LPTSTR pszExt, BOOL bImport) {
    HRESULT hr;
    HCESVC hSvc, hDev, hDevFilterKey;
    DWORD dwPro, i = 0;
    TCHAR szKeyName[64];

    // Open generic filter key.
    hr = CeSvcOpen (CESVC_FILTERS, pszExt, TRUE, &hSvc);
    if (hr)
        return hr;
    // Call routine to fill in proper keys.
    hr = RegExtensionforDevice (hSvc, pszGUID, pszExt, bImport);
    CeSvcClose (hSvc);

    // Now register for each current partner.
    while (CeSvcEnumProfiles (&hSvc, i++, &dwPro) == 0) {

        // Open key for that partner.
        hr = CeSvcOpen (CESVC_DEVICEX, (LPTSTR)dwPro, FALSE, &hDev);
        if (hr) {
            CeSvcClose (hSvc);
            return hr;
        }
        // Open filter key underneath.
        lstrcpy (szKeyName, TEXT ("Filters\\"));
        lstrcat (szKeyName, pszExt);
        hr = CeSvcOpenEx (hDev, szKeyName, TRUE, &hDevFilterKey);

        // Close this key since we don't need it anymore.
        CeSvcClose (hDev);
        if (hr) {
            CeSvcClose (hSvc);
            return hr;
        }
        // Call routine to fill in proper keys.
        hr = RegExtensionforDevice (hDevFilterKey, pszGUID, pszExt,
                                    bImport);
        // Close filter\extension key.
        CeSvcClose (hDevFilterKey);
    }
    return hr;
}
```

To register a file filter with the routines, you would call *RegFileExtension*. This routine first calls *RegExtensionforDevice* to register the file filter for future partners under HKEY_LOCAL_MACHINE. Then the routine enumerates each currently registered partner and registers the filter for those devices. The GUID and file extension for *RegFileExtension* are passed as strings. An example call would be

```
RegFileExtension ("{2b06f7a1-088e-11d2-93f1-204c4f4f5020}",
                  ".tst", TRUE);
```

For the other parts of the registry initialization, registering file extensions and registering the class library, a simple REG file will do. A REG file is a text file that contains the keys and values to merge into the registry. Following is an example REG file that registers a class library for converting TST files into PTS files on the Windows CE device.

```
REGEDIT4

[HKEY_CLASSES_ROOT\CLSID\{2b06f7a1-088e-11d2-93f1-204c4f4f5020}]
@="CEFileFilter Example"
[HKEY_CLASSES_ROOT\CLSID\{2b06f7a1-088e-11d2-93f1-204c4f4f5020}\DefaultIcon]
@="TstFilt.dll,-100"
[HKEY_CLASSES_ROOT\CLSID\{2b06f7a1-088e-11d2-93f1-204c4f4f5020}\InProcServer32]
@="e:\\CEBOOK\\11. Connecting to the Desktop\\TstFilt\\Debug\\TstFilt.dll"
"ThreadingModel"="Apartment"
[HKEY_CLASSES_ROOT\CLSID\{2b06f7a1-088e-11d2-93f1-204c4f4f5020}\PegasusFilter]
"Import"=""
"Description"="TstFilt: Copy a .tst file with no conversion."
"NewExtension"="pts"

[HKEY_CLASSES_ROOT\.tst]
@="tstfile"
[HKEY_CLASSES_ROOT\tstfile]
@="TstFilt: Desktop TST File"
[HKEY_CLASSES_ROOT\tstfile\DefaultIcon]
@="e:\\CEBOOK\\11. Connecting to the Desktop\\TstFilt\\Debug\\TstFilt.dll,-100"
[HKEY_CLASSES_ROOT\ptsfile]
@="TstFilt: HPC TST File"
[HKEY_CLASSES_ROOT\ptsfile\DefaultIcon]
@="e:\\CEBOOK\\11. Connecting to the Desktop\\TstFilt\\Debug\\TstFilt.dll,-101"
```

Now that we've learned how to register a file filter, let's look into building one.

The File Filter Interfaces

Windows CE file filters are COM in-proc servers that export an *ICeFileFilter* interface. The filter can also optionally export an *ICeFileFilterOptions* interface. Mobile Devices indirectly calls these two interfaces using the OLE object manager when it needs to convert a file. When stripped of all the COM paraphernalia, implementing a file filter is nothing more that implementing three functions, two of which are quite trivial.

The *ICeFileFilter* interface has the following methods:

- *ICeFileFilter::NextConvertFile* Called to convert a file
- *ICeFileFilter::FilterOptions* Called to display a dialog box for filter options during setup
- *ICeFileFilter::FormatMessage* Called to convert an error code into a text message to be displayed to the user

ICeFileFilter::NextConvertFile

The primary method of a file filter is *NextConvertFile*. This method is called by the Mobile Devices program when a file needs to be converted from its PC format to its Windows CE format or the reverse. The method actually keeps being called until you tell it to stop. This allows a file filter to create multiple output files for every input file it converts.

The prototype for this method is

```
HRESULT ICeFileFilter::NextConvertFile (int nConversion,
                             CFF_CONVERTINFO *pci,
                             CFF_SOURCEFILE *psf,
                             CFF_DESTINATIONFILE *pdf,
                             volatile BOOL *pbCancel,
                             PR_ERROR *perr);
```

The first parameter, *nConversion*, is a count value that's incremented each time the method is called for a single file. This means that the first time *NextConvertFile* is called to convert the file FOO.BAR, *nConversion* is 0. After you return from *NextConvertFile*, Mobile Devices calls *NextConvertFile* again, specifying the same input file, FOO.BAR, and the *nConversion* parameter is set to 1. Most file filters simply return the error code ERROR_NO_MORE_ITEMS, which tells Mobile Devices that you've completed converting the file. On the other hand, you can continue to process the conversion of FOO.BAR in the second, third, and subsequent calls. Mobile Devices continues to call *NextConvertFile*, specifying the same input file until you return ERROR_NO_MORE_ITEMS.

The next parameter, *pci*, is a pointer to a CFF_CONVERTINFO structure, which give you general information about the conversion as well as providing a pointer to the *ICeFileFilterSite* interface. The structure looks like this:

```
typedef struct {
    BOOL bImport;
    HWND hwndParent;
    BOOL bYesToAll;
    ICeFileFilterSite *pffs;
} CFF_CONVERTINFO;
```

The first field, *bImport*, is set to TRUE if the file is being copied from the PC to the Windows CE device. The *hwndParent* parameter is the handle of a window that you can use as the parent window for any dialog boxes that need to be displayed. The *bYesToAll* field should be set to TRUE if you're copying more than one file. This flag indicates whether the Yes To All button is displayed in the overwrite files dialog box. Finally, the *pffs* field contains a pointer to an *ICeFileFilterSite* interface. This interface provides the functions used by the file filter to open and close the source and destination files.

ICeFileFilterSite has the following methods:

- *ICeFileFilterSite::OpenSourceFile* Opens the source file
- *ICeFileFilterSite::OpenDestinationFile* Opens the destination file
- *ICeFileFilterSite::CloseSourceFile* Closes the source file
- *ICeFileFilterSite::CloseDestinationFile* Closes the destination file
- *ICeFileFilterSite::ReportProgress* Updates the modeless dialog box that indicates the progress of the conversion
- *ICeFileFilterSite::ReportLoss* Causes a dialog box to be displayed that reports to the user that data was lost in the conversion

The *OpenSourceFile* and *OpenDestinationFile* methods of *ICeFileFilterSite* return pointers to *IStream* or *IStorage* interfaces that are used to read and write these files. The *IStream* interface is used if the file is opened as a standard flat file while the *IStorage* interface is returned if the file is opened as an OLE compound document.

The next parameter of *NextConvertFile*, *psf*, is a pointer to a CFF_SOURCEFILE structure that gives you information about the source file used in the conversion. The structure is defined as

```
typedef struct {
    TCHAR szFullpath[_MAX_PATH];
    TCHAR szPath[_MAX_PATH];
```

```
    TCHAR szFilename[_MAX_FNAME];
    TCHAR szExtension[_MAX_EXT];
    DWORD cbSize;
    FILETIME ftCreated;
    FILETIME ftModified;
} CFF_SOURCEFILE;
```

The *szFullPath* field contains the fully qualified filename of the source file. The next three fields contain the parsed components of the same name. The *cbSize* parameter contains the size of the source file, while the *ftCreated* and *ftModified* fields contain the time the file was created and last modified.

The *pdf* parameter points to a CFF_DESTINATIONFILE that defined the particulars of the recommended destination filename. The structure is defined as

```
typedef struct {
    TCHAR szFullpath[_MAX_PATH];
    TCHAR szPath[_MAX_PATH];
    TCHAR szFilename[_MAX_FNAME];
    TCHAR szExtension[_MAX_EXT];
} CFF_DESTINATIONFILE;
```

The structure has the same first four fields as the CFF_SOURCEFILE structure. The difference is that the name in the CFF_DESTINATIONFILE structure is a recommended name. You can override the name of the destination file in the *OpenDestinationFile* method of *ICeFileFilterSite.* To do this, use the suggested path of the destination file contained in *szPath* and append the name and extension with the suggested modifications. Pass this new name to the *pszFullPath* parameter in *OpenDestinationFile.* The file filter example at the end of the chapter uses this technique to rename the destination file.

The next parameter of *NextConvertFile* is *pbCancel*, a pointer to a BOOL. The *pbCancel* parameter points to a boolean that is changed to FALSE if the user pressed the Cancel button on the modeless dialog box that's reporting the progress of the conversion. The file filter must check this value periodically to see whether the user has canceled the conversion.

The last parameter, *perr*, points to an error value that's returned by the *NextConvertFile* method. If *NextConvertFile* returns the error code E_FAIL, the value pointed to by *perr* is used as the error code for the routine. This code is then passed back to the filter for interpretation when you call *FormatMessage*.

ICeFileFilter::FormatMessage

The *FormatMessage* method closely follows the syntax of the *FormatMessage* system call that formats messages using an error code and either the system message table or a string table from a module. For many uses, you can simply pass the call directly from *ICeFileFilter::FormatMessage* to the Win32 function *FormatMessage*.

ICeFileFilter::FormatMessage has the prototype

```
HRESULT ICeFileFilter::FormatMessage (DWORD dwFlags,
                             DWORD dwMessageId,
                             DWORD dwLanguageId, LPTSTR lpBuffer,
                             DWORD nSize, va_list *Arguments,
                             DWORD *pcb);
```

While the parameter list looks daunting, the best way to handle this method is to create a message resource in the filter and pass the call directly to Win32's *FormatMessage* with the addition of the flag FORMAT_MESSAGE_FROM_HMODULE to the *dwFlags* parameter. The only additional processing is to copy the number of bytes returned by Win32's *FormatMessage* and set the byte count in a variable pointed to by the parameter *pcb*. An example would be

```
//----------------------------------------------------------------------
// FormatMessage - Called to format error messages
//
STDMETHODIMP MyFileFilter::FormatMessage (DWORD dwFlags,
                            DWORD dwMessageId, DWORD dwLanguageId,
                            LPTSTR lpBuffer, DWORD dwSize,
                            va_list *args, DWORD *pcb) {
    DWORD cMsgLen;

    // Pass the error code on to the Win32 FormatMessage.  Force look
    // into message table of filter by ORing dwFlags with
    // FORMAT_MESSAGE_FROM_HMODULE.
    cMsgLen = ::FormatMessage (dwFlags | FORMAT_MESSAGE_FROM_HMODULE,
                               hInst, dwMessageId, dwLanguageId,
                               lpBuffer, dwSize, args);
    if (cMsgLen)
        *pcb = cMsgLen;
    else
        return E_FAIL;

    return NOERROR;
}
```

If you're going to use custom filter error messages, you should define them using a constant combined with the macro CF_DECLARE_ERROR. This macro ensures that the error value you choose won't conflict with the standard Win32 error constants. In addition to defining the constants, you associate a string with the constant by including a message table resource in your filter. This, combined with the FORMAT_MESSAGE_FROM_HMODULE flag when you're calling Win32's *FormatMessage*, causes your message text to be used for your error constants. If the error value returned isn't one you defined, *FormatMessage* then looks in the system message table for a matching error message.

ICeFileFilter::FilterOptions

The final method of *ICeFileFilter* is *FilterOptions*. This method is prototyped as

```
HRESULT IPegasusFileFilter::FilterOptions (HWND hwndParent);
```

The only parameter is a handle to a window that should be used as the parent window for the dialog box. Windows CE Services calls this method when the user requests that the Options dialog box be displayed. However, none of the current versions of Windows CE Services support this Options button—so while you need to support this method, you can't depend on the user being able to gain access to any dialog box displayed by this method.

The *ICeFileFilterOptions* Interface

Windows CE file filters can support one other interface, *ICeFileFilterOptions*. This interface has, aside from the *IUnknown* methods, only one method: *SetFilterOptions*. The *SetFilterOptions* method enables Windows CE Services to tell the file filter whether it can display a modal dialog box during the conversion process. This is necessary because some conversions might take place in the background, where such displays of dialog boxes wouldn't be appropriate.

SetFilterOptions is prototyped as

```
HRESULT SetFilterOptions (CFF_CONVERTOPTIONS* pco);
```

The only parameter is a pointer to a CFF_CONVERTOPTIONS structure, which is defined as

```
typedef struct {
    ULONG   cbSize;
    BOOL    bNoModalUI;
} CFF_CONVERTOPTIONS;
```

While it may seem that using a structure to pass one Boolean is overkill, the use of a structure with a *size* field at the start lets Microsoft think about extending this structure while remaining backward compatible with older file filters.

The DivFile Filter Example

The example shown on the next page is a Windows CE file filter that detects when the user is copying files larger than 100 KB to a Windows CE device and splits the file into separate files on that device. If the file is larger than 100 KB and the version of

Windows CE is earlier than 2.1, the DivFile filter splits the file into multiple parts so that it can be stored in the object store of the device. Although the actual limit for files in Windows CE 2.0 and earlier is 4 MB, the 100-KB limit gives you an opportunity to see the splitting in action without having to wait for a file larger than 4 MB to be copied across to a Windows CE device.

The filter defines two new file types, TST for a file on the PC and PTS for *pocket test*, a sample file type on a Windows CE device. For this example, the splitting function is performed only on TST files larger than 100 KB. The result is a series of files on the Windows CE device, each with a number appended to the original filename and a new file type of PTS. The PTS files can be copied back to the PC unaltered and then rejoined using a binary copy operation, as in

```
copy /b file_1.pts+file_2.pts+file_3.pts+file_4.pts original.tst
```

The first file in this example isn't a source or include file; it's a registry file that registers the file filter, DivFile.reg. Note that since I'm not using an install program that can enumerate the various Windows CE devices already partnered, this filter won't be used until a new device is partnered with the PC or a device is attached as a guest of Windows CE Services. Also, the Explorer doesn't recognize the new file types until the system is rebooted—or more precisely, until the desktop is restarted. DivFile.reg is shown in Figure 11-8.

```
REGEDIT4

[HKEY_CLASSES_ROOT\CLSID\{2b06f7a1-088e-11d2-93f1-204c4f4f5020}]
@="DivFile Sample"
[HKEY_CLASSES_ROOT\CLSID\{2b06f7a1-088e-11d2-93f1-
204c4f4f5020}\DefaultIcon]
@="copy.dll,-100"
[HKEY_CLASSES_ROOT\CLSID\{2b06f7a1-088e-11d2-93f1-
204c4f4f5020}\InProcServer32]
@="C:\\Programming Windows CE\\Chap11\\DivFile\\Debug\\DivFile.dll"
"ThreadingModel"="Apartment"
[HKEY_CLASSES_ROOT\CLSID\{2b06f7a1-088e-11d2-93f1-
204c4f4f5020}\PegasusFilter]
"Import"=""
"Description"="DivFile: Copy a .tst file with no conversion."
"NewExtension"="pts"

[HKEY_CLASSES_ROOT\.tst]
@="tstfile"
[HKEY_CLASSES_ROOT\tstfile]
@="DivFile: Desktop TST File"
```

Figure 11-8. *The DivFile.reg file filter.*

```
[HKEY_CLASSES_ROOT\tstfile\DefaultIcon]
@="C:\\ Programming Windows CE\\Chap11\\DivFile\\Debug\\DivFile.dll,-100"

[HKEY_CLASSES_ROOT\.pts]
@="ptsfile"
[HKEY_CLASSES_ROOT\ptsfile]
@="DivFile: HPC TST File"
[HKEY_CLASSES_ROOT\ptsfile\DefaultIcon]
@="C:\\ Programming Windows CE\\Chap11\\DivFile\\Debug\\DivFile.dll,-101"

[HKEY_LOCAL_MACHINE\SOFTWARE\Microsoft\Windows CE Services\Filters\.tst]
"DefaultImport"="{2b06f7a1-088e-11d2-93f1-204c4f4f5020}"
[HKEY_LOCAL_MACHINE\SOFTWARE\Microsoft\Windows CE Services\Filters\.tst\
    InstalledFilters]
"{2b06f7a1-088e-11d2-93f1-204c4f4f5020}"=""
```

The registry file shown here uses the path to the copy of the DivFile.dll on my machine; you'll need to modify the path for your machine. Also, the GUID I generated should be replaced with one you create using GUIDGEN.EXE. The lines in this registry file are grouped into four sections. The first section registers the COM server DLL, DivFile.DLL. The second and third groups of lines register the file types TST and PTS. Finally, the last group of lines registers the file filter in the generic section of Windows CE Services' entries in the registry. You could easily write an install program to automatically register the file filter with the currently partnered Windows CE devices, using the routines I presented earlier in the chapter.

The next file in the example is DivFile.def. The def file describes the exported functions from the DLL. I don't use the declspec macro used in the earlier examples here because of the predefined type definitions of the functions *DllGetClassObject* and *DllCanUnloadNow*. Figure 11-9 shows DivFile.def.

```
;
;Standard COM library DEF file
;
LIBRARY   DIVFILE.DLL

EXPORTS
   DllCanUnloadNow      @1 PRIVATE
   DllGetClassObject    @2 PRIVATE
```

Figure 11-9. *The DivFile.def program.*

Finally, we get to the source files for the example, DivFile.rc, DivFile.h, and DivFile.cpp shown in Figure 11-10 on the following page. The resource file declares two icon files that are used for the TST and PTS file types. The header file contains the class definitions for my derivations of the *ICeFileFilter* and *IClassFactory* objects. And last but not least, DivFile.cpp is filled mainly with code to support the requirements of a COM server.

DivFile.rc

```
//======================================================================
// Resource file
//
// Written for the book Programming Windows CE
// Copyright (C) 1998 Douglas Boling
//======================================================================

100 ICON "PCSide.ico"
101 ICON "CESide.ico"
```

DivFile.h

```
//======================================================================
// Header file
//
// Written for the book Programming Windows CE
// Copyright (C) 1998 Douglas Boling
//======================================================================

// Returns number of elements
#define dim(x) (sizeof(x) / sizeof(x[0]))

// **** Start of Generic COM declarations ****

//======================================================================
// MyClassFactory - Object declaration
//
class MyClassFactory : public IClassFactory {

private:
    long m_lRef;

public:
    MyClassFactory();
    ~MyClassFactory();

    // IUnknown methods
    STDMETHODIMP QueryInterface (THIS_ REFIID riid, LPVOID *ppv);
```

Figure 11-10. *DivFile source code files.*

```
    STDMETHODIMP_(ULONG) AddRef (THIS);
    STDMETHODIMP_(ULONG) Release (THIS);
    // IClassFactory methods
    STDMETHODIMP CreateInstance (LPUNKNOWN pUnkOuter, REFIID riid,
                                 LPVOID *ppv);
    STDMETHODIMP LockServer (BOOL fLock);
};

// **** End of Generic OLE declarations ****

//----------------------------------------------------------------------
// Defines used by the DLL
//
#define BUFFSIZE        4096

#define FILESIZELIMIT   (100*1024)
#define FILEBREAKSIZE   (100*1024)

//======================================================================
// MyFileFilter - Object declaration
//
class MyFileFilter : public ICeFileFilter {

private:
    long m_lRef;
    BOOL m_fBreakFile;
    ULONG m_ulTotalMoved;

public:
    MyFileFilter();
    ~MyFileFilter();

    // IUnknown methods
    STDMETHODIMP QueryInterface (THIS_ REFIID riid, LPVOID *ppvObj);
    STDMETHODIMP_(ULONG) AddRef (THIS);
    STDMETHODIMP_(ULONG) Release (THIS);

    // ICeFileFilter methods
    STDMETHODIMP NextConvertFile (THIS_ int nConversion,
                      PFF_CONVERTINFO *pci, PFF_SOURCEFILE *psf,
                      PFF_DESTINATIONFILE *pdf,
                      volatile BOOL *pbCancel, PF_ERROR *perr);
    STDMETHODIMP FilterOptions (THIS_ HWND hwndParent);
```

(continued)

Figure 11-10. *continued*

```
    STDMETHODIMP FormatMessage (THIS_ DWORD dwFlags, DWORD dwMessageId,
                                DWORD dwLanguageId, LPTSTR lpBuffer,
                                DWORD dwSize, va_list *args, DWORD *pcb);
};
```

DivFile.cpp

```
//======================================================================
// DivFile - A Windows CE file filter DLL
//
// Written for the book Programming Windows CE
// Copyright (C) 1998 Douglas Boling
//======================================================================
#include <windows.h>                    // For all that Windows stuff

#define INITGUID
#include <initguid.h>                   // GUID defines
#include <replfilt.h>                   // Required for file filters
#include <rapi.h>                       // Required for RAPI functions

#include "DivFile.h"

HINSTANCE hInst;                        // DLL instance handle
long g_DllCnt = 0;                      // Global DLL reference count

// Replace this GUID with your own!
// {2B06F7A1-088E-11d2-93F1-204C4F4F5020}
static const GUID CLSID_MyCopyFilter =
{0x2b06f7a1, 0x88e, 0x11d2, {0x93,0xf1,0x20,0x4c,0x4f,0x4f,0x50,0x20}};

//======================================================================
// DllMain - DLL initialization entry point
//
BOOL WINAPI DllMain (HINSTANCE hinstDLL, DWORD dwReason,
                     LPVOID lpvReserved) {
    hInst = hinstDLL;
    return TRUE;
}
//======================================================================
// DllGetClassObject - Exported function called to get pointer to
// Class factory object
//
```

```
STDAPI DllGetClassObject (REFCLSID rclsid, REFIID riid, LPVOID *ppv) {
    MyClassFactory *pcf;
    HRESULT hr;

    // See if caller wants us....
    if (IsEqualCLSID (rclsid, CLSID_MyCopyFilter)) {

        // Create class factory object.
        pcf = new MyClassFactory();
        if (pcf == NULL)
            return E_OUTOFMEMORY;

        // Call class factory's query interface method.
        hr = pcf->QueryInterface (riid, ppv);
        // This will cause an object delete unless interface found.
        pcf->Release();
        return hr;
    }
    return CLASS_E_CLASSNOTAVAILABLE;
}
//======================================================================
// DllCanUnloadNow - Exported function called when DLL can unload
//
STDAPI DllCanUnloadNow () {

    if (g_DllCnt)
        return S_FALSE;

    return S_OK;
}
//**********************************************************************
// MyClassFactory Object implementation
//----------------------------------------------------------------------
// Object constructor
MyClassFactory::MyClassFactory () {

    m_lRef = 1;     // Set ref count to 1 on create.
    g_DllCnt++;
    return;
}
//----------------------------------------------------------------------
// Object destructor
MyClassFactory::~MyClassFactory () {
    g_DllCnt--;
    return;
}
```

(continued)

Figure 11-10. *continued*

```
//----------------------------------------------------------------------
// QueryInterface - Called to see what interfaces this object supports
STDMETHODIMP MyClassFactory::QueryInterface (THIS_ REFIID riid,
                                             LPVOID *ppv) {

    // If caller wants our IUnknown or IClassFactory object,
    // return a pointer to the object.
    if (IsEqualIID (riid, IID_IUnknown) ||
        IsEqualIID (riid, IID_IClassFactory)){

        *ppv = (IClassFactory *)this;     // Return pointer to object.
        AddRef();                 // Inc ref to prevent delete on return.
        return NOERROR;
    }
    *ppv = NULL;
    return (E_NOINTERFACE);
}
//----------------------------------------------------------------------
// AddRef - Increment object ref count.
STDMETHODIMP_(ULONG) MyClassFactory::AddRef (THIS) {
    ULONG cnt;

    cnt = (ULONG)InterlockedIncrement (&m_lRef);
    return cnt;
}
//----------------------------------------------------------------------
// Release - Decrement object ref count.
STDMETHODIMP_(ULONG) MyClassFactory::Release (THIS) {
    ULONG cnt;

    cnt = (ULONG)InterlockedDecrement (&m_lRef);
    if (cnt == 0) {
        delete this;
        return 0;
    }
    return cnt;
}
//----------------------------------------------------------------------
// LockServer - Called to tell the DLL not to unload even if use cnt 0
STDMETHODIMP MyClassFactory::LockServer (BOOL fLock) {
    if (fLock)
        InterlockedIncrement (&g_DllCnt);
    else
        InterlockedDecrement (&g_DllCnt);

    return NOERROR;
}
```

```
//----------------------------------------------------------------------
// CreateInstance - Called to have class factory object create other
// objects
STDMETHODIMP MyClassFactory::CreateInstance (LPUNKNOWN pUnkOuter,
                                              REFIID riid,
                                             LPVOID *ppv) {
    MyFileFilter *pMyff;
    HRESULT hr;

    if (pUnkOuter)
        return (CLASS_E_NOAGGREGATION);

    if (IsEqualIID (riid, IID_IUnknown) ||
        IsEqualIID (riid, IID_ICeFileFilter)) {

        // Create file filter object.
        pMyff = new MyFileFilter();
        if (!pMyff)
            return E_OUTOFMEMORY;

        // See if object exports the proper interface.
        hr = pMyff->QueryInterface (riid, ppv);
        // This will cause an object delete unless interface found.
        pMyff->Release ();
        return hr;
    }
    return E_NOINTERFACE;
}
//*******************************************************************
// MyFileFilter Object implementation
//----------------------------------------------------------------------
// Object constructor
MyFileFilter::MyFileFilter () {

    m_lRef = 1;     // Set ref count to 1 on create.
    return;
}
//----------------------------------------------------------------------
// Object destructor
MyFileFilter::~MyFileFilter () {
    return;
}
//----------------------------------------------------------------------
// QueryInterface - Called to see what interfaces this object supports
```

(continued)

Figure 11-10. *continued*

```
STDMETHODIMP MyFileFilter::QueryInterface (THIS_ REFIID riid,
                                             LPVOID *ppv) {

    // If caller wants our IUnknown or IID_ICeFileFilter object,
    // return a pointer to the object.
    if (IsEqualIID (riid, IID_IUnknown) ||
        IsEqualIID (riid, IID_ICeFileFilter)){

        // Return pointer to object.
        *ppv = (ICeFileFilter *)this;
        AddRef();                   // Inc ref to prevent delete on return.
        return NOERROR;
    }
    *ppv = NULL;
    return (E_NOINTERFACE);
}
//----------------------------------------------------------------------
// AddRef - Increment object ref count.
STDMETHODIMP_(ULONG) MyFileFilter::AddRef (THIS) {
    ULONG cnt;

    cnt = (ULONG)InterlockedIncrement (&m_lRef);
    return cnt;
}
//----------------------------------------------------------------------
// Release - Decrement object ref count.
STDMETHODIMP_(ULONG) MyFileFilter::Release (THIS) {
    ULONG cnt;

    cnt = (ULONG)InterlockedDecrement (&m_lRef);
    if (cnt == 0)
        delete this;
    return cnt;
}
//----------------------------------------------------------------------
// NextConvertFile - Called to convert the next file
STDMETHODIMP MyFileFilter::NextConvertFile (int nConversion,
                            CFF_CONVERTINFO *pci, CFF_SOURCEFILE *psf,
                            CFF_DESTINATIONFILE *pdf,
                            volatile BOOL *pbCancel, CF_ERROR *perr) {
    IStream *pstreamSrc;
    IStream  *pstreamDest;
    ICeFileFilterSite *pffs;
    CEOSVERSIONINFO vi;
    DWORD cBytesRemaining, cBytesRead, cCopySize;
```

```
    LARGE_INTEGER largMov;
    TCHAR szNewName[MAX_PATH];
    PBYTE pBuff;
    HRESULT hr;
    int i;

    // If first call for file, see if too large to fit in object store.
    if (nConversion == 0) {
        m_fBreakFile = FALSE;
        m_ulTotalMoved = 0;
        // If import to CE and file > 4 MB, see if too big for
        // object store.
        if ((pci->bImport) && psf->cbSize > FILESIZELIMIT) {

            vi.dwOSVersionInfoSize = sizeof (vi);
            CeGetVersionEx (&vi);
            // If version < 2.1, ask user
            // if we should break file.
            i = (vi.dwMajorVersion << 8) | vi.dwMinorVersion;
            if (i < 0x20a) {
                i = MessageBox (pci->hwndParent,
                            TEXT ("The file being copied is too \
large for the object store, would you like to break it into separate \
files?"),
                            TEXT ("Size Filter"), MB_YESNO);
                if (i == IDYES)
                    m_fBreakFile = TRUE;
                else {
                    *perr = HRESULT_TO_PFERROR (hr,ERROR_ACCESS_DENIED);
                    return E_FAIL;
                }
            }
        }
    } else if (m_fBreakFile) {

        if ((UINT)(nConversion * FILEBREAKSIZE) > psf->cbSize)
            return HRESULT_FROM_WIN32(ERROR_NO_MORE_ITEMS);
    } else
        return HRESULT_FROM_WIN32(ERROR_NO_MORE_ITEMS);

    // Allocate buffer for transfer.
    pBuff = (PBYTE)LocalAlloc (LPTR, BUFFSIZE);
    if (!pBuff) {
        *perr = HRESULT_TO_PFERROR (hr, E_OUTOFMEMORY);
        return E_FAIL;
    }
```

(continued)

Figure 11-10. *continued*

```
    // Get pointer to FileFilterSite interface.
    pffs = pci->pffs;

    // Open source file.
    hr = pffs->OpenSourceFile (PF_OPENFLAT, (PVOID *)&pstreamSrc);

    if (!SUCCEEDED (hr)) {
        LocalFree (pBuff);
        *perr = HRESULT_TO_PFERROR (hr, ERROR_ACCESS_DENIED);
        return E_FAIL;
    }
    // Seek to part of file for this section.
    if (m_fBreakFile) {
        largMov.HighPart = 0;
        largMov.LowPart = nConversion * FILEBREAKSIZE;
        hr = pstreamSrc->Seek (largMov, STREAM_SEEK_SET, NULL);

        // Modify destination name to mark part.  New name becomes
        // old name with a number appended for each part.
        wsprintf (szNewName, TEXT ("%s%s_%d.%s"),
                  pdf->szPath, pdf->szFilename, nConversion,
                  pdf->szExtension);

        hr = pffs->OpenDestinationFile (PF_OPENFLAT, szNewName,
                                        (PVOID *)&pstreamDest);
        if (!SUCCEEDED (hr)) {
            LocalFree (pBuff);
            pffs->CloseSourceFile (pstreamSrc);
            *perr = HRESULT_TO_PFERROR (hr, ERROR_ACCESS_DENIED);
            return E_FAIL;
        }

    } else
        // Open destination file with default name.
        hr = pffs->OpenDestinationFile (PF_OPENFLAT, NULL,
                                        (PVOID *)&pstreamDest);
    if (!SUCCEEDED (hr)) {
        LocalFree (pBuff);
        pffs->CloseSourceFile (pstreamSrc);
        *perr = HRESULT_TO_PFERROR (hr, ERROR_ACCESS_DENIED);
        return E_FAIL;
    }

    // Copy data.
    cCopySize = min (psf->cbSize - m_ulTotalMoved, FILEBREAKSIZE);
```

```
    for (cBytesRemaining = cCopySize; cBytesRemaining > 0; ) {
        // Read the data.
        i = min (BUFFSIZE, cBytesRemaining);
        hr = pstreamSrc->Read (pBuff, i, &cBytesRead);
        if (cBytesRead == 0)
            break;

        // See if user canceled the transfer.
        if (*pbCancel) {
            hr = ERROR_CANCELLED;
            break;
        }

        // Write the data and update bytes remaining.
        hr = pstreamDest->Write (pBuff, cBytesRead, NULL);
        if (!SUCCEEDED (hr))
            break;

        // Update transfer totals.
        m_ulTotalMoved += cBytesRead;
        cBytesRemaining -= cBytesRead;

        // Tell the user how far we've gotten.
        pffs->ReportProgress (m_ulTotalMoved/psf->cbSize * 100);
    }
    // Close files and clean up.
    pffs->CloseSourceFile (pstreamSrc);
    pffs->CloseDestinationFile (TRUE, pstreamDest);
    LocalFree (pBuff);

    if (hr == ERROR_CANCELLED)
        return HRESULT_FROM_WIN32 (ERROR_CANCELLED);

    if (!SUCCEEDED (hr)) {
        *perr = hr;
        return E_FAIL;
    }
    return NOERROR;
}
//----------------------------------------------------------------------
// FilterOptions - Called to indicate the file filter options
STDMETHODIMP MyFileFilter::FilterOptions (HWND hwndParent) {
    MessageBox (hwndParent, TEXT ("Filter Options Box"), TEXT ("Title"),
                MB_OK);
    return NOERROR;
}
```

(continued)

Figure 11-10. *continued*

```
//----------------------------------------------------------------------
// FormatMessage - Called to format error messages
//
STDMETHODIMP MyFileFilter::FormatMessage (DWORD dwFlags,
                            DWORD dwMessageId, DWORD dwLanguageId,
                            LPTSTR lpBuffer, DWORD dwSize,
                            va_list *args, DWORD *pcb) {
    DWORD cMsgLen;

    // Pass the error code on to the Win32 FormatMessage.  Force look
    // into message table of filter by ORing dwFlags with
    // FORMAT_MESSAGE_FROM_HMODULE.
    cMsgLen = ::FormatMessage (dwFlags | FORMAT_MESSAGE_FROM_HMODULE,
                               hInst, dwMessageId, dwLanguageId,
                               lpBuffer, dwSize, args);
    if (cMsgLen)
        *pcb = cMsgLen;
    else
        return E_FAIL;

    return NOERROR;
}
```

The code that does the actual work of the file filter is contained in *NextConvertFile*. The routine uses the value in *nConversion* to see whether this is the first time it is being called to convert the file. If so, the routine checks the file size to see whether it's bigger than the arbitrary file size limit. If so, the user is asked if the file should be split into multiple files.

The routine creates individual destination files by specifying a new name for the destination file when the routine calls *OpenDestinationFile*. For files that are split, the routine generates each new filename by appending a number to the end of the original filename. Note that the routine takes care to preserve the suggested path for the destination file. This path specifies the temporary directory on the PC that Windows CE Services uses before copying the converted file down to the Windows CE device. At this point, the source file is copied to the new destination file up to the limit of the destination file size. The files are then closed, and *NextConvertFile* returns.

Windows CE Services calls *NextConvertFile* again, this time with *nConversion* incremented. The routine opens a new destination file and the old source file, then seeks to an offset in the source file that matches the last byte read in the previous call. The new data is then copied, and the routine again returns.

This process of calling *NextConvertFile* is continued until the routine determines that all the source file has been copied into the various destination files. At this point, the routine returns ERROR_NO_MORE_ITEMS, which ends the conversion process for the file.

Now I come to the end of my explanation of the PC-side Windows CE Services. In the next two chapters, I'll return to the Windows CE–side of things to look at the shell. The Windows CE shell varies widely across the different platforms. The Handheld PC shell looks on the surface like a standard Windows 95 shell, although the programming interface is much simpler. The Palm-size PC shell, on the other hand, is new and unique.

COM ISN'T A FOUR-LETTER WORD

At this point, I've written 705 pages in a modern Windows programming book, and I have yet to explicate COM. It's amazing in this day and age that we've actually programmed almost an entire Windows system without COM. That avoidance ends here because COM is used extensively on the PC side of the Windows CE data synchronization interfaces.

COM is the acronym for Component Object Model. In brief, COM is formally defined as *a binary standard for defining objects*. The classical definition of an object is *data surrounded by a collection of functions, usually called methods, which act on the data*. Sometimes people stretch this classical object definition when they talk about COM. It works out that the only internal data state that some COM objects have is a use count variable. That kind of COM object simply provides an interface that's used for some purpose or another. Plenty of COM objects do maintain some internal data but this condition isn't a requirement of a COM object.

Many people have written and argued about COM. Various programmers think of COM as the Second Coming, the ultimate programming concept, or even the key to World Peace. On the other hand, others think of COM as the devil incarnate, a complex unworkable mess, or most evil of all, a way to keep dozens of authors employed writing books trying to explain it. In my mind, COM is simply a tool. Many books have been written about COM, but only one, *Mr. Bunny's Guide to Active X*, captures the essence of COM. Check it out if you get the opportunity.

In the Appendix, "COM Basics," I touch ever so lightly on the subject of COM. I talk only about a few interfaces, and then only to the extremely shallow depth necessary to accomplish our task at hand, synchronizing data between a PC and a Windows CE device. This treatment doesn't do justice to COM nor is it meant to. I'm just trying to use a tool to accomplish a job.

Part IV

ADVANCED TOPICS

Chapter 12

Shell Programming —Part 1

One of the unique aspects of Windows CE is that different Windows CE platforms have different shells. The shell for the Handheld PC is significantly different from the shell for the Palm-size PC. Despite differences, the parts of the shell that are the same (and there are plenty of common shell components), share the underlying API.

The shells used by the H/PC and H/PC Pro derive from the Windows 95 and 98 shells. To the user, the look is almost pure Windows 95. That is, of course, by design. The folks at Microsoft figured that having the Windows CE shell resemble the Windows 95 shell would flatten the user's learning curve and enhance the acceptability of Windows CE devices.

The shell used by the Palm-size PC keeps some of the more basic aspects of the Windows 95 shell. Gone are the Explorer and the familiar desktop icons. In place of the Explorer is the Active Desktop, which displays data from applications directly on the desktop. But while the Explorer is gone, the taskbar, with its familiar Start button, remains. The interface for the taskbar, common to both desktops, is the same. Both systems also use special directories and the shell *namespace,* which I'll talk about shortly.

So although the Windows CE shell resembles the Windows 95 shell, it's not as flexible. Most of the powerful interfaces available under Windows 95, such as the ability to drag and drop objects between programs, are either only partially implemented or not implemented at all. The goal of the programmers of the Windows CE 2.0 shell seemed to be to implement as few of the native COM interfaces as possible while still retaining the ability to contain the Internet viewing capabilities of an embedded Internet Explorer in the shell. That said, the current Windows CE shell does use some COM interfaces. It's just that those interfaces aren't the ones available on the desktop.

This chapter covers the concept of the shell namespace and the shell's use of special directories. This chapter also explains how to work with the taskbar as well as how to create shortcuts. And although the Notification API and the console aren't strictly part of the shell, this chapter covers them, too. Windows CE provides a powerful notification interface that allows applications to schedule themselves to run at a certain time or when some system event occurs. The code that implements the notification API was moved from the shell to the base operating system in Windows CE 2.1. This allows the notification functions to be used in the embedded versions of Windows CE where only a minimal shell is provided. The Windows CE console, on the other hand, was introduced in Windows CE 2.1. Windows CE doesn't support the full character mode API found in Windows NT, but you can write fairly complete console applications.

For those of you who are working with the embedded version of Windows CE 2.1 and later, most of what's covered in this chapter (with the exception of the Notification API and console applications) won't help you. The embedded version of Windows CE 2.1 includes only a bare minimum shell that has neither a taskbar nor an Explorer, and doesn't include many of the DLLs that support the shell. This means that you'll have to employ third-party developers or write your own shell to perform any shell-like functions.

WORKING WITH THE SHELL

Because the H/PC and Palm-size PC shells are derived from the Windows 95 shell, I must cover some system definitions first introduced with Windows 95. In general, while the concepts remain the same, the implementation is completely different under the covers.

The Shell Namespace

From Windows 95 on, the Windows shell has used the concept of a shell namespace. The Windows CE shell also uses the namespace concept to track the objects in the shell. Simply put, the shell namespace is the entire collection of the operating system's objects, files, directories, printers, control panel applets, and so forth. The idea is that by addressing files the same way as control panel applets, the shell makes it easy to deal with the diverse collection of objects.

A *folder* is simply a collection of objects. A *directory* is a collection of files on a disk. A folder generalizes and extends the directory concept, in that a folder doesn't merely contain files, but can include other objects such as control panel objects, printers, or remote connection links. Each object in a folder is called an *item*. Items are identified by an *item ID*.

The item ID is a data structure that uniquely identifies the item in the folder. Since folders also have identifiers, an individual item can be uniquely defined by means of a list of item IDs that identify the item, its folder, and the parent folders of the folder. Think of this list of item identifiers as a completely specified pathname of a file. A system might have many files named *foobar*, but only one in a specific directory. This list of item IDs is appropriately called an *ID list*. A pointer to such a list is a *pointer to an ID list*, frequently abbreviated as *pidl*, which is generally and rather unfortunately pronounced *piddle*. Shell functions usually reference items in the shells by their *pidls*. There is, of course, a translation function that converts a *pidl* to a filename.

With the release of the Palm-size PC, the developers faced a problem. The *pidl* concept is powerful, but implementing and maintaining *pidls* didn't seem worth the trouble, given the limited need the Palm-size PC shell has for them. But because some of the shell functions use *pidls* to remain compatible with the H/PC, the Palm-size PC has to implement *pidls*. The solution is for the Palm-size PC shell to "fake" *pidl*s. The necessary APIs use a value typed as a *pidl* but the actual implementation is a constant, not a pointer to an item ID list. This strategy doesn't much affect you as you program the Palm-size PC, but you should be aware of it.

Special Folders

The Windows CE shell, like the shells for Windows 95 and Windows NT 4.0, has a set of folders that are treated differently from normal directories in the file system. An example of this is the recycle bin, which is simply a hidden directory to which the shell moves files and directories when the user deletes them. Another example is the Programs folder, which contains a set of shortcuts that are then displayed on the Start menu.

The list of special folders changes with each shell. The Windows 95, Windows 98, and Windows NT 4.0 shells have a different set of special folders from those of the Windows CE shells. The shells implemented on the Palm-size PC and H/PC each implement their own subset of special folders. Fortunately, the function to return the location of a specific special folder is the same on all these systems. That function, *ShSpecialFolderLocation*, is prototyped as

```
HRESULT SHGetSpecialFolderLocation (HWND hwndOwner, int nFolder,
                                    LPITEMIDLIST *ppidl);
```

The first parameter is a handle to a window that owns any dialog box the shell needs to display during the processing of this function. The second parameter is a constant that specifies the directory you're requesting. The two main shells for Windows CE support different subsets of the constants defined by Windows. Below are the lists of constants supported by the H/PC and the Palm-size PC.

On the Handheld PC

- *CSIDL_BITBUCKET* The location of the recycle bin.
- *CSIDL_DESKTOP* The folder that stores the objects that appear on the desktop. Note that the use of this constant is different than under Windows 95.
- *CSIDL_FONTS* The folder that contains the system fonts.
- *CSIDL_DRIVES* The root of the file system.
- *CSIDL_PROGRAMS* The folder that contains the items shown in the Programs submenu of the Start menu.
- *CSIDL_PERSONAL* The default folder in which to save documents.
- *CSIDL_FAVORITES* The folder that contains shortcuts to favorite items.
- *CSIDL_STARTUP* The folder that contains programs or shortcuts to programs that will be launched when the system is restarted.
- *CSIDL_RECENT* The folder that contains the list of recently used documents.

On the Palm-size PC

- *CSIDL_DRIVES* The root of the file system.
- *CSIDL_PROGRAMS* The folder that contains the items shown in the Programs submenu of the Start menu.
- *CSIDL_STARTUP* The folder that contains programs or shortcuts to programs that will be launched when the system is restarted.
- *CSIDL_FONTS* The folder that contains the system fonts.
- *CSIDL_FAVORITES* The folder that contains shortcuts to favorite items.
- *CSIDL_STARTMENU* The folder that contains the items shown in the Start menu.
- *CSIDL_PERSONAL* The default folder in which to save documents.

The final parameter in *SHGetSpecialFolderLocation*, *pidl*, is a pointer to an ITEMIDLIST pointer that receives a pointer to the folder's item ID list.

The *pidl* that is returned by *SHGetSpecialFolderLocation* can be translated to a standard file path using this function:

```
BOOL WINAPI SHGetPathFromIDList (LPCITEMIDLIST pidl,
                                 LPTSTR pszPath);
```

The two parameters for this function are a *pidl* and a pointer to a buffer that receives the path of the folder specified by the *pidl*. This buffer must be at least MAX_PATH characters in length.

If you needed only to call *SHGetSpecialFolderLocation* and follow that by calling *SHGetPathFromIDList* to get the path, life would be simple. Unfortunately, the process isn't that simple. On systems other than the Palm-size PC, the *pidl* that's returned by *SHGetSpecialFolderLocation* points to a buffer that has been allocated by the shell. You need to call the shell back to free this buffer after you're finished with the ID list. You free this buffer using an *IMalloc* interface provided by the shell.

The *IMalloc* interface contains methods that allow an application to allocate, free, and otherwise manipulate memory in the local heap of the *IMalloc* provider. In the case of the shell, a pointer to its *IMalloc* interface can be acquired with a call to *SHGetMalloc*. The function is prototyped as

```
HRESULT SHGetMalloc (LPMALLOC *ppMalloc);
```

Once you have a pointer to the interface, you can call the *Free* method to free any ID lists returned by *ShGetSpecialFolderLocation*. On systems other than the Palm-size PC, the process can be encapsulated in the following routine:

```
INT MyGetSpecialDirectory (HWND hWnd, INT nFolderID,
                           LPTSTR lpDir) {
    int rc;
    LPITEMIDLIST pidl;
    LPMALLOC lpMalloc = NULL;

    // Get the Shell Malloc interface to be able to free the pidls.
    rc = SHGetMalloc (&lpMalloc);
    if (rc != NOERROR)
        return rc;

    // Ask the shell for the specified folder's pidl.
    rc = SHGetSpecialFolderLocation (hWnd, nFolderID, &pidl);
    if (rc == NOERROR) {
        // Translate the pidl to a directory name.
        SHGetPathFromIDList (pidl, lpDir);
```

(continued)

```
        // Free the idlist.
        IMalloc_Free(lpMalloc,pidl);
    }

    // Free shell's IMalloc interface.
    IMalloc_Release(lpMalloc);
    return rc;
}
```

This routine calls *SHGetMalloc* to receive a pointer to the shell's *IMalloc* interface. You then make calls to *SHGetSpecialFolderLocation* and *SHGetPathFromIDList* to get the folder and translate it into a directory name. Next you call the *Free* method of *IMalloc* using a macro defined for C-compiled programs. The methods of most COM interfaces have macros defined for C-compiled programs if your application isn't written in C++. Finally you call the *Release* method of *IMalloc* to free the interface.

As I mentioned earlier, the Palm-size PC doesn't formally implement *pidls*. Instead, *SHGetSpecialFolderLocation* returns a constant, typed as a *pidl*, that can then be passed to *SHGetPathFromIDList* to get a directory name. Had the developers also implemented a dummy *IMalloc* interface for the shell, the process for getting the location of a special folder would be identical. Instead, the current version of the Palm-size PC shell doesn't implement an *IMalloc* interface. Although you could simply remove any references to the *IMalloc* interface, a better solution would be something like the following routine:

```
INT MyGetSpecialDirectory (HWND hWnd, INT nFolderID,
                           LPTSTR lpDir) {
    int rc;
    LPITEMIDLIST pidl;
    BOOL fUseIMalloc = TRUE;
    LPMALLOC lpMalloc = NULL;

    // Attempt to get the Shell Malloc interface.
    rc = SHGetMalloc (&lpMalloc);
    if (rc == E_NOTIMPL)
        fUseIMalloc = FALSE;
    else if (rc != NOERROR)
        return rc;

    rc = SHGetSpecialFolderLocation (hWnd, nFolderID, &pidl);
    if (rc == NOERROR) {
        // Translate the idlist to a directory name.
        SHGetPathFromIDList (pidl, lpDir);
        // Free the idlist.
        if (fUseIMalloc)
            IMalloc_Free(lpMalloc,pidl);
    }
```

```
    // Free shell's IMalloc interface.
    if (fUseIMalloc)
        IMalloc_Release(lpMalloc);
    return rc;
}
```

Shortcuts

Shortcuts are small files that, when opened, launch an application or open a document in another folder. The idea behind shortcuts is that you could have an application located in one directory but you might want to be able to launch it from other directories. Since the shell uses the contents of special directories to define what is in the Start menu and on the desktop, placing a shortcut in one of those special directories allows an application to appear in the Start menu or on the desktop.

While the concept of shortcuts was taken from Windows 95, the method of creating them was not. Instead of using a COM interface, as is done under Windows 95, you create a shortcut in Windows CE using the following function:

```
BOOL SHCreateShortcut (LPTSTR szShortcut, LPTSTR szTarget);
```

The first parameter specifies the name and location of the shortcut. This name should be a fully qualified filename with an extension of LNK. The second parameter is the fully qualified filename of the application you want to start or the file you want to open. The function returns TRUE if successful.

You can determine the contents of a shortcut by calling this function:

```
BOOL SHGetShortcutTarget (LPTSTR szShortcut, LPTSTR szTarget,
                          int cbMax);
```

The first parameter is the filename of the shortcut. The remaining two parameters are the buffer that receives the target filename of the shortcut and the size of that buffer.

Configuring the Start Menu

Shortcuts come into their own when you're customizing the Start menu. When the Start button is clicked, the taskbar looks in its special folder and creates a menu item for each item in the folder. Subfolders contained in the special folder become submenus on the Start menu.

The Start menu of the H/PC is limited in that you can't customize the Start menu itself. You can, however, modify the Programs submenu and the submenus it contains. To add an item to the Programs submenu of the H/PC Start menu, you place a shortcut in the folder returned after you called *SHGetSpecialFolderLocation* with the folder constant CSIDL_PROGRAMS. For example, look at the short code fragment on the next page; it lists the Calc program in the Programs submenu of the Start directory on an H/PC.

```
INT rc;
TCHAR szDir[MAX_PATH];

rc = MyGetSpecialDirectory (hWnd, CSIDL_PROGRAMS, szDir);
if (rc == NOERROR) {
    lstrcat (szDir, TEXT ("\\Calc.lnk"));
    SHCreateShortcut (szDir, TEXT ("\\windows\\calc.exe"));
}
```

This fragment uses the routine *MyGetSpecialDirectory*, which I listed earlier in the chapter, to return the folder used by the Programs submenu. Once that's found, all that is required is to append the necessary LNK extension to the name of the link and call *SHCreateShortcut* specifying the location of CALC.EXE.

The Start menu of the Palm-size PC is more flexible than the H/PC's because you can add items directly to the Start menu itself. To accomplish this, add shortcuts to the folder returned with *SHGetSpecialFolderLocation* and the constant CSIDL_STARTMENU. From that folder, you can use the standard *FindFirstFile* and *FileNextFile* functions to determine the structure of the Start menu.

Recent Documents List

A feature of the Start menu since it was introduced in Windows 95 is the Documents submenu. This menu lists the last 10 documents that were opened by applications in the system. This list is a convenient place in which users can reopen recently used files. The system doesn't keep track of the last-opened documents. Instead, an application must tell Windows that it has opened a document. Windows then prunes the least recently opened document on the menu and adds the new one.

Under Windows CE, the function that an application calls to add a document to the recently used list is

```
void SHAddToRecentDocs (UINT uFlags, LPCVOID pv);
```

The first parameter can be set to one of two flags, SHARD_PATH or SHARD_PIDL. If *uFlags* is set to SHARD_PATH, the second parameter points to the fully qualified path of the document file. If SHARD_PIDL is specified in *uFlags*, the second parameter points to a pointer to an ID list. If the second parameter is 0, all items in the recently used document menu are deleted.

THE TASKBAR

The taskbar interface under Windows CE is almost identical to the taskbar interface under Windows 95 and Windows NT 4.0. I've already talked about how you can configure the items in the Start menu. The taskbar also supports *annunciators*, those tiny icons on the far right of the taskbar. The taskbar icons are programmed by the identical methods used in Windows 95. The only limitation under the current Windows CE shell is that it doesn't support tool tips on the taskbar icons.

Programs can add, change, and delete taskbar icons using this function:

```
BOOL Shell_NotifyIcon (DWORD dwMessage, PNOTIFYICONDATA pnid);
```

The first parameter, *dwMessage*, indicates the task to accomplish by calling the function. This parameter can be one of the following three values:

- *NIM_ADD* Adds an annunciator to the taskbar
- *NIM_DELETE* Deletes an annunciator from the taskbar
- *NIM_MODIFY* Modifies an existing annunciator on the taskbar

The other parameter points to a NOTIFYICONDATA structure, which is defined as

```
typedef struct _NOTIFYICONDATA {
    DWORD cbSize;
    HWND hWnd;
    UINT uID;
    UINT uFlags;
    UINT uCallbackMessage;
    HICON hIcon;
    WCHAR szTip[64];
} NOTIFYICONDATA;
```

The first field, *cbSize*, must be filled with the size of the structure before a call is made to *Shell_NotifyIcon*. The *hWnd* field should be set to the window handle that owns the icon. This window receives messages notifying the window that the user has tapped, double-tapped, or moved her pen on the icon. The *uID* field identifies the icon being added, deleted, or modified. This practice allows an application to have more than one icon on the taskbar. The *uFlags* field should contain flags that identify which of the remaining fields in the structure contain valid data.

When you're adding an icon, the *uCallbackMessage* field should be set to a message identifier that can be used by the taskbar when notifying the window of user actions on the icon. This value is usually based on WM_USER so that the message value won't conflict with other messages the window receives. The taskbar looks at this field only if *uFlags* contains the NIF_MESSAGE flag.

The *hIcon* field should be loaded with the handle to the 16-by-16-pixel icon to be displayed on the taskbar. You should use *LoadImage* to load the icon because *LoadIcon* doesn't return a small format icon. The taskbar looks at this field only if the NIF_ICON flag is set in *uFlags*. Finally, the *szTip* field would contain the tooltip text for the icon on other Windows systems but is ignored by the current Windows CE shells.

Managing a taskbar icon involves handling the notification messages the taskbar sends and acting appropriately. The messages are sent with the message identifier you defined in the call to *Shell_NotifyIcon*. The *wParam* parameter of the message contains the ID value of the taskbar icon that the message references. The *lParam* parameter contains a code indicating the reason for the message. These values are actually the message codes for various mouse events. For example, if the user taps on your taskbar icon, the *lParam* value in the notification message will be WM_LBUTTONDOWN, followed by another message containing WM_LBUTTONUP.

The TBIcons Example Program

The TBIcons program demonstrates adding and deleting taskbar annunciator icons. Figure 12-1 shows the TBIcons window. The buttons at the bottom of the window allow you to add and delete icons from the taskbar. The list box that takes up most of the window displays the callback messages as the taskbar sends them. In the taskbar, you can see two icons that TBIcons has added. The list box contains a list of messages that have been sent by the taskbar back to the TBIcons window.

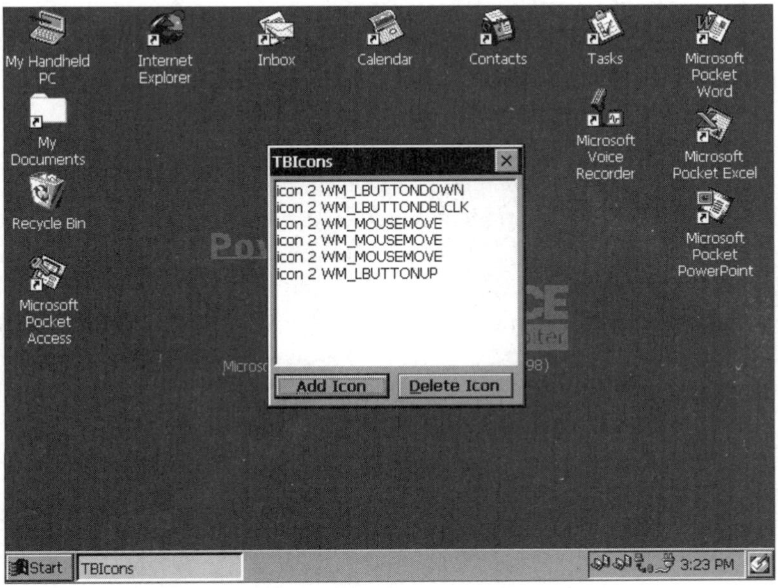

Figure 12-1. *The Windows CE desktop with a TBIcons window.*

The source code for TBIcons is shown in Figure 12-2. The program uses a dialog box as its main window. The routines that add and delete taskbar icons are *DoMainCommandAddIcon* and *DoMainCommandDelIcon*. Both these routines simply fill in a NOTIFYICONDATA structure and call *Shell_NotifyIcon*. The routine that handles the notification messages is *DoTaskBarNotifyMain*. This routine is called when the window receives the user-defined message MYMSG_TASKBARNOTIFY, which is defined in TBIcons.h as *WM_USER+100*. Remember that dialog boxes use some of the WM_USER message constants, so it's a good practice not to use the first hundred values above WM_USER to avoid any conflicts.

TBIcons.rc

```
//======================================================================
// Resource file
//
// Written for the book Programming Windows CE
// Copyright (C) 1998 Douglas Boling
//======================================================================
#include "windows.h"
#include "TBIcons.h"                            // Program-specific stuff

//----------------------------------------------------------------------
// Icons and bitmaps
//
ID_ICON ICON   "TBIcons.ico"                    // Program icon

//----------------------------------------------------------------------
TBIcons DIALOG discardable  25, 5, 120, 110
STYLE  WS_OVERLAPPED | WS_VISIBLE | WS_CAPTION | WS_SYSMENU |
       DS_CENTER | DS_MODALFRAME
CAPTION "TBIcons"
BEGIN
    LISTBOX                   IDD_OUTPUT,   2,   2, 116,  90,
                           WS_TABSTOP | WS_VSCROLL | LBS_NOINTEGRALHEIGHT
    PUSHBUTTON "&Add Icon", IDD_ADDICON,   2,  95,  55,  12, WS_TABSTOP
    PUSHBUTTON "&Delete Icon",
                            IDD_DELICON, 61,  95,  55,  12, WS_TABSTOP
END
```

TBIcons.h

```
//======================================================================
// Header file
//
// Written for the book Programming Windows CE
// Copyright (C) 1998 Douglas Boling
//======================================================================
```

Figure 12-2. *TBIcons source code.* *(continued)*

Figure 12-2. *continued*

```
// Returns number of elements
#define dim(x) (sizeof(x) / sizeof(x[0]))

//----------------------------------------------------------------------
// Generic defines and data types
//
struct decodeUINT {                             // Structure associates
    UINT Code;                                  // messages
                                                // with a function.
    BOOL (*Fxn)(HWND, UINT, WPARAM, LPARAM);
};
struct decodeCMD {                              // Structure associates
    UINT Code;                                  // menu IDs with a
    LRESULT (*Fxn)(HWND, WORD, HWND, WORD);     // function.
};
//----------------------------------------------------------------------
// Generic defines used by application

#define  ID_ICON              1

#define  IDD_ADDICON          10                // Control IDs
#define  IDD_DELICON          11
#define  IDD_OUTPUT           12

#define MYMSG_TASKBARNOTIFY  (WM_USER + 100)

//----------------------------------------------------------------------
// Function prototypes
//
void Add2List (HWND hWnd, LPTSTR lpszFormat, ...);

// Window procedures
BOOL CALLBACK MainDlgProc (HWND, UINT, WPARAM, LPARAM);

// Message handlers
BOOL DoInitDlgMain (HWND, UINT, WPARAM, LPARAM);
BOOL DoCommandMain (HWND, UINT, WPARAM, LPARAM);
BOOL DoTaskBarNotifyMain (HWND, UINT, WPARAM, LPARAM);

// Command functions
LPARAM DoMainCommandExit (HWND, WORD, HWND, WORD);
LPARAM DoMainCommandAddIcon (HWND, WORD, HWND, WORD);
LPARAM DoMainCommandDelIcon (HWND, WORD, HWND, WORD);
```

TBIcons.c

```
//======================================================================
// TBIcons - Taskbar icon demonstration for Windows CE
//
// Written for the book Programming Windows CE
// Copyright (C) 1998 Douglas Boling
//======================================================================
#include <windows.h>                 // For all that Windows stuff
#include "TBIcons.h"                 // Program-specific stuff

//----------------------------------------------------------------------
// Global data
//
const TCHAR szAppName[] = TEXT ("TBIcons");
HINSTANCE hInst;                     // Program instance handle
INT nIconID = 0;                     // ID values for taskbar icons
BOOL fPalm = FALSE;

// Message dispatch table for MainWindowProc
const struct decodeUINT MainMessages[] = {
    WM_INITDIALOG, DoInitDlgMain,
    WM_COMMAND, DoCommandMain,
    MYMSG_TASKBARNOTIFY, DoTaskBarNotifyMain,
};
// Command Message dispatch for MainWindowProc
const struct decodeCMD MainCommandItems[] = {
    IDOK, DoMainCommandExit,
    IDCANCEL, DoMainCommandExit,
    IDD_ADDICON, DoMainCommandAddIcon,
    IDD_DELICON, DoMainCommandDelIcon,
};
//======================================================================
// Program entry point
//
int WINAPI WinMain (HINSTANCE hInstance, HINSTANCE hPrevInstance,
                    LPWSTR lpCmdLine, int nCmdShow) {
    hInst = hInstance;

    // Display dialog box as main window.
    DialogBoxParam (hInstance, szAppName, NULL, MainDlgProc, 0);
    return 0;
}
```

(continued)

Figure 12-2. *continued*

```
//======================================================================
// Message handling procedures for main window
//----------------------------------------------------------------------
// MainDlgProc - Callback function for application window
//
BOOL CALLBACK MainDlgProc (HWND hWnd, UINT wMsg, WPARAM wParam,
                           LPARAM lParam) {
    INT i;
    //
    // Search message list to see if we need to handle this
    // message.  If in list, call procedure.
    //
    for (i = 0; i < dim(MainMessages); i++) {
        if (wMsg == MainMessages[i].Code)
            return (*MainMessages[i].Fxn)(hWnd, wMsg, wParam, lParam);
    }
    return FALSE;
}
//----------------------------------------------------------------------
// DoInitDlgMain - Process WM_INITDIALOG message for window.
//
BOOL DoInitDlgMain (HWND hWnd, UINT wMsg, WPARAM wParam, LPARAM lParam){
    TCHAR szType[256];

    SystemParametersInfo (SPI_GETPLATFORMTYPE, dim(szType), szType, 0);
    if (lstrcmp (szType, TEXT ("Palm PC")) == 0) {
        fPalm = TRUE;
        PostMessage (hWnd, WM_COMMAND,
                     MAKELONG (IDD_ADDICON, BN_CLICKED), 0);
    }
    return 0;
}
//----------------------------------------------------------------------
// DoCommandMain - Process WM_COMMAND message for window.
//
BOOL DoCommandMain (HWND hWnd, UINT wMsg, WPARAM wParam, LPARAM lParam){
    WORD idItem, wNotifyCode;
    HWND hwndCtl;
    INT  i;

    // Parse the parameters.
    idItem = (WORD) LOWORD (wParam);
    wNotifyCode = (WORD) HIWORD (wParam);
    hwndCtl = (HWND) lParam;
```

```
    // Call routine to handle control message.
    for (i = 0; i < dim(MainCommandItems); i++) {

        if (idItem == MainCommandItems[i].Code) {
            (*MainCommandItems[i].Fxn)(hWnd, idItem, hwndCtl,
                                       wNotifyCode);
            return TRUE;
        }
    }
    return FALSE;
}
//----------------------------------------------------------------------
// DoTaskBarNotifyMain - Process MYMSG_TASKBARNOTIFY message for window.
//
BOOL DoTaskBarNotifyMain (HWND hWnd, UINT wMsg, WPARAM wParam,
                          LPARAM lParam) {
    TCHAR szText[128];

    SetForegroundWindow (hWnd);
    wsprintf (szText,
              TEXT ("icon %d "), wParam);
    switch (lParam) {
    case WM_MOUSEMOVE:
        lstrcat (szText, TEXT ("WM_MOUSEMOVE"));
        break;
    case WM_LBUTTONDOWN:
        lstrcat (szText, TEXT ("WM_LBUTTONDOWN"));
        break;
    case WM_LBUTTONUP:
        lstrcat (szText, TEXT ("WM_LBUTTONUP"));
        break;
    case WM_LBUTTONDBLCLK:
        lstrcat (szText, TEXT ("WM_LBUTTONDBLCLK"));
        break;
    }
    Add2List (hWnd, szText);
    return 0;
}
//======================================================================
// Command handler routines
//----------------------------------------------------------------------
// DoMainCommandExit - Process Program Exit command.
//
```

(continued)

Figure 12-2. *continued*

```
LPARAM DoMainCommandExit (HWND hWnd, WORD idItem, HWND hwndCtl,
                          WORD wNotifyCode) {
    NOTIFYICONDATA nid;

    // Delete any remaining taskbar icons.
    memset (&nid, 0, sizeof nid);
    nid.cbSize = sizeof (NOTIFYICONDATA);
    nid.hWnd = hWnd;
    while (nIconID) {
        nid.uID = nIconID--;
        Shell_NotifyIcon (NIM_DELETE, &nid);
    }

    EndDialog (hWnd, 0);
    return 0;
}
//----------------------------------------------------------------------
// DoMainCommandAddIcon - Process Add Icon button.
//
LPARAM DoMainCommandAddIcon (HWND hWnd, WORD idItem, HWND hwndCtl,
                             WORD wNotifyCode) {
    NOTIFYICONDATA nid;

    nIconID++;
    nid.cbSize = sizeof (NOTIFYICONDATA);
    nid.hWnd = hWnd;
    nid.uID = nIconID;
    nid.uFlags = NIF_ICON | NIF_MESSAGE;   // NIF_TIP not supported
    nid.uCallbackMessage = MYMSG_TASKBARNOTIFY;
    nid.hIcon = LoadImage (hInst, MAKEINTRESOURCE (ID_ICON),
                           IMAGE_ICON, 16,16,0);
    nid.szTip[0] = '\0';

    Shell_NotifyIcon (NIM_ADD, &nid);
    return 0;
}
//----------------------------------------------------------------------
// DoMainCommandDelIcon - Process Del Icon button.
//
LPARAM DoMainCommandDelIcon (HWND hWnd, WORD idItem, HWND hwndCtl,
                             WORD wNotifyCode) {
    NOTIFYICONDATA nid;

    // Leave one icon on for Palm-size PC, so user can get back to the
    // window. Otherwise, don't delete an icon if none currently exists.
```

```
    if ((fPalm && (nIconID == 1)) || (nIconID == 0))
        return 0;

    memset (&nid, 0, sizeof nid);
    nid.cbSize = sizeof (NOTIFYICONDATA);
    nid.hWnd = hWnd;
    nid.uID = nIconID--;

    Shell_NotifyIcon (NIM_DELETE, &nid);
    return 0;
}
//----------------------------------------------------------------------
// Add2List - Add string to the report list box.
//
void Add2List (HWND hWnd, LPTSTR lpszFormat, ...) {
    int i, nBuf;
    TCHAR szBuffer[512];

    va_list args;
    va_start(args, lpszFormat);

    nBuf = _vstprintf(szBuffer, lpszFormat, args);
    i = SendDlgItemMessage (hWnd, IDD_OUTPUT, LB_ADDSTRING, 0,
                            (LPARAM)(LPCTSTR)szBuffer);
    if (i != LB_ERR)
        SendDlgItemMessage (hWnd, IDD_OUTPUT, LB_SETTOPINDEX, i,
                            (LPARAM)(LPCTSTR)szBuffer);
    va_end(args);
}
```

THE OUT OF MEMORY DIALOG BOX

Because Windows CE applications are almost always running in a limited memory environment, it seems likely that they'll need an Out Of Memory dialog box. The standard Windows CE shells give you just such a dialog box as a system service. Figure 12-3 on the following page shows this dialog box on a Casio E-10 Palm-size PC.

The advantage of using the system-provided Out Of Memory dialog box is that you don't have to create one yourself in what, by definition, is already a low-memory condition. The dialog box provided by the system is also correctly configured for the proper screen size and local language. To display an Out Of Memory dialog box, you call this function:

```
int SHShowOutOfMemory (HWND hwndOwner, UINT grfFlags);
```

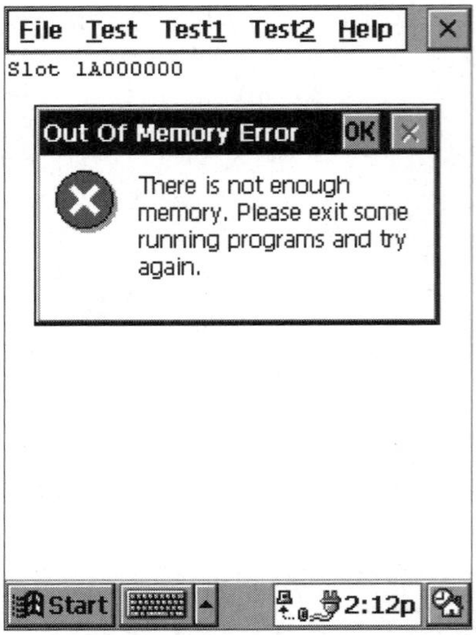

Figure 12-3. *The Windows CE Out Of Memory dialog box.*

The two parameters are the owner window and *grfFlags*, which must be set to 0. In the latest versions of Windows CE, this function has been moved from the shell so that it's available to embedded systems designed with the Embedded Toolkit (ETK).

NOTIFICATIONS

One area in which Windows CE exceeds the Windows 98 and Windows NT API is the notification interface. Windows CE applications can register to be launched at a predetermined time or when any of a set of system events occur. Applications can also register a *user notification*. In a user notification, the system notifies the user at a specific time without the application itself being launched at that time.

In Windows CE 2.1, the notification interface was moved from the shell to the base system. The advantage of this change is that this interface is now available for embedded systems.

User Notifications

A Windows CE application can schedule the user to be notified at a given time using the *CeSetUserNotification* function. When the time of the notification occurs, the system alerts the user by displaying a dialog box, playing a wave file, or flashing an external LED. Windows CE also displays the icon of the application that set the notification on the taskbar. The user has the option of acknowledging the notification either by clicking OK on the notification dialog box, pressing the Notify button on the system case, if one is present, or tapping on the application's taskbar annunciator icon, which launches the application that registered the notification. After a user notification has been set, you can modify it by making another call to *CeSetUserNotification*.

Setting a user notification

CeSetUserNotification is prototyped as

```
HANDLE CeSetUserNotification (HANDLE hNotification,
                         TCHAR *pwszAppName, SYSTEMTIME *lpTime,
                         PCE_USER_NOTIFICATION lpUserNotification);
```

The *hNotification* parameter is set to 0 to create a new notification. To modify a notification already registered, you should set *hNotification* to the handle of the user notification that you want to modify. The *pswzAppName* parameter specifies the name of the owning application. If this application has a small icon (16-by-16-pixel) image in its primary icon, that icon will be displayed as the taskbar annunciator icon when the notification occurs. The *lpTime* parameter is a pointer to a SYSTEMTIME structure that specifies the time for the notification to occur. The *lpUserNotification* parameter points to a CE_USER_NOTIFICATION structure that describes how the user is to be notified. This structure is defined as

```
typedef struct UserNotificationType {
    DWORD ActionFlags;
    TCHAR *pwszDialogTitle;
    TCHAR *pwszDialogText;
    TCHAR *pwszSound;
    DWORD nMaxSound;
    DWORD dwReserved;
} CE_USER_NOTIFICATION;
```

The *ActionFlags* field of this structure contains a set of flags that define how the user is notified. The flags can be any combination of the following:

- *PUN_LED* Flash the external LED.
- *PUN_VIBRATE* Vibrate the device.
- *PUN_DIALOG* Display a dialog box.
- *PUN_SOUND* Play a wave file.
- *PUN_REPEAT* Repeat the wave file for 10 to 15 seconds.

The fact that these flags are defined doesn't mean that all systems implement all these actions. Most Windows CE devices can't vibrate and a few don't even have an external LED. There isn't a defined method for determining the notification capabilities of a device, but as I'll presently show you, the system provides a dialog box that's customized by the OEM for the capabilities of each device.

The remainder of the fields in the structure depend on the flags set in the *ActionFlags* field. If the PUN_DIALOG flag is set, the *pwszDialogTitle* and *pwszDialogText* specify the title and text of the dialog that's displayed. The *pwszSound* field is loaded with the filename of a wave file to play if the PUN_SOUND flag is set. The *nMaxSound* field defines the size of the *pwsSound* field.

Configuring a user notification

To give you a consistent user interface for choosing the method of notification, Windows CE provides a dialog box to query the user how he wants to be notified. To display the user configuration dialog box, you call this function:

```
BOOL CeGetUserNotificationPreferences (HWND hWndParent,
                                   PCE_USER_NOTIFICATION lpNotification);
```

This function takes two parameters—the window handle of the parent window for the dialog box and a pointer to a CE_USER_NOTIFICATION structure. You can initialize the CE_USER_NOTIFICATION structure with default settings for the dialog before *CeGetUserNotificationPreferences* is called. When the function returns, this structure is filled with the changes the user made. *CeGetUserNotificationPreferences* returns TRUE if the user clicked on the OK button to accept the changes and FALSE if an error occurred or the user canceled the dialog box.

This function gives you a convenient method for configuring user notifications. The dialog box lets you have check boxes for playing a sound, displaying another dialog box, and flashing the LED. It also contains a combo box that lists the available wave files that the user can choose from if he wants sound. The dialog box doesn't have fields to allow the user to specify the text or title of the dialog box if one is to be displayed. That text must be provided by the application.

Acknowledging a user notification

A user notification can be cleared by the application before it times out by calling

```
BOOL CeClearUserNotification (HANDLE hNotification);
```

Once a user notification has occurred, it must be acknowledged by the user. The user can tap the OK button on the notification dialog box or press the notification button on the H/PC or Palm-size PC case. A third alternative is for the user to tap on the taskbar icon of the program that registered the notification. This icon is displayed by the system when the notification is made. In this case, Windows CE launches the application.

If the user taps on the taskbar icon, the notification isn't automatically acknowledged. Instead, an application should programmatically acknowledge the notification by calling this function:

```
BOOL CeHandleAppNotifications (TCHAR *pwszAppName);
```

The one parameter is the name of the application that was launched due to the taskbar icon tap. Calling this function removes the dialog box, stops the sound, turns off the flashing LED, and removes the application's annunciator icon from the taskbar.

When the system starts an application due to a notification, it passes a command line argument to indicate why the application was started. For a user notification, this argument is the command line string *AppRunToHandleNotification* followed by a space, and the handle of the notification. Instead of using the literal string for comparison, notify.h, which is the include file that contains the notification API, includes defines for the command line strings. The constant for *AppRunToHandleNotification* is APP_RUN_TO_HANDLE_NOTIFICATION.

As a general rule, an application started by a notification should first check to see whether another instance of the application is running. If so, the application should communicate to the first instance that the notification occurred and terminate. This saves memory because only one instance of the application is running. The code fragment below shows how this can be easily accomplished.

```
INT i;
HWND hWnd;
HANDLE hNotify;
TCHAR szText[128];

if (*lpCmdLine) {
    pPtr = lpCmdLine;
    // Parse the first word of the command line.
    for (i = 0; i < dim(szText) && *lpCmdLine > TEXT (' '); i++)
        szText[i] = *pPtr++;
    szText[i] = TEXT ('\0');

    // Check to see if app started due to notification.
    if (lstrcmp (szText, APP_RUN_TO_HANDLE_NOTIFICATION) == 0) {
        // Acknowledge the notification
        GetModuleFileName (hInst, szText, sizeof (szText));
        CeHandleAppNotifications (szText);

        // Get handle off the command line.
        hNotify = (HANDLE)_wtol (pPtr);

        // Look to see if another instance of the app is running.
        hWnd = FindWindow (NULL, szAppName);
        if (hWnd) {
            SendMessage (hWnd, MYMSG_TELLNOTIFY, 0, (LPARAM)hNotify);
            // This app should terminate here.
            // return 0;
        }
    }
}
```

This code first looks to see whether a command line parameter exists and if so, whether the first word is the keyword indicating that the application was launched by the system in response to a user notification. If so, the notification is acknowledged and the application looks for an instance of the application already running, using *FindWindow*. If found, the routine sends an application-defined message to the main window of the first instance and terminates. Otherwise, the application can take actions necessary to respond to the user's tap of the program icon on the taskbar.

Timer Event Notifications

To run an application at a given time without user intervention, use a *timer event notification*. The function that creates a timer event notification is this one:

```
BOOL CeRunAppAtTime (TCHAR *pwszAppName, SYSTEMTIME *lpTime);
```

The two parameters are the name of the application to launch and a pointer to a SYSTEMTIME structure to set the time to launch the application. Only one timer event notification can be set for any one application. Calling *CeRunAppAtTime* a second time with a new time simply replaces the first notification with the second. A timer notification can be cleared by passing a NULL pointer in the *lpTime* parameter.

When the timer notification is activated, the system powers on, if currently off, and launches the application with a command line parameter of APP_RUN_AT_TIME. As with the user notification, the application should check to see whether another instance of the application is running and pass the notification on if one is running. Also, an application should be careful about creating a window and taking control of the machine during a timer event. The user might object to having his game of solitaire interrupted by another application popping up because of a timer notification.

System Event Notifications

Other times, you might want an application to be automatically started. Windows CE supports a third type of notification, known as a *system event notification*. This notification starts an application when one of a set of system events occurs, such as after the system has completed synchronizing with its companion PC. To set a system event notification use this function:

```
BOOL CeRunAppAtEvent (TCHAR *pwszAppName, LONG lWhichEvent);
```

As with the timer event notification, the first parameter is the name of the application to launch. The second parameter is a constant indicating which event to monitor. The flags are the following:

- *NOTIFICATION_EVENT_NONE* Clear event notifications.

- *NOTIFICATION_EVENT_SYNC_END* Notify when sync complete.
- *NOTIFICATION_EVENT_DEVICE_CHANGE* Notify when a PCMCIA device is added or removed.
- *NOTIFICATION_EVENT_RS232_DETECTED* Notify when an RS232 connection is detected.
- *NOTIFICATION_EVENT_TIME_CHANGE* Notify when the system time is changed.
- *NOTIFICATION_EVENT_RESTORE_END* Notify when a device restore is complete.

For each of these events, the application is launched with a specific command line parameter indicating why the application was launched. In the case of a device change notification, the NOTIFICATION_EVENT_DEVICE_CHANGE command line string is followed by either */ADD* or */REMOVE* and the name of the device being added or removed. For example, if the user inserts a modem card, the command line for the notification would look like this:

```
AppRunDeviceChange /ADD COM3:
```

A number of additional system events are defined in notify.h but at this point, none are currently supported.

Once an application has registered for a system event notification, Windows CE will start the application again if the event that caused the notification is repeated. To stop being notified, an application must call *CeRunAppAtEvent* and pass its name and NOTIFICATION_EVENT_NONE in the *lWhichEvent* parameter.

The MyNotify Example Program

The following program, MyNotify, demonstrates each of the notification functions that allow you to set user notifications, system notifications, and timer notifications. The program presents a simple dialog box that has four buttons. The first two buttons allow you to configure and set a user notification. The second two buttons let you set system and timer notifications. The gap above the buttons is filled with the command line, if any, that was passed when the application started. It's also used to display a message when another instance of MyNotify is started due to a user notification. Figure 12-4 on the following page shows two MyNotify windows. The one in the foreground was launched because of a user notification, while the one in the background displays a message, indicating it was sent a message from the other instance of the application.

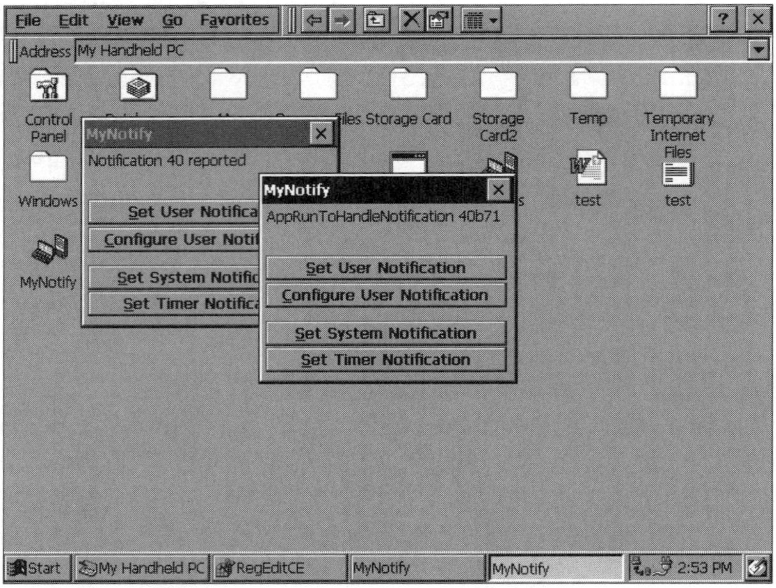

Figure 12-4. *The MyNotify window.*

The source code for MyNotify is shown in Figure 12-5. The notification code is confined to the button handler routines. The code is fairly simple: for each type of notification, the appropriate Windows CE function is called. When asked to configure a user notification, the application calls *CeGetUserNotificationPreferences*. The program gives you one additional dialog box with which to configure the system notifications.

MyNotify.rc

```
//======================================================================
// Resource file
//
// Written for the book Programming Windows CE
// Copyright (C) 1998 Douglas Boling
//======================================================================
#include "windows.h"
#include "MyNotify.h"                              // Program-specific stuff

//----------------------------------------------------------------------
// Icons and bitmaps
//
ID_ICON ICON   "MyNotify.ico"                      // Program icon
//----------------------------------------------------------------------
```

Figure 12-5. *The MyNotify program.*

```
// Main window dialog template
//
MyNotify DIALOG discardable  25, 5, 120,  85
STYLE  WS_OVERLAPPED | WS_VISIBLE | WS_CAPTION | WS_SYSMENU |
       DS_CENTER | DS_MODALFRAME
CAPTION "MyNotify"
BEGIN
    LTEXT "",                IDD_OUTPUT,   2,   2, 115,  21
    PUSHBUTTON "&Set User Notification",
                             IDD_ADDUSERNOT,   2,  25, 115,  12, WS_TABSTOP
    PUSHBUTTON "&Configure User Notification",
                             IDD_CFGUSERNOT,   2,  38, 115,  12, WS_TABSTOP

    PUSHBUTTON "&Set System Notification",
                             IDD_ADDSYSNOT,   2,  56, 115,  12, WS_TABSTOP
    PUSHBUTTON "&Set Timer Notification",
                             IDD_ADDTIMENOT,   2,  69, 115,  12, WS_TABSTOP
END
//----------------------------------------------------------------------
// Set system event notification dialog box dialog template.
//
SysNotifyConfig DIALOG DISCARDABLE  0, 0, 139, 87
STYLE DS_MODALFRAME | WS_POPUP | WS_CAPTION | WS_SYSMENU
EXSTYLE WS_EX_CAPTIONOKBTN
CAPTION "Notify On..."
BEGIN
    AUTOCHECKBOX "Sync End",          IDC_SYNC_END,   7,   7, 121,  10,
                                           WS_TABSTOP
    AUTOCHECKBOX "Device Change",IDC_DEVICE_CHANGE,   7,  22, 121,  10,
                                           WS_TABSTOP
    AUTOCHECKBOX "Serial Connection Detected",
                                IDC_SERIAL_DETECT,   7,  37, 121,  10,
                                           WS_TABSTOP
    AUTOCHECKBOX "System Time Change",
                                  IDC_TIME_CHANGE,   7,  52, 121,  10,
                                           WS_TABSTOP
    AUTOCHECKBOX "Restore End",     IDC_RESTORE_END,   7,  67, 121,  10,
                                           WS_TABSTOP
END
```

MyNotify.h

```
//======================================================================
// Header file
//
// Written for the book Programming Windows CE
```

(continued)

Figure 12-5. *continued*

```
// Copyright (C) 1998 Douglas Boling
//======================================================================
// Returns number of elements
#define dim(x) (sizeof(x) / sizeof(x[0]))

//----------------------------------------------------------------------
// Generic defines and data types
//
struct decodeUINT {                             // Structure associates
    UINT Code;                                  // messages
                                                // with a function.
    BOOL (*Fxn)(HWND, UINT, WPARAM, LPARAM);
};
struct decodeCMD {                              // Structure associates
    UINT Code;                                  // menu IDs with a
    LRESULT (*Fxn)(HWND, WORD, HWND, WORD);     // function.
};

// Define function not supported under Windows CE.
#ifndef IsDlgButtonChecked
#define IsDlgButtonChecked(a, b)\
                           SendDlgItemMessage (a, b, BM_GETCHECK, 0, 0)
#endif
//----------------------------------------------------------------------
// Generic defines used by application

#define  ID_ICON            1

#define  IDD_ADDUSERNOT     10                  // Control IDs
#define  IDD_CFGUSERNOT     11
#define  IDD_ADDSYSNOT      12
#define  IDD_ADDTIMENOT     13
#define  IDD_OUTPUT         14

#define  IDC_SYNC_END       20
#define  IDC_DEVICE_CHANGE  21
#define  IDC_SERIAL_DETECT  22
#define  IDC_TIME_CHANGE    23
#define  IDC_RESTORE_END    24

#define MYMSG_TELLNOTIFY    (WM_USER + 100)

//----------------------------------------------------------------------
// Function prototypes
//
void Add2List (HWND hWnd, LPTSTR lpszFormat, ...);
```

```
// Window procedures
BOOL CALLBACK MainDlgProc (HWND, UINT, WPARAM, LPARAM);
BOOL CALLBACK SetEventNotifyDlgProc (HWND, UINT, WPARAM, LPARAM);

// Message handlers
BOOL DoInitDialogMain (HWND, UINT, WPARAM, LPARAM);
BOOL DoCommandMain (HWND, UINT, WPARAM, LPARAM);
BOOL DoTellNotifyMain (HWND, UINT, WPARAM, LPARAM);

// Command functions
LPARAM DoMainCommandExit (HWND, WORD, HWND, WORD);
LPARAM DoMainCommandAddUserNotification (HWND, WORD, HWND, WORD);
LPARAM DoMainCommandConfigUserNotification (HWND, WORD, HWND, WORD);
LPARAM DoMainCommandAddSysNotification (HWND, WORD, HWND, WORD);
LPARAM DoMainCommandAddTimerNotification (HWND, WORD, HWND, WORD);
```

MyNotify.c

```
//======================================================================
// MyNotify - Demonstrates the Windows CE Notification API
//
// Written for the book Programming Windows CE
// Copyright (C) 1998 Douglas Boling
//======================================================================
#include <windows.h>                 // For all that Windows stuff
#include <notify.h>                  // For notification defines
#include "MyNotify.h"                // Program-specific stuff

//----------------------------------------------------------------------
// Global data
//
const TCHAR szAppName[] = TEXT ("MyNotify");
HINSTANCE hInst;                     // Program instance handle

CE_USER_NOTIFICATION g_ceun;         // User notification structure
TCHAR szDlgTitle[128] = TEXT ("Notification Demo");
TCHAR szDlgText[128] = TEXT ("Times Up!");
TCHAR szSound[MAX_PATH] = TEXT ("alarm1.wav");

// Message dispatch table for MainWindowProc
const struct decodeUINT MainMessages[] = {
    WM_INITDIALOG, DoInitDialogMain,
    WM_COMMAND, DoCommandMain,
    MYMSG_TELLNOTIFY, DoTellNotifyMain,
};
```

(continued)

Figure 12-5. *continued*

```
// Command Message dispatch for MainWindowProc
const struct decodeCMD MainCommandItems[] = {
    IDOK, DoMainCommandExit,
    IDCANCEL, DoMainCommandExit,
    IDD_ADDUSERNOT, DoMainCommandAddUserNotification,
    IDD_CFGUSERNOT, DoMainCommandConfigUserNotification,
    IDD_ADDSYSNOT, DoMainCommandAddSysNotification,
    IDD_ADDTIMENOT, DoMainCommandAddTimerNotification,
};
//======================================================================
// Program entry point
//
int WINAPI WinMain (HINSTANCE hInstance, HINSTANCE hPrevInstance,
                    LPWSTR lpCmdLine, int nCmdShow) {
    INT i;
    TCHAR szText[MAX_PATH];
    WCHAR *pPtr;
    HANDLE hNotify;
    HWND hWnd;

    hInst = hInstance;

    if (*lpCmdLine) {
        pPtr = lpCmdLine;
        // Parse the first word of the command line.
        for (i = 0; (i < dim(szText)-1) && (*pPtr > TEXT (' ')); i++)
            szText[i] = *pPtr++;
        szText[i] = TEXT ('\0');

        // Check to see if app started due to notification.
        if (lstrcmp (szText, APP_RUN_TO_HANDLE_NOTIFICATION) == 0) {
            // Ack the notification
            GetModuleFileName (hInst, szText, sizeof (szText));
            CeHandleAppNotifications (szText);

            // Get handle off the command line.
            hNotify = (HANDLE)_wtol (pPtr);

            // Look to see if another instance of the app is running.
            hWnd = FindWindow (NULL, szAppName);
            if (hWnd) {
                SendMessage (hWnd, MYMSG_TELLNOTIFY, 0,
                             (LPARAM)hNotify);
                // I should terminate this app here, but I don't so you
                // can see what happens.
                // return 0;
```

```
            }
        }
    }
    // Do a little initialization of CE_USER_NOTIFICATION.
    memset (&g_ceun, 0, sizeof (g_ceun));
    g_ceun.ActionFlags = PUN_DIALOG;
    g_ceun.pwszDialogTitle = szDlgTitle;
    g_ceun.pwszDialogText = szDlgText;
    g_ceun.pwszSound = szSound;
    g_ceun.nMaxSound = sizeof (szSound);

    // Display dialog box as main window.
    DialogBoxParam (hInstance, szAppName, NULL, MainDlgProc,
                    (LPARAM)lpCmdLine);
    return 0;

}
//======================================================================
// Message handling procedures for main window
//----------------------------------------------------------------------
// MainDlgProc - Callback function for application window
//
BOOL CALLBACK MainDlgProc (HWND hWnd, UINT wMsg, WPARAM wParam,
                           LPARAM lParam) {
    INT i;
    //
    // Search message list to see if we need to handle this
    // message.  If in list, call procedure.
    //
    for (i = 0; i < dim(MainMessages); i++) {
        if (wMsg == MainMessages[i].Code)
            return (*MainMessages[i].Fxn)(hWnd, wMsg, wParam, lParam);
    }
    return FALSE;
}
//----------------------------------------------------------------------
// DoInitDialogMain - Process WM_INITDIALOG message for window.
//
BOOL DoInitDialogMain (HWND hWnd, UINT wMsg, WPARAM wParam,
                       LPARAM lParam) {

    if (*(LPTSTR)lParam)
        Add2List (hWnd, (LPTSTR)lParam);
    return FALSE;
}
//----------------------------------------------------------------------
```

(continued)

Figure 12-5. *continued*

```
// DoCommandMain - Process WM_COMMAND message for window.
//
BOOL DoCommandMain (HWND hWnd, UINT wMsg, WPARAM wParam, LPARAM lParam){
    WORD idItem, wNotifyCode;
    HWND hwndCtl;
    INT  i;

    // Parse the parameters.
    idItem = (WORD) LOWORD (wParam);
    wNotifyCode = (WORD) HIWORD (wParam);
    hwndCtl = (HWND) lParam;

    // Call routine to handle control message.
    for (i = 0; i < dim(MainCommandItems); i++) {
        if (idItem == MainCommandItems[i].Code) {
            (*MainCommandItems[i].Fxn)(hWnd, idItem, hwndCtl,
                                       wNotifyCode);
            return TRUE;
        }
    }
    return FALSE;
}
//----------------------------------------------------------------------
// DoTellNotifyMain - Process MYMSG_TELLNOTIFY message for window.
//
BOOL DoTellNotifyMain (HWND hWnd, UINT wMsg, WPARAM wParam,
                       LPARAM lParam) {
    Add2List (hWnd, TEXT ("Notification %d reported"), lParam);
    return 0;
}
//======================================================================
// Command handler routines
//----------------------------------------------------------------------
// DoMainCommandExit - Process Program Exit command.
//
LPARAM DoMainCommandExit (HWND hWnd, WORD idItem, HWND hwndCtl,
                          WORD wNotifyCode) {
    EndDialog (hWnd, 0);
    return 0;
}
//----------------------------------------------------------------------
// DoMainCommandAddUserNotification - Process Add User Notify button.
//
```

```
LPARAM DoMainCommandAddUserNotification (HWND hWnd, WORD idItem,
                                         HWND hwndCtl, WORD wNotifyCode) {
    SYSTEMTIME st;
    TCHAR szExeName[MAX_PATH], szText[128];
    HANDLE hNotify;

    // Initialize time structure with local time.
    GetLocalTime (&st);
    // Do a trival amount of error checking.
    if (st.wMinute == 59) {
        st.wHour++;
        st.wMinute = 0;
    } else
        st.wMinute++;

    GetModuleFileName (hInst, szExeName, sizeof (szExeName));
    // Set the notification.
    hNotify = CeSetUserNotification (0, szExeName, &st, &g_ceun);
    if (hNotify) {
        wsprintf (szText, TEXT ("User notification set for %d:%02d"),
                  st.wHour, st.wMinute);
        MessageBox (hWnd, szText, szAppName, MB_OK);
    }
    return 0;
}
//----------------------------------------------------------------------
// DoMainCommandConfigUserNotification - Process Config user
// notification button.
//
LPARAM DoMainCommandConfigUserNotification (HWND hWnd, WORD idItem,
                                         HWND hwndCtl, WORD wNotifyCode) {
    CeGetUserNotificationPreferences (hWnd, &g_ceun);
    return 0;
}
//----------------------------------------------------------------------
//  DoMainCommandAddSysNotification - Process Add Sys notify button.
//
LPARAM DoMainCommandAddSysNotification (HWND hWnd, WORD idItem,
                                        HWND hwndCtl,  WORD wNotifyCode) {

    DialogBox (hInst, TEXT ("SysNotifyConfig"), hWnd,
               SetEventNotifyDlgProc);
    return 0;
}
//----------------------------------------------------------------------
```

(continued)

Figure 12-5. *continued*

```
// DoMainCommandAddTimerNotification - Process add timer notify button.
//
LPARAM DoMainCommandAddTimerNotification (HWND hWnd, WORD idItem,
                                          HWND hwndCtl,  WORD wNotifyCode) {
    SYSTEMTIME st;
    TCHAR szExeName[MAX_PATH], szText[128];

    // Initialize time structure with local time.
    GetLocalTime (&st);
    // Do a trivial amount of error checking.
    if (st.wMinute == 59) {
        st.wHour++;
        st.wMinute = 0;
    } else
        st.wMinute++;

    GetModuleFileName (hInst, szExeName, sizeof (szExeName));
    // Set the notification.
    if (CeRunAppAtTime (szExeName, &st)) {
        wsprintf (szText, TEXT ("Timer notification set for %d:%d"),
                  st.wHour, st.wMinute);
        MessageBox (hWnd, szText, szAppName, MB_OK);
    }
    return 0;
}
//----------------------------------------------------------------------
// Add2List - Add string to the report list box.
//
void Add2List (HWND hWnd, LPTSTR lpszFormat, ...) {
    int i, nBuf;
    TCHAR szBuffer[512];

    va_list args;
    va_start(args, lpszFormat);

    nBuf = _vstprintf(szBuffer, lpszFormat, args);
    i = SendDlgItemMessage (hWnd, IDD_OUTPUT, WM_SETTEXT, 0,
                            (LPARAM)(LPCTSTR)szBuffer);
    va_end(args);
}
//======================================================================
// SetEventNotifyDlgProc - Callback function for Event dialog box
//
```

```
BOOL CALLBACK SetEventNotifyDlgProc (HWND hWnd, UINT wMsg,
                                     WPARAM wParam,
                                     LPARAM lParam) {
    LONG lEvent;
    TCHAR szExeName[MAX_PATH];

    switch (wMsg) {
    case WM_COMMAND:
        {
            WORD idItem = LOWORD (wParam);
            switch (idItem) {
            case IDOK:
                lEvent = 0;

                // IsDlgButtonChecked isn't defined in Win CE, so
                // a macro has been defined.
                if (IsDlgButtonChecked (hWnd, IDC_SYNC_END) == 1)
                    lEvent |= NOTIFICATION_EVENT_SYNC_END;

                if (IsDlgButtonChecked (hWnd, IDC_SERIAL_DETECT) == 1)
                    lEvent |= NOTIFICATION_EVENT_RS232_DETECTED;

                if (IsDlgButtonChecked (hWnd, IDC_DEVICE_CHANGE) == 1)
                    lEvent |= NOTIFICATION_EVENT_DEVICE_CHANGE;

                if (IsDlgButtonChecked (hWnd, IDC_TIME_CHANGE) == 1)
                    lEvent |= NOTIFICATION_EVENT_TIME_CHANGE;

                if (IsDlgButtonChecked (hWnd, IDC_RESTORE_END) == 1)
                    lEvent |= NOTIFICATION_EVENT_RESTORE_END;

                // Set the notification.
                GetModuleFileName (hInst, szExeName,
                   sizeof (szExeName));
                CeRunAppAtEvent (szExeName, lEvent);

                EndDialog (hWnd, 1);
                return TRUE;

            case IDCANCEL:
                EndDialog (hWnd, 0);
                return TRUE;
            }
        }
        break;
    }
    return FALSE;
}
```

When MyNotify is started, it examines the command line to determine whether it was started by a user notification. If so, the program attempts to find another instance of the application already running. If the program finds one, a message is sent to the first instance, informing it of the user notification. Because this is an example program, the second instance doesn't terminate itself as it would were it a commercial application.

CONSOLE APPLICATIONS

A console driver was added to Windows CE in version 2.1. Windows CE doesn't support the character mode API supported by Windows NT. Instead, a Windows CE console application just uses the standard C library I/O functions, such as *printf* and *getc,* to read and write characters from the command line. Another major difference between command line applications on Windows CE and on other versions of Windows is that they use the standard *WinMain* entry point instead of the standard C entry point of *main*.

Below is a Windows CE console application that runs under Windows CE 2.1. Aside from the difference of the entry point, a Windows CE console application looks like any other standard C command line application.

```
//
// HelloCon - A simple console application
//
#include <windows.h>                   // For all that Windows stuff

// Program entry point
int WINAPI WinMain (HINSTANCE hInstance, HINSTANCE hPrevInstance,
                    LPWSTR lpCmdLine, int nCmdShow) {

    // You don't use Unicode for the stdio functions...
    printf ("Hello World\n");

    //...but you can with the 'w' versions.
    wprintf (TEXT ("Hello World\n"));
    return 0;
}
```

Windows CE console applications have access to the Win32 API. In fact, a console application can create windows, enter a message loop, and operate as if it were a standard Windows application. The difference is that the first time you call one of the *stdio* C library functions, such as *printf*, a console window is created and the result of that function will be seen in that window.

You implement consoles under Windows CE using a console driver with the appropriate device name of CON. Up to 10 console windows can be opened at any one time. The limit comes from the CON0 through CON9 naming convention used by drivers under Windows CE. Console applications don't directly open a CON driver to read and write to the window. At the current time, support for console applications is limited to a subset of the standard C library character mode functions.

Because the initialization of the console driver occurs only after the first call to an I/O library function, it's possible for a console application to run to completion and terminate without ever creating a console window for output. If you want a console window to always be created, you'll need to include a *printf* or other console input or output call to force the console to be created. You can always insert a line like

```
printf (" \b");
```

which prints a space and then backspaces over the space to force the console to be created.

The CEFind Example Program

The following program is a short console application that searches the Windows CE file system for matching file names. The program can be launched from a console window using CMD.EXE, or it can be launched from the Explorer. Because no concept of a current directory is built into Windows CE, the search always starts from the root of the file system unless a path is specified with the filename specification. Figure 12-6 shows the results of CEFind when looking for all the TrueType fonts on a system.

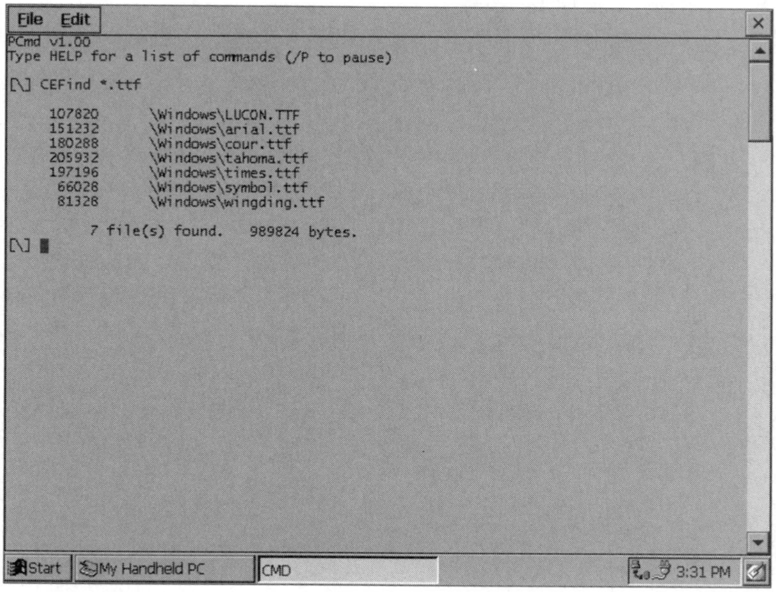

Figure 12-6. *The results of a CEFind search for TrueType font files.*

The CEFind source is contained in one file, CEFind.C, shown in Figure 12-7. The entry point is *WinMain*, which then calls *SrchDirectory*, which recursively calls itself to search each of the directories underneath the original directory.

CEFind.c

```
//======================================================================
// CEFind - A Windows CE console file search application
//
// Written for the book Programming Windows CE
// Copyright (C) 1998 Douglas Boling
//======================================================================
#include <windows.h>                    // For all that Windows stuff

// Returns number of elements
#define dim(x) (sizeof(x) / sizeof(x[0]))

int SrchDirectory (LPTSTR pszDir);
//----------------------------------------------------------------------
// Global data
//
int nTotal = 0;
int nFiles = 0;

//======================================================================
// Program entry point
//
int WINAPI WinMain (HINSTANCE hInstance, HINSTANCE hPrevInstance,
                    LPWSTR lpCmdLine, int nCmdShow) {
    TCHAR pInput[256];

    if (wcslen (lpCmdLine) == 0) {
        printf ("USAGE: CEFIND filespec\n");
        return 0;
    }
    printf ("\n");                          // Initialize the console.
    // We always start at the root.
    if (*lpCmdLine != TEXT ('\\')) {
        pInput[0] = TEXT ('\\');
    } else
        pInput[0] = L'\0';
    wcscat (pInput, lpCmdLine);

    // Perform recursive search.
    SrchDirectory (pInput);
```

Figure 12-7. *The CEFind program.*

```
    wprintf (L"\n  %9d file(s) found.   %d bytes.\n", nFiles, nTotal);
    return 0;
}
//----------------------------------------------------------------------
// SrchDirectory - Recursive routine that searches a dir and all
// child dirs for matching files
//
int SrchDirectory (LPTSTR pszDir) {
    WIN32_FIND_DATA fd;
    TCHAR szNew[MAX_PATH];
    INT i, rc, nErr = 0;
    HANDLE hFind;
    TCHAR *pPtr, *pSrcSpec;

    // Separate subdirectory from search specification.
    for (pSrcSpec = pszDir + lstrlen (pszDir); pSrcSpec >= pszDir;
         pSrcSpec--)
        if (*pSrcSpec == TEXT ('\\'))
            break;

    // Copy the search specification up to the last directory
    // separation character.
    if (pSrcSpec <= pszDir)
        lstrcpy (szNew, TEXT ("\\"));
    else {
        for (i = 0; (i < dim(szNew)-10) &&
                    ((pszDir+i) <= pSrcSpec); i++)
            szNew[i] = *(pszDir+i);
        szNew[i] = TEXT ('\0');
    }
    pPtr = szNew + lstrlen (szNew);

    // Find matching files.
    hFind = FindFirstFile (pszDir, &fd);
    if (hFind != INVALID_HANDLE_VALUE) {

        do {
            // Report all matching files.
            if (!(fd.dwFileAttributes & FILE_ATTRIBUTE_DIRECTORY)) {
                wprintf (L"  %9d\t %s%s\n", fd.nFileSizeLow, szNew,
                         fd.cFileName);
                nTotal += fd.nFileSizeLow;
                nFiles++;
            }
```

(continued)

Figure 12-7. *continued*

```
            rc = FindNextFile (hFind, &fd);
        } while (rc);

        FindClose (hFind);
    } else {
        rc = GetLastError();
        if ((rc != ERROR_FILE_NOT_FOUND)  &&
            (rc != ERROR_NO_MORE_FILES)) {
            wprintf (L"1Find Error.  Str:%s rc:%d", pszDir, rc);
            return -1;
        }
    }

    // Create generic search string for all directories.
    lstrcat (szNew, TEXT ("*.*"));

    hFind = FindFirstFile (szNew, &fd);
    if (hFind != INVALID_HANDLE_VALUE) {
        do {
            if (fd.dwFileAttributes & FILE_ATTRIBUTE_DIRECTORY) {
                // Recurse to the lower directory
                lstrcpy (pPtr, fd.cFileName);
                lstrcat (pPtr, pSrcSpec);
                nErr = SrchDirectory (szNew);
                if (nErr) break;
                *pPtr = TEXT ('\0');
            }
            rc = FindNextFile (hFind, &fd);
        } while (rc);

        FindClose (hFind);
    } else {
        rc = GetLastError();
        if ((rc != ERROR_FILE_NOT_FOUND) &&
            (rc != ERROR_NO_MORE_FILES)) {
            wprintf (L"2Find Error:%d", rc);
            return -1;
        }
    }
    return nErr;
}
```

I began this chapter by saying the Windows CE shell is interesting in that, like many parts of Windows CE, it resembles its desktop counterparts but is implemented very differently. These differences show up the most in places, such as the Explorer, where almost all of the COM interfaces are unique and private, and in console applications, where the implementation is limited to supporting a subset of standard C library calls and nothing else.

The next chapter covers the *tablet mode* shell components. These shell components were first introduced for the Palm-size PC. These components include the SIP (the supplementary input panel), and dedicated hot keys on the system. Let's take a look.

Chapter 13

Shell Programming —Part 2

A Windows CE programmer needs to understand at least three shells when programming a Windows CE device. The Handheld PC and Handheld PC Pro devices, each equipped with a keyboard and a landscape-oriented screen, use an Explorer-type shell that looks similar to the shell used by Windows 95 and Windows NT 4. The Palm-size PC and other Windows CE keyboardless devices, which come equipped with a portrait-oriented screen, use a completely different shell, one that doesn't expose the file system to the user. Each of these devices has an Active Desktop that displays information from various applications directly on the desktop. The third shell a Windows CE programmer needs to know is the one not written. This is the custom shell, written by the OEM designing an embedded device.

This chapter covers components that most directly relate to the Palm-size PC shell, although the technologies presented in this chapter aren't restricted to use in the Palm-size PC. The primary difference between the Palm-size PC and other Windows CE devices is the Palm-size PC's lack of a full hardware keyboard. In its place, is the Supplementary Input Panel, or SIP, which gives the user a way to register keystrokes directly on the screen. However, as with many Windows CE technologies, the SIP has now been generalized in Windows CE 2.1 for use on other platforms.

I'll also cover how to handle the hardware buttons that are on many Palm-size PCs. These buttons can be used two ways—to launch an application or to provide additional keys to an application while it's running. While the navigation buttons are specific to the Palm-size PC, the application launch buttons are also available on some Handheld PC and Handheld PC Pro systems as well as other Windows CE–based systems.

THE SUPPLEMENTARY INPUT PANEL

The SIP gives the user access to a keyboard's capacities on devices that don't have a keyboard or at times when the keyboard of a device isn't available to the user. Having a SIP on a Windows CE system affects the application in a couple of ways. First the screen real estate used by the SIP isn't available to the application. Second since the SIP can be displayed and hidden interactively by the user, the amount of the screen that's available to the application can change while the application is running. What doesn't change is the way an application deals with keyboard input. Characters entered by means of a SIP appear to an application in the same message-based way that keys appear if they're pressed on a hardware keyboard. That is, the same series of WM_KEYDOWN, WM_CHAR, and WM_KEYUP messages are generated by the system in response to a key being entered through a SIP.

A SIP can use a number of different *input methods* or IMs. These input methods are installable components and provide the user interface to the SIP. Two such input methods are the keyboard IM and the Jot Character recognizer IM, which are provided on the Palm-size PC.

Working with a SIP

The functions available to Windows CE applications for interaction with the SIP have changed since they were introduced with the Palm-size PC. So while Windows CE 2.1 adds a newer and more general set of functions, I'm going to present the Palm-size PC functions first, because most applications dealing with the SIP run, at this point, on the Palm-size PC. At the end of this section, I'll describe the different functions provided by Windows CE 2.1 for use with the SIP.

The primary function an application uses when dealing with the SIP on a Palm-size PC is *SHSipInfo*. This omnibus function allows an application to receive information about the current SIP settings (such as its location), set those settings, query the current default SIP, and even change the default SIP. The function is prototyped as

```
BOOL SHSipInfo (UINT uiAction, UINT uiParam, PVOID pvParam,
                UINT fWinIni);
```

The first parameter to *SHSipInfo*, *uiAction*, should be set with a flag that specifies the action you want to perform with the function. The allowable flags are these:

- *SPI_SETSIPINFO* Sets the SIP configuration including its location and its visibility
- *SPI_GETSIPINFO* Queries the SIP configuration
- *SPI_SETCURRENTIM* Sets the current default input method
- *SPI_GETCURRENTIM* Queries the current default input method

Because the behavior of *SHSipInfo* is completely different for each of the flags, I'll describe the function as if it were four different function calls. For each of the flags though, the second and fourth parameters, *uiParam* and *fWinIni*, must be set to 0.

Querying the state of the SIP

To query the current state of the SIP, you would call *SHSipInfo* with the SPI_GET-SIPINFO flag in the *uiAction* parameter. In this case, the function looks like this:

```
BOOL SHSipInfo (SPI_GETSIPINFO, 0, SIPINFO *psi, 0);
```

The third parameter must point to a SIPINFO structure, which is defined as

```
typedef struct {
    DWORD cbSize;
    DWORD fdwFlags;
    RECT rcVisibleDesktop;
    RECT rcSipRect;
    DWORD dwImDataSize;
    VOID *pvImData;
} SIPINFO;
```

The structure's first field, *cbSize*, must be set to the size of the SIPINFO structure before a call is made to *SHSipInfo*. The second field in SIPINFO, *fdwFlags*, can contain a combination of the following flags:

- *SIPF_ON* When set, the SIP is visible.
- *SIPF_DOCKED* When set, the SIP is docked to its default location on the screen.
- *SIPF_LOCKED* When set, the visibility state of the SIP can't be changed by the user.

The next two fields of SIPINFO provide information on the location of the SIP. The field *rcVisibleDesktop* is filled with the screen dimensions of the visible area of the desktop. If the SIP is docked, this area is the rectangle above the SIP. If the SIP is undocked, this rectangle contains the full desktop area minus the taskbar, if it's showing. This field is ignored when you set the SIP configuration. Some SIPs might have a docked state that doesn't run from edge to edge of the screen. In this case, the rectangle describes the largest rectangular area of the screen that isn't obscured by the SIP.

The *rcSipRect* field contains the location and size of the SIP. If the SIP is docked, the rectangle is usually the area of the screen not included by *rcVisibleDesktop*. But if the SIP is undocked, *rcSipRect* contains the size and position of the SIP while *rcVisibleDesktop* contains the entire desktop not obscured by the taskbar, including the area under the SIP. Figure 13-1 shows the relationship between *rcVisibleDesktop* and *rcSipRect*.

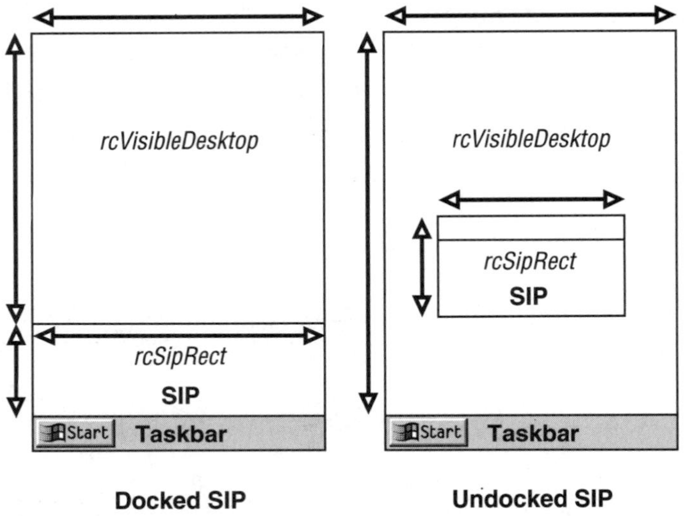

Figure 13-1. *The relationship between* rcVisibleDesktop *and* rcSipRect *in the SIPINFO structure.*

The final two fields of SIPINFO allow you to query information specific to the current input method. The format of this information is defined by the input method. To query this information, the *pvImData* field should be set to point to a buffer to receive the information and *dwImDataSize* should be set to the size of the buffer. It is up to the application to know which input methods provide what specific data. For most input methods, these two fields should be set to 0 to indicate that no IM-specific data is being queried.

Setting the SIP configuration

To set the configuration of the current SIP, you call *SHSipInfo* with the SPI_SETSIPINFO flag, as in

```
BOOL SHSipInfo (SPI_SETSIPINFO, 0, SIPINFO *psi, 0);
```

The parameters are the same as when you call to query the SIP configuration with the third parameter pointing to a SIPINFO structure. As a general rule, you shouldn't fill in the SIPINFO fields from scratch. Instead, you should call *SHSipInfo* to fill in the SIPINFO structure, modify the fields necessary to make your change, and then call *SHSipInfo* again to make the changes. That said, you really can't change much with the present version of the Palm-size PC shell. Currently, an application can't undock a SIP, move the SIP, or even dock an undocked SIP. The only state that an application can change is to show or hide the SIP by toggling the SIPF_ON flag in the *fdwFlags* field of the SIPINFO structure.

Changing the default input method

You can use *SHSipInfo* to query and to change the current SIP. To query the current SIP, you call *SHSipInfo* with the SPI_GETCURRENTIM flag in the *uiAction* parameter as in

```
BOOL SHSipInfo (SPI_SETSIPINFO, 0, CLSID *pclsid, 0);
```

In this case, the third parameter points to a CLSID variable that receives the CLSID of the current input method.

To set the current input method, call *SHSipInfo* with the *uiAction* parameter set to SPI_SETCURRENTIM, as in

```
BOOL SHSipInfo (SPI_SETSIPINFO, 0, CLSID *pclsid, 0);
```

Here again, the third parameter of *SHSipInfo* is a pointer to a CLSID value. In this case, the value must contain a CLSID of a valid input method.

Enumerating the installed input methods

The Palm-size PC has no function that enumerates the input methods that are installed on a system. So applications must iterate through the registry to find the input method DLLs. Fortunately, this isn't an onerous task because input methods are COM objects, and an input method is required to have a special key named *IsSIPInputMethod* with a default value of 1 in its COM registration key. So, to enumerate the installed input methods, all you have to do is enumerate the CLSID keys under [HKEY_CLASSES_ROOT]\CLSID. In each key that you open, look for the subkey *IsSIPInputMethod*. If you find it, the entry is the CLSID of an input method and the default value of the CLSID key is the name of the input method.

The routine that follows enumerates the installed input methods. The routine fills a buffer with a list of strings. For each input method found, the routine returns two strings, the CLSID of the input method and the input method's friendly name. The list is terminated with a null character.

```
//----------------------------------------------------------------------
// EnumerateInputMethods - Produces a list of installed input methods
// and their CLSIDs
//
int EnumerateInputMethods (LPTSTR pOut, int sMax) {
    INT i = 0, rc, nCnt = 0;
    HKEY hKey, hSubKey, hKey2;
    DWORD dwType, dwSize;

    // Open CLSID key.
    if (RegOpenKeyEx (HKEY_CLASSES_ROOT, TEXT ("CLSID"), 0,
                      0, &hKey) != ERROR_SUCCESS)
        return 0;
    sMax -= 2;                    // Make room for terminating zero.
    while (sMax > 0) {
        // Enumerate active driver list.
        dwSize = sMax;
        if (RegEnumKeyEx (hKey, i++, pOut, &dwSize, NULL, NULL,
                          NULL, NULL) != ERROR_SUCCESS)
            break;

        // Open object ID key for object.
        rc = RegOpenKeyEx (hKey, pOut, 0, 0, &hSubKey);
        if (rc != ERROR_SUCCESS)
            continue;

        // See if IsSIPMethod key present indicating an IM object.
        rc = RegOpenKeyEx (hSubKey, TEXT ("IsSIPInputMethod"), 0, 0,
                           &hKey2);

        if (rc == ERROR_SUCCESS) {
            RegCloseKey (hKey2);
            // Move output pointer beyond CLSID.
            sMax -= (lstrlen (pOut) + 1) * sizeof (TCHAR);
            if (sMax > 0)
                pOut += lstrlen (pOut) + 1;
            else
                break;
            // Get name of IM.
            dwSize = sMax;
            rc = RegQueryValueEx (hSubKey, 0, 0, &dwType,
                                  (PBYTE)pOut, &dwSize);
            RegCloseKey (hSubKey);
            if (rc != ERROR_SUCCESS) {
                *pOut = TEXT ('\0');
                RegCloseKey (hSubKey);
                RegCloseKey (hKey);
                return -1;
            }
```

```
            // Move output pointer beyond current name.
            sMax -= (int)dwSize;
            if (sMax > 0)
                pOut += lstrlen (pOut) + 1;
            nCnt++;
        }
        RegCloseKey (hSubKey);
    }
    RegCloseKey (hKey);
    // Add terminating zero.
    if (!rc)
        *pOut = TEXT ('\0');
    return nCnt;
}
```

Reacting to SIP Changes

When the user or an application displays or hides the SIP, the Palm-size PC shell sends a WM_SETTINGCHANGE message to all top-level windows. To indicate that the message was sent in response to the state of the SIP changing, the *wParam* value is set to the constant SPI_SETSIPINFO. You can then call *SHSipInfo* to determine the new state of the SIP. Note that while this message is sent to all top-level windows, only the foreground window should make any changes to the SIP. A window not in the foreground can save the indication that the SIP state has changed and respond when that window is brought to the foreground.

When the user changes the input method of the SIP, a WM_SETTINGCHANGE message is sent to all top-level windows. In this case, the *wParam* value is set to the constant SPI_SETCURRENTIM.

When a foreground application detects that the SIP has been displayed, it should ensure that the SIP doesn't obscure the location of the input caret or, in the case of a dialog box, the control that currently has focus. In most cases, this means scrolling the window or reconfiguring the dialog box so that the user can see the control even with the SIP displayed. Another option is to always have controls laid out on the top two thirds of the Palm-size PC screen because docked SIPs won't obscure this area.

Input Panels on Windows CE 2.1 Devices

One of the goals of Windows CE 2.1 was to take some of the more interesting and useful functional units of the different H/PC and Palm-size PC shells and move them into the base operating system. This would allow developers of embedded systems, who don't currently have access to those complex shells, to use those functional blocks. One of the functional blocks moved is the notification API that I talked about in Chapter 12. Another functional block is the SIP architecture. When the SIP was moved to the operating system from the shell, the API for the SIP was redesigned to be a more general

API. Because of this, SIP-aware applications written for Windows CE 2.1 need to use a different set of functions than used by their Palm-size PC cousins.

Note that the SIP API isn't the same IME API that's also supported on Windows CE 2.1. The IME API is a much more general and complex API than the relatively simple SIP needs.

The first four functions of the Windows CE 2.1 SIP API correspond directly to the four different modes of the Palm-size PC's *SHSipInfo* functions. Their prototypes are

```
BOOL SipGetInfo (SIPINFO *pSIPInfo);
BOOL SipSetInfo (SIPINFO *pSIPInfo);
BOOL SipGetCurrentIM (CLSID *pClsid);
BOOL SipSetCurrentIM (CLSID *pClsid);
```

Both *SipGetInfo* and *SipSetInfo* use the same SIPINFO structure that I described earlier in connection to the *SHSipInfo* function. Likewise, the *SipGetCurrentIM* and *SipSetCurrentIM* functions use pointers to CLSID values to identify the input methods.

A new function has been added to simplify the process of showing and hiding the SIP. Instead of using *SipGetInfo* and *SipSetInfo* to fill in a SIPINFO structure and modify the SIPF_ON flag to show or hide the SIP, you can use the *SipShowIM* function. It's prototyped as

```
BOOL SipShowIM (DWORD dwFlags);
```

The only flags that can be specified are SPIF_ON and SPIF_OFF.

Instead of your having to manually enumerate the input methods by looking through the registry, you can use a new function, *SipEnumIM*. This function is prototyped as

```
int SipEnumIM (IMENUMPROC pEnumIMProc);
```

The only parameter is a pointer to an enumeration function in your application. If you pass NULL in the *pEnumIMProc* parameter, *SipEnumIM* returns the number of input methods installed on the system. The callback function should be prototyped as

```
int SipEnumIMProc (IMENUMINFO * pIMInfo);
```

Windows CE will call the enumeration function once for each input method installed on the system. The function will be called with the parameter pointing to an IMENUMINFO structure, which is defined as

```
struct _IMENUMINFO {
    TCHAR szName[MAX_PATH];
    CLSID Clsid;
} IMENUMINFO;
```

Here again, the fields are fairly self-explanatory. The *szName* is the friendly name of the IM, while the *Clsid* field contains the CLSID value for the IM.

Another function is *SipStatus*. This function tells the caller whether the SIP component of Windows CE is installed on a system. The function is prototyped as

```
DWORD SipStatus(void);
```

The function returns SIP_STATUS_AVAILABLE if the SIP functions are available or SIP_STATUS_UNAVAILABLE if the SIP component isn't installed.

The last two functions are provided for SIP maintenance. The Palm-size PC doesn't need these functions because its shell maintains the SIP. For systems whose shells don't have knowledge of a SIP, you'll have to write an application that maintains the SIP through these functions. A better alternative would be to have your custom shell provide the SIP maintenance through these functions.

On the Palm-size PC, the taskbar maintains the button that displays and hides the SIP window. The taskbar maintains a button that displays a bitmap, which represents the current input method so that the user knows which input method is the default. On other systems, this function must be performed by another application or more likely, by a custom shell. To provide this function, the custom shell needs to know what bitmap the SIP wants displayed, while also maintaining the default rectangle for the SIP. Windows CE 2.1 gives you two functions for this purpose.

The *SipRegisterNotification* function can be called by the application that maintains the SIP. This application will then be notified when the input method changes the bitmaps that are used to represent the input method. Only one application, the application that manages the SIP, can call *SipRegisterNotification* to ask to be notified when the SIP changes state. That application will then be notified about input method changes until the system is rebooted. The function is prototyped as

```
BOOL SipRegisterNotification (HWND hWnd);
```

The only parameter is the window that will receive the notifications. That window will receive WM_IM_INFO messages when an input method initially sets or later changes its bitmaps. The *wParam* for this message contains one of the following flags, indicating what's being changed by the input method. These flags are

- *IM_POSITION* The size or position of the input method has changed.
- *IM_WIDEIMAGE* The input method has selected a new wide image.
- *IM_NARROWIMAGE* The input method has selected a new narrow image.

The *lParam* parameter contains different data, depending on the flag. For IM_POSITION, *lParam* isn't used. For IM_WIDEIMAGE and IM_NARROWIMAGE, *lParam* contains the handle to the new bitmap to be used.

The final function is also used by the custom shell or the application maintaining the SIP. It is

```
BOOL SipSetDefaultRect (RECT * pRect);
```

This function is called to set the default docked rectangle for the SIP. This allows a custom shell to define where the docked position of the SIP is to be on the screen. The only parameter is the rectangle that defines the default location. This new location won't be used until a new input method is selected either by the user or by the program.

You might want to have your SIP-aware applications that need to be cross-compatible with the Palm-size PC shell manually load the function pointers to the different SIP functions. This procedure would allow an application to run both on the Palm-size PC as well as on any embedded Windows CE 2.1 or later system. I describe how to do this in Chapter 14.

WRITING AN INPUT METHOD

Up to this point, I've talked only about the application side of dealing with SIPs. You can also design your own input method rather easily. An input method is merely a COM object that exports an *IInputMethod* interface and creates an input method window in response to requests from the input panel.

The Components of a SIP

A SIP is composed of two main components—the input panel and the input method. The input panel is supplied by the system. It creates the input panel window, provides the message loop processing for the SIP, and the window procedure for the input panel window. The input panel cooperates with the taskbar or other shell program to provide the user with the ability to switch between a number of installed input methods.

The input method is the installable portion of the SIP. It's responsible for translating pen strokes and taps into keyboard input. It's also responsible for the look and feel of the SIP while it's selected. In almost all cases, the input method creates a window that's a child of the input panel window. Within that child window, the input method draws its interface and interprets mouse messages. The input method then calls back to the input panel when it wants to generate a key event.

Each of these two components implements a COM interface that becomes the interface between them. The input method implements an *IInputMethod* interface, while the input panel implements an *IIMCallback* interface. In the interaction between the input panel and the input method, the input panel drives the interaction. For the most part, the input method simply responds to calls made to its *IInputMethod* methods. Calls are made when the input method is loaded, when it's unloaded, and when it's shown or hidden. In response, the input method must draw in its child window, interpret the user's actions, and call methods in the *IIMCallback* interface to send keys to the system or to control the input panel's window.

Input methods are implemented as COM in-proc servers. Because of this, they must conform to the standard COM in-proc server specifications. This means that an input method is implemented as a DLL that exports *DllGetClassObject* and *DllCanUnloadNow* functions. Input methods must also export *DllRegisterServer* and *DllUnregisterServer* functions that perform the necessary registry registration and unregistration for the server DLL.

Threading Issues with Input Methods

Because the input panel and input method components are so tightly interrelated, you must follow a few rules when writing an input method. While it's permissible to use multiple threads in an input method, the interaction between the input panel and the input method is strictly limited to the input panel's primary thread. This means that the input method should create any windows during calls to methods in the *IInputMethod* interface. This ensures that these windows will use the same message loop as the input panel's window. This, in turn, allows the input panel to directly call the input method's window procedures, as necessary. In addition, that same thread should make all calls made back to the *IIMCallback* interface.

In short, try not to multithread your input method. If you must, create all windows in your input method using the input panel's thread. Secondary threads can be created, but they can't call the *IIMCallbac*k interface and they shouldn't create any windows.

The *IInputMethod* Interface

The *IInputMethod* interface is the core of an IM. Using the interface's methods, an IM should create any windows, react to any changes in the parent input panel window, and provide any cleanup when it's released. The *IInputMethod* interface exports the following methods in addition to the standard *IUnknown* methods:

- *IInputMethod::Select* The user has selected the IM. The IM should create its window.
- *IInputMethod::Deselect* The user has selected another IM. The IM should destroy its window.

- *IInputMethod::Showing* The IM window is about to be displayed.
- *IInputMethod::Hiding* The IM window is about to be hidden.
- *IInputMethod::GetInfo* The system is querying the IM for information.
- *IInputMethod::ReceiveSipInfo* The system is providing information to the IM.
- *IInputMethod::RegisterCallback* The system is providing a pointer to the *IIMCallback* interface.
- *IInputMethod::GetImData* The IM is queried for IM-specific data.
- *IInputMethod::SetImData* The IM is provided IM-specific data.
- *IInputMethod::UserOptionsDlg* The IM should display an options dialog box to support the SIP control panel applet.

Let's now look at these methods in detail so that we can understand the processing necessary for each.

IInputMethod::Select

When the user chooses your input method, the DLL that contains your IM is loaded and the *Select* method is called. This method is prototyped as

```
HRESULT IInputMethod::Select (HWND hwndSip);
```

The only parameter is the handle to the SIP window that's the parent of your input method's main window. You should return S_OK to indicate success or E_FAIL if you can't create and initialize your input method successfully.

When the *Select* method is called, the IM will have just been loaded into memory and you'll need to perform any necessary initialization. This includes registering any window classes and creating the input method window. The IM should be created as a child of the SIP window because it's the SIP window that will be shown, hidden, and moved in response to user action. You can call *GetClientRect* with the parent window handle to query the necessary size of your input window.

IInputMethod::GetInfo

After the input panel has loaded your IM, it calls the *GetInfo* method. The input panel calls this method to query the bitmaps that represent the IM. These bitmaps appear in the SIP button on the taskbar. In addition, the IM can provide a set of flags and the size and location on the screen where it would like to be displayed. This method is prototyped as

```
HRESULT IInputMethod::GetInfo (IMINFO *pimi);
```

The only parameter is a pointer to an IMINFO structure that the IM must fill out to give information back to the SIP. The IMINFO structure is defined as

```
typedef struct  {
    DWORD cbSize;
    HANDLE hImageNarrow;
    HANDLE hImageWide;
    int iNarrow;
    int iWide;
    DWORD fdwFlags;
    RECT rcSipRect;
} IMINFO;
```

The first field, *cbSize*, must be filled with the size of the IMINFO structure. The next two fields, *hImageNarrow* and *hImageWide*, should be filled with handles to image lists that contain the bitmaps that will appear on the taskbar SIP button. The wide image is a 32-by-16-pixel bitmap that's used when the shell has room to display the wide SIP button on the taskbar. When space on the taskbar is constrained, the system narrows the SIP button and displays the 16-by-16 bitmap from the Narrow image list. The input method must create these image lists and pass the handles in this structure. The IM is responsible for destroying the image lists when a user or an application unloads it. You can create these image lists in the *GetInfo* method, as long as you design your application to know not to create the image lists twice if *GetInfo* is called more than once. Another strategy is to create the image lists in the *Select* method and store the handles as member variables of the *IInputMethod* object. Then when *GetInfo* is called, you can pass the handles of the already created image lists to the input panel.

The next two fields, *iNarrow* and *iWide*, should be set to the index in the image lists for the bitmap you want the SIP to use. For example, you might have two different bitmaps for the SIP button, depending on whether your IM is docked to the taskbar or is floating. You can then have an image list with two bitmaps, and you can specify the index depending on the state of your IM.

The *fdwFlags* field should be set to a combination of the flags, SIPF_ON, SIPF_DOCKED, SIPF_LOCKED, and SIPF_DISABLECOMPLETION, all of which define the state of the input panel. The first three flags are the same flags that I described earlier. When the SIPF_DISABLECOMPLETION flag is set, the auto-completion function of the SIP is disabled.

Finally, the *rcSipRect* field should be filled with the default rectangle for the input method. Unless you have a specific size and location on the screen for your IM, you can simply query the client rectangle of the parent SIP window for this rectangle. Note that just because you request a size and location of the SIP window doesn't mean that the window will have that rectangle. You should always query the size of the parent SIP window when laying out your IM window.

IInputMethod::ReceiveSipInfo

The *ReceiveSipInfo* method is called by the input panel when the input panel is shown and then again when an application moves or changes the state of the input panel. The method is prototyped as

```
HRESULT IInputMethod::ReceiveSipInfo (SIPINFO *psi);
```

The only parameter is a pointer to a SIPINFO structure that I described earlier in this chapter. When this method is called, only two of the fields are valid—the *fdwFlags* field and the *reSipRect* field. The *rcSipRect* field contains the size and location of the input panel window, while the *fdwFlags* field contains the SIPF_*xxx* flags previously described. In response to the *ReceiveSipInfo* method call, the IM should save the new state flags and rectangle.

IInputMethod::RegisterCallback

The input panel calls the *RegisterCallback* method once, after the input method has been selected. The method is prototyped as

```
HRESULT IInputMethod::RegisterCallback (IIMCallback *lpIMCallback);
```

This method is called to provide a pointer to the *IIMCallback* interface. The only action the IM must take is to save this pointer so that it can be used to provide feedback to the input panel.

IInputMethod::Showing and *IInputMethod::Hiding*

The input panel calls the *Showing* and *Hiding* methods just before the IM is shown or hidden. Both these methods have no parameters and you should simply return S_OK to indicate success. The *Showing* method is also called when the panel is moved or resized. This makes the *Showing* method a handy place for resizing the IM child window to properly fit in the parent input panel window.

IInputMethod::GetImData and *IInputMethod::SetImData*

The *GetImData* and *SetImData* methods give you a back door into the IM for applications that need to have a special communication path between the application and a custom IM. This arrangement allows a specially designed IM to provide additional data to and from applications. The two methods are prototyped as

```
HRESULT IInputMethod::GetImData (DWORD dwSize, void* pvImData);

HRESULT IInputMethod::SetImData (DWORD dwSize, void* pvImData);
```

For both of these functions, the pointer points to a block of memory in the application. The *dwSize* parameter contains the size of the block pointed to by *pvImData*.

When an application is sending data to a custom IM, it calls *SHSipInfo* with the SPI_SETSIPINFO flag. The pointer to the buffer and the size of the buffer are specified in the *pvImData* and *dwImDataSize* fields of the SIPINFO structure. If these two fields are nonzero, the input panel then calls the *SetImData* method with the pointer and the size of the buffer contained in the two parameters of the method. The input method then accepts the data in the buffer pointed to by *pvImData*. When an application calls *SHSipInfo* with the SPI_GETSIPINFO structure and nonzero values in *pvImData* and *dwImDataSize*, the input panel then calls the *GetImData* method to retrieve data from the input method.

IInputMethod::Deselect

When the user or a program switches to a different default IM, the input panel calls *Deselect*. Your input method should save its state (its location on the screen, for example), destroy any windows it has created, and unregister any window classes it has registered. It should also destroy any image lists it's still maintaining. The prototype for this method is

```
HRESULT IInputMethod::Deselect (void);
```

After the *Deselect* method is called, the SIP will unload the input method DLL.

IInputMethod::UserOptionsDlg

The *UserOptionsDlg* method isn't called by the input panel. Instead, the input panel's control panel applet calls this method when the user clicks on the Options button. The IM should display a dialog box that allows the user to configure any settable parameters in the input method. The *UserOptionsDlg* method is prototyped as

```
HRESULT IInputMethod::UserOptionsDlg (HWND hwndParent);
```

The only parameter is the handle to the window that should be the parent window of the dialog box. Because the IM might be unloaded after the dialog box is dismissed, any configuration data should be saved in a persistent place such as the registry, where it can be recalled when the input panel is loaded again.

The *IIMCallback* Interface

The *IIMCallback* interface allows an IM to call back to the input panel for services such as sending keys to the operating system. Aside from the standard *IUnknown* methods that can be ignored by the IM, only four methods are exposed by IIMCallback. These methods are

- *IIMCallback::SetImInfo* Sets the bitmaps used by the input panel as well as the location and visibility state of the input method
- *IIMCallback::SendVirtualKey* Sends a virtual key to the system

- *IIMCallback::SendCharEvents* Sends Unicode characters to the window with the current focus
- *IIMCallback::SendString* Sends a string of characters to the window with the current focus

It's appropriate that the *IIMCallback* interface devotes three of its four methods to sending keys and characters to the system because that's the primary purpose of the IM. Let's take a quick look at each of these methods.

IIMCallback::SetImInfo

The *SetImInfo* method allows the IM control over its size and location on the screen. This method can also be used to set the bitmaps representing the IM. The method is prototyped as

```
HRESULT IIMCallback::SetImInfo (IMINFO *pimi);
```

The only parameter is a pointer to an IMINFO structure. This is the same structure that the IM uses when it calls the *GetInfo* method of the *IInputMethod* interface, but I'll repeat it here for clarity.

```
typedef struct  {
    DWORD cbSize;
    HANDLE hImageNarrow;
    HANDLE hImageWide;
    int iNarrow;
    int iWide;
    DWORD fdwFlags;
    RECT rcSipRect;
} IMINFO;
```

This structure enables an IM to tell the input panel the information that the panel asked for in *GetInfo*. The IM must correctly fill in all the fields in the IMINFO structure because it has no other way to tell the input panel to look at only one or two of the fields. You shouldn't re-create the image lists when you're calling *SetImInfo*; instead, use the same handles you passed in *GetInfo* unless you want to change the image lists used by the input panel. In that case, you'll need to destroy the old image lists after you've called *SetImInfo*.

You can use *SetImInfo* to undock the input panel and move it around the screen by clearing the SIPF_DOCKED flag in *fdwFlags* and specifying a new size and location for the panel in the *rcSipRect* field. Because Windows CE doesn't provide system support for dragging an input panel around the screen, the IM is responsible for providing such a method. The sample IM I present beginning on page 766 supports dragging the input panel around by creating a gripper area on the side of the panel and interpreting the stylus messages in this area to allow the panel to be moved around the screen.

IIMCallback::SendVirtualKey

The *SendVirtualKey* method is used to send virtual key codes to the system. The difference between this method and the *SendCharEvents* and *SendString* methods is that this method can be used to send noncharacter key codes, such as those from cursor keys and shift keys, that have a global impact on the system. Also, key codes sent by *SendVirtualKey* are affected by the system key state. For example, if you send an *a* character and the Shift key is currently down, the resulting WM_CHAR message contains an *A* character. *SendVirtualKey* is prototyped as

```
HRESULT IIMCallback::SendVirtualKey (BYTE bVk, DWORD dwFlags);
```

The first parameter is the virtual key code of the key you want to send. The second parameter can contain one or more flags that help define the event. The flags can be either 0 or a combination of flags. You would use KEYEVENTF_KEYUP to indicate that the event is a key up event as opposed to a key down event and KEYEVENTF_SILENT, which specifies that the key event won't cause a key click to be played for the event. If you use *SendVirtualKey* to send a character key, the character will be modified by the current shift state of the system.

IIMCallback::SendCharEvents

The *SendCharEvents* method can be used to send specific characters to the window with the current focus. The difference between this method and the *SendVirtualKey* method is that *SendCharEvents* gives you much more control over the exact information provided in the WM_KEY*xxx* and WM_CHAR messages generated. Instead of simply sending a virtual key code and letting the system determine the proper character, this method allows you to specify the virtual key and associate a completely different character or series of characters generated by this event. For example, in a simple case, calling this method once causes the messages WM_KEYDOWN, WM_CHAR, and WM_KEYUP all to be sent to the focus window. In a more complex case, this method can send a WM_KEYDOWN, and multiple WM_CHAR messages, followed by a WM_KEYUP message.

This method is prototyped as

```
HRESULT IIMCallback::SendCharEvents (UINT uVK, UINT uKeyFlags,
                     UINT uChars, UINT *puShift, UINT *puChars);
```

The first parameter is the virtual key code that will be sent with the WM_KEYDOWN and WM_KEYUP messages. The second parameter is the key flags that will be sent with the WM_KEYDOWN and WM_KEYUP messages. The third parameter is the number of WM_CHAR messages that will be generated by this one event. The next parameter, *puShift*, should point to an array of key state flags, while the final parameter, *puChar*, should point to an array of Unicode characters. Each entry in the shift array will be joined with the corresponding Unicode character in the character array when the WM_CHAR messages are generated. This allows you to give one key on the IM keyboard a unique virtual key code and to generate any number of WM_CHAR messages, each with its own shift state.

IIMCallback::SendString

You use the *SendString* method to send a series of characters to the focus window. The advantage of this function is that an IM can easily send an entire word or sentence, and the input panel will take care of the details such as key down and key up events. The method is prototyped as

```
HRESULT IIMCallback::SendString (LPTSTR ptszStr, DWORD dwSize);
```

The two parameters are the string of characters to be sent and the number of characters in the string.

The NumPanel Example Input Method

The NumPanel example code demonstrates a simple IM. NumPanel gives a user a simple numeric keyboard including keys 0 through 9 as well as the four arithmetic operators, +, –, *, and / and the equal sign key. While not of much use to the user, NumPanel does demonstrate all the requirements of an input method. The NumPanel example is different from the standard IMs that come with the Palm-size PC in that it can be undocked. The NumPanel IM has a gripper bar on the left side of the window that can be used to drag the SIP around the screen. When a user double-taps the gripper bar, the SIP snaps back to its docked position. Figure 13-2 shows the NumPanel IM in its docked position while Figure 13-3 shows the same panel undocked.

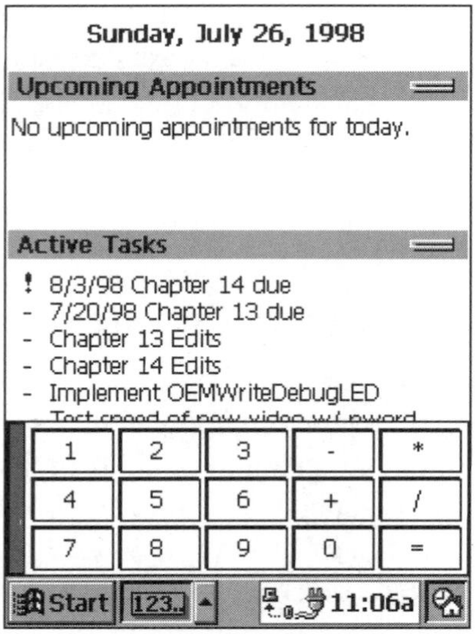

Figure 13-2. *The NumPanel IM window in its docked position.*

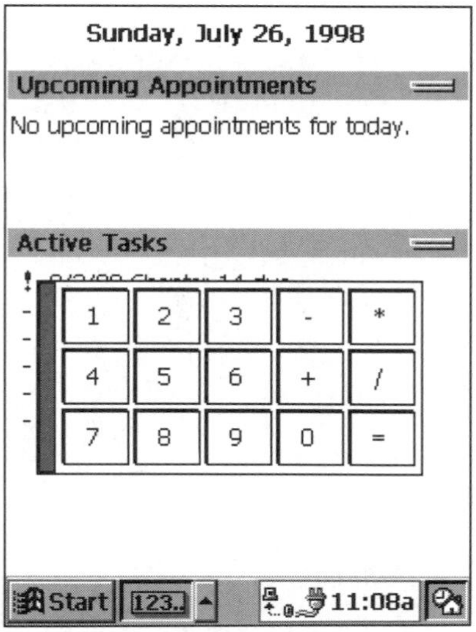

Figure 13-3. *The NumPanel IM window undocked.*

The source code that implements NumPanel is divided into two main files, NumPanel.cpp and NPWnd.c. NumPanel.cpp provides the COM interfaces necessary for the IM, including the *IInputMethod* interface and the *IClassFactory* interface. In this file as well is *DllMain*, and the other functions necessary to implement a COM in-proc server. NPWnd.c contains the code that implements the NumPanel window. This code comprises the NumPanel window procedure and the supporting message handling procedures. The source code for NumPanel is shown in Figure 13-4.

NumPanel.def

```
;
;Standard COM library DEF file
;

LIBRARY    NUMPANEL.DLL

EXPORTS
   DllCanUnloadNow      @1 PRIVATE
   DllGetClassObject    @2 PRIVATE
   DllRegisterServer    @3 PRIVATE
   DllUnregisterServer  @4 PRIVATE
```

Figure 13-4. *The NumPanel source code.* *(continued)*

Figure 13-4. *continued*

NumPanel.rc

```
//======================================================================
// Resource file
//
// Written for the book Programming Windows CE
// Copyright (C) 1998 Douglas Boling
//======================================================================
#include "windows.h"                  // For all that Windows stuff
#include "NumPanel.h"                 // Program-specific stuff

//----------------------------------------------------------------------
// Icons and bitmaps
//
ID_ICON         ICON   "NumPanel.ico" // Module icon

NarrowBmp       BITMAP "nkbd.bmp"     // Bmp used in image list
NarrowMask      BITMAP "nmask.bmp"    // Mask used in image list
WideBmp         BITMAP "widekbd.bmp"  // Bmp used in image list
WideMask        BITMAP "widemask.bmp" // Mask used in image list
```

NumPanel.h

```
//======================================================================
// Header file
//
// Written for the book Programming Windows CE
// Copyright (C) 1998 Douglas Boling
//======================================================================

#define ID_ICON         1
#define IDC_SIP         10

// **** Start of Generic COM declarations ****
//======================================================================
// MyClassFactory - Object declaration
//
class MyClassFactory : public IClassFactory {

private:
    long m_lRef;

public:
    MyClassFactory();
    ~MyClassFactory();
```

```
    //IUnknown methods
    STDMETHODIMP QueryInterface (THIS_ REFIID riid, LPVOID *ppv);
    STDMETHODIMP_(ULONG) AddRef (THIS);
    STDMETHODIMP_(ULONG) Release (THIS);

    //IClassFactory methods
    STDMETHODIMP CreateInstance (LPUNKNOWN pUnkOuter, REFIID riid,
                                 LPVOID *ppv);
    STDMETHODIMP LockServer (BOOL fLock);
};
// **** End of Generic OLE declarations ****

//======================================================================
// MyIInputMethod - Object declaration
//
class MyIInputMethod : public IInputMethod {

private:
    long m_lRef;
    HWND m_hwndParent;
    HWND m_hwndMyWnd;
    HIMAGELIST m_himlWide;
    HIMAGELIST m_himlNarrow;
    IIMCallback *m_pIMCallback;

public:
    MyIInputMethod();
    ~MyIInputMethod();

    //IUnknown methods
    STDMETHODIMP QueryInterface (THIS_ REFIID riid, LPVOID *ppvObj);
    STDMETHODIMP_(ULONG) AddRef (THIS);
    STDMETHODIMP_(ULONG) Release (THIS);

    //IInputMethod
    HRESULT STDMETHODCALLTYPE Select (HWND hwndSip);
    HRESULT STDMETHODCALLTYPE Deselect (void);
    HRESULT STDMETHODCALLTYPE Showing (void);
    HRESULT STDMETHODCALLTYPE Hiding (void);
    HRESULT STDMETHODCALLTYPE GetInfo (IMINFO __RPC_FAR *pimi);
    HRESULT STDMETHODCALLTYPE ReceiveSipInfo (SIPINFO __RPC_FAR *psi);
    HRESULT STDMETHODCALLTYPE RegisterCallback (
                                   IIMCallback __RPC_FAR *lpIMCallback);
    HRESULT STDMETHODCALLTYPE GetImData (DWORD dwSize, LPVOID pvImData);
    HRESULT STDMETHODCALLTYPE SetImData (DWORD dwSize, LPVOID pvImData);
```

(continued)

Figure 13-4. *continued*

```
    HRESULT STDMETHODCALLTYPE UserOptionsDlg (HWND hwndParent);

};
```

NPWnd.h

```
//======================================================================
// NPWnd.h - An include file
//
// Written for the book Programming Windows CE
// Copyright (C) 1998 Douglas Boling
//======================================================================

#ifdef __cplusplus
extern "C"{
#endif

// Returns number of elements
#define dim(x) (sizeof(x) / sizeof(x[0]))

struct decodeUINT {                             // Structure associates
    UINT Code;                                  // messages
                                                // with a function.
    LRESULT (*Fxn)(HWND, UINT, WPARAM, LPARAM);
};

#define MYSIPCLS        TEXT ("MyNumPanelWndCls")
#define MYMSG_METHCALL (WM_USER+100)            // Used to pass info

#define GRIPWIDTH       9                       // Width of the gripper
#define FLOATWIDTH      200                     // Width of floating wnd
#define FLOATHEIGHT     100                     // Height of floating wnd

#define CXBTNS          5                       // Num columns of buttons
#define CYBTNS          3                       // Num rows of buttons

//
// Local data structure for keypad IM window
//
typedef struct {
    DWORD dwBtnDnFlags;
    IIMCallback *pIMCallback;
    RECT rectDocked;
```

```
    BOOL fMoving;
    POINT ptMovBasis;
    POINT ptMovStart;
    IMINFO imi;
} SIPWNDSTRUCT, *LPSIPWNDSTRUCT;

LRESULT CALLBACK NPWndProc (HWND, UINT, WPARAM, LPARAM);

LRESULT CALLBACK DoCreateSip (HWND, UINT, WPARAM, LPARAM);
LRESULT CALLBACK DoSetSipInfo (HWND, UINT, WPARAM, LPARAM);
LRESULT CALLBACK DoPaintSip (HWND, UINT, WPARAM, LPARAM);
LRESULT CALLBACK DoMouseSip (HWND, UINT, WPARAM, LPARAM);
LRESULT CALLBACK DoDestroySip (HWND, UINT, WPARAM, LPARAM);

#ifdef __cplusplus
}
#endif
```

NumPanel.cpp

```
//======================================================================
// NumPanel - A Windows CE example input method
//
// Written for the book Programming Windows CE
// Copyright (C) 1998 Douglas Boling
//======================================================================
#include <windows.h>                 // For all that Windows stuff
#include <commctrl.h>                // Command bar includes
#define INITGUID
#include <initguid.h>
#include <coguid.h>
#include <aygshell.h>                // Palm-size PC shell includes
#include <sip.h>                     // SIP includes

#include "NumPanel.h"                // Local program includes
#include "NPWnd.h"                   // My IM window includes
HINSTANCE hInst;                     // DLL instance handle
long g_DllCnt = 0;                   // Global DLL reference count

// Replace this GUID with your own!
static const TCHAR szCLSIDNumPanel[] =
TEXT ("{C915FE81-24C0-11d2-93F7-204C4F4F5020}");
static const GUID CLSID_NumPanel =
{0xc915fe81, 0x24c0, 0x11d2, {0x93,0xf7,0x20,0x4c,0x4f,0x4f,0x50,0x20}};
static const TCHAR szFriendlyName[] = TEXT ("Numeric Keypad");
```

(continued)

Figure 13-4. *continued*

```
//======================================================================
// DllMain - DLL initialization entry point
//
BOOL WINAPI DllMain (HINSTANCE hinstDLL, DWORD dwReason,
                     LPVOID lpvReserved) {
    hInst = hinstDLL;
    return TRUE;
}
//======================================================================
// DllGetClassObject - Exported function called to get pointer to
// Class factory object
//
STDAPI DllGetClassObject (REFCLSID rclsid, REFIID riid, LPVOID *ppv) {
    MyClassFactory *pcf;
    HRESULT hr;

    // See if caller wants us...
    if (IsEqualCLSID (rclsid, CLSID_NumPanel)) {

        // Create IClassFactory object.
        pcf = new MyClassFactory();
        if (pcf == NULL)
            return E_OUTOFMEMORY;

        // Call class factory's query interface method.
        hr = pcf->QueryInterface (riid, ppv);
        // This will cause an obj delete unless interface found
        pcf->Release();
        return hr;
    }
    return CLASS_E_CLASSNOTAVAILABLE;
}
//======================================================================
// DllCanUnloadNow - Exported function called when DLL can unload
//
STDAPI DllCanUnloadNow () {

    if (g_DllCnt)
        return S_FALSE;
    return S_OK;
}
//======================================================================
// DllRegisterServer - Exported function called to register the server
//
STDAPI DllRegisterServer () {
    TCHAR szName[MAX_PATH+2];
```

```
    DWORD dwDisp;
    HKEY hKey, hSubKey;
    INT rc, i;

    GetModuleFileName (hInst, szName, sizeof (szName));
    // Open the key.
    rc = RegCreateKeyEx (HKEY_CLASSES_ROOT, szCLSIDNumPanel, 0,
                         TEXT (""), 0, 0, NULL, &hKey, &dwDisp);
    if (rc != ERROR_SUCCESS)
        return E_FAIL;

    // Set the friendly name of the SIP.
    RegSetValueEx (hKey, TEXT (""), 0, REG_SZ, (PBYTE)szFriendlyName,
                   (lstrlen (szFriendlyName)+1) * sizeof (TCHAR));

    // Create subkeys.
    // Set the module name of the SIP.
    rc = RegCreateKeyEx (hKey, TEXT ("InProcServer32"), 0, TEXT (""),
                         0, 0, NULL, &hSubKey, &dwDisp);
    rc = RegSetValueEx (hSubKey, TEXT (""), 0, REG_SZ, (PBYTE)szName,
                        (lstrlen (szName)+1) * sizeof (TCHAR));
    RegCloseKey (hSubKey);

    // Set the default icon of the server.
    RegCreateKeyEx (hKey, TEXT ("DefaultIcon"), 0, TEXT (""),
                         0, 0, NULL, &hSubKey, &dwDisp);
    lstrcat (szName, TEXT (",0"));
    RegSetValueEx (hSubKey, TEXT (""), 0, REG_SZ, (PBYTE)szName,
                        (lstrlen (szName)+1) * sizeof (TCHAR));
    RegCloseKey (hSubKey);

    // Set the flag indicating this is a SIP.
    RegCreateKeyEx (hKey, TEXT ("IsSIPInputMethd"), 0, TEXT (""),
                    0, 0, NULL, &hSubKey, &dwDisp);
    i = 1;
    RegSetValueEx (hSubKey, TEXT (""), 0, REG_DWORD, (PBYTE)&i, 4);
    RegCloseKey (hSubKey);

    RegCloseKey (hKey);
    return S_OK;
}
//======================================================================
// DllUnregisterServer - Exported function called to remove the server
// information from the registry
//
```

(continued)

Figure 13-4. *continued*

```
STDAPI DllUnregisterServer() {
    INT rc;
    rc = RegDeleteKey (HKEY_CLASSES_ROOT, szCLSIDNumPanel);
    if (rc == ERROR_SUCCESS)
        return S_OK;
    return E_FAIL;
}
//**********************************************************************
// MyClassFactory Object implimentation
//----------------------------------------------------------------------
// Object constructor
MyClassFactory::MyClassFactory () {
    m_lRef = 1;     //Set ref count to 1 on create
    return;
}
//----------------------------------------------------------------------
// Object destructor
MyClassFactory::~MyClassFactory () {
    return;
}
//----------------------------------------------------------------------
// QueryInterface - Called to see what interfaces this object supports
STDMETHODIMP MyClassFactory::QueryInterface (THIS_ REFIID riid,
                                             LPVOID *ppv) {

    // If caller wants our IUnknown or IClassFactory object,
    // return a pointer to the object.
    if (IsEqualIID (riid, IID_IUnknown) ||
        IsEqualIID (riid, IID_IClassFactory)) {

        *ppv = (LPVOID)this;     // Return pointer to object.
        AddRef();                // Inc ref to prevent delete on return.
        return NOERROR;
    }
    *ppv = NULL;
    return (E_NOINTERFACE);
}
//----------------------------------------------------------------------
// AddRef - Increment object reference count.
STDMETHODIMP_(ULONG) MyClassFactory::AddRef (THIS) {
    ULONG cnt;

    cnt = (ULONG)InterlockedIncrement (&m_lRef);
    return cnt;
}
```

```
//----------------------------------------------------------------------
// Release - Decrement object reference count.
STDMETHODIMP_(ULONG) MyClassFactory::Release (THIS) {
    ULONG cnt;

    cnt = (ULONG)InterlockedDecrement (&m_lRef);
    if (cnt == 0)
        delete this;
    return cnt;
}
//----------------------------------------------------------------------
// LockServer - Called to tell the DLL not to unload even if use cnt 0
STDMETHODIMP MyClassFactory::LockServer (BOOL fLock) {
    if (fLock)
        InterlockedIncrement (&g_DllCnt);
    else
        InterlockedDecrement (&g_DllCnt);
    return NOERROR;
}
//----------------------------------------------------------------------
// CreateInstance - Called to have class factory object create other
// objects
STDMETHODIMP MyClassFactory::CreateInstance (LPUNKNOWN pUnkOuter,
                                             REFIID riid, LPVOID *ppv) {
    MyIInputMethod *pMyIM;
    HRESULT hr;

    if (pUnkOuter)
        return (CLASS_E_NOAGGREGATION);

    if (IsEqualIID (riid, IID_IUnknown) ||
        IsEqualIID (riid, IID_IInputMethod)) {

        // Create file filter object.
        pMyIM = new MyIInputMethod();
        if (!pMyIM)
            return E_OUTOFMEMORY;

        // See if object exports the proper interface.
        hr = pMyIM->QueryInterface (riid, ppv);
        // This will cause an obj delete unless interface found.
        pMyIM->Release ();
        return hr;
    }
    return E_NOINTERFACE;
}
```

(continued)

Figure 13-4. *continued*

```
//**********************************************************************
// MyIInputMethod Object implementation
//----------------------------------------------------------------------
// Object constructor
MyIInputMethod::MyIInputMethod () {

    m_lRef = 1;     //Set reference count to 1 on create.
    g_DllCnt++;
    return;
}
//----------------------------------------------------------------------
// Object destructor
MyIInputMethod::~MyIInputMethod () {
    g_DllCnt--;
    return;
}
//----------------------------------------------------------------------
// QueryInterface - Called to see what interfaces this object supports
STDMETHODIMP MyIInputMethod::QueryInterface (THIS_ REFIID riid,
                                             LPVOID *ppv) {

    // If caller wants our IUnknown or IID_ICeFileFilter object,
    // return a pointer to the object.
    if (IsEqualIID (riid, IID_IUnknown) ||
        IsEqualIID (riid, IID_IInputMethod)){

        // Return pointer to object.
        *ppv = (IInputMethod *)this;
        AddRef();                  // Inc ref to prevent delete on return.
        return NOERROR;
    }
    *ppv = NULL;
    return (E_NOINTERFACE);
}
//----------------------------------------------------------------------
// AddRef - Increment object reference count.
STDMETHODIMP_(ULONG) MyIInputMethod::AddRef (THIS) {
    ULONG cnt;

    cnt = (ULONG)InterlockedIncrement (&m_lRef);
    return cnt;
}
//----------------------------------------------------------------------
// Release - Decrement object reference count.
STDMETHODIMP_(ULONG) MyIInputMethod::Release (THIS) {
    ULONG cnt;
```

```
    cnt = (ULONG)InterlockedDecrement (&m_lRef);
    if (cnt == 0) {
        delete this;
        return 0;
    }
    return cnt;
}
//----------------------------------------------------------------------
// Select - The IM has just been loaded into memory.
//
HRESULT STDMETHODCALLTYPE MyIInputMethod::Select (HWND hwndSip) {
    RECT rect;
    WNDCLASS wc;
    HBITMAP hBmp, hbmpMask;

    m_hwndParent = hwndSip;

    // Create image list for narrow (16x16) image.
    m_himlNarrow = ImageList_Create (16, 16, ILC_COLOR | ILC_MASK,
                                     1, 0);
    hBmp = LoadBitmap (hInst, TEXT ("NarrowBmp"));
    hbmpMask = LoadBitmap (hInst, TEXT ("NarrowMask"));
    ImageList_Add (m_himlNarrow, hBmp, hbmpMask);
    DeleteObject (hBmp);
    DeleteObject (hbmpMask);

    // Create image list for wide (32x16) image.
    m_himlWide = ImageList_Create (32, 16, ILC_COLOR | ILC_MASK, 1, 0);
    hBmp = LoadBitmap (hInst, TEXT ("WideBmp"));
    hbmpMask = LoadBitmap (hInst, TEXT ("WideMask"));
    ImageList_Add (m_himlWide, hBmp, hbmpMask);
    DeleteObject (hBmp);
    DeleteObject (hbmpMask);

    // Register SIP window class.
    memset (&wc, 0, sizeof (wc));
    wc.style = CS_DBLCLKS;
    wc.lpfnWndProc = NPWndProc;                    // Callback function
    wc.hInstance = hInst;                          // Owner handle
    wc.hbrBackground = (HBRUSH) GetStockObject (WHITE_BRUSH);
    wc.lpszClassName = MYSIPCLS;                   // Window class name
    if (RegisterClass (&wc) == 0) return E_FAIL;

    // Create SIP window.
    GetClientRect (hwndSip, &rect);
```

(continued)

Figure 13-4. *continued*

```
    m_hwndMyWnd = CreateWindowEx (0, MYSIPCLS, TEXT (""),
                  WS_VISIBLE | WS_CHILD | WS_BORDER, rect.left,
                  rect.top, rect.right - rect.left,
                  rect.bottom - rect.top, hwndSip, (HMENU)IDC_SIP,
                  hInst, 0);
    if (!IsWindow (m_hwndMyWnd))
        return E_FAIL;

    return S_OK;
}
//----------------------------------------------------------------------
// Deselect - The IM is about to be unloaded.
//
HRESULT STDMETHODCALLTYPE MyIInputMethod::Deselect (void) {

    // Clean up since we're about to be unloaded.
    DestroyWindow (m_hwndMyWnd);
    UnregisterClass (MYSIPCLS, hInst);
    ImageList_Destroy (m_himlNarrow);
    ImageList_Destroy (m_himlWide);
    return S_OK;
}
//----------------------------------------------------------------------
// Showing - The IM is about to be made visible.
//
HRESULT STDMETHODCALLTYPE MyIInputMethod::Showing (void) {
    return S_OK;
}
//----------------------------------------------------------------------
// Hiding - The IM is about to be hidden.
//
HRESULT STDMETHODCALLTYPE MyIInputMethod::Hiding (void) {
    return S_OK;
}
//----------------------------------------------------------------------
// GetInfo - The SIP wants info from the IM.
//
HRESULT STDMETHODCALLTYPE MyIInputMethod::GetInfo (
                                                 IMINFO __RPC_FAR *pimi) {
    pimi->cbSize = sizeof (IMINFO);
    pimi->hImageNarrow = m_himlNarrow;
    pimi->hImageWide = m_himlWide;
    pimi->iNarrow = 0;
    pimi->iWide = 0;
    pimi->fdwFlags = SIPF_DOCKED;
```

```
    pimi->rcSipRect.left = 0;
    pimi->rcSipRect.top = 0;
    pimi->rcSipRect.right = FLOATWIDTH;
    pimi->rcSipRect.bottom = FLOATHEIGHT;
    SendMessage (m_hwndMyWnd, MYMSG_METHCALL, 1, (LPARAM) pimi);
    return S_OK;
}
//----------------------------------------------------------------------
// ReceiveSipInfo - The SIP is passing info to the IM.
//
HRESULT STDMETHODCALLTYPE MyIInputMethod::ReceiveSipInfo (
                                             SIPINFO __RPC_FAR *psi) {
    // Pass the SIP info data to the window.
    SendMessage (m_hwndMyWnd, MYMSG_METHCALL, 2, (LPARAM) psi);
    return S_OK;
}
//----------------------------------------------------------------------
// RegisterCallback - The SIP is providing the IM with the pointer to
// the IIMCallback interface.
//
HRESULT STDMETHODCALLTYPE MyIInputMethod::RegisterCallback (
                                  IIMCallback __RPC_FAR *lpIMCallback) {
    m_pIMCallback = lpIMCallback;
    PostMessage (m_hwndMyWnd, MYMSG_METHCALL, 0, (LPARAM)m_pIMCallback);
    return S_OK;
}
//----------------------------------------------------------------------
// GetImData - An application is passing IM-specfic data to the IM.
//
HRESULT STDMETHODCALLTYPE MyIInputMethod::GetImData (DWORD dwSize,
                                                   LPVOID pvImData) {
    return E_FAIL;
}
//----------------------------------------------------------------------
// SetImData - An application is querying IM-specfic data from the IM.
//
HRESULT STDMETHODCALLTYPE MyIInputMethod::SetImData (DWORD dwSize,
                                                   LPVOID pvImData) {
    return S_OK;
}
//----------------------------------------------------------------------
// UserOptionsDlg - The SIP control panel applet is asking for a
// configuration dialog box to be displayed.
//
```

(continued)

Figure 13-4. *continued*

```
HRESULT STDMETHODCALLTYPE MyIInputMethod::UserOptionsDlg (
                                                     HWND hwndParent) {
    MessageBox (hwndParent, TEXT ("UserOptionsDlg called."),
                TEXT ("NumPanel"), MB_OK);
    return S_OK;
}
```

NPWnd.c

```
//======================================================================
// NPWnd - An IM window
//
// Written for the book Programming Windows CE
// Copyright (C) 1998 Douglas Boling
//======================================================================
#include <windows.h>
#define COBJMACROS
#include <aygshell.h>                // Palm-size PC shell includes
#include <sip.h>                     // SIP includes
#include <keybd.h>                   // Keyboard flag includes

#include "NPWnd.h"                  // Includes for this window

INT DrawButton (HDC hdc, RECT *prect, LPTSTR pChar, BOOL fPressed);

TCHAR g_tcBtnChar[] = {
        TEXT ('1'), TEXT ('2'), TEXT ('3'), TEXT ('-'), TEXT ('*'),
        TEXT ('4'), TEXT ('5'), TEXT ('6'), TEXT ('+'), TEXT ('/'),
        TEXT ('7'), TEXT ('8'), TEXT ('9'), TEXT ('0'), TEXT ('='),
};
UINT g_BtnVChars[] = {
        '1', '2', '3', VK_HYPHEN, VK_MULTIPLY,
        '4', '5', '6', VK_ADD, VK_SLASH,
        '7', '8', '9', '0', VK_EQUAL,
};

// Message dispatch table for SipWindowProc
const struct decodeUINT SipMessages[] = {
    WM_CREATE, DoCreateSip,
    WM_PAINT, DoPaintSip,
    MYMSG_METHCALL, DoSetSipInfo,
    WM_LBUTTONDOWN, DoMouseSip,
    WM_MOUSEMOVE, DoMouseSip,
    WM_LBUTTONUP, DoMouseSip,
```

```
    WM_LBUTTONDBLCLK, DoMouseSip,
    WM_DESTROY, DoDestroySip,
};
//======================================================================
// NPWndProc - Window procedure for SIP
//
LRESULT CALLBACK NPWndProc (HWND hWnd, UINT wMsg, WPARAM wParam,
                            LPARAM lParam) {
    INT  i;
    // Call routine to handle control message.
    for (i = 0; i < dim(SipMessages); i++) {
        if (wMsg == SipMessages[i].Code)
            return (*SipMessages[i].Fxn)(hWnd, wMsg, wParam, lParam);
    }
    return DefWindowProc (hWnd, wMsg, wParam, lParam);
}
//----------------------------------------------------------------------
// DoCreateSip - Process WM_CREATE message for window.
//
LRESULT CALLBACK DoCreateSip (HWND hWnd, UINT wMsg, WPARAM wParam,
                              LPARAM lParam) {
    LPSIPWNDSTRUCT pWndData;

    // Allocate a data structure for the SIP keyboard window.
    pWndData = LocalAlloc (LPTR, sizeof (SIPWNDSTRUCT));
    if (!pWndData) {
        DestroyWindow (hWnd);
        return 0;
    }
    memset (pWndData, 0, sizeof (SIPWNDSTRUCT));
    GetWindowRect (GetParent (hWnd), &pWndData->rectDocked);
    SetWindowLong (hWnd, GWL_USERDATA, (INT)pWndData);
    return 0;
}
//----------------------------------------------------------------------
// DoSetSipInfo - Process set information user message for window.
//
LRESULT CALLBACK DoSetSipInfo (HWND hWnd, UINT wMsg, WPARAM wParam,
                               LPARAM lParam) {
    LPSIPWNDSTRUCT pWndData;
    RECT rect;

    pWndData = (LPSIPWNDSTRUCT)GetWindowLong (hWnd, GWL_USERDATA);
    switch (wParam) {
    // Called when RegisterCallback method called
```

(continued)

Figure 13-4. *continued*

```
    case 0:
        pWndData->pIMCallback = (IIMCallback *)lParam;
        break;
    // Called when GetInfo method called
    case 1:
        pWndData->imi = *(IMINFO *)lParam;
        break;
    // Called when ReceiveSipInfo method called
    case 2:
        GetClientRect (GetParent(hWnd), &rect);
        MoveWindow (hWnd, 0, 0, rect.right - rect.left,
                    rect.bottom - rect.top, TRUE);
        break;
    }
    return 0;
}
//----------------------------------------------------------------------
// DoPaintSip - Process WM_PAINT message for window.
//
LRESULT CALLBACK DoPaintSip (HWND hWnd, UINT wMsg, WPARAM wParam,
                             LPARAM lParam) {
    HDC hdc;
    HBRUSH hOld;
    PAINTSTRUCT ps;
    RECT rect, rectBtn;
    INT i, j, k, x, y, cx, cy, cxBtn, cyBtn;
    LPSIPWNDSTRUCT pWndData;

    pWndData = (LPSIPWNDSTRUCT)GetWindowLong (hWnd, GWL_USERDATA);

    hdc = BeginPaint (hWnd, &ps);
    GetClientRect (hWnd, &rect);

    cx = (rect.right - rect.left - 3 - GRIPWIDTH) / CXBTNS;
    cy = (rect.bottom - rect.top - 3) / CYBTNS;
    cxBtn = cx - 3;
    cyBtn = cy - 3;

    // Select a brush for the gripper.
    hOld = SelectObject (hdc, GetStockObject (GRAY_BRUSH));
    Rectangle (hdc, rect.left, rect.top, rect.left + GRIPWIDTH,
               rect.bottom);
    SelectObject (hdc, hOld);

    k = 0;
    y = 3;
```

```
    for (i = 0; i < CYBTNS; i++) {
        x = 3 + GRIPWIDTH;
        for (j = 0; j < CXBTNS; j++) {
            SetRect (&rectBtn, x, y, x + cxBtn, y + cyBtn);
            DrawButton (hdc, &rectBtn, &g_tcBtnChar[k++],
                        pWndData->dwBtnDnFlags & (1 << k));
            x += cx;
        }
        y += cy;
    }
    EndPaint (hWnd, &ps);
    return 0;
}
//----------------------------------------------------------------------
// HandleGripper - Handles mouse messages over gripper bar
//
LRESULT HandleGripper (HWND hWnd, LPSIPWNDSTRUCT pWndData, UINT wMsg,
                       LPARAM lParam) {
    POINT pt;

    pt.x = (short)LOWORD (lParam);
    pt.y = (short)HIWORD (lParam);

    switch (wMsg) {
    case WM_LBUTTONDOWN:
        if (pt.x > GRIPWIDTH+3)
            return 0;
        SetCapture (hWnd);
        pWndData->fMoving = TRUE;
        pWndData->ptMovBasis = pt;
        ClientToScreen (hWnd, &pt);
        pWndData->ptMovStart = pt;
        break;

    case WM_MOUSEMOVE:
        if (!pWndData->fMoving)
            return 0;
        break;
    case WM_LBUTTONUP:
        if (!pWndData->fMoving)
            return 0;
        ReleaseCapture();
        pWndData->fMoving = FALSE;
        ClientToScreen (hWnd, &pt);
```

(continued)

Figure 13-4. *continued*

```
        if ((abs (pWndData->ptMovStart.x - pt.x) < 3) &&
            (abs (pWndData->ptMovStart.y - pt.y) < 3))
            break;
        pt.x -= pWndData->ptMovBasis.x;
        pt.y -= pWndData->ptMovBasis.y;

        pWndData->imi.rcSipRect.right = FLOATWIDTH;
        pWndData->imi.rcSipRect.bottom = FLOATHEIGHT;
        pWndData->imi.rcSipRect.left = pt.x;
        pWndData->imi.rcSipRect.top = pt.y;
        pWndData->imi.rcSipRect.right += pt.x;
        pWndData->imi.rcSipRect.bottom += pt.y;

        pWndData->imi.fdwFlags &= ~SIPF_DOCKED;
        pWndData->imi.fdwFlags |= SIPF_ON;

        IIMCallback_SetImInfo(pWndData->pIMCallback, &pWndData->imi);
        break;

    case WM_LBUTTONDBLCLK:
        if (pt.x > GRIPWIDTH+3)
            return 0;
        ReleaseCapture();
        pWndData->fMoving = FALSE;
        pWndData->imi.fdwFlags |= (SIPF_DOCKED | SIPF_ON);
        pWndData->imi.rcSipRect = pWndData->rectDocked;
        IIMCallback_SetImInfo(pWndData->pIMCallback, &pWndData->imi);
        break;
    }
    pWndData->dwBtnDnFlags = 0;   // If we moved, no buttons down.
    return 1;
}
//----------------------------------------------------------------------
// DoMouseSip - Process mouse button messages for window.
//
LRESULT CALLBACK DoMouseSip (HWND hWnd, UINT wMsg, WPARAM wParam,
                             LPARAM lParam) {
    RECT rect;
    INT i, x, y, cx, cy, nChar;
    DWORD BtnDnFlags, dwShiftFlags = 0;
    LPSIPWNDSTRUCT pWndData;
    pWndData = (LPSIPWNDSTRUCT)GetWindowLong (hWnd, GWL_USERDATA);

    // See if moving gripper or gripper tap.
    if (HandleGripper (hWnd, pWndData, wMsg, lParam))
        return 0;
```

```
    // Compute the button grid.
    GetClientRect (hWnd, &rect);
    cx = (rect.right - rect.left - 3 - GRIPWIDTH) / CXBTNS;
    cy = (rect.bottom - rect.top - 3) / CYBTNS;
    x = ((LOWORD (lParam)-3-GRIPWIDTH) / cx);
    y = ((HIWORD (lParam)-3) / cy);
    i = (y * CXBTNS) + x;    // i now contains btn index.

    // Do small amount of message-specific processing.
    switch (wMsg) {
    case WM_LBUTTONDOWN:
        SetCapture (hWnd);
        // Fall through to WM_MOUSEMOVE case.
    case WM_MOUSEMOVE:
        BtnDnFlags = 1 << i;
        break;
    case WM_LBUTTONDBLCLK:
    case WM_LBUTTONUP:
        if (pWndData->dwBtnDnFlags)
            ReleaseCapture();
        BtnDnFlags = 0;
        nChar = g_tcBtnChar[i];
        IIMCallback_SendCharEvents(pWndData->pIMCallback,
                                   g_BtnVChars[i], KeyStateDownFlag,
                                   1, &dwShiftFlags, &nChar);
        break;
    }
    // Decide how to repaint wnd. If only 1 btn changed, just
    // invalidate that rect. Otherwise, invalidate entire wnd.
    if ((wMsg == WM_MOUSEMOVE) && (BtnDnFlags !=pWndData->dwBtnDnFlags))
        InvalidateRect (hWnd, NULL, FALSE);
    else {
        i = 3+GRIPWIDTH;   // Compensate for the gripper on left side.
        SetRect (&rect, x*cx+i, y*cy, (x+1)*cx+i, (y+1)*cy);
        InvalidateRect (hWnd, &rect, FALSE);
    }
    pWndData->dwBtnDnFlags = BtnDnFlags;
    return 0;
}
//----------------------------------------------------------------------
// DoDestroySip - Process WM_DESTROY message for window.
//
LRESULT CALLBACK DoDestroySip (HWND hWnd, UINT wMsg, WPARAM wParam,
                               LPARAM lParam) {
    LPSIPWNDSTRUCT pWndData;
```

(continued)

Figure 13-4. *continued*

```
    pWndData = (LPSIPWNDSTRUCT)GetWindowLong (hWnd, GWL_USERDATA);
    LocalFree (pWndData);
    return 0;
}
//----------------------------------------------------------------------
// DrawButton - Draws a button
//
INT DrawButton (HDC hdc, RECT *prect, LPTSTR pChar, BOOL fPressed) {

    if (!fPressed) {
        SelectObject (hdc, GetStockObject (BLACK_PEN));
        SelectObject (hdc, GetStockObject (WHITE_BRUSH));
        SetBkColor (hdc, RGB (255, 255, 255));
        SetTextColor (hdc, RGB (0, 0, 0));
    } else {
        SelectObject (hdc, GetStockObject (BLACK_BRUSH));
        SelectObject (hdc, GetStockObject (WHITE_PEN));
        SetTextColor (hdc, RGB (255, 255, 255));
        SetBkColor (hdc, RGB (0, 0, 0));
    }
    Rectangle (hdc, prect->left, prect->top, prect->right,
               prect->bottom);
    Rectangle (hdc, prect->left+1, prect->top+1, prect->right+1,
               prect->bottom+1);
    DrawText (hdc, pChar, 1, prect, DT_CENTER|DT_VCENTER|DT_SINGLELINE);
    return 0;
}
```

Although NumPanel is divided into two source files, both the *IInputMethod* interface and the NumPanel window procedure run in the same thread. In response to a call to the Select method of *IInputMethod*, the NumPanel window class is registered and the window is created as a child of the IM's window. The image lists used by the IM are also created here with the handles stored in member variables in the *MyInputMethod* object. The only other work of interest performed by the code in NumPanel.cpp is the code for the *GetInfo* method. In this method, the image list handles are provided to the IM along with the requested dimensions of the undocked window. The dimensions of the docked window are provided by the system.

For three other methods, all *MyInputMethod* does is to post messages to the window procedure of the NumPanel window. In NMWnd.c, these messages are fielded in the MYMSG_METHCALL user-defined message. The three methods make available to the window a pointer to the *IIMCallback* interface and notify the NumPanel window that the window is about to be displayed or that the state of the input panel is changing.

The other code in the NumPanel window draws the keys on the window and processes the stylus taps. The *DoPaintSip* routine handles the painting. The routine draws a grid of 3 rows of 5 columns of buttons. In each button, a character is drawn to label it. A separate bit array contains the up or down state of each button. If the button is down, the background of the button is drawn in reverse colors.

Two routines—*DoMouseSip* and *HandleGripper*—handle the mouse messages. The mouse messages all initially go to *DoMouseSip*, which calls *HandleGripper*. If the routine determines that the mouse message is on the gripper or that the window is currently being dragged, *HandleGripper* handles the message. Otherwise, if the *DoMouseSip* routine determines that a mouse tap occurs on one of the buttons, it calls the *SendCharEvent* method of *IIMCallback* to send the character to the focus window.

When the window is dragged to a new location on the screen, the *HandleGripper* routine clears the SIPF_DOCKED flag and sets the new size and location of the SIP by calling the *SetImInfo* method of *IIMCallback*. When the user double-taps on the gripper, *HandleGripper* sets the SIPF_DOCKED flag and sets the SIP rectangle to the original docked rectangle that was saved when the NumPanel window was first created.

HARDWARE KEYS

The SIP isn't the only way for the user to enter keystrokes to an application. All Palm-size PCs and some Handheld PCs have additional buttons that can be assigned to launch an application or to send unique virtual key codes to applications. The Palm-size PC has an additional set of buttons known as *navigation buttons* that mimic common navigation keys such as Line Up and Line Down. These navigation keys give the user shortcuts, which allow scrolling up and down as well as access to the services of the often-used keys, Enter and Escape. Because the scrolling buttons simply send Page Up, Page Down, Line Up, and Line Down key messages, your application doesn't have to take any special action to use these keys.

The application launch buttons are another matter. When pressed, these keys cause the shell to launch the application registered for that key. Although a system is usually configured with default associations, you can override these settings by modifying the registry so that pressing a hardware control button launches your application. An application can also override the application launch ability of a specific key by having the key mapped directly to a window. In addition, you can use the hot key features of GWE to override the hardware key assignment and send a hot key message to a window.

Virtual Codes for Hardware Keys

Since the hardware control buttons are treated as keyboard keys, pressing a hardware control key results in WM_KEYDOWN and WM_KEYUP messages as well as a WM_CHAR message if the virtual key matches a Unicode character. The system mapping of these keys employs two strategies. For the navigation keys, the resulting virtual key codes are codes known and used by Windows applications so that those applications can "use" the keys without even knowing that's what they're doing. The application-launching keys, on the other hand, need virtual key codes that are completely different from previously known keys so that they won't conflict with standard key events.

Navigation key codes

As I mentioned above, the navigation keys are mapped to common navigation keys. The actual virtual key code mapping for navigation keys is shown below.

Key	*Action*	*Key Message*	*Key Code*
Action	Press	WM_KEYDOWN	OEM dependent*
Action	Release	WM_KEYUP	OEM dependent*
		WM_KEYDOWN	VK_RETURN
		WM_CHAR	VK_RETURN
		WM_KEYUP	VK_RETURN
Exit	Press	WM_KEYDOWN	OEM dependent*
	Release	WM_KEYUP	OEM dependent*
		WM_KEYDOWN	VK_ESCAPE
		WM_KEYUP	VK_ESCAPE
Rock Up	Press	WM_KEYDOWN	OEM dependent*
	Release	WM_KEYUP	OEM dependent*
		WM_KEYDOWN	VK_UP
		WM_KEYUP	VK_UP
Rock Down	Press	WM_KEYDOWN	OEM dependent*
	Release	WM_KEYUP	OEM dependent*
		WM_KEYDOWN	VK_DOWN
		WM_KEYUP	VK_DOWN

* OEM-dependent key codes differ from system to system. Some OEMs might not send these messages while others may send the messages with a virtual key code of 0.

Unfortunately, there's no reliable way of determining whether a VK_RETURN key event came from the SIP or from a hardware button. Each OEM has a different method of assigning virtual key codes to the hardware navigation buttons.

Application launch key codes

The shell manages the application launch keys named App1 through a possible App16. These keys produce a combination of virtual key codes that are interpreted by the shell. The codes produced are a combination of the left Windows key (VK_LWIN) and a virtual code starting with 0xC1 and continuing up, depending on the application key pressed. For example, App1 key produces the virtual key sequence VK_LWIN followed by 0xC1 while App2 key produces the sequence VK_LWIN followed by 0xC2.

Using the Application Launch Keys

Applications are bound to a specific application launch key through entries in the registry. Specifically, each key has an entry under [HKEY_LOCAL_MACHINE]\Software\Microsoft\Shell\Keys. The entry is the virtual key combination for that key, so for the App1 key, the entry is

```
[HKEY_LOCAL_MACHINE]\Software\Microsoft\Shell\Keys\40C1
```

The 40C1 comes from the code 0x40, which indicates the Windows key has been pressed and concatenated with the virtual key code of the application key, 0xC1. The default value assigned to this key is the fully specified path name of the application assigned to the key. A few other values are also stored under this key. The *ResetCmd* value is the path name of the application that is assigned to this key if the Restore Defaults button is pressed in the Palm-size PC's Button control panel applet. The *Name* value contains the friendly name of the key, such as Button 1 or Side Button.

The only way to change the application assigned to a key is to manually change the registry entry to point to your application. Of course, you shouldn't do this without consulting your users, since they may have already configured the application keys to their liking. The routine that follows assigns an application to a specific button and returns the name of the application previously assigned to that button. The *vkAppKey* parameter should be set to an application key virtual key code, 0xC1 through 0xCF. The *pszNewApp* parameter should point to the fully specified path name of the application you want to assign to the key.

```
//----------------------------------------------------------------------
// SetAppLaunchKey - Assigns an application launch key to an
// application
//
int SetAppLaunchKey (LPTSTR pszNewApp, BYTE vkAppKey, LPTSTR pszOldApp,
                     INT nOldAppSize) {
    TCHAR szKeyName[256];
    DWORD dwType, dwDisp;
    HKEY hKey;
    INT rc;
```

(continued)

```
    // Construct the key name.
    wsprintf (szKeyName,
        TEXT ("Software\\Microsoft\\Shell\\Keys\\40%02x"), vkAppKey);

    // Open the key.
    rc = RegCreateKeyEx (HKEY_LOCAL_MACHINE, szKeyName, 0, TEXT (""),
                         0, 0, NULL, &hKey, &dwDisp);
    if (rc != ERROR_SUCCESS)
        return -1;

    // Read the old application name.
    rc = RegQueryValueEx (hKey, TEXT (""), 0, &dwType,
                          (PBYTE)pszOldApp, &nOldAppSize);
    if (rc != ERROR_SUCCESS) {
        RegCloseKey (hKey);
        return -2;
    }
    // Set the new application name.
    rc = RegSetValueEx (hKey, TEXT (""), 0, REG_SZ, (PBYTE)pszNewApp,
                        (lstrlen (pszNewApp)+1) * sizeof (TCHAR));
    RegCloseKey (hKey);
    if (rc != ERROR_SUCCESS)
        return -3;

    return 0;
}
```

When an application button is pressed, the system doesn't check to see whether another copy of the application is already running—it simply launches a new copy. You should design your application, especially on the Palm-size PC, to check to see whether another copy of your application is already running and if so, to activate the first copy of the application and quietly terminate the newly launched copy.

You can determine whether an application is assigned to a key by calling the Palm-size PC–specific function *SHGetAppKeyAssoc*, which is prototyped as

```
Byte SHGetAppKeyAssoc (LPCTSTR ptszApp);
```

The only parameter is the fully qualified name of your application. If a key is associated with your application, the function returns the virtual key code for that key. If no key is associated with your application, the function returns 0. This function is useful because most applications, when launched by an application key, override the default action of the key so that another copy of the application won't launch if the key is pressed again.

Dynamically Overriding Application Launch Keys

A running application can override a launch key in two ways. The first method is to use the Palm-size PC–specific function *SHSetAppKeyWndAssoc*, prototyped as

```
BOOL SHSetAppKeyWndAssoc (BYTE bVk, HWND hwnd);
```

The first parameter is the virtual key code of the hardware button. The second parameter is the handle of the window that's to receive the notices of button presses. For example, a program might redirect the App1 key to its main window with the following line of code:

```
SHSetAppKeyWndAssoc (0xC1, hwndMain);
```

The window that has redirected an application might receive key messages but the virtual key codes received and the type of key messages are OEM-specific. The chief reason for using *SHSetAppKeyWndAssoc* is to prevent the button from launching an application. When you no longer want to redirect the application launch key, you can call *SHSetAppKeyWndAssoc* specifying the virtual code of the key and NULL for the window handle.

The second method of overriding an application launch key is to use the *RegisterHotKey* function. The advantage of using the *RegisterHotKey* function is that your window will receive known messages, albeit WM_HOTKEY instead of WM_KEY*xxx* messages when the key is pressed, no matter what application currently has the keyboard focus. A second, even more important reason to use *RegisterHotKey* is that this function is supported on Handheld PCs as well as on Palm-size PCs. This function is prototyped as

```
BOOL RegisterHotKey (HWND hWnd, int id, UINT fsModifiers, UINT vk);
```

The first parameter is the handle of the window that receives the WM_HOTKEY messages. The second parameter is an application-defined identifier that's included with the WM_HOTKEY message to indicate which key caused the message. The *fsModifiers* parameter should be set with flags, indicating the shift keys that must also be pressed before the WM_HOTKEY message can be sent. These self-explanatory flags are MOD_ALT, MOD_CONTROL, MOD_SHIFT, and MOD_WIN. An additional flag, MOD_KEYUP, indicates that the window will receive WM_HOTKEY messages when the key is pressed and when the key is released. When using *RegisterHotKey* on application keys, you should always specify the MOD_WIN flag because application keys always are combined with the Windows shift-modifier key. The final parameter, *vk*, is the virtual key code for the key you want as your hot key. This key doesn't have to be a hardware key code; you can actually use almost any other virtual key code supported by Windows, although assigning Shift-F to your custom fax application might make Pocket Word users a bit irate when they tried to enter a capital *F*.

When the key registered with *RegisterHotKey* is pressed, the system sends a WM_HOTKEY message to the window. The *wParam* parameter contains the ID code you specified when you called *RegisterHotKey*. The low word of *lParam* parameter contains the shift-key modifiers, MOD_*xxx*, that were set when the key was pressed, while the high word of *lParam* contains the virtual key code for the key.

The disadvantage of using *RegisterHotKey* is that if another application has already registered the hot key, the function will fail. This can be problematic on the Palm-size PC, where applications stay running until the system purges them to gain extra memory space. One strategy to employ when you want to use a hardware key temporarily—for example, in a game—would be to use *SHGetAppKeyAssoc* to determine what application is currently assigned to that key. It's a good bet that if *RegisterHotKey* failed due to some other program using it, the application assigned the application key is also the one currently running and has redirected the hot key to its window. You can then send a WM_CLOSE message to that application's main window to see whether it will close and free up the hardware key.

When you no longer need the hot key, you can unregister the hot key with this function:

```
BOOL UnregisterHotKey (HWND hWnd, int id);
```

The two parameters are the window handle of the window that had registered the hot key and the ID value for that hot key you assigned with *RegisterHotKey*.

As you can see, the Palm-size PC presents new problems and new opportunities for developers. The SIP technology, originally developed for the Palm-size PC, is already starting to migrate to other Windows CE platforms. The application launch buttons are another area of cross platform cooperation. You use the same techniques for managing these buttons on H/PCs as on Palm-size PC devices.

In the final chapter of the book, I step back from application programming and look at system programming issues. Chapter 14 explains how the different components of Windows CE work together while presenting a unified Win32-compatible API.

Chapter 14

System Programming

This chapter takes a slightly different tack from the previous chapters of the book. Instead of touring the API of a particular section of Windows CE, I'll show you Windows CE from a systems perspective.

Windows CE presents standard Windows programmers some unique challenges. First, because Windows CE supports a variety of different microprocessors and system architectures, you can't count on the tried and true IBM/Intel PC–compatible design that can be directly traced to the IBM PC/AT released in 1984. Windows CE runs on devices that are more different than alike. Different CPUs use different memory layouts and while the set of peripherals are similar, they have totally different designs.

In addition to using different hardware, Windows CE itself changes, depending on how it's ported to a specific platform. While all H/PCs of a particular version have the same set of functions, that set is slightly different from the functions provided by Windows CE for the Palm-size PC. In addition, Windows CE is designed as a collection of components so that OEMs using Windows CE in embedded devices can remove unnecessary small sections of the operating system, such as the Clipboard API.

All of these conditions make programming Windows CE unique, and I might add, fun. This chapter describes some of these cross-platform programming issues. I'll begin the chapter by describing how the system boots itself, from reset to running applications.

THE BOOT PROCESS

If you're a systems programmer, you might enjoy, as I do, seeing how a system boots up. When you think about it, booting up poses some interesting problems. How does the system load its first process when the process loader is part of that process you want to load? How do you deal with 30 different CPUs, each with its own method of initialization?

In the case of Windows CE, we have a somewhat better view of this process. Because the hardware varies radically across the different platforms, Windows CE requires that OEMs write some of the initialization code. In each instance, this initialization code is incorporated in the HAL (hardware abstraction layer), under the kernel. When an OEM builds the system for a specific hardware platform, the HAL is statically linked with the Windows CE kernel code to produce NK.exe.

Actually, the OEM writes far more than the HAL when porting Windows CE to a new platform. The OEM also writes a thin layer under the Graphics Windowing and Event Manager (GWE) to link in some of the more basic drivers used by GWE. In addition, the OEM must write a series of device drivers, from a display device driver to drivers for the keyboard, touch panel, serial, and audio devices. The actual collection of drivers is, of course, dependent on the hardware. This collection of the HAL layer plus the drivers is called the OEM Adaptation Layer, or OAL.

In any case, let's get back to the boot process. This boot process is described through the documentation and code examples provided in the Embedded Tool Kit. Our journey starts, as with any CPU, at the occurrence of a reset.

Reset

When the system is reset, the CPU jumps to the entry point of NK.exe, which is the kernel module for Windows CE.[1] The code at the entry point is actually written by the OEM, not Microsoft. This routine, written in assembler, is traditionally named *Startup* and is responsible for initializing the CPU into a known state for the kernel. Since most CPUs supported by Windows CE are embedded CPUs, they generally have a number of registers that must be set to configure the system for the speed and sometimes even the base address of memory. Startup is also responsible for initializing any caches and for ensuring that the system is in an uncached, flat addressing mode.

NK.exe

When Startup has completed its tasks, it jumps to the entry point of the kernel, *KernelStart*. This is the entry point for the Microsoft written code for NK. *KernelStart* configures the virtual memory manager, initializes the interrupt vector table to a

---

1. The program that builds the ROM image inserts the proper jump instructions, or vector, at the reset location, which causes the CPU to start executing code at the entry point of NK.

default handler, and calls down to the OEM layer to initialize the debug serial port.[2] *KernelStart* then initializes its local heap by copying the initialized heap data from ROM into system RAM, in a routine named *KernelRelocate*. Now that the local heap for NK.exe has been initialized, the code can start acting less like a loader and more like a program. The kernel then calls back down to the HAL to the *OEMInit* routine.

The job of *OEMInit*, which is customarily written in C, is to initialize any OEM-specific hardware. This includes hooking interrupts, initializing timers, and testing memory.[3] Many systems perform some initial configuration of integrated peripherals, if only to place them in a quiescent state until the driver for that peripheral can be loaded. The *OEMInit* routine is generally responsible for drawing the splash screen on the display during a boot process.

When *OEMInit* returns, the kernel calls back into the HAL to ask whether any additional RAM is available to the system. When an OEM creates a ROM image of the Windows CE files, it makes some preliminary estimates about the size and location of the RAM as well as defining the size and location of the ROM. This routine, *OEMGetExtensionDRAM*, allows the OEM to tell the kernel about additional RAM that can be used by the system. Once *OEMGetExtensionDRAM* returns, the kernel enables interrupts and calls the scheduler to schedule the first thread in the system.

FileSys.exe

At this point, the kernel looks for the file FileSys.exe and launches that application. FileSys is the process that manages the file system, the database functions, and more important at this stage, the registry. When FileSys is loaded, it looks in the RAM to see whether it can find a file system already initialized. If one is found, FileSys uses the already initialized file system. This allows Windows CE devices to retain the data in their RAM-based file systems over a reboot of the system.

If FilSys doesn't find a file system, it creates one that merges an empty RAM file system with the files on ROM. FileSys knows what files are in ROM by means of a table that's built into the ROM image by the ROM builder program, which merged all the disparate programs into one image. FileSys reads the default directory structure from a file stored on ROM, which is composed of entries suggested by Microsoft for the OEM. In addition to initializing the file system, FileSys creates default database images and a default registry. The initial images of the default databases and default registry are also defined in files in ROM written by the OEM and Microsoft. This file-driven initialization process allows OEMs to customize the initial images of the file system from the directory tree to the individual entries in the registry.

---

2. All Windows CE systems, including all H/PCs and Palm-size PCs, have a way to access a dedicated serial port used for debugging. For consumer platforms, where controlling hardware cost is critical, this debug serial port is typically on a separate "debug board" that can be plugged into a system.

3. It's the OEM's decision whether to run a RAM test when the system boots. Microsoft requires only that the system boot process is complete within 5 or so seconds.

One other feature of FileSys acts like a back door to the file system. During initialization, FileSys looks to see whether the system is connected to a debugging station, which is a PC running a program named CESH.[4] Traditionally, the connection between the PC and the Windows CE system was a parallel port link. However, starting with Windows CE 2.1, this link can be made over Ethernet or a dedicated serial link. If such a connection is found, FileSys takes the additional step of looking on the PC for files when the system asks it to load a file. In effect, this seamlessly extends the \windows directory on the Windows CE system to include any files in a specific directory on the debugging PC. This procedure allows the system to load files that aren't in the initial ROM image during the boot process. Later, when the system is running, files can be directly loaded from the PC without your first having to copy them into the object store of the Windows CE system.

Launching optional processes

Once FileSys has initialized, the system initialization can proceed. The kernel needs to wait because, at this point, it needs data from the registry to continue the boot process. Specifically, the kernel looks in the registry for values under the key [HKEY_LOCAL_MACHINE]\Init. The values in this key provide the name, order, and dependencies of a set of processes that should be loaded as part of the boot process. The processes to be launched are specified by values named *Launchxx* where the *xx* is a number defining the order of the launch. An optional value, *Dependxx*, can be used to make the launch of a process dependent on another process specified earlier in the order. For example, the following set of values was take from the registry of a Casio Handheld PC.

```
Value                Data             Comments
Launch10             SHELL.EXE

Launch20             DEVICE.EXE

Launch30             GWES.EXE
Depend30             0014             Depends on Device (0x14 == 20)

Launch50             EXPLORER.EXE
Depend50             0014 001E        Depends on Device and GWE
```

While I've listed the values in their launch order for clarity, the values don't need to be in order in the registry. The numbers embedded in the names of the values define the launch order.

The kernel loads each of the modules listed in their own process space. When a process completes its initialization successfully, it signals this event to the kernel

4. CESH is a PC-based debugging tool provided by Microsoft in the ETK. It was called PPSH, for parallel port shell, before the release of Windows CE 2.1.

by calling the function *SignalStarted* and passing the application's launch number. The kernel knows from these calls to *SignalStarted* that any dependent processes can now be launched.

What's interesting here is that each of these components of the operating system functions as a standard user-level process. Just because a process appears in this list doesn't mean that it's part of the operating system. While this launch list is generally used only by OEMs, you can insert other processes in this list, as long as the functions needed by that application have been loaded earlier in the list. For example, you could write an application that's loaded after Device and before GWES.exe as long as that application didn't make any calls to the window manager or the graphics functions until GWE is initialized. On the other hand, launching an application with a standard user interface before Explorer loads can confuse Explorer. So unless you need to launch a process to support system services, you should use Explorer to launch your applications on startup. One additional point—you *can't* separately launch an application that depends on Explorer to launch successfully because Explorer.exe doesn't call *SignalStarted* during its initialization. Now let's follow this sequence and examine each of these launched processes.

Shell.exe

Shell is an interesting process because it's not even in the ROM of most systems. Shell.exe is the Windows CE side of CESH, the command line–based monitor. Because Shell.exe isn't in the ROM, the only way to load it is by connecting the system to the PC debugging station so that the file can be automatically downloaded from the PC.

CESH uses the FileSys link to the debugging PC to communicate with the programmer. Instead of opening a file on the PC, CESH opens a console session on the PC. The CESH debugger provides a number of useful functions to the Windows CE OEM. First it gives the OEM developer a command line shell, running on a PC that can be used to launch applications, query system status, and read and write memory on the system.

CESH also lets the OEM developer manipulate a very handy feature of debug builds of Windows CE named *debug zones*. When you're developing software, it's often useful to insert debugging messages that print out information. On a Windows CE system, these debugging messages are sent via the debug serial port. The problem is that too many messages can hide a critical error behind a blizzard of irrelevant informational messages. On the other hand, Murphy says that the day after you strip all your debugging messages from a section of code, you'll need those messages to diagnose a newly reported bug. Debug zones allow the developer to interactively enable and disable sets of debug messages that are built into debug builds of Windows CE. All of the base processes bundled with Windows CE as well as all the device drivers have these debugging messages built into them. Every message is assigned to one of 16 defined debug zones for that process or DLL. So, a developer can use CESH to enable or disable each of the 16 zones for a module, which enables or disables the messages for that zone.

Shell.exe uses a Windows CE version of toolhelp.dll, so when Shell loads, it loads ToolHelp. Shell doesn't bring any additional function to Windows CE; it's just one place where Microsoft has added built-in debugging features for the OEM.

Device.exe

After Shell, the next module in the launch list is Device.exe. Notice that there's no *Depened20* line that makes the launch of Device.exe dependent on Shell.exe. That's important because Shell won't launch successfully unless the system has Shell.exe in the object store or is connected to a debug station. The job of Device.exe is to load and manage the installable device drivers in the system. This includes managing any PCMCIA Card drivers that must be dynamically loaded and freed as well.

When Device.exe loads, it first loads the PCMCIA driver. It then looks in the registry under [HKEY_LOCAL_MACHINE\BuiltIn for the list of the other drivers it must load when it initializes. This list is contained in a series of keys. The names of the keys don't matter—it's the values contained in the keys that define which drivers to load and the order in which to load them. Figure 14-1 shows the contents of the WaveDev key. The Wave driver is the audio driver.

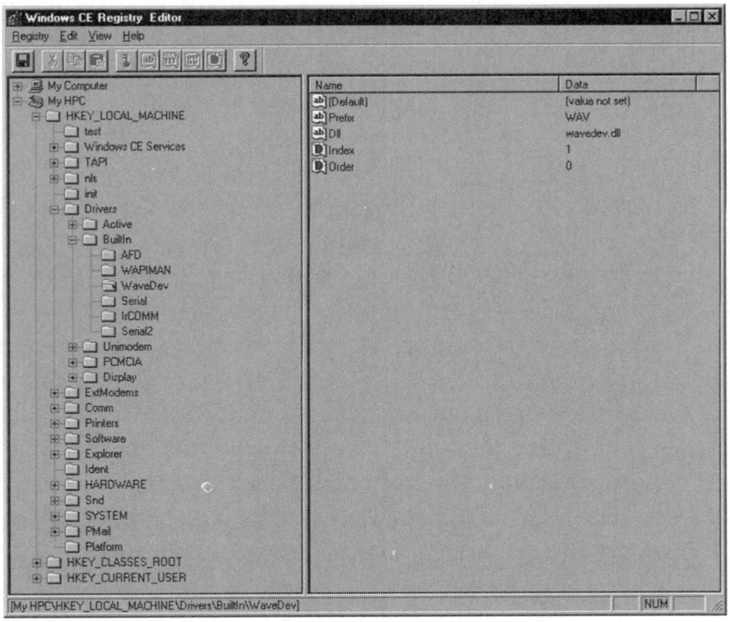

Figure 14-1. *The registry key for the Wave driver on an HP360.*

The four values under this key are the basic four entries used by a device driver under Windows CE. The Prefix value defines the three-letter name of the driver. Applications that want to open this driver use the three-letter key with the number that Windows CE appends to create the device name.

The Index value is the number that will be appended to the device name. The Dll key specifies the name of the DLL that implements the driver. This is the DLL that Device.exe loads.

The Order value allows the OEM to recommend the order in which the drivers are loaded. Device.exe loads drivers with lower Order values before drivers with higher Order values in the registry. As Device.exe reads each of the registry keys, it loads the DLL specified, calls *RegisterDevice* to register the DLL as a device driver with the system, and then unloads the DLL. The DLL stays in memory because *RegisterDevice* increments the use count of the DLL.

While this is the standard load procedure, you can use another method. If the driver key contains a value named Entry, Device loads the DLL, and then, instead of calling *RegisterDevice*, it calls the entry point in the driver named in Entry. The driver is then responsible for calling the *RegisterDevice* function on its own so that it will be registered as a driver with the system.

The Entry value allows OEMs to fine-tune the loading process for a driver, if necessary. If the Entry key is present, another key, Keep, can also be specified. Specifying the Keep key tells Device.exe not to attempt to unload the driver after it calls the driver's entry point. This allows the driver DLL to avoid calling *RegisterDevice* and therefore avoid being a driver at all. Instead, the DLL is simply loaded into the process space of Device.exe.

One of the subtle points about having Device.exe load the installable drivers is that all these drivers will execute in the same 32-MB process space of Device.exe. This coincidence allows related drivers to actually directly call entry points in each other, although the preferred method would be to formally make an IOCTL call into the other driver. You can't count on this common process arrangement in future versions of Windows CE.

GWES.exe

Referring again to the list in the registry, we see that the next module to be loaded is GWES.EXE. GWES.exe contains the GWE subsystem. As I mentioned earlier in the book, GWE stands for Graphics Windowing and Event Manager. Essentially, GWES is the graphical user interface over the top of the base operating system composed of NK, FileSys, and Device.

Because GWE forms the user interface of a graphical version of Windows CE, it's not too surprising that the drivers that directly access the user interface hardware, the keyboard, the touch panel, and the display are loaded by GWES.exe instead of

Device.exe. A "pure" operating system design would isolate these drivers with the others, down in the kernel. Given the lightweight nature of Windows CE, however, having these drivers loaded by GWE makes a faster and simpler interface for the operating system. These drivers also don't support the standard stream interface required of drivers loaded by Device.exe. Instead, each driver has a custom set of entry points called by GWES.exe.

Unlike device.exe, GWES.exe doesn't load just any set of drivers. Instead, GWE simply loads three predefined drivers: the keyboard driver, the touch panel driver, and the display driver. GWES.exe looks in the registry in the following keys to find these drivers all under the root registry key of [HKEY_LOCAL_MACHINE]:

Driver	*Registry Key Name*	*Value Name*
Keyboard	\HARDWARE\DEVICEMAP\KEYBD	DriverName
Touch Panel	\HARDWARE\DEVICEMAP\TOUCH	DriverName
Display	\SYSTEM\GDI\DRIVERS	Display

If the registry entries aren't found for a particular driver, GWES.exe uses default names for that driver. These drivers are written by the OEM and are called *native drivers* to differentiate them from the installable form of a driver loaded by Device.

In addition to the drivers loaded by GWE, the OEM also is charged with writing a small amount of system adaptation code to support GWE. This code deals with providing information about the state of the battery and an interface to the notification LED, if one is present. Although this code can be statically linked to GWE when the system is built, many OEMs isolate this code into one or more DLLs and statically link only a small amount of code that loads these DLLs.

Custom processes

At this point in the boot process, Windows CE, as an operating system, is up and running. All that's left is to launch the shell. Some OEMs, however, launch processes at this point that manage some OEM-specific tasks. Although you *can* launch other applications before you launch the Explorer, you should be careful about that, as I mentioned before. The Explorer isn't written to handle visible top-level windows that are created before the Explorer. You can see this by inserting the following lines in the init key that launches Calc before the Explorer:

```
Launch45        calc.exe
Depend45        0014 001E
```

After you insert the lines, reset your Windows CE device. Tap the desktop button on the right end of the taskbar a couple of times and you'll see the Calc window. Pressing on the Pop-Up button reduces the size of the Calc window so you can again see the Explorer underneath. Notice that the taskbar doesn't have a button for the

Calc window. Nor, if you press Alt-Tab, is Calc listed in the Active Tasks list. Figure 14-2 shows this unusual arrangement of Calc and the Explorer on an H/PC.

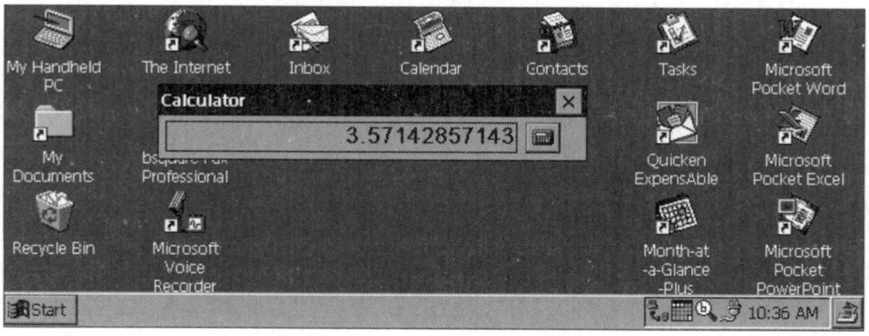

Figure 14-2. *The unusual arrangement of Calc and the Explorer.*

Because of the limitations of this arrangement, you shouldn't launch applications with a user interface before the Explorer is launched. On the other hand, if you have an application that doesn't have a user interface but you need to launch before the shell, this is the time to do it.

Explorer.exe

Finally the list is terminated by the launch of the Explorer, or Shell32.exe, if the system is a Palm-size PC. The Explorer is, of course, the shell. Although the latest versions of the Explorer add some functions to the API, the trend is to move as many functions as possible from the shell to the operating system. This allows developers of embedded systems to use those functions even if the system doesn't include the Explorer.

At this point, the location of the list of files launched during startup changes from the registry to the file system. After the Explorer initializes the desktop and the taskbar window, it looks in the \windows\startup directory and launches any executables or shortcuts contained in that directory. This is the standard, user-accessible method for launching applications when the system starts. This auto launching is part of the Explorer, so if you're building an embedded system without the Explorer, you'll have to perform this last task yourself.

Powering Up Doesn't Boot the System

One thing to always remember in Windows CE is that for most configurations, including all battery-powered systems, pressing the Power button doesn't reset the device. As I explained in Chapter 6, when the system is powered down it doesn't really turn off. Instead, the system enters an extremely low power state in which all the peripherals and the CPU power down but the state of the RAM is maintained. When a user presses the power switch, the system restores power and simply returns to the thread that was executing when the power button was originally pressed.

Battery-powered Windows CE systems are reset only when power is initially applied to the system—that is, when the first set of batteries is put in the device. Other than that, resets occur only when the user presses the reset button that's generally exposed through a pinhole somewhere on the case of the device. Memory isn't erased when a user presses the reset switch, which allows FileSys to use the Object Store that was already in RAM before the reset.

System Configuration

At this point, the system is up and running, but just what is running and how is it configured? Figure 14-3 shows the system after a reset has occurred. The diagram separates the individual processes into their memory slots. Remember that slot 0 is reserved for the currently active process. The list of DLLs that each process has loaded is shown below the name of the process.

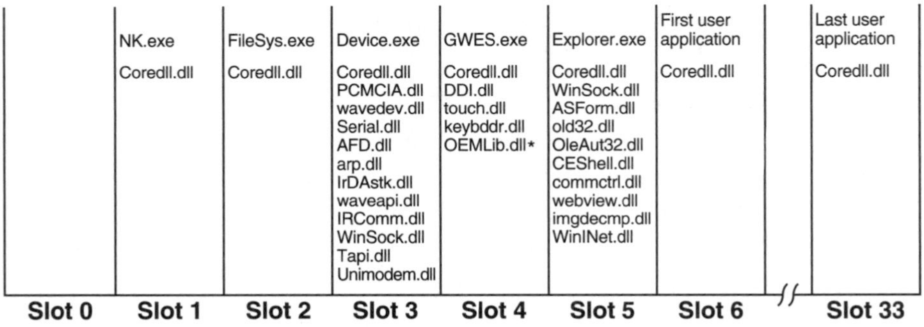

* OEMLib.dll - Most OEMs have a DLL to support battery and notification LED.

Figure 14-3. *The system configuration after the system starts up.*

Note that Coredll.dll is loaded by every process. Coredll provides the entry points for most APIs supported by Windows CE. As a call is made into Coredll.dll, it redirects the call to the appropriate server process—NK, FileSys, Device, GWE, or Explorer.

Notice that Shell.exe isn't shown in Figure 14-3. This is because when I captured the information for this figure, the Windows CE device I was using wasn't connected to a debug PC, so Shell.exe wasn't loaded.

Writing Cross-Platform Windows CE Applications

Over the years, Windows programmers have had to deal concurrently with different versions of the operating system. Part of the solution to the problem this situation posed was to call *GetVersion* or *GetVersionEx* and to act differently depending on the version of the operating system you were working with. You can't do that under Windows CE. Because of the flexible nature of Windows CE, two builds of the same version of Windows CE can have different APIs. The question remains, though, how do you support multiple platforms with a common code base? How does the operating system version relate to the different platforms?

Platforms and Operating System Versions

To understand how the different platforms relate to the different versions of Windows CE, it helps to know how the Windows CE development team is organized within Microsoft. Windows CE is supported by a core OS group within Microsoft. This team is responsible for developing the operating system, including the file system and the various communication stacks.

Coordinating efforts with the OS team are the various platform teams, working on the Handheld/PC, Palm-size PC, Auto PC, and Handheld/PC Pro as well as many other platforms yet to be announced. Each team is responsible for defining a suggested hardware platform, defining applications that will be bundled with the platform, and deciding which version of the operating system the platform will use. Because the OS team works continually to enhance Windows CE, planning new versions over time, each platform team generally looks to see what version of Windows CE will be ready when that team's platform ships.

The individual platform teams also develop the shells for their platforms. Because each team develops its own shell, many new functions or platform-specific functions first appear as part of the shell of a specific platform. Then if the newly introduced functions have a more general applicability, they're moved to the base operating system in a later version. You can see this process in both the Notification API and the SIP API. Both these sets of functions started in their specific platform group and have now been moved out of the shell and are in the base operating system.

Following is a list of the different platforms that have been released up to this point and the version of Windows CE that those platforms use.

Platform	***Windows CE version***
Original H/PC	1.00
Japanese release of H/PC	1.01
H/PC	2.00
Original Palm-size PC	2.01
Windows CE 2.1 for embedded systems	2.10
Handheld PC Pro	2.11

It's not presently difficult to remember what platform is associated with which version of Windows CE, but this task will get more difficult as more platforms are added to the list.

You can choose from a number of ways to deal with the problem of different platforms and different versions of Windows CE. Let's look at a few.

Compile-Time Versioning

The version problem can be tackled in a couple of places in the development process of an application. At compile time, you can use the preprocessor definition _WIN32_WCE to determine the version of the operating system you're currently building for. By enclosing code in an *#if* preprocessor bracket, you can cause code to be compiled for specific versions of Windows CE.

Following is an example of a routine that's tuned both for the original Palm-size PC and for other platforms equipped with a SIP that are based on Windows CE 2.1.

```
//
// Get SIP rectangle.
//
void MyGetSipRect (RECT *prect) {

#if _WIN32_WCE == 201
    SIPINFO si;

    memset (&si, 0, sizeof (si));
    si.cbSize = sizeof (SIPINFO);
    // On original Palm-size PC, use old PPC Shell function.
    SHSipInfo (SPI_GETSIPINFO, 0, &si, 0);
    *prect = si.rcSipRect;

#elif _WIN32_WCE >= 210
    SIPINFO si;

    si.cbSize = sizeof (SIPINFO);
    // On Windows CE 2.1 or later, use new function.
    SipGetInfo (&si);
    *prect = si.rcSipRect;

#else
    // Else, there isn't support for this function.
#error No SIP support.
#endif
    return;
}
```

A virtue of this code is that linker links the appropriate function for the appropriate platform. Without this sort of compile-time code, you couldn't simply put a run-time *if* statement around the call to *SHSipInfo* because the program would never load on anything but a Palm-size PC. The loader wouldn't be able to find the exported function *SHSipInfo* in Coredll.dll because it's present only in Palm-size PC versions of Windows CE.

Builds for the Palm-size PC have an additional define set named *Palm*. So you can bracket Palm-size PC code in the following way:

```
#ifdef Palm
    // Insert Palm-size PC code here.
#endif
```

The reason I didn't use the *Palm* define in the previous code is that I wanted to target specifically the original Palm-size PC, which used Windows CE version 2.01. Otherwise, if I'd used the *Palm* define, that code would be included even when I was compiling for newer versions of the Palm-size PC, which will use a newer version of Windows CE. The problem with using conditional compilation is that while you still have a common source file, the resulting executable will be different for each platform.

Explicit Linking

You can tackle the version problem other ways. Sometimes one platform requires that you call a function different from one you need for another platform you're working with but you want the same executable file for both platforms. A way to accomplish this is to explicitly link to a DLL using *LoadLibrary*, *GetProcAddress*, and *FreeLibrary*. You can then call the function as if it had been implicitly linked by the loader.

LoadLibrary is prototyped as

```
HINSTANCE LoadLibrary (LPCTSTR lpLibFileName);
```

The only parameter is the filename of the DLL. The system searches for DLLs in the following order:

1. The image of the DLL that has already been loaded in memory.
2. The statically linked DLL in ROM for a ROM-based executable.
3. The file in the path specified in *lpLibFileName* parameter.
4. The directory of the executable loading the library. (This is supported only for Windows CE 2.1 and later.)
5. The Windows directory.

6. The root directory.
7. The image of the DLL in ROM.

Notice in the search sequence above that if the DLL has already been loaded into memory, the system uses that copy of the DLL even if your pathname specifies a different file from the DLL originally loaded. Another peculiarity of *LoadLibrary* is that it ignores the extension of the DLL when comparing the library name to what's already in memory. For example, if SIMPLE.dll is already loaded in memory and you attempt to load the control panel applet SIMPLE.cpl, which is under the covers simply a DLL with a different extension, the system won't load SIMPLE.cpl. Instead the system returns the handle to the previously loaded SIMPLE.dll.

LoadLibrary returns either an instance handle to the DLL that's now loaded or 0 if for some reason the function couldn't load the library.

Once you have the DLL loaded, you get a pointer to a function exported by that DLL by using *GetProcAddress*, which is prototyped as

```
FARPROC GetProcAddress (HMODULE hModule, LPCWSTR lpProcName);
```

The two parameters are the handle of the module and the name of the function you want to get a pointer to. The function returns a pointer to the function or 0 if the function isn't found. Once you have a pointer to a function, you can simply call the function as if the loader had implicitly linked it.

When you are finished with the functions from a particular library, you need to call *FreeLibrary*, prototyped as

```
BOOL FreeLibrary (HMODULE hLibModule);
```

FreeLibrary decrements the use count on the DLL. If the use count drops to 0, the library is removed from memory.

The following routine solves that same problem I presented earlier (how to retrieve the SIP rectangle without using compile-time switches). The routine explicitly loads the two possible functions, calls the one found, and frees the libraries loaded. A more efficient application would load the libraries and query the function pointers when the program was initialized instead of performing this task each time the functions were needed.

```
// Type definitions for the function pointers.
typedef HRESULT (CALLBACK* GETSIPINFOFUNC)(SIPINFO *);
typedef HRESULT (CALLBACK* SHSIPINFOFUNC)(INT, INT, PVOID, INT);

int MyGetSipRect1 (RECT *prect) {
    HINSTANCE hCoreDll, hAGYShell;
    GETSIPINFOFUNC lpfnGetSipInfo;
```

```
    SHSIPINFOFUNC lpfnSHSipInfo;
    SIPINFO si;
    INT rc = 0;

    //Load the DLL.
    hCoreDll = LoadLibrary(TEXT("coredll.dll"));
    // If we can't load Coredll, something is really strange!
    if (!hCoreDll)
        return -2;

    // Prepare structure for call.
    memset (&si, 0, sizeof (si));
    si.cbSize = sizeof (SIPINFO);

    // Attempt to get a pointer to GetSipInfo.
    lpfnGetSipInfo = (GETSIPINFOFUNC)GetProcAddress(hCoreDll,
                                                 TEXT("GetSipInfo"));
    if (lpfnGetSipInfo) {
        // Call GetSipInfo.
        (*lpfnGetSipInfo)(&si);

    } else {
        // This DLL exports the Palm-size PC shell APIs.
        hAGYShell= LoadLibrary(TEXT("aygshell.dll"));
        if (hAGYShell) {

            // Attempt to get a pointer to SHSipInfo.
            lpfnSHSipInfo = (SHSIPINFOFUNC)GetProcAddress(
                                          hAGYShell, TEXT("SHSipInfo"));
            if (lpfnSHSipInfo) {
                (*lpfnSHSipInfo)(SPI_GETSIPINFO, 0, &si, 0);
            } else
                rc = -1;
            FreeLibrary (hAGYShell);
        } else
            rc = -1;
    }
    // At this point, one of the two functions has been called.
    if (!rc)
        *prect = si.rcSipRect;

    // Free the library.
    FreeLibrary(hCoreDll);
    return rc;
}
```

This routine can be run on any platform, but will work only with those that export one of the two get SIP information functions. On the other platforms, the routine simply returns an error code of −1.

Run-Time Version Checking

When you're determining the version of the Windows CE operating system at run time, you use the same function as under other versions of Windows—*GetVersionEx*, which fills in a OSVERSIONINFO structure defined as

```
typedef struct _OSVERSIONINFO{
    DWORD dwOSVersionInfoSize;
    DWORD dwMajorVersion;
    DWORD dwMinorVersion;
    DWORD dwBuildNumber;
    DWORD dwPlatformId;
    TCHAR szCSDVersion[ 128 ];
} OSVERSIONINFO;
```

Upon return from *GetVersionEx*, the major and minor version fields are filled with the Windows CE version. This means, of course, that you can't simply copy desktop Windows code that branches on classic version numbers like 3.1 or 4.0. The *dwPlatformId* field contains the constant VER_PLATFORM_WIN32_CE under Windows CE.

Although it's possible to differentiate platforms by means of their unique Windows CE versions numbers, you shouldn't. For example, you can identify the current Palm-size PC by its unique Windows CE version, 2.01, but newer versions of the Palm-size PC will be using different versions of Windows CE. Instead, you should call *SystemParametersInfo* with the SPI_GETPLATFORMTYPE constant, as in

```
TCHAR szPlat[256];
INT rc;

rc = SystemParametersInfo (SPI_GETPLATFORMTYPE, sizeof (szPlat),
                           szPlat, 0);
if (lstrcmp (szPlat, TEXT ("Jupiter") == 0) {
    // Running on an H/PC Pro
} else if (lstrcmp (szPlat, TEXT ("Palm PC") == 0) {
    // Running on a Palm-size PC
} else if (lstrcmp (szPlat, TEXT ("HPC") == 0) {
    // Running on an H/PC
}
```

Aside from the differences in their shells, though, the platform differences aren't really that important. The base operating system is identical in all but some fringe cases.[5] The best strategy for writing cross-platform Windows CE software is to avoid differentiating among the platforms at all—or at least as little as possible.

For the most part, discrepancies among the user interfaces for the different consumer Windows CE devices can be illustrated by the issue of screen dimension. The Palm-size PC's portrait-mode screen requires a completely different layout for most windows compared to the Handheld PC's landscape-mode screen. The Handheld PC Pro's screen is landscape, but it's at least double the height of an H/PC screen. So, instead of looking at the platform type to determine what screen layout to use, you'd do better to simply check the screen dimensions using *GetDeviceCaps*.

This has been a brief tour of some of the system issues for Windows CE. The configurability of Windows CE makes it the chameleon of operating systems, changing its API and even its size, depending on the platform. Whatever the platform differences, though, remember that underneath the covers, all configurations of Windows CE share the same basic design. Keep this in mind as you look at the wide variety of platforms developed for Windows CE.

The configurability of Windows CE makes it a powerful tool for the systems designer. Its Win32 API makes it familiar to thousands of programmers. But most of all, the Windows CE operating system is fun. Enjoy it.

---

5. For example, first generation Palm-size PCs don't support printing, so you wouldn't want to implicitly link to any printing APIs if you wanted an application that ran on both the H/PC 2 and the original Palm-size PC.

Appendix

COM Basics

To qualify as COM compliant, all an object has to have is an implicit *IUnknown* interface. In C++ talk, a COM-compliant interface must be derived from, directly or indirectly, an *IUnknown* interface. The *IUnknown* interface has three methods: *QueryInterface*, *AddRef*, and *Release*.

The methods *AddRef* and *Release* are called to increment and decrement the reference count of the COM interface. When an object is created and a pointer is returned by the object to an interface, an implicit call is made to *AddRef*. When a program no longer needs an interface, it calls *Release*, which decrements the use count for that interface. When the use count for all interfaces exposed by the object is 0, *Release* deletes the object.

The third method, *QueryInterface*, provides a way for the caller to receive a pointer to a specific interface the COM-compliant object supports. *QueryInterface* is prototyped as

```
HRESULT QueryInterface (REFIID iid, void ** ppvObject);
```

The first parameter to *QueryInterface* is an identifier to an interface that the caller is requesting. Because there are countless interfaces and new ones generated every day, this identifier needs to be unique—globally and universally unique—for all COM interfaces ever programmed. Thus, the globally unique interface identifier is abbreviated as a *GUID*, pronounced *goo-id* or *gwid* (rhymes with *squid*). If you create your own unique interface, you too will need a *GUID*. You can create your own *GUID* using the GUIDGEN utility provided with Visual C++.

The second parameter is a pointer that receives a pointer to the requested interface. So, to use an interface, the *QueryInterface* method, which must be included in any COM-compliant interface, is called to return a pointer to a specific interface exposed by the object. If the object makes a requested interface available, a pointer to that interface is returned.

USING COM INTERFACES

In many cases, applications use COM interfaces without even knowing that's what they're doing. In the RAPI stream example I used in Chapter 11, both the CE-side and the PC-side applications used an *IStream* interface. This interface is formally defined as a COM interface, but because the pointer to the interface was provided, neither the CE- nor the PC-side applications had to know anything about COM.

COM CLIENTS

However, sometimes you need to directly create and use a COM interface. In this case, the application becomes a COM client. Before an application can use the COM library, it must initialize the COM handler library by calling this function:

```
HRESULT CoInitialize (LPVOID pvReserved);
```

The only parameter is reserved and must be set to NULL. *CoInitialize* returns S_OK if the COM library was successfully initialized. You can also call *CoInitializeEx* instead of *CoInitialize* if you need to more precisely specify how the library is initialized.

To get a pointer to an interface, you then call the function

```
STDAPI CoCreateInstance (REFCLSID rclsid, LPUNKNOWN pUnkOuter,
                         DWORD dwClsContext, REFIID riid,
                         LPVOID * ppv);
```

The first parameter for this function is the class identifier of the interface or object you're trying to load. The second parameter specifies a pointer to an *IUnknown* interface if you're trying to extend an existing COM object with the new interface. In all our uses of this function, this parameter will be NULL. The third parameter is the context in which you're opening the object. For our purposes, we'll use CLSCTX_SERVER, indicating that we're loading a server object and we don't care whether that server runs in our process or in another process. The *riid* parameter specifies the interface ID of the interface to be loaded. Finally, the last parameter, *ppv*, is a pointer to a value that will receive the pointer for the interface being requested. *CoCreateInstance* returns S_OK if the function was successful.

At this point, the client has a pointer to the interface for the object and can call the methods provided by that interface. When you're finished with the object, a call should be made to the *Release* method of the object to free it.

COM Servers

On the other side of the COM fence is a COM server. A COM server is a module, EXE or DLL, which provides one or more COM interfaces. There are three types of COM servers: in-proc, which operate in the process space of the caller; local, which operate in separate process spaces; and remote, which reside on different machines from the COM clients. For all our cases, I'll stick to COM in-proc servers.

A COM server doesn't just provide a pointer to a requested interface. That would be too easy. Instead, a COM server must make available an additional interface, *IClassFactory*. *IClassFactory* is composed of the *IUnknown* methods, *QueryInterface*, *AddRef*, and *Release* along with two additional methods, *CreateInstance* and *LockServer*. It's through calling methods within *IClassFactory* that the server creates other objects provided by the server. To create an instance of an interface, the client calls the *IClassFactory CreateInstance* method. The prototype for this function is

```
HRESULT CreateInstance (IUnknown * pUnkOuter, REFIID riid,
                        void ** ppvObject);
```

If the first parameter isn't NULL, it's a pointer to the controlling *IUnknown* interface of the aggregate object. The second parameter is the CLSID for the object you want to create. Finally, the *ppvObject* parameter points to a value that receives a pointer to the interface provided by the newly created object. When *CreateInstance* is called, *IClassFactory* examines the GUID in the *riid* parameter to see what interface it identifies; if that interface is provided, *IClassFactory* creates the object that implements the interface and queries that object for a pointer to the newly created interface that it then returns.

So, just how does a client get access to *IClassFactory*? Well, if we're talking about in-proc servers, COM must fall back on functions exported from the DLL or EXE. A COM server must provide at least two exported functions—*DllGetClassObject* and *DllCanUnloadNow*. The first of these two functions is the more interesting. It's prototyped as

```
STDAPI DllGetClassObject (REFCLSID rclsid, REFIID riid,
                          LPVOID *ppv);
```

The first parameter is a class ID, which is a GUID that uniquely identifies this object. Many objects, for example, might export a file filter interface, but each will have a unique class ID. The COM server must ensure that the object's class ID matches its class ID and, if not, return an error to the caller.

The second parameter is the reference ID for the interface that the client wants. When calling *DllGetClassObject*, the reference ID usually identifies either *IUnknown* or *IClassFactory*, but it doesn't have to. The server's responsibility here is to compare the requested interface with those that are provided. If that interface is provided, a pointer to it is returned in a variable pointed to by the third parameter, *ppv*.

The other exported function is

```
STDAPI DllCanUnloadNow (void);
```

This function is called to determine whether the DLL can be removed from memory. The COM server is required to know whether any object instances are currently active. Each object tracks this information by keeping a count of the number of instances of itself currently created. This is what the *AddRef* and *Release* methods of *IUnknown* are used for. When the use count for a specific object/interface reaches 0, the *Release* method of the object deletes the object. The server must keep track of which objects are still in use and return S_FALSE from *DllCanUnloadNow* if any of the objects it serves are still in use.

One final point. Plenty of DLLs are in a system. How does the COM library know to load a specific DLL to look for a specific class? It looks in the registry. If you look in the registry under [HKEY_CLASSES_ROOT]\CLSID, you'll see hundreds of keys with class IDs for names. Each of these class ID keys has a series of subkeys that identify the DLL that implements that COM object as well as identifying other information important to the implementation of the server.

So, to sum up, when a client requests an object identified by a class ID, the COM library finds the name of the DLL that implements that object in the registry. The DLL is then loaded into memory and the exported function *DllGetClassObject* is called to confirm the class ID and to (usually) request a pointer to the object's associated *IClassFactory* object. The client then calls a method in the *IClassFactory* interface to request that an object that has a requested interface be created. If it can comply, the *IClassFactory* object creates the requested object and returns a pointer to an interface exposed by that object. Whew.

This short and almost trivial COM primer isn't meant to turn you into a COM expert. My goal is to help you identify all those extra functions implemented in the examples that use COM in this book. I strongly encourage you to learn more about COM from other books and papers. For all its complexity, COM is the wave of the present and future in Windows programming.

Index

Page numbers for tables and figures are in italics.

C

E

G

K

M

Q

R

T

W

X

Z

DOUG BOLING

Kathleen Atkins

A longtime contributing editor to *PC Magazine* and a columnist for *MIND,* Douglas Boling is known as an astute observer of the computer industry. He's an electrical engineer by training and a writer and a consultant by practice. He's a recognized authority on Windows CE and other programming topics and speaks at leading professional developer conferences.

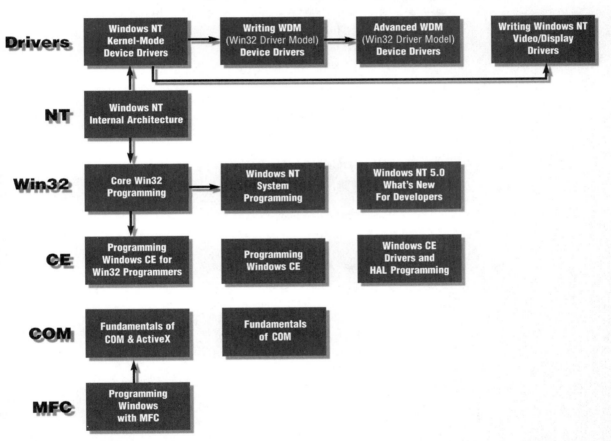

The manuscript for this book was prepared using Microsoft Word 97. Pages were composed by Microsoft Press using Adobe PageMaker 6.52 for Windows, with text in Garamond and display type in Helvetica Black. Composed pages were delivered to the printer as electronic prepress files.

Cover Graphic Designer
Tim Girvin Design, Inc.

Cover Illustrator
Glenn Mitsui

Interior Graphic Artist
Michael Victor

Principal Compositor
Elizabeth Hansford

Principal Proofreader/Copy Editor
Cheryl Penner

Indexer
Liz Cunningham

MICROSOFT LICENSE AGREEMENT

(Book Companion CD)

IMPORTANT—READ CAREFULLY: This Microsoft End-User License Agreement ("EULA") is a legal agreement between you (either an individual or an entity) and Microsoft Corporation for the Microsoft product identified above, which includes computer software and may include associated media, printed materials, and "on-line" or electronic documentation ("SOFTWARE PRODUCT"). Any component included within the SOFTWARE PRODUCT that is accompanied by a separate End-User License Agreement shall be governed by such agreement and not the terms set forth below. By installing, copying, or otherwise using the SOFTWARE PRODUCT, you agree to be bound by the terms of this EULA. If you do not agree to the terms of this EULA, you are not authorized to install, copy, or otherwise use the SOFTWARE PRODUCT; you may, however, return the SOFTWARE PRODUCT, along with all printed materials and other items that form a part of the Microsoft product that includes the SOFTWARE PRODUCT, to the place you obtained them for a full refund.

SOFTWARE PRODUCT LICENSE

The SOFTWARE PRODUCT is protected by United States copyright laws and international copyright treaties, as well as other intellectual property laws and treaties. The SOFTWARE PRODUCT is licensed, not sold.

1. **GRANT OF LICENSE.** This EULA grants you the following rights:

   a. **Software Product.** You may install and use one copy of the SOFTWARE PRODUCT on a single computer. The primary user of the computer on which the SOFTWARE PRODUCT is installed may make a second copy for his or her exclusive use on a portable computer.

   b. **Storage/Network Use.** You may also store or install a copy of the SOFTWARE PRODUCT on a storage device, such as a network server, used only to install or run the SOFTWARE PRODUCT on your other computers over an internal network; however, you must acquire and dedicate a license for each separate computer on which the SOFTWARE PRODUCT is installed or run from the storage device. A license for the SOFTWARE PRODUCT may not be shared or used concurrently on different computers.

   c. **License Pak.** If you have acquired this EULA in a Microsoft License Pak, you may make the number of additional copies of the computer software portion of the SOFTWARE PRODUCT authorized on the printed copy of this EULA, and you may use each copy in the manner specified above. You are also entitled to make a corresponding number of secondary copies for portable computer use as specified above.

   d. **Sample Code.** Solely with respect to portions, if any, of the SOFTWARE PRODUCT that are identified within the SOFTWARE PRODUCT as sample code (the "SAMPLE CODE"):

      i. **Use and Modification.** Microsoft grants you the right to use and modify the source code version of the SAMPLE CODE, *provided* you comply with subsection (d)(iii) below. You may not distribute the SAMPLE CODE, or any modified version of the SAMPLE CODE, in source code form.

      ii. **Redistributable Files.** Provided you comply with subsection (d)(iii) below, Microsoft grants you a nonexclusive, royalty-free right to reproduce and distribute the object code version of the SAMPLE CODE and of any modified SAMPLE CODE, other than SAMPLE CODE (or any modified version thereof) designated as not redistributable in the Readme file that forms a part of the SOFTWARE PRODUCT (the "Non-Redistributable Sample Code"). All SAMPLE CODE other than the Non-Redistributable Sample Code is collectively referred to as the "REDISTRIBUTABLES."

      iii. **Redistribution Requirements.** If you redistribute the REDISTRIBUTABLES, you agree to: (i) distribute the REDISTRIBUTABLES in object code form only in conjunction with and as a part of your software application product; (ii) not use Microsoft's name, logo, or trademarks to market your software application product; (iii) include a valid copyright notice on your software application product; (iv) indemnify, hold harmless, and defend Microsoft from and against any claims or lawsuits, including attorney's fees, that arise or result from the use or distribution of your software application product; and (v) not permit further distribution of the REDISTRIBUTABLES by your end user. Contact Microsoft for the applicable royalties due and other licensing terms for all other uses and/or distribution of the REDISTRIBUTABLES.

2. **DESCRIPTION OF OTHER RIGHTS AND LIMITATIONS.**

   - **Limitations on Reverse Engineering, Decompilation, and Disassembly.** You may not reverse engineer, decompile, or disassemble the SOFTWARE PRODUCT, except and only to the extent that such activity is expressly permitted by applicable law notwithstanding this limitation.
   - **Separation of Components.** The SOFTWARE PRODUCT is licensed as a single product. Its component parts may not be separated for use on more than one computer.
   - **Rental.** You may not rent, lease, or lend the SOFTWARE PRODUCT.
   - **Support Services.** Microsoft may, but is not obligated to, provide you with support services related to the SOFTWARE PRODUCT ("Support Services"). Use of Support Services is governed by the Microsoft policies and programs described in the user manual, in "on-line" documentation, and/or in other Microsoft-provided materials. Any supplemental software code provided to you as part of the Support Services shall be considered part of the SOFTWARE PRODUCT and subject to the terms and conditions of this EULA. With

respect to technical information you provide to Microsoft as part of the Support Services, Microsoft may use such information for its business purposes, including for product support and development. Microsoft will not utilize such technical information in a form that personally identifies you.

- **Software Transfer.** You may permanently transfer all of your rights under this EULA, provided you retain no copies, you transfer all of the SOFTWARE PRODUCT (including all component parts, the media and printed materials, any upgrades, this EULA, and, if applicable, the Certificate of Authenticity), **and** the recipient agrees to the terms of this EULA.
- **Termination.** Without prejudice to any other rights, Microsoft may terminate this EULA if you fail to comply with the terms and conditions of this EULA. In such event, you must destroy all copies of the SOFTWARE PRODUCT and all of its component parts.

3. **COPYRIGHT.** All title and copyrights in and to the SOFTWARE PRODUCT (including but not limited to any images, photographs, animations, video, audio, music, text, SAMPLE CODE, REDISTRIBUTABLES, and "applets" incorporated into the SOFTWARE PRODUCT) and any copies of the SOFTWARE PRODUCT are owned by Microsoft or its suppliers. The SOFTWARE PRODUCT is protected by copyright laws and international treaty provisions. Therefore, you must treat the SOFTWARE PRODUCT like any other copyrighted material **except** that you may install the SOFTWARE PRODUCT on a single computer provided you keep the original solely for backup or archival purposes. You may not copy the printed materials accompanying the SOFTWARE PRODUCT.

4. **U.S. GOVERNMENT RESTRICTED RIGHTS.** The SOFTWARE PRODUCT and documentation are provided with RESTRICTED RIGHTS. Use, duplication, or disclosure by the Government is subject to restrictions as set forth in subparagraph (c)(1)(ii) of the Rights in Technical Data and Computer Software clause at DFARS 252.227-7013 or subparagraphs (c)(1) and (2) of the Commercial Computer Software—Restricted Rights at 48 CFR 52.227-19, as applicable. Manufacturer is Microsoft Corporation/One Microsoft Way/Redmond, WA 98052-6399.

5. **EXPORT RESTRICTIONS.** You agree that you will not export or re-export the SOFTWARE PRODUCT, any part thereof, or any process or service that is the direct product of the SOFTWARE PRODUCT (the foregoing collectively referred to as the "Restricted Components"), to any country, person, entity, or end user subject to U.S. export restrictions. You specifically agree not to export or re-export any of the Restricted Components (i) to any country to which the U.S. has embargoed or restricted the export of goods or services, which currently include, but are not necessarily limited to, Cuba, Iran, Iraq, Libya, North Korea, Sudan, and Syria, or to any national of any such country, wherever located, who intends to transmit or transport the Restricted Components back to such country; (ii) to any end user who you know or have reason to know will utilize the Restricted Components in the design, development, or production of nuclear, chemical, or biological weapons; or (iii) to any end user who has been prohibited from participating in U.S. export transactions by any federal agency of the U.S. government. You warrant and represent that neither the BXA nor any other U.S. federal agency has suspended, revoked, or denied your export privileges.

DISCLAIMER OF WARRANTY

NO WARRANTIES OR CONDITIONS. MICROSOFT EXPRESSLY DISCLAIMS ANY WARRANTY OR CONDITION FOR THE SOFTWARE PRODUCT. THE SOFTWARE PRODUCT AND ANY RELATED DOCUMENTATION IS PROVIDED "AS IS" WITHOUT WARRANTY OR CONDITION OF ANY KIND, EITHER EXPRESS OR IMPLIED, INCLUDING, WITHOUT LIMITATION, THE IMPLIED WARRANTIES OF MERCHANTABILITY, FITNESS FOR A PARTICULAR PURPOSE, OR NONINFRINGEMENT. THE ENTIRE RISK ARISING OUT OF USE OR PERFORMANCE OF THE SOFTWARE PRODUCT REMAINS WITH YOU.

LIMITATION OF LIABILITY. TO THE MAXIMUM EXTENT PERMITTED BY APPLICABLE LAW, IN NO EVENT SHALL MICROSOFT OR ITS SUPPLIERS BE LIABLE FOR ANY SPECIAL, INCIDENTAL, INDIRECT, OR CONSEQUENTIAL DAMAGES WHATSOEVER (INCLUDING, WITHOUT LIMITATION, DAMAGES FOR LOSS OF BUSINESS PROFITS, BUSINESS INTERRUPTION, LOSS OF BUSINESS INFORMATION, OR ANY OTHER PECUNIARY LOSS) ARISING OUT OF THE USE OF OR INABILITY TO USE THE SOFTWARE PRODUCT OR THE PROVISION OF OR FAILURE TO PROVIDE SUPPORT SERVICES, EVEN IF MICROSOFT HAS BEEN ADVISED OF THE POSSIBILITY OF SUCH DAMAGES. IN ANY CASE, MICROSOFT'S ENTIRE LIABILITY UNDER ANY PROVISION OF THIS EULA SHALL BE LIMITED TO THE GREATER OF THE AMOUNT ACTUALLY PAID BY YOU FOR THE SOFTWARE PRODUCT OR US$5.00; PROVIDED, HOWEVER, IF YOU HAVE ENTERED INTO A MICROSOFT SUPPORT SERVICES AGREEMENT, MICROSOFT'S ENTIRE LIABILITY REGARDING SUPPORT SERVICES SHALL BE GOVERNED BY THE TERMS OF THAT AGREEMENT. BECAUSE SOME STATES AND JURISDICTIONS DO NOT ALLOW THE EXCLUSION OR LIMITATION OF LIABILITY, THE ABOVE LIMITATION MAY NOT APPLY TO YOU.

MISCELLANEOUS

This EULA is governed by the laws of the State of Washington USA, except and only to the extent that applicable law mandates governing law of a different jurisdiction.

Should you have any questions concerning this EULA, or if you desire to contact Microsoft for any reason, please contact the Microsoft subsidiary serving your country, or write: Microsoft Sales Information Center/One Microsoft Way/Redmond, WA 98052-6399.